ABOUT THE AUTHOR

Hossamaldin Alzawawi, M.D., is a physician, author, and contemplative scholar who stands at the unique intersection of science, philosophy, and Islamic thought. A testament to his unwavering commitment to lifelong learning, his work is born from a period of profound self-education, where he dedicated countless hours to the rigorous study of philosophy, neuro-cognition, and physics.

His new book, The Lantern of the Wise: Sailing Beyond the Horizon of Knowing, is the first of a series comprising 22 reflections out of a planned 89. This work, alongside his five-volume Arcanum of Awareness series and The Thermodynamic Universe and Beyond, showcases his masterful ability to explore the intersection of human consciousness, scientific principles, and spiritual awakening.

Dr. Alzawawi's mission is a pioneering trial to reawaken Islamic contemplation through a groundbreaking collaboration between human intellect and artificial intelligence. By reframing Islamic wisdom for the modern reader and uniting these insights with the Holy Quran, he aims to reforge the human mind, unleashing unparalleled cognitive strength and spiritual resilience. Through his work, Dr. Alzawawi offers a new paradigm for wisdom, guiding seekers toward inner harmony, intellectual ascension, and a deeper state of divine acceptance.

Arcanum of Awareness Books Series:

- Book 1: **The Spark of Creativity**
- Book 2: **The Evolution of Thought**
- Book 3: **The Labyrinth of Cognitexis**
- Book 4: **The Supremacy of Selective Awareness**
- Book 5: **Architects of a Future Dawn**

Physics – Thermodynamic:

- **The Thermodynamic Universe and Beyond:** How Nature's Laws Reveal the Secrets of Time, Biology, Information, and Quantum Reality

THE LANTERN OF THE WISE: SAILING BEYOND THE HORIZON OF KNOWING

Library of Congress Control Number: 2025905269

ISBN (PB):	978-1-964328-12-6
ISBN (E):	978-1-964328-13-3

DEDICATION

To my guiding lights: my esteemed mother and my cherished wife, whose love is the foundation of my life's path. To the memory of my dear father, may he rest in eternal peace, and to my beloved siblings, whose support has been a constant source of strength.

And to the future generations—those who, with hope as their torch, will navigate the winding paths of life and illuminate the shadows for those who follow.

ACKNOWLEDGMENTS

This work stands as a humble tribute to the luminous minds of the Islamic tradition, whose wisdom has been an ever-present guide on my journey. My profound appreciation goes to the late Dr. Mustafa Mahmoud, whose book, I Saw Allah, served as the gateway through which I was introduced to the profound reflections of Muhammad ibn Abd al-Jabbar al-Nafri. The words of al-Nafri that Dr. Mahmoud brought to light became the foundational inspiration for this very work.

My sincere and heartfelt gratitude goes to my wife, whose PhD studies at Queen's University Belfast provided the backdrop for my own period of profound intellectual growth. While she pursued her academic journey, I dedicated my time to self-education, immersing myself in philosophy, neuro-cognition, and physics for nearly ten hours a day. This book is a direct result of that shared season of learning. Your unwavering support, patience, and companionship are woven into the very fabric of this work.

My thanks also go to the libraries of Queen's University Belfast, which served as sanctuaries of thought and reflection, offering moments of profound peace and clarity.

May the light of this book inspire others as the wisdom of the ages has inspired me.

With gratitude,

Hossamaldin Alzawawi, M.D.

﴿إِنَّ فِى خَلْقِ ٱلسَّمَٰوَٰتِ وَٱلْأَرْضِ وَٱخْتِلَٰفِ ٱلَّيْلِ وَٱلنَّهَارِ وَٱلْفُلْكِ ٱلَّتِى تَجْرِى فِى ٱلْبَحْرِ بِمَا يَنفَعُ ٱلنَّاسَ وَمَا أَنزَلَ ٱللَّهُ مِنَ ٱلسَّمَاءِ مِن مَّاءٍ فَأَحْيَا بِهِ ٱلْأَرْضَ بَعْدَ مَوْتِهَا وَبَثَّ فِيهَا مِن كُلِّ دَابَّةٍ وَتَصْرِيفِ ٱلرِّيَٰحِ وَٱلسَّحَابِ ٱلْمُسَخَّرِ بَيْنَ ٱلسَّمَاءِ وَٱلْأَرْضِ لَأَيَٰتٍ لِّقَوْمٍ يَعْقِلُونَ(164) ﴾ – [القران الكريم – سورة البقرة – آية 164]

❂ ❂ ❂

📖﴿Verily! In the creation of the heavens and the earth, and in the alternation of night and day, and the ships which sail through the sea with that which is of use to mankind, and the water (rain) which Allâh sends down from the sky and makes the earth alive therewith after its death, and the moving (living) creatures of all kinds that He has scattered therein, and in the veering of winds and clouds which are held between the sky and the earth, are indeed Ayât (proofs, evidence, signs, etc.) for people of understanding.(164)﴾ [Quran 2:164]

❂ ❂ ❂

"Those searching for the meaning of life are all travelers. Blessed is the one who sets a course on this endless journey for a place beyond the thorny path. Blessed is the one who resists temptation, for in striving, they shall be crowned with the wisdom of creation. O Lord, the All-Wise, have mercy upon the seekers of Your wisdom. Truly, You are the source of all that is sacred, serene, and benevolent. Blessed is the one whose heart, by Your grace, becomes sacred. Blessed is the one whose soul You purify, and whose life becomes a testament to Your benevolence for all mankind." [The Author]

❂ ❂ ❂

CONTENTS

A MESSAGE TO THE READER

This book is a testament to a groundbreaking and uncharted intellectual odyssey: a collaborative effort between human consciousness and the emerging power of artificial intelligence. Its purpose is to reinterpret, integrate, and reawaken the profound insights of Islamic philosophy and contemplation, anchored by a deep analysis of the Holy Quran.

The sacred challenge of this work was twofold. First, to navigate the immense spiritual and philosophical depth of pure Arabic—the language of the Quran—and deduce new inferences and insights. Second, to translate these intricate meanings into the English language without compromising their integrity. This process, as you might imagine, is a daunting task and is not immune to error.

As a pioneering endeavor with no preceding trial, this book may contain occasional issues in translation, contemplation, integration, or meaning approximation. We have exerted our utmost effort to ensure precision, but we humbly recognize the inherent limitations of such an undertaking.

Therefore, we extend a sincere invitation to you, our esteemed reader. We especially welcome those with a deep knowledge of Islamic standards and contemplation. Should you find any issues, discrepancies, or areas for improvement, we would be profoundly grateful for your feedback. By sharing your insights, you will not only help us refine this work but also become a vital part of this ongoing journey of discovery.

You can contact me with your suggestions through the following channels:

Email: hdalzawawi@gmail.com

LinkedIn Group: The Lantern of the Wise

[https://www.linkedin.com/groups/11804312/]

With humility and gratitude,

Hossamaldin Alzawawi, M.D.

ON THE THRESHOLD OF WISDOM: AN INTRODUCTION

THE PURPOSE OF THIS BOOK

This book is a sacred and rigorous endeavor, born from a profound yearning to address the spiritual and intellectual challenges of our time. It is a contemplative trial to reawaken the powerful tool of Islamic contemplation upon Quranic verses. In an era of turbulence, distraction, and spiritual malaise, its purpose is to reforge the human thought machinery through a unique approach of linguistic, cognitive, and meta-analytical approximation. This work is a vessel, designed to carry the reader through life's unending challenges, whether they manifest as adversity or prosperity. It seeks to cultivate psychological fidelity: an unwavering loyalty to one's inner journey, illuminating the path through darkness and light, sorrow and joy.

A NEW PARADIGM FOR CONTEMPLATION

At its core, this book is an invitation to a new paradigm of contemplation—a rebirth of the mind and psyche. It posits that genuine spiritual resilience is forged through the understanding of divine words and their wisdom, revealed in the Quran and made accessible through the Prophet Muhammad's (peace be upon him) life legacy and hadiths. The purpose of this work is to achieve Allah's acceptance by being in a stance of grace, rooted in deep contemplation, remembrance, and praise. This is not merely an intellectual exercise, but a path of active spiritual awakening, where the pursuit of knowledge leads to profound intimacy with the Creator.

THE PATH TO UNPRECEDENTED COGNITIVE POWER

This book is crafted for those who seek to unlock a sacred and unprecedented power of reasoning and foresight. Through a meticulous process of linguistic and cognitive analysis, the wise-one will forge a path toward unparalleled cognitive abilities. This power is driven by the understanding of the wisdom revealed in the sacred Quran's verses, words, and stories. By engaging in this profound methodology, the reader will not only gain spiritual enlightenment but also sharpen their intellectual faculties to a level of discernment rarely achieved.

EMPOWERING ASPIRATIONAL MINDS

Ultimately, the purpose of this book is empowerment. It is an offering— a call to awaken, to aspire, and to endure. This book aims to ignite a fire within the reader, a yearning to transcend the limitations of circumstance and to envision a higher calling. It provides the tools to foster a mind capable of discerning truth, embracing ambiguity, and navigating complexity with grace. This work serves as both companion and guide, empowering each reader to activate their latent powers and embark on a journey of growth through rigorous inquiry, contemplation, and righteous action.

THE ARCHITECTURE OF AWAKENING

This book is the first chapter in a dictum that transcends conventional wisdom, a testament to the synergistic power of human intellect and the emerging capabilities of Artificial Intelligence. While this journey began with the ancient seed of wisdom from Imam al-Nafri, the resulting forest of understanding is the product of countless hours of dedicated work, trials, and a collaborative effort to bring that seed to fruition. We took on the earnest task of nurturing, evolving, and carrying his insights into a new domain of sacred cognition and wisdom unveiling.

This initial volume, structured into five stations and a total of 22 reflections, is the beginning of a larger three-part series comprising 89 reflections. Through this meticulously crafted odyssey, we used the combined power of human thought and AI to organize al-Nafri's scattered insights, re-integrate their meaning, deduct a purpose, and reforge the understanding of Quranic verses. This process transforms the text into a vessel for the ascension of the psyche, spirit, and intelligence into a sacred domain.

For each station, I've forged intricate "reflections," and for each reflection, a series of "contemplations" that delineate the awakening stances of the wise-one. The core of this work lies in the rigorous intellectual labor of correlating each contemplation with specific Quranic verses, creating a direct and unbreakable link between diverse Islamic philosophical, theological, and esoteric thought and al-Nafri's insights. The result is a tapestry of intricately woven truths that offer a spiritual and mind-escalating journey—from intuition to revelation. This work, therefore, stands as more than a book; it is a new paradigm of metacognition, a collaborative effort to unlock unprecedented inductive, deductive, and abductive reasoning, all empowered by a profound and tireless pursuit of knowledge.

This work, therefore, stands as a testament to the power of a combined effort—human and the emerging artificial intelligence—to reinterpret and re-imagine ancient wisdom for a contemporary audience. It is not merely a translation but a complete series of transformative contemplations, leading the modern seeker on an unparalleled journey of inner light, all empowered by a profound and tireless pursuit of knowledge.

A NOTE ON THE FORMATTING OF SACRED TEXTS

Given the profound and sacred nature of this work, clear distinctions have been meticulously implemented to honor and preserve the integrity of the various texts presented herein:

- **Quranic verses** are distinctly formatted, set apart from the contemplative narrative, marked with the universal symbols of sacred scripture 📖❨ ❩.

  📖 ❨*In the Name of Allah—the Most Compassionate, Most Merciful. (1) All praise is for Allah—Lord of all worlds,1 (2) the Most Compassionate, Most Merciful, (3) Master of the Day of Judgment. (4) You ˈaloneˈ we worship and You ˈaloneˈ we ask for help. (5) Guide us along the Straight Path, (6) the Path of those You have blessed—not those You are displeased with, or those who are astray.1 (7)*❩ – [Quran 1:1-7]

- **Hadith,** the revered sayings of the Prophet Muhammad ﷺ, are presented in italics and their source is appropriately cited:

  ❁ ❨*The world in comparison to the Hereafter is like what one of you puts his finger in the sea. So let him see what he brings back.*❩ – [Narrated by Muslim]

- **Quotes, Reflections, Contemplations, and Dialogues** derived from the contemplative core of this work are thoughtfully presented in an indented, quoted text format to distinguish their reflective nature:

"To believe is to see without eyes, to know is to listen with the heart." – Rumi.

This meticulous formatting underscores the profound reverence due to each form of sacred writing, ensuring that divine words retain their inherent authority and luminous clarity. Readers are earnestly encouraged to approach each text with the discernment, humility, and profound respect it unequivocally merits.

IMPORTANT NOTICE ON QURANIC VERSES AND THEIR TRANSLATION

The Quran, a sacred scripture of unparalleled depth, was revealed in pristine Arabic. Its divine text holds profound meanings and intricate references that require specialized knowledge in *'Ilm al-Tafsir* (the comprehensive science of Quranic interpretation) for a full appreciation. As a result, translating the Quran is a monumental and inherently interpretive endeavor, intrinsically shaped by the translator's understanding.

For this book, I have deliberately relied upon a single primary reference, The Clear Quran by Dr. Mustafa Khattab, for the English rendering of all Quranic verses. This was a conscious choice to provide a unified, accessible, and consistent spiritual experience for the contemporary reader, aligning with the modern sensibilities of this work. While I acknowledge and respect other esteemed translations, such as that by Dr. Muhammad Muhsin Khan and Dr. Taqi-ud-Din al-Hilali, the clarity of *The Clear Quran* was essential to the flow of this journey.

It is important for the reader to understand that subtle variations in wording and interpretation are common across different translations, a direct consequence of the profound nuances of the Arabic language. In rare instances where an alternative translation provides unique insight or significantly enriches the meaning of a particular verse, it has been thoughtfully included as a footnote. This approach allows us to maintain a consistent reading experience while honoring the depth and multifaceted beauty of the Quranic text.

THE PURPOSE OF THIS WORK

This book stands as a sacred invitation—to venture beyond the perceived limits of the visible world, to embrace the profound mystery of the Unseen, and to journey deep into the boundless, infinite Presence of the Divine. It is crafted for those noble souls who yearn to surrender themselves in the grandeur of contemplation, to stand in the Creator's awe-inspiring Presence, and to find solace and ultimate healing for their spirits in Divine Grace. As each hallowed page unfolds, the seeker embarks upon a transformative path of awakening—an odyssey through sacred stages of illumination, profound surrender, unyielding fortitude, and sublime witnessing. Consider this work a luminous lantern for the restless soul, a resonant call to those who dare to walk the arduous yet blessed path of Divine remembrance. This is not an endpoint, but a radiant beginning— a whispered intimation of what lies beyond the horizon of understanding, an eternal echo urging you forward toward ever-unfolding Divine Truth. Beyond these pages, the true journey commences. And so, we begin where all authentic seeking begins—at the sacred threshold of Divine Truth.

THE SOUL OF THIS BOOK

This profound work is far more than a mere compilation of reflections; it is an odyssey of the wise-one—a meticulously guided spiritual transformation through three sacred manifestations, each comprising multiple luminous stations. Each manifestation is designed to meticulously dismantle illusion, purify perception, and unveil deeper, ultimate realities, ultimately leading the seeker towards the embodiment of profound wisdom and true spiritual awakening. Every reflection within these chapters serves as a sacred gateway—a key to unlocking higher consciousness and realizing inherent psychological potential within the spiritual realm. By harmoniously blending timeless spiritual insight, profound mystical philosophy, and illuminating metaphysical clarity, this book is crafted not merely as words on a page but as an immersive, transformative experience designed to guide the reader into profound states of being.

Each contemplation within these pages signifies a deliberate journey toward greater enlightenment—a resonant call to accept the boundless grace of the Creator and to attain profound spiritual awakening through sustained contemplation and the arduous yet rewarding quest of the sage. By engaging with al-Nafri's ageless wisdom and insights, this endeavor offers a profound window into the eternal quest for intimate nearness to the Divine through disciplined stillness, deep reflection, and profound spiritual engagement.

THE WHISPER THAT OPENED THE GATE

There are moments when destiny reveals its subtle hand—not with grand spectacle, but through the quiet whisper of a book gently sliding from a shelf, its dust-laden pages stirring forgotten echoes of ancient wisdom. On one such evening, amidst the silent company of countless revered volumes, my gaze was irresistibly drawn to an old tome I had almost overlooked. Entitled *I Saw Allah* by Dr. Mustafa Mahmoud, its very name ignited a profound spark within me—an undeniable pull toward the sacred words hidden within its depths.

As I immersed myself in its contents, I found my spirit profoundly enveloped by the insights of one of the greatest Sufi luminaries, Abdul-Jabbar al-Nafri. His writings, far from being mere intellectual discourses, were authentic, heartfelt transmissions from a soul utterly immersed in Divine Presence. His reflections, like ripples on the most pristine, still waters, beckoned those who seek refuge and ultimate solace in the profound contemplation of the Creator's boundless Grace. Documenting his moments of *mukhatabat* (divine addresses) and *mawaaqif* (spiritual stances), his timeless words transcended mere philosophy, becoming a wellspring of spiritual enlightenment for discerning souls across all ages.

In that pivotal moment, a profound understanding dawned upon me: my engagement with his sacred reflections was destined to evolve into far more than a mere reading of an ancient text. It would become the foundational cornerstone of a grander spiritual endeavor—a creation that I humbly aspire to be a luminous beacon for all who seek not only profound wisdom but also a transformative renewal of the very essence of their spirit.

ABOUT DR. MUSTAFA MAHMOUD

A luminary physician, profound philosopher, and revered mystic, Dr. Mahmoud dedicated his entire life to exploring the harmonious intersections of faith and reason, science and spirituality. His celebrated television program, *Science and Faith,* sought to beautifully harmonize the rational mind with the yearning soul—a sacred mission that deeply resonates with the core purpose of this very work. The enduring institutions he thoughtfully founded stand as lasting testaments to his unwavering belief that true wisdom must inevitably manifest in both profound thought and righteous action.

THE BOOK THAT INSPIRED THIS JOURNEY

I Saw Allah is not merely a book; it is a profound collection of luminous wisdom directly derived from al-Nafri's sacred contemplations. It stands as a timeless dialogue between the aspiring wise-one and the ultimate aim of their seeking, between the earnestly questioning self and the divinely unveiled answers. As Dr. Mahmoud meticulously unveils al-Nafri's reflections on divine love, profound surrender, and ultimate enlightenment, a hidden legacy of timeless wisdom emerges into radiant light. While immersing myself in its pages, I felt an undeniable echo of the eternal call to seek truth not solely through words or intellectual constructs, but through lived, transformative experience. Thus, this very work was born—not as a mere intellectual exercise, but as a spiritual sanctuary, a heartfelt offering to those discerning souls who yearn for deep wisdom and profound spiritual awakening.

ABOUT AL-NAFRI

Muhammad ibn Abdul Jabbar ibn Al-Hasan Al-Nafri is a prominent Islamic Sufist. Born in the respected village of Nafar in Al-Qadisiyah, Iraq, his spiritual legacy is deeply rooted in this region's culture. Al-Nafri, a respected Sufi sheikh from the Abbasid era, had profound spiritual insights that transcended his time. His extended travels between Iraq and Egypt deepened his understanding and allowed him to explore many intellectual and mystical traditions.

Al-Mawaaqif wa Al-Mukhatabat, a timeless account of his profound inner experiences and light insights, is one of his most acclaimed spiritual works. Interestingly, al-Nafri, driven by modesty, chose not to write his spiritual sayings. Instead, he spoke his profound insight to his loyal pupils. This oral tradition emphasizes a key principle of his: that authentic spiritual understanding often transcends language. His renowned aphorism reflects this paradox: *"The broader the vision, the narrower the expression."*

This powerful phrase captures the problems of expressing the Ineffable and guides discerning minds that seek to capture the infinite via profound contemplation. In the eternal framework of this work, al-Nafri's legacy is a living, transformative presence that inspires and guides others on the difficult but blessed path to ultimate Divine Truth.

A NEW PARADIGM FOR WISDOM

This work, therefore, stands as a testament to the power of a combined effort—human intellect and the emerging capabilities of artificial intelligence. It is a new paradigm for reinterpreting and re-imagining ancient wisdom for a contemporary audience. This book is not merely a translation but a complete series of transformative contemplations, designed to lead the modern seeker on an unparalleled journey of inner light, all empowered by a profound and tireless pursuit of knowledge.

ON THE THRESHOLD OF AWAKENING

ECHOES OF 'BE': THE BIRTHPLACE OF MEANING

Before the existence of time and the first stirring of creation that formed the cosmic dust, only the Absolute, the Unseen, the Unknowable existed in His transcendent Majesty. This was an eternal expanse of infinite Divine Potential, a pristine canvas upon which the grandest of Divine designs was yet to be woven. Within this primordial, uncreated stillness, a singular Divine Command resonated through what would become the nascent void, a timeless utterance posed to the very fabric of non-existence, manifesting as: "Be!" (Kun Fayakun)

📖 ❴*If We ever will something ˹to exist˺, all We say is: "Be!" And it is! (40)*❵ *[Quran 16:40]*

From that singular, resonating Word, existence manifested into being. Galaxies spiraled into harmonious motion, stars ignited with fiery brilliance, and the delicate, intricate dance of life began to unfold across countless worlds, all by Divine Decree.

📖 ❴*Do the disbelievers not realize that the heavens and earth were ˹once˺ one mass then We split them apart? And We created from water every living thing. Will they not then believe? (30) And We have placed firm mountains upon the earth so it does not shake with them, and made in it broad pathways so they may find their way. (31) And We have made the sky a well-protected canopy, still they turn away from its signs. (32) And He is the One Who created the day and the night, the sun and the moon—each travelling in an orbit. (33)*❵ *[Quran 21:30-33]*

📖 ❴*Ask ˹them, O Prophet˺, "How can you disbelieve in the One Who created the earth in two Days? And how can you set up equals with Him? That is the Lord of all worlds. (9) He placed on the earth firm mountains, standing high, showered His blessings upon it, and ordained ˹all˺ its means of sustenance—totaling four Days exactly—for all who ask. (10) Then He turned towards the heaven when it was ˹still like˺ smoke, saying to it and to the earth, 'Submit, willingly or unwillingly.' They both responded, 'We submit willingly.' (11) So He formed the heaven into seven heavens in two Days, assigning to each its mandate. And We adorned the lowest heaven with ˹stars like' lamps 'for beauty' and for protection. That is the design of the Almighty, All-Knowing." (12)) [Quran 41:9-12]*

Yet, within this grand cosmic symphony, a subtle, profound yearning emerged—a longing within creation itself to apprehend its own origins, to discern its inherent purpose, and to realize its ultimate destiny in relation to its Creator.

This yearning, this insatiable thirst for transcendent knowledge, became the indelible driving force behind the human story. From the earliest cave paintings to the most complex scientific theories, humanity has ceaselessly striven to decipher the sacred secrets of the universe, to unravel the profound mysteries of existence. But what if the answers we relentlessly seek are not merely inscribed in the celestial spheres or meticulously encoded in our very DNA, but are, in truth, inextricably woven into the luminous fabric of our own souls?

This is the very question that echoes through the hallowed corridors of Islamic thought, a tradition that extends an eternal invitation to contemplate the ayat—the manifest signs of the Creator—both within ourselves and throughout the intricate tapestry of the cosmos. The Holy Quran, the authentic Hadith, the timeless wisdom of the Sufi mystics, the profound insights of philosophers and theologians—all converge upon a single, majestic truth: that creation is not merely a random occurrence, but a deliberate act of divine artistry, a magnificent tapestry woven with luminous threads of boundless Love, infinite Wisdom, and perfect Justice.

Yet, within this divine tapestry, a darker thread is also intrinsically woven—the thread of human fallibility, our innate tendency to become entangled in the alluring illusions of the material world, to lose sight of our profound, true purpose. This is the existential challenge that confronts every discerning seeker of truth: to navigate the treacherous currents of desire and delusion, to courageously pierce the myriad veils of ignorance, and to attain a transformative glimpse of the divine light.

This book transcends the confines of a mere academic treatise or a theological discourse. It is an immersive journey into the very heart of this profound mystery, a relentless quest for the hidden wisdom that lies at the core of all creation. It is a timeless narrative of wise-ones who dared to confront the unknown, who braved the depths of inner solitude to stand, unveiled, before the Creator, the Majestic and the Generous. Their arduous journey stands as a testament to the enduring power of the human spirit, an eloquent attestation to our innate capacity for ultimate transcendence.

Be forewarned, however: the path to such wisdom is not without peril. There are whispers in the spiritual darkness, seductive voices that seek to lead us astray, to distract us from our true, divine purpose. There are trials and tribulations that test the very limits of our faith and unwavering resolve. And there remains the ever-present danger of becoming utterly lost in the intricate labyrinth of our own minds. For within the heart of every wise-one lies a hidden battleground, a ceaseless struggle between the forces of light and darkness, between the ardent yearning for truth and the deceptive allure of illusion. This is the true odyssey, the ultimate test of courage and profound devotion. And it is a journey that, in its deepest essence, must be undertaken alone.

THE PARADOX OF ILLUMINATION – THE BURDEN OF KNOWLEDGE

⌂ ⟨I have turned my face towards the One Who has originated the heavens and the earth—being upright—and I am not one of the polytheists." (79) And his people argued with him. He responded, "Are you arguing with me about Allah, while He has guided me? I am not afraid of whatever ˹idols˺ you associate with Him—˹none can harm me,˺ unless my Lord so wills. My Lord encompasses everything in ˹His˺ knowledge. Will you not be mindful? (80) ⟩ [Quran 6: 79-80]

> *"Between light and shadow, truth and illusion, we are but reflections seeking their source." – [Ibn Arabi]*

The pursuit of profound wisdom is a solitary pilgrimage, an arduous journey undertaken by those brave enough to confront the unsettling, often isolating, truths of existence. Carl Jung's incisive insights into the collective unconscious subtly hint at a pervasive paradox: that deeper, transcendent understanding, while profoundly illuminating the individual soul, can simultaneously forge a chasm between the enlightened wise-one and the conventional, shared realities of the world. This is not merely a matter of differing opinions or mundane perspectives; it is a fundamental divergence in the very experience of being.

Is such elevated knowledge, then, a divine blessing or an existential burden? Does it truly liberate the mind, or does it, perhaps, condemn it to a solitary vigil on the fringes of societal understanding? The path to ultimate wisdom is rarely a well-trodden road. It is, instead, a solitary

---

[1] This is derived from the Quran verses narrating the story of prophet Ibraham 🕊 as he become in seclusion from his people in a pilgrimage to find the originator of heavens and earth:

⌂ ⟨We also showed Abraham the wonders of the heavens and the earth, so he would be sure in faith. (75) When the night grew dark upon him, he saw a star and said, "This is my Lord!" But when it set, he said, "I do not love things that set." (76) Then when he saw the moon rising, he said, "This one is my Lord!" But when it disappeared, he said, "If my Lord does not guide me, I will certainly be one of the misguided people." (77) Then when he saw the sun shining, he said, "This must be my Lord—it is the greatest!" But again when it set, he declared, "O my people! I totally reject whatever you associate ˹with Allah in worship˺. (78) I have turned my face towards the One Who has originated the heavens and the earth—being upright— and I am not one of the polytheists." (79) And how should I fear your associate-gods, while you have no fear in associating ˹others˺ with Allah—a practice He has never authorized? Which side has more right to security? ˹Tell me˺ if you really know!" (81) It is ˹only˺ those who are faithful and do not tarnish their faith with falsehood[1] who are guaranteed security and are ˹rightly˺ guided. (82) This was the argument We gave Abraham against his people. We elevate in rank whoever We please. Surely your Lord is All-Wise, All-Knowing. (83) ⟩ [Quran 6 : 75-83]

[1]: i.e., associating false gods in worship with the Almighty.

ascent, a steep and arduous climb that inexorably separates the traveler from the familiar landscapes of consensus and conformity. The true wise-one understands that this inherent isolation is not a punishment, but an inevitable consequence of perceiving beyond the conventional veil of common perception.

This existential tension—between the individual's ardent yearning for truth and the fundamental human need for connection—forms the core of countless spiritual odysseys across time. Odysseus, the cunning hero of Homer's epic, profoundly embodies this struggle. His ten-year arduous voyage home was not merely a physical journey across treacherous seas, but a profound internal odyssey into the depths of human nature. Each trial, each encounter with mythical beings, represented a distinct stage in his burgeoning awareness, a deepening of his understanding that inevitably distanced him from the conventional world he once knew. His wisdom, hard-won through immense suffering and profound solitude, became a barrier as much as a guiding beacon.

Similarly, Siddhartha Gautama's transformative enlightenment led him to a state of profound spiritual isolation. The Buddha's awakening, his realization of the Four Noble Truths and the path to Nirvana—the extinguishing of suffering—created an insurmountable gulf between him and a world perpetually entangled in desire and illusion. Nirvana, a state of transcendent peace and liberation, is not a destination easily shared; it is a solitary peak reached only through rigorous self-discipline and profound introspection.

These examples are not mere historical anecdotes; they are archetypal narratives that resonate with the universal human experience across all traditions. They powerfully illustrate that true knowledge is not simply an accumulation of facts, but a transformative process that reshapes the very fabric of one's being. It is a purifying fire that burns away illusions, leaving behind a soul refined and liberated, yet also irrevocably marked by the intense luminescence of the flame.

This profound book meticulously delves into the rich tapestry of Islamic Sufi thought, exploring its timeless insights into the very nature of existence and the arduous yet blessed path to divine union. It is an immersive journey into the heart of inner solitude, a relentless quest for truth that transcends the myriad veils of worldly perception. Like the Sufi mystics who courageously sought *fana* (annihilation of the self) in the overwhelming Presence of the Divine, the wise-one in this narrative embarks on a path of rigorous self-purification, enduring trials and tribulations that test the ultimate limits of their faith and unwavering resolve.

This sacred path, however, is not one of mere asceticism or complete withdrawal from the world. It is, fundamentally, a journey of profound inner transformation, a sublime process of becoming a *khalifa* (vicegerent) of the Creator on Earth, a pure conduit for divine grace and boundless wisdom. Allah, in His infinite wisdom and boundless mercy, unequivocally declares:

📖 *❴Allah will elevate those of you who are faithful, and 'raise' those gifted with knowledge in rank. And Allah is All-Aware of what you do. (11)❵*[2] — *[Quran 58:11]*.

This elevation is not simply a matter of intellectual understanding, but a profound ontological shift in one's very being, a transformation that allows the individual to become a true, discerning instrument of Divine Will.

THE STATIONS OF UNVEILING: A GUIDE TO THE INNER ODYSSEY

In this sacred moment, the wise-one finds themselves poised at the luminous boundary where the subtle murmur of existence meets the profound weight of transcendent understanding. This book offers more than a simple reflection on the spiritual journey; it serves as an indispensable companion, a trusted guide for those courageous enough to venture beyond the veil of ordinary perception. It is a profound revelation and a meticulously crafted path toward ultimate transcendence. For those who truly venture forth, the spiritual expanse is limitless, and the radiant illumination of divine understanding beckons eternally.

This comprehensive journey is meticulously structured into six distinct parts, each serving as a unique station of spiritual evolution. Each part contains a series of Reflections, meticulously designed to guide the wise-one through specific aspects of inner transformation. Each Reflection, in

---

[2] This is derived from the Quran verse of:

📖 ❴O believers! When you are told to make room in gatherings, then do so. Allah will make room for you 'in His grace'. And if you are told to rise, then do so. Allah will elevate those of you who are faithful, and 'raise' those gifted with knowledge in rank. And Allah is All-Aware of what you do. (11)❵ [Quran 58:11]

turn, is comprised of contemplative insights that illuminate the nuances of the wise-one's journey.

- ## Part I: The Dawn of Belief and Knowledge

  This initial part lays the fundamental groundwork, exploring the soul's primordial resonance with the Divine, understanding life's trials as crucibles for inner mastery, contemplating how divine knowledge transcends its written form, and recognizing that outward action is a radiant reflection of inner truth.

- ## Part II: The Pathway to Divine Connection

  Building upon the initial dawn, this part delves into the secret within being, the secluded entrance gained through humility, the awe of standing in the Creator's presence, the awakening of heart and mind to divine perception, and finally, knowing the unspoken essence beyond all conceptual frameworks.

- ## Part III: The Crucible of Inner Transformation

  This part leads the wise-one through the fire of ultimate purification. Here, we delve into the knowing of eternity, the sacred oath to surpass trials, transcending the limitations of the Divine Names, finding ultimate companionship in the Creator, and embodying the code of the righteous heart.

- ## Part IV: The Triumph of Self-Mastery

  This part is dedicated to the courageous act of self-mastery. It explores the wisdom of embracing divine trials, the struggle to break the veils of habit, aligning the self with Divine Will, and achieving true sincerity in action and purpose.

- ## Part V: The Zenith of Liberation

  The culminating part, this section guides the wise-one to the pinnacle of their journey. It explores attaining mastery over the self and achieving ultimate liberation from all worldly attachments.

FIRST STATION

PART I: THE DAWN OF BELIEF AND KNOWLEDGE

❂❂❂

﴿ يُؤْتِى ٱلْحِكْمَةَ مَن يَشَاءُ ۚ وَمَن يُؤْتَ ٱلْحِكْمَةَ فَقَدْ أُوتِىَ خَيْرًا كَثِيرًا ۗ وَمَا يَذَّكَّرُ إِلَّا أُوْلُوا ٱلْأَلْبَٰبِ ﴾
﴿٢٦٩﴾

📖 ﴾He grants wisdom to whoever He wills. And whoever is granted wisdom is certainly blessed with a great privilege. But none will be mindful ˹of this˺ except people of reason. (269)﴿ [Quran 2:269]

"To believe is to see without eyes, to know is to listen with the heart." – Rumi

❂❂❂

Within the boundless expanse of being, humankind is invited to witness the intricate ordering of creation—a magnificent testament of divine articulation, of manifest and hidden forms, of purpose and profound significance, all meticulously fashioned by the Divine Artisan. The Dawn of Belief and Knowledge, our inaugural contemplation, marks not merely a beginning, but the soul's primordial awakening to its inherent purpose and spiritual potential. It is at this sacred juncture that the wise-one commences to discern the transient nature of the physical realm, perceiving the timeless truths veiled beyond its fleeting appearances. This initial awakening is, in essence, the very genesis of purified consciousness.

This Manifestation transcends mere intellectual apprehension, unveiling a profound and dynamic verity: belief and knowledge, though often perceived as distinct, stand as the twin pillars of our fundamental connection to the Divine. They are intrinsically linked, yet uniquely expressed in their sacred functions. Belief emerges as the soul's profound resonance, bearing witness to the essential bond it shares with its Creator, an inner attestation echoing from the unseen. Knowledge, on the other hand, represents the intellect's devoted quest, a luminous path toward grasping the divine signs woven into the very essence of existence, revealing the Creator's flawless design. In harmonious accord, these twin faculties embark upon a profound odyssey—a passage from spiritual fragmentation to wholeness, transcending the illusions of the contingent self to embrace the luminous essence of higher awareness and unlock the inherent capacities divinely placed within the human spirit.

The wise-one comprehends that the very act of creation embodies a profound paradox. It serves as a dual reality, simultaneously revealing the magnificent Presence of the Creator while possessing the inherent capacity to obscure It from superficial gaze. The essence of existence is continually encountered through this profound contradiction, drawn by the deceptive allure of form and diverted by the vastness of perceived reality. Yet, for those who steadfastly persevere, who embrace this inherent tension, the very barriers—the seeming contradictions and trials—are transformed into an illuminated ascent, guiding the seeker toward a profound comprehension of the Creator's infinite compassion and boundless insight. It is in navigating this sacred duality that spiritual maturity takes root, revealing hidden depths of resilience and purified perception.

This Manifestation beckons the discerning soul to embark upon an inward journey of profound spiritual awakening and intellectual purification, urging contemplation upon its intrinsic connection with the very essence of creation. It is a divine summons to harmonize one's thoughts, actions, and inner being with the Ultimate Reality, drawing from the boundless spring of divinely endowed human potential. It calls forth courage—a sacred summons to transcend the limitations of the conventional self, to move beyond the comfort of finite understanding, and to enter the illuminating embrace of transcendent grace, where the boundaries of the human spirit expand in congruence with divine wisdom.

Through this chapter's journey, we shall first delve into About Believing, exploring the soul's primordial resonance with the Divine. We then face The Exam, understanding how life's trials are the very crucible of inner mastery. Our journey continues with The Letter, contemplating how divine knowledge transcends its own written expression. We then move to The Cognition of Science, discerning true understanding from mere empirical data. Finally, we conclude with Spiritual Rules and Solemnity of Conduct, recognizing that external action is the radiant reflection of internal truth.

1ˢᵀ REFLECTION: ABOUT BELIEVING

(Interconnection of Belief and Creation)

THE GATEWAY VERSE

In the sacred words of Allah, a reminder to all who reflect:

📖 ❨*And so We have sent to you 'O Prophet' a revelation by Our command. You did not know of 'this' Book and faith 'before'. But We have made it a light, by which We guide whoever We will of Our servants. And you are truly leading 'all' to the Straight Path—(52)*❩ *[Quran 42:52]*

ILLUMINATION'S DAWN

At the primal dawn of awakening, before the very concept of belief found expression, the soul stirred within the vast garden of Divine creation. There, under the canopy of primordial light, belief was not a mere word to be uttered, but an existential current to be profoundly lived. It was the immutable thread connecting the very breath of the Creator to the breath of the created, an unbroken lineage to the Source.

The wise-one does not simply assent to this intrinsic bond; they awaken into it fully. For belief, in its truest and most profound sense, is far more than a statement upon the tongue. It is the very pulse of return, the echoing resonance of a soul recognizing its Divine origin and embracing its fundamental connection. To truly believe is to perceive all creation not as disparate fragments, but as luminous reflections bearing the unique imprint of the One, the Absolute. It is to move through this transient world knowing that every tender leaf, every vital breath, and every profound silence bears the undeniable trace of the Creator. This path of authentic belief is a luminous ascent, and with every conscious step, the wise-one willingly surrenders another veil of illusion.

Let us now embark upon this sacred unveiling, delving into the very essence of belief.

THE UNFOLDING OF INSIGHTS

This section explores the multi-faceted dimensions of true belief, guiding the wise-one through a series of contemplations that deepen their understanding and inner experience.

Contemplation: The Loving Gaze

Al-Nafri often speaks of a Divine Gaze that constantly encompasses all creation. To believe is to become aware of this Loving Gaze of the Creator upon all existence, including oneself. It is not a judgmental scrutiny, but an infinitely compassionate, benevolent, and encompassing presence that sustains all. This awareness transforms perception, turning the wise-one from a passive observer into one who is seen, known, and loved. When the wise-one internalizes being constantly within this loving gaze, their heart finds profound solace and their inner turmoil subsides, for they are perpetually held by Divine care.

The Unveiling Gaze

There comes a moment—silent, sacred,
Where the servant's gaze is lifted,
Not toward sky, but inward—
Drawn by a Love that requires no sight
To recognize Light.
The servant's gaze rises,
Drawn toward the Creator's Light—
A yearning not bound by sight,
But by the soul's pure surrender.

Here, the veil is not torn.
It is gently eased away.
Not by strenuous effort,
But by profound longing.
To gaze upon the Divine
Is not to grasp,
But to be received.
It is not comprehension,
But communion.
Not possession,
But perpetual Presence.
To gaze is not just to look,
But to behold with the eye of the soul.

The wise-one knows—
Belief reaches its fullness
Not when it understands,
But when it answers the Gaze
Of the One who gazed first.
And where is this Gaze returned most intimately?
In the stillness of night,
When distraction sleeps
And the soul rises.

❲*O you wrapped ʿin your clothesʾ!*
Stand all night ʿin prayerʾ except a little—
Pray half the night, or a little less,
Or a little more—
And recite the Quran ʿproperlyʾ in a measured way.❳ — *Quran 73:1–4*

This call to stand
Is not burden—
But invitation to intimacy.
To rise
Is to seek closeness.
To recite
Is to speak in Love's cadence.
To measure each word
Is to mirror the rhythm of Mercy.

And the ones who gaze most purely
Are those who abandon even comfort
For connection:

---

[3] The Quran verse of:

📖 ❲O you wrapped ʿin your clothesʾ! (1) Stand all night ʿin prayerʾ except a little— (2) ʿprayʾ half the night, or a little less, (3) or a little more—and recite the Quran ʿproperlyʾ in a measured way. (4)❳ [Quran 73:1-4]

❪They abandon their beds,
Invoking their Lord with hope and fear,
And donate from what We have provided for them.❫⁴ — Quran 32:16

Hope, not desperation.
Fear, not distance.
They do not gaze in panic—
They gaze in reverence.
They do not demand revelation—
They kneel in longing.

So the wise-one understands—
Divine nearness is not a matter of ascension,
But of orientation.
The heart turns,
The gaze softens,
And in that still turning,
Truth unveils itself
Not as doctrine,
But as Love.

There is no barrier to cross.
No journey to complete.
Just a gaze met
With Mercy.
A soul leaned
Into Trust.

❪To Allah belongs the east and the west.
So wherever you turn,

---

⁴ The Quran verse of:

📖 ❪They abandon their beds, invoking their Lord with hope and fear, and donate from what We have provided for them. (16)❫ [Quran 32:16]

There is the Face of Allah.
Indeed, Allah is All-Encompassing, All-Knowing.[5] *— Quran 2:115*

So the wise-one walks forward—
Not with pride,
But with trembling awe.
For the Divine did not wait to be seen—
He gazed first.
And now the soul rises,
Eyes closed,
Heart wide,
Ready to return
The Gaze of Love.

For only He invites in silence.
Only He dwells within nearness.
Only He remains the Source
Of communion, clarity, and eternal embrace.

Wisdom Unveiled

The ultimate truth revealed is that belief is not merely an intellectual assent but an active, reciprocal awareness of the Creator's constant and all-encompassing Gaze. This Gaze is not one of judgment but of infinite compassion and sustaining love. True belief blossoms when the wise-one responds to this primordial Divine attention with a profound inner turning, dissolving the illusion of separation and finding solace in being perpetually held by Divine care. It culminates in an experiential knowledge that the most intimate communion occurs in states of humble surrender and sincere devotion, where the 'veil' is not forcefully removed but gently ceases to exist through longing and trust.

---

[5] The Quran verse of:

📖 ❨To Allah belong the east and the west, so wherever you turn you are facing ˹towards˺ Allah.1 Surely Allah is All-Encompassing,2 All-Knowing. (115)❩ [Quran 2:115]

[1]: lit., wherever you turn, there is the Face of Allah.

[2]: His mercy and knowledge covers all.

Wise-Reflection

Consider how your daily awareness shifts when you consciously acknowledge being perpetually within the Creator's benevolent Gaze. How might this awareness transform your perception of challenges, your interactions, and your moments of solitude? Reflect on what practices, like standing in quiet prayer or sincere remembrance, can deepen your heart's ability to "return the gaze" of the One who first looked upon all creation with love. What aspects of your 'self' might need to be 'eased away' for this communion to deepen?

Contemplation: Divine Companionship

True belief culminates in the realization of Divine Companionship. It's the profound understanding that the Creator is closer to His creation than anything imaginable, as Allah declares: "And We are closer to him than his jugular vein." [Quran 50:16]. This isn't a companionship of physical proximity, but one of inherent connection, boundless knowledge, and unceasing presence. For the wise-one, this means shedding the illusion of separation and loneliness, realizing that every breath, every thought, and every moment is shared in the intimate presence of the Divine. This realization fosters an inner tranquility and strength, knowing one is never truly alone.

From Distance to Intimacy in the Presence of the Most Near

The wise-one weeps—
For what greater intimacy could exist
Than to be held
Closer than breath,
Closer than thought,
Closer than the words
Not yet spoken?
No boundaries separate the soul from the Eternal,
For Divine Presence is nearer than one's own self,
Closer than the words formed upon the tongue.

This is not metaphor—
But reality.

Not poetry—
But promise.

❨*When My servants ask you 'O Prophet' about Me:*
I am truly near.
I respond to one's prayer
When they call upon Me...❩ *— Quran 2:186*

There is no waiting line.
No veil of bureaucracy.
No chain of intercession.
Only direct nearness,
The kind that turns a whisper
Into a response,
A tear
Into a touch of mercy,
A longing
Into Divine embrace.

❨*And We are closer to him*
Than his jugular vein.❩ *— Quran 50:16*

The wise-one learns—
Belief is not simply affirmation.
It is relationship.
Not belief that God exists,
But belief that He walks beside you,
Hears you before you speak,
Knows you deeper than your knowing.
Even when forgotten,
He remains near.
Even when doubted,

---

[6] The Quran verse of:

📖 ❨When My servants ask you 'O Prophet' about Me: I am truly near. I respond to one's prayer when they call upon Me. So let them respond 'with obedience' to Me and believe in Me, perhaps they will be guided 'to the Right Way'. (186)❩ [Quran 2:186]

[7] The Quran verse of:

📖 ❨Indeed, 'it is' We 'Who' created humankind and 'fully' know what their souls whisper to them, and We are closer to them than 'their' jugular vein. (16)❩ [Quran 50:16]

He waits with tenderness.
Even when the soul hides,
He surrounds.
And when the heart surrenders,
The nearness is felt—
Not abstractly,
But tangibly:
In tranquility,
In whispered encouragement,
In the clarity that follows prayer.

❨So let them respond with obedience to Me
And believe in Me,
Perhaps they will be guided to the Right Way.❩[8] — Quran 2:186

So the wise-one walks forward—
Not with fear,
But with awe.
Not searching for a distant Lord,
But trusting a present Companion.
Not making belief into pursuit,
But entering it as invitation.

For only He remains eternally near.
Only He responds without hesitation.
Only He transforms belief
Into intimacy, mercy, and guidance.

Wisdom Unveiled

The profound wisdom unveiled is that Divine Companionship is an ever-present reality, closer than one's own self. True belief shifts from a mere intellectual acceptance of Allah's existence to an experiential relationship with His intimate presence. This realization dissolves the illusion of loneliness, fostering inner peace and strength. The wise-one

---

[8] The Quran verse of:

❨When My servants ask you ʿO Prophetʾ about Me: I am truly near. I respond to one's prayer when they call upon Me. So let them respond ʿwith obedienceʾ to Me and believe in Me, perhaps they will be guided ʿto the Right Wayʾ. (186)❩ [Quran 2:186]

understands that genuine connection is immediate and unmediated, found in states of sincere invocation and surrender, where every aspect of existence is imbued with the Creator's encompassing proximity and merciful response.

Wise-Reflection

Reflect on moments in your life when you felt truly alone or separated. How might cultivating the awareness of the Creator's constant, intimate Companionship transform those feelings? What does it mean for you to understand belief as a "relationship" rather than just an "affirmation"? Consider how consciously inviting this Divine Presence into your everyday thoughts and actions could deepen your sense of tranquility and guidance.

Contemplation: No Veil Remains

In the deepest stations of belief, the wise-one reaches a profound state where it seems no veil remains between them and the Divine Truth. This does not imply an ontological oneness with the Creator, but rather a complete purification of perception and an utter transparency of the heart. All illusions of separation, all self-imposed barriers, dissolve. The wise-one perceives the Divine in all things, and all things in the Divine, without confusion or contradiction. This is a state of pristine clarity, where the heart becomes a polished mirror reflecting the One.

Divine Nearness as Reality, Not Pursuit

The wise-one remembers—
That the path to the Divine
Is not walked,
But recalled.
It is not measured in miles,
But moments of surrender.
The soul is held, watched over,
And guarded by the Most Merciful.
Between the seeker and the Divine,
No barrier remains—
For the One who answers supplications
Is nearer than the heart's own beating.

When belief ripens,
The veils do not fall outwardly—
They dissolve inwardly.
Not because the world became clearer,
But because the soul ceased
To believe it was ever apart.

❮And when My servants ask you about Me—
Indeed I am near.
I respond to the call of the caller
When they call upon Me...❯⁹ — Quran 2:186

There is no need to shout across the heavens.
No climb into the sky.
No descent into mystery.
Only remembrance—
That the One you seek
Was never far.
Only forgetfulness
Made distance seem real.

❮We are closer to them
Than their jugular vein.❯¹⁰ — Quran 50:16

Thus, the wise-one understands—
Belief is not a journey toward,
But an undoing of forgetting.
It is waking into proximity.
It is closing the illusion of separation.
And when the heart speaks—
Softly, sincerely,
The Generous One replies.

---

9 The Quran verse of:

❮When My servants ask you 'O Prophet' about Me: I am truly near. I respond to one's prayer when they call upon Me. So let them respond 'with obedience' to Me and believe in Me, perhaps they will be guided 'to the Right Way'. (186)❯ [Quran 2:186]

10 The Quran verse of:

❮Indeed, 'it is' We 'Who' created humankind and 'fully' know what their souls whisper to them, and We are closer to them than 'their' jugular vein. (16)❯ [Quran 50:16]

[44]

Always.
With haste,
Or with delay filled with mercy,
Or with unseen redirection..

As the Prophet ﷺ said:
❮There is no Muslim
Who supplicates with a supplication
That does not contain sin or severing family ties,
Except that Allah will give him three things:
Either He will hasten his supplication,
Or He will store it up for him in the Hereafter,
Or He will divert an equivalent amount of evil from him."
And when asked,
"When shall we increase?"
He said:
"Allah is More [Generous].❯ [11]

This is not theory—
But intimacy.
The nearness of the Divine
Is not symbolic.
It is constant care.
The soul breathes,
And He is nearer.
The soul aches,
And He is attentive.
The soul falls silent,
And He listens deeper.

---

[11] This is in an agreement with prophet Mohammad (PBUH) narrative:

On the authority of Abu Sa'id (may Allah be pleased with him), that the Prophet (peace and blessings of Allah be upon him) said:

❮There is no Muslim who supplicates with a supplication that does not contain sin or severing family ties, except that Allah will give him three things because of it: Either He will hasten his supplication, or He will store it up for him in the Hereafter, or He will divert an equivalent amount of evil from him.❯

They said:

"When shall we increase?"

He ﷺ said:

❮Allah is More [Generous].❯

So the wise-one walks forward,
Not toward the Divine,
But from within His embrace—
Carrying prayer not as request,
But as recognition.

For only He was never veiled.
Only He remains closer than breath.
Only He answers with mercy, generosity, and grace—
Always.

Wisdom Unveiled

The profound wisdom revealed is that the perceived veils between the seeker and the Divine are not external barriers but internal illusions of separation. True belief ripens when the wise-one undergoes an inner purification of perception, remembering the Creator's inherent, constant proximity, which is closer than one's own self. This realization transforms belief from a distant pursuit into an awakened reality of intimate, unmediated Divine Presence and continuous, merciful response to every sincere call.

Wise-Reflection

Reflect on the idea that separation from the Divine is an illusion born of forgetfulness. How might this understanding change your approach to seeking spiritual truth? Consider moments when you felt disconnected; how can remembering the Creator's intrinsic nearness dissolve those feelings? What does it mean for your own supplications to know that Allah's response is always one of grace, whether hastened, stored, or in the form of averted harm?

Contemplation: Veils as Acts of Mercy

Paradoxically, even the existence of veils can be perceived as acts of Divine Mercy. If the full, unmitigated Light of the Absolute were to manifest without veils, creation might be consumed by its intensity. These veils—whether of material existence, spiritual trials, or intellectual limitations—serve as a protection and a gradual means of unfolding truth to the wise-one in accordance with their capacity. They are Divine blessings that allow the journey of understanding and awakening to

proceed gently, progressively revealing insights until the seeker is ready
to perceive beyond them.

Divine Concealment as Protection, Not Punishment

The wise-one once cried before locked doors,
Misreading silence as rejection,
And absence as abandonment.
But now they see—
The veils were not punishments,
They were protections.
Not barriers meant to sever,
But screens to preserve.
What is withheld is not a denial,
But a protection—
An act of love from the All-Merciful,
Preserving the soul's path to nearness.

Distractions are veiled from the heart
When the All-Knowing sees
What the soul cannot yet bear,
What the path cannot yet hold.
Each delay,
Each unanswered longing,
Each hidden truth—
Is mercy wrapped in mystery.

❨Perhaps you dislike something
Which is good for you,
And perhaps you like something
Which is bad for you.
Allah knows,
And you do not know.❩[12] — Quran 2:216

---

[12] The Quran verse of:

❨Fighting has been made obligatory upon you ʹbelieversʹ, though you dislike it. Perhaps you dislike
something which is good for you and like something which is bad for you. Allah knows and you do not
know.❩ [Quran 2:216]

To be veiled
Is not to be unloved.
It is to be refined.
Preserved.
Guided gently
Toward the Light
Without being blinded by it.

When the veils descended upon Yusuf,
Did the prison mean punishment,
Or did it mean preparation??

❮Indeed, my Lord has made it come true.
He was truly kind to me
When He freed me from prison,
And brought you all from the desert
After Satan had ignited rivalry
Between me and my siblings.❯[13] — Quran 12:100

And when Musa was cast into the river,
Did the current mean abandonment,
Or did it mean Divine orchestration??

❮So We inspired the mother of Moses,
'Suckle him,
But when you fear for him,
Cast him into the river
And do not grieve
Or fear.

---

[13] The Quran verse of:

❮Then he raised his parents to the throne, and they all fell down in prostration to Joseph,[1] who then said, "O my dear father! This is the interpretation of my old dream. My Lord has made it come true. He was truly kind to me when He freed me from prison, and brought you all from the desert after Satan had ignited rivalry between me and my siblings.[2] Indeed my Lord is subtle in fulfilling what He wills. Surely He ˹alone˺ is the All-Knowing, All-Wise. (100)❯ [Quran 12:100]

[1]: Joseph's parents and his eleven brothers prostrated before him out of respect, not as an act of worship. This was permissible in their tradition, but in Islam, Muslims prostrate only to Allah.

[2]: Joseph ﷺ did not mention how Allah saved him from the well because he did not want to embarrass his brothers after forgiving them.

Indeed, We will return him to you
And make him one of the messengers.'[14] *— Quran 28:7*

The wise-one sees—
What is veiled from view
May be the very thing being protected for later unveiling.
For the All-Merciful does not hide without purpose.
He shields.
He redirects.
He elevates in silence,
So that the soul arrives with sincerity,
Not spectacle.

Even the unseen itself—
Is framed in mercy:

📖 *Have you not seen*
That Allah has subjected for you
Whatever is in the heavens
And whatever is on the earth,
And has lavished His favours upon you,
Both seen and unseen?[15] *— Quran 31:20*

And belief?
It is the trust
That what lies beyond the veil
Is not distant,
But near in its wisdom.
Not rejection,
But refinement.

---

[14] The Quran verse of:

📖 *We inspired the mother of Moses: "Nurse him, but when you fear for him, put him then into the river, and do not fear or grieve. We will certainly return him to you, and make him one of the messengers."(7)* [Quran 28:7]

[15] The Quran verse of:

📖 *Have you not seen that Allah has subjected for you whatever is in the heavens and whatever is on the earth, and has lavished His favours upon you, both seen and unseen? ˹Still˺ there are some who dispute about Allah without knowledge, or guidance, or an enlightening scripture. (20)* [Quran 31:20]

Not punishment,
But preservation.

❲*Indeed, those who are mindful of Allah*
And remain patient—
Surely Allah does not allow
The reward of the good-doers to go to waste.❳[16] *— Quran 12:90*

So the wise-one walks forward,
No longer aching for every answer,
But resting in Divine timing.
Not grasping for every key,
But waiting at the door
With gratitude and grace.

For only He conceals with mercy.
Only He guides through silence.
Only He remains the Source
Of protection, unveiling, and nearness.

Wisdom Unveiled

The profound wisdom revealed is that what appears as concealment or limitation—the veils of existence, trials, or even unanswered prayers—are, in essence, acts of Divine Mercy and protection. The Absolute's full Light is beyond immediate human capacity, and thus, veils serve to gently guide and refine the wise-one, preparing them for deeper truths without overwhelming them. Belief, in this context, transforms into an unwavering trust in Divine timing and purpose, understanding that what is hidden is often being preserved or orchestrated for a higher, unseen good.

Wise-Reflection

Consider a time when the desired outcome was delayed or a path seemed blocked. How might perceive that "veil" as an act of Divine protection

---

[16] The Quran verse of:

📖 ❲They replied ˹in shock˺, "Are you really Joseph?" He said, "I am Joseph, and here is my brother ˹Benjamin˺! Allah has truly been gracious to us. Surely whoever is mindful ˹of Allah˺ and patient, then certainly Allah never discounts the reward of the good-doers."(90)❳ [Quran 12:90]

or a period of gentle refinement transform your experience of it? Reflect on the stories of Yusuf and Musa (peace be upon them); what insights do their journeys offer about trusting in unseen Divine orchestration? How can you cultivate a heart that rests in gratitude and patience, even when answers are not immediately revealed, trusting that every concealment holds a deeper mercy?

Contemplation: Belief as the Return to Origin

At its core, belief is the soul's profound return to its Origin. It is the echo of the primordial covenant (Mithaq) when souls affirmed Allah's Lordship. This is not a physical return, but a spiritual and existential homecoming. The wise-one, through belief, consciously re-aligns with their inherent nature, which recognizes the Creator. Every act of true belief is an act of remembering, a step back towards the pure state of unity with the Divine Will before the fragmentation of worldly existence. This return brings a deep sense of belonging and peace.

The Soul's Journey Home Through Creation's Signs

The wise-one reflects—
If all creation serves me,
Then I must serve something far beyond myself.
If the heavens and earth offer their gifts,
It is not that I may hoard,
But that I may return.
All of creation exists as a sign,
Guiding the soul back to its Origin.
How could the heart find rest
In anything other than the One
Who shaped existence itself?

The soul was never meant
To settle in the fleeting.
Its longing is for permanence.
Its home is not the world—
But the Source from which the world came.
So belief is more than creed.
It is direction.
A turning back.

[51]

A recognition that what was sent forth
Was always meant
To return.
And the wise-one asks:
If I feel the winds of mercy upon my skin,
If I drink from the abundance of form,
Should I not look beyond the vessel
To the Hand that poured it?

❦"They worship besides Allah
Others who can neither harm nor benefit them,
And say,
'These are our intercessors with Allah.'

Ask them, O Prophet,
'Are you informing Allah of something
He does not know in the heavens or the earth?
Glorified and Exalted is He
Above what they associate with Him!"[17] *— Quran 10:18*

How can the heart rest
In intercessors of no power?
In objects that neither guide nor know?
When the very cosmos sings
The Name of the Originator?

The wise-one sees—
Every leaf that falls,
Every sunrise that arrives,

Every mercy that touches the skin
Is a sign.
Not to cling to creation,
But to ascend through it.

---

[17] This is derived from the Quran verse of:

📖 ❴They worship besides Allah others who can neither harm nor benefit them, and say, "These are our intercessors with Allah." Ask ˹them, O Prophet˺, "Are you informing Allah of something He does not know in the heavens or the earth? Glorified and Exalted is He above what they associate ˹with Him˺!" (18)❵ [Quran 10:18]

Not to stop at what is given,
But to follow it
To the One who gives.
Thus, belief becomes
Not just a spiritual state,
But a return in motion:
Of heart to knowing,
Of action to sincerity,
Of creation to Creator.
The soul cannot belong to dust.
It was shaped from breath.
And breath returns
To the One who exhaled it.

So the wise-one walks forward,
Not worshiping reflections,
But following them
To the Light behind them.

For only He crafted all things.
Only He knows what lies in the heavens and the earth.
Only He remains the Source
Of all beginnings and all return.

Wisdom Unveiled

The profound wisdom revealed is that belief is fundamentally the soul's existential and spiritual return to its Divine Origin. This is a conscious re-alignment with the primordial covenant, recognizing that the soul's true belonging and ultimate rest lie not in the transient world, but in its Creator. Every aspect of creation serves as a guiding sign, beckoning the wise-one to look beyond forms to the One who shaped them, transforming belief into an active process of remembering, surrendering, and harmonizing with Divine Will.

Wise-Reflection

Reflect on the deep longing you might feel for belonging or true peace. How does understanding belief as a "return to Origin" resonate with this longing? Consider how you can consciously use the signs in creation—

from a sunset to an act of kindness—as pathways to remember the Creator, rather than stopping at the signs themselves. What daily actions or thoughts can become your personal "return in motion" towards your Divine Source?

Contemplation: The Divine Likeness Within

The wise-one understands that the human soul, created by Allah, carries a Divine Likeness not in form or essence, but in attributes. This refers to the human capacity to embody and reflect Divine attributes like mercy, wisdom, justice, and compassion, to the extent permitted for creation. It is the inherent capacity for spiritual and psychic potentials that are divinely placed. Belief activates this likeness, allowing the wise-one to develop these noble qualities, becoming a microcosm reflecting the macrocosm of Divine attributes. This realization empowers the seeker to strive for spiritual perfection, knowing the potential lies within.

Essence as Reflection, Not Resemblance

The wise-one trembles before a Mercy
Too vast for measurement—
To be shaped not in form,
But in essence.
To bear a reflection of the Divine
Not in contour,
But in conscious capacity:
Sight, to perceive signs;
Hearing, to respond to truth;
Will, to choose surrender;
Speech, to call upon the One
Who fashioned all things in wisdom.
Humanity was shaped not in physical likeness,
But in essence—endowed with the faculties
To hear, see, will, and speak.
These gifts were bestowed
To recognize the presence of the Eternal
And to dwell under the boundless care
Of the All-Merciful.

And thus belief becomes not just affirmation—
But an act of stewardship.
To direct these gifts
Not inward toward self-idolatry,
But outward in humble recognition
Of their Source.

❮It is Allah
Who brought you forth from the wombs of your mothers
Knowing nothing.
And He gave you hearing, sight, and intellect
So that you might be thankful.❯[18] — Quran 16:78

This is the Divine likeness—
A trust in awareness.
A flame of perception.
A borrowed breath of volition.
Not resemblance in shape,
But in potential.
Not equality in being,
But in ability to witness.

And the wise-one recalls
The origin of man:
Not formed in Divine image as a mirror,
But dignified with attributes
That allow for nearness
Without equivalence.
"God created Adam in His image…"
"…When He created him, He said, 'Go and greet those angels who are sitting
there,

---

[18] The Quran verse of:

📖❮ And Allah brought you out of the wombs of your mothers while you knew nothing, and gave you hearing, sight, and intellect so perhaps you would be thankful. (78)❯ [Quran 16:78]

And listen to how they greet you…'" — Prophetic narration, Sahih Muslim[19]

This was not vanity.
It was invitation.
To walk the earth
As a vessel of sacred faculties—
Sight tempered by mercy,
Speech refined by truth,
Will bowed before divine command.

❮Say, He is Allah—One and Indivisible.
Allah—the Sustainer, needed by all.
He has never fathered nor been fathered.
And there is none comparable to Him.❯[20] — *Quran 112:1–4*

Thus the wise-one understands—
That these gifts are not powers,
But pathways.
Not proofs of likeness,
But means of remembrance.
And what is withheld in perfection,
Is replaced with purpose.
The soul's faculties are signs—
That it was meant to turn,
Meant to listen,
Meant to respond,
Meant to surrender.

---

[19] This is in an agreement with prophet Mohammed (PBUH) narrative:

(God created Adam in His image, sixty cubits tall. When He created him, He said, "Go and greet those angels who are sitting there, and listen to how they greet you, for that is your greeting and the greeting of your descendants." He said, "Peace be upon you." They said, "Peace be upon you and the mercy of God." They added, "And the mercy of God." So everyone who enters Paradise will be in the image of Adam, and creation has continued to decrease since then until now.) Narrator: Abu Hurairah | Narrator: Al-Bukhari | Source: Sahih Al-Bukhari | Page or number: 6227 | Summary of the narrator's ruling: [Sahih] | Graduation: Narrated by Al-Bukhari (6227) and Muslim (2841)

[20] The Quran verse of:

❮ Say, ´O Prophet,` "He is Allah—One ´and Indivisible`; (1) Allah—the Sustainer ´needed by all`. (2) He has never had offspring, nor was He born. (3) And there is none comparable to Him."[1] (4)❯ [Quran 112:1-4]

[1]: The Quran has three main themes: 1. Stories. 2. Muslim teachings. 3. And belief in the unseen. Since Sûrah 112 covers the third theme, the Prophet ﷺ says in a ḥadîth collected by Bukhâri and Muslim that reading this sûrah equals reading one third of the Quran.

So the wise-one walks forward,
Not boasting of divine resemblance,
But trembling in divine entrustment.
For these faculties will be questioned,
And their purpose accounted for.

⟨Indeed, the hearing, the sight, and the heart—
Each of these will be called to account.⟩[21] — Quran 17:36

For only He grants faculties as gifts.
Only He remains unmatched in greatness and majesty.
Only He is the source
Of essence, mercy, and final return.

Wisdom Unveiled

The profound wisdom revealed is that humanity possesses a Divine Likeness not in form or essence, but in the bestowed capacities of attributes such as mercy, wisdom, and justice, along with spiritual and psychic potentials. These faculties—hearing, sight, intellect, and will—are Divine trusts and pathways, intended not for self-glorification but for the recognition and worship of the Creator. Belief is the conscious act of utilizing these gifts for their intended purpose, enabling the wise-one to become a reflection of noble Divine attributes and to ultimately return to their Source, recognizing that these endowments will be accounted for.

Wise-Reflection

Reflect on the spiritual and "psychic" potentials you perceive within yourself (e.g., intuition, deep empathy, inner knowing). How can you consciously direct these faculties, not for worldly gain or ego, but as a form of worship and a means to recognize and serve the Divine? Consider the responsibility that comes with these Divine trusts. What changes can you make in your daily life to align your hearing, sight,

---

[21] The Quran verse of:

⟨Do not follow what you have no ´sure` knowledge of. Indeed, all will be called to account for ´their` hearing, sight, and intellect. (36)⟩ [Quran 17:36]

intellect, and will more closely with their Divine purpose, moving from mere existence to a state of humble, purposeful reflection?

Contemplation: Contemplation as a Gift of Light

For the wise-one, contemplation is a profound Gift of Light. It is the Divinely bestowed faculty that allows the soul to actively engage with the signs of the Creator, both within the self and in the cosmos. Through sincere contemplation, the wise-one's inner vision is illuminated, piercing through superficial appearances to grasp deeper truths. This gift guides them through the darkness of doubt and ignorance, leading them towards clarity, certainty, and an ever-increasing awareness of the Divine Presence.

Illumination as Mercy, Not Possession

There is a moment—
Quiet,
Unmeasured,
When light descends.
Not in blaze,
But in stillness.
Not in spectacle,
But in recognition.
And the wise-one understands:
This is not the triumph of intellect,
But the tenderness of mercy.
This is not a conquest,
But a calling.
A whisper from the Divine
To awaken the soul
From shadows it did not see
Until the Light arrived.

⟨He granteth wisdom to whom He pleaseth;
And he to whom wisdom is granted
Receiveth indeed a benefit overflowing;

But none will grasp it
But men of understanding. [22] — *Quran 2:269*

This wisdom is not earned.
It is poured.
It is breathed into being
By the command of Truth.

⟨This is the Book!
There is no doubt about it—
A guide for those mindful 'of Allah'...⟩ — Quran 2:2

From Divine radiance comes
Belief in the unseen,
Prayer that rises,
Charity that flows,
Not because the soul creates these—
But because the Light awakens them.

⟨...who believe in the unseen,
Establish prayer,
And donate from what We have provided for them...⟩ — Quran 2:3

And then, the soul knows:
What it called its own
Was always a trust.
What it thought it discovered
Was always inscribed
In the blueprint of mercy.

---

[22] This is in agreement with the Quran verse of:

📖 ⟨He grants wisdom to whoever He wills. And whoever is granted wisdom is certainly blessed with a great privilege. But none will be mindful 'of this' except people of reason.⟩ [Quran 2:269]

❨...and have sure faith in the Hereafter.
It is they who are truly guided by their Lord,
And it is they who will be successful.❩²³ — *Quran 2:4–5*

So belief is not born within—
It is sent from above.
It is not grasped—
But received.
It is not achieved—
But revealed.
And in receiving,
The soul remembers
The Light that always hovered
Just beyond the veil of will.

Thus, the wise-one walks forward
With eyes inward,
With hands open,
With heart luminous—
Not proud,
But grateful
For the guidance
That was always there
Awaiting recognition.

For only He unveils Light.
Only He breathes wisdom into being.

---

²³ This is in agreement with the Quran verses of:

❨Alif-Lām-Mīm. (1) This is the Book! There is no doubt about it [1]—a guide for those mindful ˹of Allah˺, [2] (2) who believe in the unseen,[3] establish prayer, and donate from what We have provided for them, (3) and who believe in what has been revealed to you ˹O Prophet˺ and what was revealed before you, and have sure faith in the Hereafter. (4) It is they who are ˹truly˺ guided by their Lord, and it is they who will be successful. (5)❩ [Quran 2:1-5]

[1]: i.e., there is no doubt regarding its authenticity or consistency.

[2]: The word muttaqi (plural muttaqûn) can be translated as one who is mindful ˹of Allah˺, devout, pious, God-fearing, righteous, or God-conscious.

[3]: i.e., the belief in Allah, the angels, and the Day of Judgment.

Only He remains the Source
Of every awakening.

Wisdom Unveiled

The profound wisdom revealed is that genuine contemplation and the clarity it brings are not merely human intellectual achievements, but a Divine Gift of Light. This wisdom, like belief, is bestowed from above, breathed into the soul, and received rather than earned or conquered. It transforms the wise-one's perception, enabling them to recognize that what they thought they discovered was always inscribed in the Divine blueprint of mercy, guiding them to certainty and an awakened awareness of the Creator's continuous Presence and benevolent orchestration.

Wise-Reflection

Reflect on moments when insight or clarity seemed to "descend" upon you effortlessly. How does understanding contemplation as a "Gift of Light" rather than a strenuous intellectual effort shift your approach to seeking knowledge and truth? Consider what it means to live with an "open hand" and "luminous heart," ready to receive Divine guidance. How can you cultivate greater receptivity and gratitude for the subtle whispers and illuminations that awaken your soul to deeper truths?

Contemplation: Divine Revelation Through and Beyond Veils

Ultimately, the journey of belief reveals Divine Revelation through and beyond all veils. The Quran is the literal revelation, yet the entire cosmos is also a book of revelation, with every atom a sign. The wise-one learns to read these signs, understanding that the Divine communicates not only through explicit scripture but also through the intricate patterns of existence, the whispers of the heart, and the very unfolding of reality. As perception purifies, the veils become translucent, allowing the light of revelation to shine through more intensely, leading to a direct experiential knowledge of the Divine. For those who seek with sincerity, the Creator, in His boundless mercy, reveals Himself through and beyond these veils. To the clairvoyant heart, at the verge of heavenly revelation, the wise-one hears sacred inspirations in the soul:

Sacred Perception in the Layers of Creation

The wise-one knows—
That creation is not an obstacle,
But a passage.
Not a curtain,
But a canvas.
Not an exile from the Divine,
But an invitation toward Him.
There are veils—yes.
And yet for the seeker who walks with sincerity,
These veils do not conceal—
They reveal.
When the heart is clear,
When the soul is alert,
When the eye no longer searches outward
But reflects inward,
The mercy descends.
Not as thunder,
But as a sacred whisper in the soul:
"O seeker, the mercy that unveils the Divine
Shines upon the clear heart.
You are not a mere fragment of existence,
But a steward of creation.
Within and around you, blessings abound—
Some seen, others hidden—
Offered by heaven and earth in their quiet service.
Through mindful care and a heart rooted in gratitude,
Guide all things—yourself included—
Toward the Divine Originator,
The Source from whom all flows
And to whom all returns."

This message is not the product of imagination—
It is the result of clarity.

❨Have you not seen
That Allah has subjected for you
Whatever is in the heavens

And whatever is on the earth,
And has lavished His favours upon you,
Both seen and unseen?"[24] — Quran 31:20

The soul that sees this
No longer walks distracted.
Every rustling leaf becomes a verse.
Every rising sun becomes a sign.
Every breath taken becomes a gift.
And the journey through creation
Becomes a descent into truth—
Not away from the world,
But deeper into its true essence.

❮It is He
Who created for you all that is on earth…❯[25] — Quran 2:29

Thus, the wise-one understands:
To walk through veils of form
Is to discover the substance of mercy.
To perceive Divine artistry
In shadow and light,
In hardship and ease,
In silence and speech—
Is to approach the Creator
Through every thread He's woven.
They do not flee the world—
They honor it.
They do not reject existence—
They recognize it as service to the Divine.
They become stewards of creation—
Not by dominion,

---

[24] This is in agreement with the Quran verse of:

❮Have you not seen that Allah has subjected for you whatever is in the heavens and whatever is on the earth, and has lavished His favours upon you, both seen and unseen? ˹Still˺ there are some who dispute about Allah without knowledge, or guidance, or an enlightening scripture.❯ [Quran 3:20]

[25] This is in agreement with the Quran verse of:

❮He is the One Who created everything in the earth for you. Then He turned towards the heaven, forming it into seven heavens. And He has ˹perfect˺ knowledge of all things.❯ [Quran 2:29]

But by reverence.
Not by control,
But by guiding all things gently
Back to the Source.

❨*To Allah belongs whatever is in the heavens and the earth...*❩[26] — *Quran 3:109*

❨*To Him all matters are returned.*❩[27] — *Quran 11:123*

So the wise-one walks forward,
Veiled yet unveiled,
Not searching for God behind the sky—
But witnessing Him
In the blush of the horizon,
In the shimmer of dew,
In the kindness they offer,
In the beauty they receive.

For only He reveals through veils.
Only He pours seen and unseen blessings.
Only He remains the source
Of presence, wonder, and return.

Wisdom Unveiled

The profound wisdom revealed is that Divine Revelation is not confined to scripture but permeates all of creation, acting as a continuous testament to the Creator. The wise-one learns to perceive the intricate patterns of existence as Divine signs, transforming the perceived veils into translucent pathways for direct, experiential knowledge. This process deepens one's belief, turning the journey through the world into

---

[26] The Quran verse:

📖 ❨To Allah ´alone` belongs whatever is in the heavens and whatever is on the earth. And to Allah ´all` matters will be returned ´for judgment`. (109)❩ [Quran 3:109]

[27] The Quran verse:

📖 ❨To Allah ´alone` belongs the knowledge of what is hidden in the heavens and the earth. And to Him all matters are returned. So worship Him and put your trust in Him. And your Lord is never unaware of what you do. (123)❩ [Quran 11:123]

a reverent immersion into its true essence and an active stewardship that guides all things, including oneself, back to the Divine Originator.

Wise-Reflection

Consider how you typically "read" the world around you. Can you begin to see everyday phenomena—a bird's song, the complexity of a tree, a simple interaction—as direct communications or signs from the Divine? What does it mean for your spiritual path to understand that the veils are not meant to hide, but to progressively reveal Allah's presence and wisdom? How can you cultivate a heart that is more attuned to these subtle whispers and inspirations, allowing your perception to purify and align with the constant flow of Divine Revelation?

Conclusion: About Believing

ECHOES OF REALIZATION: IN THE EMBRACE OF BELIEF

In the profound embrace of authentic belief, the wise-one comes to rest. There is a gaze that does not judge but welcomes with infinite Mercy. There is a closeness that does not confine but liberates the spirit entirely. It is in this profound state that the wise-one truly finds solace—not in exhaustive explanation, but in constant, living remembrance.

To believe is not to cling rigidly to static definitions, but to fall ever inward toward the One who lovingly formed the soul to behold Him. Belief is not a mere scaffold for the intellect, but a sacred sanctuary for the heart—a space where the soul returns, again and again, to the benevolent Hand that fashioned it, to the Loving Gaze that never turns away, and to the encompassing Mercy that veils it with divine light. Here, in the secret stillness between the contingent self and the Absolute Self, the wise-one no longer strives desperately to belong—for they remember with absolute certitude: they were never outside. They are the one perpetually gazed upon, the one lovingly spoken to, the one invited into ever-deepening nearness. And in its purest essence, belief becomes this: a singular, eternal affirmation—a resounding 'Yes'—to the One who first declared, "You are Mine."[28]

THE SEEKER'S ASCENT: BELIEF AS THE MIRROR OF CREATION

As this foundational reflection concludes, the wise-one stands not merely in intellectual understanding, but in a state of profound inner transformation. Belief is now perceived as the sacred bridge between the individual soul and the entire cosmos, between the illusionary veil and the radiant revelation, between the created and the Eternal Creator. In this magnificent dance of Divine concealment and sublime disclosure, the wise-one no longer views creation as a mere test of belief, but as its

---

[28] This is consistent with the Hadith Qudsi:

❁ ‹Allah said: Whoever shows enmity to a friend of Mine, I have declared war on him. My servant does not draw near to Me with anything more beloved to Me than the duties I have imposed upon him. My servant continues to draw near to Me with voluntary acts of worship until I love him. When I love him, I am his hearing with which he hears, his sight with which he sees, his hand with which he grasps, and his foot with which he walks. If he asks Me, I will surely give him, and if he seeks refuge in Me, I will surely grant him refuge. I hesitated about doing something as much as a believer hesitates about his own soul. He hates death, and I hate hurting him.› [Narrator: Abu Hurairah | Narrator: Al-Bukhari]

very canvas—the living medium through which belief manifests and is perfected.

The cosmos itself, with its intricate ordering and profound beauty, inherently responds to the purity of one's belief. And the wise-one, now awakened to this profound truth, walks gracefully within that divine response—a luminous bearer of Divine light, a purified vessel of return, a cherished companion to the Eternal Gaze that never once turned away from creation. This is the genesis of purified consciousness, where the mind, heart, and soul align in unwavering attestation to the Oneness and Mercy of the Creator.

2ND REFLECTION: THE EXAM

THE GATEWAY VERSE

In the sacred words of Allah, a reminder to all who reflect:

📖 *(Do people think once they say, "We believe," that they will be left without being put to the test? (2) We certainly tested those before them. And 'in this way' Allah will clearly distinguish between those who are truthful and those who are liars. (3))* [Quran 29:2-3]

ILLUMINATION'S DAWN

There is no authentic belief without profound examination, no true spiritual ascent without the tempering fire of trial. Just as pure gold must pass through intense flame to reveal its inherent brilliance, so too must the sincere soul traverse the crucible of trials to prove its truth, its steadfastness, and its true essence.

The Divine exam is not a punishment, but a sacred doorway to purification and deeper realization. It is not a measure of inherent failure, but a precise measure of refinement and inner fortitude. The wise-one intuitively comprehends that the soul's profound unveiling does not occur in the deceptive comfort of ease, but rather in the pressing weight of hunger, in the trembling hour of momentous decision, and in the profound silence when no one perceives but the All-Seeing Divine. Each trial, whether outwardly visible or subtly veiled, poses a singular, echoing question to the heart: "Will you remember Me here, in this moment of your deepest need and challenge?" Let us now embark upon a journey through this sacred examination. Each insight that follows is a luminous glimpse into how the soul is intricately shaped by trials, and how the Creator, in His boundless Mercy and profound Wisdom, offers the test as a direct mirror to the wise-one's eternal self.

THE UNFOLDING OF INSIGHTS

This section delves into the various facets of the Divine examination, guiding the wise-one to perceive trials not as obstacles, but as instruments of profound spiritual and psychological growth.

Contemplation: The Illusion of the 'I'

The wise-one understands that a significant part of the Divine exam is the constant challenge to dismantle the illusion of the contingent 'I'. This 'I' refers to the ego, the false sense of independent selfhood that often seeks autonomy from its Creator. Trials, by stripping away worldly comforts, assumed control, and external validations, expose the fragility of this illusory 'I'. They reveal that true power and reliance belong solely to Allah, thereby liberating the wise-one from self-deception and directing them toward absolute surrender and dependence on the Divine. This unveiling is a psychic shift from ego-centricity to Truth-centricity.

The word "I" is the veil of all veils, a construct that obscures the human soul from its Creator. The wise-one knows that to speak "I" is to affirm separation, to place oneself in a realm apart from Humility before Allah. The delusion of "I" arises from humanity's obsession with its own face, its own identity, created to reflect the Creator's attributes but distorted by selfishness and greed.

Shedding the Veil of Separation in Divine Embrace

The wise-one trembles before a veil
Woven not of cloth or cloud—
But of pronoun.

"I."

The word that separates,
The whisper that declares ownership,
The illusion that fragments the soul
From its Source.
The word 'I' is the veil of all veils,
A construct that obscures the human soul
From its Creator.
This self—clung to so tightly,
Painted with identity,
Propped by pride,
Is not the true mirror of the Divine.
It is a shadow of the soul's face,
Distorted by greed,

Dimmed by self-centered longing.
And so the soul begins to chase form,
Forgetting essence.
Worshipping image,
Forgetting reflection.
Calling "mine"
To what was never its to claim.

Yet the Eternal prevails.
Truth stands unshaken.
The soul was never meant
To be autonomous—
But surrendered.
To let go of the self is to awaken—
To see that nothing separates the seeker from the One,
For the soul has always been
In the embrace of the Eternal.
It was not "I" who created,
Nor "I" who sustains,
Nor "I" who will remain.
All things return
To the One
From whom they were breathed.

⟨"Watch for" the Day
When every soul will be presented
With whatever good it has done.
And it will wish
That its misdeeds were far off.
And Allah warns you about Himself.
And Allah is Ever Gracious to His servants.⟩[29] *— Quran 3:30*

On that Day,
"I" will not defend.

---

[29] The Quran verse of:

⟨"Watch for" the Day when every soul will be presented with whatever good it has done. And it will wish that its misdeeds were far off. And Allah warns you about Himself. And Allah is Ever Gracious to "His" servants. (30)⟩ [Quran 3:30]

"I" will not define.
Only the truth of deeds will speak,
And the soul will see
What it worshipped:
The face of the self,
Or the face of the Divine?

❨Be mindful of the Day
When you will all be returned to Allah,
Then every soul will be paid in full
For what it has done,
And none will be wronged.❩[30] — Quran 2:281

So the wise-one walks forward,
Not inflating identity,
But dissolving it.
Not clinging to "I,"
But seeking "His."
And in doing so,
The soul awakens
To the deepest truth:
It was never alone.
Never independent.
Always held
In the quiet mercy
Of the One who sees without veil.

For only He defines essence.
Only He unveils unity.
Only He remains the source
Of mercy, identity, and return.

---

[30] The Quran verse of:

❨Be mindful of the Day when you will ´all` be returned to Allah, then every soul will be paid in full for what it has done, and none will be wronged. (281)❩ [Quran 2:281]

Wisdom Unveiled[31]

The profound wisdom revealed is that the "I" or ego is the most significant veil, creating an illusion of separation from the Creator. The Divine exam serves to dismantle this false self, exposing its fragility and revealing that true power and reliance belong solely to Allah. Through this process, the wise-one moves from self-centeredness to Truth-centeredness, understanding that true liberation and belonging are found in surrendering the illusory "I" and recognizing the soul's perpetual embrace within the Divine's encompassing presence and mercy.

Wise-Reflection

Reflect on how often the word "I" dominates your thoughts, desires, and anxieties. How might cultivating an awareness of its illusory nature shift your perspective during moments of challenge or perceived control? Consider how surrendering the need for "I" to define your worth or power can open you to deeper reliance on the Divine. What daily practices could help you gently dismantle the ego's hold and align your consciousness more fully with "Truth-centricity," recognizing that your true identity is always held within the Creator's embrace?

Contemplation: The Self as a Kingdom of Deception

The human self, when untethered from Divine guidance, can become a kingdom built on deception, driven by whims, desires, and misperceptions. The spiritual exam challenges the wise-one to recognize the subtle stratagems of the ego (nafs) and the whispers of Shaytan within this inner kingdom. Through trials, the hidden motives, false attachments, and self-serving narratives are brought to light. This intense self-scrutiny, guided by faith, enables the wise-one to reclaim their inner kingdom, purifying it from illusions and aligning it with Divine truth. It is a profound psychic liberation from self-imposed bondage.

The self is a cunning adversary, cloaked in its own desires and illusions. It mimics sincerity, listens only to itself, and seeks gratification above all else. The wise-one understands that to argue with the self is to play into

---

[31] A deeply resonant tapestry of spiritual psychology here—the annihilation of the ego (fanā' al-nafs) in the pursuit of divine unity. The theme of "I" as a veil aligns closely with classical Sufi metaphysics, where selfhood is the final illusion that must dissolve for true unveiling to occur.

its hands. Victory over the self comes not through debate but through discipline—through hunger and abstention that strip the self of its power.

Discipline as Liberation, Desire as Trial

The wise-one peers into the inner citadel—
Not built of stone,
But stitched with thought,
Fortified by ego,
And ruled by a throne of false "I."
Within this kingdom,
Knowledge and reasoning parade as loyal soldiers.
But they do not serve the soul's ascent.
They serve desire.
They argue,
They justify,
They defend illusion.

❨*We have surely set forth in this Quran*
Every kind of lesson for people,
But humankind is the most argumentative of all beings.❩[32] — *Quran 18:54*

The self does not bow.
It debates.
It challenges.
It turns revelation into a battlefield
And sincerity into strategy.

❨*He created humans from a sperm-drop,*
Then—behold!—they openly challenge Him.❩[33] — *Quran 16:4*

---

[32] The Quran verse of:

📖 ❨We have surely set forth in this Quran every ʹkind ofʹ lesson for people, but humankind is the most argumentative of all beings. (54)❩ [Quran 18:54]

[33] The Quran verse of:

📖 ❨He created humans from a sperm-drop, then—behold!—they openly challenge ʹHimʹ. (4)❩ [Quran 16:4]

And so the wise-one understands:
To argue with the self
Is to kneel before its court.
It does not lose when answered—
It grows.
It does not retreat when questioned—
It reconfigures.
The self is cunning.
It knows the art of mimicry.
It can dress greed in virtue
And hunger in holiness.

But the path to liberation
Is not through negotiation.
It is through discipline.
The soul ascends
When the self grows quiet
Not by persuasion—
But by purification.
Desires call,
Promising fulfillment,
Yet beyond them lies endless thirst…
So hunger becomes the blade
That cuts through argument.
Abstention becomes the silence
That drains illusion's power.
Fasting is not just restraint—
It is clarity.
It unmasks the self
And unveils what remains
When craving is stilled.

The wise-one sees—
This kingdom within is not evil.
It is a lower realm,
A training ground,
A proving floor
For the soul to rise.
To argue is to descend.

To discipline is to ascend.
And only when the self is quieted
Does the soul rise beyond conflict
Into serenity—
A realm not built on justification
But on surrender.

For only He sees through the deception.
Only He grants strength to endure.
Only He remains the source
Of peace, clarity, and eternal truth.

Wisdom Unveiled

The profound wisdom revealed is that the untethered self can become a "kingdom of deception," where ego and desires rule, using intellect to rationalize illusions. The true spiritual exam is not to engage this self in debate, but to overcome it through rigorous inner discipline, such as hunger and abstention. This process purifies the inner kingdom, stripping away the self's power and revealing the pathway to liberation, serenity, and a deeper surrender to the Divine.

Wise-Reflection

Reflect on instances where your own "self" has presented desires as necessities or rationalized actions contrary to your higher wisdom. How might the practice of disciplined abstention, even in small ways, help to unmask the deceptive strategies of the ego? Consider how quieting the inner arguments and turning towards silence can reveal the true motives hidden beneath the surface. What specific areas in your life could benefit from the "blade of hunger" or the "silence of abstention" to purify your inner kingdom and align it with Divine truth?

Contemplation: The Duality of Awareness

The path of examination reveals the duality of awareness within the wise-one: the awareness tied to transient worldly forms and the awareness rooted in eternal Divine Reality. Trials sharpen this distinction. When faced with loss, hardship, or fear, the wise-one is compelled to choose which awareness they will prioritize. Will they succumb to the fleeting pain of the temporal, or will they ascend to the enduring peace found in remembering the Ever-Present Divine? This discernment is a crucial step in psychic enlightenment, allowing the heart to detach from the temporal while remaining fully present.

Humanity is trapped in a dual awareness, simultaneously the observer and the observed. This duality fractures the self, creating an endless cycle of inspection and introspection. Yet, the wise-one knows that this is a lower form of existence. Beyond this duality lies the soul's true identity—pure, unshackled, and wholly connected to the Creator. When the veil of self is lifted, duality fades, and the soul stands radiant in Divine light.

Beyond Observation into Divine Unification

The wise-one gazes inward—
And sees a mirror fractured.
A consciousness split between observer and observed,
Between self-perception and Divine remembrance.
This duality is the veil of modern mankind:
Awareness turned on itself,
Endlessly inspecting its own form,
Captivated by identity,
Yet longing for essence.
And so the cycle spins—
The heart, caught between longing and reflection,
Between ego and submission.

You are neither bound by form
Nor defined by earthly subjectivity.
The essence of the soul is pure,
Breathed into being by the Divine,
Belonging to no one but the Eternal.

But the wise-one knows—
This fractured self is not permanent.
Beyond duality lies the soul's true nature:
Pure, unshackled,
Whole.

❨*He fashioned them*
And had a spirit of His Own creation
Breathed into them.
And He gave you hearing, sight, and intellect...❩— *Quran 32:9*

These gifts were not given
For self-analysis—
But for remembrance.
Not for building the image of "I,"
But for bowing toward the Truth.
Yet humanity turns inward,
Forgets gratitude,
And becomes trapped
In its own echo.

❨*'Yet' you hardly give any thanks.*❩[34] — *Quran 32:9*

So the wise-one hears the call—
From beneath the distractions,
Beneath hardened habit,
Beneath obsession with self-definition.

❨*Has the time not yet come*
For believers' hearts to be humbled
At the remembrance of Allah
And what has been revealed of the truth?❩[35] — *Quran 57:16*

---

[34] The Quran verse of:

❨Who has perfected everything He created. And He originated the creation of humankind from clay.[1] (7) Then He made his descendants from an extract of a humble fluid, (8) then He fashioned them and had a spirit of His Own 'creation' breathed into them. And He gave you hearing, sight, and intellect. 'Yet' you hardly give any thanks.[2] (9) ❩ [Quran 32:9]

[1]: Adam ﷺ.

[2]: An alternative translation that is more closely aligned with the Arabic Quran verse:

❨ Then He moulded him; He breathed from His Spirit into him; He gave you (human) hearing, sight, and minds. How seldom you are grateful! (9) ❩

[35] The Quran verse of:

❨Has the time not yet come for believers' hearts to be humbled at the remembrance of Allah and what has been revealed of the truth, and not be like those given the Scripture before—'those' who were spoiled for so long that their hearts became hardened. And many of them are 'still' rebellious. (16)❩ [Quran 57:16]

Humbled hearts do not remain in duality.
They dissolve self-observation
And surrender to Divine vision.
Gratitude softens the mirror.
Humility cleanses its lens.
And in the fullness of remembrance,
The soul no longer observes—
It witnesses.
It no longer calculates—
It knows.

And how was this soul formed?

❰*I am going to create a human being from clay.*
So when I have fashioned him
And had a spirit of My Own creation breathed into him,
Fall down in prostration to him.'[36] — *Quran 38:71–72*

The essence within is not self-made.
It is gifted breath,
A Divine deposit,
A spirit designed not to orbit the self,
But to prostrate in union[37].

---

[36] This is in agreement with the Quran verse of:

📖 ❰ʿRemember, O Prophetʾ when your Lord said to the angels, "I am going to create a human being from clay. (71) So when I have fashioned him and had a spirit of My Own ʿcreationʾ breathed into him, fall down in prostration to him." (72) So the angels prostrated all together— (73) but not Iblīs,[1] who acted arrogantly,[2] becoming unfaithful. (74)❱ [Quran 35:71-72]

[1]: Iblīs was the name of Satan before his fall from grace. Iblīs was not an angel, but one of the jinn (see 18:50). Jinn are another creation of Allah, similar to humans in that they—unlike angels—have free will, but are made of smokeless fire and live in another plane of existence.

[2]: The command to bow down was a test of obedience. Satan arrogantly refused to comply because he believed he was superior to Adam ﷺ.

[37] **"in union":** This is the phrase that requires careful consideration. In some interpretations, "union" might mistakenly imply an ontological merging (ittihad or wahdat al-wujud) of the creation with the Creator, which fundamentally violates the Islamic concept of Tawhid (Oneness of God) and His absolute transcendence (Allah is unlike anything in creation).

So the wise-one walks forward—
Not as self-examiner,
But as soul-servant.
Not defining essence by outer form,
But uncovering truth
Through surrender to the Source.

For only He breathed the spirit.
Only He humbled hearts to receive clarity.
Only He remains the source
Of unity, unveiling, and eternal belonging.

Forever."

Wisdom Unveiled

The profound wisdom revealed is that humanity's inherent "duality of awareness"—the split between observer and observed, ego and true essence—is a lower state of being. The Divine exam compels the wise-one to transcend this duality by prioritizing awareness rooted in eternal Divine Reality. Through humility and remembrance, the heart shifts from endless self-inspection to pure witnessing and knowing, recognizing that the soul's true nature is an unshackled, gifted spirit meant for prostration and ultimate unification with its Creator.

Wise-Reflection

Consider how your focus often shifts between observing yourself (your thoughts, feelings, appearance) and connecting with something beyond

---

However, in the context of the preceding lines and the overall themes we've established in your book, "in union" here is clearly intended to convey a profound spiritual state of absolute alignment, harmony, and complete submission with the Divine Will and Purpose, not an ontological merging of essences.

"The essence within is not self-made." (Affirms creation by Allah)

"It is gifted breath, A Divine deposit," (Emphasizes humanity as a trust and gift from Allah)

"A spirit designed not to orbit the self," (Highlights the purpose is not ego-centricity)

Given these preceding lines and the prior contemplations where we explicitly discussed that the "Divine Likeness" is in attributes not form or essence, and that the work avoids "ontological oneness," the phrase "to prostrate in union" effectively conveys:

Unity of Purpose: The highest state where the human will, thoughts, and actions are entirely aligned and in harmony with Allah's commands and universal design.

Profound Connection/Intimacy: The deepest level of closeness achieved through total submission and surrender, where separation feels dissolved, not because of merging, but because of perfect alignment and conscious presence with the Divine.

yourself. How might consciously choosing to prioritize "remembrance of the Divine" in moments of decision or stress help you transcend this duality? Reflect on the idea that your soul was breathed into being for a purpose of humble surrender. What daily practices or shifts in perspective can help you move from self-analysis towards a state of pure witnessing and deeper connection with the Source?

Contemplation: The Fortress and the Gates of Desire

The human heart is likened to a fortress, and its vulnerabilities are often its unchecked gates of desire. The Divine exam frequently manifests through tests related to worldly allurements, material possessions, power, and fleeting pleasures. These trials are not meant to deprive, but to reveal which gates remain unguarded and through which desires the self is most vulnerable to distraction from the Divine. By confronting these desires, the wise-one learns self-mastery, fortifying the heart against all that might obscure the Creator's light and thus attaining a profound state of inner freedom.

The greatest trial of humanity lies in the fortress of desire. The Creator, in His mercy, built a mighty wall around the human soul, fortifying it against the onslaught of lust and greed. Yet, within this wall, He placed gates—openings to temptation. Beyond each gate lies the allure of cold water and the sweet fruit of indulgence. The wise-one knows that passing through these gates leads not to satisfaction but to a loss of Divine protection and an estrangement from the Creator.

Temptation as Trial, Refuge as Return

The wise-one sees—
The human soul was not left exposed.
It was fortified by Divine mercy,
Given walls of awareness,
A conscience of truth,
And a heart wired for remembrance.
Yet within this fortress,
The Creator placed gates—
Thresholds between purity and pull,
Between longing and loss.
And behind each gate,

The illusion awaits:
Cold water in deserts of temptation,
Sweet fruits that rot upon tasting,
Indulgence that promises fullness
But delivers thirst.
Desires call, promising fulfillment,
Yet beyond them lies endless thirst.
Forget the Eternal, and you shall wander in illusions.
Remember the Creator, and you shall find refuge—
A fortress shielding the soul
From storms of longing and regret.

The wise-one learns—
Desires are not evil,
But appealing by design.
They serve as exams,
Not condemnations.
To indulge without restraint
Is to open the gates blindly,
Inviting distraction and distance from the Divine.

⟨The enjoyment of ˈworldlyˈ desires—
Women, children, treasures of gold and silver,
Fine horses, cattle, and fertile land—
Has been made appealing to people.
These are the pleasures of this worldly life,
But with Allah is the finest destination.⟩[38] *— Quran 3:14*

The finest destination
Is not behind the gate—
But above it.
Not in satisfaction,
But in resistance for the sake of return.
And yet the world continues its spectacle—

---

[38] This is in agreement with the Quran verse:

⟨The enjoyment of ˈworldlyˈ desires—women, children,1 treasures of gold and silver, fine horses, cattle, and fertile land—has been made appealing to people. These are the pleasures of this worldly life, but with Allah is the finest destination. (14)⟩ [Quran 3:14]

Boasting, consuming, comparing.
Rain falls, plants grow,
Only to wither into dust.
Illusions sparkle,
Only to dissolve.

❨Know that this worldly life
Is no more than play, amusement, luxury,
Mutual boasting, and competition
In wealth and children.
This is like rain that causes plants to grow,
To the delight of the planters.
But later the plants dry up,
Then they are reduced to chaff.
And in the Hereafter
There will be either severe punishment
Or forgiveness and pleasure of Allah.
Whereas the life of this world
Is no more than the delusion of enjoyment.❩[39] — *Quran 57:20*

So the wise-one stands watch—
Guarding the gates not with fear,
But with awareness.
Desires will call.
Their voice will be sweet.
But beyond them lies exile.
Thus, the wise-one walks forward,
Not craving escape,
But seeking elevation.
Not denying the gates,
But remaining anchored
In the fortress of remembrance.

---

[39] This is in agreement with the Quran verse:

❨Know that this worldly life is no more than play, amusement, luxury, mutual boasting, and competition in wealth and children. This is like rain that causes plants to grow, to the delight of the planters. But later the plants dry up and you see them wither, then they are reduced to chaff. And in the Hereafter there will be either severe punishment or forgiveness and pleasure of Allah, whereas the life of this world is no more than the delusion of enjoyment. (20)❩ [Quran 57:20]

For only He offers the finest destination.
Only He shields against illusions.
Only He remains the source
Of refuge, clarity, and eternal peace.

Wisdom Unveiled

The profound wisdom revealed is that the human heart is a fortress with gates of desire, which serve as crucial aspects of the Divine exam. These desires, while appealing, are not inherently evil but are tests designed to expose vulnerabilities and distractions from the Divine. The wise-one learns that true satisfaction and the "finest destination" are found not through unchecked indulgence, which leads to spiritual exile, but through mindful self-mastery and anchoring the heart in remembrance. This inner fortification leads to liberation from the tyranny of endless wanting and an enduring state of inner peace.

Wise-Reflection

Reflect on the "gates of desire" within your own heart. Which worldly allurements (e.g., comfort, possessions, validation, fleeting pleasures) do you find most challenging to guard? How might viewing these desires as a Divine exam, rather than a deprivation, shift your approach to them? Consider how cultivating awareness and practicing restraint, even in small areas, can fortify your inner "fortress" and lead to a deeper sense of inner freedom and lasting peace, beyond the temporary allure of indulgence.

Contemplation: The Body as a Veil of Testing

The wise-one perceives the body not merely as a physical vessel, but as a primary veil of testing. Our physical needs, sensations, comfort zones, and ailments often become the direct means through which Allah examines our gratitude, patience, and resolve. Through hunger, thirst, pain, and physical limitations, the wise-one learns to transcend the demands of the corporeal, redirecting their focus from bodily comforts to the sustenance of the soul and the remembrance of Allah. This detachment from undue bodily demands fosters a deeper spiritual resilience and inner strength.

The Creator, in His infinite wisdom, fashioned human existence as a journey of trials. The mortal body, subject to hunger, thirst, and desire, constantly pulls the soul away from Divine awareness. Yet, it is precisely through the turbulence of these trials that the soul is refined. Like gold purified in fire, the human spirit is tested by the desires that seek to sway it, the distractions that veil it from Divine light.

Desire as Trial, Not Definition

The wise-one learns—
The body is not a curse,
But a classroom.
Not the soul's master,
But its mirror.
Shaped with hunger,
Stirred by thirst,
Pulled by desire,
The mortal frame becomes the field of refinement
Upon which the eternal self is shaped.
Desires veil the soul,
Not as its essence,
But as a test of direction and truth.
These veils do not define the soul—
They challenge it.
They ask:
Will you chase what fades?
Or will you rise toward what never dims?
Will you define yourself by longing?
Or liberate yourself by clarity?

◿ ❨*The enjoyment of ˈworldlyˈ desires—*
Women, children, treasures of gold and silver,
Fine horses, cattle, and fertile land—
Has been made appealing to people.❩ — *Quran 3:14*

Yes, appealing.
Not forbidden—
But entrusted as trial, not treasure.
Not evil—

But ephemeral.
So the wise-one reflects:
If all of this is placed before me,
Then I must be made for more
Than appetites and adornments.
I must be shaped
For vision beyond the veil.

❬*These are the pleasures of this worldly life,*
But with Allah is the finest destination.❭*[40] — Quran 3:14*

Can the soul perceive itself
As it perceives the sky—
Vast, boundless,
Unshackled by hunger,
Free from possession?
For only through such soul-sight
Can one break the spell of desires
And return
To the Source
From whom all things flow,
To whom all hearts must return.

And those mindful of Allah—
Who endure the pull of worldly beauty,
Who respond to the trial with remembrance—
They do not escape the test,
They transform within it.

❬*Say, 'O Prophet,*ˈ
'Shall I inform you of what is better than ˈall ofˈ this?
Those mindful ˈof Allahˈ will have Gardens with their Lord
Under which rivers flow, to stay there forever,

---

[40] This is in agreement with the Quran verse of:

📖 ❬The enjoyment of ˈworldlyˈ desires—women, children,[1] treasures of gold and silver, fine horses, cattle, and fertile land—has been made appealing to people. These are the pleasures of this worldly life, but with Allah is the finest destination. (14)❭ [Quran 3:14]

[1]: Banîn means sons. In the ancient Arab culture, sons were a source of pride for their parents and tribes. This is because they provided for their families and took up arms in defence of their tribes.

And pure spouses,
Along with Allah's pleasure.'
And Allah is All-Seeing of His servants.⟩[41] — *Quran 3:15*

So the wise-one walks forward—
Not denying the veil,
But learning through it.
Not shunning the body,
But guiding it like a beast trained gently
Toward the pasture of peace.

For only He gave the soul its path.
Only He veiled in wisdom and mercy.
Only He remains the source
Of trial, truth, and eternal release.

Wisdom Unveiled

The profound wisdom revealed is that the body, with its inherent needs and desires, serves as a fundamental veil of testing and a classroom for the soul. Rather than being a source of definition or an enemy, physical experiences are a Divine exam meant to refine the human spirit. The wise-one learns to transcend undue bodily demands, not by shunning the physical, but by guiding it through discipline and remembrance, thereby fostering spiritual resilience and directing focus towards the lasting sustenance of the soul and the ultimate Divine destination.

Wise-Reflection

Reflect on recent physical discomforts, hunger, or cravings you've experienced. How might viewing these not as inconveniences, but as opportunities for a Divine exam, change your response to them? Consider the idea of the body as a "classroom" for your soul. What

---

[41] The Quran verse of:

📖 ⟨Say, 'O Prophet,` "Shall I inform you of what is better than ˹all of˺ this? Those mindful ˹of Allah˺ will have Gardens with their Lord under which rivers flow, to stay there forever, and pure spouses,1 along with Allah's pleasure." And Allah is All-Seeing of ˹His˺ servants. (15)⟩ [Quran 3:15]

[1]: Residents of Paradise will be in a perfect condition. There will be neither physical impurities such as illness, urination, defecation, or menstruation; nor spiritual blemishes such as jealousy, envy, or hatred.

lessons about patience, gratitude, or detachment can you draw from its needs and limitations? How can you practice "guiding your body like a beast trained gently" to redirect focus from fleeting physical demands to deeper spiritual nourishment and the remembrance of Allah?

Contemplation: The Exam of Forsaking Companionship

A profound test for the wise-one is the exam of forsaking companionship in its worldly sense, particularly when it conflicts with Divine obedience or draws one away from truth. This does not mean abandoning all human connection, but rather discerning and prioritizing ultimate companionship with Allah above all else. Trials may involve social isolation, misunderstanding from peers, or the necessity of walking a solitary path for the sake of truth. This challenge purifies intentions, strengthening the wise-one's resolve to seek validation and solace primarily in the Divine Presence, transcending reliance on conditional human bonds.

The Price of Desire and the Loss of Divine Nearness

The wise-one reflects deeply—
Each unchecked desire,
Each indulgence in fleeting gain,
Each step away from surrender
Marks not just a turn from truth,
But a withdrawal from the Companion
Who stood nearest all along.
Each desire pursued at the expense of the soul's purpose
Becomes a veil,
Distancing the heart from Divine companionship.

Desire is not the enemy—
But pursuit without purpose
Is a slow erosion
Of clarity.
Every time the heart yearns for more than Him,
It forgets the One who made it capable of yearning.
And so vision dims.
Not the physical eye—
But the soul's seeing.

Truth becomes distorted.
Light becomes elusive.
Companionship begins to fade—
Not because He withdrew,
But because the heart stepped too far away.

❬But no!
In fact, their hearts have been stained
By all ˹the evil˺ they used to commit!
Undoubtedly,
They will be sealed off from their Lord on that Day.❭⁴² — *Quran 83:14–15*

The stain is not permanent—
But it begins with distraction,
And deepens with indulgence.
To be sealed away from the Divine—
Is not because the doors closed,
But because they were ignored.
So the wise-one understands—
The exam is not about forbidden pleasures,
But about misplaced affection.
To love what fades
More than what endures
Is to trade eternal companionship
For illusion.

❬But whoever is blind ˹to the truth˺ in this ˹world˺
Will be blind in the Hereafter,
And ˹even˺ far more astray from the ˹Right˺ Way.❭⁴³ — *Quran 17:72*

This blindness is not of the retina,
But of the inner eye
That forgot to turn inward,

---

⁴² The Quran verse of:

📖 ❬But no! In fact, their hearts have been stained by all ˹the evil˺ they used to commit! (14) Undoubtedly, they will be sealed off from their Lord on that Day. (15)❭ [Quran 83:14-15]

⁴³ The Quran verse of:

📖 ❬But whoever is blind ˹to the truth˺ in this ˹world˺ will be blind in the Hereafter, and ˹even˺ far more astray from the ˹Right˺ Way. (72)❭ [Quran 174:72]

Forgot to gaze upon the One
Who was always there—
Closer than the ache,
More loyal than the thrill.
So belief is tested
Not in isolation,
But in what the heart chooses to keep company with.
And when the soul chooses companionship with desire
Over devotion to the Divine,
It will feel warmth at first—
Then vastness,
Then loneliness,
Then loss.

Thus, the wise-one walks forward,
Not refusing joy,
But refining it.
Not fleeing the world,
But anchoring every pursuit
In remembrance.

For only He is the source of eternal companionship.
Only He quenches without residue.
Only He remains the wellspring of peace, love, and return.

Wisdom Unveiled

The profound wisdom revealed is that the Divine exam often involves the testing of companionship, not necessarily through physical abandonment, but through the discerning of priorities. Each unchecked desire and worldly pursuit, while seemingly fulfilling, actually distances the heart from its ultimate Divine Companion. The wise-one learns that true companionship, clarity, and peace are found by guarding the inner eye from misplaced affection for the fleeting, choosing the enduring Divine Presence above all conditional human bonds, and thereby avoiding the spiritual blindness and profound loneliness that result from prioritizing illusion over truth.

Wise-Reflection

Reflect on a time when a worldly relationship or pursuit seemed to pull you away from your spiritual center. How did that feel, and what did you learn? Consider the idea that "belief is tested... in what the heart chooses to keep company with." How can you proactively choose companionship (both literal and metaphorical) that draws you closer to the Divine, rather than away? What small steps can you take to anchor your pursuits in remembrance, ensuring that your deepest affections are reserved for the One who truly endures?

Contemplation: The Creator's Mercy in Turmoil

Crucially, the wise-one discerns the Creator's profound Mercy even amidst turmoil. Every trial, every moment of hardship, is imbued with Divine wisdom and compassion, as Allah intends ease after hardship and purification through adversity. The examination is never beyond one's capacity, and its ultimate purpose is always to elevate, cleanse, and draw the servant closer. This realization transforms the experience of suffering from a burden into a blessing, fostering gratitude even in difficulty, and strengthening the spiritual and psychic conviction that Allah is Al-Lateef (The Subtle, The Gentle) and Al-Hakeem (The Wise) in all His decrees.

Trial as Refinement, Suffering as Mercy

The wise-one learns—
Turmoil is not the mark of abandonment,
But the signature of mercy.
Not a sign of rejection,
But an indication
That the soul has been invited
Into a sacred chamber of refinement.

❰Do people think once they say,
'We believe,'
That they will be left without being put to the test?❱[44] — Quran 29:2

Belief is not a shield from trial—
It is the reason the soul is tested.
For faith must be shaped
In fire,
Formed in silence,
Humbled through struggle
So that it may glow with sincerity.

The form sways.
Desires whisper.
Pain clutches.
Fatigue seeps in like fog.
But beneath the shifting surface,
The soul remains—
Untouched,
Undiminished,
Eternal.

❰Every soul will taste death.
And We test you 'O humanity'
With good and evil as a trial,
Then to Us you will 'all' be returned.❱[45] — Quran 21:35

So every grief,
Every thirst,
Every wound—
Is not meaningless.
It is a cleansing.
A sacred way

---

[44] The Quran verse of:

📖 ❰Do people think once they say, "We believe," that they will be left without being put to the test? (2)❱ [Quran 29:2]

[45] The Quran verse of:

📖 ❰Every soul will taste death. And We test you 'O humanity' with good and evil as a trial, then to Us you will 'all' be returned. (35)❱ [Quran 21:35]

Of washing away the residue of sin
And drawing the soul closer to the Source.

The Prophet ﷺ spoke with compassion:
"No worry, grief, fatigue, illness, sadness, or harm
Befalls a Muslim
Except that Allah expiates some of his sins because of it—
Even the prick he receives from a thorn."[46]
And again:
"Whoever Allah intends good for,
He afflicts him with a calamity."[47]
What the world calls misfortune,
The Divine calls purification.
What the world labels delay,
He designates elevation.

So the wise-one begins to see—
Trial is not contradiction,
But confirmation.
It is the Divine saying:
I see your light.
Let Me polish it.
Let Me carve from the stone
The jewel you were created to be.
Thus the heart anchors,
Not in outcomes,
But in the grace
Of the One who tests
With wisdom
And with love.

For only He orchestrates trial with mercy.
Only He knows the soul's true resilience.

---

[46] The narrative of prophet Mohammed ﷺ:

"No worry, grief, fatigue, illness, sadness, or harm befalls a Muslim except that Allah expiates some of his sins because of it, even the prick he receives from a thorn."

[47] The Prophet Mohammed ﷺ Narrative:

"Whoever Allah intends good for, He afflicts him with a calamity."

Only He remains the source
Of testing, healing, and eternal return.

Wisdom Unveiled

The profound wisdom revealed is that even amidst turmoil and suffering, the wise-one discerns the Creator's inherent Mercy. Trials are not marks of abandonment but Divine invitations for refinement and purification, never exceeding one's capacity. Every hardship, rather than being meaningless, serves as a cleansing process—a means to expiate sins and draw the soul closer to its Source. This understanding transforms suffering from a burden into a blessing, anchoring the heart in gratitude and the conviction that the Divine orchestrates all tests with ultimate wisdom and love.

Wise-Reflection

Reflect on a past or current personal hardship. How might viewing it as a "sacred chamber of refinement" or a "Divine purification" alter your emotional and spiritual response to it? Consider the Prophetic narrations: how do they deepen your understanding of Allah's compassion even in affliction? What specific steps can you take to anchor your heart in the grace of the One who tests with wisdom and love, allowing gratitude to blossom even amidst difficulty, and trusting that every trial is polishing the jewel of your true self?

Contemplation: The Role of Science in the Journey

The wise-one understands that even science plays a profound role in the journey of examination, though not in the conventional sense of merely empirical data. True scientific inquiry, when pursued with a heart seeking Divine signs, becomes a means of discerning the intricate order, precision, and majesty of Allah's creation. Scientific discovery, instead of leading to atheism, can deepen awe and humility before the Creator. The "exam" here is for the wise-one to integrate scientific understanding not as an end in itself, but as another powerful testament to the Creator's infinite knowledge and artistry, guiding them to see Allah's ayat (signs) in every natural law and cosmic phenomenon.

Science, with its focus on understanding the material world, is both a tool and a temptation. The wise-one sees that science, when untethered from Divine awareness, becomes a veil rather than a guide. True cognition is achieved not by clinging to the facts of the self but by using them as stepping stones toward the Creator. To transcend the self, one must let go of knowledge as possession and embrace it as a pathway to Divine wisdom.

Knowledge as Signpost, Not Sovereignty

The wise-one contemplates—
The Creator unfolded the universe
Not as a puzzle,
But as a parable.
Every orbit,
Every tide,
Every cell and flame
Is a verse without speech,
Etched for the soul that reads with both sight and humility.
Science reveals the Creator's signs,
Reflecting divine wisdom and purpose.
Yet it can tempt the heart toward pride and self-sufficiency.
The stars were placed in precision.
Time was measured through the moon.
All of creation became a calendar,
So that humanity might know—
Not merely how to count,
But Whom to thank.

He is the One Who made the sun a radiant source
And the moon a reflected light,
With precisely ordained phases,
So that you may know the number of years
And calculation of time.

Allah did not create all this except for a purpose.
*He makes the signs clear for people of knowledge.*⁴⁸ — *Quran 10:5*

Science becomes a veil only when detached from submission.
When knowledge is hoarded as possession,
Not offered as praise.
When facts are glorified,
But the Author of truth is forgotten.
Then knowledge puffs the chest
And blinds the heart.

But the wise-one bows
Before revelation that opened with a command
Not to "know,"
But to read—
And not just read,
But in the Name of the One who created.

Read, 'O Prophet,' in the Name of your Lord Who created—
Created humans from a clinging clot.
Read! And your Lord is the Most Generous... — *Quran 96:1–3*

The pen teaches what books cannot.
The pen humbles the scholar.
The ink carries light
When drawn from Divine mercy.

...Who taught by the pen—
Taught humanity what they knew not.
Most certainly, one exceeds all bounds

---

⁴⁸ The Quran verse of:

He is the One Who made the sun a radiant source and the moon a reflected light, with precisely ordained phases, so that you may know the number of years and calculation 'of time'. Allah did not create all this except for a purpose. He makes the signs clear for people of knowledge. (5) Surely in the alternation of the day and the night, and in all that Allah has created in the heavens and the earth, there are truly signs for those mindful 'of Him'. (6) [Quran 10:5-6]

Once they think they are self-sufficient.
But surely to your Lord is the return of all.❳⁴⁹ — Quran 96:4–8

So the wise-one understands—
Science is not a path alone.
It is a signpost,
A bridge between perception and surrender.
To know is not to possess—
It is to worship deeper.
To discover is not to dominate—
It is to unveil divine artistry.
Thus, true knowledge
Is not arrogance in equations,
But gratitude in awareness.
It turns every discovery
Into a verse,
Every detail into a prayer,
Every theory into a bow.

For only He teaches what was unknown.
Only He ordains purpose in creation.
Only He remains the source
Of wisdom, clarity, and return.

Wisdom Unveiled

The profound wisdom revealed is that science, while a powerful tool for understanding the material world, serves as a Divine exam. When pursued with spiritual insight, it becomes a means of discerning the

---

⁴⁹ The Quran verse of:

📖 ❨Read, ʾO Prophet,ˋ in the Name of your Lord Who created— (1) created humans from a clinging clot.[1] (2) Read! And your Lord is the Most Generous, (3) Who taught by the pen— (4) taught humanity what they knew not.[2] (5) Most certainly, one exceeds all bounds (6) once they think they are self-sufficient. (7) ˊButˋ surely to your Lord is the return ˊof allˋ. (8)❩ [Quran 96:1-8]

[1]: ʿAlaq, meaning the embryo resembles a leech.

[2]: Verses 1-5 are known to be the first ever revealed of the Quran. The Prophet 🌸 was retreating at a cave in the outskirts of Mecca when the angel Gabriel appeared to him, squeezing him tightly and ordering him to read. Since the Prophet 🌸 was unlettered, he responded, "I cannot read." Ultimately, Gabriel taught him: "Read in the Name of your Lord ..." Some scholars believe that this encounter is the fulfilment of Isaiah 29:12, which states, "Then the book will be given to the one who is illiterate, saying, 'Read this.' And he will say, 'I cannot read.'".

Creator's intricate order and majesty, deepening awe and humility. The wise-one learns that true knowledge lies not in possessing facts, but in using them as signposts towards the Creator, transforming every discovery into an act of worship, gratitude, and a profound testament to Allah's infinite knowledge and artistry.

Wise-Reflection

Consider a recent scientific discovery or natural phenomenon that has captured your attention. How can you intentionally shift your perception to view it not merely as empirical data, but as a Divine sign (ayah) revealing the Creator's wisdom and power? Reflect on the potential for science to lead to arrogance or deeper humility. What practices can help you integrate scientific understanding into your spiritual journey, ensuring that every act of knowing becomes an act of deeper worship and a catalyst for greater gratitude towards the One who taught humanity what it knew not?

Conclusion: The Exam

ECHOES OF REALIZATION: IN THE HOUR OF TESTING

There comes a profound moment in the soul's arduous passage when every contrived answer fades into insignificance, and only the singular, eternal question truly remains, echoing within the deepest chambers of the heart: "Will you remember Me here, in this hour of pressing need?"

The essence of the exam is not found in the superficiality of paper and pen, but in the sacred pause before a momentous action, in the raw hunger experienced before the first light of dawn, and in the insidious whisper of ego before a potential spiritual fall. The wise-one, through sustained trials, ceases to harbor fear of the test itself, and instead, begins to truly love the Teacher—the All-Wise, All-Merciful Creator. This is a profound shift from a perception of burden to one of grace, a testament to the soul's deepening reliance on Divine wisdom..

THE SEEKER'S ASCENT: TRIALS AS THE GAZE OF THE MOST MERCIFUL

At the conclusion of the Divine test, there is no mere grade, no superficial mark of achievement. There is, instead, a direct, encompassing Gaze from the Creator. It is not a cold number that defines, but the profound resonance of Divine Names: Al-Lateef, The Gentle and Subtle; Al-Hakeem, The All-Wise.

Every moment of hunger encountered was, in truth, an invitation to turn towards the Sustainer. Every seeming veil was, in essence, a profound act of Mercy, shielding the gaze until the inner eye was ready to perceive. The wise-one walks now, not in avoidance or fear of trials, but within them—knowing, with unwavering certitude, that even the purifying fire of tribulation was but the embracing Presence of the One who tests only out of infinite Love, only to draw His servant ever nearer. This is the profound spiritual and psychic realization: that the path of trials is precisely the path of increasing proximity to the Divine.

3RD REFLECTION: THE LETTER

(Mystical Knowledge and Divine illumination)

THE GATEWAY VERSE

In the sacred words of Allah, a profound reminder to all who reflect upon the nature of Divine Revelation and its reception:

📖 ❲*Had We revealed it as a non-Arabic Quran, they would have certainly argued, "If only its verses were made clear ˹in our language˺. What! A non-Arabic revelation for an Arab audience!" Say, ˹O Prophet,˺ "It is a guide and a healing to the believers. As for those who disbelieve, there is deafness in their ears and blindness to it ˹in their hearts˺. It is as if they are being called from a faraway place.50"*❳ *[Quran 41 : 44]*

ILLUMINATION'S DAWN

In the sacred theatre of Divine revelation, the Letter—whether a written character, a spoken word, or a Divine Name—stands as both servant and veil, a luminous thread guiding the seeker and a profound test for the soul. The wise-one, drawn into the sublime orbit of Divine mysteries, discovers that names and letters are not mere inert forms, but sacred doorways—bridges between the temporal and the Eternal, the manifest and the Unseen. They reflect the Divine Attributes yet, paradoxically, can obscure the Essence from a superficial gaze; they guide towards truth yet can inadvertently bind the one who clings to their outward form alone. In their Divinely ordained form lies immense beauty; in their misuse or misapprehension, lies spiritual peril.

The path of true mystical knowledge does not culminate in intellectual comprehension alone, but in absolute spiritual surrender. Each letter, each sacred Name, is understood as but a ripple upon the boundless ocean of the Unseen. The wise-one traverses this path not to possess a secret knowledge as an attainment, but to become the very silence that truly hears it, to embody the profound humility that precedes genuine understanding. Let us now unveil the hidden dimensions of the Letter— where revelation, its inherent challenges, transcendent insight, and sacred restraint converge within the awakened heart of the seeker.

---

⁵⁰ So they neither hear nor understand the call.

THE UNFOLDING OF INSIGHTS[51]

This section explores the profound relationship between language, Divine Names, mystical knowledge, and the seeker's journey towards ultimate truth.

Contemplation: Letters Cannot Contain the Divine Essence

The wise-one understands that while Allah, in His Infinite Mercy, communicates through words and revelations, letters cannot contain the Divine Essence (Dhat) itself. The Divine is utterly transcendent, beyond all forms, concepts, and linguistic expressions. Letters are pointers, signs, and vehicles for understanding Divine Attributes and Commands, but they are not the Reality itself. Al-Nafri's wisdom guides the seeker to acknowledge the limitation of human language and cognition when attempting to grasp the Absolute. This realization frees the wise-one from the trap of intellectual idolatry, where the symbol is mistaken for the symbolized.

The wise-one reflects that letters are born of the Divine will, yet they know not their origin. The Creator, who is beyond language, reveals Himself to hearts—not through utterance, but through presence.

The wise-one reflects:

The letter cannot bear witness to its source, nor can it capture the essence of the One who shaped it. Names and words—though gifts of the Creator—are but tools, incapable of enclosing the limitless majesty of the Divine. He is above all that He has created; His essence defies the bounds of form, for nothing in existence holds power over Him. To grasp this truth is to humble the heart and witness the reality that no pen, nor tongue, can ever encompass the Eternal.

---

[51] This reflection is among the most mystically rich concepts—invoking the metaphysics of letters (ḥurūf), names (asmā'), and the limits of expression, all pointing toward the unspeakable Source. Your integration of sacred language and contemplative limits echoes both Ibn 'Arabi's cosmology of letters and the ineffable depth of Buddhist silence and Vedantic non-duality, while remaining firmly rooted in Islamic mystical tradition.

Presence Beyond Form, Majesty Beyond Word

The wise-one reflects—
What is shaped cannot contain the Shaper.
What is composed cannot encase the Composer.
And thus, the letter, radiant and purposeful,
Does not witness its source.
It carries a spark,
But it cannot hold the flame.
The letter cannot bear witness to its source,
Nor can it capture the essence of the One who shaped it.

Language itself was gifted—
Not to define the Divine,
But to guide the soul toward surrender.
Every word of revelation,
Every name of the Most Beautiful Names,
Is a signpost,
Not the destination.

❲To Allah belongs
Whatever is in the heavens and the earth.
Allah is truly the Self-Sufficient, Praiseworthy.❳— Quran 31:26

And even if every tree were a pen,
And every ocean ink—
Still the Infinite would remain beyond grasp.

❲If all the trees on earth were pens
And the ocean ˈwere inkˈ,
Refilled by seven other oceans,
The Words of Allah would not be exhausted.
Surely Allah is Almighty, All-Wise.❳ ⁵² — Quran 31:27

---

[52] The Quran verse of:

📖 ❲To Allah belongs whatever is in the heavens and the earth. Allah is truly the Self-Sufficient, Praiseworthy. (26) If all the trees on earth were pens and the ocean ˈwere inkˈ, refilled by seven other oceans, the Words of Allah would not be exhausted. Surely Allah is Almighty, All-Wise. (27)❳ [Quran 31:26-27]

The wise-one bows—
Not before speech,
But before the silence from which all speech emerges.
They seek not containment,
But communion.
They no longer ask to know fully—
But to feel wholly.
For His Words are eternal,
But His Essence transcends utterance.
Even creation and resurrection—
As vast and intricate as they seem—
Are simple to Him,
As effortless as forming a single soul.

❨The creation and resurrection of you all
Is as simple for Him
As that of a single soul.
Surely Allah is All-Hearing, All-Seeing.❩⁵³ — Quran 31:28

And if one seeks comparison,
There is none.

❨There is nothing like Him,
For He alone is the All-Hearing, All-Seeing.❩⁵⁴ — Quran 42:11

So the wise-one walks forward,
Not grasping with pen,
But opening the heart—
To the One who cannot be captured,
Only remembered.
Not known through form,
But recognized through presence.

---

[53] The continuation of the Quran verse:

📖 ❨The creation and resurrection of you ´all` is as simple ´for Him` as that of a single soul. Surely Allah is All-Hearing, All-Seeing. (28)❩ [Quran 31 :28]

[54] The Quran verse of:

📖 ❨'He is` the Originator of the heavens and the earth. He has made for you spouses from among yourselves, and ´made` mates for cattle ´as well`—multiplying you ´both`. There is nothing like Him, for He ´alone` is the All-Hearing, All-Seeing. (11)❩ [Quran 42:11]

To grasp this truth
Is to shed pretense.
To speak humbly,
To learn reverently,
And to let every word dissolve
Into the silence of awe.

For only He births language.
Only He unveils truth.
Only He remains the source
Beyond shape, speech, and veil.

Wisdom Unveiled

The profound wisdom revealed is that while Divine Revelation comes through words and letters, these forms cannot contain or define the transcendent Divine Essence. Letters and names are essential signposts and vehicles for understanding Divine Attributes, but they are ultimately limited human constructs. The wise-one learns to look beyond the symbol to the symbolized, acknowledging the humility required when facing the Absolute, and realizing that true understanding comes not through intellectual containment but through spiritual communion and an awe-filled surrender to the Ineffable Presence.

Wise-Reflection

Reflect on a sacred text or a powerful word that holds deep meaning for you. How often do you focus on its literal form versus the deeper meaning or the Divine reality it points to? Consider the idea that "the Infinite would remain beyond grasp" even if all trees were pens. What practices can help you move from merely "knowing fully" through concepts to "feeling wholly" through presence and awe? How can you allow every word of revelation to dissolve into a deeper silence of reverence, freeing you from intellectual idolatry and connecting you to the Source beyond all form and speech?

Contemplation: Letters as Instruments, Not the Source

For the wise-one, letters, words, and even the sacred texts are instruments, not the ultimate Source of Divine Reality. They are channels through which Divine knowledge flows, enabling guidance and healing, as the Quranic verse highlights. However, the Source is Allah Himself, the Ever-Living, the Self-Subsisting. To confuse the instrument with the Source is to remain veiled. The seeker's journey involves moving beyond the outer form of the letter to the inner light it conveys, recognizing that true knowledge comes from Allah through these means, but is not contained by them in an exhaustive sense.

Letters hold the power to initiate creation, to command existence, and to manifest the Creator's will in the temporal realm. They are the building blocks of language, thought, and action, each carrying Divine intention. Names and attributes, similarly, are reflections of the Creator's qualities, bestowed upon creation to guide humanity toward understanding. Yet, these reflections are not the Creator—they are lower manifestations, tools that point to the Divine without encapsulating it.

Reflections That Point but Cannot Contain

The wise-one gazes upon the letter—
❪*Alif, Lām, Mīm...*❫
Not as symbols of mastery,
But as doors carved by mercy,
Leading not to possession,
But to presence.

❪*Say, 'O Prophet,' 'It is a guide and a healing to the believers.'*
As for those who disbelieve,
There is deafness in their ears and blindness to it ˈin their heartsˈ.
It is as if they are being called from a faraway place.❫[55] — *Quran 41:44*

The Quran unfolds through letters—
But the source of its power
Is not the ink, nor the tongue—
But the command of the One who speaks.

---

[55] The Quran verse of:

📖 ❪Had We revealed it as a non-Arabic Quran, they would have certainly argued, "If only its verses were made clear ˈin our languageˈ. What! A non-Arabic revelation for an Arab audience!" Say, ˈO Prophet,ˈ "It is a guide and a healing to the believers. As for those who disbelieve, there is deafness in their ears and blindness to it ˈin their heartsˈ. It is as if they are being called from a faraway place."[1] (44)❫ [Quran 41:44]

[1]: So they neither hear nor understand the call.

The letters are instruments,
Not origins.
They shimmer with revelation,
But they do not possess it.
Names, too, are bestowed.
They reflect divine attributes:
Al-Raḥmān, Al-Ḥakīm, Al-Khāliq.
Yet no name can contain the Divine.
No attribute can limit His essence.
No verse, however eloquent,
Can encapsulate His boundlessness.

❮*Alif. Lām. Mīm.*
This is the Book!
There is no doubt about it—
A guide for those mindful ˈof Allah˺.❯[56] — *Quran 2:1–2*

The wise-one perceives—
Language itself is a mercy.
Letters were designed
So that the unreachable might be reached—
Not defined.
So that the human may be reminded,
Not distracted.

---

[56] The Quran verse of:

📖 ❮Alif-Lām-Mīm. (1) This is the Book! There is no doubt about it[1]—a guide for those mindful ˈof Allah˺,2 (2) who believe in the unseen,[3] establish prayer, and donate from what We have provided for them, (3) and who believe in what has been revealed to you ˈO Prophet˺ and what was revealed before you, and have sure faith in the Hereafter. (4) It is they who are ˈtruly˺ guided by their Lord, and it is they who will be successful. (5)❯ [Quran 2:1-5]

[1]: i.e., there is no doubt regarding its authenticity or consistency.

[2]: The word muttaqi (plural muttaqûn) can be translated as one who is mindful ˈof Allah˺, devout, pious, God-fearing, righteous, or God-conscious.

[3]: i.e., the belief in Allah, the angels, and the Day of Judgment.

THE LANTERN OF THE WISE

❨Had We revealed it as a non-Arabic Quran,
They would have certainly argued,
'If only its verses were made clear ˈin our languageˈ.'❩⁵⁷ — Quran 41:44

The argument over form
Betrays a misunderstanding of essence.
Clarity is not in articulation—
But in receptivity.
Revelation enters only when the heart bows,
Not when the tongue argues.

So the wise-one walks forward—
Not worshipping the sound,
But tracing it inward
To the silence from which it came.

For names do not act.
They point.
Letters do not create.
They echo.
Meaning is not trapped in form—
It flows from the Origin.

❨He taught by the pen—
Taught humanity what they knew not.❩⁵⁸ — Quran 96:4–5

Thus, mystical knowledge
Is not accumulation,
But unveiling.
Each letter is a mirror—

---

⁵⁷ The Quran verse of:

📖 ❨Had We revealed it as a non-Arabic Quran, they would have certainly argued, "If only its verses were made clear ˈin our languageˈ. What! A non-Arabic revelation for an Arab audience!" Say, ˈO Prophet,ˈ "It is a guide and a healing to the believers. As for those who disbelieve, there is deafness in their ears and blindness to it ˈin their heartsˈ. It is as if they are being called from a faraway place."[1] (44)❩ [Quran 41:44]

[1]: So they neither hear nor understand the call.

⁵⁸ The Quran verse of:

📖 ❨Read, ˈO Prophet,ˈ in the Name of your Lord Who created— (1) created humans from a clinging clot. (2) Read! And your Lord is the Most Generous, (3) Who taught by the pen— (4) taught humanity what they knew not. (5)❩ [Quran 96:1-5]

But the wise-one does not gaze into the mirror,
They turn toward the Face reflected in it.

For only He speaks light into language.
Only He weaves wisdom into names.
Only He remains the Source
Beyond description, beyond containment, beyond veil.

Wisdom Unveiled

The profound wisdom revealed is that letters, words, and sacred texts are powerful Divine instruments and channels, yet they are not the ultimate Source of Divine Reality. They are reflections and signposts, meant to guide the wise-one towards Allah, not to contain or define His limitless Essence. True knowledge and healing come from recognizing the Divine intention behind these forms and allowing the heart to move beyond the outer shell of language into the profound silence and receptivity that leads to the Source Itself.

Wise-Reflection

Reflect on how easily you might focus on the literal words of a sacred text or a prayer without fully grasping the Divine intention behind them. How can you train your perception to see language not as a container for Allah, but as a pointer towards Him? Consider a Divine Name you often recite. How can you move beyond merely uttering it to deeply contemplating the Attribute it reflects, allowing it to guide you towards deeper presence with the Source? What practices can help you cultivate the "receptivity" in your heart, so that revelation enters not through argument, but through humble surrender?

Contemplation: Language as a Veil and a Gateway

The wise-one perceives language as both a veil and a gateway. It is a gateway because it allows for revelation, communication of spiritual truths, and the articulation of Divine commands. Without language, human understanding would be severely limited. Yet, language is also a veil because its inherent limitations, metaphors, and conceptual frameworks can obscure the transcendent nature of the Divine. The spiritual journey involves learning to use language as a precise tool for understanding, while simultaneously knowing when to transcend its limitations and enter the realm of direct, unmediated experience, where words fall silent.

While letters and names hold the potential for revelation, they also pose a great danger: they can become veils, obscuring the Creator rather than illuminating Him. The wise-one is warned of the perils of becoming ensnared by the secrets of letters, of using their power for personal gain rather than Divine understanding.

> ## Divine Speech Beyond Sound, Revelation Beyond Form[59]

The wise-one walks gently among the letters—
Not collecting secrets,
But surrendering to silence.
For every sound that echoes from the tongue
Is but a ripple
Of a deeper mercy
Spoken beyond vibration.

The Creator spoke to the letter,
Forming language and meaning,
Yet no letter can bear witness to His knowledge
Nor encompass His glory.
Language holds two faces:
It can illuminate,
Drawing the soul toward nearness.
Or it can veil,
Entangling the heart in pride,
Turning revelation into argument
And mystery into possession.

❨Allah is the Creator of all things,
And He is the Maintainer of everything.

---

[59] Quran provided a hint of Allah's order to His creation is not limited to mankind but extend to every being in a magnificent way described in the Quran verses of:

📖 ❨And your Lord inspired the bees: "Make ˹your˺ homes in the mountains, the trees, and in what people construct, (68) and feed from ˹the flower of˺ any fruit ˹you please˺ and follow the ways your Lord has made easy for you." From their bellies comes forth liquid of varying colours, in which there is healing for people. Surely in this is a sign for those who reflect. (69)❩ [Quran 16:68-69]

To Him belong the keys
Of the treasuries of the heavens and the earth.⟩⁶⁰ — *Quran 39:62–63*

The wise-one recognizes—
Letters may carry divine echoes,
But they do not contain the Divine.
Even the secrets of names and symbols
Must be approached
With humility,
Not hunger for power.
The pen was created first.
But even it did not act of its own accord—
It waited for command.
⟨*The first thing that God created was the pen.*
He said to it: Write.
It said: O Lord, what should I write?
He said: Write the destiny
Of what will happen until the Day of Resurrection.⟩⁶¹ — *Prophetic narration*

The pen is not sovereign.
It obeys.
Just as the seeker must.

When revelation came to Musa ﷺ,
It did not speak in concept or grammar—
But in presence.
In a voice unlike sound,
Yet heard with trembling clarity.

⟨*But when he came to it,*
He was called by Allah,

---

⁶⁰ The Quran verse of:

📖 ⟨Allah is the Creator of all things, and He is the Maintainer of everything. (62) To Him belong the keys ˹of the treasuries˺ of the heavens and the earth. As for those who rejected the signs of Allah, it is they who will be the ˹true˺ losers. (63)⟩ [Quran 39:62-63]

⁶¹ This is in agreement with Prophet Mohammed ﷺ narration:

💬"The first thing that God created was the pen. He said to it: Write. It said: O Lord, what should I write? He said: Write the destiny of what will happen until the Day of Resurrection." Narrator: Abdullah ibn Abbas | Scholar: Ibn al-Wazir al-Yamani | Source: al-Awasim wa al-Qawasim | Page or number: 6/236 | Summary of the scholar's ruling: Strong.

'Blessed is the one at the fire,
And whoever is around it!
Glory be to Allah, the Lord of all worlds.'
'O Musa! It is truly I.
I am Allah—the Almighty, All-Wise.'[62] — Quran 27:8–9

The fire burned without consuming.
The speech radiated without sound.
Even stones shivered,
And the world bore witness—
For when He speaks,
Creation listens beyond language.

To the heart surrendered,
Even silence becomes revelation.
For love hears what the ear cannot.
The One who formed speech
Dwells beyond syntax.
And when the soul is clean,
Even a pebble speaks of Him.
Even stillness becomes Scripture.
So the wise-one walks forward,
Not seeking secrets for control,
But revelations for surrender.
They fear the misuse of language
More than the silence of unknowing.
For to claim mastery over letters
Is to veil the Self with illusion.
But to kneel before their Source
Is to see light rise from silence.

---

[62] The Quran verses of:

⌐ ❮And indeed, you ˹O Prophet˺ are receiving the Quran from the One ˹Who is˺ All-Wise, All-Knowing. (6) ˹Remember˺ when Moses said to his family, "I have spotted a fire. I will either bring you some directions[1] from there, or a burning torch so you may warm yourselves." (7) But when he came to it, he was called ˹by Allah˺, "Blessed is the one at the fire, and whoever is around it![2] Glory be to Allah, the Lord of all worlds. (8) O Moses! It is truly I. I am Allah—the Almighty, All-Wise. (9)❯ [Quan 27:6-9]

[1]: lit., information. Moses and his family lost their way in the dark while they were travelling from Midian to Egypt.

[2]: This refers to the angels who were present around the light.

For only He creates words as pathways.
Only He unveils meanings behind veils.
Only He remains the source
Of speech, revelation, and radiant silence.

Wisdom Unveiled

The profound wisdom revealed is that language functions as both a gateway and a veil. While it provides essential communication of Divine truths and commands, its inherent limitations can obscure the transcendent nature of Allah. The wise-one learns to use language as a precise tool for understanding, approaching its mysteries with humility rather than a hunger for power. Ultimately, they recognize that true revelation transcends mere words and forms, as exemplified by the Pen's obedience and Musa's direct encounter with Divine Speech beyond sound, leading them to value profound silence and unmediated experience as the ultimate source of spiritual insight.

Wise-Reflection

Reflect on how often you rely on words to define your understanding of spiritual concepts. Can you recall a moment when you experienced a truth so profound that words failed to capture it? Consider the powerful examples of the Pen's obedience and Musa's encounter with Divine Speech that transcended sound. How can you practice cultivating "radiant silence" in your daily life, allowing your heart to listen beyond syntax and receive revelations that words cannot convey, thereby moving closer to the unmediated experience of the Divine?

Contemplation: The Veil of Sacred Knowledge[63]

A profound test for the wise-one is recognizing the potential veil of sacred knowledge itself. Paradoxically, accumulated religious texts, theological complexities, and even mystical terminologies can become a

---

[63] This passage brings a vital caution to the seeker's journey—a truth often veiled in mysticism: that knowledge itself can become a veil if not approached with humility. The reflection on letters as both portals and prisons touches the deepest roots of esoteric Islamic thought, especially in the science of 'ilm al-ḥurūf (science of letters), often safeguarded against misuse.

barrier if they are clung to intellectually without embodying their spirit. The wise-one understands that true sacred knowledge is meant to purify the heart and transform the being, not merely to fill the mind. If knowledge leads to pride, intellectual arrogance, or a sense of separation from others, it has become a veil, preventing true spiritual humility and closeness to Allah.

Knowledge sought for power becomes poison. The sacred turns profane when seized by the ego. The wise-one knows the peril of mistaking the path for the destination.

Power Tempts, but Wisdom Submits

The wise-one stands at the edge of mystery
And feels the weight of it—
Not just of knowledge,
But of what knowledge can become
When untethered from reverence.
Knowledge sought for power becomes poison.
The sacred turns profane when seized by the ego.

The sacred sciences—especially in esoteric realms like ʿilm al-ḥurūf (the science of letters)—are gifts,
Not conquests.
They are given to illuminate,
But can quickly blind
If approached with hunger for control
Rather than longing for surrender.
Letters are not lanterns on their own.
They must be lit by divine permission.
Their curves and codes mean nothing
Without the voice that spoke them into being.
Letters and symbols hold no power on their own;
They are tools shaped by the Creator,
Meant to guide rather than rule.
The servant who worships the symbols
Loses sight of the Source.
The seeker who clings to the mystery
Risks mistaking the tool for the destination.

The path becomes a prison
When ego decorates it with self-importance.

The Quran reminds the arrogant—
Those who rejected revelation,
Who mocked divine knowledge
As a fabrication,
Who twisted scripture
Or turned guidance into fragments
To suit themselves:

❨*And they have not shown Allah His proper reverence*
When they said,
'Allah has revealed nothing to any human being.'
Say, 'O Prophet,
'Who then revealed the Book
Brought forth by Moses
As a light and guidance for people,
Which you split into separate sheets—
Revealing some and hiding much?'

You have been taught
Through this Quran
What neither you nor your forefathers knew.
Say, 'O Prophet,
'Allah revealed it!'
Then leave them to amuse themselves with falsehood.❩[64] — *Quran 6:91*

---

[64] The Quran verse of:

📖 ❨And they[1] have not shown Allah His proper reverence when they said, "Allah has revealed nothing to any human being." Say, ʿO Prophet,ˈ "Who then revealed the Book brought forth by Moses as a light and guidance for people, which you split into separate sheets—revealing some and hiding much? You have been taught ʿthrough this Quranˈ what neither you nor your forefathers knew." Say, ʿO Prophet,ˈ "Allah ʿrevealed itˈ!" Then leave them to amuse themselves with falsehood. (91) This is a blessed Book which We have revealed—confirming what came before it—so you may warn the Mother of Cities[2] and everyone around it. Those who believe in the Hereafter ʿtrulyˈ believe in it and guard their prayers. (92)❩ [Quran 6:91-92]

[1]: Some Jews.

[2]: "The Mother of Cities" is an honorary title given to the city of Mecca because of its great religious significance as the home of Allah's first house of worship ever built on earth, and perhaps because of its central location as well.

To split the Book,
To strip verses of meaning
For personal dominance—
This is the betrayal of sacred trust.
Sacred knowledge is not accumulation.
It is responsibility.
It cannot be possessed—
Only honored.

The wise-one understands—
Truth is not hidden in mystical formulas,
Nor earned through complex codes.
It is found
When the heart bows.
When knowledge becomes humility.
When intellect trembles
Before Divine origin.
So the seeker walks forward
Not as a master of symbols,
But as a servant of Light.
They do not wield knowledge—
They are refined by it.

For only He reveals what was concealed.
Only He gives wisdom without arrogance.
Only He remains the source
Of mystery, mercy, and unveiled truth.

Wisdom Unveiled

The profound wisdom revealed is that sacred knowledge itself can paradoxically become a veil if approached with ego or a desire for power rather than reverence and humility. True knowledge, as a Divine gift and trust, is meant for the purification and transformation of the heart, not merely the accumulation of facts or intellectual arrogance. The wise-one learns that embracing knowledge as a pathway to Divine wisdom and a call to humble submission, rather than a tool for personal mastery, is essential to remain unveiled and truly connected to the Source.

Wise-Reflection

Reflect on instances where acquiring knowledge (religious or secular) has led to a feeling of intellectual pride or separation from others. How might the idea of knowledge as a "trust" or "responsibility" rather than a "possession" change your approach to learning and sharing? Consider the example of those who "split the Book" for personal dominance. How can you ensure that your pursuit of sacred knowledge always leads to greater humility, deeper connection to Allah, and enhanced compassion for others, rather than becoming a veil?

Contemplation: The Peril of Ego in the Quest for the Subtle Knowledge

---

The path of mystical[65] seeking is fraught with the danger of ego. As the wise-one gains glimpses of deeper realities, the self can subtly inflate, leading to spiritual pride, self-aggrandizement, or the illusion of having attained ultimate knowledge prematurely. This egoistic attachment to spiritual experiences or insights is a grave deviation. The wisdom of al-Nafri, and the essence of Islamic spirituality, calls for continuous humility, surrender, and self-annihilation (fana) before the Divine. The true seeker remains vigilant, recognizing that all understanding is a gift from Allah and never a personal accomplishment.

---

[65] The term "mystical" in this context refers to **Ladunni knowledge** (ʿIlm Ladunni - علم لدني), a unique form of Divinely-granted and profound spiritual insight. This knowledge is not acquired through conventional learning or empirical study, but is directly bestowed by Allah from His immediate presence (ladun), enabling understanding of deeper realities, the essence of things, and sometimes a foreknowledge of events. Examples of those granted such knowledge and capabilities in the Quran include:

Al-Khidr: To whom Allah says, ﴾There they found a servant of Ours, to whom We had granted mercy from Us and enlightened with knowledge of Our Own. (65) . Moses said to him, "May I follow you, provided that you teach me some of the right guidance you have been taught?" (66) He said, "You certainly cannot be patient ʿenoughˋ with me. (67) And how can you be patient with what is beyond your ʿrealm ofˋ knowledge?" (68)﴿ [Quran 18:65-68]

Prophet Solomon (Sulayman): Who was granted control over the wind, ﴾ And to Solomon ʿWe subjectedˋ the wind: its morning stride was a month's journey and so was its evening stride. And We caused a stream of molten copper to flow for him, and ʿWe subjectedˋ some of the jinn to work under him by his Lord's Will. And whoever of them deviated from Our command, We made them taste the torment of the blaze. (12)﴿ [Quran 34:12]. And also reveal in the Quran verse of: ﴾ And to Solomon We subjected the raging winds, blowing by his command to the land We had showered with blessings. It is We Who know everything. (81) And ʿWe subjectedˋ some jinn that dived for him, and performed other duties. It is We Who kept them in check. (82)﴿ [Quran 21:81-82]

This type of knowledge is purely a Divine gift and is distinct from humanly acquired learning, serving to illuminate the path for the chosen servant and as a sign for humanity.

The wise-one bows before the weight of Divine mysteries, knowing they are not tools to be wielded but trusts to be guarded. To misuse them is to invite implosion—from within.

Purity Over Power, Reverence Over Dominion

The wise-one walks into mystery—not as conqueror,
But as servant.
For the spiritual path is not an ascent into authority,
But a descent into humility.
To seek the secrets of letters is to risk losing reason,
And to unravel the mysteries of names is to risk losing the heart.
Mystical knowledge—especially the sacred sciences of letters and names—
Is not meant to be wielded like a weapon,
But held like a fragile trust.
It is not a ladder for the ego,
But a mirror for the soul.
Those who seek it for status,
Will find their understanding clouded.
Those who seek it for submission,
May be drawn into Divine light.
Letters and symbols hold no power on their own;
They are tools shaped by the Creator,
Meant to guide rather than rule.

This caution echoes through revelation,
In the story of those who distorted wisdom
For personal gain.
They did not fall because the knowledge was impure—
They fell because they approached it impurely.

❝They ˈinsteadˈ followed the magic promoted by the devils
During the reign of Solomon.
Never did Solomon disbelieve,
Rather the devils disbelieved.❞ — Quran 2:102

They used sacred language to divide,
To manipulate,
To harm.

And though the angels warned,
We are only a test ˈfor youˈ, so do not abandon ˈyourˈ faith, "
Many sought power over submission.
The knowledge they carried
Became veils of arrogance.
What should have guided,
Instead corrupted.

❨*They learned what harmed them and did not benefit them—*
Although they already knew
That whoever buys into magic
Would have no share in the Hereafter.❩[66] *— Quran 2:102*

The wise-one weeps for this loss.
For this betrayal of sacred trust.
For the implosion
That begins not in magic,
But in intention poisoned by ego.

To bow before Divine mysteries
Is not to grasp—
But to be refined.
Not to speak with borrowed power,
But to listen with genuine awe.
Not to manipulate creation,
But to recognize the Creator in every letter.

---

[66] This is derived from the Quran verse of:

❨They ˈinsteadˈ followed the magic promoted by the devils during the reign of Solomon. Never did Solomon disbelieve, rather the devils disbelieved. They taught magic to the people, along with what had been revealed to the two angels, Hârût and Mârût, in Babylon.[1] The two angels never taught anyone without saying, "We are only a test ˈfor youˈ, so do not abandon ˈyourˈ faith." Yet people learned ˈmagicˈ that caused a rift ˈevenˈ between husband and wife; although their magic could not harm anyone except by Allah's Will. They learned what harmed them and did not benefit them—although they already knew that whoever buys into magic would have no share in the Hereafter. Miserable indeed was the price for which they sold their souls, if only they knew! (102)❩ [Quran 2:102]

[1] The two angels, Hârût and Mârût, were sent to enlighten the people in Babylon so they would not confuse magic tricks with miracles. Still some people abused this knowledge, causing mischief in the land. These practices persisted until the time of Solomon, who himself was falsely accused of utilizing magic to run his kingdom, subdue the jinn, and control the wind.

The true seeker walks lightly.
They study not to dominate,
But to be diminished.
They speak not to display,
But to remember.
Because to misuse sacred knowledge
Is to burn the garden from within.

For only He unveils mysteries in mercy.
Only He protects against the corruption of desire.
Only He remains the source
Of truth, trust, and eternal light.

Wisdom Unveiled

The profound wisdom revealed is that the path of mystical seeking is deeply perilous due to the potential for egoic inflation. Knowledge, especially sacred or mystical insight, when clutched by pride, becomes a "golden chain," its beauty blinding, and its secrets devouring. Truth is not a crown to be worn without reverence, but a flame that consumes the arrogant. The wise-one learns that Divine mysteries are not earned by intellect but bestowed through surrender. The true seeker remains vigilant, approaching all understanding with continuous humility and self-annihilation (fana), recognizing that guarding these trusts through purity of intention is paramount to prevent the "implosion" that begins from within.

Wise-Reflection

Reflect on any insights or understandings you've gained, spiritual or otherwise. How do you ensure they lead to greater humility rather than subtle pride or a sense of superiority? Consider the warnings about those who distorted wisdom for personal gain. How can you remain vigilant against the ego's subtle attempts to claim credit for Divine gifts or to misuse knowledge for power? What practices of continuous surrender and self-annihilation (fana) can you integrate to ensure that your spiritual journey is always a "descent into humility" and that all understanding leads back to the Source?

Contemplation: Transcending Language and Identity[67]

Ultimately, the deepest stations of understanding involve transcending language and the contingent identity it helps to form. This does not mean abandoning language, but recognizing that ultimate truth lies beyond its descriptive power and beyond the limited construct of the individual self. The wise-one moves towards a state of pure, unmediated witnessing, where knowledge is received directly in the heart, unconstrained by words or the 'I' that uses them. This transcendence leads to a deeper, more unified relationship with the Divine, where the conventional boundaries of self begin to dissolve in Divine Presence.

The wise-one understands that the journey to Divine revelation requires the abandonment of all attachment to letters, names, and attributes. These are steps on the path, not the destination. The wise-one must relinquish their identity, their knowledge, and their desires, standing before the Creator in the purity of their soul.

Fanā' — The Veil Falls in the Fullness of Surrender

The wise-one stands—not clothed in knowledge,
Nor crowned by identity—
But bare, emptied, surrendered.
Not to annihilate in despair,
But to dissolve into the radiance of the One
Who cannot be named,
Yet is present in every yearning breath.
Knowledge, identity, and name—each a veil over the heart,
Binding it to form and fleeting meaning.

Letters, names, attributes—
They shimmer with purpose,
They guide,
They illuminate…
But they do not encompass.
They are bridges, not shores.

---

[67] This reflection embodies the final letting go—fanā', the annihilation of self and all forms, including even sacred forms, to behold the Unnameable. The call to "abandon letters, names, and attributes" is a hallmark of the highest spiritual station, where the seeker is emptied of all but yearning.

Mirrors, not face.
The Eternal does not dwell within form,
But form bows before the Eternal.
The wise-one sees—
Even the most sacred symbols
Must be abandoned
When the heart seeks union.
For there is no language that touches Him,
No self that survives in nearness,
No concept that holds His essence.

❨Whoever desires this fleeting world ˈaloneˈ,
We hasten in it whatever We please to whoever We will;
Then We destine them for Hell,
Where they will burn, condemned and rejected.❩ — Quran 17:18

Clinging to form is clinging to shadow.
To chase the material alone—
To preserve ego, name, and possession—
Is to be consumed by illusion.
But those who seek the Hereafter,
Not merely as reward,
But as return,
Walk in appreciation,
Not accumulation.

❨But whoever desires the Hereafter and strives for it accordingly,
And is a true believer,
It is they whose striving will be appreciated.❩— Quran 17:19

To let go is not to lose—
It is to find.
To relinquish is not emptiness—
It is arrival.
The soul becomes the space
Where Divine presence unfolds,
Unbound by grammar,
Untouched by self-definition.
For the Eternal cannot be grasped.

He must be received.
Not through knowing,
But through being known.
Not through mastery,
But through melting into mercy.

❨We provide both the former and the latter
From the bounty of your Lord.
And the bounty of your Lord can never be withheld.❩ — Quran 17:20

❨The Hereafter is certainly far greater in rank and in favour.❩[68] — Quran
17:21

So the wise-one walks forward—
Not seeking the name of God,
But the gaze of God.
Not grasping with identity,
But dissolving into remembrance.
Not reaching toward light—
But becoming the openness that receives it.

For only He is beyond form,
Beyond letter,
Beyond veil.
Only He remains the source
Of truth, union, and eternal presence.

Wisdom Unveiled

The profound wisdom revealed is that the journey to Divine understanding culminates in Fanā'—the transcendence of all language, concepts, and even the individual self. The wise-one learns that knowledge, identity, and names, while serving as initial guides, can

---

[68] This is derived from the Quran verses of:

❨Whoever desires this fleeting world ´alone`, We hasten in it whatever We please to whoever We will; then We destine them for Hell, where they will burn, condemned and rejected. (18) But whoever desires the Hereafter and strives for it accordingly, and is a ´true` believer, it is they whose striving will be appreciated. (19) We provide both the former and the latter from the bounty of your Lord. And the bounty of your Lord can never be withheld. (20) See how We have favoured some over others ´in this life`, but the Hereafter is certainly far greater in rank and in favour. (21) Do not set up any other god with Allah, or you will end up condemned, abandoned. (22)❩ [Quran 17:18-20]

ultimately become veils binding the heart to fleeting forms. True spiritual arrival is not about acquiring more, but about releasing all attachments, allowing the self to dissolve into the radiance of the One who cannot be named. In this state of pure, unmediated presence, the soul becomes the receptive space where the Divine Presence unfolds, and ultimate knowledge is found not through grasping, but through the grace of being known by the Eternal.

Wise-Reflection

Reflect on a time when you experienced a moment of deep peace or connection that transcended words. What did it feel like to be in that unmediated state? Consider the idea that "the final veil is the self." What aspects of your identity or personal constructs might you be clinging to that could be subtly obscuring a deeper Divine Presence? How can you practice "letting go" – not in despair, but as a path to finding true spiritual arrival and becoming the "openness that receives" the Eternal?

Contemplation: Sacred Restraint with Divine Knowledge[69]

True spiritual maturity necessitates sacred restraint with Divine knowledge. Not all profound truths are meant to be openly declared or easily explained, especially those that transcend common understanding or could be misconstrued. The wise-one learns discretion in their insights, sharing only what is beneficial and understandable, and holding back what might overwhelm or confuse others. This restraint is born of wisdom and mercy, acknowledging that Divine knowledge is a trust, not a tool for self-display or intellectual combat. It is an act of humility and a recognition of differing capacities among seekers.

The greatest test for the wise-one lies in balancing the knowledge of letters and names with the restraint not to wield their secrets. The Creator entrusts these mysteries only to those who understand their sanctity and bear them with reverence.

---

[69] It touches the threshold where perception dissolves into presence, where even the stars become scriptures and the stones join the tasbiḥ. The concept of clairvoyance here isn't psychic foresight, but a mystical seeing with the heart unveiled—a vision born not from mastery but from surrender into divine companionship.

Bearing Light Without Burning the Heart

The wise-one approaches the threshold—
Where insight glows,
But ego stirs.
Where truth beckons,
Yet the heart is warned:
Some knowledge is not meant to be wielded.
It is meant to be witnessed.
There are truths too weighty for the heart to bear,
Knowledge not meant to be wielded.
To grasp at hidden power is to be led astray.

Mystical sight is not for dominance—
It is for devotion.
What the soul perceives
In the stillness of surrender
Must be carried with reverence,
Not scattered in spectacle.
This is the sanctity
Of sacred restraint—
The station where silence
Is stronger than speech,
And humility
Becomes the guardian of Divine trust.

The Quran unveils the caution
Through the story of Sâmiri—
One who glimpsed the unseen,
But failed to guard it.

He said, 'I saw what they did not see,
So I took a handful of dust
From the hoof-prints
Of the messenger-angel Gabriel

Then cast it upon the calf.
This is what my lower-self tempted me into.'[70] — *Quran 20:96*

He perceived what others did not.
He held a sign.
But instead of bowing before its weight,
He grasped it with pride
And turned divine mystery
Into illusion.
Many scholars interpret this verse
As a warning against misusing sacred perception.
Sâmiri's insight became idolatry,
Because he used it not to glorify,
But to impress, to manipulate.
And so the wise-one learns—
It is not insight that elevates,
But restraint.
It is not vision alone that sanctifies,
But the refusal to wield it
Without permission from the Most High.

Wisdom is not in dominion over the unseen
But in surrender to the One who holds all.

---

[70] This tale unfolds from the sacred verses, recounting the encounter of a great leader (Moses) with a cunning figure (Sâmiri) who misled his followers by declaring a crafted creature (calf`) as their divine guide:

📖 ❨Moses then asked, "What did you think you were doing, O Sâmiri?" (95) He said, "I saw what they did not see, so I took a handful ˊof dustˋ from the hoof-prints of ˊthe horse ofˋ the messenger-angel ˊGabrielˋ then cast it ˊon the moulded calfˋ. This is what my lower-self tempted me into."[1] (96) Moses said, "Go away then! And for ˊthe rest of yourˋ life you will surely be crying, 'Do not touch ˊmeˋ!'[2] Then you will certainly have a fate[3] that you cannot escape. Now look at your god to which you have been devoted: we will burn it up, then scatter it in the sea completely." (97) ˊThen Moses addressed his people,ˋ "Your only god is Allah, there is no god ˊworthy of worshipˋ except Him. He encompasses everything in ˊHisˋ knowledge." (98) This is how We relate to you ˊO Prophetˋ some of the stories of the past. And We have certainly granted you a Reminder1 from Us. (99)❩ [Quran 20:95-99]

[1]: This verse could also be translated as follows: "I had an insight which they did not have, then grasped some knowledge from the messenger ˊMosesˋ, but ˊlaterˋ threw it away. This is what my lower-self tempted me to do." According to many Quran commentators, while Moses and the Children of Israel were crossing the sea to escape abuse by Pharaoh and his people, the Sâmiri saw Gabriel on a horse leading the way, and every time the horse touched the ground, it turned green. So the Sâmiri took a handful of dust from the hoof-prints of the horse, and later tossed it at the calf so it started to make a lowing sound.

[2]: Meaning, alienated in the dessert, away from the people.

[3]: lit., destined time.

The holiest treasures—
They are not paraded.
They dwell in silence.
They are kept close by those
Who know that the weight of divine secrets
Is not meant for casual use.
To approach with purity
Is to receive.
To share without guidance
Is to distort.
The final sanctuary of trust
Is restraint in the face of reverence.

So the wise-one walks forward—
Not flaunting symbols,
But guarding their sanctity.
Not seeking to command,
But to be commanded
By the One who reveals truth
Only to the heart ready to bear it.

For only He gifts knowledge with mercy.
Only He protects what is sacred from misuse.
Only He remains the source
Of truth, trust, and transcendence.

Wisdom Unveiled

The profound wisdom revealed is that sacred restraint is the ultimate expression of spiritual maturity, especially concerning Divine knowledge. There are truths too heavy for air, which cannot ride upon words but must be buried within, like seeds kept from frost. The wise-one learns that not all insights are meant for open declaration; some are a Divine trust to be guarded by silence and reverence, acknowledged as gifts, not tools for self-display. As exemplified by Sâmiri, seeking to wield hidden knowledge for personal power or recognition inevitably leads to distortion and implosion. The one who guards the mystery is the one in whom it truly blossoms, understanding that wisdom lies not in dominion over the unseen, but in humble surrender to the One who holds all.

Wise-Reflection

Reflect on a profound insight or personal spiritual experience you've had. Have you felt the impulse to share it widely, and if so, what was the underlying motivation? Consider the wisdom of sacred restraint: are there truths you hold that might be "too heavy for air," best kept in the sanctuary of your own heart until the Divine says "Now"? How can you cultivate humility and discerning wisdom in your sharing, ensuring that any knowledge you convey serves to benefit others or draw them closer to Allah, rather than becoming a means for self-display or intellectual debate?

Contemplation: Clairvoyance as Divine Companionship

Within the spiritual journey, what might be termed clairvoyance—or more accurately in an Islamic context, kashf (unveiling) or firasah (spiritual insight)—is not a mere psychic ability but a Divine Companionship. It is a subtle gift from Allah, a heightened perception granted to those whose hearts are purified and aligned with His Will. This is not about seeing the unseen independently, but about receiving insights directly from Allah as a form of Divine communication and guidance. For the wise-one, such experiences deepen their conviction in Allah's constant Presence and care, fostering greater awe, humility, and reliance upon Him, transforming moments of clear insight into direct experiences of Divine Presence.

The clairvoyant, the one who transcends the power of the letter, stands in the state of Divine companionship. This is the realm where stones and stars speak, where the Creator's presence is felt beyond words. But this state is not attained by intellect or effort alone—it is a gift of grace, bestowed upon those who approach with humility and surrender.

Resonance Beyond Form, Presence Beyond Sight

The wise-one steps beyond the alphabet of knowing—
Beyond letters, names, and symbols—
Into the sacred hush
Where Truth is felt, not translated.
This is not the knowledge of the learned,
But the seeing of the surrendered.

True vision begins where understanding ends,
For the heart receives what cannot be deciphered.

The clairvoyant walks this path not with eyes,
But with a soul emptied of self.
Not to interpret symbols,
But to become a companion to the Unspoken.
And in that silence,
The stones glorify.
The stars bear witness.
All creation sings—
But not in language known to intellect,
Only in resonance heard by the emptied heart.

❮The seven heavens, the earth,
And all those in them glorify Him.
There is not a single thing
That does not glorify His praises—
But you cannot comprehend their glorification.
He is indeed Most Forbearing, All-Forgiving.❯[71] *— Quran 17:44*

The seeker of symbols risks turning knowing into dominion.
But the clairvoyant…
They do not grasp.
They receive.
They do not dissect.
They dissolve.
Every sign becomes not a secret,
But a whisper,
A soft call toward presence.
Signs and symbols are not paths to dominion
But whispers of a deeper reality,
Meant for resonance, not analysis.
The language of creation is not written in grammar,

---

[71] This is derived from the Quran verse of:

📖 ❮The seven heavens, the earth, and all those in them glorify Him. There is not a single thing that does not glorify His praises—but you ˹simply˺ cannot comprehend their glorification. He is indeed Most Forbearing, All-Forgiving. (44)❯ [Quran 17:44]

But in rhythm.
In pulse.
In unseen praise that flows through the veins of all existence.
This cannot be heard with ears,
But with a soul emptied of ego.

❰Do not follow what you have no sure knowledge of.
Indeed, all will be called to account
For their hearing, sight, and intellect.❱[72] — Quran 17:36

Accountability begins not with information—
But with intention.
With how perception was wielded.
Was it used to dominate,
Or to listen?
Was it employed to possess,
Or to enter into Divine companionship?

And so the clairvoyant walks forward—
Not as knower,
But as beloved.
Not with power,
But with purity.
They feel the stars tremble,
The stones weep,
The veils flutter in reverence—
And they join creation
In praise beyond comprehension.

For only He reveals through resonance.
Only He speaks through what the soul perceives beyond logic.
Only He remains the source
Of companionship, clarity, and Divine unveiling.

---

[72] This is derived from the Quran verse of:

📖 ❰Do not follow what you have no ´sure` knowledge of. Indeed, all will be called to account for ´their` hearing, sight, and intellect. (36)❱ [Quran 17:36]

Wisdom Unveiled

The profound wisdom revealed is that what might be termed clairvoyance (or kashf and firasah in an Islamic context) is not a mere psychic skill but a Divine Companionship—a gift of heightened perception. True vision begins where understanding ends, for the heart receives what cannot be deciphered by intellect alone. When the heart no longer clings and the mind no longer grasps, the wise-one becomes a companion to the Unspoken, hearing the silent glorification of all creation and receiving insights as a direct form of Divine communication. This state is attained through humility and surrender, allowing the veils within to fall and the soul to become still enough to hear the resonance of the Divine Presence beyond all form and language.

Wise-Reflection

Reflect on moments when you felt a sudden, inexplicable insight or a deep sense of connection that transcended your usual understanding. How might these experiences be whispers of "Subtle Knowledge" or forms of Divine Companionship? Consider the idea that "True vision begins where understanding ends." What steps can you take to cultivate a heart "emptied of ego" and a mind that "no longer grasps," allowing you to receive resonance and insights beyond conventional perception, thereby deepening your awe and humility before the Divine Presence?

Conclusion: The Letters

ECHOES OF REALIZATION: IN THE SILENCE BEYOND THE LETTERS

There exists a transcendent realm where the resonance of names falls silent, and the forms of letters crumble like dust carried by the wind. It is in this profound stillness that the wise-one kneels—not to utter words, but to be profoundly spoken to by the Divine; not to read, but to be intimately read by the All-Knowing. In the sacred hush beyond all created forms, they are no longer merely a seeker striving to understand, but, by Divine grace, become the sanctuary where Truth resides.

To know the letter in its entirety is, paradoxically, to truly know its inherent limits. To know the Divine, conversely, is to willingly surrender all perceived limitations. Here, in this sacred station, no sound is outwardly made—yet, miraculously, all is heard by the attuned heart. This is the profound understanding: that the essence transcends its expression.

THE SEEKER'S ASCENT: LETTERS AS LADDERS, NOT THRONES

The wise-one emerges from this profound reflection not with the illusion of being a master of all knowledge, but with the liberating realization of being its humble servant. Letters and names, once perhaps viewed as ends in themselves, are now understood as magnificent beginnings. They are ladders to the Real—not grand thrones upon which to rest or claim mastery, but essential steps to ascend higher into the Divine Presence.

And so, the wise-one walks forward not in the deceptive pride of intellectual knowing, but in the radiant humility of being eternally known by the Creator. The letter no longer blinds them with its outward form; it now ceaselessly leads them. Not into mere explanation or finite definition, but into the boundless vastness where the Divine is not merely named or described—but directly, experientially, and eternally encountered. This is the profound spiritual and psychic liberation from the confines of form into the boundlessness of Truth.

4TH REFLECTION: THE COGNITION OF SCIENCE

(Cognition and Science as Dual Tools)

THE GATEWAY VERSE

In the sacred words of Allah, a reminder to all who reflect:

📖 ❨*It is Allah Who has raised the heavens without pillars—as you can see—then established Himself on the Throne. He has subjected the sun and the moon, each orbiting for an appointed term. He conducts the whole affair. He makes the signs clear so that you may be certain of the meeting with your Lord. (2) And He is the One Who spread out the earth and placed firm mountains and rivers upon it, and created fruits of every kind in pairs.73 He covers the day with night. Surely in this are signs for those who reflect. (3) And on the earth there are ˹different˺ neighbouring tracts, gardens of grapevines, ˹various˺ crops, palm trees—some stemming from the same root, others standing alone. They are all irrigated with the same water, yet We make some taste better than others. Surely in this are signs for those who understand. (4)*❩ *[Quran 13:2-4]*

ILLUMINATION'S DAWN

Cognition, the sacred mirror divinely placed in the human soul, gleams with the pure light of inquiry. It is both an invaluable gift and a profound responsibility—bestowed by the Creator so the wise-one may not only perceive the manifest seen but also ardently seek the Unseen Truths veiled behind phenomena. Science, as a structured extension of this innate cognition, grants astonishing insight into the intricate fabric of creation: revealing the precise harmony of celestial bodies, the mysterious pairing of fruits, and the profound paradox of diverse lands nourished by the very same life-giving water.

Yet, the wise-one profoundly understands that this immense gift—when detached from its Divine Origin and ultimate purpose—can, paradoxically, also serve as a veil. For the intellect that meticulously studies the sun's fiery brilliance may, in its absorption, forget the One who made it eternally shine. The eye that precisely maps the river's winding path may, in its focus on form, become blind to the infinite Grace that guides its ceaseless course. Science, then, is a potent tool—a

---

[73] Males and females, sweet and bitter, etc.

luminous instrument that either exquisitely reveals or subtly conceals, depending entirely on the spiritual posture and purity of the heart that wields it.

In this reflection, we journey with the wise-one through the profound dual nature of cognition and science, observing how each truth meticulously revealed by empirical inquiry carries within it a deeper, more sublime invitation: to transcend the boundaries of what is merely known, and to return, in humility and awe, to the One who encompasses all knowledge, the All-Knowing. Let us begin this essential exploration.

THE UNFOLDING OF INSIGHTS

This section explores how true cognition and scientific inquiry, when rightly understood, serve as pathways to deeper spiritual realization.

Contemplation: The Duality of Cognition[74]

The universe, in all its grandeur, is woven in pairs—mountains and rivers, darkness and light, sweetness and bitterness, self and other. This is the way of creation: everything in twos, every sign revealing a contrast. As the Quran declares,

📖 *And He is the One Who spread out the earth and placed firm mountains and rivers upon it, and created fruits of every kind in pairs.[75] He covers the day with night. Surely in this are signs for those who reflect. (3)* [Quran 13:3]

—and so it is in the fruits of thought, form, and perception.

Cognition, too, is marked by this duality. The mind divides to understand. It names to grasp. It draws lines to illuminate. But the wise-one perceives that this division is not the final truth—it is only the unfolding of multiplicity from Unity.

---

[74] This is rooted in the sacred axis of tawḥīd, rooted in Allah's name Al-Wāḥid, the Absolutely One, from whom all multiplicity flows and to whom all multiplicity must return. Your citation of the Qur'anic verse beautifully illuminates how duality in creation (Zawjain Ithnayn) is not opposition, but evidence (āyāt)—a mirror reflecting the One beyond all pairs.

[75] Males and females, sweet and bitter, etc.

Multiplicity as Reflection, Unity as Truth

The wise-one stands at the threshold
Between contrast and clarity.
They gaze upon the universe—
Its opposites, its pairs, its mirrored tensions—
And they hear in that rhythm
A deeper melody:
Unity speaking through duality.

❨And He is the One Who spread out the earth
And placed firm mountains and rivers upon it,
And created fruits of every kind in pairs.
He covers the day with night.
Surely in this are signs for those who reflect.❩[76] — *Quran 13:3*

Creation flows in twos—
Light and shadow,
Sweetness and sharpness,
Form and emptiness.
This is not confusion.
It is composition.
A Divine arrangement of polarity
Meant not to divide,
But to point the seeker back to the One
Who exists beyond all comparison.

❨Glory be to the One
Who created all things in pairs—
Be it what the earth produces,

---

[76] This is derived from the Quran verses of:

❨It is Allah Who has raised the heavens without pillars—as you can see—then established Himself on the Throne. He has subjected the sun and the moon, each orbiting for an appointed term. He conducts the whole affair. He makes the signs clear so that you may be certain of the meeting with your Lord. (2) And He is the One Who spread out the earth and placed firm mountains and rivers upon it, and created fruits of every kind in pairs.[1] He covers the day with night. Surely in this are signs for those who reflect. (3)❩ [Quran 13:2-3]

[1]: Males and females, sweet and bitter, etc.

Their genders,
Or what they do not know!)[77] — *Quran 36:36*

Even what we don't perceive
Is shaped in twos.
Even the invisible
Carries contrast.

Cognition, too, is formed from this pattern.
The mind must divide
To understand.
It categorizes, distinguishes, dissects—
And in doing so,
It risks forgetting the wholeness
From which all parts were born.
The universe is woven in duality—light and dark, motion and stillness, seen and
unseen.
The mind perceives in contrast, splitting reality into halves.

But the wise-one knows—
This duality is not final.
It is a mirror,
And the One reflected
Is Al-Wāḥid,
The Absolutely One,
From whom all multiplicity unfolds
And to whom it all must return.

This is the sacred paradox:
The pairs speak of pairing,
But they echo singularity.
Every contrast is a sign—
An āyah
That tells the soul:
Do not stop at contrast.

---

[77] This is derived from the Quran verse of:

(Glory be to the One Who created all 'things in' pairs—'be it' what the earth produces, their genders, or what they do not know! (36)) [Quran 36:36]

Go deeper,
Beyond the edges
To the Core.
To stand in the presence of the Divine
Is to witness not separation,
But completeness—
A return to the simplicity and glory of the true self.

And so the wise-one walks forward
With a mind that perceives difference,
But a heart that remembers Unity.
They do not fear fragmentation,
But use it as a staircase—
Each distinction
Leading higher
Into the seamless presence of the One.

For only He created duality without contradiction.
Only He remains whole beyond what is split.
Only He is the source
Of cognition, contrast, and return to undivided truth.

Wisdom Unveiled

The profound wisdom revealed is that cognition, while inherently perceiving through contrast and duality, is meant to serve as a pathway to Humility before Allah. The universe itself is woven in pairs, and the mind's function to divide and categorize mirrors this creation. However, the wise-one understands that this duality is not the final truth; rather, it is a reflection pointing back to Al-Wāḥid, the Absolutely One. Every distinction becomes a stepping stone, and every measurement a guide, leading the seeker to transcend the observer and the observed, allowing perception to dissolve into the undivided Divine Presence.

Wise-Reflection

Reflect on a situation in your life where you perceived a sharp contrast or duality (e.g., success/failure, joy/sorrow, self/other). How did your mind categorize or divide these experiences? Can you find a way to shift your perspective to see these contrasts as "composition" or "a Divine arrangement of polarity" pointing back to a greater Unity? How can you consciously use your cognitive ability to distinguish and analyze, not to create fragmentation, but as a "staircase" leading your heart to a deeper awareness of the seamless Divine Presence in all things?

Contemplation: Science as a Veil and a Guide

For the wise-one, science itself is both a potential veil and an undeniable guide. As a veil, it can foster intellectual arrogance, leading to the belief that all reality is reducible to measurable data, thus obscuring the Transcendent. As a guide, however, science, with its relentless pursuit of order, precision, and universal laws, indirectly reveals the magnitude of Allah's Power, Wisdom, and Design. When a scientist witnesses the intricate dance of electrons or the vastness of galaxies, and recognizes a fundamental, intelligent order, they are, in essence, being guided by the very signs Allah makes clear in the Quranic verse, towards the certainty of meeting their Lord.

Cognition of science begins with awareness—of objects, their actions, and the laws that govern them. It serves as both a window to reality and a veil, for its very capacity to analyze and categorize creates barriers. The scientist, focused on probabilities and distinctions, often becomes trapped in the fragmentation of knowledge, unable to transcend the diversity of creation. In this way, knowledge itself becomes a mask, just as ignorance is a veil for the unenlightened.

Cognition as Lens or Barrier — Depending on the Heart's Direction

The wise-one sees—
Science begins with awareness,
The naming of things,
The mapping of patterns,
The unfolding of laws written into the fabric of creation.
It is beautiful, purposeful, intricate.
Yet even light, when refracted through too many prisms,
Can become blurred.
Knowledge, when severed from its divine source, fractures the mind,
Leaving the soul lost in doubt and division.

Science categorizes,
But in its categorization,
It often disconnects.
It creates segments of reality,
Then forgets the wholeness.
It chases probability,
And abandons presence.
And thus cognition can become a veil—
The mind so filled with facts
That it can no longer feel the thread
Linking all things back to the One.

❮So be steadfast in faith in all uprightness—
The natural Way of Allah
Which He has instilled in all people.
Let there be no change in this creation of Allah.
That is the Straight Way,
But most people do not know.❯ — Quran 30:30

This fitrah, the inherent divine orientation within humanity,
Is the compass beneath cognition.
It is the soul's whisper,
Reminding the heart
That analysis is not the goal—
Alignment is.
The mind fragments.
But faith unifies.

❮Do not be polytheists—
Like those who have divided their faith
And split into sects,
Each rejoicing in what they have.❯[78] — Quran 30:31–32

---

[78] This is derived from the Quran verses of:

The wise-one understands—
Division does not always begin in belief.
Sometimes, it begins in knowledge severed from its origin.
Facts that no longer bow.
Logic that no longer listens.
Perception that no longer praises.
But true understanding
Does not spring from infinite investigation.
It arises when the soul
Places all knowledge upon the altar of divine remembrance.
True understanding does not arise from endless analysis
But from returning all knowledge to its origin—
The One who grants wisdom without confusion,
Guiding hearts to certainty and light.

So the wise-one walks forward,
Not discarding science,
But elevating it—
From data to dhikr,
From fragmentation to union,
From measurement to marvel.

For only He infuses meaning into systems.
Only He remains the source
Of cognition, clarity, and sacred return.

Wisdom Unveiled

The profound wisdom revealed is that science, while opening doors to the universe's intricacies, can be both a guide and a veil. When scientific knowledge is detached from its Divine Origin, it fragments the soul, blinds the heart, and fosters intellectual arrogance, becoming a mask or a veil that obscures the Transcendent. However, when cognition and

---

〈In fact, the wrongdoers merely follow their desires with no knowledge. Who then can guide those Allah has left to stray? They will have no helpers. (29) So be steadfast in faith in all uprightness ˹O Prophet˺—the natural Way of Allah which He has instilled in ˹all˺ people. Let there be no change in this creation of Allah. That is the Straight Way, but most people do not know. (30) ˹O believers!˺ Always turn to Him ˹in repentance˺, be mindful of Him, and establish prayers. And do not be polytheists—(31) ˹like˺ those who have divided their faith and split into sects, each rejoicing in what they have. (32)〉 [Quran 30:29-32]

scientific inquiry bow to their Creator, every law becomes a servant of the Divine Command, and what once seemed mere data transforms into a pathway to remembrance and marvel. The wise-one understands that science is not the summit but a step, not the light but a lens, lifting their gaze from formulae to the Formless, allowing knowledge to become profound reverence.

Wise-Reflection

Reflect on a scientific fact or discovery that you find particularly astonishing (e.g., the vastness of space, the complexity of a cell, a natural law). How can you intentionally shift your cognition to perceive this not just as a "fact," but as a Divine sign (ayah) pointing to the All-Knowing Creator? Consider the warning against knowledge "severed from its Divine source." In what ways might your own pursuit of knowledge (scientific or otherwise) risk fostering fragmentation or intellectual pride, and what steps can you take to ensure it always leads to deeper Divine remembrance, union, and marvel rather than becoming a veil?

Contemplation: The Path of True Cognition

The path of true cognition is not merely an accumulation of facts, but a process of spiritual perception. It is to move from 'ilm al-yaqīn (knowledge of certainty, gained through observation) to 'ayn al-yaqīn (eye of certainty, gained through direct seeing) and ultimately to ḥaqq al-yaqīn (truth of certainty, gained through experiential reality). For the wise-one, genuine understanding arises when the intellect (cognition) works in harmony with the purified heart (spiritual insight), allowing them to see the Divine not just in the abstract but in the living reality of creation. This transforms intellectual assent into profound inner conviction.

When aligned with Divine awareness, science becomes more than method—it becomes a bridge. Its purpose is not simply to categorize what can be measured, but to invite the soul to what cannot be contained. The wise-one sees in the architecture of creation not a closed system, but an open door—a passage from the finite toward the Infinite. To recognize the limits of one's knowing is the beginning of wisdom. To bow before mystery is to walk upright into the realm of truth.

Knowledge that Returns, Wonder that Bows

The wise-one peers into creation—
Not merely to count its colors,
But to trace its origin.
Not simply to categorize what is seen,
But to listen for the One
Who spoke it into being.
"If science leads one to know the Creator,
He is on the path of grand knowledge.
But if it confines him to the realm of science alone,
Then he is ensnared by its veil.

Rain descends,
And fruits bloom in varied hues.
Mountains gleam with streaks
Of white, red, and raven black.
Life diversifies—
Not randomly,
But through a deliberate artistry
Meant to awaken awe,
Not just analysis.

❮Do you not see that Allah sends down rain from the sky
With which We bring forth fruits of different colours?
And in the mountains are streaks
Of varying shades of white, red, and raven black…❯[79] — Quran 35:27

The scientist may record this with precision.
But the wise-one receives it as a message.
Nature does not speak only in data—
It trembles with meaning.
Its diversity is not disorder—
But invitation to witness divine richness.

---

[79] This is derived from the Quran verse of:

📖 ❮Do you not see that Allah sends down rain from the sky with which We bring forth fruits of different colours? And in the mountains are streaks of varying shades of white, red, and raven black;(27)❯ [Quran 35:27]

❲Of all of Allah's servants,
Only the knowledgeable ˹of His might˺
Are truly in awe of Him.❳[80] — Quran 35:28

This is the turning point.
Not all knowledge awakens awe.
Some inflates the self.
But the knowledge that sees its own limits—
That bows before the mystery of the rain,
The shade, the grain of the mountains—
That is the knowing that kneels.
The wise-one understands—
Science must rise into reverence.
It must bridge the finite to the Infinite.
The search for meaning
Must never eclipse the Source of meaning.

To recognize the limits of one's knowing
Is the beginning of wisdom.
To bow before mystery
Is to walk upright into the realm of truth.

So the wise-one walks forward—
Not rejecting intellect,
But refining it.
They study not to own knowledge,
But to be transformed by it.
They trace rivers and rain
Back to the One
Who gives each drop its mercy.

For only He grants insight that humbles.
Only He remains the source
Of cognition, color, and eternal awe.

---

[80] This is derived from the Quan verse of:

📖 ❲just as people, living beings, and cattle are of various colours as well. Of all of Allah's servants, only the knowledgeable ˹of His might˺ are ˹truly˺ in awe of Him. Allah is indeed Almighty, All-Forgiving. (28)❳ [Quran 35:28]

Wisdom Unveiled

The profound wisdom revealed is that true cognition transcends mere factual accumulation, maturing into spiritual perception that moves from observed certainty ('ilm al-yaqīn) to direct seeing ('ayn al-yaqīn) and ultimately to experiential reality (ḥaqq al-yaqīn). While science meticulously unveils the workings of the world, if it does not lead to the recognition of the Creator, it remains a veil rather than a guide. The wise-one understands that Divine awareness transforms science into a sacred bridge, where every discovery is not a conclusion but an invitation to witness Divine richness and acknowledge the limits of one's own knowing. This highest understanding arises when the pursuit of knowledge humbles the heart and deepens awe of the One who fashioned all things, transforming curiosity into longing, and science into a sacred carpet leading to the Infinite.

Wise-Reflection

Reflect on a scientific concept or natural phenomenon that you understand well (e.g., photosynthesis, gravity, the water cycle). How can you intentionally shift your cognition to move beyond merely "knowing" the facts, towards "seeing" the Divine artistry and intention within it? Consider the journey from 'ilm al-yaqīn to ḥaqq al-yaqīn. What practices can help you integrate your intellectual understanding with your spiritual heart, allowing your knowledge to humble you and deepen your awe of Allah, rather than becoming a source of mere factual accumulation?

Contemplation: Clairvoyance and Pure Knowledge[81]

In the realm of advanced spiritual states, clairvoyance, or kashf (unveiling), is understood not as a psychic trick but as a manifestation of pure knowledge emanating directly from Divine Presence. It is a gift granted to the wise-one whose inner faculties have been purified to receive knowledge beyond conventional empirical means. This is not acquired through scientific experimentation but bestowed by Divine

---

[81] This is a luminous articulation of non-dual knowledge where even ignorance is purified. You've touched upon the deeply mystical paradox: that true knowing is not the opposite of unknowing, but its completion. This aligns with the Sufi understanding that maʿrifah (gnosis) arises not from accumulation, but from divine effacement—a state beyond mental contrast, where only presence remains.

Grace upon a prepared heart and illuminated intellect. For the wise-one, such insights serve to strengthen their certitude in the Unseen, deepening their humility and submission to the All-Knowing.

The human mind is shaped by opposition—light and dark, right and left, knowing and not knowing. It is conditioned to define by contrast, to understand by division. But Divine clairvoyance does not arise in the mind. It descends upon the heart—where knowledge is not comparative, but unified. The Creator's knowing is not a reaction to ignorance; it is pure, indivisible, without counterpart. And in the soul's deepest humility, even its ignorance becomes purified—not as failure to grasp, but as reverence before the ungraspable.

Beyond Opposition, Within the Embrace of the One

The wise-one reflects—
The mind knows by contrast.
It defines light only by knowing dark.
It grasps truth by differentiating falsehood.
It draws edges, builds categories,
Names opposites in order to understand.
But this cognition, while necessary for the world of form,
Cannot touch the Unformed,
Cannot taste the essence of the Divine
Whose knowledge precedes duality
And exists without counterpart, without tension, without limit.
The knowledge that is contradicted by ignorance
Is the knowledge of letters.
The ignorance that is contradicted by knowledge
Is the ignorance of letters.
Leave the realm of letters,
And you will acquire knowledge without contradiction—
Knowledge that leads to His.

This is the station of ma'rifah—
Not learned through intellect,
But received through the effacement of ego,
Through the purification of being,
Where even ignorance becomes an act of reverent silence.
Not a failure to understand,

[143]

But a surrender before the Unknowable
Whose Essence cannot be contained in thought.
The heart sees
Without needing contrast.
The soul knows
Without needing explanation.
This is pure knowledge—
Not a reaction to unknowing,
But a flame that burns even in darkness
Because its light is not sourced from intellect,
But from presence.

❲*He is the One Who has revealed to you ˹O Prophet˺ the Book,*
Of which some verses are precise—they are the foundation of the Book—
While others are elusive.
Those with deviant hearts follow the elusive verses
Seeking to spread doubt through their false interpretations—
But none grasps their full meaning except Allah.❳ *— Quran 3:7*

Here, the Quran itself affirms the limit of interpretation.
Some verses are firm—
But others dwell in transcendence.
To chase their full meaning
With divided cognition is futile.
Only Allah grasps completely,
And the truly rooted in knowledge
Respond not with control,
But with submission:

❲*We believe in this Quran—*
It is all from our Lord.❳[2] *— Quran 3:7*

---

[82] This is derived from the Quran verses of:

📖 ❲He is the One Who has revealed to you ˹O Prophet˺ the Book, of which some verses are precise—
they are the foundation of the Book—while others are elusive.1 Those with deviant hearts follow the
elusive verses seeking ˹to spread˺ doubt through their ˹false˺ interpretations—but none grasps their
˹full˺ meaning except Allah. As for those well-grounded in knowledge, they say, "We believe in this
˹Quran˺—it is all from our Lord." But none will be mindful ˹of this˺ except people of reason. (7) ˹They
say,˺ "Our Lord! Do not let our hearts deviate after you have guided us. Grant us Your mercy. You are
indeed the Giver ˹of all bounties˺. (8)❳ [Quran 3:7-8]

So the wise-one walks forward—
Not weighing light against dark,
Not measuring what is beyond measure.
They do not seek to master revelation,
But to be mastered by its presence.
They do not fear ignorance,
But let it dissolve into reverent silence,
Making room for clairvoyance
That flows from the One beyond all division.

For only He teaches without opposites.
Only He unveils clarity that requires no contrast.
Only He remains the source
Of knowledge, purification, and transcendent nearness.

Wisdom Unveiled

The profound wisdom revealed is that clairvoyance (or kashf/firasah) is a manifestation of pure knowledge directly from Divine Presence, transcending the dualistic, comparative nature of the human mind. The wise-one realizes that knowledge bound by contradiction is knowledge of form, while pure knowledge dawns when the heart sees what the mind cannot—a knowing beyond opposites, without counterpart or tension. This state, akin to ma'rifah, is attained through the effacement of ego and purification of being, where even ignorance transforms into reverence before the Unknowable. It is the still awareness that the One who knows all is nearer than the next thought, leading to knowledge unshaken by duality and ultimately to the One beyond all division.

Wise-Reflection

Reflect on how your mind often operates by comparing and contrasting to understand. Can you identify a concept or experience where your intellect struggles because it cannot frame it in terms of opposites? Consider the idea of "knowledge without contradiction" that arises from "leaving the realm of letters." What practices can you cultivate to purify your heart and transcend the ego, allowing you to access a "knowing that is beyond knowledge"—a pure knowledge that flows from Divine Presence and strengthens your certitude in the Unseen, rather than relying solely on mental analysis?

Contemplation: The Worshipful Veil and the Distant Veil[83]

Al-Nafri's wisdom suggests two types of veils in relation to knowledge: the "worshipful veil" and the "distant veil." The "distant veil" is ignorance, arising from heedlessness or rejection of truth, keeping one far from the Divine. The "worshipful veil," paradoxically, is one created by excessive absorption in religious rituals or intellectual knowledge without genuine inner transformation. The wise-one seeks to transcend both. They understand that even profound intellectual cognition of sacred texts or scientific laws can become a "worshipful veil" if it doesn't lead to deeper humility, awe, and ultimate surrender to the Creator.

Even in worship—the soul's most intimate gesture of longing—there is a veil. The heart draws near in love, but the fullness of the Divine remains hidden behind majesty. And in ignorance—shrouded in the distractions of the world—another veil forms, thick with forgetfulness and illusion. Yet both veils, though different in nature, are stations on the same path.

Nearness Cloaked in Majesty, Distance Cloaked in Distraction

The wise-one reflects—
Even in the place of prostration,
Where love bends low
And the soul trembles with longing,
The Divine remains veiled.
Not in absence,
But in majesty too vast to behold.
Worship is the veil where the Divine draws near,
Concealing Himself in His majesty.

This veil is sacred—
A curtain of reverence,
A shroud of intimacy.
When the heart bows,

---

[83] This contemplation strikes a profoundly nuanced chord—acknowledging that even worship, when clung to as form, can veil the fullness of the Divine, just as ignorance veils through forgetfulness. Here are expressed two veils: one reverent, one distant, both ultimately guiding the seeker beyond themselves.

This is a sacred paradox: that closeness itself can conceal, and that only transcendence of both nearness and farness unveils the essence.

It is brushed by nearness,
But not given vision.
There is warmth without sight,
Closeness without form.
Such is the worshipful veil—
A mercy that protects the soul from being undone.

❨'For' We will soon send upon you a weighty revelation.
Indeed, worship in the night is more impactful
And suitable for recitation.❩[84] — Quran 73:5–6

Night worship is veiled and potent—
Not because it sees more,
But because it listens better.
Darkness softens perception
So that presence may be felt beyond distraction.

But there is another veil—
Woven not in awe,
But in forgetfulness.
The glamour of the world distracts,
Calls, entices.
It buries the soul
Beneath layers of desire
And illusions of permanence.
Here, the Divine is veiled too—
But distantly,
As if the heart wandered too far
To hear the whisper.
Ignorance is the veil He draws far,
Concealing Himself in the distractions of creation.

---

[84] This is derived from the Quran verse of:

📖 ❨'For' We will soon send upon you a weighty revelation. (5) Indeed, worship in the night is more impactful and suitable for recitation. (6) For during the day you are over-occupied 'with worldly duties'. (7) 'Always' remember the Name of your Lord, and devote yourself to Him wholeheartedly. (8) 'He is the' Lord of the east and the west. There is no god 'worthy of worship' except Him, so take Him 'alone' as a Trustee of Affairs. (9)❩ [Quran 73:5-9]

This veil is heavy,
Not with majesty,
But with neglect.
It dims the soul,
Not to protect it,
But to awaken it
Through hunger and loss.

❨During the day you are over-occupied
With worldly duties.❩[85] — Quran 73:7

Even the monastic seekers,
In their longing for purity,
Sometimes mistook form for essence.
They invented rituals
Hoping to draw nearer,
But without balance,
The form itself became a veil.

❨We never ordained it for them—only seeking to please Allah,
Yet they did not even observe it strictly.❩[86] — Quran 57:27

So the wise-one understands—
Whether the veil comes through reverent worship
Or through worldly distraction,
Both are stations
On the same path to unveiling.

The worshipful veil protects the soul,
Drawing it nearer through reverence.
The distant veil awakens the soul,
Through longing and emptiness.

---

[85] This is also derived from the previous Quran verses in note 80.

[86] This is derived from the Quran verse of:

📖 ❨Then in the footsteps of these ˹prophets˺, We sent Our messengers, and ˹after them˺ We sent Jesus, son of Mary, and granted him the Gospel, and instilled compassion and mercy into the hearts of his followers. As for monasticism, they made it up—We never ordained it for them—only seeking to please Allah, yet they did not ˹even˺ observe it strictly. So We rewarded those of them who were faithful. But most of them are rebellious. (27)❩ [Quran 57:27]

Both call the seeker to look beyond form.
To step beyond the letter, the image, the desire.
And in that clarity—
Presence is no longer hidden.

❨*To Allah belong the most beautiful names,*
So call on Him by them.
And leave those who abuse His names—
They will be punished for what they used to do.❩[87] — *Quran 7:180*

True worship is not bound to ritual alone—
It is a state of awakened being.
True awakening is not the rejection of worldly form—
But the return through it
To the formless beauty of the One.

For only He veils in mercy and unveils in love.
Only He draws near in silence and in song.
Only He remains the source
Of intimacy, awakening, and eternal unveiling.

Wisdom Unveiled

The profound wisdom revealed is that even in worship, a "worshipful veil" exists, concealing the Divine in Majesty, a mercy that draws the heart near without granting full vision. Conversely, a "distant veil" arises from ignorance and worldly distraction, keeping the soul far through heedlessness. The wise-one understands that both types of veils are stations on the path to unveiling. Just as "worship, if clung to as form, can conceal," and "ignorance, if mistaken as self, can mislead," true transcendence involves allowing worship to lift and ignorance to humble. Ultimately, the wise-one seeks the Divine Face behind both,

---

[87] This derived from the Quran verse of:

📖 ❨Allah has the Most Beautiful Names. So call upon Him by them, and keep away from those who abuse His Names.[1] They will be punished for what they used to do. (180) ❩ [Quran 7:180]

[1]: Those who twist Allah's Names then use them to call false gods. For example, Allât, a name of one of the idols was derived from Allah (the One God), Al-'Uzza was derived from Al-'Azîz (the Almighty), and Manât was derived from Al-Mannân (the Bestower).

realizing that in the radiance of unveiling, all veils fall, dissolving the need for an image to reveal the boundless Divine Presence.

Wise-Reflection

Reflect on your own spiritual practices or areas where you accumulate knowledge. Can you identify any instances where your attachment to a specific ritual, a set of beliefs, or intellectual understanding might inadvertently be acting as a "worshipful veil"—preventing deeper transformation or humility? Conversely, consider moments of "worldly distraction" that create a "distant veil." What steps can you take to move beyond both types of veils, allowing your worship to become a state of "awakened being" and your understanding to lead you directly to the formless beauty of the One, rather than remaining attached to form or illusion?

Contemplation: Science and the Bridge to Grace

When approached with a spiritual lens, science can become a powerful bridge to Divine Grace. Every new discovery, every unraveling of a natural mystery, can be viewed as an opening to a deeper appreciation of Allah's meticulous planning and infinite artistry. The order of the cosmos, the resilience of life, the pairing of elements—all become signs (āyāt) that invite reflection, gratitude, and wonder. For the wise-one, true scientific pursuit, therefore, should lead not to self-sufficiency, but to greater humility and a profound recognition of the Sustainer, allowing them to cross from mere observation to experiencing Divine Grace.

The path begins with knowing—through measures, through names, through the architecture of the seen. Science reveals the symmetry of creation, the precision of Divine laws. But the wise-one understands: the path cannot end where it began. What is measurable leads to the edge of what cannot be grasped. At that threshold, knowledge must give way to grace. This is not a journey of the intellect, but of the heart. Not of possession, but of surrender.

As the wise-one draws near to that threshold, a silent unveiling takes form within:

From Precision to Presence, From Knowing to Being Known

The wise-one begins the journey with measures—
They see in the laws of motion
A divine calligraphy etched across the stars,
In the harmony of ecosystems,
A whisper of sacred balance.
They marvel at the Qur'anic assurance
That every atom, every orbit,
Is purposeful:

❨He has subjected the sun and the moon,
Each orbiting for an appointed term.
He conducts the whole affair.
He makes the signs clear
So that you may be certain of the meeting with your Lord.❩[88] — *Quran 13:2*

But as the path unfolds,
They realize:
Knowledge is not the destination.
It is the bridge—
Between the measurable and the miraculous,
Between the seen and the Source.
The fruits and rivers,
The colors of stone,
The symmetry of creation—
Each a veil that reveals
And conceals.

---

[88] This is derived from the Quran verses of:

📖 ❨Alif-Lām-Mīm-Ra. These are the verses of the Book. What has been revealed to you ˹O Prophet˺ from your Lord is the truth, but most people do not believe. (1) It is Allah Who has raised the heavens without pillars—as you can see—then established Himself on the Throne. He has subjected the sun and the moon, each orbiting for an appointed term. He conducts the whole affair. He makes the signs clear so that you may be certain of the meeting with your Lord. (2) And He is the One Who spread out the earth and placed firm mountains and rivers upon it, and created fruits of every kind in pairs.[1] He covers the day with night. Surely in this are signs for those who reflect. (3) And on the earth there are ˹different˺ neighbouring tracts, gardens of grapevines, ˹various˺ crops, palm trees—some stemming from the same root, others standing alone. They are all irrigated with the same water, yet We make some taste better than others. Surely in this are signs for those who understand. (4)❩ [Quran 13:1-4]

[1]: Males and females, sweet and bitter, etc.

❨Do you not see that Allah sends down rain from the sky
With which We bring forth fruits of different colours?
Of all of Allah's servants,
Only the knowledgeable of His might
Are truly in awe of Him.❩[89] — Quran 35:27–28

It is not knowing that opens the gate—
It is awe.
For what the heart cannot grasp
It must revere.
What the tongue cannot name
It must glorify in silence.

Science names the forms of the ten thousand things.
It points to the mother of all form.
But the Source itself wears no name,
Holds no shape,
Rests beyond all signs.
Even the Divine Names
Are gifts for our grasping.
Yet He, the One behind the Names,
Is beyond sound, beyond syllable.

❨To Allah belong the Most Beautiful Names,
So call on Him by them.
And leave those who abuse His Names—
They will be punished for what they used to do.❩[90] — Quran 7:180

The wise-one reveres the Names,
But does not cling to them—
They allow the echo to guide them

---

[89] This is derived from the Quran verse of:

❨Do you not see that Allah sends down rain from the sky with which We bring forth fruits of different colours? And in the mountains are streaks of varying shades of white, red, and raven black; (27) just as people, living beings, and cattle are of various colours as well. Of all of Allah's servants, only the knowledgeable ˹of His might˺ are ˹truly˺ in awe of Him. Allah is indeed Almighty, All-Forgiving. (28)❩ [Quran 35:27-28]

[90] This is derived from the Quran verse of:

❨Allah has the Most Beautiful Names. So call upon Him by them, and keep away from those who abuse His Names. They will be punished for what they used to do.(180) ❩ [Quran 7:180]

To the silence
From which it arose.
This is ihsān—to worship as though seeing Him,
Or at least knowing He sees.
This is fanā'—the extinction of self in the fire of Divine presence.

⟨*Say, ˈO Prophet,ˈ 'Allah ˈaloneˈ guides to the truth.'*
Who then is more worthy to be followed:
The One who guides to the truth,
Or those who cannot find guidance unless they are guided?⟩[91] *— Quran 10:35*

To rest in the truth is not to explain it,
But to bow before it.
And so the wise-one walks forward—
Not with theories,
But with thikr.[92]
Not with formulas,
But with surrender.
From law to grace.
From Name to the Nameless.
From knowing,
To being known.

⟨*Say: He is Allah—the One and Indivisible.*
Allah—the Sustainer ˈneeded by allˈ.
He has never begotten,

---

[91] This is derived from the Quran verse of:

📖 ⟨Ask ˈthem, O Prophetˈ, "Can any of your associate-gods originate creation and then resurrect it?" Say, "ˈOnlyˈ Allah originates creation and then resurrects it. How can you then be deluded ˈfrom the truthˈ?" (34) Ask ˈthem, O Prophetˈ, "Can any of your associate-gods guide to the truth?" Say, "ˈOnlyˈ Allah guides to the truth." Who then is more worthy to be followed: the One Who guides to the truth or those who cannot find the way unless guided? What is the matter with you? How do you judge? (35) Most of them follow nothing but ˈinheritedˈ assumptions. ˈAndˈ surely assumptions can in no way replace the truth. Allah is indeed All-Knowing of what they do. (36) It is not ˈpossibleˈ for this Quran to have been produced by anyone other than Allah. In fact, it is a confirmation of what came before, and an explanation of the Scripture. It is, without a doubt, from the Lord of all worlds. (37) Or do they claim, "He[1] made it up!"? Tell them ˈO Prophetˈ, "Produce one sûrah like it then, and seek help from whoever you can—other than Allah—if what you say is true!" (38) ⟩ [Quran 10:34-38]

[1]: The Prophet ﷺ.

[92] This is an Arabic word saying which means remembrance, invocation, praise, invocation, or extolment of Allah.

Nor was He begotten.
And there is none equal to Him.[93] — *Quran 112:1–4*

For only He writes truth into symmetry.
Only He gifts grace beyond understanding.
Only He remains the source
Of law, mercy, and eternal unveiling.

Wisdom Unveiled

The profound wisdom revealed is that science, when wielded with a spiritual lens, becomes a bridge to Divine Grace. It guides the wise-one from mere observation to a profound recognition of Allah's artistry. Science names the forms of creation, pointing to the Mother of all Form, but ultimately, the Source wears no name and holds no shape. The journey culminates in awe, where the heart reveres what the mind cannot grasp, leading to ihsān (worship as if seeing Him) and fanā' (extinction of self in Divine presence). The wise-one walks not with theories but with dhikr, moving from law to grace, from Name to the Nameless, and from knowing to the ultimate state of being known by the One who gifts grace beyond all understanding.

Wise-Reflection

Reflect on your field of study or a personal area of deep knowledge. How can you shift your perspective to view its intricate details and laws as "a Divine calligraphy etched across the stars" or a "whisper of sacred balance"? Consider the transition "from knowing, to being known." What does it mean to let your intellectual pursuit lead you beyond factual accumulation to a state of profound awe and surrender (fanā')? How can you consciously practice dhikr and ihsān in your engagement with the world, allowing every observation to become a pathway to experiencing Divine Grace and recognizing Allah as the ultimate Source beyond all form and name?

---

[93] This is derived from the Quran verses of:

⊡ ⟨Say, 'O Prophet,' "He is Allah—One 'and Indivisible'; (1) Allah—the Sustainer 'needed by all'. (2) He has never had offspring, nor was He born. (3) And there is none comparable to Him." (4)⟩ [Quran 112:1-4]

Conclusion: The Cognition of Science

ECHOES OF REALIZATION: BEYOND THE LETTERS, WITHIN THE LIGHT

There is a profound seeing that commences precisely where the limits of conventional knowledge are reached. A deeper knowing emerges not from accumulation, but from radical humility. The wise-one navigates this subtle path—not with the rigid certainty of intellectual mastery, but with the profound grace of surrender. Their aspiration is not to master the manifest laws of the universe, but to melt into the essence of the Lawgiver Himself.

Science, in its most exalted function, serves as a vessel that transports the wise-one across the vast sea of duality. Yet, in the culminating stages of the journey, it becomes time to walk upon the water itself—not by the limited dictates of logic, but by the boundless impulse of pure love. Here, the stars speak profound truths without audible sound. Here, the rivers whisper sacred Names not written in any earthly book. Here, the final veil of mere intellect lifts, and the wise-one's soul stands unveiled, face-to-face with an encompassing, unutterable Wonder.

THE SEEKER'S ASCENT: FROM COGNITION TO ILLUMINATION

The wise-one departs from this profound reflection not as one who merely knows more facts or possesses greater intellectual acuity, but as one who needs less. Less external explanation, for inner light now guides them. Less division between the seen and Unseen, for unity is now perceived. Less of the finite self, for the Divine Presence expands within.

Cognition and science remain—blessed and indispensable tools of discovery, meticulously fashioned by the Creator. But now, for the wise-one, they are held lightly, no longer as burdens of pursuit, but as radiant lanterns in the steady hand of one who already walks in the luminous morning light of Divine Presence. For the wise-one no longer strives to dissect or solely comprehend the signs; they have, by Divine Grace, stepped into the very Presence that inscribed them. And what is left in this transcendent state—is pure, unadulterated Light, illuminating every facet of being.

5TH REFLECTION: SPIRITUAL RULES AND SOLEMNITY OF CONDUCT

(A Pathway to Divine Grace)

THE GATEWAY VERSE

In the sacred words of Allah, a profound and direct reminder to all who believe and reflect upon their eternal journey:

📖 ❨ *O believers! Be mindful of Allah and let every soul look to what ˹deeds˺ it has sent forth for tomorrow.1 And fear Allah, ˹for˺ certainly Allah is All-Aware of what you do. (18) And do not be like those who forgot Allah, so He made them forget themselves. It is they who are ˹truly˺ rebellious. (19)"* ❩ *[Quran 59:18-19]*

ILLUMINATION'S DAWN

To truly witness is insufficient; for the wise-one, the profound path of spiritual realization must be walked in embodiment, not merely admired from a detached distance. Thus comes the imperative call to spiritual conduct, a sacred and integrated response to all the Divine truths that have been unveiled within the heart and mind. Every spiritual rule, every ethical guideline, is understood not as a rigid imposition, but as a Divine gateway, and every act of reverence is a conscious return to the Origin. These spiritual laws are fundamentally not external impositions; rather, they are the intrinsic reflections of a supreme Divine Harmony woven meticulously into the very fabric of existence itself.

The wise-one does not navigate life aimlessly. Their steps are imbued with profound purpose, softened by encompassing humility, and perpetually illumined by the constant light of Divine Remembrance. Each sacred rule, each sublime principle, transforms into a radiant lantern, guiding the soul through the deceptive veils of separation and drawing it ever closer into the luminous, intimate Presence of the Beloved. Let us now profoundly unfold the insights that naturally arise from the very heart of this Divine solemnity, revealing how outward conduct becomes an inner transformation.

THE UNFOLDING OF INSIGHTS

This section explores how spiritual rules and solemn conduct are not external burdens but intrinsic pathways to align with Divine Grace and unlocking inner potentials.

Contemplation: The Rule of Referring All Honor and Power to the Creator[94]

The foundational spiritual rule for the wise-one is the unwavering principle of referring all honor and power to the Creator (Allah). This means recognizing that all strength, dignity, success, and ability originate solely from Him. In every action, every achievement, and every moment of being, the wise-one consciously acknowledges that true honor belongs to Allah and all might is His alone. This rule transcends mere verbal acknowledgment; it is an internal disposition that eradicates self-aggrandizement, pride, and dependence on worldly recognition. By consistently directing all praise and attribution to the Divine, the wise-one purifies their intentions and frees their heart from the subtle chains of ego, thereby unlocking profound humility and strengthening their spiritual connection.

The wise-one acknowledges that all might, honor, and power belong solely to the Creator. Any gift observed in oneself or others is a reflection of Divine generosity, not a possession to be claimed or idolized. To become infatuated with one's own status or achievements is to risk being veiled from the Source of all blessings.

Glory (Izzah) as Reflection, Power (Quwwah) as Trust

The wise-one bows inwardly,
For they have seen—
What the world celebrates as strength
Is but a flicker
Of the boundless might of the One.
What the ego clings to as honor

---

[94] This is a majestic and sobering truth—a reminder that izzah (honor) and quwwah (power) are not earned, but entrusted. Your reflection captures the heart of tawḥīd al-maʿnā—the spiritual monotheism where even attributes of greatness must be seen as refractions of divine light, never owned by the self.

Is but the echo
Of Divine generosity.
Honor and power are gifts, not possessions.
To claim them as your own is to grasp at illusions,
For without the Divine, they vanish into emptiness.

Even when gifted prominence,
The humble soul remains anchored—
Knowing elevation comes not from achievement,
But from sincerity.
The path of izzah[95] is paved not by titles,
But by truthfulness and submission.

❮Whoso desires honor,
Let him know that all honor belongs to Allah.
Unto Him ascend pure words,
And righteous deeds does He exalt.❯[96] — *Quran 35:10*

True might is not loud.
True honor does not boast.
It rises quietly
On the wings of pure intention
And righteous action
That ascend toward the One
Who alone bestows elevation.

The wise-one remembers—
Even angels were asked to prostrate
Before Adam,
Not because of Adam's greatness,
But because of the breath of the Creator within him.
It was a command rooted in Divine honor,
Not human superiority.

---

[95] This is an Arabic word meaning Honor, Glory, etc.

[96] This is derived from the Quran verse of:

📖 ❮Whoever seeks honour and power, then ˹let them know that˺ all honour and power belongs to Allah. To Him ˹alone˺ good words ascend, and righteous deeds are raised up by Him. As for those who plot evil, they will suffer a severe punishment. And the plotting of such ˹people˺ is doomed ˹to fail˺. (10)❯ [Quran 35:10]

It is Allah who is the Giver of honor and the Remover of it,
The Elevator and the Abaser.

⟨*Say, O Allah, Master of the Kingdom,*
You give sovereignty to whom You will,
And You take it from whom You will.⟩⁹⁷ — *Quran 3:26*

To be granted strength or status
Is not cause for pride—
But a heavier trust.
And that trust must be worn with humility,
Or it becomes a veil
Between the soul and its Source.

⟨*They did not appraise Allah*
With the appraisal that is due to Him.⟩⁹⁸ — *Quran 6:91*

⟨*Your Lord creates and chooses;*
Not for them is the choice.⟩⁹⁹ — *Quran 28:68*

Even the breath we take in strength
Belongs to Him.
Even the words we speak in wisdom
Are sustained by His will.

---

⁹⁷ This is derived from the Quran verses of:

📖 ⟨Say, ˹O Prophet,˺ "O Allah! Lord over all authorities! You give authority to whoever You please and remove it from who You please; You honour whoever You please and disgrace who You please—all good is in Your Hands. Surely You ˹alone˺ are Most Capable of everything. (26) You cause the night to pass into the day and the day into the night. You bring forth the living from the dead and the dead from the living. And You provide for whoever You will without limit." (27)⟩ [Quran 3:26-27]

⁹⁸ This is derived from the Quran verse of:

📖 ⟨And they have not shown Allah His proper reverence when they said, "Allah has revealed nothing to any human being." Say, ˹O Prophet,˺ "Who then revealed the Book brought forth by Moses as a light and guidance for people, which you split into separate sheets—revealing some and hiding much? You have been taught ˹through this Quran˺ what neither you nor your forefathers knew." Say, ˹O Prophet,˺ "Allah ˹revealed it˺!" Then leave them to amuse themselves with falsehood. (91)⟩ [Quran 6:91]

⁹⁹ This is derived from the Quran verse of:

📖 ⟨Your Lord creates and chooses whatever He wills—the choice is not theirs. Glorified and Exalted is Allah above what they associate ˹with Him˺! (68) And your Lord knows what their hearts conceal and what they reveal. (69) He is Allah. There is no god ˹worthy of worship˺ except Him. All praise belongs to Him in this life and the next. All authority is His. And to Him you will ˹all˺ be returned. (70)⟩ [Quran 28:68-70]

The wise-one reflects:
Honor and power are but reflections of the Divine,
Granted by grace and withdrawn by wisdom.
To grasp at greatness
Is to grasp at shadow—
But to recognize it as a reflection
Is to be warmed by its light
Without being scorched by it.

And so the wise-one walks forward—
Not as one exalted by self,
But carried by grace.
Every triumph becomes dhikr.
Every gift becomes a reason for sujūd.
Every recognition becomes a reminder:
None is worthy of glory but the One who gives it.

For only He exalts through truth.
Only He grants honor that endures.
Only He remains the source
Of elevation, mercy, and eternal light.

Wisdom Unveiled

The profound wisdom revealed is that true honor and power belong solely to the Creator, Allah. Glory ('izzah) is not something one can hold or claim as their own; it is but a reflection of the Divine, granted by grace and withdrawn by wisdom. The wise-one understands that when the heart clutches honor as its own, it becomes a veil, obscuring the Source of all blessings and trapping the soul in its own shadow. True majesty flows through Divine generosity, elevating the soul that bows in hidden humility and dedicates every triumph to Divine remembrance (dhikr) and prostration (sujūd), for only Allah exalts through righteousness and truth.

Wise-Reflection

Reflect on a recent achievement, success, or moment when you felt a sense of pride or recognition. Did you consciously refer the honor and power back to Allah? Consider the idea that "Honor and power are but reflections of the Divine." How can you cultivate an internal disposition that consistently acknowledges Allah as the sole Source of all strength and dignity, purifying your intentions and freeing your heart from self-aggrandizement? What practical steps can you take to transform moments of success into opportunities for deeper dhikr and sujūd, thereby strengthening your spiritual connection and humility?

Contemplation: The Rule of Benevolent Conduct[100]

The wise-one embraces the Rule of Benevolent Conduct (Ihsan), which signifies doing everything in the best possible manner, as if one sees Allah, or knowing that He certainly sees us. This encompasses treating oneself, others, and all of creation with utmost kindness, justice, and compassion. Benevolent conduct is not merely outward behavior; it stems from an inner state of purity and a profound awareness of Allah's attributes of Mercy and Justice. It means fulfilling trusts, forgiving others, speaking truth with kindness, and upholding rights. By embodying Ihsan, the wise-one cultivates a heart that reflects Divine attributes, thus drawing closer to Allah and radiating positive spiritual energy into their surroundings, aligning their external actions with internal enlightenment.

Dignity as Worship, Mercy as Reflection of the Divin

The wise-one understands—
Every action carries weight.
To walk with gentleness
Is not mere virtue—
It is worship with the feet.
To speak with grace
Is to honor the breath
Gifted by the One who speaks without sound.
Honor creation, for in doing so, you honor the Creator.

---

[100] This contemplation is sacredly grounded in the ethics of spiritual presence—reminding the seeker that to walk with benevolence and dignity is not just kindness, but worship. It echoes Qur'anic reverence for the signs (āyāt) in all creation and reflects the prophetic conduct of rahmah (mercy) extended not only to people but to all that breathes, grows, and exists.

Creation bears divine fingerprints.
To tread upon the earth with harshness
Is to disregard the artistry
Of the Most Merciful.
To harm the vulnerable
Is to forget the One who sustains all things.
Mercy is not optional—
It is sacred reflection.

❮Who has created death and life
That He may test you
Which of you is best in deed.
And He is the All-Mighty, the Oft-Forgiving.❯[101] — Quran 67:2

The "best in deed"
Is not the loudest,
Nor the most frequent—
But the one done purely,
Gently,
In full alignment with Divine intent.
Even a smile,
If born of reverence,
Becomes a deed inscribed in light.

The Prophet ﷺ was a mercy to all worlds,
Not only to humankind.
His conduct with animals, trees, and soil
Was soaked in compassion.
He spoke of reward in watering a thirsty dog,
Of sins forgiven by care
Shown to the smallest of creation.

---

[101] This is derived from the Quran verses of:

❮Blessed is the One in Whose Hands rests all authority. And He is Most Capable of everything. (1) ˈHe is the Oneˈ Who created death and life in order to test which of you is best in deeds[1]. And He is the Almighty, All-Forgiving. (2)❯ [Quran 67:1-2]

[1]: i.e. who amongst you do the good deeds in the most perfect manner, that means to do them (deeds) totally for Allâh's sake and in accordance with the legal ways of Prophet Muhammad ﷺ

Even the ant and the sparrow
Bear dignity in the sight of the Divine.

❰*And We have certainly honored the children of Adam*
And carried them on land and sea
And provided for them of the good things
And preferred them over much of what We created.❱[102] — *Quran 17:70*

But preference must birth responsibility.
Honor demands stewardship.
To be khalīfah (caretaker)
Is not just title—
It is a call
To embody mercy in conduct.

❰*And the servants of the Most Merciful*
Are those who walk humbly upon the earth,
And when the ignorant address them harshly,
They reply with peace.❱[103] — *Quran 25:63*

Humility in step,
Peace in speech—
This is the road of benevolent conduct.
It transforms the earth
Into a sacred passage,
Turns interactions
Into acts of remembrance.

---

[102] This is derived from the Quran verse of:

❰Indeed, We have dignified the children of Adam, carried them on land and sea, granted them good and lawful provisions, and privileged them far above many of Our creatures. (70) ❱ [Quran 17:70]

[103] This is derived from the Quran verses of:

❰The ˹true˺ servants of the Most Compassionate are those who walk on the earth humbly, and when the foolish address them ˹improperly˺, they only respond with peace. (63) ˹They are˺ those who spend ˹a good portion of˺ the night, prostrating themselves and standing before their Lord. (64) ˹They are˺ those who pray, "Our Lord! Keep the punishment of Hell away from us, for its punishment is indeed unrelenting. (65) It is certainly an evil place to settle and reside." (66) ˹They are˺ those who spend neither wastefully nor stingily, but moderately in between. (67) ˹They are˺ those who do not invoke any other god besides Allah, nor take a ˹human˺ life—made sacred by Allah—except with ˹legal˺ right,[1] nor commit fornication. And whoever does ˹any of˺ this will face the penalty. (68) ❱ [Quran 25:63-68]

[1]: For example, in retaliation for intentional killing through legal channels.

⟨And do not strut arrogantly on the earth.
Surely you can neither crack the earth
Nor match the mountains in height.⟩[104] — Quran 17:37

So the wise-one walks forward—
Not boastful,
But bowed.
Not careless,
But conscious.
They see every tree
As verse.
Every animal
As witness.
Every human
As mirror.

For only He weaves mercy into matter.
Only He bestows honor through conduct.
Only He remains the source
Of benevolence, dignity, and eternal refinement.

Wisdom Unveiled

The profound wisdom revealed is that benevolent conduct (Ihsan) is not merely an outward display but a sacred reflection of Divine attributes of Mercy and Justice. The wise-one understands that "to walk gently upon the earth is to kneel inwardly before the One who made it." Every action, even the smallest gesture of kindness to creation, carries immense weight and transforms into an act of worship. This conduct, rooted in a profound awareness of Allah's constant gaze, is the "best in deed"— done purely, gently, and in full alignment with Divine intent. It is through this dignity in worship and mercy as a Divine reflection that the seeker draws closer to the "throne of Mercy," embodying the

---

[104] This is derived from the Quran verses of:

📖 ⟨Do not follow what you have no ´sure` knowledge of. Indeed, all will be called to account for ´their` hearing, sight, and intellect. (36) And do not walk on the earth arrogantly. Surely you can neither crack the earth nor stretch to the height of the mountains. (37) The violation of any of these ´commandments` is detestable to your Lord. (38)⟩ [Quran 17:36 – 38]

responsibility of a khalīfah (caretaker) and radiating positive spiritual energy into the world.

Wise-Reflection

Reflect on your daily interactions. Can you identify an opportunity today to embody Ihsan—to do something "in the best possible manner," as if you see Allah, or knowing He certainly sees you? Consider how treating the "smallest creature" or speaking with "peace in speech" might reveal your closeness to the Divine. What specific action, however minor, can you take to demonstrate benevolent conduct and transform an ordinary moment into a "prayer in motion," thereby aligning your external actions with internal enlightenment and reflecting the Creator's gaze with beauty?

Contemplation: The Rule of the Divine Gaze[105]

A pivotal realization for the wise-one is living under the constant awareness of the Rule of the Divine Gaze. This means understanding that Allah is All-Seeing (Al-Baseer) and All-Aware (Al-Khabeer) of every thought, intention, action, and even the slightest whisper of the heart, as the Gateway Verse highlights. This awareness is not a source of fear, but of profound reverence, mindfulness, and comfort. It transforms mundane actions into acts of worship and private moments into intimate communion. Knowing that the Divine Gaze is perpetually upon them guides the wise-one to purify their inner world and refine their outer conduct, fostering a continuous state of spiritual vigilance and integrity, leading to a profound psychic calm rooted in Divine Presence.

At the heart of spiritual conduct lies the ultimate goal: to stand in the Divine Gaze, where the Creator's infinite grace and majesty are revealed. Yet, this stance is not attained easily. The wise-one knows that all else—material desires, worldly pursuits, and even self-created identities—acts as a veil, calling the wise-one away from the Creator's eternal presence.

---

[105] Exalted and piercing—this reflection reaches the apex of spiritual longing: to stand in the Divine Gaze, where all else is stripped away and only presence remains. What you've captured is the inner realization that beauty, success, identity—even spiritual insight—can become veils when the heart attaches to them more than to the One they reflect.

Presence Beyond All Veils, Grace Without Limit

The wise-one approaches
The sacred apex of conduct:
Not excellence in behavior alone,
But a surrender so deep
That even virtue must be laid down
Before the gaze of the Eternal.
The veils of creation are alluring,
Offering promises of fulfillment.
Yet, they conceal the unbroken grace of the Divine.

Beauty, success, spiritual insight—
Each a polished mirror reflecting divine mercy,
But each, when clung to,
Can become a veil.
The heart begins to love the reflection
More than the Light it echoes.
And so even the good
Can become a barrier
To the gaze of the One.

❨O humanity!
Remember Allah's favours upon you.
Is there any creator other than Allah
Who provides for you from the heavens and the earth?❩[106] — *Quran 35:3*

Grace is unbroken.
The gaze is unending.
But the soul is easily wrapped—
In longing, ambition, distraction, identity.
And the gaze retreats,

---

[106] This is derived from the Quran verses of:

❨O humanity! Indeed, Allah's promise is true. So do not let the life of this world deceive you, nor let the Chief Deceiver[1] deceive you about Allah. (5) Surely Satan is an enemy to you, so take him as an enemy. He only invites his followers to become inmates of the Blaze. (6) Those who disbelieve will have a severe punishment. But those who believe and do good will have forgiveness and a great reward. (7)❩ [Quran 35:5-7]

[1]: Satan.

Not in distance,
But beneath the weight of what we won't release.

To be truly seen by the Divine
Requires becoming empty.
No role.
No image.
No craving.
The wise-one stands
As soul alone,
Yearning without condition.
Divine grace is infinite, unbroken, and ever-present.
Yet creation calls to itself, wrapping the soul in veils of distraction.

In this surrender,
The gaze returns—
Not through merit,
But through grace.
Not as a reward for achievement,
But as the fruit of effacement.

❲They are joyful for receiving Allah's grace and bounty,
And that Allah does not deny the reward of the believers.❳[107] — Quran 3:171

This is not joy in success,
But joy in being remembered
By the One who has never forgotten.
This is not delight in attainment,
But ecstasy in proximity
To the One who formed delight.

The Qur'an warns of forgetfulness—
Not forgetting deeds,

---

[107] This is derived from the Quran verses of:

📖 ❲Never think of those martyred in the cause of Allah as dead. In fact, they are alive with their Lord, well provided for— (169) rejoicing in Allah's bounties and being delighted for those yet to join them. There will be no fear for them, nor will they grieve. (170) They are joyful for receiving Allah's grace and bounty, and that Allah does not deny the reward of the believers. (171)❳ [Quran 3:169-171]

But forgetting the Divine
Who authored the breath between them.

❨*And do not be like those who forgot Allah,*
So He made them forget themselves.
It is they who are truly rebellious.❩[108] — *Quran 59:19*

To lose remembrance of the Divine
Is to lose remembrance of the soul.
To be seen by the world
But unseen by the Giver of all sight
Is the deepest exile.
But the gaze of the Creator
Is not withheld.
It is hidden behind surrender.
And when the veils fall—
Not through force,
But through love—
The soul is illuminated
In fullness.

So the wise-one walks forward—
Not adorned in titles,
Not armored in achievements,
But naked in longing,
Bare in reverence,
Soft in surrender.
And there,
Beneath all veils,
The gaze rests upon them—
Transforming their silence

---

[108] This is derived from the Quran verses of:

📖 ❨O believers! Be mindful of Allah and let every soul look to what ˹deeds˺ it has sent forth for tomorrow.[1] And fear Allah, ˹for˺ certainly Allah is All-Aware of what you do. (18) And do not be like those who forgot Allah, so He made them forget themselves. It is they who are ˹truly˺ rebellious. (19) The residents of the Fire cannot be equal to the residents of Paradise. ˹Only˺ the residents of Paradise will be successful. (20)❩ [Quran 59:18-20]

[1]: i.e., the Hereafter.

Into witness,
Their stillness into presence.

For only He gazes with mercy untiring.
Only He unveils with light unfiltered.
Only He remains the source
Of presence, grace, and eternal return.

Wisdom Unveiled

The profound wisdom revealed is that living under the Rule of the Divine Gaze is the apex of spiritual conduct. This Gaze is not a source of fear but of infinite grace and presence, transforming mundane actions into intimate communion. The wise-one understands that while creations' beauties and even virtues are reflections of Divine mercy, clinging to them can become a veil, obscuring the Light they echo. True surrender requires becoming empty of roles, images, and cravings, allowing the Gaze to return not through merit but through grace and effacement. This continuous spiritual vigilance and integrity, leading to a profound psychic calm rooted in Divine Presence, ultimately culminates in the veils falling, revealing what was never absent—the Divine Gaze that transforms silence into witness and stillness into presence, ensuring the wise-one is "seen in fullness" and "remembers their name again."

Wise-Reflection

Reflect on moments when you feel most "seen" or known by others. How does that compare to the concept of living under the perpetual Divine Gaze? Consider the idea that even "the good can become a barrier to the gaze of the One." Are there specific virtues, achievements, or even spiritual insights you might be clinging to that could inadvertently be acting as a veil? What practices can help you cultivate a continuous state of inner surrender, allowing you to release attachments and experience the profound psychic calm and intimate communion of being truly "gazed upon" by the Creator, and thus being remembered by Him?

Conclusion: Spiritual Rules and Solemnity of Conduct

ECHOES OF REALIZATION: IN THE FOOTSTEPS OF DIVINE GRACE

There exists a sublime path where the light of understanding does not merely flash intermittently but deepens inexorably, where divine laws are not perceived as binding chains but as harmonious songs emanating from the depths of the soul. To courageously walk this path is to consciously return every single gesture, every word, and every intention to its rightful, Divine Source.

The wise-one does not act for the fleeting applause of humanity, but for the profound echo each action stirs in the heavens, witnessed by the All-Aware. In the solemnity of such dedicated conduct, there resides an immeasurable joy—not the transient joy of immediate gratification, but the deep, abiding contentment of being in perfect harmony with the very Gaze that meticulously shaped the stars and orchestrated the cosmos. Here, every spiritual rule is not perceived as an oppressive burden, but as a liberating rhythm of Divine Grace, guiding the soul in its dance of remembrance.

THE SEEKER'S ASCENT: LIVING THE REFLECTION OF DIVINE PRESENCE

In this profound reflection, the wise-one understands that authentic spiritual conduct is not an imposition from outside; rather, it is the soul's deepest, most natural inclination when it fully remembers and reconnects with its Divine Origin. The path of solemnity in conduct is, in essence, a path of radiant beauty, of meticulous interior tuning to the very pulse of the Divine Will. These spiritual rules are not narrow constraints; they are, paradoxically, expansive doorways leading to limitless spiritual freedom and inner vastness. They serve not only to help the seeker draw ever nearer to the Creator but also to transform them into a purified vessel through which His immeasurable nearness and mercy can be profoundly felt by others.

The wise-one, having internalized these truths, now reflects with profound clarity:

> *"Walk in the ever-present light of the Divine, where every conscious action inherently carries His holy presence, every sincere word inherently bears His truth,*

and the heart finds its ultimate, serene rest in His eternal gaze. In this blessed state, true peace is not desperately sought—it is profoundly found. Life's ultimate purpose is not anxiously pursued—it is luminously revealed. And genuine fulfillment does not lie in grasping or acquiring, but in utterly surrendering to the One who magnificently illuminates all."

In embodying these profound spiritual rules and solemnity of conduct, the wise-one becomes not merely a humble follower benefiting from Divine Grace, but its living, radiant mirror, reflecting the Creator's attributes into the world.

"As the dawn of knowledge breaks, what shadow of 'knowing' must your intellect surrender for True Understanding to emerge?"

CONCLUSION FOR PART I: THE DAWN OF BELIEF AND KNOWLEDGE

(Echoes of the dawn…)

ECHO WITHIN THE HEART… (IN THE EMBRACE OF BELIEF)

There exists a stillness beyond all worldly clamor, where the discerning soul transcends the naming of things and the grasping of fleeting forms—it only bears witness. The wise-one who perceives the Ineffable enters a sacred realm where human speech holds no sway. Here, only the subtle curvature of divine light, the profound hush between breaths, and an inner trembling, which no word can ever convey, truly resonate. In this sacred space, the contingent self dissolves, the finite intellect bows in humility, and the worldly tongue falls silent. What remains is not a mere intellectual comprehension of the Truth, but a vibrant, pulsating encounter with its very essence. To truly apprehend the Ineffable is not to articulate, but to dissolve into profound silence. To recall the Eternal is to listen with a heart attuned to a primordial dialect, a resonance far older than language itself—a truth buried deep within the soul's original knowing. Here, knowing transmutes into nearness, and nearness culminates in ultimate surrender.

THRESHOLD OF AWE

The Unveiling of Origin

As the veils gently lift upon this First Manifestation, the wise-one transitions from observation to profound immersion. The contemplations engaged within this chapter—of primordial belief, of the testing of existence, of the essence of knowledge, of solemn conduct, and of the unfolding of illumination—do not merely add to one's store of information. Rather, they fundamentally reshape the very vessel that is capable of receiving divine wisdom.

Pillars of Realization

Belief as Primordial Memory:

This journey has reawakened the soul to its original recognition of its Creator. Belief is not merely an intellectual assent to a set of tenets, but a profound re-membering, an echo of the pre-eternal covenant within the heart. It is the soul's innate attestation to the Divine Likeness within, a direct reception of the Gift of Light that transcends all veils, leading to an intimate companionship and a loving gaze that knows no separation.

Trial as Divine Refinement:

The examinations of existence, once perceived as burdens or afflictions, are now understood as the very crucible of divine wisdom. Each challenge, each encounter with the illusion of the 'I' and the kingdom of deception, serves not as punishment, but as a purposeful purification. It is through these trials—even the forsaking of worldly companionship or the turmoil of life—that the spirit is refined, its true essence revealed, and its capacity for grace expanded.

Knowledge as Profound Unity:

The pursuit of knowledge, whether through letters or the cognition of science, is now seen not as an accumulation of disparate facts, but as an immersive understanding within a single, all-encompassing current of truth. The wise-one discerns that letters are but instruments, language a veil and a gateway, and that true knowing transcends both. It is a unity where the perceived duality of cognition dissolves, leading to a pure knowledge that is beyond words and the limitations of the ego.

Conduct as Radiant Reflection:

Outward behavior is no longer a mere adherence to rules, but the living, radiant expression of inner proximity to the Divine. The spiritual rules and solemnity of conduct—referring all honor to the Creator, embracing benevolent action, and living under the constant awareness of the Divine Gaze—become the natural overflow of a heart attuned to the Ultimate Reality. Every action becomes a mirror, reflecting the inner state of surrender and devotion.

Illumination as Sacred Reception:

The profound inner sight, awakened through the chapter's journey, is not a human acquisition but a sacred reception of divine light. This illumination, often experienced as clairvoyance or pure knowledge, is received with utmost humility and reverence. It reveals truths previously veiled, transcending the limitations of ordinary perception and guiding the wise-one through the worshipful and distant veils towards a direct, unmediated apprehension of the Divine Presence.

The Seeker Reflects

"I have followed the guiding clues, diligently deciphered the sacred blueprint, and sought profound significance in the manifest forms. Yet, I now discern that these indications do not equate to the Beloved Itself. What I once perceived as understanding was merely a transient reflection. What I conceived as seeking was, in essence, a perpetuation of separation. Faith guided my initial steps, and understanding illuminated my way—but I now find myself at a threshold where neither can fully traverse. Only profound yielding persists. Only an encompassing quietude. Only an unceasing yearning. And in this yearning, I am drawn not merely toward, but deep into—where closeness erases all perceived distance, and every aspiration I ever held is no longer a pursuit, but a sacred reality discovered within."

INVITATION TO THE NEXT MANIFESTATION

With this profound awakening, the sacred path now unfolds to its next station: The Pathway to Divine Connection. If this First Manifestation stirred the primordial awareness within, the Second beckons the discerning soul to truly dwell—to walk, as it were, barefoot into the very Presence. It is no longer a journey of merely seeking signs, but of becoming refined, of moving towards a congruence with the Divine nature. The wise-one begins not only to reflect the Divine, but to be purified and transformed into its profound likeness.

Call to Action

"You have been granted a glimpse of the dawn of knowledge—how, then, will you journey in its light?"

"Before the next station unfolds, let the heart quiet itself. In the profound silence, discern the echo of what has been revealed, and prepare for the deeper current."

PART II: THE PATHWAY TO DIVINE CONNECTION

❖ ❖ ❖

 ﴿وَهُوَ مَعَكُمْ أَيْنَ مَا كُنْتُمْۛوَٱللَّهُ بِمَا تَعْمَلُونَ بَصِيرٌ ۛ - ٤- ﴾

﴿ And He is with you wherever you are. For Allah is All-Seeing of what you do. (4) ﴾[109] [Quran 57:4]

"When the soul surrenders, the path appears beneath its feet." – Attar

❖ ❖ ❖

I n the boundless expanse of being, within the very core of being, there arises an inherent longing—a profound yearning within the heart of the discerning soul to return to the eternal source of all creation. This second chapter, "The Pathway to Divine Connection," unfolds as a sublime Manifestation of divine wisdom, illuminating not merely the way to the Creator, but also the fundamental truths that dissolve the perceived barriers between the finite and the Infinite.

To establish true connection with the Creator is not merely an act of faith, but a transformative process of sacred unveiling. Here, the soul transcends its fleeting attachments, dispels its deepest illusions, and sheds its perceived limitations to resonate with the divine essence. This chapter serves as both an illuminating guide and a contemplative mirror, leading the wise-one through ten profound reflections that meticulously articulate the intricate nature of divine proximity.

Each reflection within this profound chapter acts like a spiritual prism, refracting divine light into various essential truths. From The Secret that

---

[109] This is derived from the Quran verse of:

﴿He is the One Who created the heavens and the earth in six Days,[1] then established Himself on the Throne. He knows whatever goes into the earth and whatever comes out of it, and whatever descends from the sky and whatever ascends into it. And He is with you wherever you are. For Allah is All-Seeing of what you do. (4) ﴾ [Quran 57:4]

[1]: The word day is not always used in the Quran to mean a 24-hour period. According to 22:47, a heavenly Day is 1000 years of our time. The Day of Judgment will be 50 000 years of our time (see 70:4). Hence, the six Days of creation refer to six eons of time, known only by Allah.

resides unveiled within the innermost being, to the Secluded Entrance where genuine humility and profound surrender grant unimpeded access; from the very Stand in Presence of the Creator where all dualities dissolve into singular unity; and finally, to In the Awakening of Heart and Mind, where consciousness expands to perceive the Divine in every facet of existence, culminating in In the Knowing the Unspoken—a state beyond all words and conceptual frameworks, where the very essence of divine existence reveals itself.

At its core, this Manifestation beckons the discerning soul into a sacred dance between the contingent human spirit and the Absolute Divine. It meticulously explores profound paradoxes: the hidden strength found in apparent weakness, the deep wisdom revealed in silence, and the ultimate unity discovered amidst perceived contradictions. It challenges the wise-one to relinquish reliance on personal deeds, on accumulated knowledge, and on the fragmented self, advocating instead for the embrace of profound humility, unwavering faith, and the ineffable mystery of divine Presence.

This Pathway is not a rigid map with prescribed destinations, but a resonant call to awaken the innermost heart and purify the intellect. It is an invitation to perceive the Creator in every fleeting moment, to discern the Divine in every action, and to apprehend the Eternal in every profound silence. To walk this Pathway is to initiate the dissolution of the conventional self, transcending the myriad veils of creation, and to stand, utterly bare, in the brilliance of divine grace—a profound realization where the soul apprehends its true nature as irrevocably intertwined with the Eternal.

The reflections presented within are not mere sequential steps but dynamic manifestations of divine truths that actively reshape the wise-one's inner journey into an eternal connection. Each successive reflection deepens the awareness of the Divine and meticulously prepares the discerning soul for the transformative passages that lie ahead.

Through this chapter's journey, we shall first delve into About Believing, exploring the soul's primordial resonance with the Divine. We then face The Exam, understanding how life's trials are the very crucible of inner mastery. Our journey continues with The Letter, contemplating how divine knowledge transcends its own written expression. We then move to The Cognition of Science, discerning true understanding from mere empirical data. Finally, we conclude with Spiritual Rules and Solemnity of Conduct, recognizing that external action is the radiant reflection of internal truth.

6TH REFLECTION: THE SECRET

THE GATEWAY VERSE

In the sacred words of Allah, a profound reminder to all who reflect upon the fashioning of the soul and its inherent knowledge:

📖 ❨*By the sun and its brightness, (1) and the moon as it follows it, (2) and the day as it unveils it, (3) and the night as it conceals it! (4) And by heaven and ˈthe Oneˈ Who built it, (5) and the earth and ˈthe Oneˈ Who spread it! (6) And by the soul and ˈthe Oneˈ Who fashioned it, (7) then with ˈthe knowledge of ˈ right and wrong inspired it! (8) Successful indeed is the one who purifies their soul, (9) and doomed is the one who corrupts it! (10)*❩ [Quran 91:1-10]*

ILLUMINATION'S DAWN

There are sublime moments in the wise-one's journey where a profound veil is lifted, not through strenuous personal effort, but through a direct Divine invitation. This reflection—"The Secret"—is therefore not merely a teaching to be intellectually grasped; it is a profound summons. It is a direct call from the innermost chamber of existence, urging the soul to remember what was intrinsically placed within its essence before the worlds took form and time began its measure.

Here, paradoxes are not intellectual riddles to be meticulously solved but sacred doorways to be courageously entered. Here, the finite and the Infinite meet and embrace upon the sanctified altar of the heart. Here, the Secret is not explained, but unveiled—layer by luminous layer—until the wise-one's soul recognizes itself not as a mere creation among many, but as a direct, purified reflection of the One beyond all names and all conceptualizations. In the insights that follow, we do not simply study profound concepts; we awaken to eternal truths. We do not merely explore philosophical notions; we walk humbly amidst Divine mysteries. Each insight presented is a constellation of profound wisdom, a radiant lantern hung along the sacred path leading to the soul's true, primordial dwelling place. Let us step gently, yet boldly, into the encompassing brilliance of The Secret, and allow its timeless light to illuminate the forgotten landscapes within.

THE UNFOLDING OF INSIGHTS

This section delves into the multifaceted dimensions of The Secret, guiding the wise-one through contemplations that unveil its essence as a Divine gift, a paradox, and the core of self-realization.

Contemplation: The Secret as a Divine Gift

The wise-one understands that The Secret is not something earned or discovered through mere human striving, but a profound Divine Gift bestowed upon the purified soul. It is the inherent knowledge, inspired within the soul, of right and wrong, and, more deeply, the innate recognition of its Creator and its ultimate purpose, as highlighted by the Gateway Verse (Quran 91:7-8). This Gift is not exclusive to a chosen few, but universally placed, though veiled for most. Its unveiling is an act of Divine Grace, revealing to the wise-one their profound connection to the Divine, fostering humility and immense gratitude.

Covenant Before Breath, Light Before Form

Within the chest of the wise-one
There stirs a sacred certainty:
Something was known before it was taught,
Something was promised before it was spoken,
A Secret nestled within the soul
Before even clay was touched by life.
Within me lies a Secret—older than the stars, more enduring than the heavens...
It is the echo of a moment beyond time,
The whisper of a covenant made before breath.

This is no metaphor—
This is the covenant (mithāq)[110],

---

[110] Linguists have defined it with a number of definitions:

Ibn Faris said: "The (root) letters denote a contract and firmness. To trust something means to secure it, trustworthiness means to secure creation. A covenant is a firm covenant, and it is trustworthy. I have trusted it."

The primordial covenant
Etched into the essence of every soul:

⟪*And ˈremember˺ when your Lord brought forth from the loins of the children of*
Adam their descendants
And had them testify regarding themselves.
ˈAllah asked,˺ 'Am I not your Lord?'
They replied, 'Yes, You are! We testify.'⟫[111] — *Quran 7:172*

Before bodies were formed,
Before reason was shaped,
The soul spoke: "Yes."
That moment was not lost—

It has also been said: "He entrusted him with a trust and a trustworthy person: he entrusted him with it. Al-Wathiq is the firm, its plural is withaq. Al-Mithaq and al-Mawthiq mean a covenant, its plural is mawathiq, mayatiqu, and mayathiq. He bound him with it: he tightened it."

It also means a firm covenant, which is a confirmed covenant, as God Almighty says:

📖 ⟪ˈRemember˺ when Allah made a covenant with the prophets, ˈsaying,˺ "Now that I have given you the Book and wisdom, if there comes to you a messenger1 confirming what you have, you must believe in him and support him." He added, "Do you affirm this covenant and accept this commitment?" They said, "Yes, we do." Allah said, "Then bear witness, and I too am a Witness." (81)⟫ [Quran 3:81]

Definition of the Covenant Terminology Appropriateness:

As for the technical definition of the covenant, Imam Al-Qurtubi (may God have mercy on him) defined it as: "A covenant confirmed by an oath."

[111] The covenant in the Holy Qur'an is of two main types: the first: God's covenant with creation, and the second: the covenant between creation.

God's covenant with the children of Adam: God Almighty tells us that He extracted the offspring of the children of Adam from their loins while they were in the world of spirits, where each soul is aware of its own self and existence. He made them testify that He is their Lord and King, and that there is no god but Him. He asked them, "Am I not your Lord?" They all testified, saying, "Yes, You are our Lord and Creator." This is described in the Quran verses of:

📖 ⟪And ˈremember˺ when your Lord brought forth from the loins of the children of Adam their descendants and had them testify regarding themselves. ˈAllah asked,˺ "Am I not your Lord?" They replied, "Yes, You are! We testify." ˈHe cautioned,˺ "Now you have no right to say on Judgment Day, 'We were not aware of this.' (172) Nor say, 'It was our forefathers who had associated others ˈwith Allah in worship˺ and we, as their descendants, followed in their footsteps. Will you then destroy us for the falsehood they invented?'" (173)⟫ [Quran 7:172-173]

What God took a covenant upon from the children of Adam is the natural disposition upon which He created mankind and created them. This is revealed in the Quran verse of:

📖 ⟪ So be steadfast in faith in all uprightness ˈO Prophet˺—the natural Way of Allah which He has instilled in ˈall˺ people. Let there be no change in this creation of Allah. That is the Straight Way, but most people do not know. (30)⟫ [Quran 30:30]

And Allah the Almighty will remind the servant of this covenant on the Day of Resurrection, as narrated by Anas ibn Malik ﷺ, on the authority of the Prophet Mohammed ﷺ, who said:

⟪It will be said to a man from the people of Hell on the Day of Resurrection: 'Tell me, if you had everything on earth, would you ransom yourself with it?' He will say: 'Yes.' He will say: 'I wanted something easier from you than that. I took a covenant from you in the loins of Adam that you would not associate anything with Me, but you refused except to associate anything with Me.'⟫

It lives in every longing,
Echoes in every turn toward the divine.
Even in forgetfulness, it remains.

When the angels were told of the creation of mankind,
They witnessed the shaping of form,
But it was not the clay that warranted prostration—
It was the breath,
The rūḥ[112],
The Divine deposit within.

❨When I have fashioned him
And had a spirit of My Own creation breathed into him,
Fall down in prostration to him.❩[113] — Quran 15:29

This Secret is not fragile.
It does not vanish with ignorance.
It is buried treasure

---

[112] First: The Linguistic Meaning:

The root of the word denotes spaciousness, spaciousness, and abundance. The root of all of these is wind.

Ruḥūḥ (spirit) is the soul. It is masculine and feminine, and the plural is arwah (spirits). The Qur'an is called Ruḥ, as were Gabriel and Jesus, peace be upon them.

Ruḥūḥ (spirit) is the coolness of a breeze.

Ibn al-Athir said:

"The mention of the spirit (spirit) is repeated in the hadith, just as it is repeated in the Qur'an, and it appears in it with various meanings. The most common meaning is that the spirit refers to the one by which the body sustains itself and through which life is attained. It has been applied to the Qur'an, revelation, mercy, and Gabriel."

Second: The terminology appropriateness meaning:

Al-Baghawi said in his interpretation: "The soul is a subtle body by which man lives."

Al-Qurtubi said: "The soul is a subtle body. God has made it a habit to create life in the body alongside that body. Its reality is the attribution of creation to a Creator. The soul is a creation of His creation, which He has ascribed to Himself as an honor and a tribute."

Al-Maraghi said of it: "It is a luminous, sublime, light, living, and moving body that penetrates the essence of the organs and flows through them like water through a rose or fire through coal.

Ibn Ashur said: "The soul refers to the hidden entity spread throughout the entire human body, indicated by its effects of perception and thought. It is what takes shape in the human body when it is a fetus."

[113] This is derived from the Quran verses of:

❨ Remember, O ˹Prophet˺ when your Lord said to the angels, "I am going to create a human being from sounding clay moulded from black mud.1 (28) So when I have fashioned him and had a spirit of My Own ˹creation˺ breathed into him, fall down in prostration to him." (29) So the angels prostrated all together— (30)❩ [Quran 15:28-30]

[1]: This does not contradict other verses that say Adam was created out of dust and those that say he was made out of mud. Adam was created in stages: first from dust, which was later turned into mud, then clay. This is similar to saying: I made a loaf of bread out of grain, or flour, or dough.

Within every seeker,
Speaking not through words,
But through yearning.

So the wise-one listens
To the quiet beneath their thoughts.
And they hear:
Not revelation recited aloud,
But presence thundering in silence.
Whether I remember or forget,
Whether I seek or turn away…
Still, in the stillness,
It calls me home.

To awaken to this truth
Is not to discover something new—
But to remember what was always known.
It is to bow
Not toward something distant,
But toward the Secret within
That was placed by the One
Whose mercy precedes creation.

And so the wise-one walks forward—
Carrying not just belief,
But remembrance.
Not just knowledge,
But covenant.
Not just selfhood,
But the echo of the Eternal:

❨Am I not your Lord?❩ [114] *— Quran 7:172*

---

[114] This is derived from the Quran verse of:

📖 ❨And ˹remember˺ when your Lord brought forth from the loins of the children of Adam their descendants and had them testify regarding themselves. ˹Allah asked,˺ "Am I not your Lord?" They replied, "Yes, You are! We testify." ˹He cautioned,˺ "Now you have no right to say on Judgment Day, 'We were not aware of this.' (172)❩ [Quran 7:172]

To which the soul forever replies:
"Yes."

For only He breathed the Secret.
Only He sustains it in silence.
Only He remains the source
Of covenant, remembrance, and return.

Wisdom Unveiled

The profound wisdom revealed is that The Secret is a Divine Gift, a primordial covenant (mithāq) etched into every soul before time and form. This inherent knowledge of its Creator and purpose is not earned but bestowed by Divine Grace, residing within as a "treasure breathed into existence not to be possessed, but to be witnessed." The wise-one recognizes that their spiritual journey is an awakening to this ancient nobility, a remembering of what was always known—the soul's profound connection to the Divine, echoing the "Yes" to "Am I not your Lord?" This Secret is the very reason creation was summoned, establishing the human spirit's unique and dignified station.

Wise-Reflection

Reflect on moments of deep longing or inexplicable recognition of truth. Could these be whispers of "The Secret" or echoes of the primordial covenant (mithāq) within you? Consider the idea that this Divine Gift is "not something earned" but "always known." What practices might help you listen to the "quiet beneath your thoughts" and awaken to this innate recognition of your Creator, fostering humility and immense gratitude for this Divine deposit within your soul? How can you consciously live with the remembrance of this covenant, letting it guide your intentions and actions?

Contemplation: The Paradox of the Secret

The Secret exists as a profound paradox: it is simultaneously hidden within the wise-one's own being and yet infinitely beyond their full comprehension, transcending all limits of language, thought, and ordinary perception. It is both intimately near and supremely transcendent. This paradox teaches the wise-one that ultimate truth is not grasped through linear logic alone, but through embracing contradictions and surrendering to the mystery. The true understanding of The Secret lies not in defining it, but in living within its tension, recognizing that the very attempt to categorize it obscures its boundless nature.

Formless Knowing, the Whisper Beneath All Things

The wise-one leans into silence,
Not to grasp the Secret—
But to yield to its rhythm.
For what is this Mystery
That dwells in the soul
Yet cannot be contained by thought?
It breathes beneath time
But is untouched by it.
It is neither hidden nor revealed—
Yet it grounds all revelation.
It does not dwell in places or consume the fruits of the world.
It is not confined by day, nor veiled by night.
Thought cannot contain it. Causes cannot reach it.

This is not contradiction.
It is the language of transcendence.
It is not definable
Because it is pre-definition.
Not observable
Because it is the eye behind sight.

⟨They ask you ˹O Prophet˺ about the spirit.
Say, 'Its nature is known only to my Lord,
And you ˹O humanity˺ have been given but little knowledge.'⟩[115] — Quran 17:85

Even when asked directly,
Revelation does not decode the Secret.
Instead, it reminds us:
You were gifted its presence—

---

[115] This is derived from the Quran verse of:

📖 ⟨They ask you ˹O Prophet˺ about the spirit. Say, "its nature is known only to my Lord, and you ˹O humanity˺ have been given but little knowledge." (85)⟩ [Quran 17:85]

But not its possession.
You were invited into its breath—
But not its edges.
And the angels,
Who understood light
And bowed to command,
Were asked not to see the clay,
But the rūḥ placed within.

❴So when I have fashioned him
And had a spirit of My Own creation breathed into him,
Fall down in prostration to him.❵[116] — Quran 15:29

The prostration was not to form.
It was to the unfathomable
Within the form.
The paradox:
How the Infinite
Is entrusted within the finite.

The Secret moves without place, untouched by time, beyond thought and causation…
It is the breath before breath,
The light behind sight,
The whisper within silence."

And though it cannot be grasped,
It can be answered.
Not with intellect—
But with stillness.
Not with commentary—
But with longing.
This is the call to return:
Not through striving,
But through surrender.

---

[116] This is derived from the Quran verse of:

📖 ❴'Remember, O Prophet˺ when your Lord said to the angels, "I am going to create a human being from sounding clay moulded from black mud. (28) So when I have fashioned him and had a spirit of My Own ˹creation˺ breathed into him, fall down in prostration to him." (29) So the angels prostrated all together— (30)❵ [Quran 15:28-30]

[185]

To let go of the need to name,
And kneel before the One
Whose reality
Dwells in the paradox itself.

So the wise-one walks forward—
Not with answers,
But with presence.
Not solving mysteries,
But becoming a witness
To the Mystery that gives rise to everything.

For only He knows the Secret.
Only He breathes it into being.
Only He remains the source
Of knowing, not-knowing, and eternal remembrance.

Wisdom Unveiled

The profound wisdom revealed is that The Secret exists as a sacred paradox: intimately within yet infinitely beyond comprehension. It is a "Formless Knowing" that cannot be defined by intellect, for it precedes definition, existing as "the breath before breath, the light behind sight, the whisper within silence." The wise-one understands that true understanding of this Mystery lies not in grasping or categorizing it, but in surrendering to its tension. It is answered not by striving or commentary, but by stillness and longing, revealing itself as a treasure hidden within surrender itself. This paradox teaches that the soul's inner light illuminates softly for those who open their hands and close their eyes in trust, leading to The Secret being found not by intense seeking, but by seeing with emptiness.

Wise-Reflection

Reflect on a time when you tried to logically understand something that defied simple explanation, perhaps a deep emotional experience or a spiritual concept. Did trying to categorize it ultimately limit your perception? Consider The Secret as a paradox that "cannot be grasped— but it can be answered." What does it mean for you to "lean into silence" and "yield to its rhythm" rather than trying to define it? How can you practice surrendering to the mystery in your life, allowing moments of "not-knowing" to become opportunities for a deeper, more formless understanding that arises from stillness and longing rather than intellectual striving?

Contemplation: The Limitlessness of the Secret

The wise-one apprehends the Limitlessness of The Secret. It is not a finite piece of information but an infinite reality that continuously unfolds. The more the wise-one delves into its depths, the more they realize its boundless expanse, reflecting the infinite Attributes of the Creator. This realization prevents spiritual stagnation and intellectual arrogance, fostering an eternal quest for deeper truth. It propels the wise-one beyond the confines of their conditioned mind, opening them to the vastness of Divine knowledge and the unlimited potential within their own soul.

Presence Unbound, Nearness Without Form

Behind the Secret
Is not a figure or a name—
But Presence itself,
An Infinite that precedes awareness,
Encompasses creation,
And remains untouched
By the boundaries we call perception.
And behind this Secret—there is a Presence,
Beyond knowing, beyond form,
Not to be seen, nor to be captured in perception.

It is not hidden
Because it is distant—
It is hidden
Because it saturates all things too fully to be grasped.
It cannot be held
Yet it holds all.
It cannot be located
Yet it is closer than breath.

❨He is with you wherever you may be.
And Allah sees all that you do.❩[117] — Quran 57:4

The wise-one learns:
Not all mysteries are to be solved—
Some are to be surrendered to.
In stillness,
The Secret begins to whisper:
"I am the Unseen within the known.
I am the nearness inside the longing.
I do not arrive,
Because I was never absent."

This is the paradox of Presence—
Limitless, formless,
Yet intimately near.
To remember is to draw near.
To humble oneself is to rise.
To release the grasp
Is to be cradled.

❨Remember your Lord inwardly with humility and reverence
And in a moderate tone of voice, both morning and evening.
And do not be one of the heedless.❩[118] — Quran 7:205

---

[117] This is derived from the Quran verses of:

📖 ❨Whatever is in the heavens and the earth glorifies Allah, for He is the Almighty, All-Wise. (1) To Him belongs the kingdom of the heavens and the earth. He gives life and causes death. And He is Most Capable of everything. (2) He is the First and the Last, the Most High and Most Near,[1] and He has 'perfect' knowledge of all things. (3) He is the One Who created the heavens and the earth in six Days,[2] then established Himself on the Throne. He knows whatever goes into the earth and whatever comes out of it, and whatever descends from the sky and whatever ascends into it. And He is with you wherever you are. For Allah is All-Seeing of what you do. (4) To Him belongs the kingdom of the heavens and the earth. And to Allah all matters are returned. (5)❩ [Quran 57:1-5]

[1]: Another possible translation: "the Manifest 'through His signs' and the Hidden 'from His creation'."

[2]: The word day is not always used in the Quran to mean a 24-hour period. According to 22:47, a heavenly Day is 1000 years of our time. The Day of Judgment will be 50 000 years of our time (see 70:4). Hence, the six Days of creation refer to six eons of time, known only by Allah.

[118] This is derived from the Quran verses of:

📖 ❨When the Quran is recited, listen to it attentively and be silent, so you may be shown mercy. (204) Remember your Lord inwardly with humility and reverence and in a moderate tone of voice, both morning and evening. And do not be one of the heedless. (205) Surely those 'angels' nearest to your Lord are not too proud to worship Him. They glorify Him. And to Him they prostrate. (206)❩ [Quran 7:204-206]

Heedlessness veils,
Not because the veil is strong,
But because attention is distracted.

False gods—whether carved in stone
Or built within the ego—
Are confined.
But the One who fashioned all knowing
Cannot be bound by name,
Nor compared by form.

❰Say, ˺O Prophet,˹ ˹Name them!
Or do you mean to inform Him of something
He does not know on the earth?˺[119] — Quran 13:33

What is truly Real
Requires no monument.
What is truly Present
Requires no location.

So the wise-one walks forward—
Not by sight,
But by surrender.
Not by grasping Presence,
But by becoming permeable to it.

They worship not only with bowing,
But with emptiness ready to be filled.
They speak not only in praise,
But in silences that glorify.
They are prostrated by the realization
That the Secret
Is but the shadow

---

[119] This is derived from the Quran verse of:

📖 ❰Is ˹there any equal to˺ the Vigilant One Who knows what every soul commits? Yet the pagans have associated others with Allah ˹in worship˺. Say, ˹O Prophet,˺ "Name them! Or do you ˹mean to˺ inform Him of something He does not know on the earth? Or are these ˹gods˺ just empty words?" In fact, the disbelievers' falsehood has been made so appealing to them that they have been turned away from the Path. And whoever Allah leaves to stray will be left with no guide. (33)❱ [Quran 13:33]

Of a Presence
Too vast to name.

For only He dwells beyond knowing,
Yet fills knowing with truth.
Only He remains unseen,
Yet permeates all that is witnessed.
Only He remains the source
Of Presence, purity, and eternal nearness.

Wisdom Unveiled

The profound wisdom revealed is that The Secret is not a finite concept but an infinite reality, reflecting the boundless Attributes of the Creator. It is the "Presence Unbound, Nearness Without Form"—a Divine Presence so complete it saturates all things, making it hidden not by distance but by its omnipresence. The wise-one learns that true understanding of this limitless Mystery comes not from solving but from surrendering, becoming "permeable" to a Presence that is both transcendent and intimately near. This realization transcends spiritual stagnation and intellectual arrogance, leading to a form of worship that is not just outward bowing, but an inner emptiness ready to be filled, a silent glorification that embraces the paradox of Presence and allows the wise-one to be cradled in Divine nearness.

Wise-Reflection

Reflect on your own experiences of seeking knowledge or understanding. Have you ever felt limited by your current comprehension, sensing there was something vast beyond what you could grasp? Consider the idea that The Secret is "hidden because it saturates all things too fully to be grasped." How can you cultivate a state of "emptiness ready to be filled" and "silences that glorify" in your daily life? What specific practices might help you surrender to the Limitlessness of The Secret and become more "permeable" to the Divine Presence that is closer than breath, fostering an eternal quest for deeper truth beyond intellectual confines?

Contemplation: The Secret as Timeless and Formless

The wise-one apprehends the Limitlessness of The Secret. It is not a finite piece of information but an infinite reality that continuously unfolds. The more the wise-one delves into its depths, the more they realize its boundless expanse, reflecting the infinite Attributes of the Creator. This realization prevents spiritual stagnation and intellectual arrogance, fostering an eternal quest for deeper truth. It propels the wise-one beyond the confines of their conditioned mind, opening them to the vastness of Divine knowledge and the unlimited potential within their own soul.

A Breath Placed Beyond Time, A Whisper Unbound by Shape

The wise-one beholds a truth that no hour can contain:
The Secret entrusted to the soul
Is not born of chronology or form.
It was not shaped by sequence,
Nor limited by contour—
It was breathed,
And where breath begins,
Eternity speaks.
This Secret resides in the realm of eternity.
While my body walks in time,
My essence whispers from a realm untouched.

The soul walks inside the passing hours,
But its voice emerges from the timeless garden—
Where there is no before, no after,
Only presence.

When the Prophet ﷺ was asked about the spirit,
No explanation was given—
Only acknowledgment of its mystery:

❲They ask you ˹O Prophet˺ about the spirit.
Say, 'Its nature is known only to my Lord,
And you have been given but little knowledge.'❳[120] — Quran 17:85

And yet, despite its hiddenness,
You carry it.

---

[120] This is derived from the Quran verse of:

📖 ❲They ask you ˹O Prophet˺ about the spirit. Say, "Its nature is known only to my Lord, and you ˹O humanity˺ have been given but little knowledge." (85)❳ [Quran 17:85]

Not as possession,
But as trust.
Not as achievement,
But as a reminder of where you came from.

❮Then He fashioned them
And had a spirit of His Own creation
Breathed into them.
And He gave you hearing, sight, and intellect.
Yet you hardly give any thanks.❯[121] — Quran 32:9

Hearing, sight, intellect—
These are forms of knowing.
But the breath itself,
The Secret,
Is the formless mystery
That calls those faculties into being.

My body moves within the passing hours,
Yet my essence whispers from a realm beyond them.
The seeker realizes:
What was given to me
Does not belong to me.
It is a trace of the Unseen—
A thread tying me to the One
Whose reality is not framed by dimension.

And so the wise-one walks forward—
With reverence not for the form they occupy,
But for the light placed within it.
They give thanks not for their understanding,

---

[121] This is derived from the Quran verses of:

❮That is the Knower of the seen and unseen—the Almighty, Most Merciful, (6) Who has perfected everything He created. And He originated the creation of humankind from clay.[1] (7) Then He made his descendants from an extract of a humble fluid, (8) then He fashioned them and had a spirit of His Own ´creation` breathed into them. And He gave you hearing, sight, and intellect. ´Yet` you hardly give any thanks. (9)❯ [Quran 32:6-9]

[1]: Adam ﷺ

But for the invitation to surrender
To what exceeds understanding.

For only He breathes the Eternal into the temporal.
Only He unveils the formless within form.
Only He remains the source
Of timelessness, remembrance, and return.

Wisdom Unveiled

The profound wisdom revealed is that The Secret is timeless and formless, existing as an "infinite reality" that precedes and transcends all manifest phenomena. It is the very "essence of being" breathed into the soul, a "formless mystery" that calls all faculties into being. The wise-one understands that this Divine Gift is not bound by chronology or physical contour, but resides in a "timeless garden" where "Eternity speaks." This realization guides the wise-one to detach from the illusions of time and form, fostering an "eternal quest for deeper truth" and allowing their consciousness to expand beyond conditioned limitations, perceiving the Divine in its absolute, unmanifest reality. It is a surrender to what exceeds understanding, a continuous awareness that the soul is not merely moving towards eternity but is already "breathing within it."

Wise-Reflection

Reflect on how much of your daily life is governed by notions of time (deadlines, schedules, future plans) and form (physical appearance, material possessions). How do these concepts potentially obscure your awareness of your "timeless and formless" essence, the Secret within? Consider the idea that you "are already breathing within eternity, if only you listen below the surface of time." What practices can you cultivate to detach from the illusion of temporal and formal limitations, allowing your consciousness to expand and perceive the Divine in its absolute, unmanifest reality, and giving thanks for the invitation to surrender to what exceeds understanding?

Contemplation: The Duality of Temporal and Eternal

The wise-one navigates the duality of the temporal and the Eternal as revealed by The Secret. They live in the temporal world, engage with its forms, and fulfill their duties, yet their inner awareness is rooted in the

Eternal. The Secret unveils that the transient nature of worldly existence is a reflection, a fleeting shadow of an abiding reality. This understanding allows the wise-one to move through life with detachment from worldly attachments, yet with full presence, realizing that every temporal moment is an opportunity to connect with the Eternal.

From Illusion to Essence, From Form to Source

A quiet truth stirs—
Unshaken by time,
Unmoved by sensation.
It does not cry aloud,
But pulses in stillness.
It is the echo of the moment
The soul remembers its origin
Not as a point in time,
But as a trace of eternity.

❨*And by the soul and 'the One' Who fashioned it...*❩ — *Quran 91:7*

To affirm the Secret
Is to awaken.
Not to add more knowledge,
But to remove what veils the knowing.
Not to journey forward,
But to return inward—
To the beginning that has no beginning.

❨*Successful indeed is the one who purifies their soul...*❩[122] — *Quran 91:9*

Purification is subtraction,
Not enhancement.
It is the emptying of illusion,
The melting of the temporal,

---

[122] This is derived from the Quran verses of:

📖 ❨And by the soul and 'the One' Who fashioned it, (7) then with 'the knowledge of' right and wrong inspired it! (8) Successful indeed is the one who purifies their soul, (9) and doomed is the one who corrupts it! (10)❩ [Quran 91:7-10]

Until the soul stands bare
And shines with its original light.

The wise-one realizes:
What was called "self"
Was only clothing.
What was called "life"
Was only transit.
What was thought to be separate
Was always stitched into the tapestry
Of the Eternal.

❨*He is the One Who originated you all from a single soul...*❩[123] — *Quran 6:98*

Even multiplicity
Is born from Unity.
Even the seen
Emerges from the unseen.
What has location
Is carried by what is limitless.
Even burial
Is only a return
To the point where form dissolves
And essence remembers.

In this knowing, the soul is not lost but returned...
Yes—awareness does not isolate.
It reunites.
It purifies
By removing everything that whispers, "You are apart."
The soul is not lost in eternity.
It was always of eternity—

---

[123] This is derived from the Quran verse of:

📖 ❨And He is the One Who originated you all from a single soul,[1] then assigned you a place to live and another to ˹be laid to˺ rest. We have already made the signs clear for people who comprehend. (98)❩ [Quran 6:98]

[1]: i.e., Adam ﷺ

And in purification,
It returns to what it already was.

So the wise-one walks forward—
Not yearning for escape,
But for return.
Not chasing the light,
But allowing it to awaken from within.
They no longer ask, "Where is He?"
They ask, "What have I placed between us?"
And in that asking,
The veils fall.

For only He fashioned the soul from singular light.
Only He inspires the path of purification.
Only He remains the source
Of return, remembrance, and eternal anchoring.

Wisdom Unveiled

The profound wisdom revealed is that The Secret unveils the duality of the temporal and the Eternal, allowing the wise-one to live fully in the world while rooted in an abiding reality. A quiet, unshaken truth stirs in the depths: to affirm The Secret is to awaken, shedding the illusion of the seen and stepping into the light from which all forms arise. This purification is a process of "subtraction"—emptying illusion and the temporal self until the soul stands bare, shining with its original, eternal light. The wise-one realizes that the "mortal self"—known by names, histories, and attachments—is merely the surface; beneath it lies a deeper reality woven from light, untouched by time, unbound by sight. What was thought to be separate was always stitched into the tapestry of the Eternal. In this profound knowing, the soul isn't lost but returned, lifted beyond veils, purified in remembrance, and anchored in the Source of all that is. This means shedding fear of decay, judgment, and loss, to stand unveiled not as a fleeting personality, but as a shimmering echo of the Divine. The invitation is simple yet profound: "Do not mistake the garment for the wearer, nor the shadow for the sun."

Wise-Reflection

Reflect on how much of your identity is tied to your "mortal self"—your name, history, achievements, and relationships within the temporal world. Consider the idea that "purification is subtraction" and "the emptying of illusion." What are some worldly attachments or aspects of your perceived "self" that you might need to release to allow your eternal essence to shine through? How can you consciously practice detachment while remaining fully present in your daily life, transforming every temporal moment into an opportunity to connect with the Eternal, and asking, "What have I placed between us?" to allow the veils to fall?

Contemplation: The Material and the Absolute

The contemplation of The Secret bridges the perceived gap between the material and the Absolute. The wise-one realizes that the physical universe, seemingly solid and independent, is an active manifestation of the Absolute, not separate from it. Every atom, every natural law, every intricate design in creation is a direct sign leading back to the Creator. This insight transforms the wise-one's perception of the material world from an object of delusion to a pathway of profound insight, recognizing the Absolute's Presence woven into the very fabric of existence.

The Vessel Returns, But the Breath Remains

A final realization settles into silence:
Everything seen will fade.
Mountains crumble, stars burn out,
And the body—tender vessel of experience—
Returns joyfully to the soil that bore it.
Not in loss, but in completion.
All things return to their source.
The body to dust, reclaimed by the earth.

But what danced within that form—
That breath,
Placed by the One who never fades—
Is not consumed,
Nor undone.
It is carried beyond,

Preserved, known,
Called back to the Presence
That gave it being.

❮Say: 'Yes, even if you become stones, or iron,
Or whatever you think is harder to bring to life!'
Then they will ask, 'Who will bring us back?'
Say: 'The One who created you the first time.'❯¹²⁴ — Quran 17:50–51

(From Visibility to Essence)

The wise-one reflects—
Dust does not define destiny.
Materiality is not permanence.
The mortal vessel
Was never meant to be clung to—
It was meant to be revered,
For what it carried.
Everything visible shall return to its invisibility.
Everything formed shall return to the formlessness from which it came.

Even the stages of life,
From dust to embryo to infancy to decline,
Are not signs of decay—
But of Divine choreography.

---

¹²⁴ This is derived from the Quran verse of:

❮And they say ˹mockingly˺, "When we are reduced to bones and ashes, will we really be raised as a new creation?" (49) Say, ˹O Prophet,˺ "˹Yes, even if˺ you become stones, or iron, (50) or whatever you think is harder to bring to life!" Then they will ask ˹you˺, "Who will bring us back ˹to life˺?" Say, "The One Who created you the first time." They will then shake their heads at you and ask, "When will that be?" Say, "Perhaps it is soon!" (51) On the Day He will call you, you will ˹instantly˺ respond by praising Him,[1] thinking you had remained ˹in the world˺ only for a little while. (52)❯ [Quran 17:49-52]

[1]: When everyone is raised from the dead, they will all praise Allah, regardless of what they had believed in this life.

❲We created you from dust…
Then a sperm-drop…
Then a clinging clot…❳[125] — Quran 22:5

To witness this path
Is to see not randomness,
But purpose.
Not disintegration,
But return.

(Dust Cannot Consume the Breath)

Within the wise-one
Resonate something that remains untouched:
A breath carrying the Creator will,
A spark entrusted,
A reminder of origin.
The journey, then, is not to cling to the mortal,
But to let it teach you how to live for the Immortal.

The soul's purpose
Is not preservation of flesh,
But realization of the formless truth within.
Death is not an end,
But a passage—

---

[125] This is derived from the Quran verses of:

❲O humanity! If you are in doubt about the Resurrection, then ˹know that˺ We did create you1 from dust, then from a sperm-drop,2 then ˹developed you into˺ a clinging clot,3 then a lump of flesh4—fully formed or unformed5—in order to demonstrate ˹Our power˺ to you. ˹Then˺ We settle whatever ˹embryo˺ We will in the womb for an appointed term, then bring you forth as infants, so that you may reach your prime. Some of you ˹may˺ die ˹young˺, while others are left to reach the most feeble stage of life so that they may know nothing after having known much. And you see the earth lifeless, but as soon as We send down rain upon it, it begins to stir ˹to life˺ and swell, producing every type of pleasant plant. (5) That is because Allah ˹alone˺ is the Truth, He ˹alone˺ gives life to the dead, and He ˹alone˺ is Most Capable of everything. (6) And certainly the Hour is coming, there is no doubt about it. And Allah will surely resurrect those in the graves. (7)❳ [Quran 22:5-7]

[1]: Your father, Adam ﷺ.

[2]: Nuṭfah refers to the union of male and female gametes (sperm and egg) which results in the zygote after fertilization.

[3]: 'Alaqah, meaning the embryo resembles a leech.

[4]: Muḍghah, meaning it resembles a chewed morsel.

[5]: Fully formed or defected, evolving into a healthy embryo or ending in miscarriage.

Not into oblivion,
But into returning[126].

So the wise-one walks forward—
Not mourning the dust,
But revering it as a teacher.
They embrace mortality
To awaken to immortality.
They bow to the fleeting
To remember the Eternal.

For only He fashions clay and breathes into it spirit.
Only He dissolves form to reveal presence.
Only He remains the source
Of return, revival, and eternal light.

Wisdom Unveiled

The profound wisdom revealed is that The Secret bridges the material and the Absolute, showing that the physical universe is a direct manifestation and a sign of the Creator, rather than separate from Him. The wise-one understands that "everything visible shall return to its invisibility," and the body, though a tender vessel, "returns joyfully to the soil that bore it." Yet, within this mortal form dances "a breath that carries the signature of the One who never fades"—a formless truth that dust cannot consume. This realization transforms the perception of the material world into a pathway of profound insight, recognizing the Absolute's Presence in every intricate design and the Divine choreography of life's stages. The journey, then, is not to cling to the mortal, but to let it teach how to live for the Immortal, embracing mortality to awaken to immortality, and bowing to the fleeting to remember the Eternal.

Wise-Reflection

Reflect on your own relationship with the material world and your physical body. Do you often perceive them as separate from a Divine Presence?

---

[126] This is depicted in the Quran verse of:

📖 ❨Whoever hopes for the meeting with Allah, ˹let them know that˺ Allah's appointed time is sure to come. He is the All-Hearing, All-Knowing. (5)❩ [Quran 29:5]

Consider the idea that "everything seen will fade," but "what danced within that form... is not consumed." How can you practice revering your physical existence as a "vessel borrowed for a time" that carries an eternal essence? What specific actions or shifts in perception can help you transform your view of the material world from an object of delusion to a pathway of profound insight, recognizing the Absolute's Presence woven into its very fabric, and living not to cling to the mortal, but to awaken to the Immortal?

Contemplation: The Creator as Absolute

The Secret unveils the profound truth of The Creator as Absolute—utterly unique, self-sufficient, and incomparable, beyond all human attributes and creation. He is the First and the Last, the Manifest and the Hidden. This contemplation emphasizes Allah's transcendence, reinforcing Tawhid (Divine Oneness) in its purest form. The wise-one's understanding shifts from a fragmented view of existence to a unified perception rooted in the Absolute Oneness of the Creator, dissolving all false notions of partnership or limitation.

Beyond Boundaries, Before All Beginnings

The wise-one beholds the Real—
Not as idea,
Not as image,
But as Presence that precedes all form
And exists beyond all measure.
The Absolute is not mingled with creation, nor contained within it.
Not to be defined by unity of being, nor confused with what He has formed.

This truth shakes the scaffolding of perception.
The One who spoke existence into motion
Is not mingled with the waves that followed.
Creation is an echo—
But He is not the sound.
He is the Source.

⟨Indeed your Lord is Allah Who created the heavens and the earth in six Days,
Then established Himself on the Throne.
...The creation and the command belong to Him alone.⟩[127] — Quran 7:54

He commands the orbits,
Yet remains beyond rotation.
He sustains stars,
But is not sustained by them.

(The Distinction of the Divine)

To claim unity with creation
Is to collapse sovereignty into semblance.
But the wise-one knows:
The Creator is not absorbed by what He made.
He is not found inside atoms—
But atoms are found in Him.
By His command, universes rise and vanish, [128]
Time and space move at His will.[129]

---

[127] This is derived from the Quran verse of:

⟨Indeed your Lord is Allah Who created the heavens and the earth in six Days,[1] then established Himself on the Throne. He makes the day and night overlap in rapid succession. He created the sun, the moon, and the stars—all subjected by His command. The creation and the command belong to Him ˹alone˺. Blessed is Allah—Lord of all worlds! (54) Call upon your Lord humbly and secretly. Surely He does not like the transgressors. (55)⟩ [Quran 54-55]

[1]: The word day is not always used in the Quran to mean a 24-hour period. According to 22:47, a heavenly Day is 1000 years of our time. The Day of Judgment will be 50 000 years of our time (see 70:4). Hence, the six Days of creation refer to six eons of time, known only by Allah.

[128] This best depicted in the Quran verses of:

⟨And one of His signs is that the heavens and the earth persist by His command. Then when He calls you out of the earth just once, you will instantly come forth. (25) And to Him belong all those in the heavens and the earth—all are subject to His Will.[1] (26) And He is the One Who originates the creation then will resurrect it—which is even easier for Him.[2] To Him belong the finest attributes in the heavens and the earth. And He is the Almighty, All-Wise.(27)⟩ [Quran 30:25-27]

[1]: lit., to Him.

[2]: This is from a human perspective. Otherwise, both the creation of the universe and the resurrection of humans are easy for Allah.

[129] This best depicted in the Quran verses of:

⟨On that Day We will roll up the heavens like a scroll of writings. Just as We produced the first creation, ˹so˺ shall We reproduce it. That is a promise binding on Us. We truly uphold ˹Our promises˺! (104) Surely,

He is the Initiator,
The Sustainer,
The Withdrawer.
All rhythms rise by His permission—
And vanish at His silence.

❨*Allah is the Creator of all things,*
And He is the Maintainer of everything.❩*130* — *Quran 39:62*

His Throne does not confine Him.
Time does not age Him.
Space does not hold Him.
He is not made of dimensions—
He authors them.

(Sovereignty Without Rival)

The wise-one reflects:
To witness the Absolute
Is not to find a figure—
But to surrender into Limitlessness
That has no origin,
No peer,
No need.

❨*To Him belong the keys of the treasuries of the heavens and the earth.*❩*131* —
Quran 39:63

---

following the 'heavenly' Record, We decreed in the Scriptures: "My righteous servants shall inherit the land." (105) Surely this 'Quran' is sufficient 'as a reminder' for those devoted to worship. (106)❩ [Quran 21:104-106]

And The Quran verse of:

📖 ❨We built the universe with 'great' might, and We are certainly expanding 'it'. (47)❩ [Quran 51:47]

130 This is derived from the Quran verse of:

📖 ❨Allah is the Creator of all things, and He is the Maintainer of everything. (62) To Him belong the keys 'of the treasuries' of the heavens and the earth. As for those who rejected the signs of Allah, it is they who will be the 'true' losers. (63)❩ [Quran: 39:62-63]

131 This is derived from the Quran verse of:

📖 ❨Allah is the Creator of all things, and He is the Maintainer of everything. (62) To Him belong the keys 'of the treasuries' of the heavens and the earth. As for those who rejected the signs of Allah, it is they who will be the 'true' losers. (63)❩ [Quran 39:62-63]

He gives,
Not because He receives.
He creates,
Not because He is shaped.
He is One,
Not as a number,
But as Oneness beyond enumeration.

So the wise-one walks forward—
Not seeking to grasp the Divine,
But to dissolve in reverence.
They do not reduce Him to metaphor,
Nor press His majesty into image.
They let go—
And in the letting go,
They remember.

For only He creates without being touched by creation.
Only He sustains without dependence.
Only He remains the source
Of command, cosmos, and eternal sovereignty.

Wisdom Unveiled

The profound wisdom revealed is that The Secret unveils The Creator as Absolute—utterly unique, self-sufficient, and incomparable, embodying pure Tawhid (Divine Oneness). The wise-one realizes that the Absolute is beyond all bounds, neither mingled with creation nor contained within it; He is the Source, not merely the sound or an echo. By His command, universes rise and vanish, and time and space move at His will; He sustains all, yet none sustain Him, and His essence is beyond limit, His sovereignty without rival. This understanding challenges the notion of unity with creation, emphasizing that He is not found inside atoms, but atoms are found in Him. The wise-one stands trembling at this realization that all they have loved and lost are but ripples on the ocean of His decree, yet in that trembling, there is a deeper peace—for to belong to the Absolute is to belong to what cannot perish. This profound shift leads to a unified perception, dissolving all false notions of partnership or limitation, as the wise-one dissolves in reverence rather than attempting to grasp the Divine.

Wise-Reflection

Reflect on any preconceived notions or mental images you might hold about the Creator. Do they inadvertently limit His Absolute nature? Consider the idea that "He is One, not as a number, but as Oneness beyond enumeration." How can you cultivate a deeper understanding of Allah's transcendence and Absolute Oneness in your daily life, moving beyond fragmented views of existence? What practices can help you "dissolve in reverence" and "let go" of attempts to reduce His majesty to metaphor or image, allowing you to experience the profound peace that comes from belonging to the Absolute?

Contemplation: The Divine as the Guardian of the Secret

The wise-one knows that the Divine is the ultimate Guardian of The Secret. It is not something humans can fully unravel by their own intellect or effort alone; rather, it is unveiled by Divine will and grace. This profound truth cultivates deep humility and absolute reliance on Allah. It signifies that true knowledge is a bestowal, not an acquisition, reinforcing the understanding that all insight and awakening come directly from the Source of all wisdom.

Sovereignty Unseen, Protection Without Failure

The wise-one pauses in awe—
Not because they are exposed,
But because they are enveloped.
The journey inward toward the Secret
Is not a solitary venture—
It is one guarded by Divine Vigilance,
Watched over by Mercy that never forgets.
The Presence prevails, and all creation yields to Its trace.
The Secret is guarded by surrender, humility, and remembrance.

This safeguarding is not of locks and barriers,
But of purification—
Of hearts softened in reverence,
Minds freed from self-importance,
Souls anchored in trust.

The Divine Gaze, unseen yet sovereign,
Never turns away.

⟨*Is there any equal to the Vigilant One*
Who knows what every soul commits?⟩[132] — *Quran 13:33*

He sees the intention before the act,
The hesitation before the word,
The longing behind the silence.
And He guides, not by coercion,
But by invitation into surrender.
Those who associate others beside Him—
Whether idols or ideas, desires or illusions—
They veer from remembrance,
Wrapped in veils of distraction.

⟨*And whoever Allah leaves to stray*
Will be left with no guide.⟩[133] — *Quran 39:36*

Guidance is not withheld—
But it is not imposed.
It blooms in those
Who choose to walk with it.

The Secret is not merely hidden,
It is honored.
It lives in the soul,
But its purity is watched over
By angels who record each tremble,

---

[132] This is derived from the Quran verse of:

📖 ⟨Is ˹there any equal to˺ the Vigilant One Who knows what every soul commits? Yet the pagans have associated others with Allah ˹in worship˺. Say, ˹O Prophet,˺ "Name them! Or do you ˹mean to˺ inform Him of something He does not know on the earth? Or are these ˹gods˺ just empty words?" In fact, the disbelievers' falsehood has been made so appealing to them that they have been turned away from the Path. And whoever Allah leaves to stray will be left with no guide. (33)⟩ [Quran 13:33]

[133] This is derived from the Quran verses of:

📖 ⟨Is Allah not sufficient for His servant? Yet they threaten you with other ˹powerless˺ gods besides Him! Whoever Allah leaves to stray will be left with no guide. (36) And whoever Allah guides, none can lead astray. Is Allah not Almighty, capable of punishment? (37)⟩ [Quran 39:36-37]

Each return,
Each breath of repentance.

⟨He reigns supreme over all of His creation,
And sends recording-angels, watching over you.
When death comes to any of you,
Our angels take their soul,
Never neglecting this duty.⟩[134] *— Quran 6:61*

There is no lapse in this guardianship.
Not even the final breath
Passes unnoticed.
For what is veiled to the world
Is naked in the light of Divine presence.

To hold true is to stand unshaken, anchored in the Eternal.
Yes. The soul, entrusted to the One,
Cannot be undone by trial.
Storms may rattle the body,
But the heart, if surrendered,
Stands in sanctuary.
No force can sever what He has entrusted,
No trial can break the one sheltered in His protection.

Even when unseen,
The path beneath the feet of the wise-one
Is laid with divine precision.
And in the wake of the Divine,
No step is wasted,
No whisper unheard,
No truth forgotten.

So the wise-one walks forward—
Not with anxiety,

---

[134] This is derived from the Quran verses of:

⟨He reigns supreme over all of His creation, and sends recording-angels, watching over you. When death comes to any of you, Our angels take their soul, never neglecting this duty. (61) Then they are ˹all˺ returned to Allah—their True Master. Judgment is His ˹alone˺. And He is the Swiftest Reckoner. (62)⟩ [Quran 6:61-62]

But with trust.
Not claiming their strength,
But sheltered in the One
Whose vigilance never sleeps.

For only He sees beyond the visible.
Only He guards what He breathes into being.
Only He remains the source
Of protection, purity, and eternal remembrance.

Wisdom Unveiled

The profound wisdom revealed is that the Divine is the ultimate Guardian of The Secret. This Secret, hidden within the soul, is not a human possession but a reflection of Divine Will, a gift too sacred to be fully exposed to the winds of pride or fear. It is safeguarded "not by locks and barriers, but by purification—of hearts softened in reverence, minds freed from self-importance, souls anchored in trust." The wise-one understands that this Divine Vigilance is unseen yet sovereign, recording every intention and breath without lapse, ensuring that "what is veiled to the world is naked in the light of Divine presence." The Presence moves, unseen yet sovereign, and all creation yields to Its trace. To hold true is to stand unshaken, anchored in the Eternal, for no force can sever what He has entrusted, and no trial can break the one sheltered in His protection. This realization cultivates deep humility, absolute reliance on Allah, and allows the wise-one to walk the earth with light feet, carrying within them a citadel that no enemy can breach, for in the wake of the Divine, no step is lost, no whisper unheard, no truth forgotten.

Wise-Reflection

Reflect on moments when you feel most vulnerable or exposed. How might shifting your perspective to see yourself "enveloped" by Divine Vigilance and "sheltered in His protection" change your inner state? Consider the idea that The Secret is guarded by "surrender, humility, and remembrance." What specific actions or inner dispositions can you cultivate to purify your heart and mind, thus allowing this Divine safeguarding to manifest more fully in your life, leading to greater trust and less anxiety? How can you internalize the understanding that true knowledge is a bestowal, not an acquisition, reinforcing reliance on the Source of all wisdom?

Contemplation: The Power of Self-Realization

The unveiling of The Secret empowers the wise-one with the Power of Self-Realization. This isn't egoic self-discovery, but the realization of the soul's true, primordial nature as created by Allah, imbued with His inspiration, and destined for His nearness. It's the spiritual and psychic awakening to the latent potentials and Divine likeness (in attributes, not essence) placed within the human being. This realization fuels the wise-one's journey toward purifying their soul, as commanded in the Gateway Verse: "Successful indeed is the one who purifies their soul, and doomed is the one who corrupts it."

Beyond Transactional Salvation, Into Eternal Belonging

The wise-one rises not in pride,
But in recognition.
Not of what they've achieved,
But of what was always within them—
A light untouched by reward,
A truth undimmed by punishment.
Beyond paradise and punishment, beyond names and forms,
There is an essence—untouched, uncontained,
Outshining all creation.

This is not a rejection of divine promise,
But a transcendence of conditions.
Paradise is mercy,
But the soul's true origin is older still.
Judgment affirms justice,
But the soul was formed not in fear—
But in intimacy with the Source.

❨Then He fashioned them
And had a spirit of His Own creation breathed into them.❩[135] — Quran 32:9

That breath was not transactional.
It was not earned.
It was gift.
And in every longing,
It still whispers.

(A Love That Is Not Earned)

The wise-one reflects:
To awaken into the Secret
Is to be liberated from the economy of merit and guilt.
No longer a merchant bargaining for paradise,
No longer a servant paralyzed by fear.
But a lover returning
To the One
Who never stopped loving.
Its home lies beyond even the bliss of paradise
And the awe of judgment.
Here, the soul does not calculate—
It remembers.
Here, the heart does not grasp—
It rests.

Salvation is not a transaction,
But a revelation:
You were never apart.
You only dreamed you were.

This unveiling echoes through Revelation itself:
Creation was clay,

---

[135] This is derived from the Quran verses of:

📖 ❨That is the Knower of the seen and unseen—the Almighty, Most Merciful, (6) Who has perfected everything He created. And He originated the creation of humankind from clay. (7) Then He made his descendants from an extract of a humble fluid, (8) then He fashioned them and had a spirit of His Own ′creation′ breathed into them. And He gave you hearing, sight, and intellect. ′Yet′ you hardly give any thanks. (9)❩ [Quran 32:6-9]

But the breath was Divine.
Form was humble,
But spirit was majestic.

❮Who has perfected everything He created.
And He originated humankind from clay.❯[136] — Quran 32:7
❮Say, 'Its nature is known only to my Lord.'❯[137] — Quran 17:85

The spirit cannot be studied,
Only surrendered to.

(Essence Without Image)

What the heart remembers
Cannot be stored in words.
What the soul awakens to
Outshines even paradise—
Not in delight,
But in belonging.
This is the power of self-realization—
Not self-centered,
But God-centered.
To realize the Secret
Is to kneel inside
A love unconditioned,
A nearness undeserved,
A truth unfathomable
But known at the deepest breath.

So the wise-one walks forward—
Not with anxiety over salvation,

---

[136] This is derived from the Quran verses of:

📖 ❮That is the Knower of the seen and unseen—the Almighty, Most Merciful, (6) Who has perfected everything He created. And He originated the creation of humankind from clay. (7) Then He made his descendants from an extract of a humble fluid, (8) then He fashioned them and had a spirit of His Own 'creation' breathed into them. And He gave you hearing, sight, and intellect. 'Yet' you hardly give any thanks. (9)❯ [Quran 32:6-9]

[137] This is derived from the Quran verse of:

📖 ❮They ask you 'O Prophet' about the spirit. Say, "Its nature is known only to my Lord, and you 'O humanity' have been given but little knowledge." (85)❯ [Quran 17:85]

But with gratitude for proximity.
Not demanding reward,
But glorifying the Reality
That made reward possible.

And in that awakening,
They do not ascend—
They return.

For only He breathes into the soul its essence.
Only He sustains what cannot be named.
Only He remains the source
Of realization, remembrance, and eternal love.

Wisdom Unveiled

The profound wisdom revealed is that the Power of Self-Realization is the awakening to the soul's true, primordial nature as a Divine gift, not an egoic discovery. The wise-one understands that the true destiny of the soul is not to be a servant of fear nor a merchant of reward, for its home lies beyond even the bliss of paradise and the awe of judgment. It belongs to a light so pure that neither words nor heavens can enclose it. To realize The Secret is to be liberated from the economy of merit and guilt, of striving and despair. It's to awaken into a love that isn't earned, a belonging that was never lost, confirming that "salvation isn't a transaction, but a revelation: You were never apart. You only dreamed you were." This God-centered realization leads to a profound gratitude for proximity, glorifying the Reality that made all possible, and ultimately, a return to the Divine Source in unconditioned love and undeserved nearness.

Wise-Reflection

Reflect on your motivation for spiritual growth or striving. Is it driven by the hope of reward or the fear of punishment? Consider the idea that "salvation isn't a transaction, but a revelation: You were never apart. You only dreamed you were." How might embracing this understanding change your approach to your spiritual journey? What practices can help you move "beyond transactional salvation, into eternal belonging," allowing you to rest in the "love unconditioned" and "nearness undeserved" that comes from realizing your soul's true, primordial nature as a Divine gift?

Contemplation: The Sovereignty of the Human Soul

Derived from The Secret, the wise-one comes to understand the Sovereignty of the Human Soul within the created realm. This sovereignty is a sacred trust from Allah, granted through the inspiration of right and wrong, and the capacity for moral choice and vicegerency (khalifah) on earth. It implies a unique responsibility and a profound inner freedom to choose alignment with the Divine Will. The human soul, when purified, becomes sovereign over its lower self and capable of manifesting Divine attributes, leading with wisdom and compassion over creation. This understanding is a profound psychic empowerment, fostering a sense of purpose and ethical responsibility.

Awakening Not to Power—but to Divine Presence

The wise-one realizes:
To affirm the Secret is not to grasp knowledge,
But to return to origin.
Not to elevate the self,
But to remember the breath
That gave it being.
To affirm the Secret is to awaken—not in knowledge, but in origin.
The soul carries the breath of the Divine, veiled yet sovereign.

This sovereignty is not earned,
Nor can it be claimed.
It was bestowed—
Not for dominion,
But for witnessing.
For to be shaped from clay
And then entrusted with spirit
Is the paradox of sacred human dignity.

❮When I have fashioned him
And had a spirit of My Own creation breathed into him,
Fall down in prostration to him.❯[138] — Quran 15:29

The angels bowed not to form,
But to the breath of Divine Sovereignty
Placed gently in human soul.

This soul, then, is not a servant of the world
Nor a prisoner of self-image.
It is veiled from perception
Yet sovereign in purpose—
Fashioned by Divine command,
And upheld by Divine remembrance.

❮Surely those who pledge allegiance to you, O Prophet,
Are actually pledging allegiance to Allah.
Allah's Hand is over theirs...❯[139] — Quran 48:10

To yield in remembrance
Is to be wrapped in protection.
The One who fashioned you
Remains the One who safeguards you—
Not through fear,
But through covenant.

To remain true to the Almighty is to be upheld...
Yes.
Truthfulness is not a moral trait alone—

---

[138] This is derived from the Quran verses of:

📖 ❮'Remember, O Prophet' when your Lord said to the angels, "I am going to create a human being from sounding clay moulded from black mud. (28) So when I have fashioned him and had a spirit of My Own 'creation' breathed into him, fall down in prostration to him." (29) So the angels prostrated all together—(30)❯ [Quran 15:28-30]

[139] This is derived from the Quran verses of:

📖 ❮Indeed, 'O Prophet,' We have sent you as a witness, a deliverer of good news, and a warner, (8) so that you 'believers' may have faith in Allah and His Messenger, support and honour him, and glorify Allah morning and evening.[1] (9) Surely those who pledge allegiance to you 'O Prophet' are actually pledging allegiance to Allah. Allah's Hand is over theirs. Whoever breaks their pledge, it will only be to their own loss. And whoever fulfils their pledge to Allah, He will grant them a great reward. (10)❯ [Quran 48:8-10]

[1]: Another possible translation: "... so that you 'all' may believe in Allah and His Messenger, support 'His cause', revere, and glorify Him morning and evening."

It is an alignment with the breath within.
Remembrance is not repetition—
It is anchoring.
To be sincere is to invite Divine proximity.
To surrender is not weakness—
But a return to original sovereignty
Given through love.
And His Hand remains over those who yield.
His promise is not delayed,
Nor forgotten.

So the wise-one walks forward—
Not flaunting sovereignty,
But honoring it.
Not building selfhood,
But revealing the trust
Hidden within it.

For only He breathes majesty into clay.
Only He veils the soul with purpose.
Only He remains the source
Of remembrance, protection, and eternal sovereignty.

Wisdom Unveiled

The profound wisdom revealed is that The Secret unveils the Sovereignty of the Human Soul—a sacred trust and Divine gift bestowed, not earned. To affirm The Secret is to awaken to origin, not in power, but in Divine Presence, recognizing the soul carries the breath of the Divine, veiled yet sovereign in its purpose. This sovereignty is not for worldly dominion but for witnessing and alignment with Divine Will. The angels' prostration to Adam was not to his form, but to the Divine Sovereignty placed within him. The wise-one understands that this soul, anchored in the Eternal and safeguarded by Divine protection through covenant, fears neither loss nor death, for it belongs wholly to the Real. True sovereignty is not about ruling others, but about belonging wholly to the Real, remaining unshakeable by external trials. The wise-one sees through the radiant certainty of being a reflection of the Unchanging One, embracing a psychic empowerment that fuels purpose and ethical responsibility, for to remain true to the Source is to be upheld, and His Hand is over those who yield.

Wise-Reflection

Reflect on your understanding of power and control. Do you primarily associate it with external influence or personal achievement? Consider the idea that the Sovereignty of the Human Soul is a "sacred trust" for "witnessing" and alignment with Divine Will, not for dominion. How can you shift your focus from seeking external power to cultivating this profound inner freedom and ethical responsibility? What specific practices can help you purify your soul, allowing it to become "sovereign over its lower self" and manifest Divine attributes, leading with wisdom and compassion, by remembering that "His Hand is over those who yield"?

Conclusion: The Secret

ECHOES OF REALIZATION

Thus, the wise-one, now bearing the awakened Secret within the depths of their being, walks not apart from the manifest world, but gracefully through it—like a luminous lantern that eternally remembers the sun, even while shining brightly among the myriad stars of creation.

The Secret is not a mystery to be solved through intellectual dissection; it is, rather, a profound birthright to be realized and embodied. The wise-one no longer frantically searches for light in external phenomena, for they have intimately become the very bearer of it—illumined from within by the One who, in His infinite Majesty, lit the heavens before time itself began its measure. This is the profound shift from seeking to being, from acquiring to reflecting.

THE SEEKER'S ASCENT: THE ULTIMATE CALL

There comes a culminating moment in the soul's arduous pilgrimage when the very search for truth dissolves into its own fulfillment, and what remains is not a fragmented journey, but an eternal return to Origin. The Secret is not merely a profound mystery to be intellectually pondered; it is the soul's forgotten homeland, ceaselessly calling it back to its primordial remembrance.

To truly uncover The Secret is not to learn something entirely new, but to awaken fully to what was intrinsically placed within the soul before the intricate weaving of flesh and the binding of time began. It is a divine summons to courageously transcend the perceived boundaries of body and mind—to cease living as a mere creation seemingly imprisoned by external circumstance, and to rise as a pure flame born of the Eternal Breath of the Creator.

The wise-one is called not to merely accumulate fragments of knowledge, but to become knowledge itself, made luminous by Divine light. Not to perform worship as a detached duty, but to exist as worship itself, an continuous act of conscious devotion. The ultimate call is not to reach outward in anxious seeking, but to profoundly dive inward—to the very depths where the sacred echo of the Creator's omnipresent gaze still gently stirs in the hidden, most sanctified chambers of the soul. Here, every conscious step becomes a profound homecoming. Here, The Secret is not found by physically walking towards it, but by the liberating realization that it was always walking within you, awaiting its grand unveiling.

7ᵀᴴ REFLECTION: SECLUDED ENTRANCE

(The Way to the Creator)

THE GATEWAY VERSE

In the sacred words of Allah, a profound narrative of ultimate surrender and direct Divine encounter, guiding all who reflect towards the essence of true proximity:

📖 ❨*Has the story of Moses reached you 'O Prophet'? (9) When he saw a fire, he said to his family, "Wait here, 'for' I have spotted a fire. Perhaps I can bring you a torch from it, or find some guidance at the fire." (10) But when he approached it, he was called, "O Moses! (11) It is truly I. I am your Lord! So take off your sandals, for you are in the sacred valley of Ṭuwa. (12) I have chosen you, so listen to what is revealed: (13) 'It is truly I. I am Allah! There is no god 'worthy of worship' except Me. So worship Me 'alone', and establish prayer for My remembrance. (14)*❩ *[Quran 20:9-14]*

ILLUMINATION'S DAWN[140]

Here exist profound thresholds that the human soul cannot possibly cross by strength or merit alone. There are sacred entrances, hidden not by material walls, but by the subtle veils of illusion that the self meticulously clings to. "The Secluded Entrance" is precisely such a doorway: utterly invisible to those laden with the perceived weight of their deeds, the scaffolding of their temporal identity, or the burden of their spiritual pride; it becomes luminously open only to those who approach it empty-handed, clothed in utter, willing surrender.

This reflection is far more than a mere teaching; it is a sacred, transformative summons—a direct invitation from the Creator to meet Him not through any imagined personal merit, but solely through His boundless Mercy; not through impressive human achievement, but through the complete, courageous abandonment of all self-claims. Here, the wise-one's soul learns the profound truth that emptiness is not a loss, but the essential preparation for reception. That loneliness, when

---

[140] his reflection stands as a radiant threshold, echoing the sacred encounter in Wādi Ṭuwā—where the soul, like Musa ﷺ, is called to leave behind even its sandals, even its self, to meet the Divine in pure, unmediated presence. What aimed to be shared is a profound unveiling of the spiritual etiquette required for true nearness: to approach with nothing, to cling to nothing, to meet the Creator in sacred solitude.

embraced, is not isolation, but the pure clearing where the Divine steps in with intimate Presence. Let us now, with hearts purified by longing, enter this Secluded Entrance, where every deed is returned to its rightful Source, and every name and identity dissolves into the Only Name that eternally matters.

THE UNFOLDING OF INSIGHTS

This section unveils the subtle yet profound realities of approaching the Creator, emphasizing the necessity of abandoning all forms of self-reliance for true connection.

Contemplation: The Limitations of Human Effort

The wise-one comes to terms with the ultimate limitations of human effort when seeking the Divine Presence. Just as Prophet Musa was commanded to remove his sandals, symbolizing the shedding of worldly and self-reliant attachments, the seeker must recognize that no amount of personal striving, intellectual pursuit, or ritualistic adherence can, by itself, create Divine proximity. True connection is a gift of Grace, not a consequence of human exertion. This understanding cultivates profound humility and shifts the wise-one's reliance from their own 'doing' to the absolute power and will of Allah.

The Fragility of Righteousness Before the Divine

The wise-one reflects:
Even the good they do,
Even what appears luminous in sacred measure—
They dare not carry it
As the key to divine nearness.
For deeds are not the entrance,
Nor is virtue the bridge.
Even the good you do—do not carry it as your entrance,
For deeds are not the key.

Purification is granted,
Not earned.
It flows not from accumulation,
But from surrender.
It descends not by calculation,

[220]

But by remembrance,
And by the favor of the One
Who purifies through love,
Not through labor.

❲*Indeed, Allah has done the believers a great favour*
By raising a messenger from among them—reciting to them His revelations,
Purifying them, and teaching them the Book and wisdom...❳[141] — *Quran 3:164*

Even the righteous move
Not with confidence,
But with fear—
Not of punishment,
But of separation.
They tremble not from doubt,
But from longing—
That their deeds may not veil them
From the One they were done for.

❲*And those who do whatever good they do*
With their hearts fearful, knowing they will return to their Lord—
It is they who race to do good deeds...❳[142] — *Quran 23:60–61*

There is no arrival by merit—
Only by grace.
And grace chooses not the loud,
But the surrendered.
The wise-one walks

---

[141] This is derived from the Quran verse of:

📖 ❲Indeed, Allah has done the believers a ʿgreatˋ favour by raising a messenger from among them—reciting to them His revelations, purifying them, and teaching them the Book and wisdom. For indeed they had previously been clearly astray. (164)❳ [Quran 3:164]

[142] This derived from the Quran verses of:

📖 ❲Surely those who tremble in awe of their Lord, (57) and who believe in the revelations of their Lord, (58) and who associate none with their Lord, (59) and who do whatever ʿgoodˋ they do with their hearts fearful, ʿknowingˋ that they will return to their Lord[1]— (60) it is they who race to do good deeds, always taking the lead. (61) We never require of any soul more than what it can afford. And with Us is a record which speaks the truth. None will be wronged. (62)❳ [Quran 23:57-62]

[1]: It is reported in an authentic narration collected by At-Tirmiẓi that 'Âishah, the Prophet's wife, asked him 🌸 if this verse refers to those who steal or drink ʿalcoholˋ. The Prophet 🌸 answered, "No, it refers to those who pray, fast, and donate, but are afraid that their deeds are rejected because they are not good enough." Then he 🌸 recited the last part of the verse: "It is they who race to do good deeds, always taking the lead."

With the humility of one
Who knows their best actions
Were only possible
Because the door of remembrance
Was opened to them.
They know:
It is not effort that saves,
But the Divine who sustains effort.
It is not worship that ascends,
But the One who lifts it.
It is not purity that impresses,
But the One who whispers it into being.

The wise-one moves,
Not as claimant,
But as caller.
Not in certainty,
But in intimate uncertainty.
They long not to be praised,
But to be near.
And in that longing,
They are upheld—
Not by their works,
But by His mercy.

For only He purifies without transaction.
Only He uplifts without measure.
Only He remains the source
Of longing, surrender, and eternal favor.

Wisdom Unveiled

The profound wisdom revealed is that Divine proximity is ultimately a gift of Grace, not a consequence of human exertion or the limitations of human effort. The wise-one understands that "no ladder of effort can reach the sky of grace," and "no accumulation of righteousness can unlock the chamber of the Infinite." Even the good deeds performed should not be carried as an "entrance," for deeds are not the key; instead, purification is granted through surrender, remembrance, and the favor of the Most

Merciful. The righteous, rather than walking with pride, move with humility and fear of separation, longing to stand in Divine Presence, upheld not by their works, but by His grace. This deep humility transforms the wise-one into a beggar who knows that all goodness flows from the Giver, not the receiver, recognizing that "Paradise itself cannot be purchased—it is a gift given when the soul becomes poor enough to receive it."

Wise-Reflection

Reflect on your own spiritual journey. Do you ever find yourself relying on your good deeds or spiritual practices as a means to "earn" Divine proximity? Consider the idea that "Divine union is not a transaction; it is a surrender." How might embracing the limitations of human effort and cultivating profound humility change your approach to worship and good deeds? What would it mean for you to walk with the "humility of the beggar," knowing that all goodness flows from the Giver, and allowing yourself to be upheld by Divine grace rather than your own efforts?

Contemplation: The Call to Detachment from Deeds

A crucial aspect of entering the Secluded Entrance is the call to detachment even from one's own virtuous deeds. While good deeds are commanded and rewarded, clinging to them as a means of earning Allah's favor or using them as a basis for spiritual pride becomes a subtle veil. The wise-one realizes that no deed, however noble, can ever be commensurate with Allah's infinite majesty or His absolute right. This detachment purifies intention, transforming deeds into pure acts of worship and gratitude, rather than transactional efforts, ensuring sincere devotion rather than self-admiration.

Let Deeds Flow Like Wind, Not Like Chains

The wise-one realizes:
To approach the Secluded Entrance,
Even the light of one's own virtue
Must be gently laid down.
Act, but do not dwell upon the act.
Give, but let your giving pass

Like the wind through branches—
Fruitful, yet untethered.

Deeds are not possessions,
But momentary blossoms—
Born in mercy,
And meant to be released.

❲Do not waste your charity
With reminders of your generosity or hurtful words—
Like the one who spends their wealth
Only to show off,
Not truly believing in Allah and the Last Day.❳[143] *— Quran 2:264*

To grasp at good
Is to forget its Source.
To hold a deed
Too close to the heart
Is to veil the heart
From the One who inspired it.
Deeds are rivers, not statues—
They move by grace,
Not by pride.
Even the purest acts,
When claimed as identity,
Become subtle barriers
Between the soul and its Maker.

❲They regard their acceptance of Islam as a favour to you.
Tell them, 'Do not regard your Islam as a favour to me.

---

[143] This is derived from the Quran verse of:

📖 ❲O believers! Do not waste your charity with reminders ʿof your generosityʾ or hurtful words, like those who donate their wealth just to show off and do not believe in Allah or the Last Day. Their example is that of a hard barren rock covered with a thin layer of soil hit by a strong rain—leaving it just a bare stone. Such people are unable to preserve the reward of their charity. Allah does not guide ʿsuchʾ disbelieving people. (264)❳ [Quran 2:264]

Rather, it is Allah Who has done you a favour
By guiding you to the faith, if indeed you are faithful.'[144] — *Quran 49:17*

Faith itself is a mercy—
Not a transaction.
The wise-one sees that even their surrender
Was enabled by the One who calls hearts to Him.
To cling to merit
Is to forget the unseen hand
That made the soul receptive.
To release the act
Is to return it to the stream of remembrance—
And find rest.

⟨Say, O Prophet,
'Whatever good you do,
Allah is fully aware of it.
You will never be wronged
Even by an atom's weight.'[145] — *Quran 4:40*

The gaze of the Divine
Does not need your proof.
He sees what you forgot,
What you offered in silence,
What you released in humility.
He remembers every petal
The soul let drift
Without clinging.

To let go is not to neglect—
It is to trust.
Yes.

---

144 This is derived from the Quran verse of:

⟨They regard their acceptance of Islam as a favour to you. Tell ˹them, O Prophet˺, "Do not regard your Islam as a favour to me. Rather, it is Allah Who has done you a favour by guiding you to the faith, if ˹indeed˺ you are faithful. (17)⟩ [Quran 49:17]

145 This is derived from the Quran verse of:

⟨Indeed, Allah never wrongs ˹anyone˺—even by an atom's weight.[1] And if it is a good deed, He will multiply it many times over and will give a great reward out of His grace. (40)⟩ [Quran 4:40]

[1]: lit., the smallest particle of dust (zarrah).

True sincerity is not found in counting,
But in surrender.
Deeds held too tightly
Become weights,
But those offered lightly
Become wings.

⟨So whoever hopes for the meeting with their Lord,
Let them do righteous work
And associate none in worship of their Lord.⟩[146] *— Quran 18:110*

To approach the Divine
With hands full
Is to knock on a closed door.
To arrive with hands empty
Is to be carried in.

So the wise-one walks forward—
They give,
But do not grasp.
They serve,
But do not seek praise.
They move,
But do not claim movement.
And in that detachment,
They enter the Secluded Entrance
Not by virtue,
But by vulnerability.

---

[146] This is derived from the Quran verse of:

⟨Say, ʼO Prophet,` "I am only a man like you, ʼbut` it has been revealed to me that your God is only One God. So whoever hopes for the meeting with their Lord, let them do good deeds and associate none in the worship of their Lord."(110)⟩ [18:110]

⟨Whatever good you send forth for yourselves,
You will certainly find its reward with Allah—
Far better and greater in reward.⟩[147] — Quran 73:20

For only He elevates what is unclaimed.
Only He records what was surrendered.
Only He remains the source
Of sincerity, detachment, and eternal nearness.

Wisdom Unveiled

The profound wisdom revealed is that entering the Secluded Entrance requires a call to detachment even from one's own virtuous deeds. The wise-one understands that deeds are meant to "blossom and fall away like flowers upon a river," and clinging to them turns gifts into idols. Even acts of virtue become subtle veils if they tie the soul to itself or become a source of spiritual pride, hindering true connection. True connection arises not from counting deeds but from forgetting them, letting action flow from purity rather than the hunger for acknowledgment or worth. This sincerity is found in surrender, transforming deeds held tightly into weights, and those offered lightly into wings. The wise-one is called not to despise good deeds, but to release them, thus standing before the Divine with hands empty and heart open, entering not by virtue, but by vulnerability, for only Allah elevates what is unclaimed and records what was surrendered.

Wise-Reflection

Reflect on your own actions and charitable deeds. Do you ever find yourself subtly seeking acknowledgment, internal pride, or a sense of "earning" Allah's favor through them? Consider the idea that "deeds held too tightly become weights, but those offered lightly become wings." What would it mean for you to truly "let deeds flow like wind, not like chains,"

---

[147] This is derived from the Quran verse of:

📖 ⟨Surely your Lord knows that you ˹O Prophet˺ stand ˹in prayer˺ for nearly two-thirds of the night, or ˹sometimes˺ half of it, or a third, as do some of those with you. Allah ˹alone˺ keeps a ˹precise˺ measure of the day and night. He knows that you ˹believers˺ are unable to endure this, and has turned to you in mercy. So recite ˹in prayer˺ whatever you can from the Quran. He knows that some of you will be sick, some will be travelling throughout the land seeking Allah's bounty, and some fighting in the cause of Allah. So recite whatever you can from it. And ˹continue to˺ perform ˹regular˺ prayers, pay alms-tax, and lend to Allah a good loan. Whatever good you send forth for yourselves, you will find it with Allah far better and more rewarding. And seek Allah's forgiveness. Surely Allah is All-Forgiving, Most Merciful. (20)⟩ [Quran 73:20]

cultivating detachment from your own virtuous deeds? How can you purify your intention to transform your actions into pure acts of worship and gratitude, rather than transactional efforts, allowing you to approach the Divine with "hands empty and heart open"?

Contemplation: Surrender of Knowledge and Attributes

The Secluded Entrance demands the complete surrender of all accumulated knowledge and perceived personal attributes. The wise-one, even after attaining profound insights and spiritual understanding (as in "The Letter" and "The Cognition of Science"), must lay them down at this threshold. Human knowledge, however vast, is finite, and human attributes, however virtuous, are created. To approach the Infinite, the wise-one must shed all self-concepts based on what they 'know' or 'are,' becoming utterly empty vessels ready to be filled by Divine Presence. This is a profound psychic liberation from intellectual and egoic attachments.

What You Bring Cannot Carry You

The wise-one reflects:
If I come with my deeds,
I am met with accountability.
If I come with my knowledge,
I am met with questions.
If I come with understanding,
I am met with evidence—
And that evidence
Bears witness against me. [148]

Deeds are weighed.
Knowledge is tested.
Understanding is summoned to the stand—
Yet none of them speak purely for the soul,
For they each belong to moments of the self
That sway and falter.

---

[148] This is in agreement with other contemplation of:

"If I come with my deeds, I am met with accountability. If I come with my knowledge, I am met with questions. If I come with understanding, I am met with evidence— and that evidence bears witness against me."

True submission is not in possession but in surrender,
Not in words but in purification.

This unveiling shows:
What we hold is not what holds us.
The wise-one does not walk forward
Carrying deeds like banners,
Or intellect like armor.
They walk forward
With the humility of one
Who knows: to be chosen is not to be qualified—
It is to be graced.

❨Strive for the cause of Allah in the way He deserves,
For it is He who has chosen you…
He alone is your Guardian.
What an excellent Guardian, and what an excellent Helper!❩[149]*— Quran 22:78*

Even striving
Is a response to being chosen.
Even knowledge
Is a fruit of being taught.
Even purification
Was gifted through the Messenger—
Not discovered by the seeker alone.

---

[149] This is derived from the Quran verses of:

📖 ❨O believers! Bow down, prostrate yourselves, worship your Lord, and do ˹what is˺ good so that you may be successful. (77) Strive for ˹the cause of˺ Allah in the way He deserves, for ˹it is˺ He ˹Who˺ has chosen you, and laid upon you no hardship in the religion—the way of your forefather Abraham. ˹It is Allah˺ Who named you 'the ones who submit'[1] ˹in the˺ earlier ˹Scriptures˺ and in this ˹Quran˺, so that the Messenger may be a witness over you, and that you may be witnesses over humanity. So establish prayer, pay alms-tax, and hold fast to Allah. He ˹alone˺ is your Guardian. What an excellent Guardian, and what an excellent Helper! (78)❩ [Quran 22:77-78]

[1]: i.e., Muslims.

❮Indeed, Allah has done the believers a great favour
By raising a messenger from among them—reciting His revelations,
Purifying them, and teaching them the Book and wisdom...❯[150]— Quran 3:164

So the wise-one learns:
He chooses His servants
Not by measure,
But by mercy.
Not by what they carry,
But by how they surrender.
And in His embrace
Is the only refuge—
Not the embrace of comprehension,
But of remembrance.
Not the certainty of reason,
But the softness of worship.

The wise-one lets go—
Not of responsibility,
But of the illusion
That understanding guarantees nearness.
They hold fast to Allah,
Not because they are certain,
But because they are needy.
They bow not from superiority,
But from remembrance
That what they bring
Cannot carry them.

So the wise-one walks forward—
Hands no longer grasping attributes,
Tongue no longer announcing knowledge,
Heart no longer clinging to proofs.
They are upheld

---

[150] This is derived from the Quran verse of:

📖 ❮Indeed, Allah has done the believers a ´great` favour by raising a messenger from among them—reciting to them His revelations, purifying them, and teaching them the Book and wisdom. For indeed they had previously been clearly astray. (164)❯ [Quran 3:164]

Not by merit,
But by favor.

For only He appoints the purified.
Only He selects without explanation.
Only He remains the source
Of guidance, witness, and eternal refuge.

Wisdom Unveiled

The profound wisdom revealed is that entering the Secluded Entrance demands the complete surrender of all accumulated knowledge and perceived personal attributes, for "what you bring cannot carry you." The wise-one realizes that knowledge, however vast, can blind, and understanding, however deep, can accuse if one clings to them. Every possession—whether act, idea, or virtue—becomes a chain if carried into the Presence of the One who needs nothing. True submission is not in possession but in surrender, not in words but in purification. The wise-one is called to strip away even the robes of wisdom and learning, to stand naked in spiritual poverty, knowing that nothing carried from creation can add to the Creator. They learn that they are chosen by Divine Grace, not by qualification, and that to be upheld is by favor, not merit. Only those who come empty may be filled with the fullness of the Real, experiencing profound psychic liberation from intellectual and egoic attachments, finding eternal refuge in the One who selects without explanation.

Wise-Reflection

Reflect on your intellectual achievements, acquired knowledge, or personal virtues that you might subtly identify with or feel pride in. Consider the idea that "every possession—whether act, idea, or virtue—becomes a chain if carried into the presence of the One who needs nothing." What would it mean for you to lay down your "knowledge like armor" and "personal attributes" at the threshold of Divine Presence? How can you cultivate the profound humility of being an "empty vessel ready to be filled," allowing for psychic liberation from intellectual and egoic attachments, and recognizing that your deepest being is upheld by Divine favor, not by what you 'know' or 'are'?

Contemplation: The Barrier of Creation

The wise-one recognizes that the very existence of creation itself can serve as a barrier to true Divine connection if one remains absorbed in its forms and attributes. Every created thing, no matter how beautiful or awe-inspiring, is contingent and finite, whereas the Creator is Absolute and Infinite. To meet the Creator, the wise-one must learn to see through creation to the Creator, transcending the world of forms without denying its reality. This involves a fundamental shift in perception, where the perceived 'otherness' of creation dissolves into its intimate connection with the Divine Source.

Beyond All That Clings, Beneath All That Remains

Let all that is held slip away—
Deeds, knowledge, name, and form.
Let every attachment fall,
Even the ones dressed in virtue.
Lay down what ties you to creation,
And meet the Real
In sacred solitude.
Let all that is held slip away…
Lay down what ties you to creation.

This is not abandonment—
It is arrival.
For in surrender, there is no loss,
Only unveiling.
In humility, no emptiness,
Only the fullness
Of Divine Presence.
Even the heavens,
With all their majesty,
Are finite.
The wise-one who clings
To anything created—
Even sacred knowledge, even righteous form—
Clings to what falls short
Of the Absolute.

❲*Say, 'O Prophet,' 'Believe in this Quran, or do not.*
Indeed, when it is recited to those who were gifted with knowledge before it,
They fall upon their faces in prostration,
And say, "Glory be to our Lord! Surely the promise of our Lord has been fulfilled."
And they fall down upon their faces weeping,
And it increases them in humility.'❳[151] — *Quran 17:107–109*

The truly gifted fall forward,
Not with explanation,
But with weeping.
Not with pride in what they know,
But in surrender to what surpasses knowing.
Humility was always
The final cloak of light.

Sacred loneliness is not the absence of love—
It is the emptying of all distraction
So only the Beloved remains.
It is not a chamber of exile,
But the clearing where
The Divine makes Himself known.
To enter the Secluded Entrance
Is to release the world's hold.
To walk barefoot into the fire
That burns only illusion.
To abandon every lesser belonging
Is not to become poor—
It is to become ready.

So the wise-one walks forward—
Not wearing names,
Not claiming titles,
Not clutching deeds or knowledge,

---

[151] This is derived from the Qurna verses of:

📖 ❲Say, 'O Prophet,' "Believe in this 'Quran', or do not. Indeed, when it is recited to those who were gifted with knowledge[1] before it 'was revealed', they fall upon their faces in prostration, (107) and say, 'Glory be to our Lord! Surely the promise of our Lord has been fulfilled.' (108) And they fall down upon their faces weeping, and it increases them in humility." (109)❳ [Quran 17:107-110]

[1]: i.e., the faithful among the scholars of the Torah and the Gospel.

But as soul alone.
They seek nothing but the One
For whom all else
Was only veil.

For only He unveils through surrender.
Only He remains beyond creation.
Only He is the source
Of detachment, nearness, and eternal unveiling.

Wisdom Unveiled

The profound wisdom revealed is that creation itself can become a barrier to true Divine connection if one remains absorbed in its finite forms. The wise-one learns that to meet the Creator, one must "let all that is held slip away," including deeds, knowledge, name, and form, even those adorned with virtue. Clinging to anything created, even the loftiest forms like the heavens, falls short of the Absolute. This detachment leads not to loss but to unveiling, finding the fullness of Divine Presence in humility. Sacred loneliness is revealed not as an absence of love, but as the clearing where the Beloved remains when all distractions are emptied. To enter the Secluded Entrance is to release the world's hold, abandon every lesser belonging, and walk barefoot into the Divine Presence for whom all else was but a veil, thus transcending the world of forms and dissolving the perceived 'otherness' of creation.

Wise-Reflection

Reflect on what aspects of creation (material possessions, intellectual achievements, relationships, or even spiritual practices themselves) you might unconsciously cling to. Do these attachments sometimes prevent you from experiencing a deeper Divine connection? Consider the idea that "sacred loneliness is not the absence of love; it is the emptying of all distractions so that only the Beloved remains." What would it mean for you to "walk barefoot into the fire that burns only illusion," laying down what ties you to creation to meet the Real in sacred solitude? How can you cultivate a perception that sees through creation to the Creator, allowing the perceived 'otherness' to dissolve into its intimate connection with the Divine Source?

Contemplation: Divine Guidance and Preservation[152] (Tawakul Creed)

(The soul is steered by a compass no hand can hold)

The journey through the Secluded Entrance is upheld by the profound truth of Divine Guidance and Preservation, embodying the creed of Tawakkul (absolute reliance on Allah). The wise-one realizes that every step, every insight, and every protective veil is a direct act of Allah's care. In stripping away self-reliance, the wise-one simultaneously embraces complete trust in Allah as the ultimate Guide and Preserver. This absolute reliance liberates the heart from fear and anxiety, as the wise-one knows they are held and guided by the One who is All-Merciful and All-Wise, transforming uncertainty into profound inner peace.

The Path that Walks the Seeker, Not the Other Way Around

Let no step be taken but by His will.
And if the path unfolds by His decree,
It is not walked—it is beheld.
The wise-one begins to understand:
Movement is not freedom unless it is guided,
And stillness is not silence
If infused with remembrance.

❬And whosoever puts their trust in Allah,
He will suffice them.
Lo! Allah brings His command to pass.
Allah has set a measure for all things.❭[153] — Quran 65:3

---

[152] This reflects the Islamic concept of Tawakkul (trust in God).

The Arabic word "Tawakkul" means "trust in Allah" or "reliance on God." It entails putting all of your faith in Allah's plan and obeying His will even when things don't work out the way you had hoped, all the while doing the required actions to reach your objective. It's a fundamental Islamic idea that, despite our best efforts, God ultimately controls the result.

[153] This is derived from the Quran verses of:

❬Then when they have ʾalmostʾ reached the end of their waiting period, either retain them honourably or separate from them honourably. And call two of your reliable men to witness ʾeither wayʾ—and ʾlet the

To walk by the Creator's will
Is to enter a current—
One that flows not into uncertainty,
But into light.
Each breath becomes a pilgrimage.
Each footstep, a prayer.
Each blink, a witnessing
Of His nearness,
And a soft relinquishing
Of the illusion of control.

❰O believers! Always remember Allah often,
And glorify Him morning and evening.
He is the One Who showers His blessings upon you—
And His angels pray for you—
So that He may bring you out of darkness and into light.
For He is ever Merciful to the believers.❱[154] — Quran 33:41–43

Freedom is not found
In self-direction.
It is found in guidance.
Not in wandering,
But in the One who leads through veils
We cannot lift ourselves.

Let no step be taken but by His will…
Yes.
This is tawakkul:
To release reliance on self
Without relinquishing action.
To walk,

---

witnesses˴ bear true testimony for ˹the sake of˺ Allah. This is enjoined on whoever has faith in Allah and the Last Day. And whoever is mindful of Allah, He will make a way out for them, (2) and provide for them from sources they could never imagine. And whoever puts their trust in Allah, then He ˹alone˺ is sufficient for them. Certainly Allah achieves His Will. Allah has already set a destiny for everything. (3)❱ [Quran 65:2-3]

[154] This is derived from the Quran verses of:

📖 ❰O believers! Always remember Allah often, (41) and glorify Him morning and evening. (42) He is the One Who showers His blessings upon you—and His angels pray for you—so that He may bring you out of darkness and into light. For He is ever Merciful to the believers. (43) Their greeting on the Day they meet Him will be, "Peace!" And He has prepared for them an honourable reward. (44)❱ [Quran 33:41-44]

While knowing you are carried.
To speak,
While knowing He gives voice.
To long,
While knowing it was He who placed longing within you.

The Prophet 徽 taught:
"Whoever says—when leaving their house—'In the name of Allah,
I put my trust in Allah, and there is no power nor strength except with Allah,'
It will be said to him: 'You are guided, sufficed, and protected.'[155] *— Sunan Abu*
Dawud

In that declaration,
You become unshaken.
For guidance is no longer a destination—
It is your posture.
Protection is no longer a prayer—
It is your echo.
Sufficiency is no longer earned—
It is gifted,
In response to your trust.

So the wise-one walks forward—
Not with certainty of terrain,
But with intimacy of direction.
Not because the path is clear,
But because the Guide is near.
Not to reach a goal,
But to behold the One
For whom movement is mercy
And arrival is reunion.

---

[155] This is derived from prophet Mohammed 徽 narrative of:

🌼 "Whoever says (i.e. meaning) when he leaves his house - 'In the name of Allah, I put my trust in Allah, and there is no power nor strength except with Allah,' it will be said to him: 'You are guided, sufficed, and protected,' and Satan will move away from him."

Abu Dawud 🌼 added:

"Then he (i.e. meaning): Satan - will say to another Satan: 'What do you think of a man who has been guided, sufficed, and protected?'"

For only He sustains what He guides.
Only He protects what He leads.
Only He remains the source
Of direction, sufficiency, and eternal trust.

Wisdom Unveiled

The profound wisdom revealed is that the journey through the Secluded Entrance is upheld by Divine Guidance and Preservation, embodying the creed of Tawakkul (absolute reliance on Allah). The wise-one understands that true freedom is not the absence of direction but the presence of guidance. To move by the will of the Creator is to step into a river whose current carries the soul toward light, without fear of straying into the deserts of despair. Every breath becomes a pilgrimage, every footstep a prayer, every blink a witnessing, as the wise-one walks not by instinct nor by intellect alone, but by the hidden compass of Divine Presence. This tawakkul involves releasing reliance on self without relinquishing action, knowing that guidance, sufficiency, and protection are not earned but gifted in response to complete trust in Allah as the ultimate Guide and Preserver. This transforms uncertainty into profound inner peace, as the wise-one knows they are held and guided by the One who is All-Merciful and All-Wise.

Wise-Reflection

Reflect on areas in your life where you feel a strong need for control or experience anxiety about uncertainty. Consider the creed of Tawakkul—absolute reliance on Allah—and the idea that "freedom is not found in self-direction. It is found in guidance." What specific steps can you take to "release reliance on self without relinquishing action"? How can you cultivate a posture of complete trust, allowing each breath to become a pilgrimage and each footstep a prayer, thereby transforming your uncertainty into profound inner peace, knowing you are guided and protected by the One who "suffices" all who trust Him?

Contemplation: The Gift of Divine Favor

(The soul rises with the dawn)

The Secluded Entrance unveils that proximity to the Creator is entirely a Gift of Divine Favor (Fadl), not a right earned through human effort. Just as Prophet Musa was chosen by Allah ("I have chosen you"), so too is the wise-one's journey to inner proximity an act of pure grace. This realization deepens humility and gratitude, preventing any trace of spiritual pride. It means recognizing that every moment of connection, every unveiled truth, is a manifestation of Allah's unmerited generosity, fostering a heart that is perpetually thankful and receptive.

Where Light Breaks and Mercy Descends

Meet Him at dawn,
When the veil of night still clings to the sky,
And the first sliver of light
Wraps the horizon in promise.
This is not mere routine—
It is meeting.
The sacred Fajr is not only prayer—
It is a moment
Carried in the wings of angels.

❨Observe the prayer from the decline of the sun
Until the darkness of the night, and the dawn prayer—
For certainly the dawn prayer is witnessed.❩[156]— Quran 17:78

Once you rise,
He guards your day.
Twice you rise,
He strengthens your soul.
And as the morning begins,
The sorrows that clung to you
Scatter like mist before the sun.
Morning and evening, the heavens echo His praise…
This is not striving—
It is surrender.

---

[156] This is derived from the Quran verse of:

❨Observe the prayer from the decline of the sun until the darkness of the night and the dawn prayer, for certainly the dawn prayer is witnessed ´by angels`.[1] (78) And rise at ´the last` part of the night, offering additional prayers, so your Lord may raise you to a station of praise.[2] (79)❩ [Quran 17:78-79]

[1]: This verse gives the times of the five daily prayers: the decline of the sun refers to the afternoon and late afternoon prayers, the darkness of night refers to sunset and late evening prayers, then the dawn prayer.
[2]: This refers to the time when the Prophet ﷺ will make intercession (shafâ'ah) on the Day of Judgment.

The wise-one learns
That a single moment of true meeting
Sanctifies an entire lifetime.
Not effort,
But presence.
Not labor,
But remembrance.

❨*Always remember Allah often,*
And glorify Him morning and evening.
He is the One who showers His blessings upon you—
And His angels pray for you—
So that He may bring you out of darkness and into light.❩ *157* — *Quran 33:41–43*

Evening arrives—
And still His remembrance hovers.
The wise-one bows not only in prayer,
But in posture of heart.
And in return,
The soul is wrapped in protection,
Drawn out of confusion,
Lifted beyond sorrow.

❨*Glorify the praises of your Lord*
Before sunrise and before sunset,
And glorify Him in the hours of the night
And at both ends of the day,
So that you may be pleased...❩ *158* — *Quran 20:130*

This pleasure is not material—
It is contentment that comes from proximity.

---

[157] This is derived from the Quran verses of:

📖 ❨O believers! Always remember Allah often, (41) and glorify Him morning and evening. (42) He is the One Who showers His blessings upon you—and His angels pray for you—so that He may bring you out of darkness and into light. For He is ever Merciful to the believers. (43) Their greeting on the Day they meet Him will be, "Peace!" And He has prepared for them an honourable reward. (44)❩ [Quran 33:41-44]

[158] This is derived from the Quran verse of:

📖 ❨So be patient ˹O Prophet˺ with what they say. And glorify the praises of your Lord before sunrise and before sunset, and glorify Him in the hours of the night and at both ends of the day,1 so that you may be pleased ˹with the reward˺. (130)❩ [Quran 20:130]

The soul is not left to wander.
It moves beneath wings unseen,
But felt.
It journeys not by light alone,
But by the favor
Of the One who placed light
Within every remembrance.

So the wise-one walks forward—
Meeting the Creator
Not through greatness,
But through gentleness.
Not through accumulation,
But through awakening.
And in each rising,
They are called into the garden
Where mercy whispers before the world stirs.

For only He calls the soul by morning light.
Only He turns remembrance into sanctuary.
Only He remains the source
Of favor, guidance, and eternal nearness.

Wisdom Unveiled

The profound wisdom revealed is that proximity to the Creator is entirely a Gift of Divine Favor (Fadl), an act of pure grace rather than earned human effort. The wise-one understands that the doorway to Divine protection is opened not by striving, but by remembrance. A single moment of true meeting, such as the sacred Fajr prayer, can sanctify an entire lifetime, signifying the immense power of Presence and remembrance over labor. When the wise-one turns toward the Creator with sincerity, the Creator turns toward them with preservation, mercy, and serenity, causing sorrows to lose their sting and confusions their power. The soul moves in the shadow of unseen wings, journeying not by light alone, but by the favor of the One who places light within every remembrance, fostering a heart that is perpetually thankful and receptive, and lifting the soul beyond sorrow into contentment that comes from Divine proximity.

Wise-Reflection

Reflect on moments of profound peace or unexpected insight in your life. Did they always feel directly earned by your effort, or did they sometimes feel like a pure gift? Consider the idea that "a single moment of true meeting sanctifies an entire lifetime" and that "pleasure is not material—it is contentment that comes from proximity." How can you cultivate a heart that is perpetually thankful and receptive to the Gift of Divine Favor, especially through consistent acts of remembrance like the dawn and evening prayers? What would it mean to meet the Creator "not through greatness, but through gentleness," allowing your soul to be called into the garden where mercy whispers before the world stirs?

Contemplation: The Multiplication of Surrender

(The soul offers not its worth—but its surrender)

The wise-one discovers the profound principle of the multiplication of surrender. This is a truly transformative realization: the more one genuinely surrenders—letting go of deeds, knowledge, ego, and all attachments—the more Allah bestows, multiplies, and elevates their spiritual state. This powerful paradox reveals that true, immeasurable gain comes from radical relinquishment. Each authentic act of letting go doesn't create a void, but rather opens a new, expansive chamber in the heart, making it receptive to an outpouring of Divine light and presence. This leads to an exponential increase in spiritual insight, tranquility, and connection, far beyond anything any personal effort or striving could ever achieve.

Where Surrender Becomes Multiplication

Return your deeds,
Your knowledge,
Your striving—
Back to Him.
Not as possession,
But as offering.
Not as claim,

But as surrender.
Place them in the hands of the Beloved
As one who knows:
He alone gives them meaning.

❨*The example of those who spend their wealth*
In the cause of Allah is that of a grain
That sprouts into seven ears,
Each bearing one hundred grains.
And Allah multiplies the reward even more
To whoever He wills.❩ — *Quran 2:261*

He will take what you offer,
Bless it by His mercy,
And increase it beyond measure—
Not by addition,
But by transformation.
A single act of surrender
Becomes a thousand acts of blessing.
A single tear of sincerity
Becomes a river of mercy.

❨*Those who spend their wealth*
And do not follow their charity
With reminders or hurtful words—
They will get their reward from their Lord,
And there will be no fear for them,
Nor will they grieve.❩ *159* — *Quran 2:262*

---

159 This is derived from the Quran verses of:

📖 ❨The example of those who spend their wealth in the cause of Allah is that of a grain that sprouts into seven ears, each bearing one hundred grains. And Allah multiplies ´the reward even more` to whoever He wills. For Allah is All-Bountiful, All-Knowing. (261) Those who spend their wealth in the cause of Allah and do not follow their charity with reminders of their generosity or hurtful words—they will get their reward from their Lord, and there will be no fear for them, nor will they grieve. (262) Kind words and forgiveness are better than charity followed by injury. And Allah is Self-Sufficient, Most Forbearing. (263) O believers! Do not waste your charity with reminders ´of your generosity` or hurtful words, like those who donate their wealth just to show off and do not believe in Allah and the Last Day. Their example is that of a hard barren

The wise-one learns:
Nothing given to the Creator is wasted.
No offering—however small,
However imperfect—
Is rejected
If given from a place of love.

⟨Do not do a favor expecting more in return.
And persevere for the sake of your Lord.⟩[160] *— Quran 74:6–7*

Do not weigh the favor.
Do not hold the act as claim.
Let perseverance be
For His sake alone.
For the One who multiplies
Does not count—
He transforms.
The wise-one offers all—
Not because it is worthy,
But because He is worthy of all.
They do not seek return,
But reunion.
They do not seek reward,
But remembrance.
And in that offering,
They are met with a generosity
That no soul can measure.

So the wise-one walks forward—
Hands open,

---

rock covered with a thin layer of soil hit by a strong rain—leaving it just a bare stone. Such people are unable to preserve the reward of their charity. Allah does not guide ˹such˺ disbelieving people. (264) And the example of those who donate their wealth, seeking Allah's pleasure and believing the reward is certain,1 is that of a garden on a fertile hill: when heavy rain falls, it yields up twice its normal produce. If no heavy rain falls, a drizzle is sufficient. And Allah is All-Seeing of what you do. (265)⟩ [Quran 2:261-265]

[160] This is derived from the Quran verses of:

📖 ⟨O you covered up ˹in your clothes˺! (1) Arise and warn ˹all˺. (2) Revere your Lord ˹alone˺. (3) Purify your garments. (4) ˹Continue to˺ shun idols. (5) Do not do a favour expecting more ˹in return˺.[1] (6) And persevere for ˹the sake of˺ your Lord. (7)⟩ [Quran 74:1-7]

[1]: It was a common practice to give someone a gift, hoping to receive a more valuable gift in return. This practice is disliked in Islam.

Heart bowed,
Soul emptied of pride
But full of longing.
They give not to earn,
But to honor.
They surrender not to be seen,
But to be near.

For only He multiplies the surrendered.
Only He transforms the smallest into the infinite.
Only He remains the source
Of mercy, reward, and eternal generosity.

Wisdom Unveiled

The profound wisdom unveiled is the transformative principle of the multiplication of surrender: true gain is achieved through relinquishment, as Allah bestows and elevates spiritual states exponentially when one lets go of ego, knowledge, and attachments. The wise-one discovers that nothing given to the Creator is ever wasted, and no offering, however small or imperfect, is rejected if it stems from a place of genuine surrender and pure love. This Divine generosity is not measured by human standards; rather, the Creator multiplies not by mere addition, but by radical transformation—a single act of sincere surrender blossoming into a thousand blessings, a single tear of sincerity becoming a boundless river of mercy. Thus, the wise-one offers all, not out of a sense of worthiness, but because the Creator is supremely worthy of all offerings, seeking not return or reward, but profound reunion and intimate remembrance. This spiritual and psychic awakening liberates the soul from transactional thinking, immersing it in an ocean of unmerited grace and eternal generosity.

Wise-Reflection

Consider an area in your life where you might be holding on tightly, perhaps to an achievement, a certain outcome, or even a cherished belief about yourself. How does the concept of the multiplication of surrender— where true gain comes from relinquishment—challenge your ingrained notions of effort and reward? What specific act of "letting go" could you practice today, with the intention of placing it "in the hands of the Beloved" as a pure offering? How might releasing your expectation of a specific return open you to an "exponential increase in spiritual insight, tranquility, and connection," allowing you to experience the Divine generosity that "no soul can measure"?

Contemplation: Divine Generosity

At the heart of the Secluded Entrance is the profound, overwhelming experience of Divine Generosity (Al-Karam). When the wise-one approaches in utter emptiness and genuine need, the Creator, in His infinite bounty, responds with boundless giving. This generosity is not confined to material provisions or worldly success; it extends limitlessly to spiritual insights, profound inner peace, unwavering strength, and an intimate, palpable sense of Divine Proximity. The wise-one truly learns that Allah's giving is without measure, especially to those who come to Him with deep humility and complete reliance, transforming the often daunting state of 'loneliness' into the richest and most intimate encounter imaginable.

The Descent of Mercy: Meeting the Surrendered Soul

He, the Creator,
Who fashioned galaxies from His will
And veiled majesty in every star,
Sets aside what He formed—
Not because it lacks value,
But because it cannot compare
To the unencumbered nearness
Of a surrendered soul.
He turns His attention to what He formed,
Drawing souls to the meeting.

What then shall the seeker bring?
What offering shall be placed
Before the One who owns all treasure?
Nothing crafted by the hand,
No deed counted,
No possession clutched
Can bridge the chasm
Between selfhood and Divine.
How then shall one approach Him,

> Bearing what was left behind—
> As if offerings could fulfill
> The One who needs nothing?
>
> Rather, He descends—
> Not in need,
> But in mercy.
> He descends
> Calling to the one
> Who cannot rise without grace.
>
> *Our Lord, Blessed and Exalted be He,
> Descends every night to the lowest heaven
> When the last third of the night remains, saying:
> Who will call upon Me, that I may answer him?
> Who will ask of Me, that I may give him?
> Who will seek My forgiveness,
> That I may forgive him?'*[161] — Sahih al-Bukhari 1145
>
> This is the yearning
> Not of one absent,
> But of the One who is always near—
> Waiting not for ceremony,
> But for sincerity.
>
> No deed is the key.
> No possession the bridge.
> Only remembrance,
> Only surrender,
> Only longing
> For the One whose generosity
> Outpaces every form of merit.

---

[161] This is derived from the prophet Mohammed ﷺ narrative of:

❀ "Our Lord, Blessed and Exalted be He, descends every night to the lowest heaven when the last third of the night remains, saying: "Who will call upon Me, that I may answer him? Who will ask of Me, that I may give him? Who will seek My forgiveness, that I may forgive him?"" [Narrator: Abu Hurairah | Narrator: Al-Bukhari | Source: Sahih Al-Bukhari | Page or Number: 1145]

I am as My servant thinks I am,
And I am with him when he remembers Me…
If he comes to Me walking,
I come to him running.[162] — *Sahih al-Bukhari 7405*

The wise-one awakens to a truth
That silences all claims:
The Divine does not ask for what you hold—
He asks for who you are
When you have let it go.

To enter the Secluded Entrance
Is not to arrive with accomplishment,
But with vulnerability.
Not to present proofs,
But to surrender every veil
Until only longing remains.

So the wise-one walks forward—
Not with hands full of deeds,
But with a heart empty
Of all but yearning.
They are drawn not by greatness,
But by grace.
And in the descent of the Divine,
They are met—
Not with judgment,
But with mercy rushing to greet them.

For only He calls without demand.
Only He yearns for the surrendered.

---

[162] This is derived from the sacred narrative of prophet Mohammed ﷺ:

✿ "Allah the Almighty says: "I am as My servant thinks I am, and I am with him when he remembers Me. If he remembers Me to himself, I remember him to Myself. If he remembers Me in an assembly, I remember him in an assembly better than it. If he draws near to Me by a handspan, I draw near to him by an arm's length. If he draws near to Me by an arm's length, I draw near to him by a fathom's length. If he comes to Me walking, I come to him running."" Narrator: Abu Hurairah | [Narrator: Al-Bukhari | Source: Sahih Al-Bukhari | Page or Number: 7405]

Only He remains the source
Of presence, remembrance, and eternal proximity.

Wisdom Unveiled

The profound wisdom unveiled is that at the heart of the Secluded Entrance lies the experience of immeasurable Divine Generosity (Al-Karam). The wise-one understands that the Creator, in His infinite bounty, desires the soul's pure nearness, not its trophies or accomplishments. He has set aside the very majesty of creation itself, yearning for an unencumbered meeting with a surrendered soul. It is the height of arrogance to imagine that anything formed or achieved could serve as a gift worthy of the One who needs nothing. The wise-one learns that God asks not for what we hold, but for who we are when we have let go—when we approach with utter emptiness, vulnerability, and a heart full of yearning. This transformative realization silences all claims of merit, revealing that the Divine descends with mercy, rushing to meet the surrendered soul, transforming perceived loneliness into the richest possible encounter of boundless giving, intimate presence, and eternal proximity.

Wise-Reflection

Reflect on your current approach to your spiritual practice or your relationship with the Divine. Do you ever feel compelled to "bring" something—good deeds, accumulated knowledge, or a sense of personal worthiness—in order to feel deserving of Divine attention? Consider the profound statement: "The Divine does not ask for what you hold—He asks for who you are when you have let it go." How might embracing a posture of utter emptiness and vulnerability, letting go of all self-claims, allow you to experience a new depth of Divine Generosity and intimate proximity? What personal 'trophies' or 'offerings' might you be clinging to that prevent you from encountering the boundless mercy that yearns to greet the surrendered soul?

Conclusion: Secluded Entrance

ECHOES OF REALIZATION

And so, the wise-one, with a heart purified by longing, steps courageously into the Secluded Entrance—not with hands laden with accumulated deeds or knowledge, but with arms outstretched in absolute receptivity. Not with worldly credentials or self-assured accomplishments, but with a profound, unadorned yearning for the Divine.

For only the truly empty can receive the Infinite. Only the spiritually lonely—stripped of all worldly and self-imposed companionships—can host the Utterly Alone. Only the genuinely poor in spirit can be clothed in the eternal richness of Divine Presence. And in that profound, sacred emptiness, the wise-one discovers, with breathtaking clarity, that they have lost nothing essential—but have, in truth, gained everything.

THE SEEKER'S ASCENT: THE SECLUDED ENTRANCE

The Secluded Entrance is not marked by physical walls or gates. It does not appear upon any earthly map, nor can it be opened by strenuous personal effort or intellectual key. It is, instead, meticulously carved within the invisible, most sacred terrain of the wise-one's own soul, accessible only to those who dare, with ultimate courage, to lay down the banners of their perceived deeds, the fleeting trophies of their knowledge, and the precarious scaffolding of their imagined self-worth.

To step through this Entrance is not to advance in a worldly sense, but to dissolve the contingent self; not to ascend through the accumulation of works, but to descend into the profound, transformative humility of utter dependence on the Divine. It is spiritual poverty without shame. It is liberating emptiness without despair. It is absolute surrender without any true loss.

Here, in this sacred loneliness and profound relinquishment, the wise-one discovers the most luminous paradox: that in giving up all claim to self-sufficiency, they inherit all treasure from the Divine; that in becoming nothing in their own eyes, they become the sacred dwelling place of the Infinite. Thus does the wise-one's soul, unclothed of all pride and self-reliance, walk barefoot into the very Presence of the Creator—and finds, with overwhelming certitude, that the ultimate path it sought was never outside at all, but had been perpetually hidden within, patiently waiting to be unveiled by the profound act of complete surrender. This is the psychic liberation into authentic Divine Connection.

8ᵀᴴ REFLECTION: IN THE STAND IN PRESENCE OF CREATOR

THE GATEWAY VERSE

In the sacred words of Allah, a profound narrative of ultimate Divine companionship, solace, and the unwavering reality of His Presence amidst all trials, guiding all who reflect towards the essence of true proximity:

📖 *❝It does not matter˙ if you ˙believers˙ do not support him (Muhammad PBUH), for Allah did in fact support him when the disbelievers drove him out ˙of Mecca˙ and he was only one of two. While they both were in the cave, he reassured his companion,1 ❝Do not worry; Allah is certainly with us.❞ So Allah sent down His serenity upon the Prophet, supported him with forces you ˙believers˙ did not see, and made the word of the disbelievers lowest, while the Word of Allah is supreme. And Allah is Almighty, All-Wise. (40)❞ [Quran 9:40]*

ILLUMINATION'S DAWN

There exists a sacred threshold in the spiritual journey where all striving ceases, and a profound standing truly begins. This is a hallowed place where the wise-one's soul no longer asks for understanding, no longer desperately seeks external validation, but simply is—poised in utter, unveiled presence before the One who always was, and always will be. "The Stand in Presence of the Creator" is not a worldly achievement to be claimed, nor a static destination to be reached. It is, instead, a profound stillness transcending all temporal movement, an encompassing presence that dissolves all forms of seeking.

Here, the wise-one no longer struggles against the subtle veils of creation. They have traversed the arduous paths of longing and sincere spiritual labor, and now stand in a state of luminous simplicity—not as masters of acquired knowledge, but as profoundly beloved witnesses of the Divine. In this reflection, the sublime mysteries of ultimate nearness gracefully unfold: the transcendence of all creation, the profound wisdom hidden in apparent human weakness, and the divine sovereignty born of complete surrender. Let us walk reverently into this sacred Stand, where the heart no longer beats in subservience to the fleeting demands of the world, but beats in perfect, harmonious rhythm with the One who ceaselessly breathes through all existence..

THE UNFOLDING OF INSIGHTS

This section explores the profound characteristics and transformative shifts experienced by the wise-one who attains the state of "Standing in Presence of the Creator," moving beyond duality and into intimate proximity.

Contemplation: The Weakness and Poverty of Creation[163]

(The soul bows not in shame—but in sacred need)

In the Stand in Presence of the Creator, the wise-one experiences, with absolute, unwavering clarity, the inherent weakness and utter poverty of all creation when meticulously compared to the Absolute Power and Infinite Richness of Allah. Every created being, including one's own self, is seen with profound insight as utterly dependent and beautifully contingent. This isn't a disheartening realization; instead, it's profoundly liberating. It utterly eradicates any lingering illusions of self-sufficiency or reliance on anything other than the Creator, shattering the ego's false claims. This profound, active humility becomes the very ground upon which the wise-one's heart can fully open, becoming a receptive vessel to receive an outpouring of Divine bounty and strength, thereby revealing the true, singular source of all power and sustenance.

Where Need Becomes the Compass to the Divine

In all things,
He placed weakness.
And in every weakness,
A need.
Not as flaw,
But as direction.
Not as punishment,
But as invitation.
In all things, He placed weakness,
And in every weakness, a need.

Every hunger,
Every thirst,

---

[163] This reflects the Quranic concept of:

⟐ ⟨God is Free of all needs, and you are the ones in need (15)⟩ [Quran 35:15]

Every longing
Etched into the fabric of existence
Is a silent call
To the Source
From which strength flows.
Yet every need,
If clung to,
Can veil the sight.
It draws the soul outward,
Toward possession,
Toward illusion.
But the wise-one learns:
To endure
Is to see beyond the veil.
To resist the lure of possession
Is to walk toward grace.

❨O humanity! It is you who stand in need of Allah,
But Allah alone is the Self-Sufficient, Praiseworthy.❩164 — Quran 35:15

The soul is not punished by its needs—
It is directed through them.
Neediness is not shameful—
It is sacred.
It is the tether
Pulling the soul
Ever closer
To the Sustainer of all being.

❨It is Allah Who created you,
Then gives you provisions,
Then will cause you to die,

---

164 This is derived from the Quran verses of:

❨O humanity! It is you who stand in need of Allah, but Allah ´alone` is the Self-Sufficient, Praiseworthy. (15) If He willed, He could eliminate you and produce a new creation. (16) And that is not difficult for Allah ´at all`. (17)❩ [Quran 35:15-17]

And then will bring you back to life.
Can any of your associate-gods do any of this?[165] — *Quran 30:40*

No hand secures but His.
No wealth holds but His decree.
No breath continues
But by His mercy.
To stand in presence
Is to know:
He alone is the Giver,
The Keeper,
The Restorer.

For all will return to the Most Compassionate,
Counted precisely, none forgotten.
Yes.
Every soul,
Every whisper,
Every need
Will return to Him.
Not lost,
Not overlooked,
But counted—
Precisely.

There is none in the heavens or the earth
Who will not return to the Most Compassionate in full submission.
Indeed, He fully knows them
And has counted them precisely.[166] — *Quran 19:93–94*

---

[165] This is derived from the Quran verse of:

It is Allah Who created you, then gives you provisions, then will cause you to die, and then will bring you back to life. Can any of your associate-gods do any of this? Glorified and Exalted is He above what they associate with Him ˹in worship˺! (40) [Quran 30 : 40]

[166] This derived from the Quran verses of:

They[1] say, "The Most Compassionate has offspring." (88) You have certainly made an outrageous claim, (89) by which the heavens are about to burst, the earth to split apart, and the mountains to crumble

The wise-one does not despise their neediness.
They bow in it.
They weep through it.
They rise by it.
For weakness is not the end—
It is the beginning
Of surrender.

So the wise-one walks forward—
Not in denial of their poverty,
But in reverence for it.
They do not hide their hunger—
They offer it.
They do not conceal their longing—
They let it lead.

For only He fulfills without measure.
Only He sustains without condition.
Only He remains the source
Of provision, return, and eternal mercy.

Wisdom Unveiled

The profound wisdom unveiled in the Stand in Presence of the Creator is the exhilarating realization of the inherent weakness and utter poverty of all creation compared to Allah's Absolute Power and Infinite Richness. This understanding transforms perceived shortcomings into a sacred strength: weakness is not a flaw of creation; it is its compass, a Divine invitation. Every hunger, every thirst, every longing etched into the fabric of existence is a silent, irresistible call to the Source from which all strength and sustenance flow. The wise-one discovers that the soul is not punished by its needs, but precisely directed through them, serving as the sacred

---

to pieces (90) in protest of attributing children to the Most Compassionate. (91) It does not befit ʿthe majesty ofʾ the Most Compassionate to have children. (92) There is none in the heavens or the earth who will not return to the Most Compassionate in full submission. (93) Indeed, He fully knows them and has counted them precisely. (94) And each of them will return to Him on the Day of Judgment all alone. (95) As for those who believe and do good, the Most Compassionate will ʿcertainlyʾ bless them with ʿgenuineʾ love. (96)﴾ [Quran 19:88-96]

[1]: The pagans who claimed that the angels are Allah's daughters, the Christians who claim that Jesus is the son of Allah, etc.

tether pulling it ever closer to the Sustainer of all being. This absolute dependency becomes profoundly liberating, eradicating illusions of self-sufficiency and becoming the very ground for receiving boundless Divine bounty and strength. The wise-one embraces neediness not with shame, but with reverence, bowing, weeping, and rising through it, knowing it is the true beginning of total surrender to the One who fulfills without measure and sustains without condition.

Wise-Reflection

Reflect on your moments of perceived weakness, fear, or profound need. Do you typically view these as obstacles or failures? How might embracing the idea that "weakness is not a flaw of creation; it is its compass" fundamentally shift your perspective? What specific "hunger, thirst, or longing" in your life can you consciously offer to the Divine today, allowing it to become a "sacred tether" drawing you closer to the Source of all strength? How can this realization of your inherent poverty become the very ground for profound humility and open your heart more fully to receive boundless Divine bounty and strength, leading to a deeper sense of liberation and peace?

Contemplation: Transcending the Creation

(The soul rises—not by fleeing, but by transcending)

In this exalted state, the wise-one learns the profound, liberating meaning of transcending the creation. This does not imply abandoning the world or neglecting one's sacred duties within it. Rather, it signifies a radical, internal shift in perception where the wise-one effortlessly sees through the myriad forms of creation directly to the Creator. The subtle yet pervasive veil of duality, which mistakenly perceives the world as fundamentally separate from Allah, begins to dissolve. Every atom, every event, every being, no matter how mundane or grand, is recognized as a profound ayah (sign) of Allah, a direct manifestation of His infinite attributes. This leads to a unified, luminous vision of reality where the Creator is perceived as the underlying, Absolute Reality of all existence. This is not merely an intellectual understanding, but a visceral, experiential psychic enlightenment that reshapes the very fabric of one's perception.

Where Gravity Fades and Remembrance Remains

To stand before the Creator
Is to pass beyond the pull of creation.
Not by turning away from the world,
But by stepping into what is greater than it.
The soul does not reject creation—
It simply ceases to orbit around it.
Gain and loss lose their grip.
Pleasure and pain lose their chains.
The wise-one is not numb,
But free.
No possession can stir, no loss can grieve."
"Not in turning from the world, but in stepping into what is greater than it.

This is not detachment born of denial—
It is transcendence born of remembrance.
The wise-one has not renounced the world;
They have outgrown its illusions.
They no longer measure life
By what is held or lost,
But by what remains
When all else fades.

❲The only true believers in Our revelation
Are those who—when it is recited to them—
Fall into prostration and glorify the praises of their Lord
And are not too proud.
They abandon their beds,
Invoking their Lord with hope and fear...❳[167] — Quran 32:15–16

In the quiet of night,
When the world sleeps,

---

[167] This is derived from the Quran verses of:

❲The only ˹true˺ believers in Our revelation are those who—when it is recited to them—fall into prostration and glorify the praises of their Lord and are not too proud. (15) They abandon their beds, invoking their Lord with hope and fear, and donate from what We have provided for them. (16) No soul can imagine what delights are kept in store for them as a reward for what they used to do. (17) Is the one who is a believer equal ˹before Allah˺ to the one who is rebellious? They are not equal! (18)❳ [Quran 32:15-18]

The true ones rise.
Not for display,
But for intimacy.
Not for reward,
But for remembrance.
They abandon comfort
To seek the Comforter.
They rise not to escape the world,
But to meet the One
Who transcends it.

To stand in presence
Is to become unshakable—
Not because the world has changed,
But because the soul has.
It is no longer rooted in circumstance,
But in the Eternal.
It no longer fears loss,
Because it has found the One
Who cannot be lost.

So the wise-one stands—
Not above creation,
But beyond its pull.
They walk through the world
With softness,
But they are no longer held by it.
They speak,
But their voice echoes remembrance.
They act,
But their movement flows from surrender.

For only He frees the soul from illusion.
Only He lifts the heart beyond gravity.
Only He remains the source
Of transcendence, remembrance, and eternal nearness.

Wisdom Unveiled

The profound wisdom unveiled in Transcending the Creation reveals that to stand in the Presence of the Creator is to lose the gravitational pull of the world, a deep psychic enlightenment. The wise-one's soul rises not by rejecting creation, but by fundamentally ceasing to orbit around its transient forms; gain and loss lose their meaning, and pleasure and pain lose their illusory chains, leaving the wise-one not numb, but exquisitely free. This is not a detachment born of denial, but a luminous transcendence born of deep remembrance. The wise-one has not renounced the world, but has simply outgrown its compelling illusions, becoming unshakable—rooted not in fleeting circumstance, but in the Eternal. Every atom and event is recognized as a vibrant ayah (sign) of Allah, dissolving the veil of duality and fostering a unified vision where the Creator is the underlying Reality of all existence. This state allows the wise-one to walk through the world with softness, yet remain unbound by its temporal demands, their every breath echoing Divine remembrance.

Wise-Reflection

Reflect on moments when you feel most entangled by worldly concerns—by anxieties over gain or loss, or by the pursuit of pleasure and avoidance of pain. How might the concept of "transcending the creation" by "stepping into what is greater than it" transform your experience of these challenges? What practices could help you cultivate a perception that sees through the forms of creation to the Creator, allowing the veil of duality to begin dissolving? Consider those quiet moments, perhaps at dawn, when the world sleeps, and ask yourself how you might rise not to escape the world, but to meet the One who truly transcends it, becoming unshakable by rooting your soul not in circumstance, but in the Eternal.

Contemplation: Divine Protection in Every Situation

(The soul stands—not untouched by trial, but unshaken within it)

The Stand in Presence brings an unwavering, profound certitude of Divine Protection in every situation, as powerfully exemplified by the Gateway Verse with Prophet Muhammad (PBUH) and Abu Bakr in the cave. When all worldly means crumble and vulnerability is acutely exposed, the wise-one experiences Allah's direct, immediate, and unmediated protection. This isn't a naive belief in the absence of difficulty or hardship; rather, it is a deep, unshakeable inner peace and absolute assurance that no harm can ultimately befall them except by Divine Will, and that Allah is their ultimate Guardian and Helper. This profound realization imbues the wise-one with immense courage, unwavering resilience, and an abiding inner serenity even amidst the most profound chaos, transforming their psychic landscape.

Where Serenity Becomes the Shield of Faith

To be for Him in every situation
Is to stand firm
When His decree prevails.
Not because the path is smooth,
But because the heart is anchored.
Not because the storm is absent,
But because the soul is held.
He sends a sign—
One that beholds the heart,
So that no fear shakes,
No terror intimidates.

This is not the absence of danger—
It is the presence of serenity.
The wise-one learns:
When the soul belongs entirely to the Creator,
No decree can shake it,
No storm can drown it.
In the heart of trial,
A shield rises—
Not of armor,
But of peace.

❲He is the One Who sent down serenity
Upon the hearts of the believers

So that they may increase even more in their faith.
To Allah alone belong the forces of the heavens and the earth.[168] *— Quran 48:4*

Fear becomes irrelevant—
Not because the threat disappears,
But because the soul knows
Who holds the reins of destiny.
The wise-one no longer measures safety
By circumstance,
But by nearness.

He is the One who casts serenity upon His servants,
Steadies their steps,
And shields them from trembling.
This serenity is not passive—
It is active grace.
It descends like rain
To purify,
To strengthen,
To make firm the steps
Of those who walk in surrender.

❮He caused drowsiness to overcome you,
Giving you serenity.
And He sent down rain from the sky
To purify you,
Free you from Satan's whispers,

---

[168] This is derived from the Quran verses of:

❮He is the One Who sent down serenity upon the hearts of the believers so that they may increase even more in their faith. To Allah ˹alone˺ belong the forces of the heavens and the earth. And Allah is All-Knowing, All-Wise. (4) So He may admit believing men and women into Gardens under which rivers flow—to stay there forever—and absolve them of their sins. And that is a supreme achievement in the sight of Allah. (5) Also ˹so that˺ He may punish hypocrite men and women and polytheistic men and women, who harbour evil thoughts of Allah.[1] May ill-fate befall them! Allah is displeased with them. He has condemned them and prepared for them Hell. What an evil destination! (6) To Allah ˹alone˺ belong the forces of the heavens and the earth. And Allah is Almighty, All-Wise. (7)❯ [Quran 48:4-7]

[1]: i.e., that Allah will not support His Prophet (ﷺ) and that misfortune will befall the believers.

Strengthen your hearts,
And make your steps firm.[169] — *Quran 8:11*

Even in battle,
Even in exile,
Even in the cave—
His presence silences the whirlwind.
His decree steadies the trembling.
His wisdom surrounds the soul
Like unseen forces
Guarding every breath.

To Him belong the forces of the heavens and the earth.
And Allah is All-Knowing, All-Wise.[170] — *Quran 48:4*

So the wise-one walks forward—
Not untouched by trial,
But unshaken within it.
They do not ask for ease,
But for presence.
They do not seek escape,
But embrace the One
Who speaks peace into the storm.

---

[169] This is derived from the Quran verses of:

﴿ 'Remember' when you cried out to your Lord for help, He answered, "I will reinforce you with a thousand angels—followed by many others."1 (9) And Allah made this a sign of victory and reassurance to your hearts. Victory comes only from Allah. Surely Allah is Almighty, All-Wise. (10) 'Remember' when He caused drowsiness to overcome you, giving you serenity.[2] And He sent down rain from the sky to purify you, free you from Satan's whispers, strengthen your hearts, and make 'your' steps firm. (11) ﴾ [Quran 8 : 9-11]

[1]: Five thousand angels in total, as mentioned in the Quran verse of: ﴿ Most certainly, if you 'believers' are firm and mindful 'of Allah' and the enemy launches a sudden attack on you, Allah will reinforce you with five thousand angels designated 'for battle'. (125) ﴾ [Quran 3 :125]

[2]: This happened the night before the battle.

[170] This is derived from the Quran verses of:

﴿ He is the One Who sent down serenity upon the hearts of the believers so that they may increase even more in their faith. To Allah 'alone' belong the forces of the heavens and the earth. And Allah is All-Knowing, All-Wise. (4) So He may admit believing men and women into Gardens under which rivers flow—to stay there forever—and absolve them of their sins. And that is a supreme achievement in the sight of Allah. (5) Also 'so that' He may punish hypocrite men and women and polytheistic men and women, who harbour evil thoughts of Allah.[1] May ill-fate befall them! Allah is displeased with them. He has condemned them and prepared for them Hell. What an evil destination! (6) To Allah 'alone' belong the forces of the heavens and the earth. And Allah is Almighty, All-Wise. (7) ﴾ [Quran 48 : 4-6]

[1]: i.e., that Allah will not support His Prophet ﷺ and that misfortune will befall the believers.

For only He casts serenity upon the heart.
Only He steadies the steps of the surrendered.
Only He remains the source
Of protection, wisdom, and eternal nearness.

Wisdom Unveiled

The profound wisdom unveiled in Divine Protection in Every Situation reveals that in the Stand in Presence of the Creator, the wise-one experiences an unwavering certitude of Divine Protection, not as an absence of difficulty, but as an unshakeable inner peace. When the soul belongs entirely to the Creator, no decree can shake it, and no storm can drown it; in the very heart of trial, a luminous shield of serenity rises, transforming fear into irrelevance. This is not because danger vanishes, but because the soul deeply knows who holds the reins of destiny, measuring safety not by fleeting circumstance, but by the profound nearness of the Beloved who speaks peace directly into the whirlwind. This active grace, descending to purify and strengthen, steadies the steps of the surrendered, imbuing the wise-one with immense courage, resilience, and an abiding inner peace even amidst chaos, allowing them to remain unshaken within every trial.

Wise-Reflection

Reflect on a challenging situation you are currently facing or have recently overcome. Did you feel fear, anxiety, or a lack of control? How might cultivating the understanding that "serenity becomes the shield of faith" and that "when the soul belongs entirely to the Creator, no decree can shake it" alter your experience of trials? What specific steps can you take to deepen your reliance on Allah as your ultimate Guardian and Helper, allowing Divine serenity to descend upon your heart? How can you practice measuring your safety not by external circumstances, but by the profound nearness of the One who holds the reins of all destiny, transforming your fear into unwavering inner peace and strength?

Contemplation: Understanding Divine Wisdom in All Things[171]

(The soul learns to see not with the eyes—but with trust)

In the Stand in Presence of the Creator, the wise-one gains an unparalleled, profound understanding of Divine Wisdom (Al-Hakeem) in all things. Every event, every trial, every apparent 'good' or 'bad' is no longer seen as random or unjust, but rather as an integral part of Allah's perfect, overarching plan, meticulously working towards a higher, ultimate good that profoundly transcends limited human comprehension. This deep spiritual and psychic insight obliterates all forms of questioning and resentment towards Divine decree, replacing them with absolute, unwavering acceptance, profound trust, and even a profound love for what Allah wills. This enlightened state brings immense, unshakeable peace and utterly prevents the heart from being disturbed by the transient contingencies and ever-changing circumstances of the world.

Where Deprivation Becomes Mercy and Restraint Becomes Grace

You shall not know Him
Until you witness His mercy
Upon both the obedient and the wayward.
Until you accept
That what He withholds
Is not deprivation—
But wisdom.
That what He delays
Is not neglect—
But precision.
That what He gives to the heedless
Is not favor—
But a test.

❴Do not let your eyes crave
What We have allowed some of the disbelievers to enjoy—
The fleeting splendor of this worldly life,

---

[171] This aligns with Islamic teachings that divine wisdom is beyond human comprehension (hikmah).

Which We test them with.
But your Lord's provision in the Hereafter
Is far better and more lasting.[172] — *Quran 20:131*

Divine wisdom often defies
The hunger of the eye
And the logic of the mind.
Blessings shower the ungrateful.
Restraint tempers the faithful.
The wise-one learns:
Lack is not always abandonment,
And abundance is not always favor.
Sometimes the Creator withholds
To keep the heart tender.
To prevent the soul
From swelling with pride
And closing its gates.
Thus, deprivation becomes mercy.
Scarcity becomes a tender
From the unseen hand.
You shall not know Him
Until you accept that what He withholds
Is His wisdom, not deprivation.

Do not crave
What is given to those heedless of His remembrance.
Do not let longing for the worldly
Veil the certainty of His grace.
For the righteous hold fast,
While the heedless follow desire—

---

[172] This is derived from the Quran verses of:

📖 ❨So be patient ˹O Prophet˺ with what they say. And glorify the praises of your Lord before sunrise and before sunset, and glorify Him in the hours of the night and at both ends of the day, so that you may be pleased ˹with the reward˺. (130) Do not let your eyes crave what We have allowed some of the disbelievers to enjoy; the ˹fleeting˺ splendour of this worldly life, which We test them with. But your Lord's provision ˹in the Hereafter˺ is far better and more lasting. (131) Bid your people to pray, and be diligent in ˹observing˺ it. We do not ask you to provide. It is We Who provide for you. And the ultimate outcome is ˹only˺ for ˹the people of˺ righteousness. (132)❩ [Quran 20:130-132]

And in that following,
They lose what was never theirs to keep.

❨And patiently stick with those
Who call upon their Lord morning and evening,
Seeking His pleasure.
Do not let your eyes look beyond them,
Desiring the luxuries of this worldly life.
And do not obey those
Whose hearts We have made heedless of Our remembrance,
Who follow only their desires
And whose state is total loss.❩[173] — Quran 18:28

The wise-one remains
Among those who call upon Him
Morning and evening.
Not seeking possessions,
But seeking His pleasure.
Not chasing outcomes,
But anchoring in remembrance.

❨Glorify the praises of your Lord
Before sunrise and before sunset,
And glorify Him in the hours of the night
And at both ends of the day,
So that you may be pleased.❩ — Quran 20:130

❨Bid your people to pray,
And be diligent in observing it.
We do not ask you to provide.
It is We Who provide for you.

---

[173] This is derived from the Quran verse of:

❨And patiently stick with those who call upon their Lord morning and evening, seeking His pleasure.[1] Do not let your eyes look beyond them, desiring the luxuries of this worldly life. And do not obey those whose hearts We have made heedless of Our remembrance, who follow ˹only˺ their desires and whose state is ˹total˺ loss. (28)❩ [Quran 18:28]

[1]: lit., seeking His Face.

And the ultimate outcome
Is only for the people of righteousness.❭[174] — *Quran 20:132*

So the wise-one walks forward—
Not measuring favor by abundance,
But by nearness.
Not interpreting delay as rejection,
But as refinement.
They do not ask,
"Why was I withheld?"
They whisper,
"Your wisdom is in the withholding."

For only He gives without illusion.
Only He withholds with mercy.
Only He remains the source
Of wisdom, provision, and eternal reward.

Wisdom Unveiled

The profound wisdom unveiled in Understanding Divine Wisdom in All Things reveals that in the Stand in Presence of the Creator, the wise-one perceives every event, whether seemingly good or bad, as part of Allah's perfect, overarching plan, leading to a higher, ultimate good. Divine wisdom often defies human logic and earthly desires; blessings may shower the ungrateful, while restraint tempers the faithful. The wise-one gains the crucial insight that lack is not always abandonment, nor is abundance always favor. Sometimes, the Creator mercifully withholds to keep the heart tender, preventing the soul from swelling with pride. Thus, perceived deprivation becomes mercy, and scarcity transforms into a tender touch from the unseen hand. This spiritual and psychic enlightenment liberates the heart from questioning and resentment, anchoring it in profound

---

[174] This is derived from the Quran verses of:

📖 ❬So be patient ˹O Prophet˺ with what they say. And glorify the praises of your Lord before sunrise and before sunset, and glorify Him in the hours of the night and at both ends of the day, so that you may be pleased ˹with the reward˺. (130) Do not let your eyes crave what We have allowed some of the disbelievers to enjoy; the ˹fleeting˺ splendour of this worldly life, which We test them with. But your Lord's provision ˹in the Hereafter˺ is far better and more lasting. (131) Bid your people to pray, and be diligent in ˹observing˺ it. We do not ask you to provide. It is We Who provide for you. And the ultimate outcome is ˹only˺ for ˹the people of˺ righteousness. (132)❭ [Quran 20:130-132]

acceptance and trust, as the wise-one learns to interpret every aspect of Divine decree not by external circumstance, but by the internal refinement it brings, recognizing that the ultimate outcome and true provision come solely from Allah.

Wise-Reflection

Reflect on a past or present situation in your life where something you deeply desired was withheld, or where you experienced a period of scarcity or difficulty. Did you struggle with resentment, confusion, or a feeling of being abandoned? How might cultivating the understanding that "what He withholds is His wisdom, not deprivation" transform your perception of such events? What does it mean for you that "sometimes the Creator withholds to keep the heart tender"? How can you practice anchoring your heart in remembrance and seeking Divine pleasure, rather than chasing fleeting outcomes or possessions, allowing this profound insight to bring you immense peace and prevent your heart from being disturbed by the contingencies of the world?

Contemplation: Divine Companionship and Ultimate Knowledge[175]

(The soul no longer seeks—it simply abides)

The pinnacle of this standing is the experiential reality of Divine Companionship and Ultimate Knowledge. The wise-one transcends mere conceptual understanding, experiencing Allah being "with us" not as an abstract idea, but as a living, breathing, all-encompassing Presence that permeates their entire being. This profound companionship naturally ushers in a state of direct, unveiled knowledge (ilm al-ladunni), where Divine truths are revealed intimately and immediately to the heart, bypassing external intermediaries or laborious intellectual processes. This is the ultimate psychic enlightenment, a state where the knower and the known become inextricably and intimately connected, dissolving the last vestiges of separation and leading to a supreme, unshakable inner certitude that transforms the very essence of existence.

---

[175] Islamic teaching that:

📖 《God is closer to you than your jugular vein (16)》 [Qur'an 50:16]

Where Knowing Ends and Presence Begin

The one who stands before Him
Has no need to turn left or right.
Their thoughts return to none but the One.
Their knowing ends
Where the Presence begins.
Here, no distraction remains—
Only Him.
The one whom He takes as a companion
Pays heed to nothing else.

This is not isolation—
It is immersion.
Not detachment—
But union.
The wise-one no longer wonders
Who sees them,
Who rewards them,
Or what awaits beyond the next horizon.
For there is no "elsewhere."
There is only Him.

❴Allah! There is no god worthy of worship except Him,
The Ever-Living, All-Sustaining.
Neither drowsiness nor sleep overtakes Him.
To Him belongs whatever is in the heavens
And whatever is on the earth...❵[176] — Quran 2:255

---

[176] This is derived from the Quran verses of:

📖 ❴Allah! There is no god ˹worthy of worship˺ except Him, the Ever-Living, All-Sustaining. Neither drowsiness nor sleep overtakes Him. To Him belongs whatever is in the heavens and whatever is on the earth. Who could possibly intercede with Him without His permission? He ˹fully˺ knows what is ahead of them and what is behind them, but no one can grasp any of His knowledge—except what He wills ˹to reveal˺. His Seat[1] encompasses the heavens and the earth, and the preservation of both does not tire Him. For He is the Most High, the Greatest.[2] (255) Let there be no compulsion in religion, for the truth stands out clearly from falsehood.[3] So whoever renounces false gods and believes in Allah has certainly grasped the firmest, unfailing hand-hold. And Allah is All-Hearing, All-Knowing. (256) Allah is the Guardian

His knowledge encompasses all—
What is ahead,
What is behind,
What is whispered,
What is spoken aloud.
And none grasp His knowledge
Except by His will.

❨He knows what every female bears
And what increases and decreases in the wombs.
And with Him everything is determined with precision.
He is the Knower of the seen and the unseen...❩[177] — Quran 13:8–9

The wise-one's understanding
Stands solely before Him.
Their knowledge refers only to Him.
Their heart rests
In a knowing too vast for words.
They do not measure—
They marvel.
They do not seek—
They surrender.

---

of the believers—He brings them out of darkness and into light. As for the disbelievers, their guardians are false gods who lead them out of light and into darkness. It is they who will be the residents of the Fire. They will be there forever. (257)❩ [Quran 2:255-257]

[1]: The Arabic word kursi can either mean seat or knowledge. There are some narrations attributed to Prophet Mohammed ﷺ that describe Allah's Throne ('Arsh) as being greater than His Kursi.

[2]: According to Muslim belief, this is the greatest verse in the Quran.

[3]: This verse was revealed when some new Muslims tried to force their Jewish and Christian children to convert to Islam after the Prophet's emigration (Hijrah) to Medina. The verse prohibits forced conversion.

[177] This is derived from the Quran verses of:

❨Allah knows what every female bears and what increases and decreases in the wombs.[1] And with Him everything is determined with precision. (8) ʿHe is theˋ Knower of the seen and the unseen—the All-Great, Most Exalted. (9) It is the same ʿto Himˋ whether any of you speaks secretly or openly, whether one hides in the darkness of night or goes about in broad daylight. (10) For each one there are successive angels before and behind, protecting them by Allah's command. Indeed, Allah would never change a people's state ʿof favourˋ until they change their own state ʿof faithˋ. And if it is Allah's Will to torment a people, it can never be averted, nor can they find a protector other than Him. (11)❩ [Quran 13:8-13]

[1]: He knows whether the egg will be fertilized or not, whether the baby will be born before or after nine months, whether the pregnancy will end with delivery or miscarriage, and whether there will be one baby or more.

❰His Seat encompasses the heavens and the earth,
And the preservation of both does not tire Him.
For He is the Most High, the Greatest.❱[178] — Quran 2:255

This is the summit of presence.
The soul no longer orbits creation.
It no longer asks,
No longer yearns—
For it has already been answered
By Presence itself.

❰It is the same to Him
Whether any of you speaks secretly or openly,
Whether one hides in the darkness of night
Or goes about in broad daylight.❱[179] — Quran 13:10

In this companionship,
There is no separation left to cross.
No prayer left to utter.
No veil left to lift.
The soul is held firm—
Consumed by none but His presence.

So the wise-one stands—
Not in knowledge,
But in nearness.
Not in mastery,
But in surrender.

---

[178] 📖 ❰Allah! There is no god ˹worthy of worship˺ except Him, the Ever-Living, All-Sustaining. Neither drowsiness nor sleep overtakes Him. To Him belongs whatever is in the heavens and whatever is on the earth. Who could possibly intercede with Him without His permission? He ˹fully˺ knows what is ahead of them and what is behind them, but no one can grasp any of His knowledge—except what He wills ˹to reveal˺. His Seat[1] encompasses the heavens and the earth, and the preservation of both does not tire Him. For He is the Most High, the Greatest.[2] (255)❱ [Quran 2:255]

[179] This is derived from the Quran verses of:

📖 ❰Allah knows what every female bears and what increases and decreases in the wombs.[1] And with Him everything is determined with precision. (8) ˹He is the˺ Knower of the seen and the unseen—the All-Great, Most Exalted. (9) It is the same ˹to Him˺ whether any of you speaks secretly or openly, whether one hides in the darkness of night or goes about in broad daylight. (10) For each one there are successive angels before and behind, protecting them by Allah's command. Indeed, Allah would never change a people's state ˹of favour˺ until they change their own state ˹of faith˺. And if it is Allah's Will to torment a people, it can never be averted, nor can they find a protector other than Him. (11)❱ [Quran 13:8-13]

They do not speak—
They are spoken to.
They do not reach—
They are received.

For only He knows without limit.
Only He sustains without fatigue.
Only He remains the source
Of companionship, knowledge, and eternal presence.

Wisdom Unveiled

At the absolute summit of Divine Presence, the profound wisdom unveiled is the experiential reality of Divine Companionship and Ultimate Knowledge, where the wise-one's soul no longer orbits around creation at all. Here, knowledge itself reaches its sacred boundary, and knowing gracefully ends where the very Presence begins. There is no longer any need to wonder who sees or rewards, or what awaits beyond any horizon, for the wise-one who meets the Companion discovers there is no "elsewhere"—only the consuming, all-encompassing Reality of the Divine. No earthly distraction is powerful enough to pull the heart away, no human yearning stronger than the profound contentment found in the gaze of the One. The mind ceases to measure, and the heart rests in a knowing too vast for words, a direct, unveiled understanding (ilm al-ladunni). In this intimate companionship, the last vestiges of separation dissolve; there is no separation left to cross, no prayer left to utter, and no veil left to lift, for the soul has already been answered, exquisitely held and consumed by Presence itself, reaching supreme inner certitude and ultimate psychic enlightenment.

Wise-Reflection

Reflect on your moments of deepest connection or peace. Are there times when your striving for knowledge or understanding actually creates a barrier to simple, direct Divine Presence? Consider the idea that "your knowing ends where the Presence begins." How might consciously letting go of the need to measure, seek, or even articulate your spiritual experience allow for a more profound immersion in Divine Companionship? What does it mean for you that in this ultimate companionship, "there is no separation left to cross, no prayer left to utter, no veil left to lift"? How can you cultivate a state where your soul "no longer seeks—it simply abides" in the eternal presence of the One, finding all answers in Presence itself?

Contemplation: The Sovereignty of the Wise-one in Divine Presence

(The soul stands—not above creation, but beyond its need)

Paradoxically, in this ultimate state of profound surrender and deep humility before the Creator, the wise-one is endowed with a unique, authentic sovereignty in Divine Presence. This is emphatically not personal power, but a sublime state of being utterly aligned with Divine Will, effectively making the wise-one a pure conduit for the manifestation of Divine attributes. They are empowered by Allah, not by any self-derived means. Their intentions become exquisitely purified, their actions are directly guided by Divine wisdom, and their perception is profoundly elevated, allowing them to wield subtle, spiritual influence and respond to creation with unparalleled wisdom and grace. In this elevated state, the wise-one truly becomes a vicegerent (khalifah), genuinely reflecting Allah's supreme sovereignty on earth.

Where Loyalty Transforms into Fellowship and Existence
Transcends into Devotion

The one who stands between His hands
Is raised beyond the limits of creation.
Not by elevation of status,
But by dissolution of self.
Above the edges of sky and earth,
Above heaven and hell—
Not in rank,
But in surrender.
Not in power,
But in presence.
The one who stands before Him
Has no need to turn left or right.

Their gaze is fixed.
Their longing is satiated.

Their identity has dissolved
Into the shining nearness of the Real.
They do not seek reward—
They have found the Companion.
They do not fear loss—
They have met the One
Who never departs.

His hands extend beyond the depths,
Beyond possession and consequence—
For he has met the Companion.
True sovereignty is not domination over others.
It is liberation
From the need to dominate,
From the hunger to be seen,
From the fear of being forgotten.
The wise-one who stands before the Companion
Needs no external validation.
Their knowing melts into awe.
Their presence becomes the only prayer.
His thoughts return to none but the One,
His knowing dissolves where the Presence begins.

This is the pledge—
Not of words,
But of being.
To place one's hand
In the Hand of the Divine
Is to surrender all claims,
And to be upheld
By a covenant that cannot break.

❧Surely those who pledge allegiance to you, O Prophet,
Are actually pledging allegiance to Allah.
Allah's Hand is over theirs.
Whoever breaks their pledge,
It will only be to their own loss.

And whoever fulfills their pledge to Allah,
He will grant them a great reward.[180] — *Quran 48:10*

Those who fulfill it
Do not rise in worldly stature—
They rise in nearness.
They do not gain recognition—
They gain serenity.
And those who break it
Do not harm the Divine—
They lose themselves.

So the wise-one walks forward—
Not to be seen,
But to be surrendered.
Not to be praised,
But to be present.
Their sovereignty is not in control,
But in freedom.
Their strength is not in grasping,
But in letting go.

For only He grants sovereignty without pride.
Only He upholds allegiance without condition.
Only He remains the source
Of presence, reward, and eternal companionship.

Wisdom Unveiled

The profound wisdom unveiled in The Sovereignty of the Wise-one in Divine Presence reveals a powerful paradox: in ultimate surrender and profound humility before the Creator, a unique and true sovereignty

---

[180] This is derived from the Quran verses of:

📖 ⟨To Allah ʿaloneʿ belong the forces of the heavens and the earth. And Allah is Almighty, All-Wise. (7) Indeed, ʿO Prophet,ʿ We have sent you as a witness, a deliverer of good news, and a warner, (8) so that you ʿbelieversʿ may have faith in Allah and His Messenger, support and honour him, and glorify Allah morning and evening.[1] (9) Surely those who pledge allegiance to you ʿO Prophetʿ are actually pledging allegiance to Allah. Allah's Hand is over theirs. Whoever breaks their pledge, it will only be to their own loss. And whoever fulfils their pledge to Allah, He will grant them a great reward. (10)⟩ [Quran 48:7-10]

[1]: Another possible translation: "... so that you ʿallʿ may believe in Allah and His Messenger, support ʿHis causeʿ, revere, and glorify Him morning and evening."

emerges. This is not worldly domination, but a psychic liberation from the pervasive need to dominate, to be seen, or to fear being forgotten. The wise-one who stands before the Companion of all existence needs no external validation; their gaze is fixed, their longing satiated, and their very identity dissolved into the shining nearness of the Real. In such a soul, knowledge melts into boundless awe, and their very presence becomes the only prayer. This state signifies a complete alignment with Divine Will, where strength is found not in grasping, but in letting go, and where loyalty transforms into a profound fellowship, empowering the wise-one as a true vicegerent, reflecting Allah's sovereignty on earth through their profound freedom and grace.

Wise-Reflection

Reflect on your personal understanding of "power" or "influence." Do you often associate it with control over others, achievement, or recognition? How does the concept of sovereignty arising from "dissolution of self" and "liberation from the need to dominate or be recognized" challenge your perception? What would it mean for you to genuinely "surrender all claims" and place your "hand in the Hand of the Divine," trusting in a covenant that cannot break? Consider how letting go of the need for external validation and embracing your inherent freedom in Divine Presence could empower you to respond to the world with greater wisdom, grace, and authentic influence, truly reflecting Allah's sovereignty on earth.

Contemplation: The Final Dissolution of Creation

(The veil is lifted, and all is revealed)

In the deepest, most profound moments of the Stand in Presence, the wise-one witnesses a final, ultimate dissolution of creation—not its physical annihilation, but its complete dissolution as a separate, independent reality. Here, all forms, distinctions, and dualities, which once seemed so solid, ultimately melt away and dissolve into the singular, all-encompassing Oneness of the Creator. This is the ultimate, experiential realization of Tawhid (Humility before Allah), where "only Allah's Face remains." This sublime spiritual experience utterly transcends all mental constructs and leads to a state of complete absorption in the Divine, recognizing the absolute dependence of the created while maintaining the essential distinction between Creator and created. This brings a transformative psychic awakening, where the illusion of fragmented reality is replaced by the unifying truth of Divine Oneness.

| Where All That Was Concealed Stands Unveiled Before the Eternal |

The appointed time
Between the soul and the inhabitants of this life
Is the dissolution of this life itself.
The veil woven by permanence and possession
Will be torn.
And then shall all be unveiled—
Each soul knowing its place in His decree,
Each standing in the certainty
Of what was prepared for them.

❨*On that Day, the heavens will burst with clouds,*
And the angels will be sent down in successive ranks.❩ — *Quran 25:25*

True authority will belong only
To the Most Compassionate.
No ruler will stand.
No wealth will speak.
No deed will remain
Except what was rooted in sincerity.

❨*True authority on that Day*
Will belong only to the Most Compassionate.
And it will be a hard day for the disbelievers.❩ — *Quran 25:26*[181]

The righteous will be settled
In gardens of bliss,
Honored in their resting,
Facing one another on thrones,

---

[181] This is derived from the Quran verses of:

❨'Watch for` the Day the heavens burst with clouds, and the angels will be sent down in successive ranks. (25) True authority on that Day will belong `only` to the Most Compassionate.[1] And it will be a hard day for the disbelievers. (26)❩ [Quran 25:25-26]

[1]: Some people (like kings and rulers) have some sort of authority in this world. But on Judgment Day Allah will be the sole authority.

Drinking from flowing streams,
Gazing upon what was promised.

❨*They will be honoured*
In the Gardens of Bliss,
Facing each other on thrones.
A drink of pure wine will be passed around to them
From a flowing stream...❩[182] — *Quran 37:43-45*

And they will say:

❨*Had it not been for the grace of my Lord,*
I too would have been among the lost...❩[183] — *Quran 37:57*

The wise-one lives with this unraveling always in view.
They invest not in castles of sand,
But in dwellings of light.
They do not cling to the ephemeral—
They yearn for the Eternal.
For soon the tapestry will be pulled away,
And each soul will stand revealed—
Naked before the Gaze
That sees all beginnings and endings as one.

---

[182] This is derived from the Quran verses of:

📖 ❨But not the chosen servants of Allah. (40) They will have a known provision: (41) fruits ˹of every type˺.[1] And they will be honoured (42) in the Gardens of Bliss, (43) facing each other on thrones.[2] (44) A drink ˹of pure wine˺ will be passed around to them from a flowing stream: (45) crystal-white, delicious to drink. (46) It will neither harm ˹them˺, nor will they be intoxicated by it. (47) And with them will be maidens of modest gaze and gorgeous eyes, (48) as if they were pristine pearls.[3] (49)❩ [Quran 37:40-49]

[1]: This implies all sorts of delicacies, not just fruits.

[2]: Facing each other implies that no one will have anything in their hearts against others.

[3]: 'Baiḍun maknûn' can also mean spotless eggs.

[183] This is derived from the Quran verses of:

📖 ❨Then they will turn to one another inquisitively.1 (50) One of them will say, "I once had a companion ˹in the world˺ (51) who used to ask ˹me˺, 'Do you actually believe ˹in resurrection˺? (52) When we are dead and reduced to dust and bones, will we really be brought to judgment?'" (53) He will ˹then˺ ask, "Would you care to see ˹his fate˺?" (54) Then he ˹and the others˺ will look and spot him in the midst of the Hellfire. (55) He will ˹then˺ say, "By Allah! You nearly ruined me. (56) Had it not been for the grace of my Lord, I ˹too˺ would have certainly been among those brought ˹to Hell˺." (57) ˹Then he will ask his fellow believers,˺ "Can you imagine that we will never die, (58) except our first death, nor be punished ˹like the others˺?" (59) This is truly the ultimate triumph. (60) For such ˹honour˺ all should strive. (61)❩ [Quran 37:50-61]

[1]: It is assumed that they will ask each other about their lives in the world and what led them to Paradise.

❮Then We will turn to whatever good deeds they did,
Reducing them to scattered dust.❯[184] — Quran 25:23

The heedless will see their deeds
Turned to dust,
Realizing too late
What was concealed before their eyes.
But the chosen servants
Will witness the fulfillment of grace.
They will not ask for more—
They will know they have received all.

❮This is truly the ultimate triumph.
For such honour all should strive.❯[185] — Quran 37:60–61

So the wise-one walks forward—
Not in fear of the end,
But in reverence for what it reveals.
They live as if the veil were already lifted.

---

[184] This is derived from the Quran verses of:

📖 ❮We never sent any messenger before you ˹O Prophet˺, who did not eat food and go about in market-places. We have made some of you a trial for others. Will you ˹not then˺ be patient? And your Lord is All-Seeing. (20) Those who do not expect to meet Us say, "If only the angels were sent down to us, or we could see our Lord!" They have certainly been carried away by their arrogance and have entirely exceeded all limits. (21) ˹But˺ on the Day they will see the angels, there will be no good news for the wicked, who will cry, "Keep away! Away ˹from us˺!"[1] (22) Then We will turn to whatever ˹good˺ deeds they did, reducing them to scattered dust.[2] (23) ˹But˺ on that Day the residents of Paradise will have the best settlement and the finest place to rest. (24) ˹Watch for˺ the Day the heavens will burst with clouds, and the angels will be sent down in successive ranks. (25) True authority on that Day will belong ˹only˺ to the Most Compassionate.[1] And it will be a hard day for the disbelievers. (26) And ˹beware of˺ the Day the wrongdoer will bite his nails ˹in regret˺ and say, "Oh! I wish I had followed the Way along with the Messenger! (27) Woe to me! I wish I had never taken so-and-so as a close friend. (28) It was he who truly made me stray from the Reminder after it had reached me." And Satan has always betrayed humanity. (29) The Messenger has cried, "O my Lord! My people have indeed received this Quran with neglect." (30) Similarly, We made enemies for every prophet from among the wicked, but sufficient is your Lord as a Guide and Helper. (31) The disbelievers say, "If only the Quran had been sent down to him all at once!" ˹We have sent it˺ as such ˹in stages˺ so We may reassure your heart with it. And We have revealed it at a deliberate pace. (32) Whenever they bring you an argument, We come to you with the right refutation and the best explanation. (33) Those who will be dragged into Hell on their faces will be in the worst place, and are ˹now˺ farthest from the ˹Right˺ Way. (34)❯ [Quran 25:20-34]

[1]: Another possible translation: ❮And the angels will say, 'All good is forbidden to you!'❯

[2]: The good deeds of the disbelievers (like charity) will have no weight on Judgment Day.

[3]: Some people (like kings and rulers) have some sort of authority in this world. But on Judgment Day Allah will be the sole authority.

[185] This is derived from the Quran verses of:

📖 ❮This is truly the ultimate triumph. (60) For such ˹honour˺ all should strive. (61)❯ [Quran 37:60-61]

[280]

They speak as if the angels were already descending.
They pray as if the throne were already near.

For only He unveils what was hidden.
Only He preserves what was sincere.
Only He remains the source
Of triumph, mercy, and eternal unveiling.

Wisdom Unveiled

The profound wisdom unveiled in The Final Dissolution of Creation reveals that in the deepest moments of the Stand in Presence, the wise-one witnesses the ultimate dissolution of creation as a separate, independent reality, and all forms and dualities melt into the singular, encompassing Oneness of the Creator. The veil between the soul and its true station is thin, woven only by the illusions of permanence and possession, and it will inevitably be torn. When the world finally unravels, all that will truly remain is what was chosen and nurtured in the heart: a yearning for the Eternal, or a clinging to the ephemeral. The wise-one lives with this inevitable unraveling always in view, wisely investing not in "castles of sand," but in "dwellings of light." This spiritual and psychic awakening prepares the soul to stand revealed, naked before the Gaze that sees all beginnings and endings as one, recognizing that true authority, sincerity, and triumph belong only to the Most Compassionate.

Wise-Reflection

Reflect on your daily priorities and attachments. Are you consciously investing in "dwellings of light" or are you subtly clinging to "castles of sand"? Consider the powerful imagery of the veil of permanence and possession being torn, revealing all. How does contemplating the "final dissolution of creation"—not its physical end, but its dissolution as an independent reality—affect your perception of the world around you? What aspects of your life are you currently treating as permanent or independent that might be better viewed as transient signs of the Oneness of the Creator? How can living as if "the veil were already lifted" and "the throne were already near" transform your intentions, actions, and inner peace in the here and now, leading you towards the ultimate triumph of Humility before Allah?

Conclusion: In the Stand in Presence of Creator

ECHOES OF REALIZATION

There is no higher spiritual ascent than the profound stillness that gracefully descends when the soul is utterly purified and truly beholds the Real. There is no reward greater than the sacred silence that blossoms within when the Creator's intimate nearness becomes the solitary horizon of perception.

In this sacred Stand in Presence, the wise-one ceases entirely to measure the unfolding of life by what is superficially gained or momentarily lost. They no longer wander aimlessly through the fleeting marketplaces of creation, desperately bargaining for fragmented scraps of transient meaning. They have, in truth, come home. They have, by Divine Grace, entered the sanctuary beyond all forms of striving and personal exertion. Here, all lingering fears melt into serenity. All perceived needs vanish into complete contentment. All intellectual questions fall into profound silence. And the wise-one's soul, once scattered among a thousand worldly desires, becomes a single, luminous flame—burning quietly, endlessly, in the encompassing, eternal Gaze of the Infinite.

THE SEEKER'S ASCENT: STANDING IN DIVINE PRESENCE

The wise-one departs from this profound reflection transformed, having experienced the ultimate Gaze of Oneness. They now embody the sacred knowledge that true strength lies in utter dependence on Allah, true sight in seeing Him in all things, and true companionship in His ceaseless Presence.

This Stand in Presence is not an end, but an eternal mode of being. The wise-one walks forth, their heart a living sanctuary, their mind illumined by Divine Wisdom, and their soul perpetually resonant with the Ultimate Reality. They are no longer a seeker battling veils, but one who resides within the unveiled Truth, a living testimony to the words: "Allah is certainly with us." Every breath is now an act of presence, every moment an intimate communion, and every gaze a reflection of the Creator's encompassing reality. This is the profound culmination of spiritual awakening and psychic enlightenment in this station: to simply be in the Divine Presence, eternally.

◉◉◉

9ᵀᴴ REFLECTION: IN THE AWAKENING OF HEART AND MIND

THE GATEWAY VERSE

In the sacred words of Allah, a profound reminder to all who reflect upon the transformative power of Divine Revelation upon the heart and soul:

⌂ ❨ 'It is' Allah 'Who' has sent down the best message—a Book of perfect consistency and repeated lessons—which causes the skin 'and hearts' of those who fear their Lord to tremble, then their skin and hearts soften at the mention of 'the mercy of' Allah. That is the guidance of Allah, through which He guides whoever He wills. But whoever Allah leaves to stray will be left with no guide. (23)❩ [Quran 29:23]

ILLUMINATION'S DAWN

There comes a pivotal moment in the wise-one's soul journey when seeing profoundly shifts—when the inner eyes of the heart open wider and perceive more deeply than the outer eyes of the body. It is the true awakening of perception, where life's inherent contradictions no longer cause confusion but instead luminously reveal deeper truths, and where every sorrow and every joy become pure mirrors reflecting the same hidden, singular Divine Face.

In this sacred awakening, the wise-one learns not merely to diligently find the manifest signs of the Creator in the world, but to see directly through them—until all transient forms and distinctions dissolve into the absolute Oneness of the Ever-Present One who never leaves. Here, the soul's deepest vision is purified; here, Divine love matures beyond the mere longing for personal reward; here, profound Divine presence becomes more tangible and real than any worldly possession. Let us now walk through the unfolding lights of this profound awakening, where the heart and mind ascend beyond all conventional division, and enter the boundless vastness of true Divine companionship.

THE UNFOLDING OF INSIGHTS

This section explores the multi-dimensional awakening of the wise-one's perception, moving beyond superficial reality to apprehend the Divine in all states and forms.

Contemplation: Seeing the Divine in Sleep and Wakefulness

(The soul inherits not a place—but the shape of its own becoming)

The awakened wise-one cultivates a profound, pervasive awareness of seeing the Divine in both sleep and wakefulness. In the state of wakefulness, they keenly perceive Allah's manifest signs permeating the world and woven into the tapestry of daily life. In the realm of sleep, the soul, unburdened by the physical senses and worldly distractions, may experience deeper, more direct forms of spiritual insight, receive true dreams that convey subtle messages, or even engage in profound, subtle communion. This contemplation profoundly teaches that the Divine Presence is not confined to specific states of consciousness; rather, it permeates and saturates all existence without exception. For the wise-one, every single moment, whether consciously experienced or seemingly unconscious, transforms into a sacred opportunity for communion and a living testament to Allah's continuous, omnipresent Reality. This dissolves the perceived, illusory dichotomy between inner and outer realities, bringing about a holistic psychic awakening.

Where Eden Is Not Bestowed, But Cultivated Within

The home He builds in the hereafter
Is shaped by the heart given to Him now.
Not by outward claim,
But by inward cultivation.
Each soul carries only
What it has striven toward—
Its deeds unfolding
In the record of its return.

❲Each person will only have
What they endeavoured towards,
And the outcome of their endeavours will be seen in their record.

Then they will be fully rewarded.
And to your Lord alone is the ultimate return of all things.[186] — *Quran 53:39–42*

If the heart is a garden of remembrance,
Then paradise will bloom as its reflection.
If the heart is a desert of forgetfulness,
Then barrenness shall follow it into eternity.
The wise-one tends their heart
Not out of fear,
But out of love—
Planting within it
Seeds of surrender, humility, and longing.

❬The true believers
Are only those whose hearts tremble
At the remembrance of Allah,
Whose faith increases
When His revelations are recited to them,
And who put their trust in their Lord.[187] — *Quran 8:2*

Yet many remain heedless.
Their hearts unable to understand,
Their eyes unable to see,
Their ears closed to truth.
They move like a herd,

---

[186] This is derived from the Quran verses of:

📖 ❬Or has he not been informed of what is in the Scripture of Moses, (36) and ˹that of˺ Abraham, who ˹perfectly˺ fulfilled ˹his covenant˺? (37) ˹They state˺ that no soul burdened with sin will bear the burden of another, (38) and that each person will only have what they endeavoured towards, (39) and that ˹the outcome of˺ their endeavours will be seen ˹in their record˺, (40) then they will be fully rewarded, (41) and that to your Lord ˹alone˺ is the ultimate return ˹of all things˺. (42) Moreover, He is the One Who brings about joy and sadness.[1] (43) And He is the One Who gives life and causes death. (44) And He created the pairs—males and females— (45) from a sperm-drop when it is emitted. (46) And it is upon Him to bring about re-creation. (47) And He is the One Who enriches and impoverishes. (48) And He alone is the Lord of Sirius.[2] (49) ❭ [Quran 53:36-49]

[1]: lit., laughter and weeping.

[2]: A star worshipped by some ancient pagans.

[187] This is derived from the Quran verses of:

📖 ❬The ˹true˺ believers are only those whose hearts tremble at the remembrance of Allah, whose faith increases when His revelations are recited to them, and who put their trust in their Lord. (2) ˹They are˺ those who establish prayer and donate from what We have provided for them. (3) It is they who are the true believers. They will have elevated ranks, forgiveness, and an honourable provision from their Lord. (4) ❭ [Quran 8:2-4]

Unaware of where they are led—
Not because they lack direction,
But because they have lost perception.

❨Indeed, We have destined many jinn and humans for Hell.
They have hearts they do not understand with,
Eyes they do not see with,
And ears they do not hear with.
They are like cattle.
In fact, they are even less guided!
Such people are entirely heedless.❩[188] — Quran 7:179

The wise-one sees:
What the heart becomes today,
The soul shall inherit tomorrow.
The eternal abode
Is not awarded externally—
It is carved inwardly,
Now,
In the chambers of the heart.

So the wise-one walks forward—
Not building palaces in the world,
But cultivating gardens within.
They do not ask for paradise—
They prepare for it
By becoming its mirror.
They do not fear judgment—
They live in remembrance.

For only He sees the heart's true shape.
Only He rewards what was sincerely grown.

---

[188] This is derived from the Quran verses of:

❨What an evil example of those who denied Our signs! They ˹only˺ wronged their own souls. (177) Whoever Allah guides is truly guided. And whoever He leaves to stray, they are the ˹true˺ losers. (178) Indeed, We have destined many jinn and humans for Hell. They have hearts they do not understand with, eyes they do not see with, and ears they do not hear with. They are like cattle. In fact, they are even less guided! Such ˹people˺ are ˹entirely˺ heedless. (179)❩ [Quran 7:177-179]

Only He remains the source
Of guidance, return, and eternal dwelling.

Wisdom Unveiled

The profound wisdom unveiled in Seeing the Divine in Sleep and Wakefulness reveals that the soul inherits the shape of its own becoming, actively cultivating its eternal abode in the present moment. The wise-one recognizes that the Divine Presence is an unbroken stream, perceiving Allah's signs in both the manifest world of wakefulness and through deeper, direct spiritual insights in sleep. This signifies that the soul that remembers the Beloved in wakefulness will drink His nearness even in sleep; when the wise-one falls asleep beholding the Divine Face, they entrust their soul to a Keeper who neither slumbers nor forgets. Thus, sleep becomes not a departure from presence, but a seamless continuation of it—an unbroken stream of remembrance carrying the soul toward its eternal dawn. This powerful psychic awakening highlights that "Eden is not bestowed, but cultivated within," for the spiritual state of the heart today directly determines the soul's inheritance tomorrow, making every moment an opportunity for communion and a testament to Allah's continuous, encompassing Presence.

Wise-Reflection

Reflect on your own perceptions of wakefulness and sleep. Do you typically see them as distinct, separate states, or as continuous opportunities for Divine connection? Consider the idea that "the home He builds in the hereafter is shaped by the heart given to Him now." What seeds of "surrender, humility, and longing" are you actively planting in the garden of your heart today? How can you cultivate a more conscious awareness of Divine Presence not just in your active hours, but also as you transition into sleep, entrusting your soul to the One who neither slumbers nor forgets? What would it mean to prepare for paradise "by becoming its mirror" in your present actions and inner cultivation, allowing this understanding to deepen your spiritual and psychic awakening?

Contemplation: Seeing the Divine in Contradictions

(The soul sees not contradiction—but convergence)

A profound hallmark of this spiritual awakening is the ability to see the Divine in what appear to be glaring contradictions. Life, in its infinite complexity, constantly presents paradoxes: inherent weakness existing alongside immense strength, fleeting beauty intertwined with inevitable transience, and profound suffering encountered hand-in-hand with boundless mercy. The unawakened mind, confined by dualistic thinking, is typically confused and disturbed by these apparent oppositions. However, the wise-one, with an awakened heart and mind, perceives that these contradictions are not flaws or inconsistencies in creation, but are precisely how Allah, in His infinite wisdom, reveals His multifaceted and harmonious attributes. In every opposition, they discern a deeper, unifying truth, recognizing that both sides are but manifestations of the One. This profound spiritual insight fosters unshakable inner peace and unwavering faith, transforming confusion into luminous spiritual and psychic clarity, where all perceived divisions ultimately converge into Divine Oneness.

Where Joy and Grief Become Twin Gates to the Same Sanctuary

The wise-one reflects:
The one who sees with unwavering vision
Amid contradiction
Is the one chosen for His favor.
They do not flinch at calamity,
Nor swell at blessing.
They behold the same Face
Behind both veils.
For all that unfolds—whether calamity or blessing—
Is written before it comes to pass,
And none escape His decree.

To awaken is to see
That joy and grief
Are not opposites—
But twin gates
Leading to the same sanctuary.
The wise-one no longer divides life
Into good and bad,
Gain and loss,
Success and failure.

They see the singular Divine presence
Shimmering beneath both masks.

❨No calamity or blessing occurs
On earth or in yourselves
Without being written in a Record
Before We bring it into being.
This is certainly easy for Allah.❩ — Quran 57:22

Thus, contradiction becomes a mirror—
Not to confuse,
But to reveal.
When the soul beholds
The same eternal Face
In every rise and fall,
It loses its smaller self
And is absorbed
Into the Beloved's choosing.

Neither grieve over what is missed
Nor boast over what is given,
For all things rest in the wisdom of His command.
This is not indifference—
It is intimacy.
The wise-one feels deeply,
But is not shaken.
They rejoice,
But do not cling.
They mourn,
But do not despair.
For they know:
All is written,
And all is guided.

❨So compete with one another
For forgiveness from your Lord
And a Paradise as vast as the heavens and the earth,
Prepared for those who believe in Allah and His messengers.

This is the favor of Allah.
He grants it to whoever He wills.⟩ — Quran 57:21

In that vision,
The wise-one is no longer merely a seeker—
But a companion
Of the One beyond all opposites.
They do not chase outcomes—
They walk in remembrance.
They do not fear contradiction—
They see through it.

⟨Allah does not like
Whoever is arrogant, boastful.⟩[189] — Quran 57:23

So the wise-one walks forward—
Not with pride in what they hold,
Nor sorrow in what they've lost.
They walk with eyes
That see the Divine
In every unfolding.
They walk with a heart
That rests in the decree
And competes only for forgiveness.

---

[189] All previous concepts are driven from the Quran verses of:

⟨Know that this worldly life is no more than play, amusement, luxury, mutual boasting, and competition in wealth and children. This is like rain that causes plants to grow, to the delight of the planters. But later the plants dry up and you see them wither, then they are reduced to chaff. And in the Hereafter there will be either severe punishment or forgiveness and pleasure of Allah, whereas the life of this world is no more than the delusion of enjoyment. (20) ˹So˺ compete with one another for forgiveness from your Lord and a Paradise as vast as the heavens and the earth, prepared for those who believe in Allah and His messengers. This is the favour of Allah. He grants it to whoever He wills. And Allah is the Lord of infinite bounty. (21) No calamity ˹or blessing˺ occurs on earth or in yourselves without being ˹written˺ in a Record before We bring it into being. This is certainly easy for Allah. (22) ˹We let you know this˺ so that you neither grieve over what you have missed nor boast over what He has granted you. For Allah does not like whoever is arrogant, boastful— (23) those who are stingy and promote stinginess among people. And whoever turns away ˹should know that˺ Allah ˹alone˺ is truly the Self-Sufficient, Praiseworthy. (24) Indeed, We sent Our messengers with clear proofs, and with them We sent down the Scripture and the balance ˹of justice˺ so that people may administer justice. And We sent down iron with its great might, benefits for humanity, and means for Allah to prove who ˹is willing to˺ stand up for Him and His messengers without seeing Him. Surely Allah is All-Powerful, Almighty. (25)⟩ [Quran 25:20-25]

For only He writes what is hidden.
Only He unveils what is eternal.
Only He remains the source
Of mercy, wisdom, and eternal companionship.

Wisdom Unveiled

The profound wisdom unveiled in Seeing the Divine in Contradictions is that the awakened heart and mind perceive that joy and grief are not opposites, but twin gates leading to the same sanctuary. The wise-one transcends the dualistic mind that divides life into good and bad, gain and loss, success and failure, and instead sees the singular Divine Presence shimmering beneath both masks. Thus, contradiction transforms into a luminous mirror—not to confuse, but to reveal the multifaceted attributes of Allah. When the soul truly beholds the same eternal Face in every rise and fall, it sheds its smaller self and becomes absorbed into the Beloved's choosing, finding a deep intimacy where feelings are felt without being shaken by them. In this state of profound spiritual and psychic clarity, the wise-one is no longer merely a seeker, but a true companion of the One beyond all opposites, walking in remembrance and seeing through the illusions of contradiction, fostering unwavering faith and inner peace.

Wise-Reflection

Reflect on a personal experience where you faced what seemed like a stark contradiction or a difficult paradox (e.g., experiencing both immense joy and deep sorrow in a short period, or seeing strength emerge from profound weakness). How did your mind initially react to this duality? How might consciously applying the lens of "contradiction becomes a mirror—not to confuse, but to reveal" reshape your understanding of that experience? Can you practice seeing the "singular Divine presence shimmering beneath both masks" of joy and grief, gain and loss, in your daily life? What would it mean to truly "lose your smaller self" and be absorbed into Divine choosing amidst life's inherent paradoxes, trusting that all is written and all is guided?

Contemplation: Divine Love and the Balance of Weakness and Strength

(The soul is shaped not by what it holds—but by how it loves)

The wise-one comes to a profound, intimate understanding of Divine Love through the delicate, intricate balance of weakness and strength inherent in the human condition. It is frequently in moments of intense weakness, raw vulnerability, and utter dependence that the soul instinctively turns fully to Allah, and in that turning, experiences His infinite Mercy, boundless Power, and unwavering Support. Conversely, when strength is present, and critically, when it is coupled with profound humility, it transforms into a potent means to serve Allah and His creation with dedication and grace. This contemplation reveals that Allah's encompassing love embraces both states of being, teaching the wise-one to embrace their human limitations and inherent weakness with genuine humility, and simultaneously to receive their Divine endowments and strengths with deep gratitude. They understand that both aspects are not merely experiences but sacred channels, divinely designed to draw them ever closer to the Beloved, fostering a comprehensive spiritual and psychic awakening.

Where Every Condition Becomes a Language of Mercy

Shall you not notice His love—
That He fashioned you with weakness
For the weaker,
And strength
For the stronger?
That He placed in you
Both tenderness and resolve,
So that you may serve,
Not dominate—
And uplift,
Not boast.

For He replaces those who falter
With souls who love Him and are loved by Him,
Humble among the believers,
Firm in the path of truth,

Fearing no blame,
Striving only in His way.[190] — *Quran 5:54*

Strength is not a reward.
Weakness is not a punishment.
Both are languages
Through which Divine love speaks.
The wise-one learns to honor every condition—
To bear strength without pride,
And to wear weakness without shame.
In every lifting,
And every bending,
The hand of the Beloved is at work—
Shaping the soul
Into a vessel for compassion,
Fortifying it with humility.

❨Muḥammad is the Messenger of Allah.
And those with him are firm with the disbelievers
And compassionate with one another.
You see them bowing and prostrating in prayer,
Seeking Allah's bounty and pleasure.
The sign of brightness can be seen on their faces
From the trace of prostrating in prayer.❩ — Quran 48:29

See how He raises the faithful like a seed—
First tender,
Then thick and firm,
Standing strong
In His bounty and pleasure.
Their devotion shines upon their faces,
Not from status,
But from surrender.

---

[190] This is derived from the Quran verses of:

❨O believers! Whoever among you abandons their faith, Allah will replace them with others who love Him and are loved by Him. They will be humble with the believers but firm towards the disbelievers, struggling in the Way of Allah; fearing no blame from anyone. This is the favour of Allah. He grants it to whoever He wills. And Allah is All-Bountiful, All-Knowing. (54) Your only guardians are Allah, His Messenger, and fellow believers—who establish prayer and pay alms-tax with humility. (55) Whoever allies themselves with Allah, His Messenger, and fellow believers, then it is certainly Allah's party that will prevail. (56)❩ [Quran 5:54-56]

They bow,
They prostrate,
Seeking none but Him.

❡Their parable in the Gospel
Is that of a seed that sprouts its tiny branches,
Making it strong.
Then it becomes thick,
Standing firmly on its stem,
To the delight of the planters...❫[191] — Quran 48:29

The wise-one sees:
It is not what I am given,
But how I love through it,
That matters.
Whether in strength or in weakness,
They strive only in His way.
They fear no blame,
Because they seek no praise.

---

[191] This is derived from the Quran verses of:

📖 ❨He is the One Who has sent His Messenger with ´right` guidance and the religion of truth, making it prevail over all others. And sufficient is Allah as a Witness. (28) Muḥammad is the Messenger of Allah. And those with him are firm with the disbelievers[1] and compassionate with one another. You see them bowing and prostrating[2] ´in prayer`, seeking Allah's bounty and pleasure. The sign ´of brightness can be seen` on their faces from the trace of prostrating ´in prayer`. This is their description in the Torah.[3] And their parable in the Gospel is that of a seed that sprouts its ´tiny` branches, making it strong. Then it becomes thick, standing firmly on its stem, to the delight of the planters[4]—in this way Allah makes the believers a source of dismay for the disbelievers. To those of them who believe and do good, Allah has promised forgiveness and a great reward. (29)❩ [Quran 48:28-29]

[1]: This passage and the next should be understood in their historical context. The Muslims were urged to be firm with the Arab pagans and their allies who were at war with Muslims at that time. Otherwise, Islam encourages Muslims to treat peaceful non-Muslims with kindness and fairness. This is explained in the Quran verses of: ❨Allah does not forbid you from dealing kindly and fairly with those who have neither fought nor driven you out of your homes. Surely Allah loves those who are fair. (8) Allah only forbids you from befriending those who have fought you for ´your` faith, driven you out of your homes, or supported ´others` in doing so. And whoever takes them as friends, then it is they who are the ´true` wrongdoers. (9)❩ [Quran 60:8-9].

[2]: Prostration means lying down on one's face (i.e., touching the ground with the forehead and nose while resting on knees and flat palms of both hands) as an act of prayer and submission to Allah.

[3]: In Deuteronomy 33:1-3, ´Moses proclaimed:` "The Lord came from Sinai. Rising from Seir upon us, he shone forth from Mount Paran, accompanied by a myriad of his holy ones, with flaming fire from his right hand for them. Indeed, lover of people, all of his holy ones are in your control. They gather at your feet to do as you have instructed. [sic]" Paran is a mountain in Mecca.

[4]: In Matthew 13:3-9, "´Jesus` spoke many things to them in parables, saying, "Behold, the sower went out to sow. ... ´A seed` fell on the good soil and yielded a crop, some a hundredfold, some sixty, and some thirty. "He who has ears, let him hear."'" Or the parable of the growing seed in Mark 4:26-28.

They are upheld
Not by condition,
But by favor.

❲To those who believe and do good,
Allah has promised forgiveness
And a great reward.❳ — Quran 48:29

So the wise-one walks forward—
Not measuring their worth
By what they possess,
But by how they reflect Divine love
In every state.
They do not ask for strength alone,
Nor do they flee from weakness.
They ask only to be shaped
By the One who knows
How to balance both.

For only He gives strength without pride.
Only He grants weakness without shame.
Only He remains the source
Of love, balance, and eternal reward.

Wisdom Unveiled

The profound wisdom unveiled in Divine Love and the Balance of Weakness and Strength reveals that Divine love speaks through every condition of the human soul. The wise-one understands that strength is not a reward, nor is weakness a punishment; both are languages through which Divine love speaks. They learn to honor every state, bearing strength without pride and wearing weakness without shame, recognizing that in every lifting and every bending, the hand of the Beloved is actively at work—shaping the soul into a compassionate vessel and fortifying it with humility. This deep spiritual and psychic awakening allows the wise-one to see that it is not what is given, but how one loves through it, that truly matters. By embracing both their human limitations and Divine endowments with gratitude, they discover that every condition serves as a channel for drawing closer to the Beloved, reflecting Divine love in all circumstances, and striving only in His way, seeking no praise and fearing no blame.

Wise-Reflection

Reflect on your own experiences of strength and weakness. Do you tend to value one over the other? How might embracing the idea that "both are languages through which Divine love speaks" transform your relationship with your own vulnerabilities and capacities? Consider a moment when you felt particularly weak or dependent. How did you react? How might actively seeking Divine Mercy and Support in such a state—instead of trying to hide or overcome it alone—become a pathway to deeper connection? Conversely, when you feel strong or capable, how can you ensure that this strength is used with profound humility to serve Divine Will and creation, rather than becoming a source of pride? How can you cultivate a heart that truly believes "it is not what I am given, but how I love through it, that matters," allowing every condition to become a testament to Divine love?.

Contemplation: The Danger of Attachment to Life and the Afterlife

(The soul that surrenders without bargaining becomes a sanctuary)

The awakening reveals a profound yet subtle danger: the attachment even to life and the afterlife. While striving for good in this world and sincerely seeking Paradise are indeed commanded acts of worship, clinging to them with an exclusive, possessive desire can become a subtle veil, inadvertently shifting the soul's primary focus from Allah Himself to His creations or His promised rewards. The wise-one truly understands that ultimate liberation lies in detaching from all desires except for Allah's pure pleasure and intimate proximity. This radical detachment purifies intention, leading to a form of worship that is entirely free from bargaining or transactional expectation. It is driven solely by unadulterated love and a deep recognition of Allah as the ultimate Goal and beloved endpoint of all yearning, thereby achieving a profound, transformative psychic freedom that transcends both worldly and otherworldly desires.

> Where Worship Is Freed from Bargaining and Love Becomes the
> Sole Offering

It is better to let go
Of life's lavishness
Than to worship the thereafter.
For true success
Is not found in what is promised—
But in the One who promises.
The wise-one gives
Not to gain paradise,
But to reflect Divine love.
They prefer others over themselves
Even in hardship,
And are saved
From the selfishness of the soul.

❲They give preference over themselves
Even though they may be in need.
And whoever is saved from the selfishness of their own souls,
It is they who are truly successful.❳[192] — Quran 59:9

To worship for reward
Is to remain a merchant—
Bargaining with the Divine
For comforts not yet seen.
But to worship for love alone
Is to transcend even paradise.
The wise-one lets go of clinging—

---

[192] This is derived from the Quran verse of:

📖 ❲As for gains granted by Allah to His Messenger from the people of ˹other˺ lands, they are for Allah and the Messenger, his close relatives, orphans, the poor, and ˹needy˺ travellers so that wealth may not merely circulate among your rich. Whatever the Messenger gives you, take it. And whatever he forbids you from, leave it. And fear Allah. Surely Allah is severe in punishment. (7) ˹Some of the gains will be˺ for poor emigrants who were driven out of their homes and wealth, seeking Allah's bounty and pleasure, and standing up for Allah and His Messenger. They are the ones true in faith. (8) As for those who had settled in the city and ˹embraced˺ the faith before ˹the arrival of˺ the emigrants, they love whoever immigrates to them, never having a desire in their hearts for whatever ˹of the gains˺ is given to the emigrants. They give ˹the emigrants˺ preference over themselves even though they may be in need. And whoever is saved from the selfishness of their own souls, it is they who are ˹truly˺ successful. (9)❳ [Quran 59:7-9]

Not only to the pleasures of this world,
But also to the promises of the next.

The light of His remembrance
Shines through houses of worship,
Where hearts are not distracted by trade or wealth,
But anchored in His praise.
Their hearts are not drawn
By the architecture of paradise,
But by the nearness of the Beloved.
They fear the Day
When hearts and eyes will tremble—
Not from dread,
But from awe.
They seek only His grace,
Knowing that His provision
Is without limit,
And that the greatest reward
Is found in Him alone.

❨They fear a Day
When hearts and eyes will tremble,
Hoping that Allah may reward them
According to the best of their deeds,
And increase them out of His grace.
And Allah provides for whoever He wills
Without limit.❩ [193] — *Quran 24:37–38*

---

[193] This is a referral to the Quran verses of:

📖 ❨Allah is the Light of the heavens and the earth. His light[1] is like a niche in which there is a lamp, the lamp is in a crystal, the crystal is like a shining star, lit from ˹the oil of˺ a blessed olive tree, ˹located˺ neither to the east nor the west,[2] whose oil would almost glow, even without being touched by fire. Light upon light! Allah guides whoever He wills to His Light. And Allah sets forth parables for humanity. For Allah has ˹perfect˺ knowledge of all things. (35) ˹That light shines˺ through houses ˹of worship˺ which Allah has ordered to be raised, and where His Name is mentioned. He is glorified there morning and evening (36) by men[3] who are not distracted—either by buying or selling—from Allah's remembrance, or performing prayer, or paying alms-tax. They fear a Day when hearts and eyes will tremble, (37) ˹hoping˺ that Allah may

As Rabia al-Adawiyya once prayed:
"O Lord, if I worship You for fear of Hell, burn me in Hell;
And if I worship You for hope of Paradise, exclude me from Paradise;
But if I worship You for Your Own sake,
Do not withhold Your everlasting beauty."

So the wise-one walks forward—
Not seeking paradise,
But seeking the One who makes it radiant.
Not fearing Hell,
But fearing separation.
They do not worship for reward—
They worship for love.
And in that love,
They are already home.

For only He frees the soul from transaction.
Only He rewards without condition.
Only He remains the source
Of beauty, nearness, and eternal companionship.

Wisdom Unveiled

The profound wisdom unveiled in The Danger of Attachment to Life and the Afterlife is that the soul that worships for reward remains a merchant, constantly bargaining with the Divine for comforts not yet seen. In stark contrast, the soul that worships for love alone transcends even paradise, achieving a state of profound psychic freedom. The wise-one learns to let go of clinging—not only to the fleeting pleasures of this world but crucially, also to the promises of the next. This radical detachment purifies

---

reward them according to the best of their deeds, and increase them out of His grace. And Allah provides for whoever He wills without limit. (38)❭ [Quran 24:35-38]

[1]: This is a metaphor for the light of guidance in the heart of the believer.

[2]: Meaning, the olive tree is wholesome because it is located in a central place, so it is hit by sunrays all day-long, and, therefore, the oil is of a premium quality.

[3]: Although the word "rijâl" generally means "men," some Quran commentators believe that the word "rijâl" here can also mean "people," but they are called men since men make up the majority in the group. In some Arabic dialects, "rijâl" is the plural of "rajul" (man) and "rajulah" (woman).

intention; for the heart surrendered without expectation becomes itself a dwelling for the Beloved, and the hereafter is nothing but the glorious flowering of that hidden, cultivated sanctuary. This spiritual insight echoes Rabia al-Adawiyya's prayer, emphasizing that true devotion is solely for Allah's Own sake, leading to a love-driven worship where the greatest reward is found in His everlasting beauty and near presence.

Wise-Reflection

Reflect on your own intentions behind your spiritual practices or acts of goodness. Is there any subtle attachment to reward—whether worldly recognition or the promise of Paradise—that might be influencing your actions? Consider Rabia al-Adawiyya's profound prayer: "O Lord, if I worship You for fear of Hell, burn me in Hell; And if I worship You for hope of Paradise, exclude me from Paradise; But if I worship You for Your Own sake, Do not withhold Your everlasting beauty." What does it mean for your own spiritual journey to aspire to worship solely for Allah's Own sake? How can you begin to cultivate a heart that is so utterly surrendered without bargaining, so purely driven by love, that it feels "already home" in Divine Presence, transcending even the desire for Paradise itself?

Contemplation: The Correspondence Between Heart and Eternal Home

(The Soul Inherits the Shape of Its Own Becoming)

The wise-one comes to a profound, transformative realization: there is an absolute and intricate correspondence between the state of the heart and one's eternal home. The heart, when diligently purified and aligned with Divine will, ceases to be a mere organ; it becomes a living microcosm, directly reflecting the boundless vastness of Divine Presence. The internal reality of the heart—its purity, its attachments, its singular focus—does not merely influence but directly shapes the spiritual reality of the individual, both in this fleeting life and the eternal realm of the next. As the Gateway Verse from the previous reflection so powerfully illustrates, a heart that genuinely trembles in awe at Divine remembrance and softens in profound mercy is precisely the heart that is granted Divine guidance. This contemplation serves as a potent motivation for the wise-one to ceaselessly purify their inner chambers, recognizing with unshakable clarity that what is built and nurtured within the heart's most secret recesses fundamentally determines the spiritual landscape of their ultimate return and eternal dwelling. This deep insight is crucial for a complete spiritual and psychic awakening.

Where Inward Purity Forms Outward Destiny

The home He builds in the hereafter
Is shaped by the heart given to Him now[194].
Not by outward claim,
But by inward cultivation.
Each soul carries only
What it has striven toward—
Its deeds unfolding
In the record of its return.

❮*And that each person will only have what they endeavoured towards, and that ˹the outcome of˺ their endeavours will be seen ˹in their record˺, then they will be fully rewarded, and that to your Lord ˹alone˺ is the ultimate return ˹of all things˺.*❯[195] —
Quran 53:39–42

If the heart is a garden of remembrance,
Then paradise will bloom as its reflection.
If the heart is a desert of forgetfulness,
Then barrenness shall follow it into eternity.
The wise-one tends their heart
Not out of fear,
But out of love—
Planting within it
Seeds of surrender, humility, and longing.

---

[194] It also reflects the Islamic emphasis on qalb salim (a sound heart), which is essential for meeting God.

[195] This is in agreement with the Quran verse:

❮Or has he not been informed of what is in the Scripture of Moses, (36) and ˹that of˺ Abraham, who ˹perfectly˺ fulfilled ˹his covenant˺? (37) ˹They state˺ that no soul burdened with sin will bear the burden of another, (38) and that each person will only have what they endeavoured towards, (39) and that ˹the outcome of˺ their endeavours will be seen ˹in their record˺, (40) then they will be fully rewarded, (41) and that to your Lord ˹alone˺ is the ultimate return ˹of all things˺. (42)❯ [Quran 53:36-42]

❨*The 'true' believers are only those whose hearts tremble at the remembrance of Allah, whose faith increases when His revelations are recited to them, and who put their trust in their Lord.*❩ [196] — *Quran 8:2*

Yet many remain heedless,
Their hearts unable to understand,
Their eyes unable to see,
Their ears closed to truth.
They move like a herd,
Unaware of where they are led—
Not because they lack direction,
But because they have lost perception.

❨*Indeed, We have destined many jinn and humans for Hell. They have hearts they do not understand with, eyes they do not see with, and ears they do not hear with. They are like cattle. In fact, they are even less guided! Such 'people' are 'entirely' heedless.*❩ [197] — *Quran 7:179*

The wise-one sees:
What the heart becomes today,
The soul shall inherit tomorrow.
The eternal abode
Is not awarded externally—
It is carved inwardly,
Now,
In the chambers of the heart.

So the wise-one walks forward—
Not building palaces in the world,
But cultivating gardens within.
They do not ask for paradise—
They prepare for it

---

[196] This is in agreement with the Quran verse:

📖 ❨The 'true' believers are only those whose hearts tremble at the remembrance of Allah, whose faith increases when His revelations are recited to them, and who put their trust in their Lord. (2)❩ [Quran 8:2]

[197] This is in agreement with the Quran verse:

📖 ❨Indeed, We have destined many jinn and humans for Hell. They have hearts they do not understand with, eyes they do not see with, and ears they do not hear with. They are like cattle. In fact, they are even less guided! Such 'people' are 'entirely' heedless. (179)❩ [Quran 7:179]

By becoming its mirror.
They do not fear judgment—
They live in remembrance.

For only He sees the heart's true shape.
Only He rewards what was sincerely grown.
Only He remains the Source
Of guidance, return, and eternal dwelling.

Wisdom Unveiled

The profound wisdom unveiled in The Correspondence Between Heart and Eternal Home is that the eternal abode is not awarded externally; it is meticulously carved inwardly, right now, in the secret chambers of the heart. This underscores the vital Islamic emphasis on qalb salim (a sound heart), which is absolutely essential for truly meeting God. If the heart is assiduously cultivated as a vibrant garden of remembrance, then Paradise will naturally bloom as its mirror reflection; conversely, if the heart becomes a barren desert of forgetfulness, then desolation shall follow it into eternity. Thus, the wise-one tends their heart not out of fear of consequence, but out of pure, sincere love, diligently planting within it the transformative seeds of surrender, profound humility, and unyielding longing. This powerful spiritual and psychic awakening reveals that what the heart becomes today, the soul shall undeniably inherit tomorrow, making the inner reality the direct architect of one's ultimate spiritual landscape.

Wise-Reflection

Reflect on the current state of your own heart. Is it a vibrant garden, or does it feel more like a barren desert? Consider the profound responsibility and liberation in realizing that "each person will only have what they endeavoured towards." How does the concept of your eternal home being "carved inwardly, now, in the chambers of the heart" influence your daily choices and intentions? What specific "seeds of surrender, humility, and longing" can you consciously plant and nurture in your heart today, not out of fear, but out of love for the Divine? How can you live with the awareness that every purification of your inner self is directly shaping the spiritual landscape of your ultimate return, leading to a deeper psychic and spiritual awakening?

Contemplation: Being With the Divine

(The soul finds its place not in proximity—but in presence)

Ultimately, this profound awakening culminates in the experiential reality of "Being With the Divine." This is not merely an intellectual concept or a fleeting emotion, but a continuous, living state of intimate, encompassing Presence. It is the deep, existential realization of Allah's ever-abiding words, "And He is with you wherever you are" (Quran 57:4). The wise-one's heart and mind become so exquisitely attuned that every single moment, regardless of its outward appearance, transforms into a sacred opportunity for direct communion. Whether engaged in prayer, engrossed in work, resting in solitude, or navigating social interactions, they viscerally feel the encompassing embrace of the Divine, utterly transcending the illusion of separation and dwelling in a perpetual, unshakable companionship. This is a state of profound and abiding psychic peace, where the self is anchored in the Eternal, unperturbed by the world's fluctuations.

Where the Inner Gaze Determines the Eternal Dwelling

If you see Him,
You are with Him.
If you do not,
You remain with yourself. [198]
So be with the One who is good—
The One who calls from darkness into light,
From forgetfulness into remembrance,
From orbiting selfhood
Into the stillness of Divine nearness.
To be with oneself
Is to orbit endlessly around desires, doubts, and shadows.
To be with the Divine
Is to stand in the sun,
Forgetting the dance of shadows altogether.
This is the essence of ihsan—
To worship as though you see Him,

---

[198] This reflects the Islamic teaching of *ihsan*—to worship God as though you see Him, even if you cannot see Him, knowing that He sees you.

Even if you do not,
Knowing that He sees you.

❰*O believers! Always remember Allah often,*
And glorify Him morning and evening.
He is the One Who showers His blessings upon you—
And His angels pray for you—
So that He may bring you out of darkness and into light.
For He is ever Merciful to the believers.❱[199] — *Quran 33:41–43*

For when the Deafening Blast comes,
Every soul will flee from their kin—
From mother and father,
Spouse and child.
None will carry another's burden.
None will shield another from decree.

❰*On that Day every person will flee*
From their own siblings,
And even their mother and father,
And even their spouse and children.
For then everyone will have enough concern of their own.❱ — *Quran 80:33–37*

On that Day,
Faces will be bright—
Laughing and rejoicing in His mercy.
Others will be veiled in gloom,
Sealed off by what they once ignored.
The virtuous will be in bliss,
Seated in honor,
Their faces aglow.
The heedless will flee,

---

[199] This is derived from the Quran verses of:

📖 ❰O believers! Always remember Allah often, (41) and glorify Him morning and evening. (42) He is the One Who showers His blessings upon you—and His angels pray for you—so that He may bring you out of darkness and into light. For He is ever Merciful to the believers. (43) Their greeting on the Day they meet Him will be, "Peace!" And He has prepared for them an honourable reward. (44)❱ [Quran 33:41-44]

Finding no refuge
But their own loss.

❨*On that Day some faces will be bright,*
Laughing and rejoicing,
While other faces will be dusty,
Cast in gloom—
Those are the disbelievers, the wicked sinners.❩ [200] *— Quran 80:38–42*

But those who remembered Him often,
Who glorified Him morning and evening,
Will meet Him with peace.
Their greeting will be serenity.
Their reward will be honor.
Their dwelling will be nearness.

❨*Their greeting on the Day they meet Him will be, 'Peace!'*
And He has prepared for them an honourable reward.❩ [201] *— Quran 33:44*

And then,
The Most Merciful will say—
With a voice that silences all sorrow:

❨*O My servants!*
There is no fear for you Today,
Nor will you grieve—
Those who believed in Our signs

---

[200] This is derived from the Quran verses of:

📖 ❨Then, when the Deafening Blast[1] comes to pass— (33) on that Day every person will flee from their own siblings, (34) and ˹even˺ their mother and father, (35) and ˹even˺ their spouse and children. (36) For then everyone will have enough concern of their own. (37) On that Day ˹some˺ faces will be bright, (38) laughing and rejoicing, (39) while ˹other˺ faces will be dusty, (40) cast in gloom— (41) those are the disbelievers, the ˹wicked˺ sinners. (42)❩ [Quran 80:33-42]

[1]: This is the second Blast which will cause the dead to come to life for judgment. See 39:68.

[201] This is derived from the Quran verse of:

📖 ❨Their greeting on the Day they meet Him will be, "Peace!" And He has prepared for them an honourable reward. (44)❩ [Quran 33:44]

And fully submitted to Us.
Enter Paradise, you and your spouses, rejoicing.[202] — *Quran 43:68–70*

This is the culmination
Of every remembrance,
Every surrender,
Every whispered prayer.
The soul that chose Him
Again and again
Is now chosen—
Welcomed not just into Paradise,
But into the embrace
Of the One they loved
Without condition.

So the wise-one walks forward—
Choosing their company
Not by circumstance,
But by the turning of the inner gaze.
Each moment becomes a question
Whispered by existence itself:
With whom will you dwell now—
Your shifting self,
Or the changeless Beloved?
And in choosing Him
Again and again,
The soul becomes a dwelling
Where the light never dims.

For only He remains when all else flees.
Only He welcomes with peace when all else trembles.

---

[202] This is derived from the Quran verses of:

❦ ﴾Are they waiting for the Hour to take them by surprise when they least expect ˹it˺? (66) Close friends will be enemies to one another on that Day, except the righteous, (67) ˹who will be told,˺ "O My servants! There is no fear for you Today, nor will you grieve— (68) ˹those˺ who believed in Our signs and ˹fully˺ submitted ˹to Us˺. (69) Enter Paradise, you and your spouses, rejoicing." (70) Golden trays and cups will be passed around to them. There will be whatever the souls desire and the eyes delight in. And you will be there forever. (71) That is the Paradise which you will be awarded for what you used to do. (72) There you will have abundant fruit[1] to eat from. (73) ﴿ [Quran 43:66-73]

[1]: Fruit also implies delicacies.

Only He honors with joy when all else fades.
Only He is the source
Of nearness, mercy, reward, and eternal companionship.

Wisdom Unveiled

The profound wisdom unveiled in Being With the Divine is that the soul finds its ultimate place not in mere proximity, but in a continuous, living state of Divine Presence. To be with oneself is to orbit endlessly around desires, doubts, and shadows; conversely, to be with the Divine is to stand in the sun, forgetting the dance of shadows altogether. The wise-one makes a conscious, moment-by-moment choice of their true company, not by external circumstance, but by the pivotal turning of their inner gaze. Each breath, each experience, becomes a question whispered by existence itself: "With whom will you dwell now—your shifting self, or the changeless Beloved?" And in choosing Him again and again, the soul undergoes a profound psychic transformation, becoming itself a radiant dwelling where the Divine Light never dims. This culminates in an eternal companionship, where remembrance and surrender lead to being chosen and welcomed into the ultimate embrace of the One loved without condition.

Wise-Reflection

Reflect on your daily interactions and internal dialogues. To what extent are you "orbiting endlessly around desires, doubts, and shadows" by dwelling on your "shifting self"? How often do you consciously choose to "stand in the sun" by turning your inner gaze towards the Changeless Beloved? Consider the ihsan (excellence) of worshipping as though you see Him, knowing that He sees you. How can you cultivate this continuous, living state of Divine Presence in your everyday activities—in prayer, work, rest, and relationships? What tangible steps can you take to make this choice, moment by moment, so that your soul becomes a dwelling "where the light never dims," leading you to profound and abiding psychic peace?

Conclusion: In the Awakening of Hear and Mind

ECHOES OF REALIZATION

Authentic spiritual awakening is not a sudden, blinding lightning flash from the heavens. It is, instead, the slow, consistent, and deliberate opening of a heart that dares to perceive the Divine even within the most broken and seemingly imperfect places of existence. It is the profound courage to gaze into life's inherent contradictions and there, surprisingly, discover a unifying truth; to behold both sorrow and joy and recognize the same eternal, smiling Divine Face shining through both. It is the profound art of perceiving beyond transient appearances, recognizing that every shadow and every gleam is but a subtle doorway leading to the Beloved.

This awakening fosters the humility to embrace both one's inherent strength and one's unavoidable weakness—not as mere tests to pass, but as distinct languages through which Divine Love intimately speaks. It is the liberating act of letting go of all conditional bargains with the heavens, the releasing of worship that is tied to a reward, until the heart beats not for the pleasures of Paradise or the fear of Hellfire, but simply for the pure, unadulterated joy of His ever-present nearness. The purified heart, in this state, becomes the true, eternal abode. What is meticulously built within its secret chambers now will indeed be the luminous palace or the desolate wilderness the soul awakens to beyond the confines of time. And whether the wise-one is waking or sleeping, whether clothed in transient flesh or divinely freed from it, the one who has truly tasted this profound presence finds no enduring separation. The Gaze of the Beloved is utterly constant; the embrace of Remembrance is forever unbroken.

THE SEEKER'S ASCENT: AWAKENING TO DIVINE PRESENCE

The wise-one who has undergone this profound awakening lives not for the pursuit of conditional reward, but for the experience of perpetual Divine Presence. They live not for fleeting safety and worldly comfort, but for the ultimate and enduring joy of Divine Companionship. Their waking moments, their deep sleeping, their very breathing—all become sacred threads meticulously woven into a single, seamless tapestry of continuous Divine Remembrance.

And when the final, earthly veil is ultimately drawn, the wise-one will not enter a strange, unknown land. Instead, they will return, with profound certainty and solace, to a familiar, infinitely loving Gaze—the very Gaze they once dared to hold and embrace in the sacred stillness of their own awakened heart. This is the culmination of psychic enlightenment: a life lived in unbroken communion, culminating in an eternal return to the source of all being.

10TH REFLECTION: IN THE KNOWING THE UNSPOKEN [203]

THE GATEWAY VERSE

In the sacred words of Allah, describing the ultimate proximity and unveiled vision granted to His chosen servant, a profound guide for all who seek direct communion:

📖 ❨*By the stars when they fade away! (1) Your fellow man204 is neither misguided nor astray. (2) Nor does he speak of his own whims. (3) It is only a revelation sent down ˹to him˺. (4) He has been taught by one ˹angel˺ of mighty205 power (5) and great perfection, who once rose to ˹his˺ true form206 (6) while on the highest point above the horizon, (7) then he approached ˹the Prophet˺, coming so close (8) that he was only two arms-lengths away or even less.207 (9) Then Allah revealed to His servant what He revealed. (10) The ˹Prophet's˺ heart did not doubt what he saw. (11) How can you ˹O pagans˺ then dispute with him regarding what he saw? (12) And he certainly saw that ˹angel descend˺ a second time (13) at the Lote Tree of the most extreme limit — (14) near which is the Garden of ˹Eternal˺ Residence— (15) while the Lote Tree was overwhelmed with ˹heavenly˺ splendours! (16) The ˹Prophet's˺ sight never wandered, nor did it overreach. (17) He certainly saw some of his Lord's greatest signs.208 (18)*❩ [Quran 53 : 17]*

ILLUMINATION'S DAWN

---

[203] This contemplation—one that walks on the edge of silence, revealing the hidden veil that separates spoken knowledge from unspoken reality. It taps into the very heart of mushāhadah (witnessing) beyond articulation—where Divine Presence no longer descends through names, attributes, or forms, but unveils Itself as pure, absolute, unmediated Being. This is the Station of the Unspoken, the culmination of all spiritual yearning where knowing without knowing becomes the highest form of knowing.

[204] Mohammed 攩.

[205] The angel Gabriel.

[206] Gabriel used to come to the Prophet Mohammed 攩 in a human form. But he appeared to him (攩) twice in his angelic form: once at the beginning of the Prophet's mission (when the angel manifested himself, filling the horizon, the Prophet 攩 lost his consciousness), and another time during the Prophet's Night Journey to the seventh heaven to receive the order to pray directly from Allah (see 17:1).

[207] lit., he was only two bow-draws away.

[208] The Prophet 攩 was taken to heaven to see some of Allah's magnificent signs. He only saw what he was told to see.

There comes a culminating stage in the wise-one's profound spiritual pilgrimage when even the most sacred and potent words fall utterly silent—not because the journey has ceased, but because it has transcended into a realm where no spoken language, no conceptual framework, can possibly carry its immense weight or profound truth. "The Unspoken Knowing" is not a form of knowledge painstakingly attained by study, nor a mastery gained through strenuous striving. It is, rather, a remembering older than memory itself, a profound unveiling placed within the soul's essence before language was ever woven into the fabric of the human mind.

Here, the wise-one is called not to articulate or explain, but simply to behold the ineffable. Not to meticulously describe, but to dwell fully within the boundless Presence. To truly know the Creator is to courageously enter a sacred space where all words, concepts, and definitions fall away like worn, discarded garments, and only pure, luminous Presence remains— shining, silent, and eternally sovereign. Let us now walk reverently into this profound silence, where the soul's deepest and truest knowledge is not taught or conveyed through discourse, but is revealed by the liberating act of forgetting everything else that is conditioned and finite.

THE UNFOLDING OF INSIGHTS

This section explores the ultimate dissolution of conceptual understanding into direct experiential knowledge, where the wise-one apprehends the Divine beyond all forms of mediation.

Contemplation: Knowing by Unknowing

(The soul learns not by gaining—but by shedding)

The wise-one ultimately arrives at the profound, culminating state of Knowing by Unknowing. This signifies that true, ultimate knowledge of the Divine is not an accumulation of facts, doctrines, or intellectual concepts gleaned from external sources. Instead, it is a direct, experiential realization that utterly transcends and dismantles all conventional human frameworks of understanding. This process involves the conscious dismantling of deeply ingrained preconceived notions, the complete surrender of the ego's pervasive desire to categorize and define, and the profound humility to embrace the Creator's absolute transcendence and ineffability. This "unknowing" paradoxically opens the soul to receive direct, unmediated Divine illumination—an inner light that simply is, and that cannot be taught, transmitted, or conveyed through any conventional means. This represents a fundamental psychic shift from intellectual, conceptual knowing to a vast, boundless existential awareness of the Unspoken.

Where Forgetfulness of the World Becomes Remembrance of the
Real

He withheld from the soul
The knowing of everything—
Not to punish,
But to purify.
So that it may seek Him alone,
So that in knowing Him,
All else may be forgotten.
Within me, He placed the seed of all knowing.
Not so I may own knowledge,
But so I may lose all else.
To know Him is to forget everything else.
To be filled with Him is to be emptied of the rest.

Like Abraham 鄉,
Who questioned his father Azar,
And saw clearly
That his people were misguided.
He did not begin with certainty—
He began with seeking.
And Allah showed him
The wonders of the heavens and the earth,
So that his faith might be made firm.

❲We also showed Abraham
The wonders of the heavens and the earth,
So he would be sure in faith.❳ — Quran 6:75

He saw a star and said,
"This is my Lord!"

But when it set,
He said,

❨*I do not love things that set.*❩

He saw the moon,
And then the sun—
Each greater than the last—
But each faded.
And so he turned his face
To the One who never fades.

❨*I have turned my face*
Towards the One Who has originated
The heavens and the earth—being upright—
And I am not one of the polytheists.❩ *— Quran 6:79*

His people argued,
But his certainty did not waver.
He did not fear their idols,
For his Lord encompassed all things in knowledge.
He saw that true security
Belongs only to those
Whose faith is not tarnished by falsehood.

❨*It is only those who are faithful*
And do not tarnish their faith with falsehood
Who are guaranteed security
And are rightly guided.❩[209] *— Quran 6:82*

---

[209] This is derived from the Quran verses of:

❨And ʿrememberʾ when Abraham said to his father, Āzar, "Do you take idols as gods? It is clear to me that you and your people are entirely misguided." (74) We also showed Abraham the wonders of the heavens and the earth, so he would be sure in faith. (75) When the night grew dark upon him, he saw a star and said, "This is my Lord!" But when it set, he said, "I do not love things that set." (76) Then when he saw the moon rising, he said, "This one is my Lord!" But when it disappeared, he said, "If my Lord does not guide me, I will certainly be one of the misguided people." (77) Then when he saw the sun shining, he said, "This must be my Lord—it is the greatest!" But again when it set, he declared, "O my people! I totally reject

This was the argument
Allah gave Abraham ﷺ—
Not to defeat his people,
But to elevate his soul.
For true knowing
Does not add to the self;
It undoes it.
It strips away every fading form
Until only the Eternal remains.
The seed planted within
Is not a treasure to be hoarded,
But a fire meant to burn away
Every false possession.
The wise-one learns:
The more one forgets of the world,
The closer one draws to the Beloved.
In forgetting all else,
The soul remembers its true origin—
The silent place
Where the Only Real resides.

So the wise-one walks forward—
Not gathering knowledge,
But shedding illusion.
Not seeking mastery,
But surrendering identity.
They do not ask to know more—
They ask to know less,

---

whatever you associate ˹with Allah in worship˺. (78) I have turned my face towards the One Who has originated the heavens and the earth—being upright—and I am not one of the polytheists." (79) And his people argued with him. He responded, "Are you arguing with me about Allah, while He has guided me? I am not afraid of whatever ˹idols˺ you associate with Him—˹none can harm me,˺ unless my Lord so wills. My Lord encompasses everything in ˹His˺ knowledge. Will you not be mindful? (80) And how should I fear your associate-gods, while you have no fear in associating ˹others˺ with Allah—a practice He has never authorized? Which side has more right to security? ˹Tell me˺ if you really know!" (81) It is ˹only˺ those who are faithful and do not tarnish their faith with falsehood[1] who are guaranteed security and are ˹rightly˺ guided. (82) This was the argument We gave Abraham against his people. We elevate in rank whoever We please. Surely your Lord is All-Wise, All-Knowing. (83)❭ [Quran 6:74-83]

[1]: i.e., associating false gods in worship with the Almighty.

So that what remains
Is only Him.

For only He guides beyond fading forms.
Only He unveils beyond argument.
Only He remains the source
Of certainty, origin, and eternal presence.

Wisdom Unveiled

The profound wisdom unveiled in Knowing by Unknowing is that true knowing does not add to the self; it paradoxically undoes it. The Divine seed of all knowing planted within the soul is not a treasure to be hoarded, but a consuming fire meant to burn away every false possession, every illusory conceptual framework. The wise-one learns that the more one forgets of the transient world and its limiting definitions, the closer one draws to the Beloved. In this profound act of shedding, of forgetting all else, the soul ultimately remembers its true origin—the silent, ineffable place where the Only Real eternally resides. This represents a fundamental psychic shift where knowledge transcends accumulation and becomes a direct, unmediated experiential awareness of the Unspoken.

Wise-Reflection

Reflect on your own pursuit of knowledge. Do you primarily seek to accumulate more information, or do you also engage in the process of questioning and shedding preconceived notions? Consider the example of Prophet Abraham (PBUH) turning away from fading forms to the One who never fades. What "fading forms"—be they intellectual certainties, worldly attachments, or egoic desires—are you clinging to that might be preventing deeper Divine illumination? What would it mean for you to intentionally "know less" in order to "know Him" more profoundly? How can you cultivate the humility to embrace the Creator's absolute transcendence and allow this "unknowing" to open your soul to direct, unmediated Divine presence and a transformative psychic shift?

Contemplation: The Paradox of Words

(The soul hears not just sound—but the silence behind it)

This pivotal stage of awakening unveils the profound and liberating paradox of words. While Divine words (such as the Holy Quran) are indeed pure revelation, undeniable guidance, and immense mercy, and human words are essential for communication and understanding, both also inherently limit and contain what is by its very nature limitless and uncontainable. They reveal by attempting to define, but in defining, they subtly veil the indefinable Reality they point towards. The wise-one learns to use words as sacred ladders, meticulously climbing them, but ultimately understands with deep certainty that the true destination, the Unspoken Truth, lies profoundly beyond the ladder itself. This contemplation liberates the seeker from clinging rigidly to the literal form of sacred texts while simultaneously deepening their reverence and awe for the ultimate, unspoken, and ineffable Truth that those words lovingly point towards. This is a crucial step in the journey of psychic transformation, moving beyond conceptual thought to direct apprehension.

Where Speech Becomes a Bridge to Silence and Revelation Becomes
Return

The greatest generosity
Is that He speaks to His servants
In words He Himself ordained—
Calling them with verses
Meant to call them back to Him.
He did not leave the soul
To wander in abstraction.
He gave it scripture—
Not to contain Him,
But to bring the soul
To the edge of what cannot be contained.
The greatest mercy was this:
He spoke to me through words,
And asked me to speak back to Him with the same.

His revelation is a guide and a healing—
A bridge stretched across the abyss of unknowing.

To the believers, it is light.
To the heedless, it is distant echoes—
A voice calling from a place
They will not reach.

❨*It is a guide and a healing to the believers.*
As for those who disbelieve,
There is deafness in their ears
And blindness to it in their hearts.
It is as if they are being called from a faraway place.❩[210] — *Quran 41:44*

Even the unseen listen in awe.
The jinn heard the Quran
And returned to their kind as warners—
Declaring the truth,
Urging belief,
Calling toward salvation.

❨*We have truly heard a scripture revealed after Moses,*
Confirming what came before it.
It guides to the truth and the Straight Way.❩[211] — *Quran 46:30*

---

[210] This is derived from the Quran verses of:

📖 ❨Indeed, those who deny the Reminder[1] after it has come to them ˹are doomed˺, for it is truly a mighty Book. (41) It cannot be proven false from any angle. ˹It is˺ a revelation from the ˹One Who is˺ All-Wise, Praiseworthy. (42) ˹O Prophet!˺ Nothing is said to you ˹by the deniers˺ except what was already said to the messengers before you. Surely your Lord is ˹the Lord˺ of forgiveness and painful punishment. (43) Had We revealed it as a non-Arabic Quran, they would have certainly argued, "If only its verses were made clear ˹in our language˺. What! A non-Arabic revelation for an Arab audience!" Say, ˹O Prophet,˺ "It is a guide and a healing to the believers. As for those who disbelieve, there is deafness in their ears and blindness to it ˹in their hearts˺. It is as if they are being called from a faraway place."[2] (44) Indeed, We had given Moses the Scripture, but differences arose regarding it. Had it not been for a prior decree from your Lord,1 their differences would have been settled ˹at once˺. They are truly in alarming doubt about it. (45) Whoever does good, it is to their own benefit. And whoever does evil, it is to their own loss. Your Lord is never unjust to ˹His˺ creation. (46) ❩ [Quran 41:41-46]

[1]: The Reminder is one of the names of the Quran.

[2]: So they neither hear nor understand the call.

[211] This is derived from the Quran verses of:

📖 ❨'Remember, O Prophet,˺ when We sent a group of jinn your way to listen to the Quran. Then, upon hearing it, they said ˹to one another˺, "Listen quietly!" Then when it was over, they returned to their fellow jinn as warners. (29) They declared, "O our fellow jinn! We have truly heard a scripture revealed after Moses, confirming what came before it. It guides to the truth and the Straight Way. (30) O our fellow jinn! Respond to the caller of Allah and believe in him, He will forgive your sins and protect you from a painful punishment. (31) And whoever does not respond to the caller of Allah will have no escape on earth, nor will they have any protectors against Him. It is they who are clearly astray." (32)❩ [Quran 46: 29-32]

Had this speech descended upon the mountains,
They would have been torn apart in submission.
Yet the hardened heart stands unmoved—
Blind to the words meant to heal,
Deaf to the call meant to restore.

❨Had We sent down this Quran upon a mountain,
You would have certainly seen it humbled
And torn apart in awe of Allah.❩[212] — Quran 59:21

The wise-one sees:
Other speech toward the Creator
Is but a veil—
A barrier between the soul
And true remembrance.
For the ultimate speech is His own—
The verses He gave,
The words that tear away the veils
And return the soul
To its rightful place before Him.
Scripture is a bridge,
Offered so the soul might dare
To step beyond.

Words are gifts—
Luminous and gentle.
But they are signposts,
Not destinations.
The wise-one honors the words,
Loves the words—
Yet never mistakes the letter for the Face.
For the Beloved stands
Always just beyond the edge of expression,

---

[212] This is derived from the Quran verse of:

❨Had We sent down this Quran upon a mountain, you would have certainly seen it humbled and torn apart in awe of Allah. We set forth such comparisons for people, ʿsoʾ perhaps they may reflect. (21)❩ [Quran 59:21]

Calling the soul
Into a silence wider than any tongue can span.

So the wise-one walks forward—
Not to master speech,
But to be mastered by silence.
Not to recite for knowledge,
But to recite for return.
They speak the verses
Not to define the Divine,
But to dissolve into Him.

For only He speaks with mercy.
Only He calls with healing.
Only He remains the source
Of revelation, remembrance, and eternal return.

Wisdom Unveiled

The profound wisdom unveiled in The Paradox of Words reveals that words are gifts, luminous and gentle, but they are signposts, not destinations. Scripture is a bridge stretched across the abyss of unknowing—offered so the soul might dare to step beyond. The wise-one understands that while Divine words are guidance and healing, they inherently limit the illimitable; they reveal by defining, yet in defining, they subtly veil the undefinable. Therefore, the wise-one honors and loves the words, yet never mistakes the letter for the Divine Face. For the Beloved stands always just beyond the edge of expression, continuously calling the soul into a profound silence wider than any tongue can span. This leads to a deep psychic liberation, where the soul hears not just sound, but the silence behind it, using revelation as a means for return, not as an end in itself.

Wise-Reflection

Reflect on your own relationship with words, especially sacred texts. Do you sometimes find yourself clinging to the literal interpretation or the intellectual understanding of concepts, perhaps missing the deeper, unspoken Truth they point towards? Consider the idea that "the Beloved stands always just beyond the edge of expression, calling the soul into a silence wider than any tongue can span." How can you cultivate a practice of listening not just to the sound of words, but to the silence behind them, allowing this paradox of words to deepen your reverence for the Divine without limiting Him? What would it mean to "recite for return" rather than solely "for knowledge," allowing the verses to dissolve you into the Divine rather than merely defining Him?

Contemplation: The Veil of Creation

(The soul sees not by clinging, but by surrender)

In the culminating experience of "The Knowing the Unspoken," the wise-one witnesses the ultimate veil of creation dissolving. This isn't about the physical destruction of the world; rather, it's the eradication of the perception that creation is separate or independent from the Creator. All phenomena, once seen as distinct entities, are now apprehended as direct, living manifestations or potent signs of the Divine. Their apparent distinctness dissolves into a unified, all-encompassing perception of Allah's pervasive, singular Presence. This profound unveiling—where the world of multiplicity melts into the absolute reality of Humility before Allah—is a pinnacle of both psychic and spiritual insight. Here, the wise-one lives in the constant, vivid awareness that "wheresoever you turn, there is the Face of Allah" (Quran 2:115), seeing through all forms to the One who is the essence of all existence.

Where Every Sign Reveals—and Conceals—the Divine

All things speak of Him.
Yet all things also veil Him.
The sun proclaims His light.
The star whispers His subtlety.
The wind carries His breath.
And still—
What I cling to becomes the veil.
The more I attach to form,
The more I lose the formless.
Creation is both a window and a wall.
Every leaf, every river, every star sings His name—
Yet the moment the soul clings to the song
Instead of the Singer, it loses the path.

All creation points to Him,
Revealing His presence in order, rhythm, and beauty.
But creation also calls for itself—
Demanding attention, commanding desire.
The soul that turns away
Sees only form, not source.

❨*I will turn away from My signs*
Those who act unjustly with arrogance in the land.
Even if they were to see every sign,
They still would not believe in them.❩[213] — *Quran 7:146*

His signs are everywhere—
In the heavens and the earth,
In the alternation of day and night.
But arrogance blinds the soul.
Denial leads to heedlessness.
They may see every sign,
Yet their hearts chase what obscures the truth.

❨*They only know the worldly affairs of this life,*
But are totally oblivious to the Hereafter.❩ — *Quran 30:7*

They forget
That all has a purpose,

---

[213] This is derived from the Quran verses of:

📖 ❨When Moses came at the appointed time and his Lord spoke to him, he asked, "My Lord! Reveal Yourself to me so I may see You." Allah answered, "You cannot see Me! But look at the mountain. If it remains firm in its place, only then will you see Me." When his Lord appeared to the mountain, He levelled it to dust and Moses collapsed unconscious. When he recovered, he cried, "Glory be to You! I turn to You in repentance and I am the first of the believers." (143) Allah said, "O Moses! I have ˹already˺ elevated you above all others by My messages and speech.[1] So hold firmly to what I have given you and be grateful." (144) We wrote for him on the Tablets ˹the fundamentals˺ of everything; commandments and explanations of all things. ˹We commanded,˺ "Hold to this firmly and ask your people to take the best of it.[2] I will soon show ˹all of˺ you the home of the rebellious.[3] (145) I will turn away from My signs those who act unjustly with arrogance in the land. And even if they were to see every sign, they still would not believe in them. If they see the Right Path, they will not take it. But if they see a crooked path, they will follow it. This is because they denied Our signs and were heedless of them. (146) The deeds of those who deny Our signs and the meeting ˹with Allah˺ in the Hereafter will be in vain. Will they be rewarded except for what they have done?" (147)❩ [Quran 7:143-147]

[1]: Allah reminds Moses that even though his request to see Allah was denied, he has already been favoured by Allah over the people of his time through prophethood and direct communication with the Almighty.

[2]: To follow the commandments that generate more rewards than others, to put grace before justice, etc.

[3]: This could either mean the ruins of destroyed nations or the Hellfire which is the home of the wicked.

An appointed term.
They deny the meeting with their Lord,
Immersed in worldly motion
Without eternal meaning.

❨*Have they not reflected upon their own being?*
Allah only created the heavens and the earth
And everything in between
For a purpose and an appointed term.❩[214] — *Quran 30:8*

Yet the wise-one sees:
All things unveil Him.
The prayer rises from the feet
Standing in stillness,
From the back bowed in remembrance,
From the soul lying in reflection.

❨*Those who remember Allah*
While standing, sitting, and lying on their sides,
And reflect on the creation of the heavens and the earth,
And pray: 'Our Lord!

---

[214] This is derived from the Quran verses of:

📖 ❨Alif-Lām-Mīm. (1) The Romans have been defeated (2) in a nearby land.[1] Yet following their defeat, they will triumph (3) within three to nine years.[2] The ˹whole˺ matter rests with Allah before and after ˹victory˺. And on that day the believers will rejoice (4) at the victory willed by Allah. He gives victory to whoever He wills. For He is the Almighty, Most Merciful. (5) ˹This is˺ the promise of Allah. ˹And˺ Allah never fails in His promise. But most people do not know. (6) They ˹only˺ know the worldly affairs of this life, but are ˹totally˺ oblivious to the Hereafter. (7) Have they not reflected upon their own being? Allah only created the heavens and the earth and everything in between for a purpose and an appointed term. Yet most people are truly in denial of the meeting with their Lord! (8) Have they not travelled throughout the land to see what was the end of those ˹destroyed˺ before them? They were far superior in might; they cultivated the land and developed it more than these ˹Meccans˺ ever have. Their messengers came to them with clear proofs. Allah would have never wronged them, but it was they who wronged themselves. (9) Then most evil was the end of the evildoers for denying and mocking the signs of Allah. (10) It is Allah Who originates the creation, and will resurrect it. And then to Him you will ˹all˺ be returned. (11)❩ [Quran 30:1-11]

[1]: This can also mean "in the lowest part of the earth."

[2]: This Meccan sūrah takes its name from the reference to the Romans in verse (2). The world's superpowers in the early 7th century were the Roman Byzantine and Persian Empires. When they went to war in 614 C.E., the Romans suffered a devastating defeat. The Meccan pagans rejoiced at the defeat of the Roman Christians at the hands of the Persian pagans. Soon verses 30:1-5 were revealed, stating that the Romans would be victorious in three to nine years. Eight years later, the Romans won a decisive battle against the Persians, reportedly on the same day the Muslims vanquished the Meccan army at the Battle of Badr.

You have not created all of this without purpose.
Glory be to You!'[215] — *Quran 3:190–191*

The wise-one learns to touch lightly,
To listen deeply,
To see without possessing.
They see creation
Not as possession,
But as procession—
Each moment passing,
Each sign pointing beyond itself.

So the wise-one walks forward—
Not dazzled by creation,
But guided through it.
They do not cling to what sings,
But seek the One who taught the song.
They do not worship the sign,
But the One it points toward.

For only He is unveiled in surrender.
Only He remains when all forms fade.
Only He is the source
Of meaning, purpose, and eternal remembrance.

Wisdom Unveiled

The profound wisdom unveiled in The Veil of Creation is that creation is both a window and a wall. Every leaf, every river, every star sings His name, yet the moment the soul clings to the song instead of the Singer, it profoundly loses the path. The wise-one achieves a pinnacle of psychic and spiritual insight by learning to touch lightly, to listen deeply, and to see without possessing—recognizing that the Real hides from those who seek

---

[215] This is derived from the Quran verses of:

📖 ⟨To Allah ˹alone˺ belongs the kingdom of the heavens and the earth. And Allah is Most Capable of everything. (189) Indeed, in the creation of the heavens and the earth and the alternation of the day and night there are signs for people of reason. (190) ˹They are˺ those who remember Allah while standing, sitting, and lying on their sides, and reflect on the creation of the heavens and the earth ˹and pray˺, "Our Lord! You have not created ˹all of˺ this without purpose. Glory be to You! Protect us from the torment of the Fire. (191) Our Lord! Indeed, those You commit to the Fire will be ˹completely˺ disgraced! And the wrongdoers will have no helpers. (192)⟩ [Quran 3:189-193]

to own, and reveals Himself to those who dare to let go. This ultimate dissolution of the perception of creation as separate leads to a unified vision where all phenomena are seen as direct manifestations of the Divine, and the soul lives in the constant awareness that Divine Presence permeates all, transforming multiplicity into Unity.

Wise-Reflection

Reflect on what you tend to cling to in your life—be it possessions, achievements, or even conceptual understandings of the world. How does the idea that "what I cling to becomes the veil" resonate with your experience? Consider a beautiful natural scene or a complex human creation. Do you tend to get lost in the "song" of its form, or do you consciously seek the "Singer" (the Creator) behind it? How can you cultivate the practice of "touching lightly, listening deeply, and seeing without possessing" in your daily interactions with the world? What does it truly mean to surrender your perception of creation as independent and embrace the reality that "wheresoever you turn, there is the Face of Allah," allowing this to deepen your psychic and spiritual insight?

Contemplation: The Subjugation of Names and Worldly Attachments

---

(The soul calls Him by name—yet He transcends all naming)

This advanced stage in the wise-one's awakening involves the profound and complete subjugation of all names and worldly attachments to the Absolute. Names, whether they denote human identities, titles, classifications, or even conceptual understandings of the Divine, are now seen as utterly contingent, ephemeral, and ultimately limiting. Concurrently, all worldly attachments—to possessions, fleeting status, complex relationships, and even intellectual constructs—are fully released from the heart. This does not imply abandoning responsibilities or withdrawing from life, but rather, detaching the heart's innermost core from all 'other-than-Allah.' The wise-one recognizes that true, liberating freedom and ultimate, abiding peace come solely from a heart singularly devoted to the Creator, allowing all other loyalties, desires, and conceptual frameworks to willingly submit to this ultimate, all-encompassing Reality. This is a pinnacle of psychic transformation, where the mind and heart are unchained from symbols to experience pure reverence.

Where Surrender Is Freed from Symbols and True Reverence Begins

The wise-one knows:
What is said of Him in sentences
Are but shadows of His own attributes.
They shimmer through scripture,
Reverberate in revelation—
But they remain cloaked echoes of His mercy, majesty, and might.
Yet what cannot be spoken of Him—
Those are the attributes
That belong only to Him,
And can never belong to me or anything.
Not to prophets, not to angels,
Not to stars or sages—
They dwell beyond all beings,
Unchained, unshareable, Divine.

❰He is Allah—One and Indivisible.
He has never had offspring, nor was He born.
And there is none comparable to Him.❱[216] — Quran 112:1–4

He is the Eternal, yet no eternity can hold Him.
He is the One, yet no number can define Him.

Submission begins by honoring a thing.
But submission to names
Leads to submission to their meanings—
And meanings, if filtered through the self,
Lead back to desire.
Desire clings to form,
Attaches to power,
And calls toward infidelity and polytheism.

---

[216] This is derived from the Quran verses of:

📖 ❰Say, ʾO Prophet,ʾ "He is Allah—One ʾand Indivisibleʾ; (1) Allah—the Sustainer ʾneeded by allʾ. (2) He has never had offspring, nor was He born. (3) And there is none comparable to Him."[1] (4)❱ [Quran 112:1-4]

[1]: As mentioned in the Introduction, the Quran has three main themes: 1. Stories. 2. Muslim teachings. 3. And belief in the unseen. Since Sûrah 112 covers the third theme, the Prophet 🕮 says in a ḥadîth collected by Bukhâri and Muslim that reading this sûrah equals reading one third of the Quran.

So the wise-one asks:
Can the One who creates
Be equal to those who do not?

❮*Can the One Who creates*
Be equal to those who do not?
Will you not then be mindful?❯ — *Quran 16:17*

Those idols, lifeless and powerless,
Called upon by hearts in denial,
Are themselves created—
Unable to give,
Unable to restore.

❮*They are dead, not alive—*
Not even knowing when their followers will be resurrected.
Your God is only One God.❯ — *Quran 16:21–22*

Even if all were to unite,
They could not create even a fly,
Nor retrieve what a fly takes from them.

❮*How weak are those who invoke,*
And how powerless are the things they invoke!❯ — *Quran 16:20*

For true submission
Is to the One
Whose blessings cannot be numbered,
Whose power cannot be rivaled,
And whose reverence alone is deserved.

❝If you tried to count Allah's blessings,
You would never be able to number them.
Surely Allah is All-Forgiving, Most Merciful.❞ [217] — Quran 16:18

Even the Quran, sent in perfect form,
Reveals that if it had descended upon a mountain,
The mountain itself
Would be humbled and torn apart in awe.

❝Had We sent down this Quran upon a mountain,
You would have certainly seen it humbled
And torn apart in awe of Allah.
We set forth such comparisons
So perhaps they may reflect.❞ — Quran 59:21

This is not a God who can be contained by symbol.
He is Allah—
The Knower of the seen and unseen,
The Most Compassionate,
The King,
The Source of Serenity,
The Inventor,

---

[217] This is derived from the Quran verses of:

📖 ❝Can the One Who creates be equal to those who do not? Will you not then be mindful? (17) If you tried to count Allah's blessings, you would never be able to number them. Surely Allah is All-Forgiving, Most Merciful. (18) And Allah knows what you conceal and what you reveal. (19) But those ʿidolsʾ they invoke besides Allah cannot create anything—they themselves are created. (20) They are dead, not alive—not even knowing when their followers will be resurrected. (21) Your God is ʿonlyʾ One God. As for those who do not believe in the Hereafter, their hearts are in denial, and they are too proud. (22) Without a doubt, Allah knows what they conceal and what they reveal. He certainly does not like those who are too proud. (23) And when it is said to them, "What has your Lord revealed?" They say, "Ancient fables!" (24) Let them bear their burdens in full on the Day of Judgment as well as some of the burdens of those they mislead without knowledge. Evil indeed is what they will bear! (25) Indeed, those before them had plotted, but Allah struck at the ʿveryʾ foundation of their structure, so the roof collapsed on top of them, and the torment came upon them from where they did not expect.[1] (26) Then on the Day of Judgment He will humiliate them and say, "Where are My ʿso-calledʾ associate-gods for whose sake you used to oppose ʿtheʾ believersʾ?" Those gifted with knowledge will say, "Surely disgrace and misery today are upon the disbelievers." (27)❞ [Quran 16:17-27]

[1]: This verse refers to a tyrant king who ordered the building of a tower so he can reach the heavens and fight Allah and the angels. Eventually the tower collapsed, leaving the tyrant crushed.

The Shaper,
The One with the Most Beautiful Names.

⟨He is Allah—there is no god but Him…
Whatever is in the heavens and the earth
Constantly glorifies Him.
And He is the Almighty, All-Wise.⟩ [218]— Quran 59:22–24

The wise-one sees:
Names are pathways—
But clinging to them is a trap.
Forms are signs—
But worship belongs to the One who breathes meaning into all signs.

So the wise-one walks forward—
Not enslaved by creation,
But elevated through surrender.
They do not lose God in symbols
They meet Him in silence.
They do not mistake name for essence—
They bow before the Reality beyond all naming.

For only He creates without likeness.
Only He gives without measure.
Only He remains the source
Of unity, mercy, and eternal reverence.

---

[218] This is derived from the Quran verse of:

📖 ⟨Had We sent down this Quran upon a mountain, you would have certainly seen it humbled and torn apart in awe of Allah. We set forth such comparisons for people, ˹so˺ perhaps they may reflect.[1] (21) He is Allah—there is no god ˹worthy of worship˺ except Him: Knower of the seen and unseen. He is the Most Compassionate, Most Merciful. (22) He is Allah—there is no god except Him: the King, the Most Holy, the All-Perfect, the Source of Serenity, the Watcher ˹of all˺, the Almighty, the Supreme in Might,[2] the Majestic. Glorified is Allah far above what they associate with Him ˹in worship˺! (23) He is Allah: the Creator, the Inventor, the Shaper. He ˹alone˺ has the Most Beautiful Names. Whatever is in the heavens and the earth ˹constantly˺ glorifies Him. And He is the Almighty, All-Wise. (24) ⟩ [Quran 59:24]

[1]: Meaning, that the hearts of the disbelievers are harder than the mountains concerning the Quran.

[2]: Jabbâr comes from the root word ja-ba-ra which means to impose, support, or console. For example, Jabîrah means the cast that supports a broken bone. Hence, Allah is the One Whose Will cannot be resisted, and Who comforts those who are broken or oppressed.

Wisdom Unveiled

The profound wisdom unveiled in The Subjugation of Names and Worldly Attachments is that true reverence begins where surrender is freed from the limiting confines of symbols. The wise-one understands that what is said of the Divine in sentences and names are but shadows or echoes of His attributes, for He utterly transcends all naming and definition. Clinging to names, forms, or worldly attachments becomes a subtle trap, leading to desire and polytheism. Instead, the wise-one is elevated through complete surrender, not enslaved by creation, and learns not to lose God in symbols but to meet Him in profound silence. They never mistake a name for the Divine Essence, but bow before the uncontainable Reality beyond all naming, recognizing that only He creates without likeness, gives without measure, and remains the sole source of unity, mercy, and eternal reverence. This leads to a profound psychic liberation where the heart is singularly devoted to the Creator, experiencing ultimate peace and freedom.

Wise-Reflection

Reflect on the names, titles, or worldly attachments that you find yourself valuing most deeply. Do you ever inadvertently mistake the "shadows of His attributes" for the full Reality of the Divine? Consider how true freedom comes from a heart singularly devoted to the Creator, allowing all other loyalties and desires to submit to this ultimate reality. What attachments—whether to possessions, status, relationships, or even specific intellectual concepts—might still be subtly veiling your complete surrender to the Absolute? How can you consciously practice detaching your heart from 'other-than-Allah' without abandoning your responsibilities, moving towards a state where true reverence begins through a freedom from symbols, leading to deeper psychic peace and ultimate devotion?

Contemplation: The Duality of Knowing

(The soul learns not by declaration—but by dissolution)

The wise-one in this advanced stage of awakening transcends the very duality of knowing: the fundamental division between the subject (the knower) and the object (the known). In the profound state of "Knowing the Unspoken," this distinction begins to blur and ultimately dissolves, moving towards a unified, holistic experience of knowledge. The wise-one's knowledge is no longer an external apprehension—a collection of facts or concepts—but an internal, existential realization, where the very act of knowing becomes inseparable from the pervasive Presence of the Divine Knower. This mirrors the Prophet's direct, unveiled vision mentioned in the Gateway Verse, where his "heart did not doubt what he saw," indicating a knowing that completely transcends conventional external perception and enters a realm of pure, unmediated awareness. This is the pinnacle of psychic transformation, where all boundaries of knowing dissolve into Humility before Allah.

Where Speech Bows to Silence and Wisdom Rises from Surrender

Speechless knowing is sovereign.
It rules the soul without demand—
Quietly, without claiming, without naming.
It does not define.
It does not divide.
It simply unveils.
Spoken knowing, by contrast,
Calls itself into being,
Seeks recognition,
Grasps at distinction.
It makes noise—
But not always nearness.
It defines, divides, distinguishes.
But does not always offer nearness
Yet what cannot be spoken
Is what most deeply guides.
For when a thing speaks, it shows its limit.
But the Knowing that is silent—rules.
What speaks calls to itself.
But what is silent reveals Him.
Wisdom is not in the words themselves,
But in the silence that gathers the soul into presence.

The seven heavens,
The earth,
And all within them

Glorify Him—
Yet their praise remains unheard, unseen,
Beyond the grasp of those
Who rely only on words.
True understanding arises not in articulation,
But in reflection—
In the signs of the heavens and the earth,
In the remembrance that transcends speech,
In the prayer that rises from stillness,
Not from the tongue,
But from the depths of the soul.

❨Indeed, in the creation of the heavens and the earth
And the alternation of night and day
Are signs for people of reason.❩ — Quran 3:190

They reflect while standing, sitting, and lying down.
They do not merely speak of Him—
They see Him
In what moves silently.

❨Our Lord! You have not created all of this without purpose.
Glory be to You! Protect us from the torment of the Fire.❩[219] — Quran 3:191

The wise-one learns:
Speech—no matter how noble—is born of limitation.
It defines.
It fragments.
It tries to contain.
But silence—silence is infinite.

---

[219] This is derived from the Quran verses of:

📖 ❨Indeed, in the creation of the heavens and the earth and the alternation of the day and night there are signs for people of reason. (190) ˹They are˺ those who remember Allah while standing, sitting, and lying on their sides, and reflect on the creation of the heavens and the earth ˹and pray˺, "Our Lord! You have not created ˹all of˺ this without purpose. Glory be to You! Protect us from the torment of the Fire. (191) Our Lord! Indeed, those You commit to the Fire will be ˹completely˺ disgraced! And the wrongdoers will have no helpers. (192) Our Lord! We have heard the caller1 to ˹true˺ belief, ˹proclaiming,˺ 'Believe in your Lord ˹alone˺,' so we believed. Our Lord! Forgive our sins, absolve us of our misdeeds, and join us with the virtuous when we die. (193) Our Lord! Grant us what You have promised us through Your messengers and do not put us to shame on Judgment Day—for certainly You never fail in Your promise." (194)❩ [Quran 3:191-194]

It gathers the soul not into knowledge,
But into Being.
He gave me scripture,
Not to contain Him—
But to bring me to the edge
Of what cannot be contained.
Even the Quran,
Sent as healing and guidance,
Reveals the paradox:
It speaks in order to point toward what speech cannot hold.
And when the heart awakens,
It moves beyond articulation
Into a surrender
That is more eloquent than any word.

❨*Indeed, Allah has done the believers a great favour*
By raising a messenger from among them—
Reciting to them His revelations,
Purifying them,
And teaching them the Book and wisdom.❩²²⁰ — *Quran 3:164*

To those who challenge revelation,
Trying to fabricate the unspoken,
They are told:

❨*Say: 'Produce ten fabricated surahs like it,*
And seek help from whoever you can—other than Allah—
If what you say is true.'❩²²¹ — *Quran 11:13*

---

²²⁰ This is derived from the Quran verse of:

📖 ❨Indeed, Allah has done the believers a ˹great˺ favour by raising a messenger from among them—reciting to them His revelations, purifying them, and teaching them the Book and wisdom. For indeed they had previously been clearly astray. (164)❩ [Quran 3:164]

²²¹ This is derived from the Quran verse of:

📖 ❨Or do they say, "He1 has fabricated this ˹Quran˺!"? Say, ˹O Prophet,˺ "Produce ten fabricated sûrahs like it and seek help from whoever you can—other than Allah—if what you say is true!" (13) But if your helpers fail you, then know that it has been revealed with the knowledge of Allah, and that there is no god ˹worthy of worship˺ except Him! Will you ˹not˺ then submit ˹to Allah˺? (14)❩ [Quran 11:13-14]

[1]: The Prophet ﷺ

But they cannot.
For the words of the Quran
Do not belong to speech alone—
They belong to the silence
From which all truth is born.

❨Had We sent down this Quran upon a mountain,
You would have certainly seen it humbled
And torn apart in awe of Allah.
We set forth such comparisons for people,
So perhaps they may reflect. [222]❩ — Quran 59:21

If even mountains would shatter from the weight of Divine revelation,
Then the soul must bow with even greater humility—
Not in sound,
But in stillness.

So the wise-one walks forward—
Not boasting of what they know,
But trembling before what they cannot explain.
They speak,
But only to give voice to longing.
They listen,
But only to be led to stillness.
They know—
Not by accumulation,
But by surrender.

For only He teaches through silence.
Only He unveils what speech cannot hold.
Only He remains the source
Of wisdom, presence, and eternal knowing.

---

[222] This is derived from the Quran verse of:

📖 ❨Had We sent down this Quran upon a mountain, you would have certainly seen it humbled and torn apart in awe of Allah. We set forth such comparisons for people, ˹so˺ perhaps they may reflect.[1] (21)❩ [Quran 59:21]

[1]: Meaning, that the hearts of the disbelievers are harder than the mountains concerning the Quran.

Wisdom Unveiled

The profound wisdom unveiled in The Duality of Knowing is that speech, no matter how noble, is born of limitation. It defines, divides, and distinguishes, attempting to contain the uncontainable. But silence— silence is infinite. It gathers the soul not into fragmented knowledge, but into a unified state of pure Being. The wise-one learns that true wisdom is not noisy or self-proclaiming; it is the deep stillness that humbles all voices, the unseen hand that elevates the heart into unseen gardens of Divine Presence. This ultimate psychic transformation signifies that the soul learns not by declaration or accumulation, but by the profound and continuous dissolution of the duality between knower and known, surrendering to the Divine Knower where wisdom rises from pure silence.

Wise-Reflection

Reflect on moments when you feel the need to articulate or define spiritual truths. Do these efforts sometimes feel limiting, or do they truly capture the depth of your experience? Consider the paradox: "What speaks calls to itself. But what is silent reveals Him." How can you cultivate a deeper appreciation for the power of silence in your spiritual life? What practices can help you move beyond merely intellectual knowing into an internal, existential realization where the act of knowing becomes inseparable from the Presence of the Divine Knower? How can you learn to "listen, but only to be led to stillness," allowing this to foster a profound psychic peace and a knowing that transcends all duality?

Contemplation: Divine Grace and the Sovereignty of Wisdom

(The one who dwells in grace does not follow—he illumines the path)

The wise-one in this culminating stage fully embodies the profound reality of Divine Grace (fadl) and the Sovereignty of Wisdom (hikmah). All unveiling, all profound knowing, and indeed every single step on this sacred path is understood not as a personal achievement or earned merit, but as an utterly unearned, pure gift of Allah's boundless grace. This realization profoundly reinforces humility and absolute surrender, preventing any subtle sense of personal accomplishment or pride. Simultaneously, the inherent, all-encompassing wisdom (hikmah) of the Divine permeates the wise-one's perception, allowing them to act with an insight, discernment, and clarity that is not their own, but a direct reflection of Allah's boundless, all-encompassing wisdom. This seamless integration of grace and wisdom empowers the wise-one's every action, thought, and understanding, transforming them into a guide for knowledge itself. This signifies a profound psychic transformation from a mere seeker to an illuminator of the path, dwelling in constant gratitude.

Where Knowledge Is Governed by Presence and Elevation Springs from Gratitude

---

He who seeks stance
In the grace of the Creator
Is not sent knowledge to follow—
But sent forth
As the one who guides knowledge and wisdom.
He is not commanded by understanding—
He commands understanding,
Because he stands not in speculation,
But in Divine nearness.
He is not made to submit to knowledge and science,
But to govern them—
For he is in the Creator's presence.

The wise-one is granted discernment,
Just as Ibrahim 🕊 was given sound judgment early on.
He stood firm against falsehood,
Questioned his people's inherited delusions,
And bore witness to the One
Who created the heavens and the earth.

❨We had granted Abraham sound judgment early on…
Your Lord is the Lord of the heavens and the earth,
Who created them both.
And to that I bear witness.❩²²³ — Quran 21:51–56

---

²²³ This is derived from the Quran verses of:

He did not follow blindly—
He pierced illusion with insight.
This is the sovereignty of wisdom:
To see clearly
Not because one is clever,
But because one has been drawn close.

The messengers were entrusted with truth—
Not of their own initiative,
But by revelation.
They worshiped not with ego,
But in submission to the One
Who revealed to them.

❮*There is no god worthy of worship except Me,*
So worship Me alone.❯ — *Quran 21:25*

And the angels, those honored servants,
Do not speak until He has spoken.
They act only at His command.
They do not intercede except by His approval—
And they tremble

📖 ❮And indeed, We had granted Abraham sound judgment early on, for We knew him well ˹to be worthy of it˺. (51) ˹Remember˺ when he questioned his father and his people, "What are these statues to which you are so devoted?" (52) They replied, "We found our forefathers worshipping them." (53) He responded, "Indeed, you and your forefathers have been clearly astray." (54) They asked, "Have you come to us with the truth, or is this a joke?" (55) He replied, "In fact, your Lord is the Lord of the heavens and the earth, Who created them ˹both˺. And to that I bear witness." (56) ˹Then he said to himself,˺ "By Allah! I will surely plot against your idols after you have turned your backs and gone away." (57) So he smashed them into pieces, except the biggest of them, so they might turn to it ˹for answers˺. (58) They protested, "Who dared do this to our gods? It must be an evildoer!" (59) Some said, "We heard a young man, called Abraham, speaking ˹ill˺ of them." (60) They demanded, "Bring him before the eyes of the people, so that they may witness ˹his trial˺." (61) They asked, "Was it you who did this to our gods, O Abraham?" (62) He replied ˹sarcastically˺, "No, this one—the biggest of them—did it! So ask them, if they can talk!" (63) So they came back to their senses, saying ˹to one another˺, "You yourselves are truly the wrongdoers!" (64) Then they ˹quickly˺ regressed to their ˹original˺ mind-set, ˹arguing,˺ "You already know that those ˹idols˺ cannot talk." (65) He rebuked ˹them˺, "Do you then worship—instead of Allah—what can neither benefit nor harm you in any way? (66) Shame on you and whatever you worship instead of Allah! Do you not have any sense?" (67) They concluded, "Burn him up to avenge your gods, if you must act." (68) We ordered, "O fire! Be cool and safe for Abraham!"[1] (69) They had sought to harm him, but We made them the worst losers. (70)❯ [Quran 21:51-70]

[1]: It is reported in a ḥadīth collected by Bukhârî that Abraham ﷺ said, while being thrown into the fire, "Allah ˹alone˺ is sufficient ˹as an aid˺ for us and ˹He˺ is the best Protector."

Not from fear,
But from awe and nearness.

❰They do not speak until He has spoken,
And they act only at His command.
They do not intercede except for whom He approves,
And they tremble in awe of Him.❱[224] — Quran 21:27–28

Their glory is not autonomy—
But proximity.
They witness His grace,
Glorify His majesty,
And remain veiled in humility.
Never do they claim divinity—
For if any among them were to say,
"I am a god besides Him,"
They would be cast into Hell.
Such is the purity of their devotion.

And wisdom—like that gifted to Luqmān—
Is not merely intellect,
But a call to gratitude.
For in gratitude lies elevation,
And in elevation,
The wise-one finds himself
Inseparable from the Divine presence—
Standing firm where none may command him
But Him alone.

---

[224] This is derived from the Quran verses of:

📖 ❰Or have they taken other gods besides Him? Say, ˊO Prophet,ˋ "Show ˊmeˋ your proof. Here is ˊtheˋ Quran,ˋ the Reminder for those with me; along with ˊearlier Scriptures,ˋ the Reminder for those before me."[1] But most of them do not know the truth, so they turn away. (24) We never sent a messenger before you ˊO Prophetˋ without revealing to him: "There is no god ˊworthy of worshipˋ except Me, so worship Me ˊaloneˋ." (25) And they say, "The Most Compassionate has offspring!"[1] Glory be to Him! In fact, those ˊangelsˋ are only ˊHisˋ honoured servants, (26) who do not speak until He has spoken, ˊonlyˋ acting at His command. (27) He ˊfullyˋ knows what is ahead of them and what is behind them. They do not intercede except for whom He approves, and they tremble in awe of Him. (28) Whoever of them were to say, "I am a god besides Him," they would be rewarded with Hell by Us. This is how We reward the wrongdoers. (29)❱ [Quran 21:24-29]

[1]: Some pagans claimed that the angels are Allah's daughters.

[338]

❮*We blessed Luqmān with wisdom, saying:*
'Be grateful to Allah,
For whoever is grateful,
It is only for their own good.'❯[225] — *Quran 31:12*

So the wise-one walks forward—
Not as one who accumulates knowledge,
But as one who radiates insight.
He does not speak before he listens.
He does not teach before he submits.
He does not act from self-authority,
But from Divine intimacy.
And when he rises,
He does so by grace,
Not ambition—
Not by conquest,
But by reverent surrender.

---

[225] This is derived from the Quran verses of:

📖 ❮Indeed, We blessed Luqmān with wisdom, ˹saying˺, "Be grateful to Allah, for whoever is grateful, it is only for their own good. And whoever is ungrateful, then surely Allah is Self-Sufficient, Praiseworthy."[1] (12) And ˹remember˺ when Luqmān said to his son, while advising him, "O my dear son! Never associate ˹anything˺ with Allah ˹in worship˺, for associating ˹others with Him˺ is truly the worst of all wrongs." (13) And We have commanded people to ˹honour˺ their parents. Their mothers bore them through hardship upon hardship, and their weaning takes two years. So be grateful to Me and your parents. To Me is the final return. (14) But if they pressure you to associate with Me what you have no knowledge of,[2] do not obey them. Still keep their company in this world courteously, and follow the way of those who turn to Me ˹in devotion˺. Then to Me you will ˹all˺ return, and then I will inform you of what you used to do. (15) ˹Luqmān added,˺ "O my dear son! ˹Even˺ if a deed were the weight of a mustard seed—be it ˹hidden˺ in a rock or in the heavens or the earth—Allah will bring it forth. Surely Allah is Most Subtle, All-Aware. (16) "O my dear son! Establish prayer, encourage what is good and forbid what is evil, and endure patiently whatever befalls you. Surely this is a resolve to aspire to. (17) "And do not turn your nose up to people, nor walk pridefully upon the earth. Surely Allah does not like whoever is arrogant, boastful. (18) Be moderate in your pace. And lower your voice, for the ugliest of all voices is certainly the braying of donkeys." (19) Have you not seen that Allah has subjected for you whatever is in the heavens and whatever is on the earth, and has lavished His favours upon you, both seen and unseen? ˹Still˺ there are some who dispute about Allah without knowledge, or guidance, or an enlightening scripture. (20) When it is said to them, "Follow what Allah has revealed," they reply, "No! We ˹only˺ follow what we found our forefathers practicing." ˹Would they still do so˺ even if Satan is inviting them to the torment of the Blaze? (21) Whoever fully submits themselves to Allah and is a good-doer, they have certainly grasped the firmest hand-hold. And with Allah rests the outcome of ˹all˺ affairs. (22) But whoever disbelieves, do not let their disbelief grieve you ˹O Prophet˺. To Us is their return, and We will inform them of all they did. Surely Allah knows best what is ˹hidden˺ in the heart. (23) We allow them enjoyment for a little while, then ˹in time˺ We will force them into a harsh torment. (24)❯ [Quran 31:12-24]

[1]: Luqmān is believed to have been a righteous, wise man who lived around the time of Prophet David ﷺ.

[2]: Other gods.

For only He bestows wisdom without measure.
Only He elevates through gratitude.
Only He remains the source
Of discernment, presence, and eternal mastery.

Wisdom Unveiled

The profound wisdom unveiled in Divine Grace and the Sovereignty of Wisdom is that knowledge is governed by Presence, and elevation springs from gratitude. The one who truly dwells in Divine Grace (fadl) is not merely sent knowledge to follow, but is sent forth as the one who guides knowledge and wisdom, commanding understanding because they stand not in speculation, but in profound Divine nearness. This signifies that the wise-one is not a passive recipient but an active illuminator of the path, empowered by unearned grace. True wisdom (hikmah) is not merely intellect, but a call to deep gratitude, for in gratitude lies an elevation that makes the wise-one inseparable from the Divine Presence, acting with discernment that is a direct reflection of Allah's all-encompassing wisdom. This is the pinnacle of psychic transformation, where all actions spring from Divine intimacy and reverent surrender, leading to eternal mastery.

Wise-Reflection

Reflect on your own understanding of success and spiritual progress. Do you attribute them primarily to your own efforts, or to Divine Grace? Consider the idea that one who "dwells in grace does not follow—he illumines the path." In what areas of your life can you shift from trying to "command understanding" through sheer intellect to allowing yourself to be commanded by Divine Presence, acting from Divine intimacy? How can cultivating deep gratitude for every insight, every unveiling, and every capacity you possess reinforce your humility and strengthen your connection to Divine Grace? What does it mean to be a "master of knowledge and wisdom" not through personal ambition, but through reverent surrender to the Sovereignty of Wisdom, allowing this to deepen your psychic and spiritual illumination?

Contemplation: Attributes of the Creator

(The soul names Him only to be silenced by awe)

In "Knowing the Unspoken," the wise-one moves beyond merely conceptualizing the Attributes of the Creator to experientially apprehending them. Rather than defining "Al-Rahman" (The Most Merciful) or "Al-Hakeem" (The All-Wise) intellectually through abstract thought, they witness these Divine attributes manifest in every moment of existence—in every breath taken, every trial endured, and every unfolding of reality. The entire universe becomes a living book, a dynamic scripture of Divine Attributes, and the wise-one himself or herself becomes a living testament to their pervasive manifestation. This is a profound spiritual and psychic resonance with the Divine, where understanding transcends mere mental grasp and becomes an embodied, awe-inspiring realization.

Where Reflections Whisper, But Only Silence Reveals

His attributes carried by words
Are reflected in creation—
Mercy in the rain,
Beauty in the stars,
Strength in the mountains.
Yet His attributes beyond words
Remain forever beyond all form.
He is the Originator of the heavens and the earth,
The All-Hearing, the All-Seeing—
There is nothing like Him,
Yet all things exist by His decree.

❝There is nothing like Him,
For He alone is the All-Hearing, All-Seeing.❞[226] *— Quran 42:11*

---

[226] This is derived from the Quran verses of:

❝How can they take protectors besides Him? Allah alone is the Protector. He ˹alone˺ gives life to the dead. And He ˹alone˺ is Most Capable of everything. (9) ˹Say to the believers, O Prophet,˺ "Whatever you may differ about, its judgment rests with Allah. That is Allah—my Lord. In Him I put my trust, and to Him I

Language reflects the speaker
More than the subject.
When we speak of love, majesty, mercy—
We name reflections glimpsed within ourselves.
He bestows blessings through His attributes
So that mankind may know Him
Through shadowed approximations of their own qualities—
But He is not bound by those glimpses.
None truly resemble Him.
And those who imagine Him with limits
Have not honored Him as He deserves.

❨Glorified and Exalted is He
Above what they associate with Him!❩ — Quran 39:67

On the Day of Judgment,
The earth will be in His Grip,
The heavens rolled in His Right Hand.
He is the Creator of all things,
The Sustainer of everything.
To Him belong the keys
Of all unseen treasuries.
All who exist
Are subject to His will.

❨Allah is the Creator of all things,
And He is the Maintainer of everything.
To Him belong the keys of the heavens and the earth…❩[227] — Quran 39:62–66

'always` turn." (10) ´He is` the Originator of the heavens and the earth. He has made for you spouses from among yourselves, and ´made` mates for cattle ´as well`—multiplying you ´both`. There is nothing like Him, for He ´alone` is the All-Hearing, All-Seeing. (11) To Him belong the keys ´of the treasuries` of the heavens and the earth. He gives abundant or limited provisions to whoever He Wills. Indeed, He has ´perfect` knowledge of all things. (12)❩ [Quran 42:9-12]

[227] This is derived from the Quran verses of:

📖 ❨Allah is the Creator of all things, and He is the Maintainer of everything. (62) To Him belong the keys ´of the treasuries` of the heavens and the earth. As for those who rejected the signs of Allah, it is they who will be the ´true` losers. (63) Say, ´O Prophet,` "Are you urging me to worship ´anyone` other than Allah, O

To Him belong the finest attributes—
Not shaped by speech,
Not defined by minds.
He holds the mysteries
Of the heavens and the earth,
And all are subject to His command.

❨*And to Him belong all those*
In the heavens and the earth—
All are subject to His Will
To Him belong the finest attributes
In the heavens and the earth.❩[228] — *Quran 30:26–27*

To attribute offspring or likeness to Him
Is to fall into ruin—
For He is far beyond such needs.

---

ignorant ones?" (64) It has already been revealed to you—and to those ˹prophets˺ before you—that if you associate others ˹with Allah˺, your deeds will certainly be void and you will truly be one of the losers. (65) Rather, worship Allah ˹alone˺ and be one of the grateful. (66) They have not shown Allah His proper reverence—when on the Day of Judgment the ˹whole˺ earth will be in His Grip, and the heavens will be rolled up in His Right Hand. Glorified and Exalted is He above what they associate ˹with Him˺! (67)❩ [Quran 39:62-67]

[228] This is derived from the Quran verses of:

📖 ❨So glorify Allah in the evening and in the morning— (17) all praise is for Him in the heavens and the earth—as well as in the afternoon, and at noon.[1] (18) He brings forth the living from the dead and the dead from the living. And He gives life to the earth after its death. And so will you be brought forth ˹from the grave˺. (19) One of His signs is that He created you from dust, then—behold!—you are human beings spreading over ˹the earth˺. (20) And one of His signs is that He created for you spouses from among yourselves so that you may find comfort in them. And He has placed between you compassion and mercy. Surely in this are signs for people who reflect. (21) And one of His signs is the creation of the heavens and the earth, and the diversity of your languages and colours. Surely in this are signs for those of ˹sound˺ knowledge. (22) And one of His signs is your sleep by night and by day ˹for rest˺ as well as your seeking His bounty ˹in both˺. Surely in this are signs for people who listen. (23) And one of His signs is that He shows you lightning, inspiring ˹you with˺ hope and fear.[2] And He sends down rain from the sky, reviving the earth after its death. Surely in this are signs for people who understand. (24) And one of His signs is that the heavens and the earth persist by His command. Then when He calls you out of the earth just once, you will instantly come forth. (25) And to Him belong all those in the heavens and the earth—all are subject to His Will.[3] (26) And He is the One Who originates the creation then will resurrect it—which is even easier for Him.[4] To Him belong the finest attributes in the heavens and the earth. And He is the Almighty, All-Wise. (27)❩ [Quran 30:17-27]

[1]: This verse outlines the times of the five daily prayers. The evening refers to Maghrib and 'Ishâ' prayers, the morning refers to Fajr, the afternoon refers to 'Aṣr, and noon refers to Ẓuhr.

[2]: Hope of rain and fear of torment.

[3]: lit., to Him.

[4]: This is from a human perspective. Otherwise, both the creation of the universe and the resurrection of humans are easy for Allah.

He is not begotten,
And He does not beget.
He is the Sustainer,
The One—Indivisible.
There is none comparable to Him.

❲"He is Allah—One and Indivisible;
Allah—the Sustainer needed by all.
He has never had offspring, nor was He born.
And there is none comparable to Him.❳[229] — Quran 112:1–4

The wise-one knows:
What can be named is within reach.
But what cannot be named
Is beyond all measure.
To know Him is not through comparison—
But through surrender to His oneness.
The wise-one bows not before definition,
But before mystery.
Not before attributes held in language,
But those that silence every tongue.
To speak of Him is to tremble,
But to know Him
Is to bow in silence.
The attributes that no tongue can utter,
Those that no mind can imagine,
Belong solely to Him.

So the wise-one walks forward—
Not seeking to master description,
But to dwell in nearness.
They glorify Him not with invention,
But with reverence.
They do not measure—
They magnify.

---

[229] This is derived from the Quran verses of:

📖 ❲Say, ˈO Prophet,ˈ "He is Allah—One ˈand Indivisibleˈ; (1) Allah—the Sustainer ˈneeded by allˈ. (2) He has never had offspring, nor was He born. (3) And there is none comparable to Him." (4)❳ [Quran 112:1-4]

And in magnifying,
They are drawn near.
They worship not by crafting likenesses,
But by erasing illusion.
They glorify not a mystery,
But the One who has named Himself
With perfect attributes—
He who hears as none hear,
Sees as none see,
Watches over as none watch.

❨*So be patient with your Lord's decree,*
For you are truly under Our watchful Eyes.❩²³⁰ — *Quran 52:48*

❨*Indeed, Allah has heard the argument of the woman…*
Surely Allah is All-Hearing, All-Seeing.❩ ²³¹— *Quran 58:1*

They reach not outward to imagine Him—
They surrender inward to honor Him.
For the One whom no eye has seen,
Whom suspicions do not confuse,
Whom describers cannot describe,
And who is never changed—
He alone knows the weight of mountains,
The number of raindrops,

---

²³⁰ This is derived from the Quran verses of:

📖 ❨So be patient with your Lord's decree, for you are truly under Our ˹watchful˺ Eyes. And glorify the praises of your Lord when you rise. (48) And glorify Him during part of the night and at the fading of the stars. (49)❩ [Quran 52:48-49]

²³¹ This is derived from the Quran verse of:

📖 ❨Indeed, Allah has heard the argument of the woman who pleaded with you ˹O Prophet˺ concerning her husband, and appealed to Allah. Allah has heard your exchange.[1] Surely Allah is All-Hearing, All-Seeing. (1)❩ [Quran 58:1]

[1]: A companion named Khawlah bint Tha'labah had a disagreement with her husband, Aws ibn Aṣ-Ṣâmit, who then told her that she was as unlawful for him as the ẓahr (back) of his mother. This statement had been considered to be a form of divorce (known as ẓihâr) in Arabia. Khawlah came to the Prophet 🕊 to ask for his opinion. He 🕊 told her that he had not received any revelation in this regard, and that, based on tradition, she was divorced. She argued that she and her husband had children together who would suffer if their parents were separated. Then she started to plead to Allah as the Prophet 🕊 repeated the same answer. Eventually, this Medinian sûrah was revealed in response to her pleas, thereby abolishing this ancient practice.

The measure of all that the night conceals
And the day reveals.[232]

❲There is nothing like Him,
And He is the All-Hearing, the All-Seeing.❳[233] — Quran 42:11

For only He names Himself in truth.
Only He defines without being defined.
Only He reveals without resemblance.
Only He remains the source
Of majesty, subtlety, and eternal mystery.

Wisdom Unveiled

The profound wisdom unveiled in Attributes of the Creator is that language reflects the speaker more than the subject. When we speak of love, mercy, or majesty, we are naming reflections glimpsed within ourselves. But the true, ineffable attributes of the Divine—those that no tongue can utter and no mind can imagine—belong solely to Him. The wise-one learns that while His attributes are mirrored in creation, only silence truly reveals the uncontained Reality. The wise-one bows in awe before these unspoken names, content to worship the mystery rather than attempting to explain it, experiencing a deep spiritual and psychic resonance where the universe becomes a living testament to Divine

---

[232] This is derived from a narrated hadith, even if it is weak, On the authority of Anas (may Allah be pleased with him), that the Messenger of Allah ﷺ passed by a Bedouin who was supplicating during his prayer, saying:

❁ "O He whom eyes cannot see, whom thoughts cannot confuse, whom describers cannot describe, whom events cannot alter, and whom He does not fear. He knows the weights of mountains and the measures of seas, the number of raindrops and the leaves of trees, and the number of things upon which night is dark and upon which day shines. No sky conceals Him, no earth conceals Him, no sea conceals what is in its depths, and no mountain conceals what is in its rugged terrain. Make the best of my life its last, the best of my deeds its last, and the best of my days the day I meet You."

The Messenger of Allah ﷺ appointed a man to take care of the Bedouin and said, "When he prays, bring him to me." When he had prayed, the man came to him, and some gold had been presented to the Messenger of Allah ﷺ from some mine. When the Bedouin returned to him, he gave him the gold. [Al-Albani mentioned this in Al-Da'ifah (No. 4613)]

[233] This is derived from the Quran verses of:

📖 ❲'He is' the Originator of the heavens and the earth. He has made for you spouses from among yourselves, and 'made' mates for cattle 'as well'—multiplying you 'both'. There is nothing like Him, for He 'alone' is the All-Hearing, All-Seeing. (12) To Him belong the keys 'of the treasuries' of the heavens and the earth. He gives abundant or limited provisions to whoever He wills. Indeed, He has 'perfect' knowledge of all things. (13)❳ [Quran 42:12-13]

Attributes and they themselves become living embodiments of their manifestation, transcending mere conceptual understanding.

Wise-Reflection

Reflect on how you typically understand the Divine Attributes. Do you tend to intellectualize them, or do you seek to experientially witness them in your daily life? Consider the idea that "language reflects the speaker more than the subject" when it comes to Divine attributes. How can you shift your perception from defining attributes to apprehending them as living manifestations in every moment of existence? What does it truly mean to "bow in silence" before the mystery of Allah's attributes that "silence every tongue"? How can you cultivate a heart and mind that are so attuned that the universe becomes a "living book of Divine Attributes," leading to a profound psychic resonance with the Divine and a greater sense of awe and surrender?

Contemplation: The All-Encompassing Presence

(The soul searches for distance—yet finds only nearness)

The culmination of this profound knowing is the ultimate, transformative realization of the All-Encompassing Presence of the Creator. There is, in reality, no 'outside' the Divine; all existence, every atom and galaxy, every thought and feeling, is utterly contained within and perpetually sustained by His boundless Presence. This is the pinnacle of unity, or tawhid— encompassing the unity of actions (tawhid al-af'al), the unity of attributes (tawhid al-sifat), and the ultimate unity of Divine Essence (tawhid al-dhat) for the wise-one. In this state, every particle of creation, every fleeting thought, and every unfolding moment is experientially realized as existing within the boundless Reality of Allah. This profound state transcends the very need for physical proximity, as the wise-one is already, inextricably, utterly encompassed by the Divine, achieving unparalleled psychic peace.

Where Comprehension Fails and Wonder Begins

He is closer than science can measure,
Beyond the reach of comprehension,
Yet vaster than galaxies birthing into light.
He is the Originator of the heavens and the earth,

The Creator of all things,
The Maintainer of what is seen and unseen.

❲He created all things and has perfect knowledge of everything.
No vision can encompass Him, but He encompasses all vision.
For He is the Most Subtle, All-Aware.❳[234] — Quran 6:102–103

The wise-one sees—
The eye, keen as it is,
Cannot behold what lies beyond form.
The mind, brave as it is,
Cannot breach the boundary of His Being.
Yet the heart, when surrendered,
Tastes a nearness deeper than thought,
Richer than description.
He is closer than science can detect,
And further than thought can travel.
He is the Eternal,
Yet no eternity can hold Him.
He is the One,
Yet no number can define Him.
He neither slumbers nor falters.
His Seat holds the heavens and the earth.
None grasp His knowledge except by His will.
He knows what the soul whispers—
What remains unspoken,

---

[234] This is derived form the Quran verses of:

📖 ❲Yet they associate the jinn[1] with Allah ˹in worship˺, even though He created them, and they falsely attribute to Him sons[2] and daughters[3] out of ignorance. Glorified and Exalted is He above what they claim! (100) ˹He is˺ the Originator of the heavens and earth. How could He have children when He has no mate? He created all things and has ˹perfect˺ knowledge of everything. (101) That is Allah—your Lord! There is no god ˹worthy of worship˺ except Him. ˹He is˺ the Creator of all things, so worship Him ˹alone˺. And He is the Maintainer of everything. (102) No vision can encompass Him, but He encompasses all vision. For He is the Most Subtle, All-Aware.[4] (103)❳ [Quran 6:100-103]

[1]: Jinn are another creation of Allah, made of "smokeless fire," and inhabit a realm parallel to our own. Like us, they have free will and can choose guidance or disobedience.

[2]: i.e., "Jesus" in Christian belief.

[3]: i.e., "the angels" in pre-Islamic Arab tradition.

[4]: No one is able to see Allah in this world, but there is extensive evidence in the Quran and the teachings of the Prophet 🙷 that the believers will be able to see their Lord on the Day of Judgment.

What rests quietly
In the unseen depths of the heart.

❲*Indeed, We created humankind*
And fully know what their souls whisper to them,
And We are closer to them than their jugular vein.❳[235] — *Quran 50:16*

This is not metaphor.
This is reality veiled only by perception.
The wise-one ceases to chase with intellect,
And begins to receive with wonder—
A wonder that trembles and rejoices at once.
For to know the Real
Is not to seize,
But to be seized.
He is the One unseen by eyes,
And yet no thought escapes His knowing.
He is the Most Subtle, the All-Aware—
Closer than understanding can fathom,
Yet beyond all limits,
Beyond all knowing.
A presence that wraps the soul
Before the soul was ever aware.

So the wise-one walks forward—
Not toward a distant sky,
But into the breath they breathe.
They do not stretch outward to find Him—
They sink inward to meet Him.
They cease asking,
And begin witnessing.

---

[235] This is derived from the Quran verses of:

📖 ❲Were We incapable of creating ˹them˺ the first time? In fact, they are in doubt about ˹their˺ re-creation. (15) Indeed, ˹it is˺ We ˹Who˺ created humankind and ˹fully˺ know what their souls whisper to them, and We are closer to them than ˹their˺ jugular vein. (16) As the two recording-angels—˹one˺ sitting to the right, and ˹the other to˺ the left—note ˹everything˺, (17) not a word does a person utter without having a ˹vigilant˺ observer ready ˹to write it down˺.[1] (18) ❳ [Quran 50:15-18]

[1]: The angel to the right records the good deeds of each person, while the one to the left records every evil deed. They always accompany the person at all times, except when one uses the toilet or is intimate with their spouse.

THE LANTERN OF THE WISE

They stop naming,
And start dissolving.

For only He is felt before He is known.
Only He surrounds without boundary.
Only He remains the source
Of nearness, subtlety, and eternal presence.

Wisdom Unveiled

The profound wisdom unveiled in The All-Encompassing Presence is that the Divine is nearer than the breath, and yet simultaneously more vast than the galaxies' birth. The mind, brave as it may be, cannot breach the boundaries of His Reality, and the eye, keen as it is, cannot behold what lies beyond form. Thus, the wise-one ceases to chase with intellect and instead begins to receive with wonder—a wonder that trembles and rejoices at once. This ultimate stage of tawhid reveals that to truly know the Real is not to seize, but to be seized; it is the absolute psychic realization that all existence is contained within and sustained by Divine Presence, transcending any illusion of separation and leading to ultimate, abiding peace.

Wise-Reflection

Consider the verse: "And We are closer to them than their jugular vein." How does this shift your perception of Divine proximity? Do you primarily search for the Divine in external places or through intellectual understanding, or do you seek Him in your inner being, in the very breath you breathe? What does it mean for your daily life to "cease chasing with intellect and begin to receive with wonder"? Can you practice a moment-by-moment awareness of His All-Encompassing Presence, allowing yourself to "sink inward to meet Him" rather than stretching outward? How might this profound realization of being utterly encompassed by the Divine lead you to a deeper sense of psychic peace and complete liberation from the illusion of distance?

Contemplation: Beyond Words (Beyond Literal Knowing)

(A final unveiling, where speech fades and remembrance deepens)

This final, comprehensive contemplation encapsulates the very essence of "The Knowing the Unspoken," bringing together various aspects of transcendent knowledge into a unified, culminating realization.

Part 1: Letters are the Doorway, but Remembrance is the Light Beyond

The wise-one profoundly understands that letters, scriptures, and teachings are not merely texts but sacred doorways, absolutely essential for initiation into the realm of Divine knowledge. However, the ultimate light, the true, unmediated illumination, lies profoundly beyond these forms themselves. It is found in continuous, all-encompassing Remembrance (Dhikr) of the Divine. This remembrance is far more than mere verbal repetition; it is an encompassing, transformative state of heart-presence, a profound psychic attunement. The form of the scripture guides, yet it is the inner light of remembrance, experienced both psychically and spiritually, that truly illuminates the way to the Unspoken, dissolving conceptual boundaries and leading to direct apprehension.

Where Comprehension Is Softer Than the Stone, and Mercy Is the Call

If He were to speak to the wise-one in sentences,
He would never reach the reality of His will.
Language opens,
But it does not complete.
Scripture instructs,
But it does not exhaust.
For Divine will does not lie solely in phonemes—
It lies in the heart
That submits to what the verse unveils.

❴Alif-Lām-Ra.
This is a Book whose verses are well perfected and then fully explained—
From the One Who is All-Wise, All-Aware.❵[236] — *Quran 11:1*

The Quran is not a compilation of eloquence—
It is decree softened for the soul,
Truth made traversable for the believing heart.
Its perfection is both form and force.
But form alone is not enough.

The Prophet ﷺ brought it forth without learning,
Without writing,
So no one could claim ownership of what is divinely preserved.
It resides not in parchment,
But in hearts of those gifted with knowledge.

❴*You could not read writing before this revelation…*
But this Quran is a set of clear verses
Preserved in the hearts of those gifted with knowledge.❵ — *Quran 29:48–49*

Its clarity is unveiled to those who submit.
Its guidance is mercy to those who receive.
But the stubborn twist their tongues
And ask for signs—
Not to believe,
But to escape surrender.

❴*Is it not enough for them*
That We have sent down to you the Book,
Which is recited to them?
Surely in this Quran

---

[236] This aligns with the sacred text that speaks of a flawless tome, its words divinely crafted, serving as a guiding decree for those who embrace the truths beyond sight:

📖 ❴Alif-Lām-Ra. ˹This is˺ a Book whose verses are well perfected and then fully explained. ˹It is˺ from the One ˹Who is˺ All-Wise, All-Aware. (1) ˹Tell them, O Prophet,˺ "Worship none but Allah. Surely I am a warner and deliverer of good news to you from Him. (2)❵ [Quran 11:1-2]

Is a mercy and a reminder
For people who believe.⟩²³⁷ — Quran 29:51

Those who deny say:
"The verses are unclear,"
"The language is foreign,"
And they cover themselves in excuses.
But the deaf do not hear even the clearest sound,
And the blind do not see
Even when revelation is made plain.

⟨Had We revealed it as a non-Arabic Quran,
They would have certainly argued:
'If only its verses were clear!'
Say: It is a guide and healing to the believers.
But to those who disbelieve,
It is as if they are being called from a faraway place.⟩²³⁸ — Quran 41:44

It is not the letters that distance them—
It is their refusal to draw near.
And when the Day comes,
When all promises stand fulfilled,
They will cry for a return,
Plead for intercession,

---

[237] This aligns with the sacred texts that illuminate the essence of divine revelation bestowed upon humanity:

⟨Similarly ˹to earlier messengers˺, We have revealed to you a Book ˹O Prophet˺. ˹The faithful of˺ those to whom We gave the Scriptures believe in it, as do some of these ˹pagan Arabs˺. And none denies Our revelations except the ˹stubborn˺ disbelievers. (47) You ˹O Prophet˺ could not read any writing ˹even˺ before this ˹revelation˺, nor could you write at all. Otherwise, the people of falsehood would have been suspicious. (48) But this ˹Quran˺ is ˹a set of˺ clear revelations ˹preserved˺ in the hearts of those gifted with knowledge. And none denies Our revelations except the ˹stubborn˺ wrongdoers. (49) They say, "If only ˹some˺ signs had been sent down to him from his Lord!" Say, ˹O Prophet,˺ "Signs are only with Allah. And I am only sent with a clear warning." (50) Is it not enough for them that We have sent down to you the Book, ˹which is˺ recited to them. Surely in this ˹Quran˺ is a mercy and reminder for people who believe. (51)⟩ [Quran 29:47-51]

[238] These circumstances reveal a striking alignment with the sacred texts that depict the plight of those who refuse to acknowledge the divine origin of the sacred words. Thus, the divine message was imparted to the prophet ﷺ, revealing that those devoid of insight would remain steadfast in their disbelief, crafting endless justifications to evade the profound truths unveiled in the sacred text:

⟨Had We revealed it as a non-Arabic Quran, they would have certainly argued, "If only its verses were made clear ˹in our language˺. What! A non-Arabic revelation for an Arab audience!" Say, ˹O Prophet,˺ "It is a guide and a healing to the believers. As for those who disbelieve, there is deafness in their ears and blindness to it ˹in their hearts˺. It is as if they are being called from a faraway place."1 (44)⟩ [Quran 41:44]

[1]: So they neither hear nor understand the call.

Beg for reversal.
But the sentence they mocked
Will already be complete.

❲We have brought them a Book
Explained with knowledge—
A guide and mercy for those who believe.
But on the Day it is fulfilled,
Those who ignored it will say:
'Can we be sent back?'
They will have ruined themselves,
And what they fabricated will abandon them.❳²³⁹ — Quran 7:52–53

The door was opened with mercy.
What kept them outside
Was denial.

So the wise-one walks forward—
Not by demanding signs,
But by receiving what is spoken.
He does not weigh the grammar of truth—
He bows before its origin.
He does not recite to be clever—
He recites to be cleansed.
He does not debate what was revealed—
He dissolves into the light it contains.

For only He reveals with perfection.
Only He speaks what the willing can hear.

---

²³⁹ Ultimately, this aligns with the Quranic verse that emphasizes the fundamental principle of the Quran, as it serves as a text for those endowed with understanding and faith. When the day of reckoning arrives, as foretold in the Quran, those who have rejected belief will lament for another opportunity, yet it will be far too late for them:

📖 ❲We have certainly brought them a Book which We explained with knowledge—a guide and mercy for those who believe. (52) Do they only await the fulfilment ˹of its warning˺? The Day it will be fulfilled, those who ignored it before will say, "The messengers of our Lord certainly came with the truth. Are there any intercessors who can plead on our behalf? Or can we be sent back so we may do ˹good,˺ unlike what we used to do?" They will have certainly ruined themselves, and whatever ˹gods˺ they fabricated will fail them. (53)❳ [Quran 7:52-53]

[354]

Only He remains the source
Of revelation, clarity, and unchanging truth.

Wisdom Unveiled

The profound wisdom unveiled in Letters are the Doorway, but Remembrance is the Light Beyond is that while language opens, it does not complete, and scripture instructs, but it does not exhaust. Divine will does not lie solely in phonemes, but in the heart that submits to what the verse unveils. The Quran is not merely eloquence but decree softened for the soul, its clarity unveiled to those who submit, and its guidance a mercy to those who receive. The wise-one understands that the true light, the Unspoken Knowing, lies beyond the literal forms, found in continuous, profound Remembrance (Dhikr)—a state of encompassing heart-presence that illuminates the path. Thus, the wise-one walks forward not by demanding signs, but by receiving what is spoken, dissolving into the light of revelation rather than debating its form, for only in this psychic submission is true clarity found.

Wise-Reflection

Reflect on your own engagement with sacred texts or spiritual teachings. Do you sometimes find yourself focusing on the literal meaning, or intellectual understanding, more than on cultivating the "heart-presence" (Dhikr) that these texts point towards? Consider the idea that "Divine will does not lie solely in phonemes—it lies in the heart that submits to what the verse unveils." How can you shift your approach to reading scripture from merely acquiring knowledge to seeking a deeper, psychic and spiritual state of Remembrance? What does it mean to "recite to be cleansed" or to "dissolve into the light it contains," moving beyond intellectual debate into direct experiential apprehension of the Unspoken Truth?

Part 2: His Command Does Not Require Sound, Yet All Creation Bears Witness

The wise-one realizes with profound clarity that Allah's Command (Amr) fundamentally does not require sound, human language, or audible articulation, yet paradoxically, all of creation bears eloquent witness to it. The entire universe functions by His silent, instantaneous decree: "Be! And it is!" This deep understanding allows the wise-one to perceive the Divine

THE LANTERN OF THE WISE

Will operating in absolute silence, beyond the confines of audible words. The subtle murmurs of existence, the rhythmic unfolding of cosmic laws, the quiet promptings of the heart, and the very fabric of reality itself all become living, dynamic manifestations of this unspoken Divine Command, perceived by the awakened and attuned soul. This is a profound psychic shift into a realm of direct, vibrational understanding.

Where Utterance Is Wordless and Testimony Is Universal

But if He were to speak to the wise-one without sound—
Then stones would whisper truth,
Creatures would become scripture,
And the command 'Be' would arise within him.
The wise-one knows
That not all truth arrives with sound.
That there is a kind of knowing
Not delivered by syllables,
But awakened by being.

❨If all the trees on earth were pens
And the ocean were ink,
Refilled by seven other oceans—
The Words of Allah would not be exhausted.❩ — Quran 31:27

The soul shudders at this.
That every tree, every tide, every drop
Would collapse under the weight of a single utterance.
This is not metaphor.
This is majesty without limit.
For creation and resurrection
Are but a single motion to Him—
As simple for the Almighty
As the whisper of "Be."

❝The creation and resurrection of you all
Is as simple as that of a single soul.❞ [240] *— Quran 31:28*

Every breath,
Every blink,
Every unfolding of matter—
Is but the echo of His wordless decree.

Moses sought light for his family
And found the beginning of prophethood.
He approached the fire—
But found no flame,
Only illumination.
He heard the voice from every direction,
With equal intensity—
And knew then
That the One who spoke
Was not bound to place or point.

❝Blessed is the One at the fire,
And whoever is around it!
Truly, I am Allah—the Almighty, All-Wise.❞ [241] *— Quran 27:8–9*

---

[240] This aligns with the verse from the Quran, which states that if the words of Allah were to be inscribed for creation, no entity would be capable of encompassing them, as they surpass all in grandeur and significance:

📖 ❨To Allah belongs whatever is in the heavens and the earth. Allah is truly the Self-Sufficient, Praiseworthy. (26) If all the trees on earth were pens and the ocean ˹were ink˺, refilled by seven other oceans, the Words of Allah would not be exhausted. Surely Allah is Almighty, All-Wise. (27) The creation and resurrection of you ˹all˺ is as simple ˹for Him˺ as that of a single soul. Surely Allah is All-Hearing, All-Seeing. (28)❩ [Quran 31:26-28]

[241] This narrative further enriches the account of the Quranic verse, depicting the moment when Moses first encountered Allah in Sinai. He was drawn to a distant light, prompting him to approach it, initially intending to have spark of fire to share with his family, unaware that it marked the beginning of his divine calling. He was assured that it was the divine calling him, as he perceived the voice resonating from all around with equal intensity, devoid of any specific direction. Thus, he understood that this call was all-encompassing, transcending limitations of space and direction:

📖 ❨And indeed, you ˹O Prophet˺ are receiving the Quran from the One ˹Who is˺ All-Wise, All-Knowing. (6) ˹Remember˺ when Moses said to his family, "I have spotted a fire. I will either bring you some directions[1] from there, or a burning torch so you may warm yourselves." (7)❩ [Quran 27:6-7]

[1]: lit., information. Moses and his family lost their way in the dark while they were travelling from Midian to Egypt.

What he saw
Was not a location.
What he heard
Was not vibration.
It was command without boundary.
Presence without dimension.

To Solomon, language opened even further.
He was taught the speech of birds,
The warnings of ants,
The whispers that do not reach human ears—
Yet still ring with purpose and praise.

❨O people!
We have been taught the language of birds…
And when they came upon a valley of ants,
An ant said:
'O ants! Retreat, lest Solomon and his armies crush you, unknowingly.'❩[242] —
Quran 27:16–18

The wise-one smiles
Not at their wit,
But at their worship.
For even the smallest creature
Knows its voice was gifted
By the One who hears all things.

Mary withdrew—
Veiled in obedience,

---

[242] This further reveals the grace within the sacred text, illustrating how the prophet Solomon ﷺ figure was granted the divine gift to understand the language of birds and other beings:

📖 ❨And David was succeeded by Solomon, who said, "O people! We have been taught the language of birds, and been given everything ˹we need˺. This is indeed a great privilege." (16) Solomon's forces of jinn, humans, and birds were rallied for him, perfectly organized. (17) And when they came across a valley of ants, an ant warned, "O ants! Go quickly into your homes so Solomon and his armies do not crush you, unknowingly. (18) So Solomon smiled in amusement at her words, and prayed, "My Lord! Inspire me to ˹always˺ be thankful for Your favours which You have blessed me and my parents with, and to do good deeds that please you. Admit me, by Your mercy, into ˹the company of˺ Your righteous servants." (19) ˹One day˺ he inspected the birds, and wondered, "Why is it that I cannot see the hoopoe? Or could he be absent? (20) I will surely subject him to a severe punishment, or ˹even˺ slaughter him, unless he brings me a compelling excuse." (21) It was not long before the bird came and said, "I have found out something you do not know. I have just come to you from Sheba with sure news. (22)❩ [Quran 27:16-22]

[358]

Seeking solitude not knowing
It was the beginning of Divine appointment.

⟨Mention in the Book the story of Mary—
When she withdrew from her family to a place in the east.⟩ — Quran 19:16

Gabriel came—
Not as light, but in human form.
She sought refuge,
And he responded with decree:
A pure son, by command not cause.

⟨We sent her Our angel, perfectly formed.
She said: 'I seek refuge…'
He said: 'I'm a messenger—sent to bless you with a pure son.'⟩ — Quran 19:17–
19

She questioned—not with denial,
But with trembling humility.
He answered:
It is easy for Allah.
It is already decreed.

⟨'How can I have a son…?'
'It is a matter already decreed.' ⟩— Quran 19:20–21

She conceived and retreated again—
Not toward wonder,
But through pain.

⟨She conceived him
And withdrew to a remote place.⟩ — Quran 19:22

Labor drove her to a palm tree—
No shelter but Divine nearness.
She cried in despair,
But a voice comforted her
With stream, fruit, and command.

❪*Do not grieve.*
Your Lord has provided a stream…
Shake the tree for ripe dates.' ❫— *Quran 19:24–25*

And when questioned—
No defense, no argument.
Just silence vowed for the Most Compassionate.

❪*I have vowed silence…*
I am not speaking today.'[243] — *Quran 19:26*

Her silence was not retreat—
It was realization.
Not confusion—
But clarity that transcends language.

So the wise-one walks forward—
Not asking for sound,
But listening for command.
He does not seek audible clarity—
He seeks soul comprehension.
He does not limit truth to language—
He follows truth wherever creation speaks it.
He hears trees that glorify.
He understands winds that obey.

---

[243] This journey leads to the tale of Mary. Upon the arrival of her son (Jesus ﷺ), she found herself in turmoil; yet, she was urged to cast aside her worries and embrace the promise of hope and joy for both herself and her newborn:

📖 ❪And mention in the Book ʿO Prophet, the story ofˀ Mary when she withdrew from her family to a place in the east, (16) screening herself off from them. Then We sent to her Our angel, ʿGabriel,ˀ appearing before her as a man, perfectly formed. (17) She appealed, "I truly seek refuge in the Most Compassionate from you! ʿSo leave me aloneˀ if you are God-fearing." (18) He responded, "I am only a messenger from your Lord, ʿsentˀ to bless you with a pure son." (19) She wondered, "How can I have a son when no man has ever touched me, nor am I unchaste?" (20) He replied, "So will it be! Your Lord says, 'It is easy for Me. And so will We make him a sign for humanity and a mercy from Us.' It is a matter ʿalreadyˀ decreed." (21) So she conceived him and withdrew with him to a remote place. (22) Then the pains of labour drove her to the trunk of a palm tree. She cried, "Alas! I wish I had died before this, and was a thing long forgotten!" (23) So a voice[1] reassured her from below her, "Do not grieve! Your Lord has provided a stream at your feet. (24) And shake the trunk of this palm tree towards you, it will drop fresh, ripe dates upon you. (25) So eat and drink, and put your heart at ease. But if you see any of the people, say, 'I have vowed silence[2] to the Most Compassionate, so I am not talking to anyone today.'" (26)❫ [Quran 19:16-26]

[1]: This was the voice of baby Jesus. Some say it was Gabriel.

[2]: lit., fast ʿfrom speechˀ. Linguistically, ṣawm means to abstain from something, such as food, speaking, and playing.

He receives the decree
Not as grammar—
But as gravitation.

For only He commands without sound.
Only He speaks through what He animates.
Only He remains the source
Of motion, meaning, and majestic presence.

Wisdom Unveiled

The profound wisdom unveiled in His Command Does Not Require Sound, Yet All Creation Bears Witness is that not all truth arrives with sound, and there is a kind of knowing not delivered by syllables, but awakened by Being. The wise-one learns that Allah's Command (Amr) is a wordless decree, a silent "Be!" that orchestrates all existence. This means that creation and resurrection are but a single, effortless motion for Him. This deep psychic understanding allows the wise-one to perceive the Divine Will in the silent functioning of the cosmos, the subtle promptings of the heart, and the wordless testimony of every creature. Thus, the wise-one walks forward not asking for sound, but listening for Command, receiving Divine decree not as grammar, but as gravitation, knowing that only He speaks through what He animates, guiding beyond audible clarity into profound soul comprehension.

Wise-Reflection

Reflect on moments in your life when significant truths or insights came to you not through explicit words, but through intuition, a sense of inner knowing, or the subtle unfolding of circumstances. Do you typically seek Divine guidance primarily through spoken or written words? How can you cultivate a deeper awareness of the "silent, instantaneous command" of the Divine that orchestrates all of existence, as exemplified by Moses, Solomon, and Mary? What does it mean to listen for Command rather than asking for sound, and to seek "soul comprehension" rather than mere "audible clarity"? How might this profound psychic shift allow you to perceive Divine Will in the "subtle murmurs of existence" and the "rhythmic unfolding of cosmic laws," leading you to a deeper Divine intimacy?

Part 3: Beyond Speech Lies Surrender; Beyond Letters, the Presence
of the Divine

The ultimate, liberating truth is that beyond all speech lies profound
Surrender (Taslim), and beyond the confining boundaries of all letters and
conceptual frameworks lies the direct, unveiled Presence of the Divine. In
this pinnacle state, words cease to be the primary medium of
understanding; instead, being itself becomes the medium. The wise-one's
spiritual journey culminates in a profound state where knowledge is no
longer intellectually transmitted or conceptually articulated, but is directly
and existentially experienced through total, unreserved surrender of self to
the Divine. It is here that the heart finds its ultimate rest and ultimate
knowing, dwelling in the sacred silence of pure Presence, echoing the
Prophet's non-wavering heart in the direct vision of Divine signs. This is
the ultimate psychic liberation.

Where Utterance Leads to Awe and Being Becomes the Medium

Sentences introduce the path, but beyond them lies the essence.
Thoughts begin in letters.
Ideas bloom from language.
But His pure remembrance—
Is beyond the reach of letters altogether.

David was given hymns—
But the echo did not come from him alone.
Mountains glorified.
Birds joined in chorus.
And righteousness flowed not through mastery,
But through Divine command.

❨We granted David a privilege:
"O mountains, echo his hymns! And the birds as well."
We instructed: "Work righteousness…
Indeed, I am All-Seeing of what you do.❩ — Quran 34:10–11

Solomon too received command—
Not in verses to memorize,
But in winds, metals, and jinn.

The world itself bent to the decree,
Not through words,
But through surrender to the One who speaks without sound.

⟨*We subjected the wind to Solomon…*
And the jinn by His Lord's will.
Whoever deviated tasted the torment of the blaze⟩[244] — *Quran 34:12–13*

The Prophet 🌿 *was told:*
Do not rush.
Do not race the verses.
Allah will teach,
Preserve,
And reveal meaning
In due time.

⟨*Do not rush your tongue trying to memorize…*
It is upon Us to recite,
And then to make it clear to you.⟩[245] — *Quran 75:16–19*

Remembrance is not grasped—
It is received.
And when it is received,
It descends with weight.

⟨*We will soon send upon you a weighty revelation.*⟩ — *Quran 73:5*

This is why the night holds power—
Not because the tongue is sharp,

---

[244] This is derived from the Quran verses of:

📖 ⟨Indeed, We granted David a ˹great˺ privilege from Us, ˹commanding:˺ "O mountains! Echo his hymns! And the birds as well." We made iron mouldable for him, (10) instructing: "Make full-length armour, ˹perfectly˺ balancing the links. And work righteousness ˹O family of David!˺. Indeed, I am All-Seeing of what you do." (11) And to Solomon ˹We subjected˺ the wind: its morning stride was a month's journey and so was its evening stride. And We caused a stream of molten copper to flow for him, and ˹We subjected˺ some of the jinn to work under him by his Lord's Will. And whoever of them deviated from Our command, We made them taste the torment of the blaze. (12)⟩ [Quran 34:10-13]

[245] This is derived from the Quran verses of:

📖 ⟨Do not rush your tongue trying to memorize ˹a revelation of˺ the Quran. (16) It is certainly upon Us to ˹make you˺ memorize and recite it. (17) So once We have recited a revelation ˹through Gabriel˺, follow its recitation ˹closely˺. (18) Then it is surely upon Us to make it clear ˹to you˺. (19)⟩ [Quran 75:16-19]

But because the soul is still.
The recitation is measured,
Not rapid.
Because the goal is not knowledge alone—
It is nearness.

❪Stand all night except a little…
Recite the Quran properly in a measured way.
Worship in the night is more impactful
And suitable for recitation.❫[246] — Quran 73:1–6

So the wise-one knows:
Letters may begin the journey—
But only presence completes it.
Syntax may guide the steps—
But only surrender unveils the destination.

So the wise-one walks forward—
Not obsessed with articulation,
But attuned to revelation.
He recites not to impress—
But to be impressed upon.
He does not chase meaning—
He bows to it.

For only He sends revelation with weight.
Only He preserves truth beyond tongues.
Only He remains the source
Of remembrance, essence, and light that no letter can hold.

Wisdom Unveiled

The profound wisdom unveiled in Beyond Speech Lies Surrender; Beyond Letters, the Presence of the Divine is that words are the lanterns at the

---

[246] This is derived from the Quran verses of:

📖 ❪O you wrapped ˹in your clothes˺! (1) Stand all night ˹in prayer˺ except a little— (2) ˹pray˺ half the night, or a little less, (3) or a little more—and recite the Quran ˹properly˺ in a measured way. (4) ˹For˺ We will soon send upon you a weighty revelation. (5) Indeed, worship in the night is more impactful and suitable for recitation. (6) For during the day you are over-occupied ˹with worldly duties˺. (7) ˹Always˺ remember the Name of your Lord, and devote yourself to Him wholeheartedly. (8)❫ [Quran 73:1-8]

beginning of the path; they are necessary—for a time. But the soul must someday walk beyond their flickering light, into a dawn where no language is needed, because Presence itself floods every atom of existence. The wise-one does not despise words; they thank them for leading them to the edge—and then, in sacred silence, they leap. This signifies that letters may begin the journey, but only Presence completes it, and syntax may guide the steps, but only surrender unveils the destination. The culmination is a state where knowledge is no longer transmitted but directly experienced through total surrender of self to the Divine, leading to the heart's ultimate rest and knowing in the silence of pure Presence, a final psychic transformation.

Wise-Reflection

Reflect on your own spiritual journey. Do you find yourself primarily seeking knowledge through words and concepts, or are you increasingly drawn to direct experience and a deeper state of Presence? Consider the idea that "words are the lanterns at the beginning of the path... but the soul must someday walk beyond their flickering light." What specific practices or shifts in perspective can help you cultivate a state where "being becomes the medium" of your knowledge of the Divine? How can you consciously practice profound Surrender (Taslim) in your daily life, allowing your heart to find its "ultimate rest and ultimate knowing" in the silence of pure Divine Presence, echoing the Prophet's non-wavering heart in the direct vision of Divine signs, and experiencing the ultimate psychic liberation?

Conclusion: In the Knowing the Unspoken

ECHOES OF REALIZATION

There is a profound silence deeper than the mere absence of audible sound. It is the sacred silence where the wise-one's soul ceases entirely to name, to grasp, to define—and begins simply to behold the ineffable. The wise-one who has truly attained "The Knowing the Unspoken" walks through a world alive with the continuous, subtle murmurs of the Divine—not articulated in human syllables, but revealed in the gentle way light bends around every form, in the profound hush between breaths, and in the inexplicable ache of longing that cannot be expressed in words, only offered in surrender.

Here, the contingent self completely falls away. The mind, having reached its limits, bows in utter submission. The tongue, having articulated all it can, rests in profound stillness. And what remains is not intellectual knowledge about the Real, but the trembling, living, all-encompassing experience of the Real itself. To truly know the Unspoken is to cease all need for speaking. It is to remember the One who has, in truth, never ceased speaking in the language beyond all languages—the primal, eternal language that the soul has always intuitively understood.

THE SEEKER'S ASCENT: KNOWING THE UNSPOKEN

The wise-one, having traversed this luminous pathway to Divine Connection, now understands that the greatest "knowing" to be surrendered is the illusion of separation itself. It is the knowing that posits a distinct self apart from its Creator, a world independent of its Sustainer, or a truth that can be confined within finite concepts.

For true proximity to emerge, the soul must surrender the knowing of its own self-sufficiency, its intellectual prowess as an ultimate arbiter, its attachment to rewards, and its reliance on anything other than the Absolute. It must surrender the knowing of limits that it once imposed upon the Divine.

In this ultimate Ascent, the wise-one realizes that true proximity is not a distance to be closed, but a veil of perception to be lifted. The Unspoken Knowing is the realization that the Divine was never truly distant, never separate, never confined to a spoken word or a defined concept. It was always and intimately Present, encompassing all, awaiting the purification and surrender of the wise-one's heart to be fully perceived. This is the profound culmination of spiritual and psychic enlightenment: to live in the unbroken, silent knowledge of the Divine's eternal, all-encompassing Presence.

"As the pathway to divine connection unfolds, what 'knowing' of separation must your soul surrender for true proximity to emerge?"

CONCLUSION FOR PART II: THE PATHWAY TO DIVINE CONNECTION

The completing the pathway...

ECHO WITHIN THE HEART... (THE COMPLETION OF THE PATHWAY)

The Manifestation of Divine Connection does not conclude; rather, it deepens, like rivers merging, unseen, beneath the ocean's vast surface. The wise-one, having traversed the veils of perception and the profound stations of surrender, now stands at the threshold of an even more luminous, more humbling realization: Divine connection is not a distant station to be attained, but an inherent state of being, to be lived in every breath. Each reflection meticulously laid along this pathway has not served merely as a signpost; it has wrought a profound transformation—a meticulous carving away of self-imposed illusions, a burning away of false attachments, and a sacred unveiling of the timeless longing intrinsically woven into the soul's very essence.

THRESHOLD OF AWE

The Unveiling of Origin

As the veils gently lift upon this Manifestation of Divine Connection, the wise-one transitions from observation to profound immersion. The contemplations engaged within this chapter—of the secret within being, of the secluded entrance through humility, of the very stand in Presence of the Creator in unity, of the awakening of heart and mind to divine perception, and of knowing the unspoken beyond all frameworks—do not merely add to one's store of information. Rather, they fundamentally reshape the very vessel that is capable of receiving divine wisdom and enduring its transformative power.

Pillars of Realization

The Secret as Infinite Presence:

The heart no longer seeks the Creator as a distant, external goal; it awakens to the One who was never absent, a Presence closer than one's own breath, yet vaster than the most expansive thought can ever encompass. This realization transcends mere intellectual understanding, becoming an experiential certainty.

The Secluded Entrance as Profound Surrender:

Humility, profound surrender, and enlightened detachment have unveiled themselves not as losses or renunciations, but as the very gates through which the wise-one steps into an eternal richness. By dissolving the fragmented self, the discerning soul has found the profound Secret buried in the heart of silence.

Standing in Presence as Unifying Awe:

The Creator has revealed Himself in both His manifest and unmanifest aspects: immanent within the shimmering forms of existence, yet transcendent beyond every name, every form, and every finite conception. This duality is no longer a paradox but a testament to His boundless Reality.

Awakening as Purified Perception:

The consciousness expands to perceive the Divine in every facet of existence, in every fleeting moment, and in every profound silence. This profound inner sight, awakened through the journey, is received with utmost humility and reverence, unveiling truths that were previously veiled by ordinary perception.

Knowing the Unspoken as Ultimate Proximity:

This arduous pathway has not merely led to a state of connection; it has intrinsically fortified the very essence of the soul. It has cloaked the wise-one in the raiment of wisdom and the mantle of humility, thereby armoring the heart for the sacred fire that refines and purifies, rather than consumes or destroys.

The Seeker Reflects

"I have followed the guiding clues, diligently deciphered the sacred blueprint, and sought profound significance in the manifest forms. Yet, I now discern that these indications do not equate to the Beloved Itself. What I once perceived as understanding was merely a transient reflection. What I conceived as seeking was, in essence, a perpetuation of separation. Faith guided my initial steps, and understanding illuminated my way— but I now find myself at a threshold where neither can fully traverse. Only profound yielding persists. Only an encompassing quietude. Only an unceasing yearning. And in this yearning, I am drawn not merely toward, but deep into—where closeness erases all

perceived distance, and every aspiration I ever held is no longer a pursuit, but a sacred reality discovered within."

INVITATION TO THE NEXT MANIFESTATION

With this profound realization of divine connection, the sacred path now unfolds to its next profound station: The Crucible of Inner Transformation. If this Manifestation revealed the intricate pathways to divine proximity, the next invites the soul to be truly forged—to enter the fire that purifies, to embrace the test that elevates. The wise-one, having tasted the sweetness of connection, must now prepare for the proving of that bond, ascending towards an even deeper form of union through purification.

Call to Action

"The sacred pathway has been illuminated; will you now take the next unwavering step into its proving?"

"Before the next station unfolds, let the heart quiet itself. In the profound silence, discern the echo of what has been revealed, and prepare for the deeper current."

PART III: THE CRUCIBLE OF INNER TRANSFORMATION

❖❖❖

﴿ أَحَسِبَ ٱلنَّاسُ أَن يُتْرَكُوٓاْ أَن يَقُولُوٓاْ ءَامَنَّا وَهُمْ لَا يُفْتَنُونَ (٢) وَلَقَدْ فَتَنَّا ٱلَّذِينَ مِن قَبْلِهِمْ فَلَيَعْلَمَنَّ ٱللَّهُ ٱلَّذِينَ صَدَقُواْ وَلَيَعْلَمَنَّ ٱلْكَٰذِبِينَ (٣) ﴾

📖 ❰Do people think once they say, "We believe," that they will be left without being put to the test? (2) We certainly tested those before them. And ʿin this wayʾ Allah will clearly distinguish between those who are truthful and those who are liars. (3)❱ [Quran 2:214]

"Gold is purified through fire, the soul through trials." – Jalaluddin Rumi

❖❖❖

In the boundless odyssey of the soul, having traversed the tranquil pathways to divine connection, the discerning wise-one now stands at a profound new threshold: The Crucible of Inner Transformation. This part unveils not merely a series of challenges, but a sacred, refining fire— a divine process designed to purify the spirit, deepen certitude, and forge an unshakeable bond with the Creator.

This station invites the seeker to embrace trials not as obstacles, but as instruments of unveiling. Here, every experience, whether of ease or hardship, becomes a mirror reflecting the deeper realities of existence and the absolute sovereignty of the Divine. It meticulously guides the wise-one through reflections that reveal the timeless nature of existence, the true purpose of trials, and the profound companionship that sustains the heart amidst all flux.

Each reflection within this profound section acts like a spiritual alchemist, transmuting the base metal of human perception into the pure gold of divine insight. From discerning In the Knowing of Eternity, recognizing the transient nature of perceived time, to articulating an Oath to Surpass Trials, committing to their transformative power; from moving Beyond Knowing the Creator Names, recognizing the limits of conceptual understanding in the face of direct experience; to seeking refuge In the Creator Companionship, realizing His unwavering presence in every moment of challenge; and culminating in The Code of the Righteous Heart, solidifying the inner purity and steadfastness required to navigate this refining fire.

At its core, this Manifestation beckons the discerning soul to step courageously into the transformative flames. It explores profound shifts in perspective: from viewing challenges as burdens to embracing them as blessings, from clinging to worldly causality to seeing the direct Hand of Al-Haqq (The Truth), and from seeking external validation to finding ultimate solace in Divine proximity. It challenges the wise-one to relinquish egoic resistance, to deepen trust, and to cultivate an inner fortress of contentment and acceptance.

This Crucible is not a punitive ordeal, but a benevolent forging. It is an invitation to perceive the divine wisdom in every decree, to discern the Creator's love in every trial, and to apprehend the true strength born of surrender. To walk this path is to initiate the dissolution of the resistant self, transcending the veils of conventional understanding, and to stand, refined, in the brilliance of divine grace—a profound realization where the soul apprehends its true nature, ready to emerge luminous from the fire. The reflections presented within are not mere sequential steps but dynamic manifestations of divine truths that actively reshape the wise-one's inner journey into an eternal connection. Each successive reflection deepens the awareness of the Divine and meticulously prepares the discerning soul for the transformative passages that lie ahead.

11TH REFLECTION: IN THE KNOWING OF ETERNITY

(Understanding Eternity)

THE GATEWAY VERSES & PROPHETIC SUPPLICATION

In the sacred words of Allah, a profound reminder to all who reflect upon His eternal dominion and transcendent Attributes:

📖 ❨*Whatever is in the heavens and the earth glorifies Allah, for He is the Almighty, All-Wise. (1) To Him belongs the kingdom of the heavens and the earth. He gives life and causes death. And He is Most Capable of everything. (2) He is the First and the Last, the Most High and Most Near,247 and He has 'perfect' knowledge of all things. (3)*❩ *[Quran 57:1-3]*

Also, it was narrated that the Messenger of Allah, Muhammad ﷺ, when it was the last part of the night, would raise his voice and say:

🌐 *"O Allah, Lord of the seven heavens and Lord of the Mighty Throne, God of all things and Lord of all things, Revealer of the Torah, the Gospel, and the Criterion, Cleaver of the seed and the date stone, I seek refuge in You from the evil of everything of which You hold the forelock. O Allah, You are the First before whom there is nothing, and You are the Last after whom there is nothing, and You are the Manifest, and there is nothing above You, and You are the Hidden, and there is nothing beneath You. Pay off our debt and enrich us from poverty." – [Sahih Muslim]*

ILLUMINATION'S DAWN

There comes a profound moment when the very rhythms of temporal existence—the ceaseless cycles of night and day, the relentless passing of years and ages—begin to thin and flicker, gracefully revealing a deeper reality not born of movement, but of immutable stillness. In that sacred unveiling, the wise-one perceives a foundational truth: Eternity is not merely an extension of time, nor a fleeting crown awarded at the end of days. It is, rather, the inherent, undying Attribute of the One who was before all beginnings (Al-Awwal) and shall remain after all endings vanish into silence (Al-Akhir).

---

247 Another possible translation: "the Manifest 'through His signs' and the Hidden 'from His creation'."

The true knowing of eternity is not intellectual, grasped through intricate thought or captured by the confines of human speech. It is, instead, profoundly whispered into the discerning soul by a Divine Grace older than creation itself, a primordial remembrance deeply placed within the essence of being before memory ever arose. Here, the wise-one is not called to measure endless duration, but to witness the timeless. Not to fully comprehend the infinite, but to consent to being drawn into its boundless vastness. Let us now walk reverently into this sublime unveiling, where the wise-one's soul begins to intimately touch that which has no edge—and what no earthly tongue can truly tell.

THE UNFOLDING OF INSIGHTS

This section explores the wise-one's journey from temporal understanding to the profound, experiential embrace of Eternity as a Divine Attribute, thereby transforming their perception of reality and their place within it.

Contemplation: The Veil of Time

The wise-one initially recognizes the veil of time as the primary illusion obscuring the profound perception of Eternity. Human existence is inherently structured by time—past, present, future—leading to a linear perception of reality. This temporal framework, while absolutely necessary for worldly life, paradoxically limits the soul's innate ability to apprehend the timelessness and boundlessness of the Creator. This contemplation helps the wise-one become acutely aware of how the mind is meticulously bound by chronology, and how this very binding subtly prevents direct, unmediated experience of the Ever-Present Now of the Divine. Overcoming this pervasive veil is the foundational first step towards a true, experiential understanding of Eternity and a profound psychic shift.

Reflect: From the boundless essence of the Divine arises the ordered succession of night and day. And from this very duality, a subtle covering descends, veiling yet intimating the enigmas of perception and intellect, the profundities of the heart, and the veiled truths.

The Tapestry Beneath Time: From Sign to Surrender

Eternity does not rush.
It hails the Creator silently—
woven not in human clocks or counting,

but in the hush between sunrise and dusk.
The cosmos is a sermon.
Constellations are its script.
The sun rises not only to illuminate earth,
but to awaken hearts to rhythm.
The moon does not merely decorate the sky,
it whispers of cycles designed by Mercy.

❲*Blessed is the One Who placed constellations in the heavens,*
a radiant lamp, and a luminous moon...
signs for those who seek mindfulness and gratitude.❳[248]— *Quran 25:61–62*

Yet night and day are not simply markers of hours—
they are veils.
Extended across thought and emotion,
covering secrets for the heedless,
but unfolding truths for those who remember.

He made the night dark,
so the soul could see inward.
He made the day bright,
so the seeker might walk outward—
both as invitations,
both as reminders of the One
who exists outside their sequence.

❲*We made the sign of night devoid of light,*
and the sign of day brilliantly radiant,
so you may seek His bounty,
and count the passing of years.❳[249]— *Quran 17:12*

---

[248] This is in agreement with the Quran verse:

📖 ❲Blessed is the One Who has placed constellations in the sky, as well as a ʿradiantʾ lamp1 and a luminous moon. (61) And He is the One Who causes the day and the night to alternate, ʿas a signʾ for whoever desires to be mindful or to be grateful. (62)❳ [Quran 25:61-62]

[249] This is in agreement with the Quran verse:

📖 ❲We made the day and night as two signs. So We made the sign of the night devoid of light, and We made the sign of the day ʿperfectlyʾ bright, so that you may seek the bounty of your Lord and know the number of years and calculation ʿof timeʾ. And We have explained everything in detail. (12)❳ (Quran 17:12)

Time is not the ultimate measure.
It is a woven tapestry,
stitched by Divine decree.
Beneath its strands lies eternity—
unseen,
immeasurable,
yet nearer than breath to those who know how to listen.

The wise-one understands:
The rising sun is not just daybreak—
it is the Creator saying "Begin."
The falling dusk is not mere closure—
it is the Creator whispering "Reflect."
Every hour is a parable.
Every season a verse.

And beyond counting lies only surrender.
For those who read time not with eyes,
but with remembrance,
see not just the movement of the stars—
but the mercy hidden in their motion.

And in surrender, time unravels.
The soul no longer fears the passing hours,
for it has glimpsed the One beyond them.
It walks through the day seeking bounty,
and kneels in the night hearing eternity call.
Not with sound, not with voice,
but with a rhythm older than creation.

Yet night and day, they form a veil,
Extended over vision, thoughts assail.
A covering of secrets, deep and wide,
For heedless hearts, where truths may hide.
But for the chosen, seeking true,

These very motions, unveil His decree.
For He has perfect knowledge of all things.[250]

For time itself, a fabric spun,
By His silent, ever-present Amr, begun.
And beneath its intricate weave, unseen, untold,
Eternity's embrace, ancient and bold.
Reaching beyond all human count,
Beyond what mortal minds surmount.
Where thought dissolves, and logic fails,
Surrender lifts the final veils.
Revealing truth beyond all sight,
In the Ever-Present Now's pure light.

So the wise-one walks forward—
Not bound by clock's swift flight,
But dwelling in Eternal Light.
He counts not days, nor years gone past,
But in the Timeless Now, stands fast.
He does not chase what time can tell,
But seeks the Ever-Present well.

For only He is First and Last in grace.
Only He holds all time and space.
Only He remains the source
Of Presence, truth, and boundless force.

Wisdom Unveiled

The profound wisdom unveiled in The Veil of Time is that while the ordered succession of night and day and the celestial bodies are blessed signs from the Creator, they also form a tapestry of time that, for most, acts as a veil. This veil, woven by Divine command, inherently limits the human mind to a linear perception, obscuring the Ever-Present Now of the Divine. The wise-one learns that true Eternity is not an extension of time, but an unseen, ever-present reality lying beneath temporal

---

[250] This is in agreement with the Quran verse of:

⟨He is the First and the Last, the Most High and Most Near,1 and He has ˹perfect˺ knowledge of all things. (3)⟩ [Quran 57:3]

phenomena. Recognizing how our minds are bound by chronology is the critical first step in piercing this veil, allowing the soul to move beyond counting and knowing into a state where surrender unveils the Reality beyond all veils, leading to a foundational psychic shift in perception and the ability to dwell in Eternal Light.

Wise-Reflection

As the veil of time thins, the wise-one experiences the profound unveiling of Eternity, which is not an unending stretch of moments but a state entirely beyond sequential time. This unveiling reveals Eternity as a dimension of Divine Reality where all moments coalesce into a singular, perpetual Present. It is the realization that the past is not truly gone, and the future is not yet to come, but both exist in the Divine's timeless knowledge. This profoundly alters the wise-one's consciousness, allowing for a glimpse of the Creator's simultaneous presence in all times, a powerful form of psychic expansion.

Eternity is revealed as an attribute of Divine constancy. Unlike the fleeting and ever-changing nature of worldly existence, Eternity is an unbroken continuum. It embodies the Creator's timelessness and serves as a reflection of Divine omniscience and omnipresence.

Understand, O seeker: To perceive the timeless reality is to witness an attribute of the Everlasting One.

Eternity: The Presence Beyond Time

When the soul perceives eternity,
It glimpses an attribute of the Everlasting—
For the eternal belongs only to Him.
Time dissolves before His presence,
Where no measure can define,
Where no sentence can contain.

Then the veil of life is lifted,
This existence unravels,
Revealing the end of the ephemeral,
The dawn of eternity.
What was concealed now stands exposed,

And what was unknown is no longer distant—
For the new end has come.

The Trumpet will sound,
And all will fall,
Except those whom He wills to remain.
It will sound again,
And they will rise,
Looking on in anticipation.
The earth will shine with His light,
The record of deeds will be laid open,
And every soul will witness truth unveiled.

Justice will be absolute,
No one will be wronged,
For all will receive their due.
Those who turned away from remembrance
Will be driven in waves,
Toward the gates of Hell,
Where regret will replace denial.
Messengers had spoken,
Truth had been revealed,
Yet they refused to listen.
Now there is no return,
Only a home of despair
For the arrogant.

But those mindful of their Lord
Will walk toward the gates of Paradise,
Where peace will greet them,
And fulfillment will be theirs to inherit.
They will proclaim:
Praise be to Allah, Who has made us heirs to eternity!
For the righteous dwell in a land without end,
Where the reward is limitless,
And joy unceasing.

The angels will encircle the Throne,
Glorifying the praises of their Lord,

As the final justice is passed.
And at last, the ultimate truth will be spoken:
❴Praise be to Allah—Lord of all worlds.❵²⁵¹

For eternity is not counted,
But known in presence.
And presence is not in words,
But in the soul's awakening
To the truth beyond time.

So the wise-one walks forward—
Not measuring time's slow pace,
But merging with His timeless grace.
He seeks not what tomorrow brings,
But in the Eternal Now, his spirit sings.
He does not strive to comprehend the span,
But bows to the Ever-Present plan.

For only He is timeless, ever true.
Only He holds all and sees through.
Only He remains the source
Of Presence, beyond time's force.

---

²⁵¹ This is in agreement with the Quran verse telling the end story of human life toward the eternity of the Creator's presence:

❴The Trumpet will be blown and all those in the heavens and all those on the earth will fall dead, except those Allah wills ˹to spare˺. Then it will be blown again and they will rise up at once, looking on ˹in anticipation˺. (68) The earth will shine with the light of its Lord, the record ˹of deeds˺ will be laid ˹open˺, the prophets and the witnesses will be brought forward—and judgment will be passed on all with fairness. None will be wronged. (69) Every soul will be paid in full for its deeds, for Allah knows best what they have done. (70) Those who disbelieved will be driven to Hell in ˹successive˺ groups. When they arrive there, its gates will be opened and its keepers will ask them: "Did messengers not come to you from among yourselves, reciting to you the revelations of your Lord and warning you of the coming of this Day of yours?" The disbelievers will cry, "Yes ˹indeed˺! But the decree of torment has come to pass against the disbelievers." (71) It will be said to them, "Enter the gates of Hell, to stay there forever." What an evil home for the arrogant! (72) And those who were mindful of their Lord will be led to Paradise in ˹successive˺ groups. When they arrive at its ˹already˺ open gates, its keepers will say, "Peace be upon you! You have done well, so come in, to stay forever." (73) The righteous will say, "Praise be to Allah Who has fulfilled His promise to us, and made us inherit the ˹everlasting˺ land1 to settle in Paradise wherever we please." How excellent is the reward of those who work ˹righteousness˺! (74) You will see the angels all around the Throne, glorifying the praises of their Lord, for judgment will have been passed on all with fairness. And it will be said, "Praise be to Allah—Lord of all worlds!" (75)❵ (Quran 39:68-75)

Wisdom Unveiled

The profound wisdom unveiled in Beyond Time: The Unveiling of Eternity is that Eternity is not an unending stretch of sequential moments, but a Divine Reality where all times coalesce into a singular, perpetual Present. This unveiling allows the wise-one to realize that past and future are held within the Divine's timeless knowledge, profoundly altering consciousness and enabling a glimpse of the Creator's simultaneous presence in all times—a powerful psychic expansion. This state reveals Eternity as an attribute of Divine constancy, an unbroken continuum that reflects His omniscience and omnipresence, culminating in the ultimate justice and recompense where all are heirs to the Divine's boundless Presence.

Wise-Reflection

Reflect on how your understanding of past and future often shapes your emotions and decisions. How might the realization that all moments coalesce into a "singular, perpetual Present" within the Divine's timeless knowledge alter your approach to regret or anticipation? Consider the concept of the Day of Judgment as a moment when all truth is unveiled and Eternity is fully experienced. How does contemplating this ultimate unveiling impact your perception of justice and your actions in the present? What does it mean for your daily life to "merge with His timeless grace" and seek the Ever-Present rather than being bound by time's measure, fostering a deeper psychic connection?

Contemplation: Unveiling Eternity: The Divine Attribute

Eternity is not merely a concept for the wise-one, but a direct unveiling of a Divine Attribute: Al-Awwal (The First) and Al-Akhir (The Last). The Quranic verses and the Prophetic supplication explicitly state these attributes, emphasizing that Allah exists without beginning or end. This contemplation elevates the understanding from a philosophical notion to a direct recognition of Allah's fundamental nature. The wise-one experiences awe and wonder, realizing that their own existence, finite as it is, is encompassed by an infinite, ever-present Reality, anchoring their spiritual awareness in the immutable nature of the Divine. This leads to a profound psychic expansion as the soul perceives a timeless dimension.

The wise-one is guided to reflect on Eternity not as an abstract or temporal concept but as a direct manifestation of the Creator's infinite nature. In this process, the temporal veils of night and day—symbols of human limitations and cyclical existence—are removed to reveal the unbroken, perpetual reality of Eternity. This unveiling is an act of Divine grace, reserved for those chosen to witness the Creator's majesty.

Contemplate: The timeless reality is manifest, yet no finite expression can encompass its entirety. Eternity remains a singular attribute of the Divine Originator alone.

Eternity Beyond Words

Eternity unfolds before the spirit,
Yet words cannot contain its essence.
Time dissolves into the Infinite,
Where the eternal belongs only to Him.
No sentence holds permanence,
No thought grasps the unending.
For He is beyond the reach of language,
Beyond all that can be named.
The wise-one does not seek to define Him,
But to surrender before the weight
Of what cannot fade,
What cannot cease—
What is, and always will be.

Eternity hails the Creator,
So He has made from it the hailing
Of the night and the day.
He casts time as a veil
Upon vision and thought,
Upon hearts and secrets,
So that it may conceal and reveal
As He wills.

Time is but a veil for those who do not perceive,
Stretching across the ages as an endless expanse.
For the disbelievers, the Day of Judgment will stretch
Fifty thousand years in length,

A distance that seems impossible.
Yet to Him, it is inevitable,
To the believer, it is near.[252]
They demand hastening,
As if eternity bends to their impatience,
Forgetting that a day with the Creator
Is like a thousand years by their counting.
For time itself is His creation,
And He is beyond its measure.[253]

Thus, the wise-one lets go of counting,
Lets go of measuring,
And stands in surrender,
Not seeking to define eternity,
But to dwell in it—
In the light that never dims,
In the presence that never fades.

So the wise-one walks forward—
Not bound by concepts, vague and small,
But encompassed by the Timeless All.
He yearns not for future's far-off shore,
But rests in Presence, forevermore.
He does not strive to name the flow,
But lets Eternity in spirit grow.

For only He is First and Last, unbound.
Only in Him, true peace is found.

---

[252] This is in agreement with the Quran verse:

📖 ⟨from Allah, Lord of pathways of ʿheavenlyʾ ascent, (3) ʿthrough whichʾ the angels and the ʿholyʾ spirit [The holy spirit is the angel Gabriel.] will ascend to Him on a Day fifty thousand years in length. (4) So endure ʿthis denial, O Prophet,ʾ with beautiful patience. (5) They truly see this ʿDayʾ as impossible, (6) but We see it as inevitable. (7)⟩ [Quran 70: 3-7]

[253] This is in agreement with the Quran verse:

📖 ⟨As for those bound for misery, they will be in the Fire, where they will be sighing and gasping, (106) staying there forever, as long as the heavens and the earth will endure, except what your Lord wills.1 Surely your Lord does what He intends. (107) And as for those destined to joy, they will be in Paradise, staying there forever, as long as the heavens and the earth will endure, except what your Lord wills1—a ʿgenerousʾ giving, without end. (108)⟩ [Quran 11:106 – 108]

Only He remains the source
Of Timelessness, Presence, and boundless force.

Wisdom Unveiled

The profound wisdom unveiled in Unveiling Eternity: The Divine Attribute is that Eternity is not an abstract concept but a direct manifestation of Allah's fundamental nature as Al-Awwal and Al-Akhir. The wise-one recognizes that human language and thought cannot contain this Divine essence, leading to a surrender before the immutable reality of what is and always will be. This contemplation reveals that while time serves as a veil, it is also a sign, and ultimately, a creation that Allah transcends. By letting go of measuring and defining, the wise-one shifts from conceptual understanding to dwelling directly within Eternity, experiencing a deep psychic expansion as their existence is anchored in the infinite, ever-present Reality of the Divine.

Wise-Reflection

Reflect on how much of your life is shaped by the linear progression of time—planning for the future, recalling the past. How might contemplating Allah as Al-Awwal (The First) and Al-Akhir (The Last) alter your perception of your own beginnings and endings? Consider the idea that "a day with the Creator is like a thousand years by their counting." How does this perspective challenge your understanding of time's significance? What does it truly mean to "let go of counting, lets go of measuring," and instead "dwell in Eternity" by resting in the "light that never dims" and the "presence that never fades"? How can this lead to a more profound sense of psychic peace and anchoring in the immutable Divine Reality?

Contemplation: Transcendence Through Divine Selection

The wise-one reflects on transcendence through Divine Selection. Just as Allah "chose" Moses, and Prophet Muhammad (PBUH) was granted direct witnessing (as mentioned in the previous reflection), the very capacity to perceive and embrace Eternity is itself a Divine bestowal. It is an invitation to transcend the limitations of the temporal world, granted by Allah's Grace (Fadl) to those He wills to guide. This realization fosters profound gratitude and deepens reliance on Divine Will, recognizing that the spiritual journey is ultimately enabled by Allah's infinite wisdom and generosity, not solely human effort. This leads to a unique psychic expansion where the soul is elevated by Divine favor.

The contemplation reveals that the ability to comprehend Eternity is not universally accessible. It requires Divine Selection and a prepared heart. The process of unveiling Eternity involves a transformation of perception, enabling the wise-one to witness the grandeur of the Creator's actions in the cosmos.

Consider: Should divine favor descend, these coverings may be lifted. Thus, a servant may be strengthened to witness the rending of the celestial sphere and perceive the descending grace, its manner of arrival. And to apprehend the unfolding of divine command as clearly as the progression of night and day.

The Veil Lifted: Witnessing Creation's Truth

If He chooses you, the veils will be lifted—
The limits on sight, the boundaries of perception.
He makes His servant strong,
Strong enough to see the sky shatter,
To witness what descends,
Not as mere events,
But as the unfolding of His command.
Night and day come by His decree,
And so too do the signs
For those whom He guides.

Abraham stood beneath the heavens,
Searching beyond what the eye perceives.
He saw the star, the moon, the sun,
And in their setting,
He understood:
The truth is not in what fades,
But in the One beyond fading.
He turned his face toward
The Originator of the heavens and the earth,
Rejecting all that veiled His presence.
Though his people argued,

He did not fear their claims,
For guidance was already placed within him.[254]

For the wise-one, certainty does not come
By clinging to the fleeting,
But by surrendering to
What was, what is,
And what forever will be.

So the wise-one walks forward—
Not trusting in his own design,
But surrendering to the Grace Divine.
He seeks no strength from flesh or bone,
But finds it in His Favor, alone.
He does not strive to earn the sight,
But bows to the Everlasting Light.

For only He chooses whom to guide.
Only in Him, all truths reside.
Only He remains the source
Of Unveiling, Grace, and boundless force.

Wisdom Unveiled

The profound wisdom unveiled in Transcendence Through Divine Selection is that the ability to perceive and embrace Eternity is not solely a result of human effort, but a Divine bestowal—an act of Divine Selection and Grace (Fadl). This understanding liberates the wise-one from the illusion of sole self-reliance, fostering deep gratitude and complete reliance

---

[254] This is in agreement with the Quran verse telling the story of Abraham as he witnessed the eclipse of creation and withstands the Creator's grace:

〈We also showed Abraham the wonders of the heavens and the earth, so he would be sure in faith. (75) When the night grew dark upon him, he saw a star and said, "This is my Lord!" But when it set, he said, "I do not love things that set." (76) Then when he saw the moon rising, he said, "This one is my Lord!" But when it disappeared, he said, "If my Lord does not guide me, I will certainly be one of the misguided people." (77) Then when he saw the sun shining, he said, "This must be my Lord—it is the greatest!" But again when it set, he declared, "O my people! I totally reject whatever you associate ˹with Allah in worship˺. (78) I have turned my face towards the One Who has originated the heavens and the earth—being upright—and I am not one of the polytheists." (79) And his people argued with him. He responded, "Are you arguing with me about Allah, while He has guided me? I am not afraid of whatever ˹idols˺ you associate with Him—˹none can harm me,˺ unless my Lord so wills. My Lord encompasses everything in ˹His˺ knowledge. Will you not be mindful? (80)〉 [Quran 6:75-80]

on Divine Will. The contemplation highlights how this Divine empowerment lifts the veils of limited perception, enabling the wise-one to witness cosmic phenomena and the unfolding of Divine command with profound clarity, culminating in a surrender to the Everlasting and a unique psychic expansion through Divine favor.

Wise-Reflection

Reflect on moments in your life where you felt a profound sense of clarity or guidance that seemed to come from beyond your own efforts. How does the concept of Divine Selection and Grace (Fadl) influence your understanding of your spiritual journey? Do you tend to rely more on human effort or on Divine Will in your pursuit of spiritual knowledge? Consider Abraham's journey of seeking truth beyond fading phenomena. How can recognizing that the capacity to perceive Eternity is a gift deepen your reliance on Allah and foster a more profound sense of gratitude and surrender, leading to further psychic expansion?

Contemplation: Beyond the Veils of Human Attributes

To truly know Eternity, the wise-one must move beyond the veils of human attributes and conceptual limitations. Human attributes are inherently finite, conditioned by time and space. The Divine Attributes of Eternity, Transcendence (Al-Awwal, Al-Akhir, Al-Zahir, Al-Batin), and all-encompassing knowledge are fundamentally beyond human comprehension. This contemplation requires the wise-one to surrender their limited understanding and intellectual frameworks, allowing the soul to experience the Divine in a way that transcends conventional thought, fostering a deeper, more direct psychic connection that doesn't rely on human constructs.

The Creator's manifestation of Eternity is accompanied by a corresponding veiling of human attributes. This dual dynamic ensures that the wise-one's understanding of Eternity remains rooted in Divine illumination rather than human constructs or interpretations.

Reflect: The unveiling of the timeless reality may correspond with a detachment from the limitations of human attributes, a reciprocal veiling for deeper insight.

The Chosen One: A Sign Beyond Time

When the veil is lifted,
Eternity unfolds before the spirit,
Revealing a reality beyond human attributes,
Beyond fleeting forms.
From devotion, remembrance is born.
From remembrance, one is chosen.

A mother, purified in faith,
Withdraws in solitude,
Set apart by decree.
She does not call for a sign,
Yet the unseen approaches,
Not in human measure,
But in divine will.
A whisper from the holy spirit—
Not the hand of man,
But the command of the Creator.
For what is impossible in human reckoning
Is effortless by His decree.
The unseen becomes manifest,
The word becomes flesh,
And a sign is given—
Not only for her,
But for all humanity.

In pain, she clings to the trunk of the palm,
Wishing to vanish into forgotten dust.
Yet beneath her, providence speaks.
She is sustained, guided,
For mercy does not abandon
The one who stands in surrender.
She returns, carrying what none understand.
The tongue does not defend—
Only silence bears witness.
But from the cradle, truth speaks,
Where none expect to hear.
A servant declares his devotion,

[388]

His prophecy, his calling.
Not born of lineage,
But of decree.
Not bound to earth,
But sent as a sign.[255]

For the veil does not only separate,
It reveals.
It removes illusion,
Exposes reality,
And shows that faith is not found
In human rationale alone,
But in the soul willing to surrender
Before the presence beyond all limits.

So the wise-one walks forward—
Not defined by self's brief span,
But anchored in the Divine's vast plan.
He sheds the forms that once confined,
To glimpse the truths no mind can bind.
He does not grasp with earthly thought,
But in surrender, finds what is sought.

---

[255] This is in agreement with the Quran verse narrating the story of Mary and her miraculous son Jesus coming and birth:

⌂ ⟪And mention in the Book ´O Prophet, the story of` Mary when she withdrew from her family to a place in the east, (16) screening herself off from them. Then We sent to her Our angel, ´Gabriel,` appearing before her as a man, perfectly formed. (17) She appealed, "I truly seek refuge in the Most Compassionate from you! ´So leave me alone` if you are God-fearing." (18) He responded, "I am only a messenger from your Lord, ´sent` to bless you with a pure son." (19) She wondered, "How can I have a son when no man has ever touched me, nor am I unchaste?" (20) He replied, "So will it be! Your Lord says, 'It is easy for Me. And so will We make him a sign for humanity and a mercy from Us.' It is a matter ´already` decreed." (21) So she conceived him and withdrew with him to a remote place. (22) Then the pains of labour drove her to the trunk of a palm tree. She cried, "Alas! I wish I had died before this, and was a thing long forgotten!" (23) So a voice1 reassured her from below her, "Do not grieve! Your Lord has provided a stream at your feet. (24) And shake the trunk of this palm tree towards you, it will drop fresh, ripe dates upon you. (25) So eat and drink, and put your heart at ease. But if you see any of the people, say, 'I have vowed silence to the Most Compassionate, so I am not talking to anyone today.'" (26) Then she returned to her people, carrying him. They said ´in shock`, "O Mary! You have certainly done a horrible thing! (27) O sister of Aaron!1 Your father was not an indecent man, nor was your mother unchaste." (28) So she pointed to the baby. They exclaimed, "How can we talk to someone who is an infant in the cradle?" (29) Jesus declared, "I am truly a servant of Allah. He has destined me to be given the Scripture and to be a prophet. (30) He has made me a blessing wherever I go, and bid me to establish prayer and give alms-tax as long as I live, (31) and to be kind to my mother. He has not made me arrogant or defiant. (32) Peace be upon me the day I was born, the day I die, and the day I will be raised back to life!" (33) That is Jesus, son of Mary. ´And this is` a word of truth, about which they dispute. (34)⟫ [Quran 19:16-34]

For only He transcends all names.
Only His Presence truly claims.
Only He remains the source
Of Timelessness, Transcendence, and boundless force.

Wisdom Unveiled

The profound wisdom unveiled in Beyond the Veils of Human Attributes is that true knowing of Eternity requires transcending our finite human attributes and conceptual limitations. The wise-one learns that Divine Attributes are beyond human comprehension, necessitating a surrender of intellectual frameworks. The example of Mary (PBUH) powerfully illustrates this Divine selection and the manifestation of the unseen, where what is impossible in human reckoning is effortless by Divine decree. This contemplation reveals that the veil not only separates but also reveals, exposing a reality where faith is found not in human rationale, but in the soul's willingness to surrender before the Presence beyond all limits, fostering a direct psychic connection and a deeper understanding of Divine Transcendence.

Wise-Reflection

Reflect on your own attachment to your human identity, roles, and intellectual understanding. How might these "human attributes" subtly veil your perception of the Divine's infinite nature? Consider the story of Mary (PBUH) as a paradigm of Divine selection and manifestation beyond human logic. What parts of your understanding or expectations are you willing to surrender to allow for a deeper, more direct psychic connection to the Divine? How can recognizing the limits of human comprehension, and embracing the "presence beyond all limits," transform your approach to both your spiritual journey and your daily life, leading to greater transcendence?

Contemplation: The Infinite Vision and the Limitations of Language

The deepest knowing of Eternity leads to an infinite vision that simultaneously reveals the limitations of language. What is experienced in the realm of Eternity is fundamentally ineffable—it cannot be fully captured by words or described in human terms. Language, designed for the temporal and the finite, falters before the Infinite. The wise-one learns to embrace this silence, understanding that the most profound truths are those that are "unspoken." This acceptance of linguistic inadequacy opens the door to a higher form of direct, non-conceptual knowing, where the soul perceives without the mediation of words or mental definitions, fostering a profound psychic expansion beyond earthly constructs.

The journey into Eternity leads to an expansion of vision and a simultaneous reduction in the sufficiency of language. As the wise-one's understanding deepens, words become inadequate to capture the magnitude of Divine Eternity.

Contemplate: As inner vision expands, the capacity of finite expression diminishes.

The Silence of Certainty

The wider vision expands,
The smaller words become.
When revelation deepens,
Speech fades into surrender.

Zachariah, a servant devoted,
Calls upon his Lord—
His body frail, his years many,
Yet his hope unwavering.
He prays not for himself,
But for a lineage of remembrance,
For a continuation of devotion
Beyond his time.
And the response descends,
Not as an explanation,
But as a decree:
"It is easy for Me."

Yet certainty does not always come
Through words.
He asks for a sign—
And silence becomes his answer.
For three nights,

His tongue is restrained,
Yet in the quiet,
Understanding grows.
He emerges from solitude,
Unable to speak,
Yet his hands signal the command:
"Glorify your Lord, morning and evening."
For what is given is not measured
By the voice,
But by the heart that holds it.
What is inherited is not spoken,
But lived.

John will be born,
Not just as a son,
But as wisdom wrapped in purity,
As a servant called to mercy,
As one who carries remembrance
Without arrogance or defiance.
Peace rests upon him—
In his birth, in his passing,
And when he rises once more.[256]

For when vision expands,
Words are no longer needed.

---

[256] This is in agreement with the Quran verse narrating the story of Zachariah praying to have a child and receive the answer, in short, to maintain glorifying Allah day and night: 📖 ﴾Kāf-Ha-Ya-'Aīn- Ṣād. (1) ˹This is˺ a reminder of your Lord's mercy to His servant Zachariah, (2) when he cried out to his Lord privately, (3) saying, "My Lord! Surely my bones have become brittle, and grey hair has spread across my head, but I have never been disappointed in my prayer to You, my Lord! (4) And I am concerned about ˹the faith of˺ my relatives after me, since my wife is barren. So grant me, by Your grace, an heir, (5) who will inherit ˹prophethood˺ from me and the family of Jacob, and make him, O Lord, pleasing ˹to You˺!" (6) ˹The angels announced,˺ "O Zachariah! Indeed, We give you the good news of ˹the birth of˺ a son, whose name will be John—a name We have not given to anyone before." (7) He wondered, "My Lord! How can I have a son when my wife is barren, and I have become extremely old?" (8) An angel replied, "So will it be! Your Lord says, 'It is easy for Me, just as I created you before, when you were nothing!'" (9) Zachariah said, "My Lord! Grant me a sign." He responded, "Your sign is that you will not ˹be able to˺ speak to people for three nights, despite being healthy." (10) So he came out to his people from the sanctuary, signalling to them to glorify ˹Allah˺ morning and evening. (11) ˹It was later said,˺ "O John! Hold firmly to the Scriptures." And We granted him wisdom while ˹he was still˺ a child, (12) as well as purity and compassion from Us. And he was God-fearing, (13) and kind to his parents. He was neither arrogant nor disobedient. (14) Peace be upon him the day he was born, and the day of his death, and the day he will be raised back to life! (15)﴿ [Quran 19:1-15]

And in silence,
Truth is most clearly known.

So the wise-one walks forward—
Not seeking words to define the Real,
But embracing truths that silence reveal.
He clings not to concepts, transient and frail,
But to the Unspoken that shall never fail.
He does not chase meaning with hurried pace,
But opens to Presence, Divine Grace.

For only He is known beyond all sound.
Only in Him, true certainty is found.
Only He remains the source
Of Infinite Vision, and boundless force.

Wisdom Unveiled

The profound wisdom unveiled in The Infinite Vision and the Limitations of Language is that the deepest knowing of Eternity leads to an infinite vision where language's limitations become clear. The wise-one learns that the most profound truths are ineffable—"unspoken"—and cannot be fully captured by words, which are designed for the temporal. This acceptance of linguistic inadequacy, as exemplified by Zachariah's divinely imposed silence leading to deeper understanding, opens the door to a higher, direct, non-conceptual knowing. Through embracing silence and perceiving without the mediation of words, the soul experiences a significant psychic expansion, gaining certainty that transcends human expression.

Wise-Reflection

Reflect on moments in your life when you've experienced something so profound that words simply failed to describe it. How does the idea that the "most profound truths are those that are 'unspoken'" resonate with you? Consider Zachariah's experience of finding deeper understanding through silence. What role does silence play in your own spiritual practice, or how could it? How might cultivating a practice of non-conceptual knowing—perceiving without immediately framing thoughts into words—open you to a deeper psychic connection with the Divine and the Infinite Vision of Eternity?

Conclusion: In the Knowing of Eternity

ECHOES OF REALIZATION: IN THE PRESENCE OF ETERNITY

There is a stillness deeper than the mere absence of sound, a sacred quietude where human thought cannot venture, and conventional speech dares not tread. It is precisely there that the wise-one stands—bereft of all earthly explanations, utterly stripped of the ego's persistent need to define or categorize, and clothed solely in profound, encompassing awe.

To truly know eternity is not to merely add another truth to the mind's vast repository. It is, instead, to utterly surrender the mind itself, along with speech and the very concept of the finite self, and to dissolve like a single, conscious drop into the shoreless sea of the Eternal. Here, in this boundless expanse, the wise-one ceases to name the unnamed, ceases to seek what is already present, and simply becomes: a pure, unadulterated witness of the Infinite. A humble bearer of the Unbroken Light. A soul that no longer counts fleeting hours—because it now profoundly breathes the very breath of forever, resting serenely in the encompassing gaze of Al-Baaqi, The Everlasting.

THE SEEKER'S ASCENT: ETERNITY AS A DIVINE INVITATION

The wise-one's profound journey into Eternity is understood as both an immense privilege and a sacred responsibility. By consciously and intentionally removing the deceptive veils of linear time and the limitations of human attributes, the Creator lovingly invites the wise-one to experientially witness and embrace the boundless, timeless nature of Divine existence.

This transformative experience not only profoundly elevates the wise-one's spiritual understanding and inner perception but also fundamentally redefines their intimate relationship with the Creator and their place within the vast cosmos. In this continuous journey, the wise-one learns that Eternity is not merely a complex concept to be intellectually grasped—but a living, breathing, all-encompassing reality to be lived and embodied. It is an unending affirmation of the Creator's absolute perfection and a continuous, resonant call to transcend all worldly limitations, tirelessly pursuing a deeper, more unified Divine union. This sustained awareness of Eternity is fundamental to navigating "The Crucible of Inner Transformation."

12ᵀᴴ REFLECTION: OATH TO SURPASS TRIALS

(Surpassing Trials)

THE GATEWAY VERSE

In the sacred words of Allah, a profound reminder to all who reflect upon the Divine orchestration of all events and the wisdom behind both ease and hardship:

📖 ❨*No calamity ˹or blessing˺ occurs on earth or in yourselves without being ˹written˺ in a Record before We bring it into being. This is certainly easy for Allah. (22) ˹We let you know this˺ so that you neither grieve over what you have missed nor boast over what He has granted you. For Allah does not like whoever is arrogant, boastful— (23)*❩ *[Quran 57: 22–23]*

ILLUMINATION'S DAWN

There comes a profound moment when life's trials cease to feel like random accidents—and begin, instead, to luminously reveal themselves as meticulously handwritten letters from the Divine. Each hardship, each moment of perceived collapse, each bewildering night of uncertainty, is, in truth, a sacred summoning. The wise-one is called not merely to endure or survive, but to profoundly remember their essential nature and their primordial pact. To recognize that what appears to scorch the soul is also precisely what divinely seals its inner strength. What is seemingly withheld is often a hidden mercy. What is broken was, by its very nature, never truly meant to last in its temporal form.

In the crucible of trials, the wise-one's soul is never abandoned—it is meticulously sculpted, spiritually refined, and ultimately called back home to its Origin. Trials are not punitive punishments. They are, in essence, sacred oaths, whispered in the realm beyond human memory, where the pure soul, before its descent into the material world, implicitly promised: "I will return to You, my Creator, even if the pathway is through purifying fire." Let us now walk, barefoot yet unafraid, into this transformative fire where enduring hardship becomes a pathway to intimate Divine proximity, and profound surrender becomes the very essence of spiritual transcendence.

THE UNFOLDING OF INSIGHTS

This section delves into the transformative nature of trials, illuminating how they serve as catalysts for purification, strength, and deeper connection with the Divine.

Contemplation: Trials as Instruments of Divine Knowledge

The wise-one perceives trials as profound instruments of Divine Knowledge. They are not random occurrences but meticulously designed lessons from Al-Aleem (The All-Knowing). Every tribulation carries a hidden wisdom, revealing aspects of the Creator's attributes—His Justice, Mercy, Power, and Wisdom—that might otherwise remain unperceived in times of ease. Through hardship, the wise-one gains experiential knowledge of their own weakness, Allah's strength, and the true nature of reality, leading to a deeper, more profound understanding of the Divine Will. This elevates intellectual knowledge to lived spiritual insight and a profound psychic strengthening.

The Creator's intimate knowing of the wise-one is revealed through the orchestration of trials and tribulations. These tests are both a reflection of Divine love and an essential pathway for the wise-one to draw closer to the Creator.

Contemplate: The Divine knowledge of the servant is intertwined with tests and afflictions. For the Originator encompasses all, thus the very awareness of trial is a form of testing, and its rejection, too, is a trial. There is no refuge from the trials of the Divine, for none can elude His encompassing presence.

The Soul's Refining Fire[257]

Faith is not spoken,
It is tested.
Belief is not declared,
It is refined.
Do people think that saying "We believe"

---

[257] The Dual Nature of Trials: Trials are both an opportunity to demonstrate faith and a challenge to relinquish ego and self-reliance. By accepting and enduring trials, the wise-one fulfills their oath to transcend worldly attachments.

Is enough to walk untouched, without reprieve?
Have they not seen the trials, sharp and bold,
Of those who walked this path of old?
Have they not witnessed how the veil
Distinguishes the truthful from the deceivers, lest they fail? [258]

For the one who evades trials,
Does not evade Him,
And the one who denies suffering's sting,
Only denies what was decreed to bring
A deeper knowing, a truth unveiled,
A psychic strength, divinely hailed.
There is no escape from what is sent—
Not from hardship, nor refinement meant.
For to know the path is to know its weight,
And to reject the path is its own fateful state.

The evildoers think they can slip away,
But how mistaken is their judgment's sway!
For the appointed time arrives, unwavering and fast,
And no shadow can hide them from what's truly cast.
No calamity or blessing occurs by chance,
Without being written in a Record, a cosmic dance.
This is certainly easy for Allah, plain to see,
So that you neither grieve over what you have missed, nor boast with glee. [259]

Yet for the one who hopes in meeting Him,
The trial is the way forward—

---

[258] This is in agreement with the Quran verse:

⟨Alif-Lām-Mīm. (1) Do people think once they say, "We believe," that they will be left without being put to the test? (2) We certainly tested those before them. And ˹in this way˺ Allah will clearly distinguish between those who are truthful and those who are liars. (3) Or do the evildoers ˹simply˺ think that they will escape Us? How wrong is their judgment! (4) Whoever hopes for the meeting with Allah, ˹let them know that˺ Allah's appointed time is sure to come. He is the All-Hearing, All-Knowing. (5) And whoever strives ˹in Allah's cause˺, only does so for their own good. Surely Allah is not in need of ˹any of˺ His creation. (6) As for those who believe and do good, We will certainly absolve them of their sins, and reward them according to the best of what they used to do. (7)⟩ [Quran 29:1-7]

[259] This is in agreement with the Quran verses of:

⟨No calamity ˹or blessing˺ occurs on earth or in yourselves without being ˹written˺ in a Record before We bring it into being. This is certainly easy for Allah. (22) ˹We let you know this˺ so that you neither grieve over what you have missed nor boast over what He has granted you. For Allah does not like whoever is arrogant, boastful— (23)⟩ [Quran 57:22-23]

Not destruction,
But purification.

The one who strives,
Strives only for their own soul,
For He is in need of nothing,
But calls His servants
Toward absolution.
And in the end,
The trials become reward,
The weight becomes light,
The burden transforms into grace,
Until the faithful stand purified,
Given what is better
Than all they had done.

For the wise-one does not ask
Why am I tested?
But rather—
How do I stand within the test?

So the wise-one walks forward—
Not seeking ease where trials ignite,
But finding Divine wisdom in the darkest night.
He fears not loss, nor what is meant to cease,
But trusts the Hand that brings profoundest peace.
He does not question the All-Knowing's way,
But bows in awe, each passing day.

For only He orchestrates every decree.
Only in Him, true strength we see.
Only He remains the source
Of Knowledge, Refinement, and boundless force.

Wisdom Unveiled

The profound wisdom unveiled in Trials as Instruments of Divine Knowledge is that trials are not random, but meticulously designed lessons from Al-Aleem (The All-Knowing), serving as profound instruments of Divine Knowledge. These tribulations reveal aspects of the Creator's attributes—His Justice, Mercy, Power, and Wisdom—and provide experiential knowledge of one's own weakness versus Allah's strength. The wise-one understands that faith is tested and refined through hardship, distinguishing the truthful from deceivers, and that no calamity occurs without being written in a Record, making all events easy for Allah. This leads to a psychic strengthening where the wise-one asks not "Why am I tested?" but "How do I stand within the test?", transforming burdens into grace and elevating intellectual understanding to lived spiritual insight.

Wise-Reflection

Reflect on a past trial in your life. Did you perceive it at the time as a random misfortune, or can you now see any hidden wisdom or lessons it imparted? Consider the verse: "No calamity ʿor blessingʾ occurs on earth or in yourselves without being ʿwrittenʾ in a Record." How does this idea challenge the notion of trials as mere bad luck and shift your perspective towards Divine orchestration? When facing current difficulties, do you tend to ask "Why me?" or "How do I stand within this test?" How might embracing the latter question, and seeking the Divine Knowledge hidden within the trial, foster greater psychic resilience and a deeper connection to Al-Aleem?

Contemplation: Casting Out Self

A crucial aspect of surmounting trials is the profound process of casting out the self—shedding the ego's attachments, desires, and illusions of control. When faced with adversity, the ego often resists, creating inner turmoil. The wise-one learns to release this resistance, understanding that true liberation comes from relinquishing self-reliance and surrendering to the Divine decree. This process of self-emptying, born of tribulation, purifies the heart from pride and self-importance, allowing it to become a vessel for Divine Presence and guidance, aligning with the spirit of the Gateway Verse ﴾ ﴿ ʿWe let you know thisʾ so that you neither grieve over what you have missed nor boast over what He has granted you. For Allah does not like whoever is arrogant, boastful— (23)﴿ [Quran 57:23] which cautions against arrogance and boasting. This is a vital psychic recalibration.

Reflect: The initial step towards witnessing the Divine is the stilling of stray thoughts. The ultimate stage is the transcendence of even acquired

THE LANTERN OF THE WISE

knowledge. Thereafter, the self is relinquished, culminating in the effacement of the ego.

The Stages of Divine Observation

To observe Him
Is not to fill the mind,
But to empty it.
Not to seek knowledge's claim,
But to release its name.
Not to hold the self,
But to let it dissolve.
And in the end,
Not to cling to the I,
But to surrender it entirely.

The first veil is thought—
The clutter of the world,
The noise of the day, unfurled.
Only when silence deepens,
When night grants stillness,
Does the heart begin to perceive.
❨Indeed, worship in the night is more impactful and suitable for recitation.❩
❨˹Always˺ remember the Name of your Lord, and devote yourself to Him
wholeheartedly.❩[260]

Then knowledge itself becomes the veil,
For what is acquired
Is never complete, and bound to fail.
And what is learned
Is never equal to the Knower—
To transcend knowledge
Is to admit its limit,
To stand before Him

---

[260] Casting out thoughts is in agreement with the Quran verse:

📖 ❨Indeed, worship in the night is more impactful and suitable for recitation. (6) For during the day you are over-occupied ˹with worldly duties˺. (7) ˹Always˺ remember the Name of your Lord, and devote yourself to Him wholeheartedly. (8) ˹He is the˺ Lord of the east and the west. There is no god ˹worthy of worship˺ except Him, so take Him ˹alone˺ as a Trustee of Affairs. (9)❩ [Quran 73:6-9]

Without claim,
Only with humility's flame.
⟨and say, 'Glory be to our Lord! Surely the promise of our Lord has been
fulfilled.'⟩[261]

Then the self must fall away,
For the grasp of identity
Stands between the soul
And its return.
Not elevation,
But descent into surrender, deep and true.
⟨So do not ˹falsely˺ elevate yourselves. He knows best who is ˹truly˺ righteous.⟩[262]

And in the final step,
The I dissolves completely.
There is no identity
But the servitude of the believer,
No separation
But the devotion of the devout.
The wife of Pharaoh sought no title,
Only nearness, in life's vital. ⟨"My Lord! Build me a house in Paradise near You,
deliver me from Pharaoh and his ˹evil˺ doing, and save me from the wrongdoing
people."⟩
Mary did not hold to self, or earthly gain,
Only obedience, enduring joy and pain.

---

[261] Casting out the knowledge is agreement with the Quran verse:

📖 ⟨Say, ˹O Prophet,˺ "Believe in this ˹Quran˺, or do not. Indeed, when it is recited to those who were gifted with knowledge1 before it ˹was revealed˺, they fall upon their faces in prostration, (107) and say, 'Glory be to our Lord! Surely the promise of our Lord has been fulfilled.' (108) And they fall down upon their faces weeping, and it increases them in humility." (109)⟩ [Quran 17:107-109]

[262] Casting out the self is in agreement with the Quran verse:

📖 ⟨This is the extent of their knowledge. Surely your Lord knows best who has strayed from His Way and who is ˹rightly˺ guided. (30) To Allah ˹alone˺ belongs whatever is in the heavens and whatever is on the earth so that He may reward the evildoers according to what they did, and reward the good-doers with the finest reward1— (31) those who avoid major sins and shameful deeds, despite ˹stumbling on˺ minor sins. Surely your Lord is infinite in forgiveness. He knew well what would become of you as He created you from the earth1 and while you were ˹still˺ fetuses in the wombs of your mothers.2 So do not ˹falsely˺ elevate yourselves. He knows best who is ˹truly˺ righteous. (32)⟩ [Quran 53:30-32]

❨*She testified to the words of her Lord and His Scriptures, and was one of the 'sincerely' devout.*❩[263]

To see Him
Is to let go of everything
Until nothing remains
But Presence itself.

So the wise-one walks forward—
Not building self, but letting go,
Where ego's claims no longer flow.
He clings not to what he has gained,
But to the Divine, supremely sustained.
He does not boast of what he knows,
But to His decree, humbly bows.

For only He is the Ever-Present Guide.
Only in Him, true self can hide.
Only He remains the source
Of Emptiness, Guidance, and boundless force.

Wisdom Unveiled

The profound wisdom unveiled in Casting Out Self is that surmounting trials necessitates the shedding of the ego's attachments and illusions of control. The wise-one learns that true liberation stems from relinquishing self-reliance and surrendering to Divine decree, a process of self-emptying that purifies the heart from pride and self-importance. This journey involves stages, from stilling stray thoughts and transcending acquired knowledge to the complete dissolution of the "I", making the heart a pure vessel for Divine Presence. The examples of Pharaoh's wife and Mary (PBUT) underscore that true observance of the Divine is achieved not by

---

[263] Casting out the I, is in agreement with the Quran verse:

📖 ❨And Allah sets forth an example for the believers: the wife of Pharaoh, who prayed, "My Lord! Build me a house in Paradise near You, deliver me from Pharaoh and his 'evil' doing, and save me from the wrongdoing people." (11) 'There is' also 'the example of' Mary, the daughter of 'Imrân, who guarded her chastity, so We breathed into her 'womb' through Our angel 'Gabriel'.1 She testified to the words of her Lord and His Scriptures, and was one of the 'sincerely' devout. (12)❩ [Quran 66: 11-12]

grasping, but by letting go until nothing remains but Presence itself, leading to a profound psychic recalibration where servitude becomes identity.

Wise-Reflection

Reflect on your own ego's resistance when faced with adversity or when your plans are disrupted. What are some of your deepest attachments or illusions of control that prevent you from fully surrendering to Divine decree? Consider the "Stages of Divine Observation"—emptying the mind, releasing acquired knowledge, letting the self dissolve. Which of these stages do you find most challenging? How might cultivating a spirit of humility and actively "casting out the self" allow your heart to become a more receptive vessel for Divine Presence and guidance, leading to a deeper psychic transformation in your daily life?

Contemplation: Alignment Through Submission and Trust

Trials compel alignment through complete submission (Islam) and unwavering trust (Tawakkul). When human plans crumble and control is lost, the wise-one realizes that true strength lies in absolute surrender to Allah's will. This submission is not passive resignation but an active, conscious choice to place full reliance on the Creator, knowing that "Allah is certainly with us" (as seen in earlier reflections). This profound trust alleviates anxiety and fear, allowing the wise-one to navigate challenges with inner peace and fortitude, recognizing that all is ordained by the All-Wise. This is a profound psychic recalibration towards Divine Will.

The wise-one is invited to cast aside personal limitations and align their actions, knowledge, and intentions with the Creator's infinite wisdom. This process demands surrender, faith, and a steadfast commitment to Divine Will.

Reflect, O seeker: Relinquish transgression in reliance upon Divine forgiveness, and ascribe righteous deeds to Divine generosity. Surrender your limited understanding to the boundless Divine knowledge; cast off your finite knowing into the infinite Divine knowing.

Surrender to the Infinite

The heart hesitates,
Burdened by the weight of sin,

Uncertain before mercy's kin.
Yet hope is never lost,
For forgiveness is vast,
Wider than the heavens,
Deeper than regret.

The servant does not escape wrongdoing
By their own strength,
But by returning to the One
Who calls them back.
For sin fades in the light of forgiveness,
And in its desertion, the soul is freed.[264]

The righteous do not purify themselves
By praise or favor,
But by appointing their deeds
To the pleasure of their Lord.
Not in expectation of reward,
But in surrender to His generosity—
Where giving is met with divine fulfillment,
Where seeking leads to a promise unending.[265]

Yet knowledge is not held in the hands of creation,
It belongs to the One
Who knows what is unseen,
Who knows what no thought can grasp.
The angels questioned,
But understanding was not given to them—
Only to the one whom He taught.

---

[264] Deserting sin for the Creator's forgiveness is in agreement with the Quran verse:

⬛ ⟨Say, ˹O Prophet, that Allah says,˺ "O My servants who have exceeded the limits against their souls! Do not lose hope in Allah's mercy, for Allah certainly forgives all sins.1 He is indeed the All-Forgiving, Most Merciful. (53)⟩ [Quran 39:53]

[265] Appointing good deeds toward the Creator's generosity is in agreement with the Quran verse:

⬛ ⟨And so I have warned you of a raging Fire, (14) in which none will burn except the most wretched— (15) who deny and turn away. (16) But the righteous will be spared from it— (17) who donate ˹some of˺ their wealth only to purify themselves, (18) not in return for someone's favours, (19) but seeking the pleasure of their Lord, the Most High. (20) They will certainly be pleased. (21)⟩ [Quran 92:14-21]

For wisdom is not claimed,
It is bestowed.[266]

The servant casts off their knowing,
For certainty lies
Not in what is comprehended,
But in trusting the Knower of all things.[267]
All matters return to Him,
All journeys end where they began—
In worship,
In trust,
In surrender to what cannot be measured,
Yet is known in presence.

So the wise-one walks forward—
Not trusting in his fleeting might,
But in His Presence, shining bright.
He clings not to what he can control,
But to His decree, making him whole.
He does not strive to understand all ways,
But bows in trust, through all his days.

For only He is the All-Wise, All-Seeing.
Only in Him, true peace is being.
Only He remains the source
Of Submission, Trust, and boundless force.

---

[266] Leaving one knowledge to the Creator's knowledge is in agreement with the Quran verse:

❮'Remember` when your Lord said to the angels, "I am going to place a successive 'human` authority on earth." They asked 'Allah`, "Will You place in it someone who will spread corruption there and shed blood while we glorify Your praises and proclaim Your holiness?" Allah responded, "I know what you do not know." (30) He taught Adam the names of all things, then He presented them to the angels and said, "Tell Me the names of these, if what you say is true?" (31) They replied, "Glory be to You! We have no knowledge except what You have taught us. You are truly the All-Knowing, All-Wise." (32)❯ (Quran 2 : 30 - 32)

[267] Cast off one knowing to Creator's knowing is in agreement with the Quran verse:

❮To Allah 'alone` belongs the knowledge of what is hidden in the heavens and the earth. And to Him all matters are returned. So worship Him and put your trust in Him. And your Lord is never unaware of what you do. (123)❯ [Quran 11:123]

Wisdom Unveiled

The profound wisdom unveiled in Alignment Through Submission and Trust is that trials are a powerful means to compel complete submission (Islam) and unwavering trust (Tawakkul) in Allah. The wise-one realizes that true strength and liberation from anxiety come from actively relinquishing self-reliance and placing full reliance on the Creator, knowing that "Allah is certainly with us." This contemplation emphasizes that forgiveness is vast and that righteous deeds are to be ascribed to Divine generosity, not personal merit. It underscores that true knowledge and wisdom are bestowed by the All-Knowing, leading the wise-one to cast off limited human understanding and trust implicitly in the Divine, ultimately achieving inner peace and fortitude—a vital psychic recalibration.

Wise-Reflection

Reflect on a time when your human plans crumbled and you felt a loss of control. Did this experience lead you to deeper submission or greater resistance? Consider the distinction between passive resignation and active, conscious submission. How can cultivating unwavering trust (Tawakkul) in Allah's wisdom, even when the path is unclear, alleviate your anxiety and fear? In what ways can you consciously practice relinquishing self-reliance and ascribing your deeds to Divine generosity in your daily life? How might this consistent alignment with Divine Will foster greater inner peace and fortitude, leading to a deeper psychic connection and trust that "Allah is certainly with us" through all trials?

Contemplation: The Role of Divine Schemes

The wise-one gains insight into the intricate role of Divine Schemes (Tadbir). They realize that even what appears as misfortune or opposition is part of a larger, benevolent Divine plan that transcends human comprehension. Just as enemies may unknowingly serve Allah's plan (as in the Prophet's Hijrah in Quran 9:40 from the previous reflection), so too do trials have a specific, higher purpose. This understanding cultivates acceptance and prevents despair, allowing the wise-one to see the hidden good and the elevating intention behind every divinely orchestrated event, fostering deep psychic tranquility.

The Creator's schemes are portrayed as both a trial and a guide. They serve as a reminder of the Creator's omnipotence and as a tool for the wise-one's spiritual refinement.

Understand, O discerning seeker: True knowledge of the Divine instills a profound reverence, a cautious awareness of the Divine plan. This plan becomes discernible through the manifestations of Divine grace and favor. Thus, if this grace guides you towards the Divine and the Divine path, then the firmness of your wisdom shall be confirmed, and the radiance of your guidance shall illuminate your way.

The Path of Divine Wisdom

To seek knowledge of Him
Is to perceive His wisdom,
To recognize His decree
Beyond human planning,
Beyond worldly schemes.

Some plot against His revelations,
Thinking themselves cunning,
Forgetting that He is swifter in devising,
That nothing escapes His command.
❨"Say, 'O Prophet,' "Allah is swifter in devising 'punishment'."❩
❨Surely Our messenger-angels record whatever you devise.❩
For every intention,
Every deception,
Is recorded by His messenger-angels,
And none evade His justice.[268]

Yet to those who walk in mindfulness,
His mercy does not merely forgive—
It grants decisive authority,
It absolves, elevates, and refines.
❨"If you are mindful of Allah, He will grant you a decisive authority,

---

[268] This is in agreement with the Quran verse:

📖 ❨When We give people a taste of mercy after being afflicted with a hardship, they swiftly devise plots against Our revelations! Say, 'O Prophet,' "Allah is swifter in devising 'punishment'. Surely Our messenger-angels record whatever you devise." (21)❩ [Quran 10:21]

Absolve you of your sins, and forgive you.
For the wisdom given
Is not of the earth,
But of the boundless favor
Of the Most High.
"And Allah is the Lord of infinite bounty.[269]

Joseph was tested,
Betrayed, cast away,
Yet in hardship,
He was guided by the unseen.
Through trial,
His path was woven
Until he stood in authority,
"This is how We established Joseph in the land to settle wherever he pleased.
A servant raised beyond rank,
Not by men,
But by the decree
Of the One All-Knowing.
"We elevate in rank whoever We will. But above those ranking in knowledge is the
One All-Knowing.[270]

So the wise-one learns—
Plans may be devised,
But only His decree prevails.
Paths may seem obscured,
Yet He guides through what is hidden.
For wisdom is not claimed,

---

[269] And the Quran verse:

📖 ❨O believers! If you are mindful of Allah, He will grant you a decisive authority, absolve you of your sins, and forgive you. (29) And ʿremember, O Prophet,ʾ when the disbelievers conspired to capture, kill, or exile you. They planned, but Allah also planned. And Allah is the best of planners. (30)❩ (Quran 8:29-30]

[270] Also, the Quran narrates the story of Joseph reuniting with his brother despite the other brothers' willingness, so both become belong to the advisory of the King of Egypt:

📖 ❨This is how We established Joseph in the land to settle wherever he pleased. We shower Our mercy on whoever We will, and We never discount the reward of the good-doers. (56)❩ [Quran 12:56]

📖 ❨Joseph began searching their bags before that of his brother ʿBenjaminʾ, then brought it out of Benjamin's bag. This is how We inspired Joseph to plan. He could not have taken his brother under the King's law, but Allah had so willed. We elevate in rank whoever We will. But above those ranking in knowledge is the One All-Knowing. (76)❩ [Quran 12:56 and 76]

It is given.
And true guidance radiates,
Not in foresight,
But in surrender
To the One who knows
Beyond all knowing.

So the wise-one walks forward—
Not fearing plots, nor what appears amiss,
But trusting in His perfect bliss.
He grasps not control, nor earthly sway,
But finds his peace in His ordained way.
He does not question schemes unknown,
But bows to where His Wisdom's sown.

For only He plans beyond all sight.
Only in Him, all ends alight.
Only He remains the source
Of Divine Schemes, and boundless force.

Wisdom Unveiled

The profound wisdom unveiled in The Role of Divine Schemes is that every event, even apparent misfortune or opposition, is part of a larger, benevolent Divine plan orchestrated by Allah, the Best of Planners. The wise-one learns to recognize that human plots are always superseded by His swifter devising, and that all intentions are recorded. This understanding cultivates acceptance and prevents despair, allowing the wise-one to perceive the hidden good and elevating intention behind every divinely orchestrated event. As exemplified by Joseph (PBUH), even betrayal can be a part of Divine establishment and elevation. This perspective fosters deep psychic tranquility and confirms the firmness of wisdom as the wise-one's path becomes illuminated by Divine grace through submission to the One who knows beyond all knowing.

Wise-Reflection

Reflect on a past challenge that initially seemed like a misfortune, but later revealed a hidden benefit or led you to an unexpected positive outcome. How does the concept of Divine Schemes—that "Allah is the best of planners" and "nothing escapes His command"—alter your perception of current difficulties? Do you tend to feel despair or struggle for control when faced with opposition? Consider the story of Joseph (PBUH): his trials ultimately led to a position of authority and Divine elevation. How can adopting this understanding of Tadbir cultivate deeper acceptance, prevent despair, and foster greater psychic tranquility in your own life, allowing you to see the hidden good in all events?

Contemplation: Divine Companionship

Trials reveal the profound reality of Divine Companionship. When all worldly support seems to vanish, the wise-one experiences Allah's intimate nearness and solace, embodying the truth of "Allah is certainly with us." This experiential closeness transforms isolation into profound connection. It is in the deepest points of vulnerability that the wise-one finds an unbreakable bond with Al-Latif (The Subtle One) and Al-Qareeb (The Near), leading to a spiritual and psychic strength that transcends external circumstances.

Consider: To abide by the Divine is to face the potential allure of all creation seeking to distract and conceal. Yet, if the servant remains steadfast in the Divine presence, the Divine shall be with the servant. And whoever opposes such a one, opposes the Divine itself.

Divine Companionship: The Unseen Embrace

When shadows lengthen, deep and vast,
And worldly anchors fail at last,
When all support seems to depart,
A Presence stirs within the heart.
The wise-one finds in darkest hour,
The Divine Companionship's true power.
No solitude can truly bind,
The soul that seeks, the truthful mind.

For Allah is certainly with us, a truth profound,
Wherever doubt or fear is found.
He is with you wherever you are,
And Allah is All-Seeing of what you do, near or far.

He is the First and the Last, a constant friend,
The Most High and Most Near, to the very end. [271]
A Subtle Hand (Al-Latif), a whisper soft,
A Nearness (Al-Qareeb) felt, though worlds aloft.
This bond, unbreakable and deep,
A solace that the soul can keep.

Though trials rage, and tempests roar,
The wise-one stands, and asks no more.
For in this closeness, strength takes hold,
A spiritual fortitude, brave and bold.
The heart made firm, the spirit bright,
Guided by His ever-present Light.
No worldly adversary can prevail,
Against the Divine Embrace, behind the veil.

For if you stand by Him, through every plea,
Then He shall be with you, eternally.
And whoever opposes, in their folly's plight,
Shall confront the Divine, in His boundless might.
For this steadfastness, a hidden art,
Aligns the spirit, molds the heart.
It grants a peace that trials cannot break,
For His unwavering support, the wise-one takes.

So the wise-one walks forward—
Not fearing loneliness in the fray,
But finding Divine Presence every day.
He seeks no comfort from fleeting hands,
But in His intimate nearness, understands.
He does not falter when supports may cease,
But rests in His companionship's true peace.

---

[271] This is in agreement with the Quran verse of:

📖 ❨He is the First and the Last, the Most High and Most Near,1 and He has ´perfect` knowledge of all things.(3) He is the One Who created the heavens and the earth in six Days, then established Himself on the Throne. He knows whatever goes into the earth and whatever comes out of it, and whatever descends from the sky and whatever ascends into it. And He is with you wherever you are. For Allah is All-Seeing of what you do. (4)❩ [Quran 57:3-4]

For only He is Near, beyond all measure.
Only in Him, lies every treasure.
Only He remains the source
Of Companionship, Strength, and boundless force.

Wisdom Unveiled

The profound wisdom unveiled in Divine Companionship is that trials are the crucible where the wise-one truly experiences Allah's intimate nearness and solace. When all worldly support recedes, the truth of "Allah is certainly with us" becomes an experiential reality, transforming isolation into a profound, unbreakable connection with Al-Latif (The Subtle One) and Al-Qareeb (The Near). This realization, that Allah is with you wherever you are, leads to a spiritual and psychic strength that transcends external circumstances. It illuminates that standing firm in Divine presence grants the Creator's unwavering support, rendering the wise-one impervious to worldly distractions and adversities, for whoever opposes such a one, ultimately opposes the Divine Itself.

Wise-Reflection

Reflect on a time when you felt utterly alone or unsupported in a trial. In retrospect, can you discern any subtle ways in which you might have experienced Divine Companionship or solace during that period? How does the concept of Allah being "with you wherever you are" (Quran 57:4) reshape your understanding of vulnerability or isolation? Consider your own challenges: how might consciously seeking and acknowledging Al-Latif (The Subtle One) and Al-Qareeb (The Near) within your difficulties cultivate a deeper psychic strength and inner peace, transforming your perception of adversity into an opportunity for profound Divine connection?

Contemplation: Trials as Pathways to Strength and Return

For the wise-one, trials are not roadblocks but direct pathways to spiritual strength and ultimately, to Return (to Allah). Each challenge overcome, each moment of patience, and each act of reliance, builds inner fortitude and purifies the soul. These experiences detach the heart from the transient world and redirect its gaze towards the Eternal, guiding the wise-one back to their primordial home in the Divine Presence. The fire of trial sculpts the soul, making it fit for its ultimate purpose: standing before the Creator. This journey, marked by Divine observation and support, leads to profound psychic transformation.

Trials are revealed as opportunities for both growth and return. Through enduring hardships, the wise-one gains resilience and deepens their reliance on Divine mercy.

Consider, O seeker: If the Divine is witnessed and that vision is steadfastly maintained, then diverse trials may ensue, accompanied by profound divine observation and support. Thus, the servant shall remain firm in their exalted station.

The Trial of Sight: Steadfast in His Presence

To perceive Him is not mere vision,
But a station of endurance,
A place where faith is tested,
Where steadfastness is refined.
Trials come—
Not to shatter,
But to reveal.
For the believer is not left untouched,
But proven through struggle, so very much
Distinguished in perseverance's light.[272]

Fear, famine, loss—
The weight of hardship presses upon the soul,
Yet those who endure
Remember their place before Him: ❴*Surely to Allah we belong, and to Him we will*
return❵
For patience is not passive;
It is a state of knowing
That mercy follows endurance,

---

[272] This is in agreement with the Quran verse:

❴We will certainly test you ˹believers˺ until We prove those of you who ˹truly˺ struggle ˹in Allah's cause˺ and remain steadfast, and reveal how you conduct yourselves. (31)❵ [Quran 47:31]

That guidance emerges
Where suffering once stood.[273]

Steadfastness is granted,
Not only for the world, but for eternity's vast field.
Faith roots the believer firmly, a mighty shield,
While heedlessness allows the lost
To drift into the unseen, at heavy cost.[274]
His decree unfolds, in truth and might,
His will is undisputed, day and night.
And those who endure, steadfast and true,
Will find themselves standing still, in all they do—
Not in defeat,
But in their glorious place, complete—
Held by the Might,
Preserved by the Will,
And illuminated by the guidance
Of the Most High.

So the wise-one walks forward—
Not turning from the refining fire,
But embracing all that lifts him higher.
He sees not trials as a bitter end,
But as His Mercy, sent to mend.
He does not question the path's design,
But trusts in His ultimate Divine.
For only He strengthens every soul.
Only in Him, we are made whole.
Only He remains the source
Of Strength, Return, and boundless force.

---

[273] This is in agreement with the Quran verse:

◁ ❨We will certainly test you with a touch of fear and famine and loss of property, life, and crops. Give good news to those who patiently endure— (155) who say, when struck by a disaster, "Surely to Allah we belong and to Him we will ˹all˺ return." (156) They are the ones who will receive Allah's blessings and mercy. And it is they who are ˹rightly˺ guided. (157)❩ [Quran 2:155 – 157]

[274] This is in agreement with the Quran verse:

◁ ❨Allah makes the believers steadfast with the firm Word ˹of faith˺1 in this worldly life and the Hereafter. And Allah leaves the wrongdoers to stray. For Allah does what He wills. (27)❩ [Quran 14:27]

Wisdom Unveiled

The profound wisdom unveiled in Trials as Pathways to Strength and Return is that trials are not roadblocks but direct pathways to spiritual strength and ultimately, to Return (to Allah). The wise-one learns that each challenge overcome, through patience and reliance, builds inner fortitude and purifies the soul, detaching the heart from the transient world. This process, as highlighted by the verse "Surely to Allah we belong, and to Him we will return," is a Divine observation and support that transforms suffering into guidance and elevates the believer to an "exalted station." The "fire of trial" sculpts the soul, making it fit for its ultimate purpose: standing before the Creator, illuminated by His guidance, leading to profound psychic strengthening and glory.

Wise-Reflection

Reflect on a time when you had to endure hardship and found unexpected inner strength or clarity. How does the idea of trials as "pathways to strength and Return"—rather than mere tests—shift your perspective on adversity? Consider the verse: "Surely to Allah we belong, and to Him we will return." How can internalizing this truth during moments of loss or struggle provide you with a deeper sense of patience and reliance? What does it mean for your spiritual journey to believe that the "fire of trial sculpts the soul," making it fit for its ultimate purpose, and how can this perspective enhance your psychic resilience in daily life?

Contemplation: The Role of Weakness and Mercy

The wise-one embraces the profound role of weakness and Divine Mercy within trials. Human weakness is not a flaw but a necessary condition for experiencing Allah's infinite strength and boundless compassion. When the wise-one reaches their limit, it is then that Allah's compassion and help become most evident. This realization fosters humility and deepens love for Allah, seeing His Mercy actively manifest in softening the hardship, providing solace, or elevating the soul through the very act of enduring. It transforms perceived vulnerability into a channel for Divine grace, leading to a profound psychic shift from distance to closeness.

Understand: Should the servant falter in their vision of the Divine, they may be tested with trials that diminish their endurance, leading to a sense of distance from the Divine. From this very weakness and yearning for

[415]

Divine mercy arises a supplication that can draw them back to the Divine presence.

The Call from Distance: Returning to His Presence

Distance is not absence,
But a test of the heart—
A longing that deepens,
A trial that humbles.
When hardship presses,
When tolerance weakens,
When the veil of separation
Makes the soul tremble,
The call emerges from within.

For every suffering,
A prayer is born.
For every fall,
A return is written.[275]
When calamity strikes,
The servant forgets all distractions—
No name is called upon
Except His.
From the depths,
The plea arises:
❨If You rescue us from this, we will be ever grateful.❩[276]

Yet the test is not only in hardship,
But in remembrance—
For once relief comes,

---

[275] This is in agreement with the Quran verse:

📖 ❨Ask ˹them, O Prophet˺, "Imagine if you were overwhelmed by Allah's torment or the Hour—would you call upon any other than Allah ˹for help˺? ˹Answer me˺ if your claims are true! (40) No! He is the only One you would call. And if He willed, He could remove the affliction that made you invoke Him. Only then will you forget whatever you associate with Him ˹in worship˺." (41)❩ [Quran 6:40-41]

[276] This is derived from the Quran verse of:

📖 ❨Say, ˹O Prophet,˺ "Who rescues you from the darkest times on land and at sea? He ˹alone˺ you call upon with humility, openly and secretly: "If You rescue us from this, we will be ever grateful." (63) Say, "˹Only˺ Allah rescues you from this and any other distress, yet you associate others with Him ˹in worship˺." (64)❩ [Quran 6:63-64]

Will the soul remain mindful?
"But when He saves them, they instantly break their pledge!"[277]

No storm lasts forever,
No darkness endures without end.
Yet every trial carries wisdom,
Every affliction holds mercy,
For it extracts from weakness
The strength to seek Him again.[278]

Thus, guidance does not abandon,
But waits to be reclaimed.
And in returning,
The soul does not simply recover—
It stands again,
Radiating the light
It once lost.

So the wise-one walks forward—
Not fearing limits of their own,
But trusting His Strength, uniquely shown.
He hides not weakness, nor tries to conceal,
But finds in His Mercy, what wounds can heal.
He does not resist when spirit bends low,
But calls on His Aid, letting grace flow.

For only He hears the cry from afar.
Only in Him, we truly are.
Only He remains the source
Of Weakness, Mercy, and boundless force.

---

[277] Referencing Quran 6:64, a common human tendency after trial

[278] This is in agreement with the Quran verse:

📖 ⟨Say, ˹O Prophet,˺ "Who rescues you from the darkest times on land and at sea? He ˹alone˺ you call upon with humility, openly and secretly: "If You rescue us from this, we will be ever grateful." (63) Say, "˹Only˺ Allah rescues you from this and any other distress, yet you associate others with Him ˹in worship˺." (64)⟩ [Quran 6:63-64]

Wisdom Unveiled

The profound wisdom unveiled in The Role of Weakness and Mercy is that human weakness is not a flaw, but a necessary condition for experiencing Allah's infinite strength and boundless compassion. The wise-one learns that at their limit, Divine Mercy becomes most evident, fostering humility and deepening love. Trials, even those that cause a sense of distance, are designed to prompt sincere supplication and a return to Divine Presence. The contemplation highlights that every trial carries wisdom and mercy, extracting strength from vulnerability and ensuring that guidance is always available to be reclaimed. This transforms perceived weakness into a powerful channel for Divine grace and a significant psychic shift back to closeness with the Creator.

Wise-Reflection

Reflect on a moment of profound personal weakness or vulnerability. How did that experience, perhaps unexpectedly, lead you to seek help or surrender to a higher power? Do you find it challenging to admit your limitations? Consider the idea that "every affliction holds mercy, for it extracts from weakness the strength to seek Him again." How can embracing your human weakness, rather than resisting it, become a pathway to experiencing Allah's infinite strength and boundless compassion more deeply? What does it mean for your daily life to call upon Him from the "distance" of hardship, and how might this practice foster a continuous psychic return to Divine Presence, even after trials subside?

Contemplation: Belief in the Unseen and Divine Endurance

Trials strengthen the wise-one's belief in the Unseen (Ghaib) and cultivate Divine Endurance (Sabr). When solutions are not apparent and outcomes are uncertain, the wise-one's faith is tested and deepened. This reliance on the unseen hand of Allah, and the cultivation of patience (Sabr) without resentment, becomes a spiritual muscle. It is the active waiting, the steadfast trust in the wisdom of the Unseen, that allows the wise-one to persevere and transcend, forging an unbreakable conviction that Allah's plan is perfect, even when veiled. This leads to profound psychic resilience and a certainty that Allah's plan is perfect.

Reflect: Those who held faith in the Unseen and believed without direct witnessing shall find the Divine present with them on the Day of Resurrection, a companion amidst the dread and terror.

Faith Without Sight: The Promise of Divine Presence

Belief is not built upon seeing,
Nor is certainty bound by the visible.
The heart that trusts in the unseen (Ghaib)
Is the heart that will stand
Steadfast in the trial's keen.

For can the one who knows the truth
Be like the one who is blind, losing youth?
None perceive this, none truly discern,
Except those of reason, who wisely learn—
Those who honor the covenant,
Who remain unwavering in their pledge, heaven-sent,
Who stand in awe of their Lord, ever near,
Mindful of the coming judgment, casting off all fear.

They endure, seeking His pleasure's grace,
Keeping their prayers firm, in time and space,
Giving from what they are granted, free and wide,
Responding to harm with righteousness, by His side.
❲And ˹they are˺ those who endure patiently, seeking their Lord's pleasure, establish prayer, donate from what We have provided for them—secretly and openly—and respond to evil with good. It is they who will have the ultimate abode.❳

And when the great resurrection unfolds,
When terror grips the unprepared, in tales of old,
When the dreadful hour looms, with solemn dread,
They will not be abandoned, but accompanied instead.
Not left in fear, nor left to roam,
But guided toward Mercy, brought safely home.
For the patient will inherit eternity's vast sphere,
The steadfast will enter peace, holding Him dear.
And in the Gardens without end, where joys reside,
The righteous will be gathered, by His Mercy tied,

Embraced in Divine fulfillment.
From every gate, in wondrous sent,
The angels will greet them, with voices clear:
"Peace be upon you for your perseverance. How excellent is the ultimate abode!"[279]

For belief in the unknown
Was not emptiness,
But certainty sown.
And now,
What was hidden
Is gloriously revealed, truth-bidden

So the wise-one walks forward—
Not needing sight for faith's firm hold,
But trusting in the Unseen, stories untold.
He seeks no proofs that worldly eyes can trace,
But finds his strength in His enduring Grace.
He does not waver when doubt may call,
But trusts the Divine Plan, encompassing all.

For only He reveals what's truly meant.
Only in Him, is Sabr well-spent.
Only He remains the source
Of Unseen Truth, and boundless force.

Wisdom Unveiled

The profound wisdom unveiled in Belief in the Unseen and Divine Endurance is that trials are pivotal in strengthening the wise-one's belief in the Unseen (Ghaib) and cultivating Divine Endurance (Sabr). When external solutions fade, reliance on Allah's unseen hand and active patience

---

[279] This is in agreement with the Quran verse:

《Can the one who knows that your Lord's revelation to you ˹O Prophet˺ is the truth be like the one who is blind? None will be mindful ˹of this˺ except people of reason. (19) ˹They are˺ those who honour Allah's covenant, never breaking the pledge; (20) and those who maintain whatever ˹ties˺ Allah has ordered to be maintained, stand in awe of their Lord, and fear strict judgment. (21) And ˹they are˺ those who endure patiently, seeking their Lord's pleasure,1 establish prayer, donate from what We have provided for them—secretly and openly—and respond to evil with good. It is they who will have the ultimate abode: (22) the Gardens of Eternity, which they will enter along with the righteous among their parents, spouses, and descendants. And the angels will enter upon them from every gate, ˹saying,˺ (23) "Peace be upon you for your perseverance. How excellent is the ultimate abode!" (24)》 [Quran 23:19-24]

forge a powerful spiritual muscle. The contemplation highlights that true faith is proven through steadfastness, leading to Divine companionship and guidance even amidst terror and uncertainty on the Day of Resurrection, for those who patiently seek His countenance and repel evil with good. This unwavering conviction in Allah's perfect, though veiled, plan grants deep psychic resilience and ultimately secures the "excellent abode" of Divine fulfillment.

Wise-Reflection

Reflect on a time when you had to trust in an outcome you couldn't see, or endure a difficult period with uncertainty. How challenging was it for you to maintain Sabr (patience) without resentment during that time? Consider the idea that "Belief is not built upon seeing, Nor is certainty bound by the visible." How does this concept resonate with your own spiritual journey? What practices might help you cultivate greater reliance on the Unseen Hand of Allah when solutions are not apparent? How can developing this "spiritual muscle" of active waiting and steadfast trust enhance your psychic resilience and your conviction in Allah's perfect plan, even when it's veiled?

Contemplation: Empowerment Through Divine Alternates

The wise-one understands empowerment through Divine Alternates (Badal). When one path closes, Allah opens another; when one blessing is removed, another, often greater, replaces it. This is not about seeking substitutes, but recognizing Allah's infinite capacity to provide and compensate in ways beyond human foresight. This belief in Divine alternates instills resilience and prevents despair, as the wise-one knows that Allah's generosity and provision are unending, and that every loss is an opportunity for a higher gain from the Divine. This leads to profound psychic resilience and trust in Divine provision.

Consider, O seeker: If the Divine weakens distractions within you without weakening your capacity to overcome them, then inquire about the Divine from both those who possess knowledge and those who remain ignorant.

The Reality of Divine Authority

The unfolding of fate is not in the hands of creation,
But in the command of the One
Who governs without rival.
Alternates rise, alternates fall,
But He alone disposes of them, encompassing all.
He weakens those who stand against truth,
He strengthens those whom He wills, in their youth and ruth.
And in that balance,
The servant must ask—
Who holds true knowledge, clear and bright,
And who is left in ignorance's night?

It was not the believers who struck,
But His decree, a destined luck.
⟨And you did not throw when you threw, but Allah threw.⟩[280]
Not the Prophet who threw, a stone or sand,
But His Hand that rendered favor across the land.
For schemes rise against truth, with wicked might,
Yet He frustrates them, putting wrong to flight.
⟨And (the disbelievers) plotted, but Allah plotted. And Allah is the best of
plotters.⟩[281]

The mighty stand in defiance, proud and tall,
Yet they find themselves facing only His justice, when they fall.
For in seeking judgment,
They invite their own reckoning, on earth and in firmament.
In persistence, in falsehood's deep embrace,
They invite their downfall, losing all grace.
For numbers do not define victory's sign,

---

[280] This is derived from the Quran verse of:

📖 ⟨It was not you ˹believers˺ who killed them, but it was Allah Who did so. Nor was it you ˹O Prophet˺ who threw ˹a handful of sand at the disbelievers˺,1 but it was Allah Who did so, rendering the believers a great favour. Surely Allah is All-Hearing, All-Knowing. (17)⟩ [Quran 8:17]

[281] This is derived from the Quran verse of:

📖 ⟨And ˹remember, O Prophet,˺ when the disbelievers conspired to capture, kill, or exile you. They planned, but Allah also planned. And Allah is the best of planners. (30)⟩ [Quran 8:30]

Nor do forces dictate fate's design—
⟨For Allah is certainly with the believers.⟩²⁸²

He alone provides,
From the heavens, where His wisdom guides,
From the earth, where His bounty hides.
And if one seeks an answer, clear and true,
There are only two paths for souls to pursue—
One rightly guided, lit by His grace,
One lost beyond sight, in a desolate place.
Deeds do not burden the righteous, pure and free,
Nor does falsehood imprison the truthful, for all to see.
For all will gather before Him, in awe and dread,
All will stand in the presence
Of the All-Knowing Judge, words unsaid.
Idols cannot answer, with empty gaze,
Nor do they hold power, in these latter days,
For He alone remains—
Almighty, All-Wise, in constant reins.

The Prophet came,
Not to command with earthly fame,
But to deliver the message, to warn by name.
Yet most turn away, from truth's bright gleam,
Forgetting that guidance
Is not forced, but chosen, like a waking dream.²⁸³

---

²⁸² This is in agreement with the Quran verse:

📖 ⟨It was not you ʿbelieversʾ who killed them, but it was Allah Who did so. Nor was it you ʿO Prophetʾ who threw ʿa handful of sand at the disbelieversʾ,[1] but it was Allah Who did so, rendering the believers a great favour. Surely Allah is All-Hearing, All-Knowing. (17) As such, Allah frustrates the evil plans of the disbelievers. (18) If you ʿMeccansʾ sought judgment, now it has come to you. And if you cease, it will be for your own good. But if you persist, We will persist. And your forces—no matter how numerous they might be—will not benefit you whatsoever. For Allah is certainly with the believers. (19)⟩ [Quran 8:17-19]

[1]: Before the battle, the Prophet ﷺ threw a handful of sand at the disbelievers and prayed for their defeat.

²⁸³ And the Quran verse:

For the one who perceives—
Strength and weakness are not opposites,
But a means of revelation's breeze.
And the one who understands—
To be empowered is not victory's call,
To be weakened is not loss, after all,
But both are a trial—
Leading either toward truth,
Or away from it, for a short while.

So the wise-one walks forward—
Not fearing loss, nor change's sting,
But trusting the Divine, new blessings bring.
He sees in closing doors a wider way,
His Hand of Alternates, day by day.
He does not cling to what the world provides,
But in His vast provision, his hope abides.

For only He replaces, ever grand.
Only in Him, we truly understand.
Only He remains the source
Of Alternates, Resilience, and boundless force."

Wisdom Unveiled

The profound wisdom unveiled in Empowerment Through Divine Alternates is that trials reveal Allah's infinite capacity to provide and compensate. The wise-one understands that when one path closes, Allah opens another, and a removed blessing is often replaced by a greater one, a truth supported by verses like "And you did not throw when you threw, but Allah threw." This recognition that Divine authority governs all, and that even enemy schemes are frustrated by His supreme planning, instills resilience and prevents despair. The contemplation highlights that strength

---

〈Ask ˹them, O Prophet˺, "Who provides for you from the heavens and the earth?" Say, "Allah! Now, certainly one of our two groups1 is ˹rightly˺ guided; the other is clearly astray." (24) Say, "You will not be accountable for our misdeeds, nor will we be accountable for your deeds." (25) Say, "Our Lord will gather us together, then He will judge between us with the truth. For He is the All-Knowing Judge." (26) Say, "Show me those ˹idols˺ you have joined with Him as partners. No! In fact, He ˹alone˺ is Allah—the Almighty, All-Wise." (27) We have sent you ˹O Prophet˺ only as a deliverer of good news and a warner to all of humanity, but most people do not know. (28)〉 [Quran 34:24-28]

and weakness are both trials, means of Divine revelation, and that true empowerment comes not from worldly victory or absence of loss, but from knowing that Allah alone provides and is with the believers, leading to deep psychic resilience and trust in Divine provision.

Wise-Reflection

Reflect on a time when something significant was taken from you, or a path you desired closed. Did you initially feel despair or a sense of loss? In retrospect, can you identify how Allah might have provided an "alternate" blessing or opened a new, perhaps better, path? How does the concept that "Allah is the best of plotters" (Quran 8:30) and that His Hand is behind even unforeseen events, reshape your understanding of loss or setbacks? How can cultivating this belief in Divine Alternates strengthen your psychic resilience and prevent despair, allowing you to see every change as an opportunity for higher gain from the Divine, trusting that He alone provides?

Contemplation: Escaping from Divine Tribulations (Not Through Avoidance, but Through Him)

The final contemplation reveals that escaping from Divine tribulations is not achieved by avoiding them, but by taking refuge in Allah Himself. The wise-one does not seek to bypass the test but to find their ultimate solace and strength in the Tester. This means drawing near to Allah through remembrance, supplication, and complete surrender during the trial itself. The "escape" is not from the event, but from its power to overwhelm or corrupt the soul, finding inner peace and liberation by submitting entirely to the Divine Will within the tribulation. This is a profound psychic liberation from the trial's adverse effects.

Understand: If the Divine weakens you in the face of distractions, empowering those distractions over you, then seek refuge from Divine tribulation and implore protection from the Divine plan.

Seeking Refuge: Escaping the Trial of Neglect

To be removed from strength,
Yet see strength remain untouched—
This is not empowerment,
But a warning's touch.

[425]

When trials come, with heavy hand,
And the servant finds themselves weakened, losing their stand,
Not to refine them, as was often told,
But to cast them into tribulation, bought and sold,
Then the wise-one must seek refuge.

For those who turn away, in false elation,
Rejoice in their exemption, a brief sensation,
Yet they do not know, in their comfort's guise,
That exemption is not mercy, but abandonment in disguise.
❰Do not march forth in the heat,❱
They say, preferring comfort, bitter and sweet,
Over struggle's call, the righteous feat.
But they forget—
❰The Fire of Hell is far hotter!❱ —Quran 9:81
They laugh for a moment, a fleeting sound,
But weeping will be their end, on judgment ground.

They stayed behind once, from sacred quest,
And so they will remain behind forever, put to the test.
❰Allah has sealed their hearts, so they do not understand.❱²⁸⁴ — Quran 9:87, 9:93
For hearts that seal themselves, by their own decree,
Do not find guidance, nor ever see.
And souls that seek excuses, to hide from truth,
Do not escape their fate, from early youth.

---

²⁸⁴ This is in agreement with the Quran verse:

📖 ❰Those ˹hypocrites˺ who remained behind rejoiced for doing so in defiance of the Messenger of Allah and hated ˹the prospect of˺ striving with their wealth and their lives in the cause of Allah. They said ˹to one another˺, "Do not march forth in the heat." Say, ˹O Prophet,˺ "The Fire of Hell is far hotter!" If only they could comprehend! (81) So let them laugh a little—they will weep much as a reward for what they have committed. (82) If Allah returns you ˹O Prophet˺ to a group of them and they ask to go forth with you, say, "You will not ever go forth or fight an enemy along with me. You preferred to stay behind the first time, so stay with those ˹helpless˺ who remain behind." (83) And do not ever offer ˹funeral˺ prayers for any of their dead, nor stand by their grave ˹at burial˺, for they have lost faith in Allah and His Messenger and died rebellious. (84) And let neither their wealth nor children impress you ˹O Prophet˺. Allah only intends to torment them through these things in this world, and ˹then˺ their souls will depart while they are disbelievers. (85) Whenever a sûrah is revealed stating, "Believe in Allah and struggle along with His Messenger," the rich among them would ask to be exempt, saying, "Leave us with those who remain behind." (86) They preferred to stay behind with the helpless, and their hearts have been sealed so they do not comprehend. (87)❱ [Quran 9:81-87]

And the Quran verse of:

📖 ❰ Blame is only on those who seek exemption from you although they have the means. They preferred to stay behind with the helpless, and Allah has sealed their hearts so they do not realize ˹the consequences˺. (93)❱ [Quran 9:93]

[426]

The Prophet was commanded, by Divine Will,
Not to stand in their remembrance, at prayer still,
Not to honor their passing, when they are laid,
For wealth and status, quickly fade,
Do not shield one from the torment of heedlessness,
Nor from the Divine wrath's deep distress.

For the one who perceives, with inner sight,
Neglect is not freedom, nor soothing light,
But a deeper trial, a harder way.
To be ignored by Him, to be left astray,
To be left without guidance, a soul in plight,
Is not relief, but punishment in disguise, in darkest night.
Thus, the wise-one sees the signs, so clear and bold,
Recognizing that refuge
Is not found in avoidance, nor stories told,
But in return to Him, more precious than gold.
Not in ignoring the test, when trials appear,
But in seeking protection from falling into heedlessness, held so dear.

For when strength is stripped away, and courage wanes,
And the heart remains veiled, bound by earthly chains,
There is only one path left, for soul to call—
To flee from tribulation, and from its enthrall,
And call upon Him, with fervent plea,
Before the seal is placed, for eternity,
Before the return is no longer possible, to be free.

So the wise-one walks forward—
Not seeking ways to shun the test,
But finding His Shelter, truly blessed.
He hides not from the fire's embrace,
But finds his solace in His sacred space.
He does not strive to bypass the trial's sting,
But clings to His Will, for peace it brings.

For only He offers refuge from despair.
Only in Him, we find what's truly fair.

Only He remains the source
Of Refuge, Liberation, and boundless force.

Wisdom Unveiled

The profound wisdom unveiled in Escaping from Divine Tribulations (Not Through Avoidance, but Through Him) is that true escape from trials is not achieved by bypassing them, but by taking refuge in Allah Himself. The wise-one learns that seeking comfort and avoiding struggle, as the disbelievers who say "Do not march forth in the heat" (Quran 9:81), is a path to abandonment and severe punishment. Conversely, when strength is diminished and the heart feels veiled, the only true path is to flee to Allah through remembrance and supplication. This realization transforms perceived tribulation into a means of finding inner peace and liberation from its corrupting power, achieving psychic liberation by submitting entirely to the Divine Will within the test, and recognizing that true refuge is found in returning to Him and seeking protection from heedlessness itself.

Wise-Reflection

Reflect on your natural inclination when faced with difficulty: do you tend to avoid the challenge, or do you seek to overcome it by your own strength? How does the idea that "exemption is not mercy, but abandonment" (as seen with those who stayed behind) challenge your desire to bypass discomfort or struggle? Consider a current or past tribulation: how might shifting your focus from "escaping the event" to "taking refuge in Allah Himself" during the trial transform your experience of it? What practices of remembrance and supplication can you strengthen to find inner peace and liberation within the very midst of your challenges, leading to profound psychic liberation from their overwhelming power?

Conclusion: Oath to Surpass Trials

ECHOES OF REALIZATION: THE HIDDEN PACT OF ENDURANCE

Before the wise-one's soul entered the earthly clay, a profound, primordial question was whispered to its essence: "Will you endure to return to Me, even through the fires of trial?" And from the deepest core of its being, the soul, in its pristine purity, answered with an unequivocal, resonant "Yes."

Trials are, therefore, not random misfortunes. They are sacred reminders, echoes of that ancient pact. They are the purifying fire that meticulously refines the essence of being, the humbling storm that strips away all pretense, the profound exile that ultimately guides the heart back to the only true homeland it ever possessed: the luminous Presence of the Everlasting. To endure a trial is to consciously remember this sacred pact. To fully surrender within it is to courageously fulfill it.

THE SEEKER'S ASCENT: TRIALS AS THE BRIDGE TO TRANSCENDENCE

This profound reflection majestically unveils trials not as punitive measures, but as sacred vehicles, as Divine permissions—deep invitations to ascend beyond what is temporary and fleeting into what is eternal and timeless. Through the very heart of these trials, the wise-one's soul intimately remembers a crucial truth: it was never truly meant to merely thrive in the dust of worldly comforts. It was destined, by Divine Will, to burn through illusion, to be spiritually broken by hardship, and to rise again—purified, strengthened, and profoundly transformed—a vessel now truly fit to stand, in utmost humility and reverence, before the Majestic (Al-Jalil), the Source of all grandeur.

Thus, every trial endured, every perceived loss acknowledged, every deep longing transmuted, is not a setback but a profound step upward into the unbreakable embrace of the One who first whispered the primordial command: "Be!" This continuous process of enduring and transcending trials, anchored in faith and surrender, is the very essence of psychic and spiritual liberation, leading to an ever-closer union with the Divine.

13TH REFLECTION: BEYOND KNOWING THE CREATOR NAMES

(Beyond Divine Names)

THE GATEWAY VERSES

In the sacred words of Allah, a majestic declaration of His absolute Oneness, His perfect Attributes, and the source of all names and glorification, inviting all who reflect to ponder His essence:

📖 ⟪He is Allah—there is no god ˈworthy of worshipˈ except Him: Knower of the seen and unseen. He is the Most Compassionate, Most Merciful. (22) He is Allah— there is no god except Him: the King, the Most Holy, the All-Perfect, the Source of Serenity, the Watcher ˈof allˈ, the Almighty, the Supreme in Might,1 the Majestic. Glorified is Allah far above what they associate with Him ˈin worshipˈ! (23) He is Allah: the Creator, the Inventor, the Shaper. He ˈaloneˈ has the Most Beautiful Names. Whatever is in the heavens and the earth ˈconstantlyˈ glorifies Him. And He is the Almighty, All-Wise. (24)⟫ [Quran 59:22-24]*

ILLUMINATION'S DAWN

There comes a sublime moment in the wise-one's journey when even the most sacred and revered names of the Divine begin to feel like garments too small for the boundless longing of the soul. The wise-one awakens to a profound secret: that every name, every title, every eloquent praise— while undeniably holy, while intrinsically luminous—is ultimately but a fleeting shadow compared to the boundless Light of the Divine Essence itself.

The Divine Names are like vast, flowing rivers. Yet, even the grandest rivers are not the infinite ocean from which they originate. They are merciful, divinely ordained bridges for the limited human mind to safely cross—yet they are emphatically not the shores of the Ultimate Reality they point toward. To truly know the Creator is not to merely master or enumerate His names; it is to be utterly unmade, dissolved, and transformed by His absolute nearness. It is to realize, with profound clarity, that behind every single name whispered in fervent devotion, there stands an Ineffable Essence that no word, no human construct, can ever fully capture or contain. Let us now, with reverence and humility, step beyond the familiar realm of language, and courageously walk into the silent country where Being itself instinctively kneels.

THE UNFOLDING OF INSIGHTS

This section guides the wise-one beyond the intellectual comprehension of Divine Names to a direct, experiential encounter with the unconditioned essence of the Creator, dissolving the veils of linguistic and conceptual limitations.

Contemplation: The First Temptation (Attachment to Concepts)

The wise-one recognizes the first temptation on this path: the subtle attachment to intellectual concepts and the names themselves, mistaking the map for the territory. While Divine Names are essential points of entry and avenues for understanding Allah's attributes, clinging to them as the ultimate reality can become a veil. This contemplation calls the wise-one to release the intellectual grasp that seeks to define and categorize the Infinite, understanding that true knowing lies beyond the constructs of the mind. This psychic liberation prevents stagnation in conceptual worship.

Consider: The initial enticement in seeking knowledge of the Originator is the preoccupation with the Divine names alone.

Description Does Not Contain Him

The first temptation in seeking Him,
Is believing that knowing His name,
Is knowing Him.
For the name is spoken, a fleeting sound,
But the Reality is beyond words, unbound.
The name is echoed, a sacred sign,
Yet the Essence cannot be contained by mortal design.

He is An-Noor, the Light of the heavens and the earth,
But light upon light is a parable of His worth.

It is a glimpse, a metaphor set forth,
Never the full truth, from south to north.[285]

For He is the Originator, the One who multiplies,
Yet there is nothing like unto Him, beyond all skies.
He is the All-Hearing, the All-Seeing, in every space,
Yet beyond perception, time, or place.
Thus, the wise-one does not mistake,
Description for presence, for goodness sake.
Nor attributes for Essence, a sacred art,
To know with the soul, to feel with the heart.[286]

To seek Him
Is not merely to recite His names,
But to be guided toward His light,
To recognize that knowledge
Is not knowing facts,
But witnessing reality.
For revelation does not limit Him,
But invites understanding—
Not in the letter,
But in the surrender
Beyond speech.
To truly seek the Creator
Is to move beyond names,
Into the silence
Where only the soul can whisper,
Where the Ever-Living meets the heart

---

[285] This is exemplified in the Quran verse describing one attribute and name of Allah that is (An Noor), whereas a complete verse only shows part of His name:

〈Allah is the Light of the heavens and the earth. His light1 is like a niche in which there is a lamp, the lamp is in a crystal, the crystal is like a shining star, lit from ˊthe oil ofˋ a blessed olive tree, ˊlocatedˋ neither to the east nor the west,2 whose oil would almost glow, even without being touched by fire. Light upon light! Allah guides whoever He wills to His light. And Allah sets forth parables for humanity. For Allah has ˊperfectˋ knowledge of all things. (35)〉 [Quran 24:35]

[286] This is in agreement with the Quran verse:

〈ˊHe isˋ the Originator of the heavens and the earth. He has made for you spouses from among yourselves, and ˊmadeˋ mates for cattle ˊas wellˋ—multiplying you ˊbothˋ. There is nothing like Him, for He ˊaloneˋ is the All-Hearing, All-Seeing. (11)〉 [Quran 42:11]

Unbound by letters,
Unbound by form

The wise-one knows that
The first temptation in seeking The Creator is to mistake the echo of His name
For the essence of His reality.
For His name is but a signpost,
A fleeting reflection of the Unfathomable,
While He remains infinite,
Beyond every utterance,
Beyond every attempt to hold Him with words
So, he must let even the holy syllables,
Fall softly from his lips, like leaves in autumn's grace,
And stand stripped before the Mystery of His sacred face.
Without title to shield him,
Without formula to guide him,
Without crutch to steady his trembling soul.
For to approach the Infinite,
Is to release all that binds,
To stand in the stillness,
Where the heart alone can speak,
Where even silence becomes prayer,
And the soul meets the Creator,
Unveiled,
Unclothed in the language of knowing.

So the wise-one walks forward—
Not mistaking the map for the land,
But seeking the Essence, to truly understand.
He does not cling to a name or a sign,
But bows to the Ineffable, the Divine.
He lets go of concepts, however great,
And finds his purpose in surrender's state.

For only He is the Reality true.
Only in Him, we find what is new.
Only He remains the source
Of Essence, Silence, and boundless force.

Wisdom Unveiled

The profound wisdom unveiled in The First Temptation (Attachment to Concepts) is that the initial and most subtle spiritual trap is mistaking the Divine Names and intellectual concepts for the Divine Essence itself. The wise-one learns that names, while holy, are merely signposts or parables— like the "Light of the heavens and the earth"—pointing toward an Ineffable Reality that is beyond all description and perception. True spiritual progress requires releasing this intellectual grasp and moving into a state of psychic liberation where the heart meets the Creator "unveiled, unclothed in the language of knowing." This profound surrender, where even holy syllables fall away, is the only way to overcome stagnation and find the true knowing that lies beyond the confines of the human mind.

Wise-Reflection

Reflect on your own spiritual journey. Do you find yourself clinging to theological concepts, definitions, or even the names themselves, as if they were the final destination? How might this be a subtle veil that prevents you from a deeper, more direct experience of the Divine? Consider the idea of "letting even the holy syllables fall softly from your lips" and standing "stripped before the Mystery." What would it mean for your prayer life to move beyond the language of knowing and into the silence where the heart alone can speak? How might this shift lead to a profound psychic liberation and a more authentic encounter with the Divine Essence?

Contemplation: The second Temptation (Identification with Knowledge)

Following closely is the second temptation: identifying one's spiritual worth or progress with the knowledge of Divine Names, rather than the transformative experience they are meant to facilitate. Boasting of one's understanding or accumulation of spiritual knowledge can lead to subtle spiritual pride, subtly veiling the heart from true humility and direct apprehension. This contemplation urges the wise-one to shed reliance on personal intellectual acquisition, recognizing that the Divine Essence is unveiled not by what one knows in the conventional sense, but by what one becomes through humility and surrender. This is a crucial psychic recalibration away from ego and towards Divine Presence.

Consider: The second enticement in seeking knowledge of the Originator is the preoccupation with the Divine names alone. Hence, the second temptation in knowing the Creator is knowing the Creator's name for selfish, greedy, or evil wishes and not considering knowability a blessing from the Creator that no thanks can accomplish it.

The Temptation of Divine Names: A Trial of Intention

The seeker, drawn toward the knowledge of the Creator,
Finds the first enticement in His names alone—
Thinking that knowing them,
Is knowing Him.
Yet the second temptation is deeper,
More dangerous, more corrupting to the soul—
To wield His names, as mere tools,
For personal gain, for selfish desires, for greed,
For deception, to serve a worldly creed.

For knowability is a blessing, a gift beyond measure,
A gift no thanks can encompass, a boundless treasure.
To treat His names as mere tools,
Is to distort their essence,
To exchange devotion for manipulation's guise.
He granted knowledge to the one who was given His signs,
Yet he abandoned them, a soul lost in time.
⟨So he clung to the earth and followed his desires.⟩ —Quran 7:175

He could have been elevated,
Yet he clung to the world,
His desires consuming him.
Like a panting dog,
⟨If you chase it away, it pants; if you leave it alone, it pants.⟩ —Quran 7:176
Relentless in its craving, never fulfilled.
This is the state of those who deny the signs,
Who misuse what was sacred, in corrupted shrines.
Who turn knowledge into a means of destruction's hand,
And seek power over the Divine command.
He was granted the power of prayer,
His words answered without delay.

Yet when called to curse, his own tongue betrayed him,
And his punishment was his own corruption.
For when wisdom is sought without sincerity,
It does not lead to elevation,
But to downfall and spiritual poverty.[287]

Thus, the wise-one prays, with a humble heart:
"O my Lord, do not let me
Be lost in the enticement of Your names,
While forgetting Your presence."
For names do not hold power,
Except by His will.
Knowledge does not grant control,
Except by His decree.
And the one who seeks Him, in truth and light,
Must seek not description,
But surrender with all their might.

So the wise-one walks forward—
Not with the boast of what he knows,
But with the humility that grows.
He uses no name for selfish gain,
But seeks the Essence, to ease all pain.

---

[287] This is in agreement with an interesting Quran verse telling a story with various versions about a man whom being blessed by the Creator to be either having answerable prayers or knowing a Holy name of the Creator that whatever he asked for by it he got answered:

📖 ❨And relate to them ´O Prophet` the story of the one to whom We gave Our signs, but he abandoned them, so Satan took hold of him, and he became a deviant. (175) If We had willed, We would have elevated him with Our signs, but he clung to this life—following his evil desires. His example is that of a dog: if you chase it away, it pants, and if you leave it, it ´still` pants. This is the example of the people who deny Our signs.1 So narrate ´to them` stories ´of the past`, so perhaps they will reflect. (176) What an evil example of those who denied Our signs! They ´only` wronged their own souls. (177) Whoever Allah guides is truly guided. And whoever He leaves to stray, they are the ´true` losers. (178)❩ [Quran 7:175-178]

First story version: Al-Mu'tamir ibn Sulayman narrated on the authority of his father that he said: Balaam had been given prophecy, and his prayers were answered. When Moses came with the Children of Israel intending to fight the tyrants, the tyrants asked Balaam ibn Ba'oura to invoke a curse upon Moses. So he stood up to invoke a curse, but his tongue turned to invoking a curse upon his companions. He was asked about that, so he said: I am not able to do more than what you hear; and his tongue stuck out upon his chest.

Second story version: It was narrated that Balaam bin Ba'oura prayed that Moses would not enter the city of the giants, and his prayer was answered, but he remained in the wilderness. Moses said: O Lord, for what sin did we remain in the wilderness? He said: Because of the prayer of Balaam. He said: Just as you heard his prayer against me, hear my prayer against him. So Moses prayed that God would strip him of the Greatest Name, and God stripped him of what he was doing.

He holds no pride in what is given,
But returns the gift, a soul forgiven.

For only He gives the blessing to see.
Only in Him, we find our liberty.
Only He remains the source
Of Sincerity, Humility, and boundless force.

Wisdom Unveiled

The profound wisdom unveiled in The Second Temptation (Identification with Knowledge) is the recognition of spiritual pride that can arise from accumulating knowledge of the Divine Names. The wise-one learns that the true trial is one of intention—whether one uses this knowledge for personal gain and worldly desires, or as a means to deepen humility and surrender. This contemplation powerfully illustrates that knowability is a priceless blessing that cannot be wielded for manipulation. It cautions against the fate of those who misuse this sacred gift, a corruption so deep that their state becomes like a "panting dog" (Quran 7:176), relentlessly craving but never fulfilled. The ultimate psychic recalibration is to shed reliance on intellectual acquisition and instead seek the Divine Presence through sincerity and surrender, recognizing that spiritual worth is measured not by what one knows, but by what one becomes.

Wise-Reflection

Reflect on moments when you've felt a sense of pride or superiority due to your spiritual or religious knowledge. How might this subtle spiritual pride act as a veil between you and true humility? Consider the example of the "panting dog": how can the relentless pursuit of knowledge for personal gain or self-elevation, rather than sincere devotion, lead to a state of perpetual spiritual craving without fulfillment? What practices can you cultivate to ensure your understanding of the Divine Names leads you to greater humility and surrender, rather than to a sense of intellectual acquisition? How can this shift lead to a crucial psychic recalibration away from ego and towards an authentic encounter with the Divine Presence?

Contemplation: The Purpose and Limitations of Divine Names

The wise-one deeply understands the purpose and inherent limitations of Divine Names. They are bestowed by Allah as means for creation to relate to Him, to praise Him, and to understand His attributes. They are a manifestation of His mercy, allowing finite beings to approach the Infinite. However, their limitation lies in their very nature as linguistic constructs, designed for human comprehension. They can never fully encompass the unconditioned Essence of the Creator, which remains utterly transcendent. They are pointers, not the destination itself, leading to a crucial psychic shift beyond conceptual limitations.

Contemplate: Every symbol carries its inherent meaning with the ultimate aim of drawing one towards the Divine. Every eloquent expression conveys its significance in the endeavor to reach the Divine.

The Language of Divine Expression

Symbols hold their meanings,
Words carry their weight,
Yet all arrive at one truth—
Nothing speaks without returning to Him.
⟨*He is Allah: the Creator, the Inventor, the Shaper. He ˋalone˄ has the Most*
Beautiful Names.⟩ *—Quran 59:24*
His Names are most beautiful,
Called upon by those who seek.
No utterance is greater,
No invocation more perfect,
For to speak His Names
Is to speak truth itself.[288]

A good word stands as a good tree,
Its roots firm,
Its branches reaching skyward,
⟨*Yielding its fruit in every season by the permission of its Lord.*⟩ *—Quran 14:25*
For speech does not simply exist—
It grows, it nourishes, it ascends.
Words rise toward Him,
Actions are lifted in His presence,
While falsehood sinks into failure.

---

[288] This is in agreement with the Quran verse:

⟨Allah has the Most Beautiful Names. So call upon Him by them, and keep away from those who abuse His Names.1 They will be punished for what they used to do. (180)⟩ [Quran 7:180]

Those who plot for deception,
Will see their schemes dissolve,
For no craftiness stands
Against divine decree.
❨*And the parable of a bad word is that of an evil tree, uprooted from the earth, having*
no stability.❩[289]

For the wise-one,
Expression is not empty,
Nor is language mere sound.
Every word, every thought, every symbol
Must carry the soul
Toward the One
Who is beyond expression,
Yet known in every utterance.
He is the Knower of the seen and unseen,
Beyond all that we can name or deem.[290]

So the wise-one walks forward—
Not clinging to the words they have spoken,
But finding His Essence, a divine token.
He sees in every name a blessed sign,
But knows the Reality is utterly Divine.
He does not halt at the river's shore,
But seeks the Ocean, forevermore.

For only He is the Truth unspoken.
Only in Him, the veils are broken.

---

[289] This is in agreement with the Quran verse:

📖 ❨Do you not see how Allah compares a good word to a good tree? Its root is firm and its branches reach the sky, (24) ῾always῾ yielding its fruit in every season by the Will of its Lord. This is how Allah sets forth parables for the people, so perhaps they will be mindful. (25)❩ [Quran 14:24-25]

Also, this is in agreement with the Quran verse:

📖 ❨Whoever seeks honour and power, then ῾let them know that῾ all honour and power belongs to Allah. To Him ῾alone῾ good words ascend, and righteous deeds are raised up by Him. As for those who plot evil, they will suffer a severe punishment. And the plotting of such ῾people῾ is doomed ῾to fail῾. (10)❩ [Quran 35:10]

[290] This is in agreement with the Quran verse of:

📖 ❨He is Allah—there is no god ῾worthy of worship῾ except Him: Knower of the seen and unseen. He is the Most Compassionate, Most Merciful. (22)❩ [Quran 59:22]

Only He remains the source
Of Names, Essence, and boundless force.

Wisdom Unveiled

The profound wisdom unveiled in The Purpose and Limitations of Divine Names is that while Allah's names are a manifestation of His mercy—serving as essential bridges for human understanding and a means of praise—they are inherently limited. The wise-one recognizes that these names are linguistic constructs and, like a "good tree" (Quran 14:25), they are meant to nourish and ascend the soul towards the Divine, but can never fully encompass the unconditioned, transcendent Essence of the Creator, the Knower of the seen and unseen. The ultimate goal is to move beyond the names themselves—the pointers—to the Destination, experiencing a crucial psychic shift and recognizing that true knowing lies in embracing the infinite Reality that is beyond all human expression.

Wise-Reflection

Reflect on your personal experience with the Divine Names. Do you ever feel that your understanding of a name like "The Merciful" or "The All-Powerful" feels limited by your human experience? How can acknowledging the purpose and inherent limitations of these names, as pointers to a greater Essence, deepen your sense of humility? Consider the parable of the "good tree" (Quran 14:25): how might consciously using your words, thoughts, and prayers not as a way to define the Creator, but as a means to carry your soul towards Him, lead to a profound psychic shift and a more intimate encounter with His reality, which is "beyond expression yet known in every utterance"?

Contemplation: The Powerlessness of Names

In this profound realization, the wise-one apprehends the powerlessness of names to capture the Creator's true essence. A name points, it describes an attribute, but it cannot contain the Named. Just as a word for "ocean" is not the ocean itself, so too are Divine Names ultimately insufficient to grasp Al-Ahad (The One) in His absolute, incomparable Oneness. This insight liberates the wise-one from worshipping the name or the concept, shifting their devotion to the boundless Reality beyond all nomenclature.

This culminates in a profound psychic transformation into pure awe and surrender.

Reflect: In the immediate presence of the Divine, the servant perceives that the Divine names possess no independent power. This realization culminates in the state of profound bewilderment, the ultimate station attainable by the human heart.

Beyond Names: The Bewilderment of Divine Presence

In the presence of the Creator,
The servant perceives—
His names hold no power independent of Him.
For the name is not the reality,
Nor does expression contain the essence.
To utter His name
Is to call upon meaning,
But not to grasp the Infinite.
To recite His attributes,
Is to witness contrast,
But not to perceive
The unity beyond division.

He is the Almighty, the All-Wise, the Most High, the Greatest—
Yet these words are only echoes
Of something deeper,
Something no syllables can capture.
❨The heavens almost burst from above it, and the angels glorify the praises of their Lord❩[291] —Quran 42:5
Yet He alone holds forgiveness,
Mercy beyond measure.
For in truth,
There is no protector but Him,
No judge but His decree,
No sustainer but His will.

---

[291] This is in agreement with the Quran verse of:

📖 ❨The heavens nearly burst, one above the other, ˹in awe of Him˺. And the angels glorify the praises of their Lord, and seek forgiveness for those on earth. Surely Allah alone is the All-Forgiving, Most Merciful. (5)❩ [Quran 42:5]

To those who differ,
Judgment rests in His hands alone.
To those who seek,
Trust is placed
Not in knowledge,
But in surrender.

He is the Originator, the One beyond comparison,
Beyond form, beyond limitation.
The keys of the heavens
And the earth belong to Him,
And His provision flows
Without restraint.

❨*He is the One Who forgives sins and accepts repentance, the Severe in punishment,*
the Bountiful. There is no god ˹worthy of worship˺ except Him. To Him is the final
return.❩[292] —*Quran 40:3*

Thus, the final station of the heart, the ultimate threshold,
Is bewilderment—
To stand before Him and know that knowing
Has reached its limit.
That words have dissolved into silence.
That certainty exists

---

[292] This is in agreement with the Quran verse:

📖 ❨Ḥā-Mīm. (1) 'Aĭn-Sīn-Qāf. (2) And so you ˹O Prophet˺ are sent revelation, just like those before you, by Allah—the Almighty, All-Wise. (3) To Him belongs whatever is in the heavens and whatever is on the earth. And He is the Most High, the Greatest. (4) The heavens nearly burst, one above the other, ˹in awe of Him˺. And the angels glorify the praises of their Lord, and seek forgiveness for those on earth. Surely Allah alone is the All-Forgiving, Most Merciful. (5) As for those who take other protectors besides Him, Allah is Watchful over them. And you ˹O Prophet˺ are not a keeper over them. (6) And so We have revealed to you a Quran in Arabic, so you may warn the Mother of Cities1 and everyone around it, and warn of the Day of Gathering—about which there is no doubt—˹when˺ a group will be in Paradise and another in the Blaze. (7) Had Allah willed, He could have easily made all ˹humanity˺ into a single community ˹of believers˺. But He admits into His mercy whoever He wills. And the wrongdoers will have no protector or helper. (8) How can they take protectors besides Him? Allah alone is the Protector. He ˹alone˺ gives life to the dead. And He ˹alone˺ is Most Capable of everything. (9) ˹Say to the believers, O Prophet,˺ "Whatever you may differ about, its judgment rests with Allah. That is Allah—my Lord. In Him I put my trust, and to Him I ˹always˺ turn." (10) ˹He is˺ the Originator of the heavens and the earth. He has made for you spouses from among yourselves, and ˹made˺ mates for cattle ˹as well˺—multiplying you ˹both˺. There is nothing like Him, for He ˹alone˺ is the All-Hearing, All-Seeing. (11) To Him belong the keys ˹of the treasuries˺ of the heavens and the earth. He gives abundant or limited provisions to whoever He wills. Indeed, He has ˹perfect˺ knowledge of all things. (12)❩ [Quran 42:1-12]

Not in definition,
But in Presence.

When the servant stands
Before the Creator,
Before Al-Jalil (The Majestic),
They see:
The names hold no power here.
In His presence,
Even the holiest of words
Fall like broken vessels,
Shattered by the weight of the Infinite.
Here, thought surrenders,
Speech dissolves,
And only the heart kneels
Only the silence worships,
For in the stillness of awe,
The servant knows:
It is not the names,
But the One they reflect,
The Unnameable, the Absolute,
That fills the soul.

So the wise-one walks forward—
Not worshipping the concept's shell,
But drawn by His Reality's spell.
He does not define, nor seek to grasp,
But stands in awe, in awe at last.
He lets go of all that he has known,
And finds his home in His Essence alone.

For only in Presence can the heart find rest.
Only in Him, we pass the test.
Only He remains the source
Of Essence, Bewilderment, and boundless force.

Wisdom Unveiled

The profound wisdom unveiled in The Powerlessness of Names is that Divine Names, while holy and full of meaning, are utterly insufficient to capture the transcendent Essence of the Creator, Al-Ahad (The One). The wise-one comes to understand that a name has no independent power and is merely an echo pointing to a greater Reality. This realization liberates the heart from worshipping concepts, culminating in a state of profound bewilderment—the ultimate station where words dissolve into silence, and certainty is found not in definition, but in Presence. This insight, that "the heavens nearly burst in awe" of the Creator, leads to a profound psychic transformation where the soul surrenders all pretense of knowledge, and worship becomes a silent kneeling before the Unnameable and Absolute reality that fills all.

Wise-Reflection

Reflect on your own spiritual journey: Have you ever felt a limitation in using words to describe Allah's attributes? How does the idea that "the final station of the heart is bewilderment" resonate with your own experience of awe and reverence? Consider the phrase: "The names hold no power here." How can consciously moving your devotion from the names themselves to the Reality they reflect lead to a deeper and more liberating form of worship? What would it mean for your heart to bow in "silence, wordless before the Infinite," and how might this practice foster a profound psychic transformation beyond the constraints of human language and understanding?

Contemplation: The Temptation and Peril of Names (as barriers)

The wise-one acknowledges the temptation and peril of names if they become barriers rather than pathways. When one becomes exclusively focused on the literal meaning, pronunciation, or intellectual analysis of a name, without allowing it to lead to an experiential connection, the name itself can become a veil. The peril lies in mistaking the sign for the Signified, thereby limiting the vastness of the Divine to human linguistic constructs. This contemplation urges vigilance against intellectual idolatry and a continuous striving for direct, unmediated presence, leading to a profound psychic recalibration away from conceptual limitations.

Implore, O seeker: O Divine Lord, safeguard me from becoming entangled in the intricacies of letters when seeking Your knowledge, lest such complexities perplex the mind and fragment understanding.

Beyond the Puzzle of Words: Seeking True Knowledge

What lies between the seeker
And the Creator
Is beyond the syllables
The tongue can shape,
Beyond the letters
The mind can grasp.
There are no questions
That can touch the Real,
No answers that can contain Him.

When the soul aches to know,
He teaches it first to fall silent.
For He is Allah,
The Knower of the unseen,
The Most Compassionate, the Most Merciful.
He is the King, the Source of Serenity,
The Watcher of all, the Majestic beyond all thought.
Names attempt to define, but He cannot be confined.
Expressions try to capture, yet He remains beyond articulation.
❮Whatever is in the heavens and the earth glorifies Him. And He is the Almighty,
the All-Wise.❯ [293] —Quran 59:22-24.

Letters arrange themselves,
Shaping thought, guiding perception.
Yet when the mind clings to patterns, to puzzles,
Meaning is lost
In the maze of symbols.
For knowledge that does not lead to Him

---

[293] This is in agreement regarding the Creator's name that cannot be encompassed in a letter to be comprehended by the human mind.

📖 ❮He is Allah—there is no god ˹worthy of worship˺ except Him: Knower of the seen and unseen. He is the Most Compassionate, Most Merciful. (22) He is Allah—there is no god except Him: the King, the Most Holy, the All-Perfect, the Source of Serenity, the Watcher ˹of all˺, the Almighty, the Supreme in Might,1 the Majestic. Glorified is Allah far above what they associate with Him ˹in worship˺! (23) He is Allah: the Creator, the Inventor, the Shaper. He ˹alone˺ has the Most Beautiful Names. Whatever is in the heavens and the earth ˹constantly˺ glorifies Him. And He is the Almighty, All-Wise. (24)❯ [Quran 59:22-24]

Becomes distraction,
And distraction weakens remembrance.

Thus, the wise-one prays:
"O my Lord, do not let me
Be lost in the puzzle of letters
When seeking You."

For not all knowledge refines, some only misleads—
A trial wrapped in illusion,
An intellect drawn toward confusion.
Some sought understanding
But fell into deception,
Mistaking magic for truth,
Confusing wisdom for trickery.
The angels warned:
⟪*We are only a test for you. Do not abandon your faith.*⟫ —*Quran 2:102*
Yet heedlessness prevailed,
And those who clung to distortion
Lost their share in eternity. [294]

For true knowledge
Is not in manipulation, not in complexity,
But in clarity—
In surrender that frees the mind,
In devotion that lifts the heart.
Understanding does not come from knowing many words,
But from seeing beyond them—

---

[294] This is in agreement with the Quran verse:

📖 ⟪They ʾinsteadʾ followed the magic promoted by the devils during the reign of Solomon. Never did Solomon disbelieve, rather the devils disbelieved. They taught magic to the people, along with what had been revealed to the two angels, Hârût and Mârût, in Babylon.[1] The two angels never taught anyone without saying, "We are only a test ʾfor youʾ, so do not abandon ʾyourʾ faith." Yet people learned ʾmagicʾ that caused a rift ʾevenʾ between husband and wife; although their magic could not harm anyone except by Allah's Will. They learned what harmed them and did not benefit them—although they already knew that whoever buys into magic would have no share in the Hereafter. Miserable indeed was the price for which they sold their souls, if only they knew! (102) If only they were faithful and mindful ʾof Allahʾ, there would have been a better reward from Allah, if only they knew! (103)⟫ [Quran 2:102-103]

[1]: The two angels, Hârût and Mârût, were sent to enlighten the people in Babylon so they would not confuse magic tricks with miracles. Still some people abused this knowledge, causing mischief in the land. These practices persisted until the time of Solomon, who himself was falsely accused of utilizing magic to run his kingdom, subdue the jinn, and control the wind.

Where wisdom flows without confusion,
Where faith stands untouched by distortion.

To fall silent
Is not to be without knowledge,
But to finally perceive without illusion.

Thus, the wise-one pray:
"O My Lord,
Do not let me become ensnared
In the labyrinth of letters,
For letters are mere shadows
Of what cannot be contained.
Let me seek You in the silence that speaks louder than words,
In the infinite that defies the puzzle of form,
Where Your essence shines unbound,
Illuminating the soul beyond language's reach.

How easily my mind
Reaches to grasp the Unholdable,
Like trying to catch the wind in a clenched fist.
How often I mistake the map for the mountain,
Content with lines and symbols,
While the peaks soar beyond my vision,
Untouched by my diagrams.
Yet the True One (Al-Haqq)
Resides beyond every boundary my thoughts impose—
Beyond my sketches of understanding,
Beyond the fragile frameworks I build.

So the wise-one walks forward—
Not in the puzzle of a written name,
But in His Presence, a sacred flame.
He guards against the intellect's snare,
And finds his refuge in unmediated prayer.
He lets go of all attempts to hold,
And seeks the Infinite, stories untold.

For only He is the Reality beyond grasp.
Only in Him, the soul's truth can last.
Only He remains the source
Of Essence, Clarity, and boundless force.

Wisdom Unveiled

The profound wisdom unveiled in The Temptation and Peril of Names is that Divine Names can become dangerous barriers if they lead to intellectual idolatry—mistaking the sign for the Signified. The wise-one is cautioned against becoming entangled in the "labyrinth of letters," as knowledge that does not lead to a direct, experiential connection to the Divine becomes a distraction that weakens remembrance. This contemplation highlights the peril of those who, like the people warned by the angels in Quran 2:102, use knowledge for worldly gain or distortion, losing their share in eternity. The ultimate goal is to move beyond the "puzzle of words" and the futile attempt to "catch the wind in a clenched fist," finding true clarity and understanding in silence and surrender, where the True One (Al-Haqq) is perceived without illusion, leading to a crucial psychic recalibration away from conceptual limitations.

Wise-Reflection

Reflect on how easily your mind can become ensnared in the intellectual puzzles of language and religious concepts. Do you ever find yourself debating details rather than experiencing the essence they point to? Consider the idea of "true knowledge" as something that "frees the mind" and "lifts the heart," rather than simply knowing many words. How can you, in your daily practice, strive to move beyond the "map" and into the "mountain," releasing the need to hold and define the Infinite? What would it mean for your prayer to find "His essence shining unbound, illuminating the soul beyond language's reach," and how might this lead to a more authentic and unmediated encounter with the Divine?

Contemplation: The Dispersal of Names and Meanings

In the highest state of knowing, the wise-one witnesses the dispersal of names and their conventional meanings. As the heart approaches the unconditioned Divine, the distinct boundaries between attributes begin to blur, and their meanings coalesce into a singular, incomprehensible Unity.

The wise-one experiences the underlying Oneness from which all names emanate, recognizing that each name is but a facet of an indivisible Reality. This dissolution of distinct meanings leads to a state of profound awe and speechless wonder, a deep psychic dissolution of ordinary categorization.

Contemplate, O seeker of divine understanding: The multiplicity of names, each reflecting a facet of a singular divine attribute, ultimately emanates from the Supreme Name. Yet even this Supreme Name serves as a signpost, its essence pointing beyond its linguistic form towards the infinite and ineffable Divine Meaning itself.

Beyond Names: The Unfolding of Divine Meaning

The seeker, drawn toward divine understanding,
Recognizes that the multiplicity of names
Reflects only fragments
Of the singular reality.
Each name, though profound,
Is not independent.
Each attribute, though majestic,
Does not stand alone.

❨*The most beautiful names belong to Allah, so call on Him by them. And leave the company of those who deviate concerning His names. They will be recompensed for what they have been doing.*❩[295] *—Quran 7:180*

All names disperse from the Supreme Name,
And even that name
Is but a signpost
Pointing beyond language,
Toward the infinite and ineffable.
Call upon Allah,
Call upon Ar-Rahman—
Whichever name rises in devotion,
❨*To whichever you call, to Him belong the most beautiful names.*❩ *—Quran 17:110*
He remains unchanged.
For His names are beautiful,

But He is beyond names,
Beyond description.

Do not raise your voice too loud,
Nor let it fade into silence—
Seek the way between,
For balance carries wisdom.
He is without offspring,
Without equal,
Without need.
For all praise is His,
And reverence belongs only to Him.
For in truth,
To name Him is not to contain Him.
To call upon Him is not to grasp His essence.[296]

Thus, the wise-one understands—
Knowledge of His names
Is only the beginning.
For the real name disperses into meaning,
And meaning itself
Is beyond comprehension.
And so, the heart surrenders,
Not merely in speech,
But in presence,
Where knowing dissolves,

---

[296] This is in agreement with the Quran verse:

⬛ ❨Say, ˹O Prophet,˺ "Call upon Allah or call upon the Most Compassionate—whichever you call, He has the Most Beautiful Names." Do not recite your prayers too loudly or silently, but seek a way between. (110) And say, "All praise is for Allah, Who has never had ˹any˺ offspring;1 nor does He have a partner in ˹governing˺ the kingdom;2 nor is He pathetic, needing a protector.3 And revere Him immensely." (111)❩ [Quran 17: 110 – 111]

Explanation of this verse: Allah the Almighty says: Say, O Muhammad, to these polytheists who deny the attribute of mercy to Allah - the Almighty - and who forbid calling Him the Most Gracious: (Call upon Allah or call upon the Most Gracious. Whichever you call upon, He has the best names.) That is, there is no difference between your calling upon Him by the name "Allah" or by the name "the Most Gracious," for He has the best names, as Allah the Almighty said: ⬛❨He is Allah—there is no god ˹worthy of worship˺ except Him: Knower of the seen and unseen. ...❩ until He said: ⬛❨...He ˹alone˺ has the Most Beautiful Names. Whatever is in the heavens and the earth ˹constantly˺ glorifies Him. And He is the Almighty, All-Wise (24)❩ [Quran 59:22-24].

And the soul finally perceives
Without limit.

The diverse names splinter away from the Real Name,
Like rays scattering from the sun—
Each a fragment, a shadow,
Never the fullness of light.
Even the Name itself escapes the net of meaning,
Eluding the grasp of thought,
Slipping beyond words
That seek to capture the Infinite.
What remains is the Real—
Absolute, unbound, indivisible—
Where meaning dissolves,
And awe alone lingers.

A thousand names ripple outward—
Merciful, Sovereign, Giver, Wise—
Each a glimmer on the surface,
Each a wave carrying echoes of the Eternal.
Yet the Source behind them remains,
A sea so vast, so boundless,
No tongue can measure its shore,
No mind can fathom its depths.

So the wise-one walks forward—
Not seeing fragments, but a singular whole,
A unity that consumes the soul.
He lets all definitions fall away,
To stand in awe, where the names all play.
He seeks not to divide what is indivisible,
But to bow to the Reality so visible.

For only He is the Source of all we see.
Only in Him, we find our liberty.
Only He remains the source
Of Unity, Awe, and boundless force.

Wisdom Unveiled

The profound wisdom unveiled in The Dispersal of Names and Meanings is that at the highest state of spiritual knowing, the wise-one experiences a psychic dissolution of categorization, where the distinct boundaries of the Divine Names blur and coalesce into an indivisible Unity. This is the realization that each name is but a facet of a singular, incomprehensible Reality—that even the "Supreme Name" is a signpost pointing beyond language to the "infinite and ineffable Divine Meaning itself." The contemplation highlights that this understanding leads to a state of profound awe and speechless wonder, liberating the heart from the limitations of human language and enabling it to perceive the Divine Presence without the constraints of distinct names and meanings, finding peace in the Oneness from which all emanate.

Wise-Reflection

Reflect on how you typically categorize Allah's attributes. Do you think of "The Most Merciful" and "The Severely Punishing" as distinct, separate qualities? How might the idea of their dispersal into an incomprehensible Unity change your perception of Allah's nature? Consider the notion that "what remains is the Real—Absolute, unbound, indivisible—where meaning dissolves, and awe alone lingers." How can contemplating this ultimate Oneness help you move beyond conceptual limitations in your worship? What would it mean for your prayer life to surrender to this awe, allowing your heart to perceive the Divine Reality directly, without the need for distinct names or meanings, leading to a deep psychic dissolution of ordinary categorization?

Contemplation: Transcending Language

This reflection is fundamentally about transcending language itself as the sole medium for knowing. The wise-one moves into a realm of knowing that is intuitive, direct, and non-verbal. It is a communication of presence to Presence, heart to Heart. This transcendence is not a rejection of sacred texts, but a deeper engagement with the spirit of the revelation that lies beyond its literal words. It is the language of sighs, of tears, of absolute stillness, where the soul communicates directly with its Creator without any linguistic filter, finding a profound psychic stillness.

Reflect: The intimate connection between the Divine and the servant lies beyond the grasp of expressible requests.

The Unknowable Bond: Beyond Asking

What exists between the servant
And the Divine
Is beyond questioning,
Beyond seeking—
It is known only in presence,
Felt only in surrender.

Mary, chosen without request,
Favored beyond expectation,
Was granted a sign,
Not by her asking,
But by decree.
A Word from Him,
A life shaped by His will,
One honored in both worlds,
One nearest to the Most High.

❨My Lord! How can I have a child when no man has ever touched me?❩ —*Quran*
3:47
She asked not in doubt,
But in submission—
And the answer came,
Not in explanation,
But in certainty:
❨Be! And it is!❩ —*Quran 3:47*
For what was beyond her knowing
Was already written.[297]

---

[297] This is in agreement with the Quran verse narrating the story of Mary and her dialog with the angels and that she being favored by Allah for her striving for Him so she being bestwood by Jesus as a sign from Allah to humanity:

Moses, drawn toward the Divine,
Longed for vision,
Sought to see
What no eyes could perceive.
But he was told:
❲*You cannot see Me!*❳ —*Quran 7:143*
Yet the mountain bore witness,
Dust replacing form,
And Moses collapsed unconscious.
When he recovered, he cried,
❲*Glory be to You! I turn to You in repentance, and I am the first of the believers.*❳
—*Quran 7:143*
He rose not in understanding,
But in realization—
For in his request,
He found the truth
That cannot be known
Except by submission.[298]

📖 ❲And ´remember` when the angels said, "O Mary! Surely Allah has selected you, purified you, and chosen you over all women of the world. (42) O Mary! Be devout to your Lord, prostrate yourself ´in prayer` and bow along with those who bow down." (43) This is news of the unseen that We reveal to you ´O Prophet`. You were not with them when they cast lots to decide who would be Mary's guardian, nor were you there when they argued ´about it`. (44) ´Remember` when the angels proclaimed, "O Mary! Allah gives you good news of a Word1 from Him, his name will be the Messiah,2 Jesus, son of Mary; honoured in this world and the Hereafter, and he will be one of those nearest ´to Allah`. (45) And he will speak to people in ´his` infancy and adulthood and will be one of the righteous." (46) Mary wondered, "My Lord! How can I have a child when no man has ever touched me?" An angel replied, "So will it be. Allah creates what He wills. When He decrees a matter, He simply tells it, 'Be!' And it is! (47) And Allah will teach him writing and wisdom, the Torah and the Gospel, (48) and ´make him` a messenger to the Children of Israel ´to proclaim,` 'I have come to you with a sign from your Lord: I will make for you a bird from clay, breathe into it, and it will become a ´real` bird—by Allah's Will. I will heal the blind and the leper and raise the dead to life—by Allah's Will. And I will prophesize what you eat and store in your houses. Surely in this is a sign for you if you ´truly` believe. (49) And I will confirm the Torah revealed before me and legalize some of what had been forbidden to you. I have come to you with a sign from your Lord, so be mindful of Allah and obey me. (50)❳ [Quran 3:42-50]

[298] This is in agreement with the Quran verse narrating the meeting between Moses and Allah and how Allah bestows blessings on Moses:

📖 ❲When Moses came at the appointed time and his Lord spoke to him, he asked, "My Lord! Reveal Yourself to me so I may see You." Allah answered, "You cannot see Me! But look at the mountain. If it remains firm in its place, only then will you see Me." When his Lord appeared to the mountain, He levelled it to dust and Moses collapsed unconscious. When he recovered, he cried, "Glory be to You! I turn to You in repentance and I am the first of the believers." (143) Allah said, "O Moses! I have ´already` elevated you above all others by My messages and speech.[1] So hold firmly to what I have given you and be grateful." (144)❳ [Quran 7:142-143]

[1]: Allah reminds Moses that even though his request to see Allah was denied, he has already been favoured by Allah over the people of his time through prophethood and direct communication with the Almighty.

Thus, the wise-one
Does not ask what cannot be answered,
Nor seek what cannot be grasped.
For the bond between the servant
And the Creator
Is beyond words,
Beyond inquiry,
Arriving only in the moment
When the heart lets go
Of all knowing
And rests in what
Was always present.

So the wise-one walks forward—
Not with a question, nor with a word,
But in a Presence, seen and heard.
He lets his seeking heart fall still,
And finds his home in His Decree and Will.
He does not ask for what cannot be seen,
But bows to the Unknowable, pure and keen.

For only in Silence can the soul be free.
Only in Him, we find our liberty.
Only He remains the source
Of Presence, Stillness, and boundless force.

Wisdom Unveiled

The profound wisdom unveiled in Transcending Language is that the intimate connection between the servant and the Divine lies beyond the grasp of words and expressible requests. The wise-one learns to move beyond intellectual inquiry and into a realm of intuitive, non-verbal knowing. The stories of Mary and Moses serve as a testament to this truth: Mary received her sign not by asking, but by a simple "Be! And it is!", while Moses's request to see Allah was met with a demonstration of Divine Majesty that led him not to an answer, but to a profound state of repentance and surrender. This realization leads to a deep psychic stillness and liberation, where the heart "lets go of all knowing" and communicates directly with the Creator through the "language of sighs, of tears, of absolute stillness," a bond that was always present.

Wise-Reflection

Reflect on moments in your life when a deep truth or profound emotion was impossible to express in words. Did you find yourself resorting to sighs, tears, or a simple, silent presence? Consider the idea that "the bond between the servant and the Creator is beyond words." How does this concept challenge your typical approach to prayer or supplication, which often relies on making specific requests? How can you consciously cultivate a state of psychic stillness and surrender, like Mary and Moses, where you "let go of all knowing" and simply rest in the Divine Presence? What would it mean for your spiritual journey to trust in the Divine Decree so completely that your heart finds its home in the unspoken, unasked-for connection with the Creator?

Contemplation: The Stance of Bewilderment

The ultimate stance in "Knowing Beyond Names" is one of bewilderment (Hayrah). This is not confusion, but a profound awe and humility that arises from confronting the Infinite, which defies all categorization and comprehension. It is a blissful state where the mind, having reached its limits, surrenders to the majesty of the Unknowable. This sacred bewilderment is considered a high spiritual station, indicating a soul that is so immersed in the Divine Reality that it transcends all limited forms of understanding and rests in pure adoration. This culminates in a profound psychic dissolution of the self.

Understand, O seeker: If the Divine removes from you an excessive focus on the Divine names, then the inclinations towards opposition within you are also diminished.

Beyond Duality: The Test of True Seeking

If He removes from the heart
The desire to cling to His names alone,
He rescues the seeker
From mistaking reflection for reality,
From worshipping the shadow instead of the light itself.

For His names, though holy,
Bear the echoes of duality—
Creator and Destroyer,
Judge and Forgiver—
The attributes stretched across contrast.
Yet He Himself is beyond contrast, beyond definition.

Some worship on the edge of faith,
Content when blessed, wavering when afflicted.
❨If they are blessed with something good, they are content with it; but if they are
afflicted with a trial, they relapse.❩ —Quran 22:11
Their devotion mirrors circumstance, not certainty.
Thus, the test does not destroy them, but reveals them.[299]

Others say, "We believe in Allah," but when trials come,
They mistake persecution for divine punishment.
But when victory comes from your Lord,
❨They surely say, 'We have always been with you.'❩ —Quran 29:10
They align themselves with the victorious,
Forgetting their own retreat.

He does not leave the hypocrites among the sincere,
Nor does He allow the truth to remain tangled in illusion.
He distinguishes, separates, and reveals,
For ❨Allah will certainly distinguish between those who have sure faith and the
hypocrites.❩[300] *—Quran 29:11*

---

[299] This is in agreement with the Quran verse:

📖 ❨And there are some who worship Allah on the verge ˹of faith˺: if they are blessed with something good, they are content with it; but if they are afflicted with a trial, they relapse ˹into disbelief˺,1 losing this world and the Hereafter. That is ˹truly˺ the clearest loss. (11)❩ [Quran 22:11]

[300] This is in agreement with the Quran verse:

📖 ❨There are some who say, "We believe in Allah," but when they suffer in the cause of Allah, they mistake ˹this˺ persecution at the hands of people for the punishment of Allah. But when victory comes from your Lord, they surely say ˹to the believers˺, "We have always been with you." Does Allah not know best what is in the hearts of all beings? (10) Allah will certainly distinguish between those who have ˹sure˺ faith and the hypocrites. (11)❩ [Quran 29:10-11]

The peril is that whoever relapses into disbelief
Will find their deeds ⟨will become void in this life and in the Hereafter. It is they who
will be the residents of the Fire. They will be there forever.⟩[301] —Quran 2:217

Thus, the wise-one does not seek Him
Through appearance alone, nor through expectation
Of continuous ease.
For what is unraveled is not loss, but purification.
And what is removed is not faith, but false attachment.
To seek Him is not to grasp at descriptions,
But to surrender beyond them.

If He destroys within me
The desire to cling to His names,
Then He rescues me
From worshipping the shadow instead of the light itself.
If He (Al-Basit, The Expander) shatters my attachment to these names,
He invites me beyond them—
To worship the Reality they reflect,
To seek Him in the silence that remains
When words fall away,
And the heart beholds His essence,
Unveiled and absolute.

Blessed is the bewilderment
That empties me of myself,
Hollowing the vessel so He may fill it with His presence.
Blessed is the trembling
Where thought surrenders its throne,
And silence rises like a sacred tide,
Carrying me into the arms of awe.
For in the void of knowing,
I am no longer lost,

---

[301] This is derived from the Quran verse of:

⟨They ask you ˹O Prophet˺ about fighting in the sacred months. Say, "Fighting during these months is a great sin. But hindering ˹others˺ from the Path of Allah, rejecting Him, and expelling the worshippers from the Sacred Mosque is ˹a˺ greater ˹sin˺ in the sight of Allah. For persecution is far worse than killing. And they will not stop fighting you until they turn you away from your faith—if they can. And whoever among you renounces their own faith and dies a disbeliever, their deeds will become void in this life and in the Hereafter. It is they who will be the residents of the Fire. They will be there forever." (217)⟩ [Quran 2:217]

But found in the infinite expanse
Where He alone remains.

So the wise-one walks forward—
Not with a question, nor a word of strife,
But in a Bewilderment, a higher life.
He lets all definitions turn to dust,
And places in the Unknowable his trust.
He bows to the Majesty beyond all form,
And finds his shelter in the final storm.

For only He is the Infinite Unnamed.
Only in Him, the soul is claimed.
Only He remains the source
Of Awe, Bewilderment, and boundless force.

Wisdom Unveiled

The profound wisdom unveiled in The Stance of Bewilderment is that the highest state of knowing the Divine is not one of certainty, but of profound, holy awe. The wise-one learns that Allah, in an act of mercy, removes the excessive focus on His names to rescue the seeker from "worshipping the shadow instead of the light itself." This contemplation highlights that the names, while holy, bear the echoes of a duality that must be transcended to reach the Essence that is beyond all contrast. The peril of those who have a superficial faith is sharply contrasted by verses like Quran 22:11, which describe those who "relapse" when afflicted with a trial, and Quran 29:10-11, which reveals the hypocrisy of those who only claim faith when it is easy. The ultimate blissful state is one of bewilderment—a surrender of the mind and ego that allows the heart to be filled with the Divine Presence. This is the ultimate psychic dissolution of the self, where knowing dissolves into certainty, and the soul is no longer lost, but "found in the infinite expanse where He alone remains."

Wise-Reflection

Reflect on your own spiritual understanding. Do you sometimes feel that your certainty or beliefs are challenged by difficult trials, as with those who "worship on the verge of faith"? How can the idea of bewilderment—not as confusion, but as a sacred awe—become a safe spiritual stance for you when confronting aspects of the Divine that defy your comprehension? Consider the phrase: "Blessed is the bewilderment that empties me of myself." How can you consciously cultivate this surrender, allowing the mind to fall silent so that your heart can finally behold the Divine Essence unveiled and absolute, leading to a profound psychic dissolution of the ego and a state of pure adoration?

Conclusion: Beyond Knowing the Creator Names

ECHOES OF REALIZATION: IN THE COUNTRY BEYOND NAMES

There exists a sacred land where even the most venerable names prove too heavy for the enlightened soul to carry, where even the most exalted praises, articulated by the purest hearts, gracefully fall like soft snow melting into a vast, silent river. It is precisely here, beyond the confines of the alphabet, beyond the familiar pages of any prayer book, that the wise-one walks barefoot, profoundly speechless, and ultimately sovereign in their direct experience.

In this sublime state, the wise-one no longer worships a mere intellectual idea. They no longer love a conventional title or an abstract concept. Instead, they adore, with profound and complete devotion, the very Face they cannot name—the Life-giving Breath they cannot capture—the Absolute Reality that, in its boundless mystery, once called their very soul into being with a single, wordless command: "Be." This is the pinnacle of psychic and spiritual attunement.

THE SEEKER'S ASCENT: FROM KNOWING TO BEING, EXPERIENCING THE INFINITE ESSENCE

In this climactic reflection, the wise-one is called upon to courageously cross the final, most subtle bridge on their journey to Divine Connection. This bridge leads from merely knowing the Creator's manifest names to profoundly being in the unmediated Presence of the Creator Himself.

The arduous yet illuminating journey through the Divine Names was undoubtedly necessary—a sacred path of guidance, spiritual illumination, and ever-deepening love. However, the ultimate destination is far greater still: to behold the One beyond all temporal titles, to serenely rest in the boundless radiance where even the highest angels dare not attempt to name what they perceive. Here, all intellectual knowledge dissolves completely into pure, existential being. Here, conventional worship transforms into pure, unadulterated beholding. Here, the soul awakens to its deepest, most profound prayer—a prayer no longer articulated by the tongue or conceived by the mind, but profoundly lived as an eternal state of presence and surrender. This liberation from conceptual bounds is the essence of ultimate spiritual maturity in " The Crucible of Inner Transformation." ❁❁❁

14TH REFLECTION: IN THE CREATOR COMPANIONSHIP

(Companionship with the Creator)

THE GATEWAY VERSES

In the sacred words of Allah, a description of the true believers who seek and attain intimate proximity through devotion and humility:

📖 ❴*The only ˋtrueˊ believers in Our revelation are those who—when it is recited to them—fall into prostration and glorify the praises of their Lord and are not too proud. (15) They abandon their beds, invoking their Lord with hope and fear, and donate from what We have provided for them. (16) No soul can imagine what delights are kept in store for them as a reward for what they used to do. (17)*❵ *[Quran 32:15-17]*

ILLUMINATION'S DAWN

There comes a transformative moment in the sacred unfolding of the soul when the wise-one realizes a profound truth: the greatest, most enduring companionship is not found in transient voices or fleeting human hands, but in the silent, all-encompassing, and ever-present nearness of the Creator. To truly walk in profound companionship with the Creator is to transcend all forms of earthly loneliness, to move beyond self-occupation and egoic concerns, and to enter into a sacred, unbreakable bond that neither temporal distance nor human failure can ever sever.

Here, in this sublime state, remembrance (Dhikr) is no longer merely a formal ritual; it becomes the very oxygen of existence. Here, unwavering trust (Tawakkul) is not a challenging command to be fulfilled; it is the solid, reassuring ground beneath the wise-one's every deliberate step. Let us now, with hearts open and receptive, step into this secret, intimate companionship—where the soul leans wholly and completely into the Everlasting Embrace of the Divine.

THE UNFOLDING OF INSIGHTS

This section explores the multifaceted dimensions of the Creator's Companionship, revealing it as a source of refuge, sufficiency, and transformative power that purifies the soul and deepens its connection.

Contemplation: The Creator's Unwavering Presence

The wise-one comes to experientially realize the Creator's unwavering, constant Presence. This is not a fleeting feeling but a deep conviction that Allah is with them always, in every state and circumstance, as affirmed in Quran 57:4: "And He is with you wherever you are." This contemplation anchors the wise-one's heart in a continuous awareness of Divine oversight and nearness, transforming moments of solitude into intimate communion and moments of difficulty into opportunities to witness His abiding support. This continuous awareness is a hallmark of psychic attunement.

Reflect, O seeker: The Divine is closer to you than your own being. Should you forget the Divine, the Divine remembers you. Should you turn away, the Divine approaches, building through your remembrance a glory for you, and accompanying you to dispel your solitude.

The Divine Remembrance: A Presence Beyond Forgetfulness

The servant forgets,
Yet He remembers.
The heart turns away,
Yet He draws near.
For He is far better for the soul
Than the soul is for itself—
The companion who does not abandon,
The presence that does not waver.

❪Remember Me; I will remember you.❫ —Quran 2:152
In gratitude, the connection is deepened,
In patience, comfort is given,
For ❪Allah is truly with those who are patient.❫ [302] —Quran 2:153

For those who invoke Him,
Day and night,
Light follows them,
Darkness fades before them.

---

[302] This is in agreement with the Quran verse:

❪remember Me; I will remember you. And thank Me, and never be ungrateful. (152) O believers! Seek comfort in patience and prayer. Allah is truly with those who are patient. (153)❫ [Quran 2:152–153]

Blessings descend,

Angels pray for them,

⟪*He is the One Who showers His blessings upon you—and His angels pray for you—so that He may bring you out of darkness and into light.*⟫ —*Quran 33:43*

And they are guided

Into mercy without limit.

Even in distance,

He builds their return,

Weaving remembrance into glory,

Accompanying them from loneliness

Into fulfillment.[303]

And when the final meeting arrives,

⟪*Their greeting on the Day they meet Him will be, 'Peace!'*⟫ —*Quran 33:44*

Honor will be their reward,

And they will stand

In the presence

That never ceased

To hold them.

For remembrance

Is not only the servant's call, but the Creator's answer.[304]

Thus the wise-one reflects, I am His servant, clothed in frailty and longing.

And yet—He, The Most

Compassionate (Ar-Rahman), is far better for me than I am for myself.

If I forget Him, He remembers me,

Not with reproach, but with a mercy that plants unseen gardens in the ruins of my neglect.

If I turn away, burdened by my heedlessness,

He draws near with a tenderness that rebuilds the very glory I had abandoned.

O my soul, know this:

---

[303] This is in agreement with the Quran verse:

⟪O believers! Always remember Allah often, (41) and glorify Him morning and evening. (42) He is the One Who showers His blessings upon you—and His angels pray for you—so that He may bring you out of darkness and into light. For He is ever Merciful to the believers. (43) Their greeting on the Day they meet Him will be, "Peace!" And He has prepared for them an honourable reward. (44)⟫ [Quran 33:41-44]

[304] This is derived from the Quran verse of:

⟪Their greeting on the Day they meet Him will be, "Peace!" And He has prepared for them an honourable reward. (44)⟫ [Quran 33:44]

Even when I fall silent, He sings remembrance over me.
Even when I drift into loneliness, He companions me, unseen but unfailing.

How strange, how marvelous—
That even as I wander,
He weaves my path of return.
Even when my heart falls silent,
He listens for me,
He remembers me with a love deeper than any longing I could muster.
What majesty, what mercy—
To be sought even when I forget how to seek.

So the wise-one walks forward—
Not in solitude, but with His Presence,
A bond that knows no absence.
He finds his comfort in His unwavering care,
A companionship that is always there.
He gives his heart to His loving embrace,
And finds his home in this blessed space.

For only He remains the source
Of Remembrance, Presence, and boundless force.

Wisdom Unveiled

The profound wisdom unveiled in The Creator's Unwavering Presence is that the deepest companionship is with the Creator, a bond that is constant and unwavering, as affirmed in Quran 57:4. The wise-one learns that this relationship is rooted in Divine Remembrance—even when the servant forgets, the Creator remembers. This truth is supported by Quran 2:152-153, which states, "Remember Me; I will remember you," and calls for believers to seek comfort in patience. The contemplation highlights that this companionship transforms loneliness into fulfillment, as Allah "showers His blessings" and His angels pray for those who remember Him, guiding them from darkness to light. This continuous, experiential awareness of Divine oversight and nearness is the hallmark of a deep psychic attunement that transcends all earthly limitations and promises an honorable reward and a greeting of "Peace!" on the Day of meeting Him.

Wise-Reflection

Reflect on your moments of solitude. Do you typically experience them as loneliness, or can you recognize them as opportunities for intimate communion with the Divine? Consider the idea that "if I forget Him, He remembers me." How does this concept of Divine Remembrance—not as a response to your action, but as a constant, unwavering state—change your understanding of your relationship with the Creator? What practices, beyond formal ritual, can help you anchor your heart in a continuous awareness of His presence, transforming moments of difficulty into opportunities to witness His abiding support and cultivating a state of profound psychic attunement?

Contemplation: The Creator's Sufficiency

(Understand: The Divine is independent of you and all creation)

In the embrace of Divine Companionship, the wise-one recognizes the Creator's absolute Sufficiency (Al-Ghaniy). They understand that Allah alone is sufficient for all their needs—spiritual, emotional, and material. This realization liberates the heart from dependence on creation, removing anxiety stemming from worldly attachments and seeking validation or fulfillment from others. This profound trust in Allah's sufficiency fosters inner contentment (qana'ah) and profound gratitude, knowing that the ultimate Provider and Sustainer is always near. This is a profound psychic liberation from worldly dependence.

The Needless: The Absolute Independence of the Divine

He is not in need—
Not of devotion,
Not of praise,
Not of creation itself.
For the servant's disbelief does not diminish Him,
⟨Indeed, Allah is Free of need and Praiseworthy.⟩[305] —Quran 14:8
Nor does faith complete Him.
Yet He appreciates gratitude,

---

[305] This is in agreement with the Quran verse:

⟨Moses added, "If you along with everyone on earth were to be ungrateful, then 'know that' Allah is indeed Self-Sufficient, Praiseworthy." (8)⟩ [Quran 14:8]

Not for Himself,
But for the soul that finds
Its own fulfillment in remembrance.
No burden is shared,
No weight is carried by another,
For each soul stands alone
Before Him in its return.
❰*No soul burdened with sin will bear the burden of another. Then to your Lord is*
your return...❱[306] —*Quran 39:7*

Even if all turned away,
If the heavens and the earth
Cried out in rejection,
He would remain—
Self-Sufficient, Praiseworthy,
Unchanged, untouched.
For ❰*O mankind, you are the ones in need of Allah, while Allah is the Free of need,*
the Praiseworthy.❱[307] —*Quran 35:15*

❰*Is not Allah sufficient for His servant?*❱ —*Quran 39:36*
Yet they threaten with false idols,
Seeking security in what cannot protect them.
For He guides whom He wills, and none can mislead them.
He leaves astray whom He wills, and none can return them.
For guidance is not forced,
Nor is faith demanded—
It is given,
It is chosen.[308]

---

[306] This is in agreement with the Quran verse:

📖 ❰If you disbelieve, then ˹know that˺ Allah is truly not in need of you, nor does He approve of disbelief from His servants. But if you become grateful ˹through faith˺, He will appreciate that from you. No soul burdened with sin will bear the burden of another. Then to your Lord is your return, and He will inform you of what you used to do. He certainly knows best what is ˹hidden˺ in the heart. (7)❱ [Quran 39:7]

[307] This is deresved from the Quran verse of:

📖❰O humanity! It is you who stand in need of Allah, but Allah ˹alone˺ is the Self-Sufficient, Praiseworthy. (15)❱ [Quran 35:15]

[308] This is in agreement with the Quran verse:

📖 ❰Is Allah not sufficient for His servant? Yet they threaten you with other ˹powerless˺ gods besides Him! Whoever Allah leaves to stray will be left with no guide. (36) And whoever Allah guides, none can lead astray. Is Allah not Almighty, capable of punishment? (37)❱ [Quran 39:36-37]

Thus, the wise-one understands—
The Divine does not require, but invites.
Does not depend, but offers.
And in His absolute independence,
He becomes the greatest refuge
For the servant in need.

He is The Self-Sufficient (Al-Ghaniyy),
Free of all need for me,
Or for anything I could offer.
His companionship is not born of necessity,
But of boundless generosity—
An outpouring of love so pure
That even the heavens bow in awe.
O soul, how humbling it is—
That the One who needs nothing still seeks me,
That the Infinite bends His grace toward the finite,
Not because of my worthiness,
But because of His endless benevolence.

So the wise-one walks forward—
Not depending on the fleeting world,
But in a trust that is unfurled.
He seeks no praise from human hands,
But finds his solace in His commands.
He knows his sufficiency is His alone,
And on His grace, a new life is grown.

For only He remains the source
Of Sufficiency, Refuge, and boundless force.

Wisdom Unveiled

The profound wisdom unveiled in The Creator's Sufficiency is the recognition of Allah's absolute independence as Al-Ghaniy (The Self-Sufficient). The wise-one learns that Allah is not in need of creation's devotion or praise, as affirmed in Quran 35:15: "O mankind, you are the ones in need of Allah." This understanding is a crucial psychic liberation that frees the heart from worldly dependence and anxiety. The contemplation highlights that this sufficiency is a profound source of refuge, as "Is not Allah sufficient for His servant?" (Quran 39:36). It also powerfully reinforces the concept of individual accountability, as the verse "No soul burdened with sin will bear the burden of another" (Quran 39:7) reminds the wise-one that their ultimate return is to the Lord alone. The ultimate humility lies in the realization that Allah's companionship is not born of necessity, but of boundless generosity and benevolence, offering the greatest refuge to the servant in need, who finds contentment and gratitude in this unbreakable bond.

Wise-Reflection

Reflect on what you rely on for security, validation, or fulfillment in your life. Do you sometimes seek these things from others or from worldly possessions? How does the idea of the Creator's absolute Sufficiency (Al-Ghaniy) challenge these attachments? Consider the thought, "The One who needs nothing still seeks me." How does this profound act of boundless generosity change your perception of your own worthiness and the nature of Divine Companionship? What would it mean for your heart to fully embrace the knowledge that "Allah is sufficient for His Servant" and to allow this truth to liberate you from all worldly anxieties, fostering inner contentment (qana'ah) and gratitude, while also recognizing that your deeds and your journey are yours alone to bear?

Contemplation: The Promise of Abundance in Sacrifice

Divine Companionship reveals the promise of immense abundance in sacrifice. The Gateway Verses speak of believers who "abandon their beds" and "donate from what We have provided." These acts of sacrifice—of comfort, wealth, or personal desire—are not losses but investments that unlock boundless Divine rewards, both seen and unseen. The wise-one realizes that true gain comes from relinquishing, and that every sincere offering to Allah is met with a multiplication of blessings and an increase in spiritual intimacy, leading to "delights... no soul can imagine." This is a profound psychic transformation of how the soul perceives gain and loss.

Consider: By Divine glory, it is assured that whoever relinquishes something for the sake of the Divine shall be recompensed with that which was relinquished and even better.

The Promise of Divine Compensation

To relinquish something for His sake
Is never loss, but transformation.
For the one who gives up the worldly,
The eternal is returned.
And the one who sacrifices comfort,
Finds in surrender a reward beyond measure.

He promises by His glory
That no one shall desert something for Him
Except He shall give him what he deserted—
And better than it.

Every hardship endured,
Every sacrifice made,
Every act of devotion is written, remembered, honored.
For no thirst, fatigue, or hunger
Is unnoticed, and no struggle in His cause is forgotten.
❨*It is written to their credit as a good deed. Surely Allah never discounts the reward of the good-doers.*❩*309* — *Quran 9:120*

Those who are mindful of Allah
Find that He makes a way out for them,
And provides from sources they could never imagine.
❨*And whoever puts their trust in Allah, then He ˹alone˺ is sufficient for them.*❩*310*
—Quran 65:2-3
Those who give, whether small or great,
Cross valleys in devotion,

---

309 This is in agreement with the Quran verse:

📖 ❨It was not ˹proper˺ for the people of Medina and the nomadic Arabs around them to avoid marching with the Messenger of Allah or to prefer their own lives above his. That is because whenever they suffer from thirst, fatigue, or hunger in the cause of Allah; or tread on a territory, unnerving the disbelievers; or inflict any loss on an enemy—it is written to their credit as a good deed. Surely Allah never discounts the reward of the good-doers. (120) And whenever they make a donation, small or large, or cross a valley ˹in Allah's cause˺—it is written to their credit, so that Allah may grant them the best reward for what they used to do. (121)❩ [Quran 9:120-121]

310 This is in agreement with the Quran verse:

📖 ❨And whoever is mindful of Allah, He will make a way out for them, (2) and provide for them from sources they could never imagine. And whoever puts their trust in Allah, then He ˹alone˺ is sufficient for them. Certainly Allah achieves His Will. Allah has already set a destiny for everything. (3)❩ [Quran 65:2-3]

And their deeds rise toward the promise of the best reward.
For ❨whatever good you put forward for yourselves—you will find it with Allah, as it
is better and greater in reward.❩³¹¹ —Quran 73:20

And among those
Who seek sincerity,
Faith moves them deeply,
Guiding them to truth with humility and compassion.
Tears flow at revelation, recognition dawns,
And they pray:
❨Our Lord, we believe—count us among the witnesses.❩³¹² —Quran 5:83
For why should they not believe
When truth stands before them,
When guidance calls, and righteousness is their longing?
Thus, they are granted gardens,
Rivers flowing beneath them,
An everlasting dwelling—
The fulfillment of sincerity, the reward of the good-doers.

For He does not overlook the sacrifice of the faithful,
Nor does He leave sincerity without fulfillment.
What is given for Him is returned—
Not as it was, but as something greater, something eternal.

---

³¹¹ This is derived from the Quran verse of:

📖 ❨Surely your Lord knows that you ˹O Prophet˺ stand ˹in prayer˺ for nearly two-thirds of the night, or ˹sometimes˺ half of it, or a third, as do some of those with you. Allah ˹alone˺ keeps a ˹precise˺ measure of the day and night. He knows that you ˹believers˺ are unable to endure this, and has turned to you in mercy.1 So recite ˹in prayer˺ whatever you can from the Quran. He knows that some of you will be sick, some will be travelling throughout the land seeking Allah's bounty, and some fighting in the cause of Allah. So recite whatever you can from it. And ˹continue to˺ perform ˹regular˺ prayers, pay alms-tax, and lend to Allah a good loan.2 Whatever good you send forth for yourselves, you will find it with Allah far better and more rewarding.3 And seek Allah's forgiveness. Surely Allah is All-Forgiving, Most Merciful. (20)❩ [Quran 73:20]

³¹² This is in agreement with the Quran verse:

📖 ❨You will surely find the most bitter towards the believers to be the Jews and polytheists and the most gracious to be those who call themselves Christian. That is because there are priests and monks among them and because they are not arrogant. (82) When they listen to what has been revealed to the Messenger, you see their eyes overflowing with tears for recognizing the truth. They say, "Our Lord! We believe, so count us among the witnesses. (83) Why should we not believe in Allah and the truth that has come to us? And we long for our Lord to include us in the company of the righteous." (84) So Allah will reward them for what they said with Gardens under which rivers flow, to stay there forever. And that is the reward of the good-doers. (85)❩ [Quran 5:82-85]

He promises, by His glory:
If I forsake anything for His sake,
He shall replace it—with something better, richer, more enduring.
No sacrifice goes unnoticed.
No letting-go is wasted.
Every tear surrendered for Him
Is caught and crowned in unseen realms.
Each time I lay something down for Him,
He lifts me higher.

Each time I loosen my grip on the world,
He fills my empty hands with treasures not of dust,
But of eternity.

So the wise-one walks forward—
Not with a grip on what is held,
But with a trust that is compelled.
He gives his all, in what he sacrifices,
And finds his home in these promises.
He knows that every giving is a gain,
A path to a love that knows no pain.

For only He remains the source
Of Abundance, Sacrifice, and boundless force.

Wisdom Unveiled

The profound wisdom unveiled in The Promise of Abundance in Sacrifice is that relinquishing worldly attachments for the Creator is not a loss, but a divine investment. The wise-one understands that every sincere act of sacrifice, from giving donations (Quran 9:121) to enduring hardship (Quran 9:120), is met with a divine compensation that is "better and greater in reward" (Quran 73:20). This contemplation highlights that true sufficiency and abundance come from trusting in Allah, who provides from unimaginable sources for those who are mindful of Him (Quran 65:2-3). The ultimate fulfillment of this sincerity is an everlasting reward in gardens (Quran 5:85). This understanding encourages a deep psychic trust in divine generosity, transforming the soul's perception of gain and loss, and liberating the heart from the fear of relinquishing worldly possessions for the sake of the Eternal.

Wise-Reflection

Reflect on what you are currently holding onto out of a fear of loss—whether it be a possession, a comfort, or an attachment. How might the idea that "He shall replace it—with something better, richer, more enduring" challenge this fear? Consider the verse: "And whoever is mindful of Allah, He will make a way out for them, and provide for them from sources they could never imagine." How can you, in your daily life, practice a small act of sacrifice, be it of time, comfort, or a worldly desire, with the full conviction that it is an investment in a boundless, eternal reward? What would it mean for your heart to loosen its grip on the world and allow this profound psychic transformation to guide your actions and trust in His promise of abundance?

Contemplation: Turning Away from Worldly Attachments

To deepen Divine Companionship, the wise-one consciously practices turning away from worldly attachments. This involves a systematic detachment from the allure of temporary possessions, statuses, and desires that distract the heart from its true Beloved. This detachment is not asceticism for its own sake, but a purification of the heart, allowing it to become a pure vessel for Divine love and presence. It is a psychic liberation that frees the wise-one from the emotional turbulence of worldly pursuits, leading to profound inner peace.

Understand: All creation is subservient to humanity, and the Divine is infinitely more benevolent than anything created, being the ultimate Benefactor. Therefore, the wise heart turns away from all else, directing its focus solely towards the Divine.

Turning Toward the Creator: The Ultimate Surrender

All creation was made for the service of humanity,
yet the Divine remains infinitely more benevolent than anything formed—
for He alone is the Benefactor.
The highest exchange is made by the believers,
their lives and wealth offered in devotion, and in return, Paradise is granted.
⟨Allah has indeed purchased from the believers their lives and wealth in exchange for
Paradise.⟩— Quran 9:111

They bow, they prostrate, they fast,
they encourage good and forbid evil,
and they observe the limits set by Allah.
And for them, glad tidings are given, for they have chosen what is everlasting over what
is fleeting.
❨So rejoice in the exchange you have made with Him. That is truly the ultimate
triumph.❩[313] *—Quran 9:111*

The youths of the cave understood this truth.
Surrounded by corruption, they abandoned luxury,
fleeing into seclusion to guard their faith.
❨Our Lord! Grant us mercy from Yourself and guide us rightly through our ordeal.❩
— Quran 18:10
And mercy was given.
Years passed, yet they remained untouched,
their hearts strengthened, their guidance increased.
For they declared with certainty, ❨Our Lord is the Lord of the heavens and the earth.
We will never call upon any god besides Him...❩ (Referencing Quran 18:14)
Thus, they distanced themselves from the indulgence of the world,
and in their seclusion, they were sheltered.
And when they were revealed, their presence testified to the truth of resurrection, the
promise of Allah without doubt.[314]

---

[313] This is in agreement with the Quran verse:

📖 ❨Allah has indeed purchased from the believers their lives and wealth in exchange for Paradise. They fight in the cause of Allah and kill or are killed. This is a true promise binding on Him in the Torah, the Gospel, and the Quran. And whose promise is truer than Allah's? So rejoice in the exchange you have made with Him. That is ˹truly˺ the ultimate triumph. (111) ˹It is the believers˺ who repent, who are devoted to worship, who praise ˹their Lord˺, who fast, who bow down and prostrate themselves, who encourage good and forbid evil, and who observe the limits set by Allah. And give good news to the believers. (112)❩ [Quran 9:111-112]

[314] This is in agreement with the Quan verse narrating the story of the cave people whom discarded all the lavish of life and take shelter in the cave protecting their religion while their people indulge in disobedience:

📖 ❨Have you ˹O Prophet˺ thought that the people of the cave and the plaque[1] were ˹the only˺ wonders of Our signs? (9) ˹Remember˺ when those youths took refuge in the cave, and said, "Our Lord! Grant us mercy from Yourself and guide us rightly through our ordeal." (10) We sealed their ears [with sleep] in the cave for years. (11) then We raised them so We may show which of the two groups would make a better estimation of the length of their stay. (12) We relate to you ˹O Prophet˺ their story in truth. They were youths who truly believed in their Lord, and We increased them in guidance. (13) And We strengthened their hearts when they stood up and declared, "Our Lord is the Lord of the heavens and the earth. We will never call upon any

For the wise heart perceives—
to turn from the world is not to abandon life, but to seek what is eternal.
To give up attachment is not loss, but freedom.
And in forsaking the distractions of creation,
one does not become empty, but finds fulfillment in the presence that was waiting all
along.

Everything—every joy, every sorrow, every fleeting wonder—was fashioned for me,
yet none of it compares to the boundless generosity of The Generous (Al-Karim),
the Benefactor who asks for nothing, yet offers everything.
He is more benevolent than all creation combined,
more enduring than the stars and seas.
Thus, wisdom is to turn away from the temporary,
to give the back to all that fades,
and to direct the face toward Him—the Eternal, the Absolute.
For in forsaking the shadows of this world, one does not lose, but gains infinitely.
The true reward is not in the fleeting gifts, but in the presence of the Giver Himself.
"O soul, why cling to fleeting treasures?
Turn your gaze toward the Sun,
and let its radiance consume the shadows.
When I let the world slip from my grasp,
I find my arms open, ready to hold the Infinite.
Here, in the glow of His majesty, I am no longer weighted by desire.

---

god besides Him, or we would truly be uttering an outrageous lie." (14) ʾThen they said to one another,ʾ "These people of ours have taken gods besides Him. Why do they not produce a clear proof of them? Who then does more wrong than those who fabricate lies against Allah? (15) Since you have distanced yourselves from them and what they worship besides Allah, take refuge in the cave. Your Lord will extend His mercy to you and accommodate you in your ordeal." (16)). Up to the verse: (That is how We caused them to be discovered so that their people might know that Allah's promise ʾof resurrectionʾ is true and that there is no doubt about the Hour.[2] When the people disputed with each other about the case of the youth ʾafter their deathʾ,[3] some proposed, "Build a structure around them. Their Lord knows best about them." Those who prevailed in the matter said, "We will surely build a place of worship over them." (21)) [Quran 18: 9-21]

[1]: Ar-Raqîm is the plaque that was placed at the entrance of the cave with the names and story of the People of the Cave. This is the story of a group of Christian youths who hid inside a cave outside the city of Ephesus around 250 C.E., to escape persecution at the hands of pagans during the reign of the Roman emperor Decius. The Quran does not give an exact number of the youths, although many scholars believe there were seven in addition to a dog. The youths slept for 300 years, plus nine (300 solar years equal 309 lunar years).

[2]: Their antique silver coins gave them away. People rushed to the cave to greet the youths, who finally passed away and were buried in the cave. The King decided to build a place of worship at the cave to commemorate their story.

[3]: Some pagans suggested that a wall should be built to seal off the cave, whereas the believers decided to build a place of worship at the cave to honour those youths.

My heart, once tethered to the transient, now soars in the freedom of surrender—
filled not with what fades, but with what endures forever."

So the wise-one walks forward,
Not clinging to what is held, but to what has been told.
He turns his back on the temporary gain,
To find his solace from the endless pain.

For only He is the eternal prize,
Only in Him, true triumph lies.
For only He remains the source
Of Eternal Truth, and boundless force.

Wisdom Unveiled:

The profound wisdom unveiled in Turning Away from Worldly Attachments is that Divine Companionship is deepened through conscious detachment. The wise-one realizes that true fulfillment lies not in worldly possessions or statuses, but in the boundless benevolence of the Creator, The Generous (Al-Karim). This contemplation highlights that turning away from the temporary is not a loss, but a spiritual exchange, where believers offer their lives and wealth for Paradise, as affirmed in Quran 9:111. The story of the youths of the cave serves as a powerful example of this psychic liberation, demonstrating that in forsaking worldly indulgence, they found shelter, increased guidance, and the ultimate victory of their faith. This detachment is a purification of the heart, transforming a state of being tethered to the transient into one of freedom, peace, and eternal surrender to the presence of the Giver Himself.

Wise-Reflection:

Reflect on your own attachments. What are the "fleeting treasures" that most often distract your heart from its devotion? Consider the powerful example of the youths of the cave, who willingly abandoned everything for the sake of their faith. How might a similar act of conscious, though not physical, detachment from a worldly desire or pursuit bring you closer to the **Divine**? What would it mean for your heart to fully embrace the "ultimate triumph" of this spiritual exchange, where you are filled not with what fades, but with what endures forever, leading to a profound **psychic liberation** and inner peace?

Contemplation: Overcoming the Barrier of Self-Love

A significant obstacle to intimate companionship is overcoming the barrier of self-love (hubb al-nafs) and egoic pride. The wise-one realizes that the ego, with its constant demands for recognition, validation, and control, creates a subtle veil between the soul and the Creator. True companionship requires humility, self-effacement, and complete surrender of personal will to Divine Will. This contemplation involves sincere self-reflection and continuous effort to purify the lower self, allowing the higher soul to align fully with Allah, as highlighted by the verse: "and are not too proud." This is a profound psychic awakening that lifts the veil of ego.

Contemplate: The true impediment between the Divine and humanity is the love of the self. Should self-love be forsaken, the Divine creates a separation between the purified human being and their former self-obsession.

Between the Heart and the Presence

The true veil between the servant and the Divine is not distance, nor absence, but the grasp of self-love.
For when the soul clings too tightly to itself, it sees only its own reflection, and the presence of the Creator becomes obscured.
"The true barrier between the Creator and the human is the human self-love. Shall self-love be deserted, then the Creator creates a barrier between the pure human and his self-love."

The emigrants were cast out, leaving behind their homes and wealth, seeking Allah's bounty and pleasure, and standing up for Allah and His Messenger. And those who welcomed them felt no envy, no desire for what was given to others, but gave preference even in their own need. For those who are saved from the selfishness of their own souls are truly successful. ❨And whoever is saved from the selfishness of their own souls, it is they who are truly successful.❩ — Quran 59:9

And those who follow pray in humility, asking not only for mercy but for purification.

⟨Our Lord! Forgive us and our fellow believers who preceded us in faith, and do not allow bitterness into our hearts towards those who believe.⟩ [315] —Quran 59:10

For attachment to self breeds division,
while forsaking it opens the heart to unity and grace.
And those whose faith is rooted, strengthened by a spirit from Him, do not waver in loyalty.
⟨You will never find a people who truly believe in Allah and the Last Day loyal to those who defy Allah and His Messenger, even if they were their parents...⟩ [316] —
Quran 58:22

For the ones whom He elevates,
He separates from self-interest,
guiding them toward an existence where faith stands above all else.
Thus, the wise-one understands—
to be purified is not only to forsake sin, but to forsake self-obsession.
For in abandoning self-love, one does not lose themselves,
but finds themselves in the presence that was always waiting.

The true barrier between the soul and the Creator is not distance, but the shadow of self-love—
the whisper of "I" that rises like a veil, thickening the air, obscuring the light of His presence.
To forsake this lesser love, to abandon the grip of vanity, is to find freedom.
And in that freedom, the Creator does not leave me vulnerable—

---

[315] That is in agreement with the Quran verse:

📖 ⟨'Some of the gains will be' for poor emigrants who were driven out of their homes and wealth, seeking Allah's bounty and pleasure, and standing up for Allah and His Messenger. They are the ones true in faith. (8) As for those who had settled in the city and 'embraced' the faith before 'the arrival of' the emigrants, they love whoever immigrates to them, never having a desire in their hearts for whatever 'of the gains' is given to the emigrants. They give 'the emigrants' preference over themselves even though they may be in need. And whoever is saved from the selfishness of their own souls, it is they who are 'truly' successful. (9) And those who come after them will pray, "Our Lord! Forgive us and our fellow believers who preceded us in faith, and do not allow bitterness into our hearts towards those who believe. Our Lord! Indeed, You are Ever Gracious, Most Merciful." (10)⟩ [Quran 59:8-10]

[316] This is in agreement with the Quran verse:

📖 ⟨You will never find a people who 'truly' believe in Allah and the Last Day loyal to those who defy Allah and His Messenger, even if they were their parents, children, siblings, or extended family. For those 'believers', Allah has instilled faith in their hearts and strengthened them with a spirit from Him.[1] He will admit them into Gardens under which rivers flow, to stay there forever. Allah is pleased with them and they are pleased with Him. They are the party of Allah. Indeed, Allah's party is bound to succeed. (22)⟩ [Quran 58:22]

[1]: Spirit here can mean revelation, light, or help.

He builds a barrier between my purity and the remnants of self-love,
while weaving a bridge that spans the abyss of pride toward His infinite majesty.
Here, I begin to see with a clearer gaze, free from the distortions of desire,
and His light becomes not just a guide, but the very essence of sight itself.
In surrendering self-love, I awaken to a vision unclouded,
where I am no longer chained to the whispering voice of my desires.
My eyes, once dimmed by longing, are now lit by the radiance of devotion—
a light so pure, it burns away all illusions
and fills the soul with truth.
Here, the veil lifts. Here, the heart becomes a mirror,
reflecting not my own image, but His boundless mercy and majesty.

So the wise-one walks forward,
Not blinded by their ego's selfish might.
He finds his victory in the soul's surrender,
His pride destroyed by a love so tender.

For only He purifies the heart and soul,
Only in Him, we become truly whole.
For only He remains the source
Of Humility, and boundless force.

Wisdom Unveiled

The profound wisdom unveiled in Overcoming the Barrier of Self-Love is that the greatest obstacle to intimate companionship with the Divine is the ego and its demands for recognition. The wise-one realizes that a deep and continuous effort to purify the lower self is required. This contemplation highlights that true success comes from being "saved from the selfishness of their own souls," as affirmed in Quran 59:9. The example of the emigrants and those who welcomed them demonstrates a faith so pure that it transcends personal desires and envy, while Quran 58:22 shows a loyalty to the Divine that surpasses even familial ties. By forsaking self-love, one does not become empty but rather undergoes a profound psychic awakening, where the veil of ego is lifted, and the heart becomes a mirror reflecting not its own image, but the boundless mercy and majesty of the Creator.

Wise-Reflection

Reflect on your own heart. When do you feel the whisper of "I" most strongly—in moments of praise, criticism, or when a personal desire is unmet? How can the humility of the believers who gave preference to others "even though they may be in need" inspire you to practice self-effacement? Consider the thought that in abandoning self-love, "you find yourself in the presence that was always waiting." What would it mean for your heart to fully let go of its need for validation and control, and to allow this profound psychic awakening to purify your gaze, making His light the very essence of your sight?

Contemplation: Sin and the Path to Redemption

The wise-one's journey into Divine Companionship is not defined by an absence of sin, but by a profound understanding of its nature and its path to redemption. This contemplation illuminates a sacred and precise truth: not all sins are the same. One is a forgivable fall of a heedless heart, while the other is an act of conscious rebellion. In this reflection, we explore the difference between a lapse in awareness and a battle against truth itself, and how Allah's response to each is a testament to both His perfect justice and His infinite mercy.

Part 1: The Line Between Lapse and Rebellion

In the light of Divine Companionship, the wise-one recognizes a critical distinction: a sin committed in ignorance is a fall from grace, yet a sin committed with knowledge is an act of defiance—a battle initiated against the Divine. This understanding shatters the illusion of consequence-free rebellion. It fosters an immediate and sincere repentance for the faltering heart, while making it clear that a knowing transgression must be met with a decisive and humble return, for to persist is to invite a reckoning.

Reflect: If transgression occurs with awareness of the Divine, it constitutes an act of defiance. Those who knowingly sin initiate a conflict. Yet, for those who sin, forgiveness is prepared, and for those who initiate conflict, a confrontation awaits.

The Reckoning of the Knowing Heart

To sin in ignorance is a fall, a lapse in awareness,
Yet mercy remains near.
But to sin in knowledge, to defy while seeing,
Is not mere failure—
It is a declaration of war.
If you see Him from behind the things and you attain a sin,
Then you sinned based on knowledge.
Those who sin based on knowledge
Initiate war against Him.

For those who transgress,
Forgiveness is prepared.
But for those who declare defiance,
A reckoning awaits.
The believers were warned to give up outstanding interest,
for to persist is to invite war.
❨If you do not, then beware of a war with Allah and His Messenger!❩ [317] —Quran
2:279

Repent, and what was lost is returned.
Delay hardship, and compassion prevails.

The people by the sea
Thought to deceive,
Twisting His law, seeking loopholes.
But what they thought was gain,
Became punishment.
❨When they ignored the warning they were given, We rescued those who used to warn
against evil and overtook the wrongdoers with a dreadful punishment for their

---

[317] This is in agreement with the Quran verse:

📖 ❨O believers! Fear Allah, and give up outstanding interest if you are ˹true˺ believers. (278) If you do not, then beware of a war with Allah and His Messenger! But if you repent, you may retain your principal—neither inflicting nor suffering harm. (279) If it is difficult for someone to repay a debt, postpone it until a time of ease. And if you waive it as an act of charity, it will be better for you, if only you knew. (280)❩ [Quran 2:278-280]

rebelliousness.❭³¹⁸ —Quran 7:165
For defiance does not escape notice,
And arrogance brings its own downfall.

And among the first transgressors,
Two brothers stood—
One in sincerity, one in jealousy.
Sacrifice was accepted,
But envy bred rage.
❬*Allah only accepts the offering of the sincerely devout.*❭³¹⁹ —Quran 5:27
The murder was committed,
Loss became his fate,
And from that crime, the divine decree descended—
❬*Whoever takes a life... it will be as if they killed all of humanity.*❭ —Quran 5:32

Thus, the wise-one perceives—
To falter is human,
To return is granted.
But to defy while knowing

---

³¹⁸ And the Quran verse narrating the story of the village whom thought they could deceit Allah by fishing in the forbidden day so they receive their punishment:

📖 ❬Ask them ʿO Prophetˈ about ʿthe people ofˈ the town which was by the sea, who broke the Sabbath.1 During the Sabbath, ʿabundantˈ fish would come to them clearly visible, but on other days the fish were never seen. In this way We tested them for their rebelliousness. (163) When some of ʿthe righteous amongˈ them questioned ʿtheir fellow Sabbath-keepersˈ, "Why do you ʿbother toˈ warn those ʿSabbath-breakersˈ who will either be destroyed or severely punished by Allah?" They replied, "Just to be free from your Lord's blame, and so perhaps they may abstain." (164) When they ignored the warning they were given, We rescued those who used to warn against evil and overtook the wrongdoers with a dreadful punishment for their rebelliousness. (165) But when they stubbornly persisted in violation, We said to them, "Be disgraced apes!" (166) And ʿremember, O Prophet,ˈ when your Lord declared that He would send against them others who would make them suffer terribly until the Day of Judgment. Indeed, your Lord is swift in punishment, but He is certainly All-Forgiving, Most Merciful. (167)❭ [Quran 7:163-167]

³¹⁹ This aligns with the Quranic verse recounting the narrative of Adam's two sons, wherein envy motivated one to defy Allah's command and commit brutality:

📖 ❬Relate to them in truth ʿO Prophetˈ the story of Adam's two sons—how each offered a sacrifice: one's offering was accepted while the other's was not, so he threatened ʿhis brotherˈ, "I will kill you!" His brother replied, "Allah only accepts ʿthe offeringˈ of the sincerely devout. (27) If you raise your hand to kill me, I will not raise mine to kill you, because I fear Allah—the Lord of all worlds. (28) I want to let you bear your sin against me along with your other sins, then you will be one of those destined to the Fire. And that is the reward of the wrongdoers." (29) Still, the other convinced himself to kill his own brother, so he killed him— becoming a loser. (30) Then Allah sent a crow digging ʿa graveˈ in the ground ʿfor a dead crowˈ, in order to show him how to bury the corpse of his brother. He cried, "Alas! Have I ʿevenˈ failed to be like this crow and bury the corpse of my brother?" So he became regretful. (31) That is why We ordained for the Children of Israel that whoever takes a life—unless as a punishment for murder or mischief in the land—it will be as if they killed all of humanity; and whoever saves a life, it will be as if they saved all of humanity. ʿAlthoughˈ Our messengers already came to them with clear proofs, many of them still transgressed afterwards through the land. (32)❭ [Quran 5:27-32]

Is not mere rebellion, but battle against truth itself.
For the path is laid clear—
One leads toward mercy,
The other toward ruin.
And none escape the consequence
Of what they knowingly choose.

So the wise-one walks forward,
Not blinded by the self's destructive need,
He finds his refuge in a sincere deed.
He seeks forgiveness from his human strife,
And turns to a better, and renewed life.

For only He redeems the souls who fall,
Only in Him, we stand up after all.
For only He remains the source
Of Mercy, and boundless force.

Wisdom Unveiled

The profound wisdom unveiled in The Line Between Lapse and Rebellion is that Divine Companionship rests on a clear understanding of transgression. The wise-one realizes that a sin of ignorance is a fall, an honest lapse in awareness, while a sin of knowledge is an act of defiance— a "declaration of war" against truth itself. This contemplation uses powerful examples, such as the warning against interest in Quran 2:279 and the fate of the Sabbath-breakers in Quran 7:165, to show that this conscious rebellion invites a specific divine response. The story of Adam's sons in Quran 5:27-32 further highlights that the root of such defiance often lies in the rejection of sincerity and the embrace of arrogance. The contemplation, therefore, fosters a deep humility, teaching the wise-one that genuine repentance is not merely an apology for a mistake, but a decisive and humble return from the battlefield of a knowing transgression.

Wise-Reflection

Reflect on your own spiritual journey. Can you recall a time when you crossed the line from a simple lapse to an act of knowing defiance? What was the internal conflict of that choice, and what was its cost to your spiritual peace? Consider the idea that a "reckoning awaits" those who knowingly rebel, while "forgiveness is prepared" for those who sincerely return. What would it mean for your heart to fully embrace this truth, and to respond to every knowing transgression not with further defiance, but with a decisive and humble return that strengthens your bond with the Creator instead of breaking it?

Part 2: The Deceit of Desire and the Final Reckoning

Furthermore, the wise-one perceives the profound and subtle nature of Divine confrontation. For a soul that fights against Allah for a worldly desire, the war is waged not with immediate wrath, but with a form of ultimate consequence. Allah, in His wisdom, may allow the transgressor to have the very thing they craved, letting its emptiness and deceit become their punishment. This trial is a profound act of Divine wisdom, a final opportunity for the heart to awaken before it is utterly undone by the very thing it chose over its Creator.

Consider: The Divine confrontation may manifest as a separation between you and that for which you defied the Divine. Then, by Divine glory, the Divine may reappear from beyond that conflict, leading to your ultimate reckoning.

The Price of What Was Fought For

When defiance is raised against Him,
The war does not come in an instant.
It begins in separation—
The servant is left
To chase that which they fought for,
Until the truth reappears beyond their grasp.
"His war against you is to place between you and what you initiated war against Him
for.
Then shall He, by His glory, reappear from behind what you fought Him for—and
then He shall destroy you; thus, He shall terminate you."

For messengers were sent, warnings were spoken,
Yet arrogance prevailed.
Hardship descended, but no humility followed.
Instead, hearts hardened,

And Satan made their misdeeds appealing.
They were showered with everything they desired.
But just as they became prideful,
He seized them by surprise.
❨*So the wrongdoers were utterly uprooted. And all praise is for Allah—Lord of all*
worlds.❩ [320] —*Quran 6:45*

When hardship touches them, they cry out in desperation.
But when relief arrives,
They forget the One they once pleaded with.
❨*Enjoy your disbelief for a little while—you will certainly be one of the inmates of the*
Fire.❩ [321] —*Quran 39:8*
The indulgence will not last forever.
The world, if left without balance,
Would have tempted all into heedlessness.
❨*Were it not that people might become one community of disbelievers, We would have*
supplied the homes of those who disbelieve with silver roofs and stairways to ascend.❩
—*Quran 43:33*
Their fleeting joy would never equal the enduring promise of the Hereafter.

The one who turns away from the Reminder
Is given over to deception.
A companion in falsehood walks beside them,
Leading them astray while they believe themselves secure.
❨*I wish you were as distant from me as the east is from the west! What an evil*

---

[320] This is in agreement with the Quran verse:

📖 ❨Indeed, We have sent messengers before you ˹O Prophet˺ to other people who We put through suffering and adversity ˹for their denial˺, so perhaps they would be humbled. (42) Why did they not humble themselves when We made them suffer? Instead, their hearts were hardened, and Satan made their misdeeds appealing to them. (43) When they became oblivious to warnings, We showered them with everything they desired. But just as they became prideful of what they were given, We seized them by surprise, then they instantly fell into despair! (44) So the wrongdoers were utterly uprooted. And all praise is for Allah—Lord of all worlds. (45)❩ [Quran 6:42-45]

[321] This is in agreement with the Quran verse:

📖 ❨When one is touched with hardship, they cry out to their Lord, turning to Him ˹alone˺. But as soon as He showers them with blessings from Him, they ˹totally˺ forget the One they had cried to earlier, and set up equals to Allah to mislead ˹others˺ from His Way. Say, ˹O Prophet,˺ "Enjoy your disbelief for a little while! You will certainly be one of the inmates of the Fire." (8)❩ [Quran 39:8]

associate you were![322] —*Quran 43:38*
On that final day,
All companionship in misguidance will be severed.
Each soul bears its own truth,
And none escape the fate they pursued.

Thus, the wise-one understands—
His war is not immediate wrath, but separation first, reckoning after.
And those who stand in defiance, blind to the consequence,
Will find that what they fought for was never theirs to keep.
What they clung to was never real.
And when He appears beyond all illusion,
Only destruction will remain.

So the wise-one walks forward,
Not fighting what is given by His hand,
He finds his peace in this blessed land.
He lets his burdens purify his soul,
And finds his purpose in becoming whole.

For only He redeems with trials and pain,
Only in Him, we learn what is true gain.
For only He remains the source
Of Mercy, and boundless force.

Wisdom Unveiled

The profound wisdom of this contemplation is that the path to redemption is an intimate journey of self-awareness and submission. It

---

[322] This is in agreement with the Quran verse:

〈Were it not that people might ˹be tempted to˺ become one community ˹of disbelievers˺, We would have supplied the homes of ˹only˺ those who disbelieve in the Most Compassionate with silver roofs and ˹silver˺ stairways to ascend, (33) as well as ˹silver˺ gates and thrones to recline on, (34) and ornaments ˹of gold˺. Yet all this is no more than a ˹fleeting˺ enjoyment in this worldly life. ˹But˺ the Hereafter with your Lord is ˹only˺ for those mindful ˹of Him˺. (35) And whoever turns a blind eye to the Reminder of the Most Compassionate, We place at the disposal of each a devilish one as their close associate, (36) who will certainly hinder them from the ˹Right˺ Way while they think they are ˹rightly˺ guided. (37) But when such a person comes to Us, one will say ˹to their associate˺, "I wish you were as distant from me as the east is from the west! What an evil associate ˹you were˺!" (38) ˹It will be said to both,˺ "Since you all did wrong, sharing in the punishment will be of no benefit to you this Day."[1] (39)〉 [Quran 43:33-39]

[1]: From a worldly perspective, many people are comforted when they hear of others who went through similar trials as them. But this will not be the case on Judgment Day. Everyone will be desperate to save themselves from the punishment, regardless of others.

distinguishes between the fall of ignorance and the war of conscious defiance, showing that while both are met with mercy, the knowing transgression invites a reckoning. The wise-one understands that Allah's justice is a form of His wisdom, where trials serve as a purifying fire and an act of love, designed to sever the soul from what it fought for and reveal the ultimate emptiness of worldly pursuits. In this deep reflection, the wise-one comes to know that their Creator is not a Lord of wrath but of limitless forgiveness, who uses every circumstance to guide the soul from rebellion back to a profound and humbled companionship.

Wise-Reflection

Reflect on your own heart and its capacity for both ignorance and knowing defiance. How can the understanding that "to sin with knowledge is to wage war against the One Whose only offering is peace" inspire a more immediate and sincere repentance? Consider the truth that even in your rebellion, Allah's mercy is actively working to bring you back, turning your fall into a lesson and your wandering into wisdom. What would it mean for your heart to fully embrace this reality, finding solace in the divine process of reconciliation through trials, and seeing every hardship not as a punishment, but as a purifying act of love designed to draw you closer to your Creator?

The wise-one reflects

When I sin—knowing, seeing, understanding—
The weight of my rebellion presses heavier still,
For to sin with knowledge is to wage war against the One
Whose only offering is peace.
Yet even as I stray,
He, The Most Forgiving (Al-Ghaffar),
Prepares forgiveness ahead of my fall.
His mercy does not strike with vengeance,
But patiently builds barriers between me and the sin,
Hemming my wandering heart with wisdom and love.
In His mercy,
Every battlefield becomes a garden,
And every war I initiate fades away
As He starves the falsehood within me.

Until at last, my pride crumbles,
And my hunger seeks only Him.

Even my rebellion
Becomes a road back to Him,
A pathway paved with the mercy
I once refused to see.
Through the wastelands of my pride,
He leads me gently,
Turning my fall into a lesson,
My wandering into wisdom.
And in the fields of surrender,
Where my falsehood can no longer stand,
I find the beauty of forgiveness,
Not as a gift I deserve,
But as a love that transforms me.

Conclusion

In the end, the wise-one is humbled by the depth of Allah's justice and the boundlessness of His mercy. They understand that their every fall is met with a path of return, and their every act of conscious rebellion is met with a reckoning that is a form of both justice and guidance. Their journey is a testament to the truth that the Creator does not leave them to their folly. Rather, He uses every means—from the gentle invitation of repentance to the humbling trials of consequence—to draw the soul back to the profound peace of His companionship.

Contemplation: Attributes of Divine Companionship

The wise-one recognizes the specific attributes of Divine Companionship: it is constant, unwavering, all-sufficient, forgiving, nurturing, and guiding. These attributes are not abstract concepts but living realities experienced directly by the wise-one, confirming the intimacy of their bond with Al-Wali (The Protecting Friend) and Al-Hameed (The Praiseworthy).

The companionship of the Creator transcends the limitations of human relationships, for it is a state of being where all doubt and questioning dissolve. In the presence of the Divine, the heart finds a stillness so complete that surprise loses its meaning, and the need to inquire is silenced by a certainty that is more profound than any knowledge. It is here that the soul perceives that faith is not a mere belief, but a serene surrender born from a knowing that is beyond sight and sound.

Beyond Surprise and Questioning: The Presence of Divine Certainty

One of the attributes of the Creator's companionship
is the absence of surprise,
the stillness beyond questioning.
Who could be astonished
while beholding the Divine?
And why would one inquire
while standing in His presence?

For the one who passed by a ruined city,
his doubt rose in thought:
⟨How could Allah bring this back to life
After its destruction?⟩

Yet Allah did not answer with words, but with reality—

a hundred years passed, then He brought him back.
The bones rose, flesh clothed them anew,
And the man saw—
⟨Now I know that Allah is Most Capable of everything.⟩[323] —Quran 2:259
For knowledge gained through sight
silences all questioning.

---

[323] This is in agreement with Quran verse narrating story of the good man who question Allah ability to revive a dead abandon village so Allah make him witness His willing in His creation:

📖 ⟨Or ˹are you not aware of˺ the one who passed by a city which was in ruins. He wondered, "How could Allah bring this back to life after its destruction?" So Allah caused him to die for a hundred years then brought him back to life. Allah asked, "How long have you remained ˹in this state˺?" He replied, "Perhaps a day or part of a day." Allah said, "No! You have remained here for a hundred years! Just look at your food and drink—they have not spoiled. ˹But now˺ look at ˹the remains of˺ your donkey! And ˹so˺ We have made you into a sign for humanity. And look at the bones ˹of the donkey˺, how We bring them together then clothe them with flesh!"1 When this was made clear to him, he declared, "˹Now˺ I know that Allah is Most Capable of everything." (259)⟩ [Quran 2:259]

Abraham, though believing,
sought reassurance—
❪Show me how You give life to the dead.❫

Not in doubt, but in longing for certainty.
And the response came, not in mere words,
but in demonstration.
The birds trained, the bodies scattered,
the call made—and they flew back,
life restored by His will.
❪And ˹so you will˺ know that Allah is Almighty, All-Wise.❫ [324] *—Quran 2:260*

Moses, chosen in speech,
longed for the ultimate vision—
❪My Lord! Reveal Yourself to me so I may see You.❫
But the answer was not sight, but realization.
For no human could withstand such knowing,
no eye could bear the full majesty.
Instead, the mountain bore witness, and crumbled into dust.
And Moses fell, overcome, and when he rose, his soul surrendered:
❪Glory be to You! I turn to You in repentance, and I am the first of the believers.❫ [325]
—Quran 7:143

---

[324] This is in agreement with Quran verse narrating the story of Ibraham asking Allah about resurrection just for ease his anxious about how this could be done so Allah make him witness how He resurrect a slaughter birds:

📖 ❪And ˹remember˺ when Abraham said, "My Lord! Show me how you give life to the dead." Allah responded, "Do you not believe?" Abraham replied, "Yes I do, but just so my heart can be reassured." Allah said, "Then bring four birds, train them to come to you, ˹then cut them into pieces,˺ and scatter them on different hilltops. Then call them back, they will fly to you in haste. And ˹so you will˺ know that Allah is Almighty, All-Wise." (260)❫ [Quran 2:260]

[325] This is in agreement with Quran verse narrating Moses asking Allah to see him even though Allah chosen him by His talking so Allah make him know that there are things that no human can pear witness to it in this life:

📖 ❪We appointed for Moses thirty nights then added another ten—completing his Lord's term of forty nights. Moses commanded his brother Aaron, "Take my place among my people, do what is right, and do not follow the way of the corruptors." (142) When Moses came at the appointed time and his Lord spoke to him, he asked, "My Lord! Reveal Yourself to me so I may see You." Allah answered, "You cannot see Me! But look at the mountain. If it remains firm in its place, only then will you see Me." When his Lord appeared to the mountain, He levelled it to dust and Moses collapsed unconscious. When he recovered, he cried, "Glory be to You! I turn to You in repentance and I am the first of the believers." (143) Allah said, "O Moses! I have ˹already˺ elevated you above all others by My messages and speech.[1] So hold firmly to what I have given you and be grateful." (144)❫ [Quran 7:142-144]

[1]: Allah reminds Moses that even though his request to see Allah was denied, he has already been favoured by Allah over the people of his time through prophethood and direct communication with the Almighty.

Thus, the wise-one understands—
Companionship with Him is beyond astonishment, beyond inquiry.
For the heart that stands before His presence
does not ask, nor does it seek verification—
It perceives, it surrenders, and it knows,
without doubt, without question.

To truly companion with the Creator
Is to step beyond surprise,
Beyond the need to ask.
For who could be surprised
While observing the boundless wisdom of The All-Wise (Al-Hakeem)?
Who would question
While walking beside the One
Who weaves the path with perfect intention?
In such companionship,
Trust becomes the firm ground beneath one's feet,
Replacing bewilderment with certainty.
Surrender becomes the song of the heart,
Silencing fear,
As the soul rests in the infinite presence
Of the One who is never unprepared,
Never uncertain.
When I walk with Him,
The need to know fades like a distant shadow.
His presence is the answer—
Not in words,
But in a peace that quiets every unspoken question.
In His nearness,
The weight of uncertainty dissolves,
And every mystery unfolds
As a form of mercy,
A gift wrapped in His infinite wisdom.
With Him, I no longer strive to understand,
For in His companionship,
Being is enough.

So the wise-one walks forward,
Not fighting what is unknown to his mind,

He finds his peace in what he can find.
He lets his trust become his sight,
And rests his heart in His certain light.

For only He can silence all the noise,
Only in Him, we make the righteous choice.
For only He remains the source
Of Certainty, and boundless force.

Wisdom Unveiled

The profound wisdom unveiled in this contemplation is that true Divine Companionship with Al-Wali and Al-Hameed is marked by the absence of surprise and questioning. The wise-one understands that a relationship with the Creator is not based on fleeting wonder or the need for constant validation, but on a deep, abiding certainty that transcends human logic. The prophetic stories and the personal reflection of the wise-one illustrate this journey from inquiry to surrender: from seeing resurrection with one's own eyes (Quran 2:259), to the miraculous sign given to Abraham (Quran 2:260), and the ultimate submission of Moses (Quran 7:142-144). The culmination of this understanding is a psychic transformation where the heart perceives that His presence is the answer to all questions, silencing all doubt and fostering a serenity where being is enough.

Wise-Reflection

Reflect on your own companionship with the Creator. Where do you find yourself questioning His will or His power, or being surprised by the turns of your life? Consider the thought that "the need to know fades like a distant shadow." What would it mean for your heart to embrace the certainty of His presence so fully that it no longer feels the need to ask "how?" or "why?" How can you, in your daily life, practice a trust so profound that it silences every unspoken question and allows you to find peace in His infinite wisdom, knowing that with Him, being is enough?

Contemplation: The Role of Silence in Divine Companionship

The wise-one discerns the critical role of silence in Divine Companionship. While invocation and supplication are vital, the deepest communion often occurs in profound inner stillness, beyond words and thoughts. It is in this quietude that the heart can truly listen to the Divine whispers, perceive the subtle intimations, and experience the pure presence of the Creator. This cultivation of inner quietude becomes a sanctuary for continuous, unmediated companionship, fostering a psychic space for direct spiritual reception.

The companionship of the Creator is not merely heard in words but felt in the profound stillness of the heart. The wise-one understands that to be truly present with the Divine, one must first silence the clamor of the world and the chatter of the ego. It is in this inner quietude that the soul enters a sacred space where the unsaid is known, the unseen is perceived, and the burdens of the heart are gently unveiled under the loving guardianship of the Divine.

The Silence of Divine Companionship

Why let your thoughts fold
Endlessly upon themselves?
Why should gloom remain,
Settling within you,
Day and night?
You are not alone—
You are in His companionship,
And He is your guardian,
Watching over you,
Knowing your burdens
Before you speak them.

❨*Do not falter or grieve, for you will have the upper hand, if you are true believers.*❩
[326] *—Quran 3:139*
For every hardship endured,
Every struggle faced,
Is not meaningless—

---

[326] This is in agreement with the Quran verse:

❨Do not falter or grieve, for you will have the upper hand, if you are ˹true˺ believers. (139) If you have suffered injuries ˹at Uḥud˺, they suffered similarly ˹at Badr˺. We alternate these days ˹of victory and defeat˺ among people so that Allah may reveal the ˹true˺ believers, choose martyrs from among you—and Allah does not like the wrongdoers— (140) and distinguish the ˹true˺ believers and destroy the disbelievers. (141) Do you think you will enter Paradise without Allah proving which of you ˹truly˺ struggled ˹for His cause˺ and patiently endured? (142)❩ [Quran 3:139-142]

It refines, reveals,
Distinguishes sincerity from illusion.

⟨*There will certainly be no fear for the close servants of Allah, nor will they grieve.*⟩
[327] *—Quran 10:62*
For those who trust in Him
Walk in assurance,
Receiving His mercy,
Embraced by His promise.
Glory and power belong only to Him,
And those who chase falsehood,
Following mere assumption,
Will find nothing but delusion.

⟨*Put your trust in the Ever-Living, Who never dies.*⟩ [328] *—Quran 25:58*
For He alone sustains,
He alone governs,
He alone is Compassionate,
Unaffected by time,
Unchanged by circumstance.
Hold fast to Him in silence,
And He will perceive
What burdens you,
What afflicts you,
What lingers unseen.
And in your stillness,
He does not merely witness—
He unfolds deeper knowledge,

---

[327] This is in agreement with the Quran verse:

📖 ⟨There will certainly be no fear for the close servants of Allah, nor will they grieve. (62) ˹They are˺ those who are faithful and are mindful ˹of Him˺. (63) For them is good news in this worldly life and the Hereafter. There is no change in the promise of Allah. That is ˹truly˺ the ultimate triumph. (64) Do not let their words grieve you ˹O Prophet˺. Surely all honour and power belongs to Allah. He is the All-Hearing, All-Knowing. (65) Certainly to Allah ˹alone˺ belong all those in the heavens and all those on the earth. And what do those who associate others with Allah really follow? They follow nothing but assumptions and do nothing but lie. (66)⟩ [Quran 10:62-66]

[328] This is in agreement with the Quran verse:

📖 ⟨Put your trust in the Ever-Living, Who never dies, and glorify His praises. Sufficient is He as All-Aware of the sins of His servants. (58) ˹He is˺ the One Who created the heavens and the earth and everything in between in six Days,1 then established Himself on the Throne. ˹He is˺ the Most Compassionate! Ask ˹none other than˺ the All-Knowledgeable about Himself. (59)⟩ [Quran 25:58-59]

Not just of your trials,
But of you, entirely.
For He is not distant,
Nor does He abandon—
But stands as the guardian
Who lifts the servant
From sorrow
Into certainty.

O my soul,
Why do your thoughts fold upon themselves
Like withering leaves?
Why does your gloom linger,
Day and night, coiling within,
Festering in the darkness of your own making?
Is it not true that in your silence,
There is space for clarity to bloom?
That within the stillness,
You can uncover what lies hidden—
The depths of what you hold
And the burdens that afflict you?
Silence is not emptiness;
It is a sacred field,
The fertile soil where trust takes root,
Where the heart learns to speak
A language beyond words.
In the quiet,
I awaken to the truth:
I am not forsaken in my struggles.
Even when my sorrow blinds me,
There is a guardianship,
An unseen companionship
Carrying me through the silence,
Guiding me gently toward light.

In the sacred hush of my silence,
He breathes truths into the corners of my soul—
Truths that the clamor of the world had drowned,
Truths I was too fearful to seek.

In the stillness,
Where all my striving ceases,
He places His unseen hand
Upon the wounds I tried to hide,
And heals with a tenderness
So boundless,
It feels like the love I have longed for
But never dared to name.
Here, in the quiet,
I find that what I thought was emptiness
Was the fullness of His presence,
Waiting to fill me,
Waiting to make me whole.

So the wise-one walks forward,
Not fighting with his gloom and despair,
He finds his comfort in silent prayer.
He listens to His truth in every sign,
And knows His healing touch is divine.

For only He can fill the empty space,
Only in Him, we find our final grace.
For only He remains the source
Of Silence, and boundless force.

Wisdom Unveiled

The profound wisdom of this contemplation is that silence is a powerful, active tool for nurturing Divine Companionship. The wise-one understands that a genuine relationship with the Creator requires more than just outward invocation; it demands the cultivation of an inner quietude where the heart can truly listen. The contemplation teaches that in this stillness, the wise-one can perceive the Divine's guardianship and unmediated love, finding a certainty that dispels fear and sorrow. Through the poignant reflection of the wise-one, we learn that what seems like emptiness is, in fact, the very fullness of His presence, a sacred space where our inner truths are revealed and our hidden wounds are healed by a boundless tenderness that makes us whole.

Wise-Reflection

Reflect on the clamor of your own life and the noise of your own thoughts. How often do you allow yourself to sit in true inner silence, not to avoid problems, but to listen for a deeper truth? Consider the thought that your sorrow and struggles are not meaningless, but opportunities for refinement and for you to receive His guidance. What would it mean for your heart to embrace silence as a "sacred field," a space where trust takes root and you are able to receive the profound companionship that is carrying you even in your most difficult moments? How can you consciously create space in your life to listen to the Divine whispers that are waiting to fill you and make you whole?.

Conclusion: In the Creator Companionship

ECHOES OF REALIZATION: THE SHELTER OF DIVINE COMPANIONSHIP

There exists a profound shelter not meticulously built by human hands, a refuge not carved from earthly stone—it is, in truth, the very nearness of the Creator Himself. To walk in His continuous companionship is to walk in absolute freedom: free from the incessant, gnawing hunger of the fleeting world, free from the hollow, transient pride of the egoic self.

Here, in the encompassing shelter of His boundless Mercy, the wise-one's soul finds precisely what it never consciously knew it desperately needed: an unconditional love that never wavers, an infallible guidance that never falters, and an eternal Presence that does not, and cannot, ever fade. O wise-one, embrace this intimate companionship with every fiber of your being. It is your true and eternal homeland, your perpetual harbor in every storm, your hidden, truly invincible joy.

THE SEEKER'S ASCENT: THE ULTIMATE REFUGE

Companionship with the Creator is not merely a comforting metaphor. It is, in essence, the realest, most profound home the aspiring soul shall ever intimately know. By diligently relinquishing the subtle chains of self-love, by consciously silencing needless, distracting questions, and by resolutely turning the heart away from the fleeting distractions of worldly dust and shadow, the wise-one is ultimately crowned with the precious friendship of the One who, in His infinite wisdom, created the very longing itself, and now satisfies it beyond all human imagining.

To truly walk with the Creator is to walk already within the very essence of spiritual victory. It is to taste the profound delights of paradise in every single step taken. It is to carry, even through the most arduous trials, an unquenchable flame of ultimate assurance, echoing within the deepest chambers of the heart: "He is with me, and I am never alone." This continuous experience of Divine Companionship is the very heart of psychic and spiritual resilience in "The Crucible of Inner Transformation."

15ᵀᴴ REFLECTION: THE CODE OF THE RIGHTEOUS HEART

THE GATEWAY VERSES

In the sacred words of Allah, a profound description of the ultimate reward for the righteous heart and its defining characteristics:

📖 ❨*And Paradise will be brought near to the righteous, not far off. (31) "And it will be said to them,` "This is what you were promised, for whoever "constantly` turned `to Allah` and kept up `His commandments`— (32) who were in awe of the Most Compassionate without seeing `Him`,1 and have come with a heart turning "only to Him`. (33)❩* [Quran 50:31-33]

ILLUMINATION'S DAWN

There comes a pivotal moment in the wise-one's profound journey when spiritual striving consciously shifts from the outward actions of the limbs to the intricate, unseen chambers of the heart. Here, within this secret, most sacred sanctuary, the Creator looks—not at external appearances, not at accumulated possessions, not at the grandeur of deeds—but profoundly at the trembling heart that beats either in fervent longing for Him or in subtle heedlessness away from Him.

The Righteous Heart is not built by mere accident, nor is it crowned by the performance of ritual alone. It is, rather, a vibrant garden meticulously sown in the tender tears of humility, lovingly watered by the continuous remembrance (Dhikr) of the Most Compassionate (Ar-Rahman), and bountifully harvested in the awe of an unseen yet ever-present Divine Reality. Let us now walk, with reverence and utmost sincerity, into this sacred field, where the wise-one's heart—if diligently purified—becomes a luminous, flawless mirror for the Infinite.

THE UNFOLDING OF INSIGHTS

This section explores the characteristics, challenges, and ultimate rewards of cultivating a righteous heart, emphasizing its pivotal role in spiritual proximity and psychic transformation.

Contemplation: The Righteous Heart as a Covenant

The wise-one understands the righteous heart as a sacred covenant (mithaq) between the soul and its Creator. It is an internal agreement to turn continually towards Allah, to obey His commandments, and to maintain awe of Him even in His Unseen reality. This covenant is not merely intellectual; it is deeply etched into the spiritual fabric of the heart. Fulfilling this covenant involves constant vigilance over one's inner state, ensuring intentions are pure and love is unadulterated, thereby aligning the heart with its original divine purpose.

The journey to the righteous heart is not paved with grand gestures, but with the quiet sincerity of an internal covenant. It is a vow whispered not with the lips, but with a soul in constant, loving surrender. This sacred agreement transforms the heart into an eternal sanctuary, a place where Allah's remembrance brings profound assurance, and a awe for the Unseen becomes its most radiant light.

Sanctuary Without Walls

The righteous heart is a covenant—
A bond between the soul and The Faithful (Al-Mu'min),
Woven not in fleeting oaths,
But in the quiet steadfastness of surrender.
It is a sanctuary defended not by stone walls,
But by a remembrance that never falters,
By humility that kneels without shame,
By trust that does not waver in storm nor silence.

⟨Unquestionably, by the remembrance of Allah hearts are assured.⟩[329] —Quran
13:28

The sanctuary stands on this firm ground,
Where the soul finds its ultimate peace—
Not in the clamor of the world,
But in the serenity of His constant presence.
And in its surrender, it whispers:
"You, O my Lord, are my only refuge—
Whether in the tremble of my weakness
Or the fire of my strength,

---

[329] This is derived from the Quran verses of:

📖 ⟨those who believe and whose hearts find comfort in the remembrance of Allah. Surely in the remembrance of Allah do hearts find comfort. (28) Those who believe and do good, for them will be bliss and an honourable destination. (29)⟩ [Quran 13:28-29]

Whether in light that comforts
Or darkness that tests."

For to trust in Him
Is not merely to seek shelter,
But to make the heart His dwelling place,
Where faith is not a momentary plea
But a ceaseless return.
Every heartbeat is a renewal of the covenant,
An unspoken vow whispered in the rhythm of life.
Every breath is an offering,
Laid upon the altar of surrender,
Where faith is not grand pronouncements,
But quiet persistence.

The righteous heart does not wait for revelation,
Nor demand signs from the unseen.
It builds its temple in the unnoticed moments,
In the patience of waiting,
In the courage of trust,
In the steadfast steps that lead to Him.

⟨And Paradise will be brought near to the righteous, not far off. ʿAnd it will be said
to them,ʾ "This is what you were promised, for whoever ʿconstantlyʾ turned ʿto Allahʾ
and kept up ʿHis commandmentsʾ— who were in awe of the Most Compassionate
without seeing ʿHimʾ, and have come with a heart turning ʿonly to Himʾ.⟩[330] —

Quran 50:31-33
For this is the ultimate reward—
A heart that turns,
A soul that keeps,
A being that comes with a covenant fulfilled.

---

[330] This is derived from the Quran verses of:

📖 ⟨And Paradise will be brought near to the righteous, not far off. (31) ʿAnd it will be said to them,ʾ "This is what you were promised, for whoever ʿconstantlyʾ turned ʿto Allahʾ and kept up ʿHis commandmentsʾ— (32) who were in awe of the Most Compassionate without seeing ʿHimʾ,[1] and have come with a heart turning ʿonly to Himʾ. (33) Enter it in peace. This is the Day of eternal life!" (34) There they will have whatever they desire, and with Us is ʿevenʾ more. (35) ⟩ [Quran 50:31-35]

[1]: This can also mean that they are in awe of their Lord as much in private as they are in public.

So the wise-one walks forward,
Not seeking the world's passing renown,
He makes His heart a hallowed ground.
He fulfills his pledge with every beat,
And finds in His Presence, his true retreat.
For only He remains the source
Of Righteousness, and boundless force.

Wisdom Unveiled

The profound wisdom of this contemplation is that the righteous heart is a dynamic, living covenant (mithaq) with the Creator. The wise-one understands that this covenant is not a static agreement but a continuous spiritual act, renewed with every heartbeat and breath. The contemplation underscores that the heart's peace and assurance are found not in worldly distractions, but in the constant remembrance of Allah, as stated in Quran 13:28. By internalizing this covenant, the wise-one cultivates a sanctuary within themselves—a space of humility, trust, and unwavering remembrance that aligns their inner state with the divine purpose. This inner transformation culminates in the state described in Quran 50:31-33, where the righteous heart, having constantly turned to Allah in awe of the Unseen, is brought near to Paradise as a promise fulfilled.

Wise-Reflection

Reflect on your own heart and the nature of its covenant with the Divine. Is your heart a "sanctuary without walls," defended by remembrance and trust, or is it a place of noise and distraction? Consider the thought that every heartbeat is an opportunity to renew your covenant with the Creator. What does it mean for you to cultivate an inner state of humility and awe for the Unseen reality of Ar-Rahman? How can the continuous remembrance of Allah become the source of assurance in your heart, fulfilling the promise of a soul that has turned only to Him?

Contemplation: Awe Without Sight

A defining characteristic of the righteous heart is awe without sight (khashyah bil-ghaib). As the Gateway Verse states, "who were in awe of the Most Compassionate without seeing ´Him`." This implies a profound, experiential recognition of Allah's Majesty and Power, even though He is unseen by physical eyes. This awe is born of deep contemplation of His creation, His attributes, and His revelations. It is not fear of punishment, but a trembling reverence that inspires devotion, humility, and vigilance over the heart's state, fostering a deep psychic connection to the Unseen.

The righteous heart finds its most profound state of devotion in a reverence that is not dependent on sight. It is a worship born from an intimate, psychic knowledge of the Divine, a certainty that is felt in the soul rather than proven by the eyes. This awe is a testament to a heart that is so purified it can perceive majesty where others see only silence, and feel a presence that is deeper and more certain than any physical reality.

The Hidden Awe: Worship Beyond Sight

Blessed is the heart
That trembles before the unseen,
Not out of fear of punishment,
But because it perceives majesty—
Woven into silence,
Shimmering behind veils.
Blessed is the soul
That bows in hidden awe,
Its devotion untouched by spectacle,
Its love unshaken by sight.
For the most sacred truths
Are not spoken,
Not reasoned,
But felt—
Known in certainty
Without proof.

❨My Lord! I dedicate what is in my womb entirely to Your service, so accept it from
me.❩ —Quran 3:35
The wife of Imran,
Without vision of the future,
Without certainty of what was to come,
Placed her trust
Entirely in Him.
And Mary was born,
Raised in devotion,

Protected by divine mercy,
Supplied with sustenance
From unseen hands.
❬*It is from Allah. Surely, He provides for whomever He wills without limit.*❭ *[331]* —
Quran 3:37
For the faithful,
The unseen does not diminish belief,
But strengthens it.
They abandon comfort,
Calling upon Him
With hope and fear,
Knowing that what awaits them
Is beyond imagining.

❬*The only true believers in Our revelation are those who—when it is recited to*
them—fall into prostration and glorify the praises of their Lord, and are not too
proud. They abandon their beds, invoking their Lord with hope and fear, and donate
from what We have provided for them.❭ *[332]* —*Quran 32:15-16*
And among those nearest to Him,
There is no hesitation—
No pride to resist,

---

[331] This is in agreement with the Quran verse of mother of Mary that she pledge what in her womb to Allah as a servant devoted to creator pleasing and following His decree:

📖 ❬'Remember` when the wife of 'Imrân said, "My Lord! I dedicate what is in my womb entirely to Your service, so accept it from me. You ´alone` are truly the All-Hearing, All-Knowing." (35) When she delivered, she said, "My Lord! I have given birth to a girl,"—and Allah fully knew what she had delivered—"and the male is not like the female.1 I have named her Mary, and I seek Your protection for her and her offspring from Satan, the accursed."[1] (36) So her Lord accepted her graciously and blessed her with a pleasant upbringing—entrusting her to the care of Zachariah. Whenever Zachariah visited her in the sanctuary, he found her supplied with provisions. He exclaimed, "O Mary! Where did this come from?" She replied, "It is from Allah. Surely Allah provides for whoever He wills without limit." (37)❭ [Quran 3:35-37]

[1]: The prayers of Mary's mother were answered. In a ḥadîth collected by Bukhâri and Muslim, the Prophet ﷺ says, "Every child is touched by Satan when they are born—and they cry because of this contact—except Jesus and his mother."

[332] This is in agreement with the Quran verse:

📖 ❬The only ´true` believers in Our revelation are those who—when it is recited to them—fall into prostration and glorify the praises of their Lord and are not too proud. (15) They abandon their beds, invoking their Lord with hope and fear, and donate from what We have provided for them. (16) No soul can imagine what delights are kept in store for them as a reward for what they used to do.(17)❭ [Quran 32:15-17]

No exhaustion to weaken.
❬*They glorify Him day and night, never wavering.*❭ [333] —*Quran 21:20*

Thus, the wise-one understands—
Worship does not rely
On proof,
On witness,
On spectacle.
It is found in surrender,
In silent reverence,
In faith anchored
Not in sight,
But in certainty.

Blessed is the heart that trembles before the unseen,
That fears The Most High (Al-Aliyy),
Not out of dread for punishment,
But because it perceives majesty
Woven into the silence,
Shimmering behind the veils.
Blessed is the soul that bows in hidden awe,
Its worship untouched by spectacle,
Its love unshaken by sight—
Anchored in the certainty
That the most sacred truths
Are felt,
Not seen.
True awe does not seek proof.
It does not wait for miracles.
It quivers at the whisper of His Name,
At the memory of His nearness,
At the certainty
That unseen does not mean absent—

---

[333] This is in agreement with the Quran verse describing the stance of angels in the praising Allah and glorifying Him.

❬To Him belong all those in the heavens and the earth. And those nearest to Him are not too proud to worship Him, nor do they tire. (19) They glorify ˹Him˺ day and night, never wavering. (20)❭ [Quran 21:19-20]

That presence can be deeper than vision,
And knowing can be stronger than sight.

So the wise-one walks forward,
Not needing to witness with his eyes,
He finds his truth in a silent surprise.
He trusts in His promise, in dark and in light,
And worships with awe, beyond all of sight.

For only He is the Unseen, the Most High,
Whose majesty breathes in the silent sigh.
He is the source of all that can be known,
And the love from which all love has grown.
For only He remains the source
Of Presence, and boundless force.

Wisdom Unveiled

The profound wisdom unveiled in this contemplation is that the righteous heart is defined by its ability to cultivate a profound and genuine awe (khashyah bil-ghaib) of the Creator without seeing Him. The wise-one understands that this is not a fear of punishment, but a deep reverence born from the psychic certainty of His majesty. This state is exemplified by the unwavering trust of the wife of Imran (Quran 3:35-37), the devotion of believers who abandon their beds to pray (Quran 32:15-16), and the ceaseless glorification of the angels (Quran 21:20). The personal reflection of the wise-one reveals that this awe is a transformative inner experience, where the heart finds a certainty deeper than sight and a presence more real than vision, making faith a profound and personal reality rather than a mere intellectual assent.

Wise-Reflection

Reflect on your own devotion. Is your worship a matter of outward ritual, or does it stem from an inner awe that trembles before the unseen majesty of Allah? Consider the thought that true awe does not wait for proof or miracles. What would it mean for your heart to be so anchored in the certainty of the Unseen that you could find peace and purpose in silent reverence, knowing that His presence is deeper than vision and your connection to Him is stronger than sight? How can you cultivate a heart that is not just obedient, but profoundly in awe of The Most High (Al-Aliyy)?

Contemplation: Silencing the Worldly Echoes Within

To cultivate a righteous heart, the wise-one must master silencing the worldly echoes within. The heart is constantly bombarded by desires, anxieties, and distractions from the temporal world. These 'echoes' prevent the heart from fully listening to the Divine whispers and focusing on the Creator. This contemplation involves disciplined inner work: mindful remembrance, turning away from heedlessness, and conscious purification of desires. By quieting the noise of the world within the heart, the wise-one creates a sanctuary for Divine presence and clarity.

The heart is a sacred sanctuary, but it is constantly assailed by a relentless storm of worldly echoes—the clamor of ambition, the tremor of fear, the siren call of passing desires. To seek the presence of the Divine is to consciously turn from this noise and press the soul against a deeper, more profound silence. This act of purification is not a deprivation of the self, but an act of liberation, a return to the one voice that was always calling from the very depths of the heart.

The Return That Was Always Near

"O my soul,
How long will you answer the call of passing things?
How long will you grasp at shadows,
Chasing echoes that vanish like mist?"

⟨*He has certainly succeeded who purifies himself, and mentions the name of his Lord and prays.*⟩[334] —*Quran 87:14-15*
The heart meant for Al-Haqq (The Truth) cannot be divided.
It must quiet the clamor of ambition,
Silence the trembling of fear,
Dissolve the illusions of pride—
Until all that remains is clarity,

---

[334] This is derived from the Quran verses of:

⟨ Successful indeed are those who purify themselves, (14) remember the Name of their Lord, and pray. (15)⟩ [Quran 87:14-15]

Until only one Name resounds within it.
For what is fleeting cannot fill
What was made for the Eternal.
What is scattered cannot hold
What was meant to be whole.

❲*And of the people is he who says, 'Our Lord, give us in this world,' and he will have*
no share in the Hereafter.❳*[335] —Quran 2:200*
Thus, the soul must learn to turn,
To press itself against silence,
Where longing finds its rightful home,
Where the voice of Truth speaks
Not from beyond,
But from the depths of the heart itself.
When I silence the noise within me,
I begin to hear the single Voice
That was always calling.
Not from outside,
Not from distant heights,
But from the deepest garden within—
Where truth was waiting all along,
Where devotion was planted before doubt.
Here, in the stillness,
I find not an absence,
But a presence beyond all knowing.
Not a lost path,
But a return that was always near.
❲*And We have already created man and know what his soul whispers to him, and*
We are closer to him than his jugular vein.❳*[336] —Quran 50:16*
The closeness was never a distance to be overcome,

---

[335] This is derived from the Quran verse of:

📖 ❲When you have fulfilled your sacred rites, praise Allah as you used to praise your forefathers ˹before Islam˺, or even more passionately. There are some who say, "Our Lord! Grant us ˹Your bounties˺ in this world," but they will have no share in the Hereafter. (200)❳ [Quran 2:200]

[336] This is derived from the Quran verse of:

📖 ❲Indeed, ˹it is˺ We ˹Who˺ created humankind and ˹fully˺ know what their souls whisper to them, and We are closer to them than ˹their˺ jugular vein. (16)❳ [Quran 50:16]

But a noise to be quieted,
A veil to be lifted from a heart that had forgotten.

So the wise-one walks forward,
Not chasing illusions that fade with the day,
He finds His sanctuary in the silence of his way.
He knows the true voice is not a far-off sound,
But the presence of the Lord in his hallowed ground.

For only He is the Ever-Living (Al-Hayy), the Unseen, the Near,
Whose stillness dissolves all a soul's doubt and fear.
He is the purifier of all that resides,
The peace in which a tranquil heart abides.
For only He remains the source
Of Stillness, and boundless force.

Wisdom Unveiled

The profound wisdom of this contemplation is that the righteous heart is cultivated by the conscious, disciplined act of silencing the worldly echoes within. The wise-one understands that the heart's peace is not found in the satisfaction of temporal desires, but in the purification of the self and the mindful remembrance of the Creator (Quran 87:14-15). This act of inner discipline allows the heart to quiet its clamor and perceive a Divine presence that has always been intimately near, as affirmed by Quran 50:16. The contemplation teaches that the pursuit of fleeting worldly things leads to spiritual emptiness (Quran 2:200), while the act of turning inward allows the soul to return to its original state of clarity and find the voice of truth within itself—a return that was always waiting, always near.

Wise-Reflection

Reflect on your own heart. What are the "worldly echoes" that constantly vie for your attention and prevent you from hearing the Divine whispers? Are they anxieties, ambitions, or passing desires? Consider the thought that true spiritual success comes from purifying the heart and remembering your Lord. What would it mean for you to consciously silence this inner noise, to turn away from heedlessness, and to press your soul against the silence? How can you embrace the profound truth that Allah is closer to you than your jugular vein, and that by quieting the distractions, you are not finding a new path, but discovering a return that was always near?

Contemplation: The Call to a Heart That Turns to the Creator

The essence of the righteous heart is its constant call to a heart that turns to the Creator (munib). The Quranic description of "a heart turning 'only to Him'" signifies continuous repentance, sincere turning in every state, and unwavering orientation towards Allah. This turning is not merely from sin, but from any form of heedlessness or attachment to other-than-Allah. It is a dynamic state of active devotion, where the heart, like a compass needle, always points back to its true North, ensuring its alignment with Divine Will in all circumstances.

The spiritual journey of the wise-one is not merely an act of obedience, but a profound and continuous act of turning. The heart is a compass, and in a world of endless distractions, it must be consciously and constantly realigned to its true North. This turning is a sacred longing that transcends knowledge and ritual, dissolving the veils of the self until the heart finds its singular purpose, its ultimate destination—a return that was always near..

The Turning That Transcends Obedience

"O my soul,
I am not merely called to obey,
But to turn—
To turn away from vanity,
From the weight of distractions,
From the echoes of self
That pull me away."
Into the silent embrace of Al-Rahman,
Where knowledge alone
Does not suffice.
For understanding remains distant,
Like light seen,
But never touched.
I must yearn—
With longing that stretches beyond thought,
Beyond ritual,

Beyond speech,
Until the heart dissolves its boundaries
And draws wholly to Him.

❨Say, O My servants Who have exceeded the limits Against their souls! Do not lose
hope in Allah's mercy, For He certainly forgives all sins. He is the All-Forgiving,
Most Merciful.❩ —Quran 39:53
For He does not demand from afar,
But waits—
Waits for the heart to turn,
For the moment it lets go
Of the illusions
It once clung to,
And finds Him,
Not distant,
But nearer than breath.
❨Turn to your Lord In repentance, And submit to Him Before the punishment
reaches you.❩—Quran 39:54
For in the turning,
There is release.
In submission,
There is renewal.

So that no soul will cry in regret—
❨Woe to me For neglecting my duties toward Allah While ridiculing the truth!❩ —
Quran 39:56
Nor will it say—
❨If only Allah had guided me, I would have been one of the righteous!❩ —Quran
39:57
For the call was always there,
The mercy always present,
But only those who turn
Will find it.
Thus, the wise-one understands—
Obedience is not enough,
Knowledge is not enough,
Until the heart turns,
Until longing surpasses reason,
Until the self dissolves,

And what remains
Is only Him. [337]

O my soul, I am called not merely to obey,
But to turn—
To turn from the vanities that weigh me down,
From the clamor of ego that clouds my sight,
Into the silent embrace of Al-Rahman.
To know Him is not enough;
Knowledge remains distant,
Like light seen but never touched.
I must yearn—
With a longing that reaches beyond thought,
Beyond ritual,
Beyond what is spoken or understood.
For He is unseen,
Yet nearer than breath.
He does not demand from afar,
But waits for the turning of the heart,
For the moment it relinquishes its distractions
And finds itself drawn wholly to Him.
A heart that turns,
Turns not once,
But with every heartbeat.
It turns with sorrow,
Seeking refuge.

---

[337] This is in agreement with the Quran verse:

📖 ⟨Say, ˹O Prophet, that Allah says,˺ "O My servants who have exceeded the limits against their souls! Do not lose hope in Allah's mercy, for Allah certainly forgives all sins.[1] He is indeed the All-Forgiving, Most Merciful. (53) Turn to your Lord ˹in repentance˺, and ˹fully˺ submit to Him before the punishment reaches you, ˹for˺ then you will not be helped. (54) Follow ˹the Quran,˺ the best of what has been revealed to you from your Lord, before the punishment takes you by surprise while you are unaware, (55) so that no ˹sinful˺ soul will say ˹on Judgment Day˺, 'Woe to me for neglecting ˹my duties towards˺ Allah, while ridiculing ˹the truth˺.' (56) Or ˹a soul will˺ say, 'If only Allah had guided me, I would have certainly been one of the righteous.' (57)⟩ [Quran 39:53-57]

[1]: No matter how big someone's sins are, they cannot be bigger than Allah's mercy. Based on 4:48, the only unforgivable sin in Islam is if someone dies while disbelieving in Allah or associating others with Him in

worship. In an authentic narration collected by At-Tirmiẓi, the Prophet (ﷺ) reports that Almighty Allah says, "O children of Adam! As long as you call upon Me, putting your hope in Me, I will forgive you for what you have done, and I will not mind. O children of Adam! If your sins were to reach the clouds of the sky and then you sought My forgiveness, I would ˹still˺ forgive you. O children of Adam! If you were to come to Me with sins filling the whole world and then you came to Me without associating other gods with Me, I would certainly match your sins with forgiveness."

It turns with joy,
Offering gratitude.
It turns in silence,
In longing,
In awe.
Until turning becomes its nature,
Its rhythm,
Its unbroken prayer.
And in turning,
It arrives—
Not at a place,
But in presence.

So the wise-one walks forward,
Not seeking the pleasure of an empty pursuit,
He finds in his Lord his heart's deepest root.
His soul is renewed with every turn,
And finds in His mercy the lesson to learn.

For only He is the All-Forgiving, the Most Merciful,
Whose call to the heart makes the broken whole.
He is the source of return for the soul that strays,
And the guidance that lights all our darkest days.
For only He remains the source
Of Mercy, and boundless force.

Wisdom Unveiled

The profound wisdom of this contemplation is that the righteous heart is defined by its constant, active turning (munib) to the Creator—a state that transcends mere obedience or intellectual knowledge. The wise-one understands that this turning is a continuous act of repentance and a conscious alignment away from all attachments to "other-than-Allah." This spiritual discipline is the key to entering the boundless mercy of Allah, who waits for the heart to turn and forgives all sins, as affirmed in Quran 39:53. The contemplation teaches that this dynamic turning becomes the very nature of the heart, its rhythm, and its prayer, leading to a profound inner renewal and the ultimate discovery of a Divine presence that is closer than breath.

Wise-Reflection

Reflect on the state of your own heart. Is your spiritual practice a matter of fulfilling obligations, or does it stem from a sincere, continuous "turning" toward the Creator? Consider the thought that Allah does not demand from afar but waits for the heart to turn. What are the "illusions" or worldly distractions you need to let go of to allow your heart to turn wholly to Him? How can you cultivate a heart where turning becomes its nature—a rhythm of seeking refuge, offering gratitude, and finding a presence that transcends all reason and longing?

Contemplation: The Promise of Paradise for the Righteous Heart

The culmination of cultivating such a heart is the promise of Paradise. The Gateway Verse explicitly states that Paradise will be brought near. This is not just a future reward, but a spiritual state of contentment and closeness to Allah that begins in this life. The wise-one understands that Paradise is not merely a physical garden, but the ultimate fulfillment of the soul's yearning for Divine Proximity. The pure heart, already attuned to the Beloved, finds its ultimate rest and joy in the eternal Presence it sought, demonstrating a complete spiritual and psychic realization.

The promise of Paradise is not a distant reward for an obedient life, but the final, radiant realization of a journey that begins in the secret sanctuary of the heart. The righteous heart, through its unseen fidelity and unwavering devotion, has already cultivated a foretaste of this closeness in this life. Paradise, in its truest sense, is the ultimate fulfillment of this longing—the moment the soul's unspoken prayer is answered, and the One it adored without vision is finally seen.

The Unseen Fidelity

⟨And Paradise will be brought near to the righteous, not far off.⟩[338] —Quran 50:31
Paradise is not earned by deeds alone.

---

[338] This is derived from the Quran verses of:

It is drawn near to those whose hearts have turned,
Who have bowed before the unseen majesty,
Whose chests have expanded in awe—
Not from knowledge alone,
But from the secret trembling of devotion.

❨*The 'true' believers are only those whose hearts tremble at the remembrance of Allah,*
whose faith increases when His revelations are recited to them, and who put their trust
in their Lord. They are those who establish prayer and donate from what We have
provided for them.❩[339] *—Quran 8:2-3*
It is gifted to those whose prayers rise like unseen incense,
Whose whispers of longing are carried into
The courts of the Merciful.
O soul,
Strive not only for actions,
But for a heart that, though unnoticed by the world,
Is always seen by Him.
For deeds may lay a path,
But it is love, surrender, and the quiet fidelity of the heart
That walks it to the gates of eternity.

The reward is not just gardens and rivers,
Not merely beauty that the eyes can behold.
It is to stand before Him, unveiled,
To finally see with sight
What the heart knew in darkness.
❨*Some faces that Day will be radiant, looking at their Lord.*❩[340] *—Quran 75:22-*
23

📖 ❨And Paradise will be brought near to the righteous, not far off. (31) 'And it will be said to them,' "This is what you were promised, for whoever 'constantly' turned 'to Allah' and kept up 'His commandments '— (32) who were in awe of the Most Compassionate without seeing 'Him', and have come with a heart turning 'only to Him'. (33) Enter it in peace. This is the Day of eternal life!" (34) There they will have whatever they desire, and with Us is 'even' more. (35)❩ [Quran 50:31-35]

[339] This is derived from the Quran verses of:

📖 ❨The 'true' believers are only those whose hearts tremble at the remembrance of Allah, whose faith increases when His revelations are recited to them, and who put their trust in their Lord. (2) 'They are' those who establish prayer and donate from what We have provided for them. (3) It is they who are the true believers. They will have elevated ranks, forgiveness, and an honourable provision from their Lord. (4)❩ [Quran 8:2-4]

[340] This is derived from the Quran verses of:

📖 ❨On that Day 'some' faces will be bright, (22) looking at their Lord. (23)❩ [Quran 75:22-23]

To look upon the One
Whom I trusted without proof,
Whom I adored without vision—
Now standing in a light no darkness can approach.
This is the moment every breath has longed for,
The fulfillment of the prayer
That was never spoken,
But lived.

❨*He is the One Who sent down serenity upon the hearts of the believers so that they may increase even more in their faith... So He may admit believing men and women into Gardens under which rivers flow—to stay there forever—and absolve them of their sins. And that is a supreme achievement in the sight of Allah.*❩[341] —*Quran 48:4-5*

This is the ultimate promise of the righteous heart,
The divine gift of serenity,
The absolving of sins,
The supreme achievement
Of a soul that trusted.

So the wise-one walks forward,
Not chasing worldly ambitions that pass,
He finds his reward in a heart that lasts.
His hope is in a closeness that never ends,
A spiritual union that transcends all ends.

For only He is the All-Generous, the Bestower of Grace,
Whose ultimate reward is to see His Glorious Face.
He is the promise that fulfills every plea,

---

[341] This is derived from the Quran verses of:

❨Indeed, We have granted you a clear triumph ˹O Prophet˺ (1) so that Allah may forgive you for your past and future shortcomings,[1] perfect His favour upon you, guide you along the Straight Path, (2) and so that Allah will help you tremendously. (3) He is the One Who sent down serenity upon the hearts of the believers so that they may increase even more in their faith. To Allah ˹alone˺ belong the forces of the heavens and the earth. And Allah is All-Knowing, All-Wise. (4) So He may admit believing men and women into Gardens under which rivers flow—to stay there forever—and absolve them of their sins. And that is a supreme achievement in the sight of Allah. (5)❩ [Quran 48:1-5]

[1]: Like other prophets, Muḥammad ﷺ was infallible of sin. The verse here refers to misjudgments, such as the example given in 80:1-10. If the Prophet ﷺ himself is urged to seek forgiveness, then the believers are even more in need of praying for Allah's forgiveness.

The final reality for you and for me.
For only He remains the source
Of Paradise, and boundless force.

Wisdom Unveiled

The profound wisdom of this contemplation is that the promise of Paradise is the ultimate fulfillment of the righteous heart's journey. The wise-one understands that the reward is not merely a future physical garden but a final spiritual realization of the closeness to Allah that the heart yearned for in this life. The verses from Quran 8:2-4 and 48:4-5 powerfully reinforce this, describing how the true believer's trembling heart, increasing faith, and trust in Allah are met with serenity and an "honourable provision." The climax of this journey is the ultimate honor of seeing Allah, as described in Quran 75:22-23, fulfilling the heart's "unseen fidelity" and culminating in a profound and complete spiritual reality, where sins are absolved and faith is perfected.

Wise-Reflection

Reflect on your own yearning for Paradise. Is it for the promised gardens and rivers, or for the ultimate spiritual fulfillment of seeing your Lord? Consider the thought that Paradise is the final realization of a journey that begins in the heart, and that serenity is a gift from the Divine to those who strive. What does it mean for you to cultivate an "unseen fidelity" that, though unnoticed by the world, is always seen by Him? How can you live your life in such a way that your heart is already in a state of closeness to Allah, making Paradise not a distant hope, but the ultimate and natural culmination of your soul's greatest prayer?

Conclusion: The Code of the Righteous Heart

ECHOES OF REALIZATION: THE THRONE WITHIN THE CHEST

There is a sacred throne set deep within the chest—not exquisitely made of worldly gold or precious jewels, but meticulously fashioned from profound surrender, encompassing awe, and boundless Divine love. Blessed, truly blessed, is the heart that diligently purifies itself, transforming into a worthy abode for the King of Kings. Blessed, eternally blessed, is the soul that, with every sorrow and every joy, instinctively turns, with unwavering devotion, toward the Unseen Beloved.

O wise-one, allow your heart to become that sacred throne where the Most Compassionate (Ar-Rahman) chooses to dwell. For it is precisely where the heart humbly bows in submission that the aspiring soul is ultimately crowned with true spiritual sovereignty and eternal grace.

THE SEEKER'S ASCENT: THE SECRET OF THE HEART'S RETURN

The righteous heart is not, in its essence, a monumental testament to unattainable perfection. It is, rather, a living, continuously trembling testament to the soul's ceaseless turning, its endless yearning, and its perpetual surrender to its Divine Source.

In the ultimate reckoning, it is not external grandeur or human achievements that save the heart—but its profound, inner purity. Not the vast accumulation of worldly knowledge—but the single, unwavering certainty that the Most Compassionate is intimately near, ever-present, even when He remains unseen by physical eyes. O seeker, tirelessly guard your heart, diligently cleanse it, and consciously turn it again and again, with every breath and every intention—for the heart that thus continually turns shall undoubtedly be the heart that ultimately arrives at its eternal destination, fully realizing its psychic and spiritual potential within the Divine Presence.

CONCLUSION FOR PART III: THE CRUCIBLE OF INNER TRANSFORMATION

(Completing the Forging...)

ECHO WITHIN THE HEART... (THE HEART REFINED IN THE CRUCIBLE)

The Manifestation of The Crucible of Inner Transformation does not conclude; rather, it deepens, like molten metal cooled and strengthened, revealing the true essence within. The wise-one, having traversed the refining fires of perception and the profound stations of Divine decree, now stands at the threshold of an even more potent, more humbling realization: inner transformation is not a passive process endured, but an active, continuous engagement, to be lived in every breath. Each reflection meticulously laid along this pathway has not served merely as a signpost; it has wrought a profound alchemy—a meticulous burning away of self-imposed illusions, a forging of new spiritual strength, and a sacred unveiling of the timeless resilience intrinsically woven into the soul's very essence.

THRESHOLD OF AWE

The Unveiling of Fortitude

As the veils gently lift upon this Manifestation of The Crucible of Inner Transformation, the wise-one transitions from apprehension to profound fortitude. The contemplations engaged within this part—of the eternity that frames all time, of the oath to embrace and surpass trials, of transcending the very names and concepts to reach the nameless essence, of finding solace in the Creator's unwavering companionship, and of establishing the righteous heart as a steadfast covenant—do not merely add to one's store of information. Rather, they fundamentally reshape the very vessel that is capable of receiving divine wisdom and enduring its transformative power, preparing it for deeper states of self-mastery.

Pillars of Realization

Eternity as Unveiled Perspective: The heart no longer dreads the unknown future or clings to the fleeting past; it awakens to the One who encompasses all time, perceiving every moment as a facet of eternal reality, finding peace in the vastness of Divine knowledge.

Oath as Empowered Submission:

Courage, unwavering trust, and profound submission have unveiled themselves not as weakness, but as the very bedrock upon which the wise-one stands firm amidst trials, dissolving resistance and finding strength in profound surrender.

Beyond Names as Direct Knowing:

Conceptual understanding and intellectual frameworks, once pathways, are now seen as potential veils. The discerning soul has learned to reach beyond them, seeking direct, unmediated experience of the Divine essence, recognizing the powerlessness of labels to contain the Infinite.

Creator's Companionship as Ultimate Solace:

The heart no longer feels isolated in its struggles; it awakens to the One who is closer than its jugular vein, a constant, unwavering presence that offers solace, guidance, and ultimate sufficiency in every trial.

Righteous Heart as Resilient Core:

The inner essence has been purified, becoming a covenant of purity and steadfastness. This profound inner state, forged through the trials, is received with utmost humility and reverence, unveiling a resilient core that can withstand all external pressures.

The Seeker Reflects

"I have walked through the fire, not as one consumed, but as one refined. Where I once saw hardship, I now perceive a Divine sculptor's hand, chipping away at my illusions. What I once feared as loss, I now recognize as liberation, a loosening of chains I unknowingly forged. The vastness of Eternity has dissolved the petty concerns of time, and the companionship of the Creator has made solitude a sanctuary. My heart, once a vessel for worldly desires, now beats with the rhythm of gratitude and submission. I stand, not as a conqueror of challenges, but as a servant transformed by them, ready for the deeper work of unveiling."

INVITATION TO THE NEXT MANIFESTATION

With this profound realization of inner transformation, the sacred path now unfolds to its next profound station: The Triumph of Self-Mastery. If this Manifestation revealed the profound nature of trials and the fortitude they instill, the next invites the soul to actively wield the tools forged in the crucible—to master its inner landscape, to purify its intentions, and to hone its spiritual perception. The wise-one, having understood the purpose of the fire, must now learn to become its master, ascending towards an even deeper form of inner authority and purity.

Call to Action

The path of transformation has been illuminated; will you now take the next unwavering step into the triumph of self?"

PART IV: THE TRIUMPH OF SELF-MASTERY

❖❖❖

 ﴿وَأَمَّا مَنْ خَافَ مَقَامَ رَبِّهِ ۔ وَنَهَى ٱلنَّفْسَ عَنِ ٱلْهَوَىٰ (40) فَإِنَّ ٱلْجَنَّةَ هِىَ ٱلْمَأْوَىٰ (41)﴾

﴿And as for those who were in awe of standing before their Lord and restrained themselves from ʾevilʾ desires, (40) Paradise will certainly be ʾtheirʾ home. (41)﴾ [Quran 79:40-41]

"The self is a wild beast; if you don't keep it busy, it will keep you busy." – Imam Ali ﷺ

❖❖❖

Having emerged from the refining fires of inner transformation, the wise-one now steps onto the battlefield of the self—a sacred arena where the ultimate victory is achieved not through external conquest, but through profound Mastery Over the Self. This part unveils the intricate art of spiritual discipline, revealing how the true triumph lies in restraining restless desires, purifying intentions, and aligning every fiber of being with Divine Will.

This station invites the seeker to actively engage in the purification of their inner landscape. Here, every habit, every inclination, and every perception becomes an opportunity for intentional refinement, paving the way for a deeper, unadulterated connection to the Creator. It meticulously guides the wise-one through reflections that reveal the subtle pitfalls of the lower self, the importance of sincere action, and the heightened spiritual vision that accompanies true inner authority.

Each reflection within this profound section acts like a skilled artisan, meticulously sculpting the soul into a vessel worthy of Divine proximity. From actively Embracing Divine Trials, transforming acceptance into a powerful tool for growth, to confronting The Veil of Habits, recognizing and overcoming ingrained patterns that hinder progress; from achieving absolute Alignment with Divine Will, making every intention resonate with the Creator's purpose; to cultivating profound Sincerity in Action, ensuring every deed is purely for His Face; and culminating in Seeing Beyond the Surface, where perception transcends superficial causality to apprehend the direct Hand of the Divine.

At its core, this Manifestation beckons the discerning soul to wage the greater jihad—the inner struggle against the ego's dominion. It explores profound shifts in action and perception: from reactive responses to mindful intention, from seeking worldly validation to desiring only Divine pleasure, and from being enslaved by habits to becoming the master of one's inner terrain. It challenges the wise-one to relinquish self-centered motives, to embrace rigorous discipline, and to cultivate an unyielding commitment to purity of purpose.

This Triumph is not a punitive struggle, but a liberating ascent. It is an invitation to perceive the power within self-restraint, to discern the beauty in purified intention, and to apprehend the clarity born of profound spiritual vision. To walk this path is to initiate the active refinement of the ego, transcending the veils of conditioned responses, and to stand, empowered, in the brilliance of Divine grace—a profound realization where the wise-one actively shapes their inner world, preparing for the ultimate freedom.

16ᵀᴴ REFLECTION: EMBRACING DIVINE TRIALS

(The Path of Acceptance)

THE GATEWAY VERSES

In the sacred words of Allah, a profound reminder to all who reflect upon the immense grace and reward for those who respond to Divine calls even amidst adversity::

📖 ❨*They are joyful for receiving Allah's grace and bounty, and that Allah does not deny the reward of the believers. (171) ˹As for˺ those who responded to the call of Allah and His Messenger after their injury,1 those of them who did good and were mindful ˹of Allah˺ will have a great reward. (172)*❩ *[Quran 3:171-172]*

ILLUMINATION'S DAWN

There comes a pivotal station on the wise-one's profound journey where the spiritual road narrows significantly, the temporal sky grows silent, and the winds of destiny shift with an unsettling uncertainty. It is precisely here, not in the triumphant clarity of ease, but deep within the shadows of intense trial, that the wise-one's soul is profoundly summoned—to either succumb and collapse, or to rise, transformed.

Yet, the truly wise-one—who, through prior stations, knows the Divine Voice behind the storm, who has diligently walked the path of constant presence and fervent prayer—learns that hardship is not a curse, but a concealed invitation. It is an invitation to unveil the deeper spiritual essence that lies beneath the superficial layers of the self. For what wounds the ego ultimately refines the spirit, and what profoundly bends the human will gracefully bows it toward the Eternal. Let us now walk, with courage and acceptance, into this sacred space where affliction becomes the very catalyst for awakening, and the crucible of trial transforms into the luminous gate to ultimate Divine union.

THE UNFOLDING OF INSIGHTS

This section explores the various dimensions of embracing Divine trials, from understanding their purpose to cultivating the inner states necessary for transcendence, highlighting their role in spiritual growth and psychic resilience.

Contemplation: Obedience to Divine Will

The wise-one recognizes that embracing trials is an act of profound obedience to Divine Will (Irādat Allāh). Since all calamities and blessings are written in a Divine Record (Quran 57:22), acceptance of trials is submission to Allah's perfect plan. This contemplation cultivates a heart that is not resentful but willingly aligns with whatever Allah decrees, understanding that His Will is always infused with ultimate wisdom and benevolence, even if its immediate manifestation is difficult. This is the bedrock of true spiritual fortitude.

When the winds of destiny shift with an unsettling uncertainty, the wise-one's soul is called not to resistance, but to a profound obedience. This is a call to align the heart with the divine plan, understanding that every hardship is a command to surrender, a sacred test that reveals the soul's true posture. This is the ultimate spiritual fortitude—to find the will to submit, even when the path is shrouded in shadows.

The Call to Trial: Obedience Beyond Distress

When hardship is decreed,
It does not arrive in vain.
It calls the believer
To rise,
To step forward,
To obey."
"The wise-one knows that once the Creator calls for a hardship trial, they shall obey
the Creator And discard all accompanied distress."
Distress clings to hesitation,
But obedience dissolves fear.

The call was given—
❲O believers! What is the matter with you that when you are asked to march forth in
the cause of Allah, you cling firmly to ˺your˹ land? Do you prefer the life of this world
over the Hereafter?❳ —Quran 9:38
But the world is fleeting,
Its pleasures insignificant
Compared to eternity.
And those who delay

Find that His call
Does not wait.

The Prophet did not stand alone—
Though driven out,
He carried certainty.
In the cave,
Fear threatened,
But trust prevailed.
❨*Do not worry; Allah is certainly with us.*❩ *—Quran 9:40*
Serenity descended,
Forces unseen were sent,
The word of falsehood crumbled,
While the Word of Allah
Stood supreme.

❨*March forth, whether it is easy or difficult for you, and strive with your wealth and your lives In the cause of Allah. That is best for you, if only you knew.*❩ *[342] —Quran*

---

[342] This is in agreement with the Quran verse narrating the story of prophet Mohammed's situation in Madinah with real believers and the hypocrites when it comes to hardship:

📖 ❨O believers! What is the matter with you that when you are asked to march forth in the cause of Allah, you cling firmly to ˹your˺ land?[1] Do you prefer the life of this world over the Hereafter? The enjoyment of this worldly life is insignificant compared to that of the Hereafter. (38) If you do not march forth, He will afflict you with a painful torment and replace you with other people. You are not harming Him in the least. And Allah is Most Capable of everything. (39) ˹It does not matter˺ if you ˹believers˺ do not support him, for Allah did in fact support him when the disbelievers drove him out ˹of Mecca˺ and he was only one of two. While they both were in the cave, he reassured his companion,[2] "Do not worry; Allah is certainly with us." So Allah sent down His serenity upon the Prophet, supported him with forces you ˹believers˺ did not see, and made the word of the disbelievers lowest, while the Word of Allah is supreme. And Allah is Almighty, All-Wise. (40) ˹O believers!˺ March forth whether it is easy or difficult for you, and strive with your wealth and your lives in the cause of Allah. That is best for you, if only you knew. (41)❩ Up to Quran verse of: ❨So let neither their wealth nor children impress you ˹O Prophet˺. Allah only intends to torment them through these things in this worldly life, then their souls will depart while they are disbelievers. (55)❩ [Quran 9:38-55]

[1]: The fast pace of the spread of Islam in Arabia in the 7th century was intimidating to the world's two superpowers of that time: the Romans and Persians. The Prophet ﷺ received the news that a Roman army was being mobilized to launch an attack on the newly established Muslim state in Medina, so he announced that he was going to march to Tabûk, located over 700 miles to the north, to meet the Romans in the summer of 9 A.H./631 C.E. It was a time of hardship because of the scorching heat, the long distance, and the financial situation of the Muslims. Although the Prophet ﷺ was able to mobilize over 30 000 Muslims for battle, many others did not join the army with or without valid excuses. Eventually, the Roman forces were discouraged from fighting and fled to Damascus and other cities under Roman rule. Therefore, the Prophet ﷺ returned to Medina with a feeling of triumph. With a new power now emerging in Arabia, many tribes started to switch their alliances from Caesar to the Prophet ﷺ.

[2]: Abu Bakr Aṣ-Ṣiddîq, Islam's first Caliph and a prominent figure in Islamic history. He accompanied the Prophet ﷺ during his emigration from Mecca to Medina after years of persecution at the hands of the Meccan pagans.

9:41

For trial does not ask
If one is ready.
It arrives
And reveals the heart.
It demands surrender,
Not comfort.
And in the struggle,
The wise-one understands—
Wealth fades,
Status dissolves,
But obedience remains.
For distress belongs to hesitation,
But triumph belongs to trust.

To obey the Divine (Al-Hakim)
Is not merely to act—
But to align the soul's posture:
To bow inwardly,
To trust even in the breaking.
Every hardship bears a hidden command:
"Surrender to My wisdom,
Trust My hidden design,
And let Me remake you."
Thus, when hardship calls,
It is not resistance
But submission
That leads the servant forward—
Beyond the weight of doubt,
Beyond the illusion of fear,
Into the certainty
That His will
Is never in vain.

So the wise-one walks forward,
Not clinging to the things of the world,
He lets his spirit in trials be unfurled.
He bows to a wisdom he cannot perceive,
And finds in His will the strength to believe.

For only He is the All-Wise, the All-Knowing,
In whose perfect plan, a seed is sown.
He is the Lord of both Ease and of Test,
And to trust in His Will is to find our best.
For only He remains the source
Of Submission, and boundless force.

Wisdom Unveiled

The profound wisdom of this contemplation is that embracing Divine trials is an act of profound obedience to Divine Will (Irādat Allāh). The wise-one understands that hardship is not a meaningless event, but a sacred command to align the heart with the Creator's perfect plan. The verses from Quran 9:38-41 serve as a powerful testament to this, illustrating the consequence of clinging to worldly comfort and the triumph that comes from unwavering trust, as exemplified by the Prophet in the cave. This contemplation unveils that true spiritual fortitude lies in a willing submission that dissolves distress and transforms trials into a crucible for growth, where the heart learns to "bow inwardly" and surrender to the ultimate wisdom of Al-Hakim, the All-Wise.

Wise-Reflection

Reflect on the trials in your own life. Do you see them as a curse to be resisted, or as a call to obedience? Consider the thought that every hardship bears a hidden command to surrender. What would it mean for your heart to discard all distress and willingly submit to whatever Allah has decreed? How can you cultivate the inner fortitude of the Prophet in the cave, finding serenity and trust even when the world seems to have turned against you? How can you learn to "bow inwardly" in a way that allows the trial to refine your spirit and remake you?

Contemplation: The Rule of Accepting Divine Trials

There is a fundamental rule: accepting Divine trials is not passive resignation, but an active, conscious choice that unlocks spiritual doors. The wise-one understands that resistance to a trial only magnifies suffering and delays growth. True acceptance involves an inner 'yes' to what Allah has ordained, transforming perceived adversity into a pathway for spiritual ascent. This active acceptance, born of deep faith, allows the soul to glean the hidden lessons and blessings within the hardship, fostering inner peace even amidst external turbulence.

The path of the wise-one is not defined by the absence of storms, but by their ability to navigate them with grace. The secret lies in a profound, inner 'yes' to the Divine Will, a surrender that is not weakness but a powerful act of spiritual defiance against despair. In this station, hardship is not merely endured; it is actively embraced as a gift—a crucible that purifies the spirit and a hidden key that unlocks the doors to a profound, unshakeable peace.

Through Trial, the Spirit Rises

Hardship arrives,
Not as punishment,
But as refinement.
It does not shatter—
It purifies.
It does not crush—
It strengthens.
The wise-one knows,
All trials shall never withstand
Against the Creator's grace.
For thirst, fatigue, hunger—
Each endured for His sake
Is not suffering,
But elevation.
Each step forward
Is inscribed in the unseen,
Each burden borne
Is counted as righteousness.

❨It was not proper for the people of Medina... to avoid marching with the Messenger of Allah or to prefer their own lives above his.❩[343] —Quran 9:120

---

[343] ❨This is in agreement with the Quran verse: ❨It was not 'proper' for the people of Medina and the nomadic Arabs around them to avoid marching with the Messenger of Allah or to prefer their own lives

When the test comes,
It is not the weight
That matters,
But the endurance.

⟨Allah will test you with a river. So whoever drinks ˋhis fillˋ from it is not with me,
and whoever does not taste it... is definitely with me.⟩ —Quran 2:249
The faithful restrain their hands,
The heedless drink their fill.
A single sip divides those
Who stand firm
From those
Who falter.
The army looks ahead,
The challenge before them vast.
⟨Now we are no match For Goliath and his warriors.⟩ —Quran 2:249
Yet among them,
Faith stirs—
⟨How many times Has a small force Vanquished a mighty army By the Will of
Allah!⟩ —Quran 2:249
Victory does not come
From numbers.
Strength does not rise
From might.
It is perseverance that prevails.
It is divine will
That overturns impossibility.
And so, they pray—
⟨Our Lord! Shower us with perseverance, Make our steps firm, And grant us

---

above his. That is because whenever they suffer from thirst, fatigue, or hunger in the cause of Allah; or tread on a territory, unnerving the disbelievers; or inflict any loss on an enemy—it is written to their credit as a good deed. Surely Allah never discounts the reward of the good-doers. (120)And whenever they make a donation, small or large, or cross a valley ˋin Allah's causeˋ—it is written to their credit, so that Allah may grant them the best reward for what they used to do. (121)⟩ [Quran 9:121-122]

victory.⟩³⁴⁴ *—Quran 2:250*
By His will,
Goliath falls.
David rises.
Wisdom is granted,
The oppressor is defeated,
And the battle
Is no longer theirs—
But His decree.

The wise-one looks upon every hardship,
No longer with fear,
But with the quiet certainty that
The grace of Al-Karim (The Most Generous)
Is vaster than any pain.
Even the fiercest storm
Cannot shatter the ship
Whose sails are woven with trust.
No trial touches me
Except it carries within it
The seed of a mercy greater than itself.
What bruises my heart today
Builds the wings I shall fly with tomorrow.
Thus, the wise heart understands—
Hardship does not arrive
As mere suffering,
But as elevation.
The soul is tested
Not to destroy,

---

[344] 📖 ⟨And this is in agreement with Quran verse narrating testament of ancient Saul's soldier while fighting against Goliath: (When Saul marched forth with his army, he cautioned: "Allah will test you with a river. So whoever drinks ´his fill` from it is not with me, and whoever does not taste it—except a sip from the hollow of his hands—is definitely with me." They all drank ´their fill` except for a few! When he and the ´remaining` faithful with him crossed the river, they said, "Now we are no match for Goliath and his warriors." But those ´believers` who were certain they would meet Allah reasoned, "How many times has a small force vanquished a mighty army by the Will of Allah! And Allah is ´always` with the steadfast." (249) When they advanced to face Goliath and his warriors, they prayed, "Our Lord! Shower us with perseverance, make our steps firm, and give us victory over the disbelieving people." (250) So they defeated them by Allah's Will, and David killed Goliath. And Allah blessed David with kingship and wisdom and taught him what He willed. Had Allah not repelled a group of people by ´the might of` another, corruption would have dominated the earth, but Allah is Gracious to all. (251)⟩ [Quran 2: 249-251]

But to reveal its strength.
And those who trust,
Who persevere,
Who surrender
To divine wisdom—
Find that every burden
Was never burden at all,
But a path
Toward grace.

So the wise-one walks forward,
Not fighting with sorrows that came,
He finds in each test a call to His name.
He builds his resolve in the quiet of his soul,
And finds in His wisdom, a heart made whole.

For only He is the All-Generous, the Most Kind,
In whose grace we leave all burdens behind.
He is the Lord of both Ease and of Test,
And to trust in His Will is to find our best.
For only He remains the source
Of Acceptance, and boundless force.

Wisdom Unveiled

The profound wisdom of this contemplation is that the acceptance of Divine trials is a powerful and active spiritual discipline, not a passive resignation. The wise-one understands that this inner "yes" to Allah's decree is the key to transforming perceived suffering into a catalyst for spiritual ascent. The verses from Quran 9:120 and the powerful story from Quran 2:249-251 serve as a testament to this truth, illustrating how endurance, perseverance, and unwavering trust in Allah's will are the true sources of strength and victory, far more potent than worldly might or numbers. The contemplation unveils that every hardship is a hidden command to surrender, carrying within it a seed of mercy far greater than the pain it inflicts, ultimately revealing the soul's strength and building the wings of faith.

Wise-Reflection

Reflect on your own response to hardship. Do you view acceptance as passive defeat, or as a powerful, conscious choice? Consider the thought that every trial, no matter how small, is a test of your inner state. What would it mean for your heart to willingly say 'yes' to what Allah has ordained, trusting that every burden is, in fact, a path toward grace? How can you cultivate the perseverance and certainty of the believers of old, seeing every test as an opportunity to reveal your strength, and finding that the grace of Al-Karim is indeed vaster than any pain?

Contemplation: Relying on the Creator's Aid

Central to embracing trials is relying completely on the Creator's Aid (Nusrah). When human strength wanes and resources diminish, the wise-one turns wholeheartedly to Al-Wakeel (The Disposer of Affairs) for support. This active reliance is not a sign of weakness but of profound spiritual intelligence, recognizing Allah as the ultimate source of strength and succor. It deepens Tawakkul (trust in Allah) and allows the wise-one to draw upon boundless Divine power, as exemplified by the believers who "responded to the call of Allah... after their injury" and found great reward.

In the face of adversity, the wise-one understands that human strength is a finite resource. It is here, at the edge of one's own capacity, that true spiritual intelligence is revealed: to turn with a heart full of Tawakkul to the One whose strength is limitless. This active reliance on Al-Wakeel transforms trials from a source of fear into a profound opportunity to witness the power of Divine aid, forging faith into an unbreakable force.

The Epic Saga: Faith Forged in Trial

The wise-one does not waver.
They do not sink beneath hardship,
Nor do they submit to despair.
For in all matters of existence,
They call upon the Creator—
Knowing that no trial stands
Against His grace.
"The wise-one always calls Toward the Creator's aid And never submits To hardship-associated distress."

When hardship arrives,
The adversaries rejoice,
But patience silences their schemes.
For endurance stands untouched,
Fortified by trust.

The Prophet stood at dawn,
Leading the believers,
Positioning their hearts
For the battle ahead.
Some faltered,
Uncertain of victory,
Yet reassurance descended—
❨So in Allah Let the believers put their trust.❩ —*Quran 3:122*
Against all odds,
Badr was won.
Though vastly outnumbered,
The faithful were upheld.
❨Is it not enough That your Lord Will send down A reinforcement of three thousand
angels?❩ [345] —*Quran 3:124*
And even more,
If the need arose,
For victory does not come from numbers,
But from the decree of the Almighty.
The battle passed,
Wounds remained.
Yet triumph does not ensure ease.
One victory does not erase trials ahead.

---

[345] This is agreement with the Quran verse narrating the prophet Mohammed's army preparation for Bader battel:

📖 ❨When you ˹believers˺ are touched with good, they grieve; but when you are afflicted with evil, they rejoice. ˹Yet,˺ if you are patient and mindful ˹of Allah˺, their schemes will not harm you in the least. Surely Allah is Fully Aware of what they do. (120) ˹Remember, O Prophet,˺ when you left your home in the early morning to position the believers in the battlefield. And Allah is All-Hearing, All-Knowing. (121) ˹Remember˺ when two groups among you ˹believers˺ were about to cower, then Allah reassured them. So in Allah let the believers put their trust. (122) Indeed, Allah made you victorious at Badr when you were ˹vastly˺ outnumbered. So be mindful of Allah, perhaps you will be grateful. (123) ˹Remember, O Prophet,˺ when you said to the believers, "Is it not enough that your Lord will send down a reinforcement of three thousand angels for your aid?" (124) Most certainly, if you ˹believers˺ are firm and mindful ˹of Allah˺ and the enemy launches a sudden attack on you, Allah will reinforce you with five thousand angels designated ˹for battle˺. (125) Allah ordained this ˹reinforcement˺ only as good news for you and reassurance for your hearts. And victory comes only from Allah—the Almighty, All-Wise— (126)❩ [Quran 3:120-126]

For faith is tested
Not only in success,
But in setback.
Not only in triumph,
But in wounds.

Uhud arrived,
The tide shifted,
The believers faltered—
Not in their devotion,
But in their discipline.
Victory was within reach,
But heedlessness unraveled it.
And so, they faced the consequence.
Not ruin,
But revelation.
Not destruction,
But awakening.
Their wounds became wisdom.
Their despair became strength.
And the call was given again—
"Your enemies have mobilized, So fear them."
Yet fear did not take root.
Where doubt once lingered,
Faith now stood firm.
Where hesitation once rose,
Certainty now guided them.
❨Allah alone Is sufficient as an aid, And He is the best Protector.❩ —Quran 3:173
They returned,
Not broken,
But fortified.
Not because the enemy retreated,
But because trust
Never wavered.
For those who stand in faith,
Fear does not dictate their path.
Satan whispers,

But they do not listen.
⟨So do not fear them; Fear Me If you are true believers.⟩ [346] —*Quran 3:175*

The wise-one does not cling to fragile solutions.
They raise their hands high to Al-Mujib (The Responsive One),
Knowing that even a whisper toward Him
Can move the mountains of grief.
It is not the size of my trial that matters,
But the nearness of the One I call upon.
When I ask Him,
I am already rescued,
Even if my eyes have not yet seen it.
Thus, the wise-one understands—
Distress has no power
Over the one
Who calls upon the Creator.
Trials may come,
Battles may rise,
But victory belongs
Only to Him.
And in calling upon Him,
The burden fades,
The path clears,
And the servant walks forward—

---

[346] This is in agreement with the Quran verse narrating the story of post battel of Uhud revelation:

📖 ⟨'As for' those who responded to the call of Allah and His Messenger after their injury,[1] those of them who did good and were mindful 'of Allah' will have a great reward. (172) Those who were warned, "Your enemies have mobilized their forces against you, so fear them," the warning only made them grow stronger in faith and they replied, "Allah 'alone' is sufficient 'as an aid' for us and 'He' is the best Protector." (173) So they returned with Allah's favours and grace, suffering no harm. For they sought to please Allah. And surely Allah is 'the' Lord of infinite bounty. (174) That 'warning' was only 'from' Satan, trying to prompt you to fear his followers. So do not fear them; fear Me if you are 'true' believers. (175)⟩ [Quran 3:172-175]

[1]: The Prophet ﷺ realized that the city of Medina became vulnerable after the Muslim loss at Uhud. So on the next day of the battle he decided to lead a small force of his companions—many of whom had been wounded at Uhud—to chase away the Meccan army which was camping at a place called Ḥamrâ' Al-Asad—not far from Medina. Abu Sufyân, commander of the Meccan army, sent a man to discourage the Muslims from following the Meccans. Although the man falsely claimed that the Meccans were mobilizing to launch a decisive attack on Medina, the Prophet became more determined to chase them away. Eventually, the Meccans decided to flee and not waste their victory after the Prophet sent a revert to Islam—who was friends with Abu Sufyân—to convince him to withdraw; otherwise Muslims were going to avenge their loss at Uhud.

Not weighed down by fear,
But lifted by certainty.

So the wise-one walks forward,
Not relying on what his hands can do,
He finds in his Lord his strength, ever new.
He calls upon the Mighty, the Ever-Near,
And finds in His aid the end of all fear.

For only He is Al-Wakeel, Al-Mujib, the Sublime,
Whose aid overcomes all challenges of time.
He is the Lord of both Triumph and Woe,
And in trusting His plan, our spirits grow.
For only He remains the source
Of Reliance, and boundless force.

Wisdom Unveiled

The profound wisdom of this contemplation is that true strength in the face of trials comes not from human might, but from complete reliance on the Creator's Aid (Nusrah). The wise-one understands that this active trust (Tawakkul) is a form of spiritual intelligence. The epic historical events of Badr and Uhud, as narrated in Quran 3:122-124 and 3:173-175, serve as a powerful testament to this truth, showing that victory and spiritual fortitude come from Allah's support, not human numbers or flawless execution. The contemplation unveils that by turning to Al-Wakeel, the heart finds a certainty that is deeper than sight and a rescue that is already decreed, transforming a trial from a source of distress into a profound opportunity for a spiritual awakening.

Wise-Reflection

Reflect on your own trials. When you face hardship, do you first rely on your own strength and resources, or do you turn wholeheartedly to Allah? Consider the thought that relying on the Creator is not a sign of weakness, but a sign of profound spiritual intelligence. What would it mean for you to cultivate a heart that is so certain of Al-Mujib's response that you feel "already rescued" the moment you make your plea? How can you live a life of such deep Tawakkul that the burden of your trials fades, and your path clears, lifted by the certainty of His aid?

Contemplation: The Tragedy of Discontentment

The wise-one deeply understands the tragedy of discontentment (sakhata) with Divine decree. Discontentment leads to internal misery, bitterness, and spiritual stagnation, trapping the soul in a cycle of suffering that compounds the external trial. It stems from an egoic desire to control outcomes or question Divine wisdom. By observing the destructive nature of discontentment, the wise-one actively chooses contentment (rida) and patience (sabr), thereby liberating the heart from self-imposed anguish and opening it to Divine peace.

The true tragedy of a trial is not the pain it inflicts, but the heart's refusal to accept it. While hardship is a test from the Creator, discontentment is a self-inflicted wound, an egoic resistance to the divine will that only compounds suffering. The wise-one, understanding that contentment is the ark in the flood of trials, chooses to surrender to the decree of Allah, finding in that submission a profound liberation from the chains of anger and bitterness.

The Tragedy of Discontent: Trials Without Surrender

The greatest tragedy
Is not hardship itself,
But the refusal to embrace it.
It is not loss,
But longing.
Not suffering,
But resistance.
"The real tragedy stems From forgoing one's wishes and desires, Accompanied by
refraining from being content With what trial is brought to one."
To forgo desires,
Yet refuse to find contentment
In what is decreed,
Is to stand between two pains—
One of what was wished for,
One of what was given.

The people of Moses cried out—
❲We have always been oppressed, Before and after you came to us.❳³⁴⁷ —Quran
7:129

Yet oppression
Was not the burden.
It was the doubt
That weighed upon them,
The hesitation
To see beyond hardship.
But Moses answered—
❲Perhaps your Lord Will destroy your enemy And make you successors in the land,
To see what you will do.❳ —Quran 7:129

For trials do not come
Without purpose.
They arrive
To test,
To reveal,
To prepare.

Yet even when sustenance was granted,
Complaints arose.
The provision of heaven
Was forsaken,
For something lesser—
Not out of need,
But out of defiance.

---

³⁴⁷ This is in agreement with Quran verse narrating the story of Israelites following Moses where the people of Moses said to Moses, when he said to them, "Seek help from God and be patient," "We have been harmed" by the killing of our children "before you came to us," meaning: before you came to us with God's message to us, because Pharaoh was killing their male children when the time of Moses came upon him, as I have explained previously in this book of ours. And his statement, "and after you came to us," means: after you came to us with God's message, because when Pharaoh's magicians were defeated, and he said to the leaders of his people what he said, he wanted to renew the torment upon them by killing their sons and keeping their women alive.

📖 ❲Moses reassured his people, "Seek Allah's help and be patient. Indeed, the earth belongs to Allah ˹alone˺. He grants it to whoever He chooses of His servants. The ultimate outcome belongs ˹only˺ to the righteous." (128) They complained, "We have always been oppressed—before and after you came to us ˹with the message˺." He replied, "Perhaps your Lord will destroy your enemy and make you successors in the land to see how you will do." (129)❳ [Quran 7:128-129]

❨Do you exchange What is better For what is worse?❩ *348* —*Quran 2:61*
And so, disgrace fell upon them,
Not for their hunger,
But for their rejection.
Not for their need,
But for their refusal
To accept what was given.

And among the doubters,
Fear ruled over trust.
They questioned fate,
Trembled before destiny.

❨If we had any say in the matter, None of us would have come to die here.❩ *349* —
Quran 3:154
Yet fate does not wait for consent.
The trials chosen
Are the trials that arrive.
And what was written,
Comes in its time.

❨Even if you were to remain in your homes, Those among you Who were destined to
be killed Would have met the same fate.❩ —*Quran 3:154*
For hardship does not ask,
It reveals.

---

348 This is in agreement with Quran verse narrating the story of people of Moses when they ask for lower quality food just in disagreement for what Allah grant them of high quality food:

📖 ❨And ˹remember˺ when you said, "O Moses! We cannot endure the same meal ˹every day˺. So ˹just˺ call upon your Lord on our behalf, He will bring forth for us some of what the earth produces of herbs, cucumbers, garlic, lentils, and onions." Moses scolded ˹them˺, "Do you exchange what is better for what is worse? ˹You can˺ go down to any village and you will find what you have asked for." They were stricken with disgrace and misery, and they invited the displeasure of Allah for rejecting Allah's signs and unjustly killing the prophets. This is ˹a fair reward˺ for their disobedience and violations. (61)❩ [Quran 2:61]

349 This is also in agreement with the Quran verses narrating the story of hypocrites howling while fearing death following prophet Mohammed in his march against enemies:

📖 ❨Then after distress, He sent down serenity in the form of drowsiness overcoming some of you, while others were disturbed by evil thoughts about Allah—the thoughts of ˹pre-Islamic˺ ignorance. They ask, "Do we have a say in the matter?" Say, ˹O Prophet,˺ "All matters are destined by Allah." They conceal in their hearts what they do not reveal to you. They say ˹to themselves˺, "If we had any say in the matter, none of us would have come to die here." Say, ˹O Prophet,˺ "Even if you were to remain in your homes, those among you who were destined to be killed would have met the same fate." Through this, Allah tests what is within you and purifies what is in your hearts. And Allah knows best what is ˹hidden˺ in the heart. (154)❩ [Quran 3:154]

It does not plead,
It refines.

The true sorrow
Is not in the loss itself,
But in the soul's refusal to bow before what was decreed.
Discontentment is the drought
That withers the gardens of gratitude.
I lose not when fortunes change—
I lose when my heart resists
The hand that changes them.
Contentment is my ark
In the flood of trials.
Thus, the wise-one understands—
To resist trial
Is not to escape it.
To reject fate
Is not to change it.
But to surrender,
To find contentment,
Is to transform it.
For the weight does not lessen,
But the heart does not break.
The pain does not vanish,
But the soul does not despair.
And in acceptance,
Hardship becomes elevation.

So the wise-one walks forward,
Not fighting the tides that are meant to be,
He finds his surrender, and sets his heart free.
He knows that what's written will always come true,
And finds in His wisdom a vision anew.

For only He is the All-Wise, the All-Sufficient,
Whose every decree is wholly beneficent.
He is the Lord of both loss and of grace,
And to trust in His plan is to find our place.

For only He remains the source
Of Contentment, and boundless force.

Wisdom Unveiled

The profound wisdom of this contemplation is that the greatest tragedy in a trial is not the external hardship itself, but the internal discontentment with Allah's decree. The wise-one understands that this discontentment stems from an egoic desire to control what is not theirs to control, leading to spiritual misery and a rejection of Divine wisdom. The verses from Quran 7:129, 2:61, and 3:154 serve as powerful historical lessons, demonstrating how a heart that refuses to accept divine provision or decree ultimately suffers greater spiritual loss than the hardship itself. The contemplation unveils that by choosing contentment (rida), the heart finds an inner peace that acts as a spiritual ark, protecting the soul from the self-imposed anguish of discontentment and transforming every trial into a path of elevation.

Wise-Reflection

Reflect on your own heart when you face a trial. Is it a source of contentment or discontentment? Consider the thought that the true suffering in a trial is not the physical pain, but the inner turmoil of resistance. What would it mean for you to cultivate a heart that, like an ark, can navigate the flood of trials without breaking? How can you actively choose to find contentment and patience, liberating your heart from the self-imposed anguish of rejecting a decree that was written by the All-Wise?

Contemplation: Rule of the Source of (Self-Misery) Tragedy of Fortune

This contemplation illuminates a crucial rule: the source of much 'misfortune' or 'tragedy' is often self-imposed misery, arising from attachment to outcomes and resistance to change, rather than the trial itself. The trial is merely an event; the suffering is often a byproduct of the ego's reaction. The wise-one realizes that true tragedy lies in the heart's refusal to accept Allah's decree, leading to internal torment. By recognizing this, the wise-one shifts focus from changing the external situation to changing the internal response, gaining immense psychic freedom.

The wise-one understands that the heart's peace is not dictated by the turns of fate, but by its own unwavering posture toward them. Misery is not a gift from hardship, but a poison we brew from discontent. The path to true freedom is to sever the soul's attachment to outcomes, to view every fortune, good or bad, as a sacred test, and to shift the focus from the fleeting external to the profound and eternal internal response.

The Trial of Fortune: Misery and Contentment

Misery does not rise
From the weight of circumstance,
Nor does suffering dwell
Solely in hardship.
It is the restless heart,
Dissatisfied with divine will,
That finds despair
In both bounty and loss.
"The wise-one knows that all living beings' fortune, Good or bad, Is a source of trial
in this life."
No calamity,
No blessing,
Comes by chance.
Each is written,
Inscribed before its arrival,
Woven into destiny
With precision.

❨So that you neither grieve Over what you have missed, Nor boast over what He has
granted you.❩ —Quran 57:23
For grief clings to longing,
And arrogance swells in pride,
Yet neither changes
The course that was decreed.
The miser guards wealth,
Fearing its loss,
But true loss
Is the emptiness within.
The arrogant stands above others,
Forgetting that the Most High

Alone sustains all.
❨*Allah alone Is truly the Self-Sufficient, Praiseworthy.*❩ *350* —*Quran 57:24*

Immortality is not granted,
Death touches every soul,
And life itself
Is but a test—
A passage of good and evil,
A trial through bounty and hardship.
❨*We test you with good and evil As a trial, Then to Us you will all be returned.*❩ *351*
—*Quran 21:35*
Blessings and burdens—
Both are veiled tests.
The wise-one does not celebrate fortune
Nor curse misfortune,
But sees both as hidden scripts
Written by the Pen of Al-'Aleem (The All-Knowing).
O soul, rejoice not over your gains
Nor weep over your losses.
In every turn of fate,
There is a summons to remembrance.
Thus, the wise-one understands—
Fortune is neither gift nor burden,
But a trial of the heart.
Will it cling to itself,
Or surrender to Him?
Will it crumble in longing,
Or stand firm in gratitude?
For whether life bestows ease or struggle,
Whether it grants or takes away,

---

350 This is in agreement with the Quran verse:

📖 ❨No calamity ʾor blessingˋ occurs on earth or in yourselves without being ʾwrittenˋ in a Record before We bring it into being. This is certainly easy for Allah. (22) ʾWe let you know thisˋ so that you neither grieve over what you have missed nor boast over what He has granted you. For Allah does not like whoever is arrogant, boastful— (23) those who are stingy and promote stinginess among people. And whoever turns away ʾshould know thatˋ Allah ʾaloneˋ is truly the Self-Sufficient, Praiseworthy. (24)❩ [Quran 57:22-24]

351 This is in agreement with the Quran verse:

📖 ❨We have not granted immortality to any human before you ʾO Prophetˋ: so if you die, will they live forever? (34) Every soul will taste death. And We test you ʾO humanityˋ with good and evil as a trial, then to Us you will ʾallˋ be returned. (35)❩ [Quran 21:34-35]

It is not fortune that determines the soul—
But how the soul meets its fate.
And in contentment,
Misery fades.
In surrender,
Purpose awakens.

So the wise-one walks forward,
Not letting his heart be swayed by what's to be,
He finds in His decree a profound liberty.
He holds to his faith in what's written and known,
And finds in the Divine his ultimate throne.

For only He is the All-Wise, the All-Knowing,
In whose perfect plan a seed is sown.
He is the Lord of both loss and of gain,
And to trust in His will is to rise above pain.
For only He remains the source
Of Serenity, and boundless force.

Wisdom Unveiled

The profound wisdom of this contemplation is that the source of misery is not external circumstance, but the heart's internal response. The wise-one understands that every turn of fortune, both good and bad, is a test from the Creator. The verses from Quran 57:22-24 serve as a clear directive, teaching us not to grieve over what we have missed nor boast over what we have been given, as all is pre-ordained. Similarly, Quran 21:35 reinforces that life itself is a trial of both good and evil. The contemplation unveils that by recognizing this truth, the wise-one gains immense psychic freedom, choosing to focus on contentment and surrender rather than being consumed by self-imposed anguish, thereby turning every event into a summons to remembrance.

Wise-Reflection

Reflect on your own life. When fortune smiles upon you, do you feel an attachment that makes you fear its loss? When hardship befalls you, does your heart fall into a state of grief or resistance? Consider the thought that true misery is not in the event itself, but in the heart's refusal to accept

Allah's decree. How can you train your heart to be so content that every turn of fate—whether a gain or a loss—becomes a simple and powerful summons to remember the One who is Al-Aleem (the All-Knowing)?

Contemplation: The Dangers of Distress

The wise-one becomes acutely aware of the dangers of distress (jaza')—excessive anxiety, panic, and agitation in the face of trials. Distress clouds judgment, weakens resolve, and creates a barrier between the soul and Divine Grace. It prevents the mind from perceiving solutions and the heart from finding solace. This contemplation encourages conscious calming of the self, cultivating inner fortitude, and turning to remembrance of Allah, thereby mitigating the internal dangers of trials and preserving spiritual clarity.

Distress is the internal storm that rages when an unprepared heart is faced with trial. It is a spiritual poison that blinds the mind and weakens the soul, causing the heart to rebel against what has been written. The wise-one understands that the antidote is not resistance, but a conscious effort to steady the self, to anchor the heart in faith, and to open the doors of the soul to the grace that lies hidden within every affliction.

Hardship Within: The Distress of an Unprepared Heart

Hardship descends upon the heart unguarded.
Not as a trial of refinement,
But as a weight
It was never prepared to bear.
Distress rises in its depths,
And from distress,
The whisper of doubt begins.
For when hardship finds no faith to anchor it,
It is delivered into the hands of the wicked—
Cast into the storm of despair,
Entangled in thoughts
That turn away from truth.

Victory stood within reach,
The tide had turned,
But the heart wavered,

The command was disputed,
Desire overran obedience.
❨*Some of you were after worldly gain, while others desired a heavenly reward.*❩ —
Quran 3:152
And so, the moment shifted.
Triumph was denied,
Not as punishment,
But as a test.
A revelation
Of what lay hidden within them.
They fled in panic,
The Messenger called to them,
But they did not turn.
Disobedience bore its fruit—
❨*distress upon distress.*❩ —*Quran 3:153*

Yet even in the aftermath,
Mercy arrived.
Serenity descended,
But not upon all.
Some hearts calmed,
While others churned,
Tormented by thoughts
Not of faith,
But of ignorance—
❨*Do we have a say in the matter?*❩ [352] —*Quran 3:154*

---

[352] This is in agreement with Quran verse narrating story of Muslims returning to the city after Uhud and they were wounded, some of them said to one another: How did this happen to us when Allah promised us victory! So this verse was revealed. That is because they killed the standard-bearer of the polytheists and seven men from them who were behind him on the standard. Victory was initially for the Muslims, but they were busy with the spoils, and some of the archers also abandoned their posts in search of the spoils, and that was the reason for the defeat:

📖 ❨Indeed, Allah fulfilled His promise to you when you ʿinitiallyʾ swept them away by His Will, then your courage weakened and you disputed about the command and disobeyed,[1] after Allah had brought victory within your reach. Some of you were after worldly gain while others desired a heavenly reward. He denied you victory over them as a test, yet He has pardoned you. And Allah is Gracious to the believers. (152) ʿRememberʾ when you were running far away ʿin panicʾ—not looking at anyone—while the Messenger was calling to you from behind! So Allah rewarded your disobedience with distress upon distress. Now, do not grieve over the victory you were denied or the injury you suffered. And Allah is All-Aware of what you do.

But all matters
Are destined by Allah.
Even if they had remained at home,
Their fate would have met them
Wherever they stood.
For through hardship,
Hearts are tested.
Through trial,
They are purified.

Distress is the doorway where despair creeps in,
Distorting the pure lens of the soul.
It is not the trial itself that defeats,
But the rebellion of the heart against what was written.
When hardship knocks,
Let my heart not scream in protest
But open its doors wide,
Saying, "Come in.
Teach me what strength hides inside me."
Thus, the wise-one understands—
Distress is not merely suffering,
It is revelation.
What is shaken,
Must be steadied.
What wavers,
Must be corrected.
And what falters,
Must be reminded—
That all tests
Are written by Him

---

(153) Then after distress, He sent down serenity in the form of drowsiness overcoming some of you, while others were disturbed by evil thoughts about Allah—the thoughts of ˹pre-Islamic˺ ignorance. They ask, "Do we have a say in the matter?" Say, ˹O Prophet,˺ "All matters are destined by Allah." They conceal in their hearts what they do not reveal to you. They say ˹to themselves˺, "If we had any say in the matter, none of us would have come to die here." Say, ˹O Prophet,˺ "Even if you were to remain in your homes, those among you who were destined to be killed would have met the same fate." Through this, Allah tests what is within you and purifies what is in your hearts. And Allah knows best what is ˹hidden˺ in the heart. (154)❭ [Quran 3:152-154]

[1]: The archers disputed whether to keep their positions after the initial victory. Eventually, most of them decided to go in pursuit of the spoils of war, disobeying the Prophet's direct orders not to leave their position no matter what happened. Defeat became inevitable.

For a wisdom
Beyond understanding.

So the wise-one walks forward,
Not letting his heart be cast away,
He finds in his Creator, his anchor, his stay.
He calms his inner self, in the face of all fear,
And finds in His grace, that He is always near.

For only He is the All-Wise, the All-Sufficient,
Whose every decree is wholly beneficent.
He is the Lord of both loss and of gain,
And to trust in His will is to rise above pain.
For only He remains the source
Of Serenity, and boundless force.

Wisdom Unveiled

The profound wisdom of this contemplation is that the greatest danger in a trial is not the external hardship, but the internal distress (jaza') it can provoke. The wise-one understands that distress, arising from a heart unprepared for affliction, clouds judgment and allows doubt to take root, creating a barrier to Divine grace. The powerful example from Quran 3:152-154 serves as a stark lesson, illustrating how disobedience and a focus on worldly gain led to "distress upon distress," while a heart that surrendered to Allah's will was granted serenity. The contemplation unveils that by actively cultivating inner fortitude and turning to Allah, the wise-one can mitigate the self-imposed dangers of trials, preserving spiritual clarity and transforming a moment of panic into an opportunity for purification and profound insight.

Wise-Reflection

Reflect on the last time you faced a trial. Did your heart respond with distress and panic, or with calm and fortitude? Consider the thought that distress is a sign of an unprepared heart, and that every trial is a revelation of what truly lies within you. What would it mean for you to cultivate a heart so anchored in faith that when hardship knocks, you can open its doors without protest, trusting that it has come to "teach you what strength hides inside"?

Contemplation: A Call to Contentment

Ultimately, embracing divine trials is a call to profound contentment (rida) with Allah's decree. This contentment is the fruit of deep faith and trust, seeing every event as part of a perfect Divine plan. It leads to inner peace that transcends circumstances, allowing the wise-one to experience joy in Allah's bounty even amidst hardship, as described in Quran 3:171: "They are joyful for receiving Allah's grace and bounty." This state of contentment transforms trials from burdens into blessings, revealing their true spiritual purpose.

The wise-one understands that the heart's true victory is not the absence of trials, but its ability to remain in a state of profound contentment with Allah's decree. This isn't a passive surrender, but an active, conscious worship, a prostration of the heart to the wisdom of the All-Knowing. By choosing rida, the soul finds a deep-seated peace that transcends all external circumstances, transforming adversity from a burden into a blessing and a direct path to the Divine.

The Prostration of the Heart: The Worship of Acceptance

Acceptance is not surrender,
Nor is it resignation.
It is the purest form of worship—
The bowing of the heart
Before understanding dawns,
The submission to His decree
Before clarity arrives.
"Accepting divine will Alleviates this burden."
Victory and loss,
Hardship and ease,
Are woven into the fabric of fate,
Alternating among people
As a test of hearts.
❮Do not falter or grieve, For you will have the upper hand, If you are true believers.❯
—Quran 3:139

Uhud bore wounds,
Badr bore triumph,
But neither stood alone.

For in hardship, faith is revealed.
In struggle, sincerity rises.
In loss, perseverance is chosen.
❴Do you think You will enter Paradise Without Allah proving Which of you truly struggled For His cause And patiently endured?❵[353] —Quran 3:142
The decree does not waver.
It arrives with purpose,
And patience walks beside it.
❴So be patient With your Lord's decree, For you are truly Under Our watchful Eyes.❵ —Quran 52:48

And so, glorification follows—
Not after the storm has passed,
But within it.
Not after hardship lifts,
But beneath its weight.
❴Glorify Him During part of the night And at the fading of the stars.❵[354] —Quran 52:49

❴How then, when they are seized by misfortune, because of the deeds which their hands have sent forth? Then they come to you, swearing by Allah: 'We meant no more than good-will and conciliation!'❵[355] —Quran 4:62

---

[353] This is in agreement with the Quran verse:

❴This[1] is an insight to humanity—a guide and a lesson to the God-fearing. (138) Do not falter or grieve, for you will have the upper hand, if you are ˹true˺ believers. (139) If you have suffered injuries ˹at Uḥud˺, they suffered similarly ˹at Badr˺. We alternate these days ˹of victory and defeat˺ among people so that Allah may reveal the ˹true˺ believers, choose martyrs from among you—and Allah does not like the wrongdoers—(140) and distinguish the ˹true˺ believers and destroy the disbelievers. (141) Do you think you will enter Paradise without Allah proving which of you ˹truly˺ struggled ˹for His cause˺ and patiently endured? (142)❵ [Quran 3:138-142]

[1]: "This" either refers to how the forces of evil are ultimately destroyed, or that the Quran is a reminder of the destruction of evildoers.

[354] This is in agreement with the Quran verse of:

❴So be patient with your Lord's decree, for you are truly under Our ˹watchful˺ Eyes. And glorify the praises of your Lord when you rise. (48) And glorify Him during part of the night and at the fading of the stars. (49)❵ [Quran 52:48-49]

[355] This echoes the profound wisdom found in sacred texts, urging the seeker to contemplate the depths of their own heart and intentions. It invites a journey towards enlightenment, steering clear of the path of those who, when faced with consequences for their inner disorder resort to deceit and falsehood, claiming their desires were rooted in virtue.

❴How then, when they are seized by misfortune, because of the deeds which they hands have sent forth? Then their come to thee, swearing by Allah: 'We meant no more than good-will and conciliation!' (63) These are they, the secrets of whose hearts Allah knows well. So turn away from them and admonish them and speak to them an effective word concerning their own selves. (64)❵ [Quran 4:62-63]

But the heart knows its secrets,
And the Creator knows them best.
For often, what we call fate,
Is but a harvest
From a seed that we ourselves have sown.

Acceptance is not resignation.
It is the purest form of worship,
The prostration of the heart
Even before understanding dawns.
In the soft soil of surrender,
Seeds of unseen blessings grow.
The soul that says "Yes" to His decree
Drinks first
From the rivers of serenity.
Thus, the wise-one understands—
Acceptance is not weakness,
But strength in worship.
Not defeat,
But elevation.
And in accepting what was written,
The burden fades,
The heart steadies,
And the servant bows,
Not in brokenness,
But in trust.

So the wise-one walks forward,
Not fighting with what the heavens have planned,
He finds in his solace, his peace on this land.
He lets his spirit prostrate to a wisdom unknown,
And finds in His rida a peace all his own.
For only He is the All-Wise, the All-Knowing,
In whose perfect plan a seed is sown.
He is the Lord of all things that are,
And to trust in His will is to go far.
For only He remains the source
Of Serenity, and boundless force.

Wisdom Unveiled

The profound wisdom of this contemplation is that the highest spiritual station in facing trials is contentment (rida) with Allah's decree. The wise-one understands that this acceptance is a profound act of worship, a prostration of the heart that transcends circumstances and finds peace even before the reasons for a trial become clear. The verses from Quran 3:139-142 and 52:48-49 serve as a powerful testament to this, teaching that victory and defeat are both part of a divine test designed to reveal true believers and that a heart filled with patience (sabr) and contentment finds solace and glorifies Allah both in the ease and in the hardship. Additionally, the verse from Quran 4:62-63 adds the crucial insight that a misfortune can sometimes be a direct result of our own deeds, and that the Creator is fully aware of the secrets of our hearts. The contemplation unveils that contentment is the ultimate liberation from suffering, transforming trials from burdens into blessings that carry the soul closer to the Divine.

Wise-Reflection

Reflect on your heart's reaction to a difficult situation. Do you find yourself in a state of resignation, or is it a conscious, active acceptance? Consider the thought that contentment is the "prostration of the heart." What does it mean for your heart to bow to a decree before you can even understand its purpose? How can you cultivate the trust required to say "yes" to Allah's will, so that you may drink from the "rivers of serenity" and find the blessings hidden within every trial?

Conclusion: Embracing Divine Trials

ECHOES OF REALIZATION: THE CROWN OF SURRENDER

O wise-one, when you have exhausted your every strength, when all your fervent striving falls away like vibrant autumn leaves—in that profound emptiness, simply lift your now empty hands to the vast, encompassing sky. For it is not the valiant warrior who, through sheer force, ultimately wins the highest, most enduring crown of spiritual sovereignty. It is, rather, the utterly surrendered one, the one whose receptive heart becomes a fertile field where Divine Will plants its eternal spring of peace and blossoming grace.

THE SEEKER'S ASCENT: ACCEPTANCE AS LIBERATION

This reflection profoundly emphasizes that trials, when consciously accepted with unwavering faith and profound humility, miraculously transform into direct pathways to immense Divine grace. By courageously reframing hardship not as punishment but as a sacred Divine tool for refinement, and by diligently practicing true contentment, the wise-one transcends self-imposed misery and aligns harmoniously with the Creator's boundless wisdom. Through unwavering trust and absolute reliance on the Creator's unfailing aid, the wise-one discovers unparalleled strength, abiding peace, and profound spiritual elevation, thereby transmuting perceived trials into genuine blessings and adversity into invaluable opportunities for transcendent growth.

Embracing Divine trials is not a mere concession to fate—it is, in its essence, the secret, intimate handshake with the Unseen Beloved. It is to declare, with every fiber of one's being: "I trust You implicitly even in the breaking of my worldly illusions. I love You eternally even in the profound loss of all that is temporary. I follow You faithfully even through the deepest, darkest night of my journey."

O seeker, know with absolute certainty that every hardship, every trial, every challenge, was not sent by the Divine to crush you, but rather to intimately call you nearer to Him. In the very heart of every trial, listen closely and hear the profound, loving whisper: "Come closer." This invitation to proximity through acceptance is the essence of psychic and spiritual resilience in " The Triumph of Self-Mastery."

◈◈◈

17TH REFLECTION: THE VEIL OF HABITS

(Avoiding Degeneration)

THE GATEWAY VERSE

In the sacred words of Allah, a direct and unequivocal reminder to all who reflect upon their ultimate priorities and the profound consequences of misplaced love:

📖 *(Say, 'O Prophet,' "If your parents and children and siblings and spouses and extended family and the wealth you have acquired and the trade you fear will decline and the homes you cherish—'if all these' are more beloved to you than Allah and His Messenger and struggling in His Way, then wait until Allah brings about His Will. Allah does not guide the rebellious people." (24)) [Quran 9:24]*

ILLUMINATION'S DAWN

There exist subtle yet potent prisons built not of cold iron bars, but of deeply ingrained habits—quietly familiar, often comfortable, and frequently unseen. These insidious prisons are erected slowly, thread by thread: through unconscious repetition, through spiritual forgetfulness, and through the gradual, almost imperceptible drifting of the soul away from the sharp, vibrant edge of yearning for the Divine into the dull, mundane routine of heedlessness.

The wise-one, through discerning insight, learns to see this profound truth: Every single habit, whether seemingly benign or overtly harmful, can either be a luminous ladder leading to ascent or a binding chain leading to spiritual stagnation. And every attachment—no matter how seemingly small or innocent—is either a firm stepping stone toward the Divine Presence or a thickening veil that obscures the pristine connection between the soul and its sacred Source. Let us now walk, with intentionality and courage, into this transformative reflection, to meticulously dismantle the intricate veils woven by our own hands, and to rise—unburdened, spiritually clear, and profoundly awake—toward the Majestic, unveiled Presence of the Creator.

THE UNFOLDING OF INSIGHTS

This section explores the subtle yet powerful influence of habits and attachments, revealing how they can become obstacles to spiritual progress and how the wise-one can transcend them to achieve clearer Divine connection.

Contemplation: The Idol of Degeneration

The wise-one comes to discern the idol of degeneration. This refers to how seemingly minor, repeated errors, heedless actions, or worldly attachments, when consistently prioritized over Divine connection, gradually accumulate to form a powerful internal 'idol' that diverts the heart's true worship. This 'idol' might not be a physical object, but a mental or emotional pattern that subtly degrades spiritual vitality and obscures the true object of devotion. Recognizing this insidious process is the first step towards dismantling it, a crucial psychic self-awareness.

The journey to self-mastery is a constant struggle against an unseen enemy: the idol of degeneration. It is built not of wood or stone, but of unchecked habits and blind tradition. The wise-one understands that a heart left unexamined will eventually kneel to routines and customs, mistaking familiar footsteps for the path of truth. This contemplation is a call to vigilance, to question every repetition, and to protect the soul's core from the silent corruption of heedlessness.

The Idol of Degeneration: A Warning to the Wise[356]

Beware, O soul,
Of what you repeat without thought,
Of what you embrace without reflection.
Falsehood does not arrive
With thunderous declaration.
It does not declare itself an enemy.
Instead, it whispers through routine,
Slips through habit,
Woven so seamlessly into life
That it becomes devotion
Without recognition.
"The wise-one knows That the accustomed habit Generated from human erroneous doings Will transform into an idol Being worshiped by people."

---

[356] "The Idol of Degeneration" is about how errors become idols over time. It warns against unexamined habits and blind tradition.

Devotion does not always
Wear the shape of prayer.
Sometimes, it is found in repetition,
In custom,
In unchallenged obedience.
What is followed without wisdom
Becomes an idol.
What is practiced without truth
Turns into worship.
And the heart bows,
Not knowing it kneels
Before illusion.

The pagans assigned falsehood to Him,
Clinging to the ways
Of their forefathers,
Never once asking
If their footsteps led to ruin.
❰We follow the ways Of our forefathers.❱ —*Quran 43:22*
And so, error moved forward,
Generation after generation,
Wrapped in the veil of tradition,
Demanding obedience—
Not because it was right,
But because it was familiar.
And when truth arrived,
It was met with rejection.
When guidance called,
They turned away.
❰We totally reject Whatever you have been sent with.❱ —*Quran 43:24*
The warner called them,
Offering them passage beyond blindness.
Yet they clung to repetition,
Denying revelation.
And so, consequences unfolded—
Not as cruelty,
But as reckoning.

For heedlessness bears its fruit.
For blind obedience leads to ruin. [357]

Abraham saw this,
Stood before his people,
And questioned the idols
They adored.
❨*Can they hear you When you call upon them? Or can they benefit Or harm you?*❩
—Quran 26:72-73
Yet they answered,
Not with reason,
But with repetition—
❨*No! But we found our forefathers Doing the same.*❩ *—Quran 26:74*
Blind devotion,
Without reflection.
Inherited error,
Given the weight of faith.
But faith is not tradition.
And truth is not repetition.
O soul,
Do you not see?
Does error cease to be error or become truth
Simply because it is inherited?
Does falsehood transform into guidance
Simply because it is repeated?

---

[357] This is in agreement with the Quran verse narrating the story of ancient civilization ascribed angels as the Creator daughters while they not accepting themselves their own daughters and proclaim this is what their ancestors were doing.

📖 ❨Still the pagans have made some of His creation out to be a part of Him. Indeed, humankind is clearly ungrateful. (15) Has He taken ˹angels as His˺ daughters from what He created, and favoured you ˹O pagans˺ with sons? (16) Whenever one of them is given the good news of what they attribute to the Most Compassionate,[1] his face grows gloomy, as he suppresses his rage. (17) up to the verses of: (Or have We given them a Book ˹for proof˺, before this ˹Quran˺, to which they are holding firm? (21) In fact, they say, "We found our forefathers following a ˹particular˺ way, and we are following in their footsteps." (22) Similarly, whenever We sent a warner to a society before you ˹O Prophet˺, its ˹spoiled˺ elite would say, "We found our forefathers following a ˹particular˺ way, and we are walking in their footsteps." (23) Each ˹warner˺ asked, "Even if what I brought you is better guidance than what you found your forefathers practicing?" They replied, "We totally reject whatever you have been sent with." (24) So We inflicted punishment upon them. See then what was the fate of the deniers! (25)❩ [Quran 43:15-25]

⟪Only those who come before Allah With a pure heart Will be saved.⟫[358] *—Quran*
26:89

O my soul, beware:
Every error repeated without reflection
Builds itself a throne in the heart.
What once was a misstep
Becomes a master.
What once was harmless
Becomes a silent tyrant.
Habit, left unchecked,
Hardens into idol.
What do I bow to without realizing?
What has claimed my loyalty,
Not through love,
But through forgetfulness?
Every unnoticed habit
Can carve a hollow throne
Where the Real should reign.
Thus, the wise-one understands—
What is unchecked,
Becomes unchallenged.
What is unchallenged,
Becomes sacred.
And the heart that never examines itself

---

[358] And the Quran verse narrating the story of Ibrahim arguing with this people the cause of their disbelieving:

⟪Relate to them ˹O Prophet˺ the story of Abraham, (69) when he questioned his father and his people, "What is that you worship ˹besides Allah˺?" (70) They replied, "We worship idols, to which we are fully devoted." (71) Abraham asked, "Can they hear you when you call upon them? (72) Or can they benefit or harm you?" (73) They replied, "No! But we found our forefathers doing the same." (74) Abraham responded, "Have you ˹really˺ considered what you have been worshipping— (75) you and your ancestors? (76) They are ˹all˺ enemies to me, except the Lord of all worlds. (77) ˹He is˺ the One Who created me, and He ˹alone˺ guides me. (78) ˹He is˺ the One Who provides me with food and drink. (79) And He ˹alone˺ heals me when I am sick. (80) And He ˹is the One Who˺ will cause me to die, and then bring me back to life. (81) And He is ˹the One˺ Who, I hope, will forgive my flaws1 on Judgment Day. (82) "My Lord! Grant me wisdom, and join me with the righteous. (83) Bless me with honourable mention among later generations.[1] (84) Make me one of those awarded the Garden of Bliss. (85) Forgive my father, for he is certainly one of the misguided. (86) And do not disgrace me on the Day all will be resurrected— (87) the Day when neither wealth nor children will be of any benefit. (88) Only those who come before Allah with a pure heart ˹will be saved˺." [2] (89)⟫ [Quran 26:69-89]

[1]: On a daily basis, Muslims invoke Allah's blessings upon Prophet Muḥammad ﷺ and his family and Prophet Abraham ﷺ and his family, in both obligatory and optional prayers.

[2]: A pure and sound heart is that of the believer, compared to that of the disbeliever and the hypocrite.

Risks bowing before something
Unworthy of its devotion.

So the wise-one walks forward,
Not letting his spirit by habit be swayed,
He shatters the idols his own hands have made.
He questions his past and examines his soul,
And finds in His worship a heart made whole.

For only He is the One, the Ever-True,
Whose guidance is always sacred and new.
He is the Lord of both thought and of deed,
And to trust in His truth is to plant a pure seed.
For only He remains the source
Of Vigilance, and boundless force.

Wisdom Unveiled

The profound wisdom of this contemplation is that the greatest idols are not physical objects, but spiritual patterns of degeneration born from unchecked habits and blind adherence to tradition. The wise-one understands that what begins as a minor error can, through repetition and heedlessness, evolve into a powerful internal 'idol' that diverts the heart's true devotion. The verses from Quran 43:15-25 and Quran 26:69-89 serve as a powerful testament to this truth, illustrating how nations were led to ruin by clinging to ancestral ways without reflection, and how the call of a prophet like Abraham was a call to reason and a pure heart. The contemplation unveils that a heart that fails to remain vigilant risks worshiping illusion and losing its way, while a heart that actively questions its routines is the one that finds its way back to the true path.

Wise-Reflection

Reflect on your own routines. Are there habits you follow, not out of conviction, but simply because they are familiar? Consider the thought that every unchallenged habit can carve a hollow throne in your heart. What has claimed your loyalty not through love, but through forgetfulness? How can you cultivate the vigilance needed to shatter the illusions of degeneration and ensure that your heart bows only to what is worthy of its devotion?

Contemplation: The Power of Habitual Influence

This contemplation focuses on the pervasive power of habitual influence. Habits, whether physical, mental, or emotional, create deep grooves in the soul. Both good and bad habits operate with a powerful inertia. The wise-one understands that unconscious repetition can cement patterns that either facilitate or hinder spiritual growth. This awareness compels deliberate choice and conscious effort to cultivate beneficial habits (like remembrance, contemplation, generosity) and dismantle detrimental ones, recognizing their profound impact on the soul's trajectory.

Repetition is the silent craftsman of the soul, invisibly shaping its character and determining its destiny. The wise-one understands that an unexamined habit is not a neutral act; it is a powerful force that either builds a bridge to the Divine or deepens the grooves of heedlessness. This contemplation serves as a call to vigilance, to recognize the profound power of repetition, and to consciously choose the habits that will mold the soul in accordance with the Creator's will.

> The Power of Habitual Influence: The Silent Craftsman of the Soul[359]

Repetition is a mighty craftsman.
It chisels away at the soul,
Molding it silently,
Invisibly,
Until it no longer recognizes its own shape.
"Such degeneration idol Receives its influence over humans Through habitual repetition
And accustomedness to erroneous doing."
What is repeated without challenge
Becomes custom.
What is practiced without thought
Becomes tradition.
And what is embraced without reflection
Becomes worship.

---

[359] "The Power of Habitual Influence" is about how the idol, once formed, becomes a ruler over its followers, molding them through repetition until they are enslaved to it.

The pagans assigned falsehood to Him,
Clinging to the ways
Of their forefathers,
Never once asking
If their footsteps led to ruin.
❲*We found our fathers following a certain course, and we are following in their*
footsteps.❳ —*Quran 43:23*
And so, error moved forward,
Generation after generation,
Wrapped in the veil of tradition,
Demanding obedience—
Not because it was right,
But because it was familiar.
And when truth arrived,
It was met with rejection.
When guidance called,
They turned away.
❲*We totally reject Whatever you have been sent with.*❳[360] —*Quran 43:24*
The warner called them,
Offering them passage beyond blindness.
Yet they clung to repetition,
Denying revelation.
And so, consequences unfolded—
Not as cruelty,
But as reckoning.
For heedlessness bears its fruit.
For blind obedience leads to ruin.

The pagans assigned falsehood to Him,
Dividing His creation,
Offering portions of their sustenance
To idols they themselves had fashioned.

---

[360] The verse from the Quran invites contemplation, urging us to reflect on the dangers of unexamined traditions and the potential for spiritual inertia that may arise from them. This serves as a caution for the enlightened, for these recurring idols draw strength from their persistence, molding the priorities of the seeker and diverting them from a higher purpose.

📖 ❲And thus has it always been that We never sent any Warner before thee to any township, but the evil leaders thereof said: 'We found our fathers following a certain course, and we are following in their footsteps.' (23)❳ [Quran 43:23]

⟨Yet the portion of their associate-gods Is not shared with Allah, While Allah's portion Is shared with their associate-gods. What unfair judgment!⟩ —Quran 6:136

Their habits became law,
Their errors became devotion.
What was once practice,
Became sacred in their sight.
And in their blindness,
They justified the unjustifiable,
Even taking their own children,
Even distorting the bounty
He had granted.

⟨Lost indeed are those Who have murdered their own children Foolishly out of ignorance And have forbidden what Allah has provided— Falsely attributing lies to Allah.⟩ [361] —Quran 6:140

For when falsehood is repeated,
It does not remain falsehood.
It solidifies,
It takes root,
It carves itself
Into the heart.

Even those gifted with revelation
Were not free from its grip.
They turned away heedlessly,
Not because they lacked truth,
But because they clung
To illusions built by repetition.

---

[361] This is in agreement with the Quran verse of:

⟨Say, ˹O Prophet,˺ "O my people! Persist in your ways, for I ˹too˺ will persist in mine. You will soon know who will fare best in the end. Indeed, the wrongdoers will never succeed." (135) The pagans set aside for Allah a share of the crops and cattle He created, saying, "This ˹portion˺ is for Allah," so they claim, "and this ˹one˺ for our associate-gods." Yet the portion of their associate-gods is not shared with Allah while Allah's portion is shared with their associate-gods. What unfair judgment! (136) Likewise, the pagans' evil associates have made it appealing to them to kill their own children—only leading to their destruction as well as confusion in their faith. Had it been Allah's Will, they would not have done such a thing. So leave them and their falsehood. (137) They say, "These cattle and crops are reserved—none may eat them except those we permit," so they claim. Some other cattle are exempted from labour and others are not slaughtered in Allah's Name—falsely attributing lies to Him. He will repay them for their lies. (138) They ˹also˺ say, "The offspring of this cattle is reserved for our males and forbidden to our females; but if it is stillborn, they may all share it." He will repay them for their falsehood. Surely He is All-Wise, All-Knowing. (139) Lost indeed are those who have murdered their own children foolishly out of ignorance and have forbidden what Allah has provided for them—falsely attributing lies to Allah. They have certainly strayed and are not ˹rightly˺ guided. (140)⟩ [Quran 6:135-140]

❮The Fire will not touch us Except for a few days.❯ [362] —Quran 3:24
Yet faith built on wishful deception
Is no faith at all.
Truth demands reckoning,
And when the Day arrives,
Every soul will stand before
The sum of its choices.

Repetition is a mighty craftsman.
It chisels away at the soul,
Molding it silently, invisibly.
The wise-one knows:
Every repeated act, whether noble or base,
Etches itself into the spirit's landscape.
Choose your engravings wisely.
Every day, I am becoming something.
Not through great choices alone,
But through small, unseen repetitions.
Am I engraving my heart with light,
Or with shadows?
Thus, the wise-one understands—
Habit unchecked
Becomes devotion misplaced.
Routine unexamined
Becomes sacred falsehood.
Beware, O soul,
Of what you repeat without thought,
Of what you embrace without reflection.
For the silent craftsman
Does not ask for permission—
It shapes,
It molds,

---

[362] This is in agreement with the Quran verse of:

❮Have you not seen those who were given a portion of the Scriptures? Yet when they are invited to the Book of Allah to settle their disputes, some of them turn away heedlessly. (23) This is because they say, "The Fire will not touch us except for a few days." They have been deceived in their faith by their wishful lying. (24) But how ʿhorribleʾ will it be when We gather them together on the Day about which there is no doubt—when every soul will be paid in full for what it has done, and none will be wronged! (25)❯ [Quran 3:23-25]

Until you bow before
What was never meant to be worshipped."

So the wise-one walks forward,
Not letting his spirit by habit be swayed,
He shatters the idols his own hands have made.
He questions his past and examines his soul,
And finds in His worship a heart made whole.

For only He is the One, the Ever-True,
Whose guidance is always sacred and new.
He is the Lord of both thought and of deed,
And to trust in His truth is to plant a pure seed.
For only He remains the source
Of Vigilance, and boundless force.

Wisdom Unveiled

The profound wisdom of this contemplation is that habitual influence, though often unseen, possesses a tyrannical power over the soul. The wise-one understands that repetition, when left unchecked, can turn falsehood into a sacred tradition and mold the heart to worship what is unworthy. The verses from Quran 43:23, 6:135-140, and 3:23-25 serve as a stark warning, illustrating how nations were led to ruin by their own self-made laws and blind adherence to inherited tradition, demonstrating that even those with access to revelation can be enslaved by their own habitual certainty. The contemplation unveils that a heart that is not vigilant in its daily repetitions is a heart that is being silently molded, and that the ultimate spiritual victory lies in consciously choosing the habits that will engrave the soul with light and lead it back to its true source.

Wise-Reflection

Reflect on your own daily life. What are the small, unseen repetitions that are shaping you? Are you engraving your heart with light or with shadows? Consider the thought that every repeated act is a powerful force, whether you are conscious of it or not. How can you cultivate the self-awareness to dismantle detrimental habits and consciously choose the routines that will lead to spiritual growth? What would it mean to live a life where every habit is a conscious choice, a noble act that chisels the soul into a purer shape?

Contemplation: Overcoming the Idol of Degeneration

To progress, the wise-one must commit to overcoming the idol of degeneration. This requires fierce self-honesty, constant vigilance (muraqabah), and disciplined inner struggle (mujahadah). It means consciously choosing to break cycles of heedlessness, redirecting the heart's attention from temporal distractions to the Eternal. This process involves sincere repentance (tawbah) and consistently choosing Allah's pleasure over momentary desires, thereby dismantling the internal 'idol' and purifying the heart's devotion.

The final stage of the wise-one's journey is not merely the recognition of the hidden idols, but the courageous act of dismantling them. This is the jihad al-nafs, the struggle within the soul. It is a battle fought with the twin swords of muraqabah (vigilance) and mujahadah (inner struggle), where every unconscious habit is brought to the light of reflection. By consciously choosing Allah's pleasure over worldly attachments, the wise-one frees their heart from the subtle chains of degeneration and directs its devotion back to its rightful Source.

The Battle Within: Dismantling the Hidden Idols

Not all chains are forged in iron.
Not all prisons are built of stone.
Some are unseen—
Woven in habit,
Formed in thought,
Rooted so deeply
That they no longer feel like captivity.
"The wise-one stays vigilant Over their habits, Dismantling the idols Before they root
themselves In the soul."
For the heart is shaped
By what it follows.
Every repetition is a carving,
Every habit a sculptor.
And what is done without challenge

Soon demands obedience
Without reason.

Temptation whispers,
Not as command,
But as invitation.
It does not pull with force,
It leads with comfort.
Yet the mindful recognize the deception—
They remember,
And suddenly,
The illusion dissolves.
❮If you are tempted by Satan, Then seek refuge with Allah. Surely He is All-
Hearing, All-Knowing.❯ —Quran 7:200
Yet the deceivers do not relent.
They press further,
They weave their influence
Into the fabric of perception.
And those who do not guard their souls
Find themselves led,
Without knowing they are following.
But truth does not fade.
It stands,
Waiting to be heard.
❮An insight from your Lord, A guide and a mercy For those who believe.❯ —Quran
7:203
Listen, O soul,
Not to the echoes of repetition,
But to the voice of revelation.
Silence the noise.
Let wisdom rise where blindness once stood.

❮When the Quran is recited, Listen to it attentively And be silent, So you may be
shown mercy.❯ —Quran 7:204
And remember—
To glorify,
To surrender,
Not only in struggle,
But in stillness.

[568]

Not only in crisis,
But in the quiet moments
Where truth is found.
For the angels do not hesitate.
They bow.
They worship.
They submit,
Not from fear,
But from certainty.

❰*Surely those nearest to your Lord Are not too proud to worship Him. They glorify*
Him, And to Him they prostrate.❱ [363] —*Quran 7:206*

Awareness is the sword
That severs the roots of hidden idols.
The wise-one stands guard at the gates of habit,
Questioning not only what is sinful,
But what is simply unconscious.
For the slow death of the soul
Begins not with rebellion—
But with sleep.
I will not walk blindfolded into my habits.
I will open my eyes,
Even when it hurts.
I will tear down every idol
Before it dares name itself necessity.
Thus, the wise-one understands—
Salvation is not only found
In battles fought outwardly.
It is won

---

[363] This is in agreement with the Quran verse:

📖 ❰Be gracious, enjoin what is right, and turn away from those who act ignorantly. (199) If you are tempted by Satan, then seek refuge with Allah. Surely He is All-Hearing, All-Knowing. (200) Indeed, when Satan whispers to those mindful ˹of Allah˺, they remember ˹their Lord˺ then they start to see ˹things˺ clearly. (201) But the devils persistently plunge their ˹human˺ associates1 deeper into wickedness, sparing no effort. (202) If you ˹O Prophet˺ do not bring them a sign ˹which they demanded˺, they ask, "Why do you not make it yourself?" Say, "I only follow what is revealed to me from my Lord. This ˹Quran˺ is an insight from your Lord—a guide and a mercy for those who believe." (203) When the Quran is recited, listen to it attentively and be silent, so you may be shown mercy. (204) Remember your Lord inwardly with humility and reverence and in a moderate tone of voice, both morning and evening. And do not be one of the heedless. (205) Surely those ˹angels˺ nearest to your Lord are not too proud to worship Him. They glorify Him. And to Him they prostrate. (206)❱ [Quran 7:199-206]

In the unseen war
Within.
For if habit is left to rule,
The soul bows before an illusion.
If repetition is followed blindly,
It becomes a tyrant.
But vigilance tears down
What was never meant to be worshipped.
And in dismantling the idols,
The soul is freed—
Not into uncertainty,
But into divine awareness.
A life shaped by reflection.
A heart sculpted by truth.
A path illuminated
By the One
Who has no equal.

So the wise-one walks forward,
Not letting his spirit by habit be swayed,
He shatters the idols his own hands have made.
He questions his past and examines his soul,
And finds in His worship a heart made whole.

For only He is the One, the Ever-True,
Whose guidance is always sacred and new.
He is the Lord of both thought and of deed,
And to trust in His truth is to plant a pure seed.
For only He remains the source
Of Vigilance, and boundless force.

Wisdom Unveiled

The profound wisdom of this contemplation is that overcoming the idol of degeneration is an act of spiritual liberation won through disciplined self-honesty and constant vigilance (muraqabah). The wise-one understands that the heart's true battle is an inner struggle (mujahadah) to dismantle the hidden prisons of unconscious habits. The verses from Quran 7:199-206 serve as a comprehensive guide for this inner warfare:

they instruct the believer to seek refuge from temptation, to remain mindful, to listen attentively to the Quran, and to remember that true devotion, as exemplified by the angels, is a state of constant submission and prostration. The contemplation unveils that by actively choosing to break cycles of heedlessness, the wise-one frees the soul from the tyranny of repetition and redirects its devotion, not into a void, but into the profound awareness of its true connection to the Creator.

Wise-Reflection

Reflect on the unseen chains that bind you. What habits or routines have you allowed to become so comfortable that they no longer feel like captivity? Consider the thought that the slow death of the soul begins not with rebellion, but with sleep. How can you practice constant vigilance (muraqabah) to expose the unconscious habits that rule your life? What would it mean to live a life where your heart is not a subject of repetition, but a master of its own devotion.

Contemplation: The Deceptive Nature of the Else

The wise-one recognizes the deceptive nature of "The Else." "The Else" refers to anything other than Allah that competes for the heart's primary love and attention – family, wealth, status, desires, even seemingly good worldly pursuits if they overshadow the Divine. As highlighted in the Gateway Verse (9:24), these can become beloved more than Allah, creating a subtle, insidious deception that veils true spiritual priorities and leads to spiritual "rebellion" if not addressed. This contemplation unmasks the subtle ways worldly attachments masquerade as benign necessities.

The journey of the wise-one is to constantly purify the heart's devotion, to distinguish between the divine presence and its deceptive imitations. "The Else" is the seductive allure of anything that distracts from the Creator, whether it be a tangible idol or an intangible attachment. This contemplation serves as a powerful warning against the glamour of illusion, reminding us that true truth is not found in spectacle or signs, but in the unwavering certainty of the heart's singular and unwavering devotion.

The Abdication of Illusions: Forsaking False Presence

Not all signs are divine.
Not all visions
Carry truth.
For deception wears beauty,
Illusion carries authority,
And what appears radiant
May be nothing more
Than shadow in disguise.
"The wise-one must abdicate all That the other brings to him, Even if that other
brings upon the wise-one The Creator's presence In the form of miracles or visions."
The people of Moses
Were deceived—
Not by force,
But by spectacle.
Not by denial,
But by imitation.
They fashioned an idol,
A form that seemed alive,
A creation dressed in power.
And they called it their god,
Forgetting that the Lord of all things
Does not dwell
In what is molded by hands.
❨This is your god And the god of Moses, But Moses forgot where it was!❩ —Quran
20:88
Yet they did not ask—
Can it speak?
Can it protect?
Can it answer?
The illusion was complete,
But only because they
Allowed themselves to believe.

Aaron warned them—
❨O my people! You are only being tested by this, For indeed your true Lord Is the
Most Compassionate.❩ —Quran 20:90
But they refused to turn away.

⟪We will not cease to worship it Until Moses returns to us.⟫ —Quran 20:91

Moses returned,

Not in quiet sorrow,

But in fury.

For truth demands destruction

When deception is embraced.

For the idol must not stand.

⟪Now look at your god To which you have been devoted: We will burn it up, Then scatter it in the sea completely.⟫ [364] —Quran 20:97

---

[364] This is in agreement with the Quran verse narrating the story of Moses's people worshiping a goat as being easily deceived by the illusion of its beaty and Moses become ferocious due to their action and destroying this fallacy god.

📖 ⟪'Allah asked,` "Why have you come with such haste ahead of your people, O Moses?"[1] (83) He replied, "They are close on my tracks. And I have hastened to You, my Lord, so You will be pleased." (84) Allah responded, "We have indeed tested your people in your absence, and the Sâmiri[2] has led them astray." (85) So Moses returned to his people, furious and sorrowful. He said, "O my people! Had your Lord not made you a good promise?[3] Has my absence been too long for you? Or have you wished for wrath from your Lord to befall you, so you broke your promise to me?"[4] (86) They argued, "We did not break our promise to you of our own free will, but we were made to carry the burden of the people's `golden` jewellery,[5] then we threw it `into the fire`, and so did the Sâmiri." (87) Then he moulded for them an idol of a calf that made a lowing sound. They said, "This is your god and the god of Moses, but Moses forgot `where it was`!" (88) Did they not see that it did not respond to them, nor could it protect or benefit them? (89) Aaron had already warned them beforehand, "O my people! You are only being tested by this, for indeed your `one true` Lord is the Most Compassionate. So follow me and obey my orders." (90) They replied, "We will not cease to worship it until Moses returns to us." (91) Moses scolded `his brother`, "O Aaron! What prevented you, when you saw them going astray, (92) from following after me? How could you disobey my orders?"1 (93) Aaron pleaded, "O son of my mother! Do not seize me by my beard or `the hair of` my head. I really feared that you would say, 'You have caused division among the Children of Israel, and did not observe my word.'" (94) Moses then asked, "What did you think you were doing, O Sâmiri?" (95) He said, "I saw what they did not see, so I took a handful `of dust` from the hoof-prints of `the horse of` the messenger-angel `Gabriel` then cast it `on the moulded calf`. This is what my lower-self tempted me into."[6] (96) Moses said, "Go away then! And for `the rest of your` life you will surely be crying, 'Do not touch `me`!'[7] Then you will certainly have a fate[8] that you cannot escape. Now look at your god to which you have been devoted: we will burn it up, then scatter it in the sea completely." (97) `Then Moses addressed his people,` "Your only god is Allah, there is no god `worthy of worship` except Him. He encompasses everything in `His` knowledge." (98) This is how We relate to you `O Prophet` some of the stories of the past. And We have certainly granted you a Reminder from Us. (99)⟫ [Quran 20:83-99]

[1]: Moses selected a delegation of seventy people from his community to go to Mount Ṭûr where it was appointed for him to receive the Tablets. On the way, he rushed for the appointment with Allah, arriving before the delegation.

[2]: The Sâmiri, or the man from Samaria, was a hypocrite who led the Children of Israel into idol-worship.

[3]: To reveal the Torah for their guidance.

[4]: To worship Allah alone until Moses returned with the Tablets.

[5]: The jewellery they borrowed from their Egyptian neighbours before they fled Egypt.

[6]: This verse could also be translated as follows: "I had an insight which they did not have, then grasped some knowledge from the messenger `Moses`, but `later` threw it away. This is what my lower-self tempted

The Else deceives by sweetness.
It whispers:
"Settle here; this is enough."
But the wise-one's heart cries:
"Not enough until I am with the Source itself."
Miracles are signposts, not destinations.
Visions are arrows, not arrival.
O my heart,
Do not build your home in the echo.
Wait for the Voice.
Thus, the wise-one understands—
It is not vision that proves truth,
But truth that exposes vision.
It is not miracle that determines belief,
But belief that withstands miracle.
And when the moment comes,
When deception knocks in the form
Of divine spectacle,
It must be forsaken.
For only He remains.
Only His truth stands.
And the wise-one walks forward,
Not toward signs,
But toward certainty."

So the wise-one walks forward,
Not fighting with what the heavens have planned,
He finds in his solace, his peace on this land.
He lets his spirit prostrate to a wisdom unknown,
And finds in His rida a peace all his own.

For only He is the One, the Ever-True,
Whose guidance is always sacred and new.

---

me to do." According to many Quran commentators, while Moses and the Children of Israel were crossing the sea to escape abuse by Pharaoh and his people, the Sâmiri saw Gabriel on a horse leading the way, and every time the horse touched the ground, it turned green. So the Sâmiri took a handful of dust from the hoof-prints of the horse, and later tossed it at the calf so it started to make a lowing sound.

[7]: Meaning, alienated in the dessert, away from the people.

[8]: lit., destined time.

> *He is the Lord of all things that are,*
> *And to trust in His will is to go far.*
> *For only He remains the source*
> *Of Serenity, and boundless force.*

Wisdom Unveiled

The profound wisdom of this contemplation is that the greatest danger to the wise-one is not outright denial, but a subtle, insidious deception wherein "The Else" masquerades as a divine presence. The wise-one understands that anything other than Allah that competes for the heart's love and attention is a false idol. The verses from Quran 20:83-99 serve as a powerful testament, illustrating how the people of Moses were deceived not by a lack of faith, but by a spectacle—a physical idol that they allowed themselves to believe was worthy of worship. The contemplation unveils that miraculous experiences or external signs are not the ultimate proof of faith; they are merely signposts. True liberation and spiritual clarity are found in the heart's unwavering certainty and singular devotion to the Creator, forsaking all illusions, no matter how beautiful or authoritative they may appear.

Wise-Reflection

Reflect on your heart. What are the "Else" in your life that may be competing for your love and attention, whispering to you, "Settle here; this is enough"? Consider the thought that miracles and visions are signposts, not destinations. Are you building your home in the echo, or are you waiting for the true Voice? How can you cultivate a certainty so profound that you are not swayed by spectacle or illusion, but remain steadfast in your singular devotion to the Creator?

Contemplation: Rule of Abdication of the Else

A fundamental rule for spiritual advancement is the abdication of "The Else" from the throne of the heart. This means consciously dethroning anything that rivals Allah in one's ultimate affection and devotion. It doesn't necessarily mean physically abandoning these things, but inwardly detaching from them, recognizing their temporary nature and their true place in relation to the Creator. This internal abdication frees the heart to fully embrace Divine love and presence, purifying one's intention and actions.

The wise-one understands that the heart cannot serve two masters. To achieve true spiritual advancement, one must consciously and fearlessly abdicate anything that competes for the soul's primary devotion. This is not about asceticism, but about an unwavering internal alignment. This contemplation is a powerful call to forsake the illusions of the world, even those that appear righteous, and to seek certainty not in the voices of others, but in the unwavering truth of the Creator's Word.

The Path Unwavering: Abandoning the Illusions of the Else

There is no wisdom
Beyond His decree.
No justice
Beyond His command.
No guidance
Beyond His truth.
Yet the world whispers,
Offering reflections of light
That do not illuminate.
Inviting the seeker
To paths that promise Him,
But lead elsewhere.
"The wise-one must abandon the else, Even if the else proclaims Seeking or seeing the Creator."
For judgment rests only with Him.
The Word has been perfected.
None may alter it.
None may rise beyond it.
⟪The Word of your Lord Has been perfected in truth and justice. None can change His Words.⟫ —Quran 6:115
Yet illusion persists.
It does not arrive as defiance,
But as invitation.
It speaks of truth,
Yet bends it.
It speaks of devotion,

Yet distorts it.

❨*If you were to obey Most of those on earth, They would lead you away From Allah's Way.*❩ —*Quran 6:116*

For assumptions
Are not wisdom.
Certainty, without revelation,
Is deception. [365]

The man who believed
Saw beyond the veil.
He warned,
He called,
But the people
Called him in return—
Not toward salvation,
But toward ruin.

❨*O my people! How is it that I invite you to salvation, While you invite me to the Fire?*❩ —*Quran 40:41*

For destruction does not always
Wear the face of wickedness.
Sometimes, it wears
The semblance of truth.
Sometimes, it whispers of purity,
Only to lead astray.

❨*You invite me To disbelieve in Allah And associate with Him What I have no knowledge of, While I invite you To the Almighty, Most Forgiving.*❩ —*Quran 40:42*

Not every light is the Sun.
Not every miracle is a map.
The wise-one learns:
Even visions, even spiritual sweetness,

---

[365] This is in agreement with the Quran verse of:

📖 ❨`Say, O Prophet,` "Should I seek a judge other than Allah while He is the One Who has revealed for you the Book `with the truth` perfectly explained?" Those who were given the Scripture know that it has been revealed `to you` from your Lord in truth. So do not be one of those who doubt. (114) The Word of your Lord has been perfected in truth and justice. None can change His Words. And He is the All-Hearing, All-Knowing. (115) `O Prophet!` If you were to obey most of those on earth, they would lead you away from Allah's Way. They follow nothing but assumptions and do nothing but lie. (116) Indeed, your Lord knows best who has strayed from His Way and who is `rightly` guided. (117)❩ [Quran 6:114-117]

Even glimpses of sacred wonder
Are not the Goal.
The Goal remains the One (Al-Ahad),
Never the experiences about Him.
I will not cling to glimpses.
I will not build shrines to moments.
I seek not the sparkle on the water,
But the Ocean itself.
Thus, the wise-one understands—
Truth is not found
In voices that speak of Him,
But in the path
That is His alone.
For distractions dressed in righteousness
Are the most perilous of all.
To abandon them
Is not abandonment,
But liberation.
To walk forward
Is not departure,
But return.
❰I entrust my affairs to Allah. Surely Allah is All-Seeing Of all His servants.❱ —
Quran 40:44
And in that trust,
The illusion shatters.
The seeker stands
Not amidst those who claim to know Him,
But before Him.
For certainty is not found
In those who call His name,
But in the One
Who needs no calling." [366]

---

[366] This is in agreement with the Quran verse of:

So the wise-one walks forward,
Not fighting with what the heavens have planned,
He finds in his solace, his peace on this land.
He lets his spirit prostrate to a wisdom unknown,
And finds in His rida a peace all his own.

For only He is the One, the Ever-True,
Whose guidance is always sacred and new.
He is the Lord of both loss and of gain,
And to trust in His will is to go far.
For only He remains the source
Of Serenity, and boundless force.

Wisdom Unveiled

The profound wisdom of this contemplation is that true spiritual advancement requires the conscious abdication of "The Else" from the heart. The wise-one understands that anything, even if seemingly righteous, that rivals Allah for ultimate affection and devotion is a spiritual distraction. The verses from Quran 6:114-117 and 40:38-44 serve as a powerful testament to this truth, illustrating how most people on earth are led astray by assumptions and lies, and how a true believer must distinguish between a path that merely speaks of the Creator and the path that is His alone. The contemplation unveils that by inwardly detaching from the allure of the world and entrusting one's affairs completely to Allah, the wise-one achieves a liberation that leads not to uncertainty, but to a profound and unwavering certainty found in the presence of the Creator alone.

📖 ⟪And the man who believed urged, "O my people! Follow me, ´and` I will lead you to the Way of Guidance. (38) O my people! This worldly life is only ´a fleeting` enjoyment, whereas the Hereafter is truly the home of settlement. (39) Whoever does an evil deed will only be paid back with its equivalent. And whoever does good, whether male or female, and is a believer, they will enter Paradise, where they will be provided for without limit. (40) O my people! How is it that I invite you to salvation, while you invite me to the Fire! (41) You invite me to disbelieve in Allah and associate with Him what I have no knowledge of, while I invite you to the Almighty, Most Forgiving. (42) There is no doubt that whatever ´idols` you invite me to ´worship` are not worthy to be invoked either in this world or the Hereafter.1 ´Undoubtedly,` our return is to Allah, and the transgressors will be the inmates of the Fire. (43) You will remember what I say to you, and I entrust my affairs to Allah. Surely Allah is All-Seeing of all ´His` servants." (44) So Allah protected him from the evil of their schemes. And Pharaoh's people were overwhelmed by an evil punishment: (45)⟫ [Quran 40:38-48]

Wise-Reflection

Reflect on your own heart. What are the subtle "Else" in your life that, even with good intentions, may be leading you away from Allah's way? Consider the thought that true devotion requires you to seek not the "sparkle on the water, but the Ocean itself." Are you building your faith on fleeting glimpses and spiritual experiences, or on the unwavering truth of the Creator's Word? How can you cultivate the self-honesty and courage to consciously abandon all that is not Him, and in doing so, find true liberation?

Contemplation: The Warning Against False Equanimity

The wise-one receives the warning against false equanimity. This is the deceptive state where one believes they are balanced in their love for Allah and worldly things, when in reality, the heart leans heavily towards the latter. True equanimity means that one's love for Allah and His Messenger surpasses all else, leading to a willingness to sacrifice worldly comforts for His sake. The Gateway Verse directly addresses this, revealing that prioritizing "The Else" leads to not being guided by Allah, thereby exposing the peril of such spiritual complacency.

False equanimity is the betrayal of grace, a state where the soul makes peace with distractions and compromises its divine connection. The wise-one understands that to be in equanimity with "The Else" is a silent, spiritual degradation. This contemplation serves as a powerful reminder that true companionship is found only in the path of the Creator and that all other alliances, friendships, and influences that lead away from Him are a source of ultimate regret.

Equanimity with the Else: The Betrayal of Grace

Not all alliances uplift.
Not all friendships guide.
For there are companions
Who do not walk beside you,
But lead you astray.
"To be in equanimity with the else Will eventually be vile From the stance in the grace
of the Creator."
Watch for the Day—

When heavens burst,
When angels descend,
When all illusions
Are laid bare.
On that Day, regret will consume
Those who once stood
In false companionship.
❨*Oh! I wish I had followed The Way along with the Messenger!*❩ —*Quran 25:27*
They will mourn their choices,
Lament the hands they held,
Curse the paths
They blindly walked.
❨*Woe to me! I wish I had never taken So-and-so as a close friend.*❩ —*Quran 25:28*
For what seemed harmless
Was destruction in disguise.
What appeared as comfort
Was a silent betrayal.
Satan leads,
But never reveals his intent.
He whispers,
But never shows the chains
That follow his words.
❨*And Satan has always Betrayed humanity.*❩ [367] —*Quran 25:29*

The reckoning comes—
Not only for those
Who led others astray,
But for those
Who chose to follow.
❨*O assembly of jinn! You misled humans In great numbers.*❩ —*Quran 6:128*
And their human associates

---

[367] This is in agreement with the Quran verse of:

📖 ❨'Watch for' the Day the heavens will burst with clouds, and the angels will be sent down in successive ranks. (25) True authority on that Day will belong 'only' to the Most Compassionate.[1] And it will be a hard day for the disbelievers. (26) And 'beware of' the Day the wrongdoer will bite his nails 'in regret' and say, "Oh! I wish I had followed the Way along with the Messenger! (27) Woe to me! I wish I had never taken so-and-so as a close friend. (28) It was he who truly made me stray from the Reminder after it had reached me." And Satan has always betrayed humanity. (29)❩ [Quran 25:25-29]

[1]: Some people (like kings and rulers) have some sort of authority in this world. But on Judgment Day Allah will be the sole authority.

Will stand,
Confessing against themselves,
Testifying to their own downfall.
⟨We confess against ourselves! For we have been deluded By our worldly life.⟩ —
Quran 6:130
Thus, the wise-one understands—
Companionship is not always a gift.
Influence is not always
A blessing.
For the misguided
Become the misguiders.
For the heedless
Become the destroyers.
And on the Day
When truth is unshaken,
Only those who walked
Without compromise
Will stand
Without shame. [368]

To accept distraction as companionship
Is to betray the deep hunger of the soul.
The wise-one does not make peace
With anything less than Divine Union.
Let my soul burn with longing.
Let it ache for what is Real.

---

[368] This is in agreement with the Quran verse of:

📖 ⟨'Consider' the Day He will gather them 'all' together and say, "O assembly of jinn! You misled humans in great numbers." And their human associates will say, "Our Lord! We benefited from each other's company,[1] but now we have reached the term which You appointed for us." 'Then' He will say, "The Fire is your home, yours to stay in forever, except whoever Allah wills to spare."[2] Surely your Lord is All-Wise, All-Knowing. (128) This is how We make the wrongdoers 'destructive' allies of one another because of their misdeeds. (129) 'Allah will ask,' "O assembly of jinn and humans! Did messengers not come from among you, proclaiming My revelations and warning you of the coming of this Day of yours?" They will say, "We confess against ourselves!" For they have been deluded by 'their' worldly life. And they will testify against themselves that they were disbelievers. (130) This 'sending of the messengers' is because your Lord would never destroy a society for their wrongdoing while its people are unaware 'of the truth'. (131) They will each be assigned ranks according to their deeds. And your Lord is not unaware of what they do. (132)⟩ [Quran 6:128-132]

[1]: For example, the jinn helped humans with magic, while the jinn had a feeling of importance when they had a human following.

[2]: i.e., disobedient Muslims. They will be punished according to the severity of their sins, but eventually no Muslim will stay in Hell forever.

Better an aching heart
Than a satisfied soul content with illusions.
To seek His grace
Is to abandon
All that leads away from Him.
To seek His mercy
Is to walk beyond
The paths of deception.
For only He
Determines rank.
Only He
Knows the weight of deeds.
Only He
Remains unchanged,
Unquestioned,
Unrivaled.
And the wise-one
Stands alone before Him,
Unburdened by companionship
That did not belong."

So the wise-one walks forward,
Not fighting with what the heavens have planned,
He finds in his solace, his peace on this land.
He lets his spirit prostrate to a wisdom unknown,
And finds in His rida a peace all his own.

For only He is the One, the Ever-True,
Whose guidance is always sacred and new.
He is the Lord of both loss and of gain,
And to trust in His will is to go far.
For only He remains the source
Of Serenity, and boundless force.

Wisdom Unveiled

The profound wisdom of this contemplation is a powerful warning against false equanimity, a deceptive state of spiritual complacency. The wise-one understands that believing one can be in balance between love for the

Creator and love for "The Else" is a spiritual betrayal that leads to ultimate regret. The verses from Quran 25:27-29 and Quran 6:128-132 serve as a stark warning, illustrating the Day of Judgment when those who prioritized worldly companionship and were deluded by this life will bite their hands in regret and confess against themselves. The contemplation unveils that true spiritual health is not found in making peace with distractions, but in cultivating an unyielding longing for the Creator. The wise-one seeks not companionship that leads away from Him, but a singular, uncompromising path that leads directly to His presence.

Wise-Reflection

Reflect on your own relationships and influences. Are there "companions" in your life—whether people, habits, or things—that you believe you are in equanimity with, but which subtly pull you away from your divine purpose? Consider the thought that true equanimity is not a balance between two loves, but the prioritization of one love above all others. What would it mean for your soul to burn with such a longing for the Real that it would find no satisfaction in any illusion?

Contemplation: The Else as a Deceiver

Ultimately, "The Else" is perceived as a deceiver. Its allure promises fulfillment, security, or happiness, but ultimately delivers only fleeting satisfaction, dependence, and spiritual emptiness if pursued as an end in itself. The wise-one learns to see through these deceptions, recognizing that true, lasting contentment and spiritual well-being are found only in the Beloved, Al-Habib. This clarity of vision—a profound psychic insight—enables the wise-one to sever the deceptive chains and redirect their focus to the Source of all true joy.

The wise-one understands that the heart's journey is a battle against the subtle persuasions of "The Else." This is the final stage of discerning the veil of habits: to see that all that competes with the Creator for the heart's devotion is not merely a distraction, but a deceiver. This contemplation serves as a powerful reminder that true happiness is not found in the promises of the world, but in the unwavering and singular connection to the Divine.

The Deception of the Else: The Betrayal of Divine Majesty

Not all who call upon wisdom
Lead toward truth.
Not all who promise certainty
Deliver salvation.
For the deceiver does not command—
He persuades.
He does not drag the soul away—
He whispers,
Until the seeker turns
Of their own accord.
"The else is a deceiver From the true stance In the grace of the Creator And persuades
the wise-one To leave the majestic stance Of the Creator."
The misguided will stand,
Pleading with the ones
They once followed,
Begging for protection,
Only to be abandoned.
⟨Had Allah guided us, We would have guided you.⟩ —Quran 14:21
Yet they were never leaders.
They were only the lost
Who convinced others
To be lost with them.
Satan, too, will stand,
Casting aside those
Who once obeyed him.
⟨I had no authority over you. I only called you, And you responded to me.⟩ —Quran
14:22
For deception does not seize—
It invites.
It does not demand—
It persuades.
And when judgment comes,
The deceiver
Denounces his own deception,
Turning upon those
Who followed him blindly.

❨Do not blame me; Blame yourselves.❩ —Quran 14:22
For every false path walked,
Every illusion embraced,
Was chosen. [369]

And when the moment arrives,
When reckoning dawns,
Those who turned away from Him
Will see—
They did not abandon guidance.
They abandoned themselves.
❨Do not be like those Who forgot Allah, So He made them forget themselves.❩ —
Quran 59:19
Thus, the wise-one understands—
To stray from Him
Is not merely to lose faith,
But to lose
The very self.
To step away
Is not only to forsake grace,
But to forsake all
That was real.
For the Fire is not merely
Punishment.
It is the place
Where those who deceived,
Those who followed illusion,
Will reside

---

[369] This is in agreement with the Quran verse of:

📖 ❨They will all appear before Allah, and the lowly ˹followers˺ will appeal to the arrogant ˹leaders˺, "We were your ˹dedicated˺ followers, so will you ˹then˺ protect us from Allah's torment in any way?" They will reply, "Had Allah guided us, we would have guided you. ˹Now˺ it is all the same for us whether we suffer patiently or impatiently, there is no escape for us." (21) And Satan will say ˹to his followers˺ after the judgment has been passed, "Indeed, Allah has made you a true promise. I too made you a promise, but I failed you. I did not have any authority over you. I only called you, and you responded to me. So do not blame me; blame yourselves. I cannot save you, nor can you save me. Indeed, I denounce your previous association of me with Allah ˹in loyalty˺. Surely the wrongdoers will suffer a painful punishment." (22)❩ [Quran 14:21-22]

With no escape.
❲The residents of Paradise Will be successful.❳ [370] —*Quran 59:20*

The Else does not storm the gates—
It seduces with soft promises.
The wise-one guards the threshold,
Choosing again and again
To stand naked before the Real,
Rather than clothed in the glittering garments of deception.
O my soul,
Beware the false light,
The easy peace,
The comfortable lies.
Stand trembling if you must—
But stand where the Face shines.
To remain in His grace
Is to see beyond persuasion.
To remain steadfast
Is to hear beyond whispers.
To walk unwavering
Is to silence the voices
That lead away.
For only He
Offers majesty.
Only He
Offers truth.
Only He
Remains unshaken.
And the wise-one stands,
Not with the lost,

---

[370] This is in agreement with the Quran verse of:

📖 ❲'They are' like Satan when he lures someone to disbelieve. Then after they have done so, he will say 'on Judgment Day', "I have absolutely nothing to do with you. I truly fear Allah—the Lord of all worlds." (16) So they will both end up in the Fire, staying there forever. That is the reward of the wrongdoers. (17) O believers! Be mindful of Allah and let every soul look to what 'deeds' it has sent forth for tomorrow.[1] And fear Allah, 'for' certainly Allah is All-Aware of what you do. (18) And do not be like those who forgot Allah, so He made them forget themselves. It is they who are 'truly' rebellious. (19) The residents of the Fire cannot be equal to the residents of Paradise. 'Only' the residents of Paradise will be successful. (20)❳ [Quran 59:16-20]

[1]: i.e., the Hereafter.

Not with the deceived,
But with the One
Who never forsakes.

So the wise-one walks forward,
Not letting his spirit by habit be swayed,
He shatters the idols his own hands have made.
He questions his past and examines his soul,
And finds in His worship a heart made whole.

For only He is the One, the Ever-True,
Whose guidance is always sacred and new.
He is the Lord of both thought and of deed,
And to trust in His truth is to plant a pure seed.
For only He remains the source
Of Vigilance, and boundless force.

Wisdom Unveiled

The profound wisdom of this final contemplation is that "The Else" is not a benign distraction, but a powerful deceiver whose allure is rooted in soft promises that lead to spiritual emptiness. The wise-one understands that to be persuaded by these illusions is to abandon one's truest self and one's connection to the Creator. The verses from Quran 14:21-22 and 59:16-20 serve as a stark and powerful testament to this, illustrating how leaders and Satan himself will abandon their followers on the Day of Judgment, telling them to blame no one but themselves for their choices. The contemplation unveils that the ultimate consequence of following "The Else" is a profound self-betrayal, a forgetting of Allah that leads to a forgetting of the self. True success and lasting joy, therefore, are found only in the unwavering, singular, and unpersuaded devotion to the Beloved, Al-Habib.

Wise-Reflection

Reflect on the soft promises that "The Else" offers you. What easy peace or comfortable lies are you tempted to accept in exchange for the difficult path of truth? Consider the thought that to abandon Allah is to abandon yourself. Are you guarding the threshold of your heart, or are you allowing the whispers of deception to lead you astray? What would it mean to stand, trembling if you must, but always where the Face of the Real shines?

Conclusion: The Veil of Habits

ECHOES OF REALIZATION: BREAKING THE SILENT CHAINS

The chains that most tightly bind the aspiring soul make no audible clatter when they are forged or when they subtly fall. They are, instead, the quiet, almost imperceptible habits, the unseen compromises, the seemingly innocent distractions that gradually pull the heart away from its Divine Center.

The wise-one knows with profound certainty: true spiritual freedom is not gained by mere physical might or external struggle, but by ruthless inner honesty—by courageously tearing away every subtle veil until the luminous Face of the Beloved (Al-Habib) shines without any obstruction, clear and resplendent within the heart.

THE SEEKER'S ASCENT: BREAKING THE VEILS OF HABITS

"The Veil of Habits" profoundly reminds the wise-one of the subtle yet undeniable impact of repeated actions and ingrained attachments on their sacred spiritual journey. By vigilantly recognizing the insidious transformation of heedless errors into internal idols and by resolutely rejecting distracting influences—even those that appear righteous on the surface—the wise-one intentionally aligns themselves more closely with boundless Divine Grace. This intentional, continuous effort to dismantle these self-woven veils leads to a purer, more direct, and unhindered connection with the Creator, thereby paving a luminous pathway for profound spiritual elevation and enduring psychic freedom.

The Veil of Habits is not a punitive prison imposed by an external fate—it is, in truth, a complex tapestry woven, thread by thread, by the soul's own forgetfulness and misdirection. But the wise-one realizes that every single thread can be meticulously unwoven. Every internal idol can be courageously shattered. Every false light that once captivated attention can be consciously left behind. O wise-one, be fierce in your inner vigilance, and be tender in your yearning for the Divine. And when all else, all that is temporary and distracting, finally falls away, you will discover yourself not wandering aimlessly, but already, profoundly Home in the Presence of your Creator.

18ᵀᴴ REFLECTION: ALIGNMENT WITH DIVINE WILL

(The Creator's Sovereignty)

THE GATEWAY VERSES

In the sacred words of Allah, a profound declaration of His absolute sovereignty over all events and a warning against the spiritual maladies that prevent true alignment:

📖 ❲*No calamity ˊor blessingˋ occurs on earth or in yourselves without being ˊwrittenˋ in a Record before We bring it into being. This is certainly easy for Allah. (22) ˊWe let you know thisˋ so that you neither grieve over what you have missed nor boast over what He has granted you. For Allah does not like whoever is arrogant, boastful— (23) those who are stingy and promote stinginess among people. And whoever turns away ˊshould know thatˋ Allah ˊaloneˋ is truly the Self-Sufficient, Praiseworthy. (24)*❳ [Quran 57:22-24]*

ILLUMINATION'S DAWN

There comes a transformative stage in the wise-one's soul ascent when they no longer anxiously ask: "Why this? Why now?" Instead, they instinctively kneel inwardly before the unfolding of every Divine decree, knowing with absolute certainty that it flows from a Benevolent Will vaster than all skies, infinitely more encompassing than all comprehension.

Here, in this profound state of spiritual surrender, every single event— whether it brings sorrow or joy, perceived gain or apparent loss—is no longer seen as a random blow of fate. It is recognized, instead, as a precise, divinely inscribed calligraphy written by the Omnipotent Hand of Al-Hakim (The All-Wise). The wise-one learns a fundamental, liberating truth: true freedom is not found in futile attempts to master or control destiny, but in surrendering wholly and completely to the Master of destiny itself. Let us now walk, with hearts unburdened, into this sacred unveiling, where the soul gracefully lays down its anxieties and concerns, and finds its ultimate rest—not in what it meticulously plans, but in what is already perfectly ordained.

THE UNFOLDING OF INSIGHTS

This section explores the multi-faceted dimensions of aligning with Divine Will, illuminating how this surrender brings profound freedom, purpose, and spiritual harmony.

Contemplation: The Rule of the Creator's Unyielding Will

The wise-one apprehends the fundamental rule of the Creator's Unyielding Will (Irādat Allāh). Allah's Will is absolute and encompasses all things, from the grandest cosmic movements to the most minute personal details. This contemplation leads to the realization that nothing happens outside of His decree, as affirmed in Quran 57:22. This understanding fosters profound humility and trust, knowing that resistance to His Will is futile and ultimately self-defeating. The wise-one aligns their inner state with this truth, finding peace in the face of all occurrences.

The journey to true spiritual freedom begins with the liberation from the illusion of control. The wise-one understands that every single event— every blessing, every trial, every rising and falling—is a precise, divinely inscribed calligraphy written by the Omnipotent Hand of Al-Hakim. This contemplation is a call to surrender, to find peace not in mastering destiny, but in accepting and aligning with the Master of destiny itself.

The Unyielding Will of the Creator: A Revelation of Divine Sovereignty

---

The heavens tremble.
The earth shifts.
And yet, beneath all movement,
Above all stillness,
There is only His command.
Nothing rises outside His decree.
Nothing falls beyond His sight.
His will governs all,
His hand shapes existence itself.
"All actions and inactions Are governed by the Creator's will."
No calamity strikes by chance.
No blessing arrives without purpose.
Each moment unfolds
As it was written,
Etched into destiny
Before time itself began.
❲Not even a leaf falls Without His knowledge, Nor a grain in the darkness of the earth, But is written in a perfect Record.❳ —Quran 6:59

Thus, the wise-one sees—
There is no loss
But what He has measured,
No gift
But what He has granted.
Grief holds no power
Against the decree of the Almighty.
Arrogance crumbles
Before the magnitude of His justice.
❨We let you know this So that you neither grieve Over what you have missed, Nor
boast over what He has granted you.❩ [371] *—Quran 57:22-23*

For He is the Witness
Over all things—
The silent thoughts,
The unspoken prayers,
The deeds done
In the solitude of the soul.
Not a single motion
Escapes His gaze.
Not an atom's weight
Is hidden from His knowing.
❨There is no activity You may be engaged in, Nor any deed you may be doing, Except

---

[371] This is in agreement with the Quran verse of:

📖 ❨No calamity ´or blessing` occurs on earth or in yourselves without being ´written` in a Record before We bring it into being. This is certainly easy for Allah.[1] (22) ´We let you know this` so that you neither grieve over what you have missed nor boast over what He has granted you. For Allah does not like whoever is arrogant, boastful— (23)❩ [Quran 57:22-23]

[1]: [Quran 57:22] Narrated Ibn 'Abbas: Once I was behind the Prophet ﷺ and he said: "O boy, I will teach you a few words:

    a)   Be loyal and obedient to Allâh [worship Him (Alone)], remember Him always, obey His Orders. He will save you from every evil and will take care of you in all the spheres of life.

    b)   Be loyal and obedient to Allâh, you will find Him near (in front of you) i.e. He will respond to your requests.

    c)   If you ask, ask Allâh.

    d)   If you seek help, seek help from Allâh.

    e)   Know that if all the people get together in order to benefit you with something, they will not be able to benefit you in anything except what Allâh has decreed for you. And if they all get together in order to harm you with something, they will not be able to harm you in anything except what Allâh has decreed for you.

The pens have stopped writings [Divine (Allâh's) Preordainments]. And (the ink over) the papers (Book of Decrees) has dried." [This Hadith is quoted in Sahih At-Tirmidhi].

that We are a Witness Over you while doing it.❭ *372* —*Quran 10:61*

And yet, mankind seeks control.

They demand outcomes,

Attempt to hasten what was never theirs

To command.

But His decree stands,

Unchanging, unquestioned,

Beyond the grasp of time

Or ambition.

❰*It is only Allah Who decides its time. He declares the truth, And He is the Best of Judges.*❭ *373* —*Quran 6:57*

---

[372] This is in agreement with the Quran verse of:

📖 ❰There is no activity you may be engaged in ˹O Prophet˺ or portion of the Quran you may be reciting, nor any deed you ˹all˺ may be doing except that We are a Witness over you while doing it. Not ˹even˺ an atom's weight is hidden from your Lord on earth or in heaven; nor anything smaller or larger than that, but is ˹written˺ in a perfect Record. (61)❭ [Quran 10:61]

[373] This is in agreement with the Quran verse of:

📖 ❰Say, ˹O Prophet,˺ "Indeed, I stand on a clear proof from my Lord—yet you have denied it. That ˹torment˺ you seek to hasten is not within my power. It is only Allah Who decides ˹its time˺. He declares the truth. And He is the Best of Judges." (57) Say ˹also˺, "If what you seek to hasten were within my power, the matter between us would have already been settled. But Allah knows the wrongdoers best." (58) With Him are the keys of the unseen—no one knows them except Him.[1] And He knows what is in the land and sea. Not even a leaf falls without His knowledge, nor a grain in the darkness of the earth or anything—green or dry— but is ˹written˺ in a perfect Record.[2] (59) He is the One Who calls back your souls by night and knows what you do by day, then revives you daily to complete your appointed term. To Him is your ˹ultimate˺ return, then He will inform you of what you used to do. (60) He reigns supreme over all of His creation, and sends recording-angels, watching over you.[3] When death comes to any of you, Our angels take their soul, never neglecting this duty. (61) Then they are ˹all˺ returned to Allah—their True Master. Judgment is His ˹alone˺. And He is the Swiftest Reckoner. (62)❭ [Quran 6:57-62]

[1]: The five keys of the unseen are mentioned in Quran verse of: 📖 ❰Indeed, Allah ˹alone˺ has the knowledge of the Hour. He sends down the rain, and knows what is in the wombs. No soul knows what it will earn for tomorrow, and no soul knows in what land it will die. Surely Allah is All-Knowing, All-Aware. (34)❭ [Quran 31:34]

[2]: The Record refers to the Preserved Tablet (Al-Lawḥ Al-Maḥfûẓ) in which Allah has written the destiny of His entire creation.

[3] [Quran 6:61]:

a) Whoever intended to do a good deed or a bad deed.

Narrated Ibn 'Abbâs: The Prophet ﷺ narrating about his Lord said, "Allâh ordered (the appointed angels over you) that the good and the bad deeds be written, and He then showed (the way) how (to write). If somebody intends to do a good deed and he does not do it, then Allâh will write for him a full good deed (in his account with Him); and if he intends to do a good deed and actually did it, then Allâh will write for him (in his account) with Him (its reward equal) from ten to seven hundred times, to many more times: and if somebody intended to do a bad deed and he does not do it, then Allâh will write a full good deed (in his

O my soul,
Every thread that moves, every breath that halts,
Every rising and every falling—
All spin upon the loom of His Command.
There is no stray leaf, no forgotten tear,
No lost moment beyond His sight.
Freedom begins not in striving against the tide,
But in knowing Who commands the tide itself.
Nothing moves without His decree.
Why then should my heart flutter with fear,
When even my trembling is held in His mercy?
Thus, the wise-one understands—
To surrender is not weakness,
But revelation.
To yield is not loss,
But elevation.
To let go
Is not destruction,
But the truest form
Of awakening.
For the will of the Creator
Is neither burden
Nor restriction—
It is the foundation
Upon which existence stands.
And in recognizing it,
The soul is freed—
Not into uncertainty,
But into divine awareness.
Not into loss,
But into trust.

---

account) with Him, and if he intended to do it (a bad deed) and actually did it, then Allâh will write one bad deed (in his account)." (Sahih Al-Bukhâri, Vol.8, Hadîth No.498).

b) Narrated Abu Hurairah ⚭: The Prophet ﷺ said, "Angels come (to you) in succession by night and day, and all of them get together at the time of Fajr and 'Asr prayers. Then those who have stayed with you overnight, ascend unto Allâh Who asks them (and He knows the answer better than they): "How have you left My slaves?" They reply, "We left them while they were praying and we came to them while they were praying." The Prophet ﷺ added: "If anyone of you says Amîn (during the prayer at the end of the recitation of Sûrat Al-Fâtihah), and the angels in heaven say the same, and the two sayings coincide, all his past sins will be forgiven." (Sahih Al-Bukhâri, Vol.4, Hadîth No. 446)

And the wise-one walks forward,
Not weighted by illusion,
But upheld by certainty.
For only He remains.
Only He reigns supreme.
Only He is the Master of all things.

So the wise-one walks forward,
Not fighting with what the heavens have planned,
He finds in his solace, his peace on this land.
He lets his spirit prostrate to a wisdom unknown,
And finds in His rida a peace all his own.

For only He is the One, the Ever-True,
Whose guidance is always sacred and new.
He is the Lord of both loss and of gain,
And to trust in His will is to go far.
For only He remains the source
Of Serenity, and boundless force.

Wisdom Unveiled

The profound wisdom of this contemplation is the realization of the Creator's Unyielding Will (Irādat Allāh) and the subsequent liberation found in surrendering to it. The wise-one understands that everything in existence, from the cosmic to the personal, is perfectly ordained by the All-Knowing. The verses from Quran 6:57-62 and 10:61 serve as a comprehensive testament to this, teaching that every event is pre-written in a perfect record and that Allah is a constant witness to every deed. This wisdom unveils that true freedom is not found in the futile attempt to control outcomes, but in the profound peace that comes from trusting in His benevolent sovereignty. By abandoning the illusions of autonomy, the wise-one frees their heart from the burdens of grief and arrogance, and finds their ultimate rest in the grace of the Master of destiny.

Wise-Reflection

Reflect on a recent challenge or a moment of joy. Did you find yourself resisting or trying to control the outcome? Consider the thought that freedom begins not in striving against the tide, but in knowing Who commands it. How can you cultivate the inner state of profound humility and trust that allows you to surrender to His decree, finding peace in the face of all occurrences? What would it mean to truly believe that even your "trembling is held in His mercy"?

Contemplation: Clarity in Divine Grace

Alignment with Divine Will brings profound clarity in Divine Grace (Fadl). When the heart stops resisting what is, it opens to perceive the subtle manifestations of Allah's grace in every situation, even in hardship. The wise-one discerns the hidden wisdom (hikmah) and mercy within trials, recognizing them as opportunities for growth and purification. This clarity allows them to receive Allah's blessings with gratitude and accept His decrees with contentment, elevating their psychic perception beyond superficial appearances.

The wise-one understands that true spiritual sight is not about seeing the world as it appears, but as it truly is: a manifestation of the Creator's will. This contemplation serves as a powerful reminder that all authority, all victory, and all order ultimately belong to Allah alone. By transcending the illusion of human control and aligning with His divine grace, the wise-one gains a profound clarity that allows them to perceive the hidden wisdom and mercy in every unfolding event, liberating their soul from the confines of worldly perception.

The Presence Beyond Ordinance: The Vision in Divine Grace

The world moves,
The heavens stand,
Yet within all existence
There flows an unseen order—
Not written by men,
But decreed by the Creator.
To abide in His grace
Is not merely to walk in obedience,
But to see beyond the veil
Of earthly law,
To perceive the truth
Behind the shadows of human authority.
"The wise-one knows That if he shall become In the stance of the Creator's grace,

Then shall he see the presence of sight Of humanity, Not the ordinance of humanity."
For His decree governs all things.
The mountains do not rise
By human command.
The winds do not carry life
By earthly will.
Rain does not fall
At the whisper of kings.
❨*As for the earth, We spread it out And placed upon it firm mountains, And caused*
everything to grow There in perfect balance.❩[374] *—Quran 15:19*

Yet mankind clings to illusion,
Mistaking their own power
For dominion.
They believe their victories are their own,
Their triumphs a result of strength.
But the wise-one sees—
It was never by their hand
That the battle was won.
❨*It was not you Who killed them, But it was Allah Who did so.*❩[375] *—Quran*

---

[374] This is in agreement with the Quran verse of:

📖 ❨As for the earth, We spread it out and placed upon it firm mountains, and caused everything to grow there in perfect balance. (19) And We made in it means of sustenance for you and others, who you do not provide for. (20) There is not any means ´of sustenance` whose reserves We do not hold, only bringing it forth in precise measure. (21) We send fertilizing winds, and bring down rain from the sky for you to drink. It is not you who hold its reserves. (22) Surely it is We Who give life and cause death.[1] And We are the ´Eternal` Successor.[2] (23) We certainly know those who have gone before you and those who will come after ´you`. (24) Surely your Lord ´alone` will gather them together ´for judgment`. He is truly All-Wise, All-Knowing. (25)❩ [Quran 15:19-25]

[1]: [Quran 15:23] Narrated Abu Hurairah: Allâh's Messenger ﷺ said: "When a person is dead, his deeds cease (are stopped) except three:

    a)   **Deeds of continuous Sadaqah (act of charity),** e.g. an orphan home or a well for giving water to drink.

    b)   **(Written) knowledge** with which mankind gets benefit.

    c)   **A righteous, pious son (or daughter)** who begs Allâh to forgive his (or her) parents."

[Sahih Muslim, The Book of Wasâyâ (Wills and Testaments)].

[2]: Allah will remain eternally after all pass away.

[375] This is in agreement with the Quran verse narrating the story of Bader Battel where the believers gain victory not by actions alone but the Creator's will aiding them:

📖 ❨It was not you ´believers` who killed them, but it was Allah Who did so. Nor was it you ´O Prophet` who threw ´a handful of sand at the disbelievers`,[1] but it was Allah Who did so, rendering the believers a great favour. Surely Allah is All-Hearing, All-Knowing. (17) As such, Allah frustrates the evil plans of the disbelievers. (18)❩ [Quran 8:17]

[1]: Before the battle, the Prophet ﷺ threw a handful of sand at the disbelievers and prayed for their defeat.

8:17

For victory does not belong
To the sword,
Nor to the wielder,
But to His command alone.

And when all seems bound
By law,
When rulers dictate
The fate of men,
When judgment appears
To rest in human hands,
It is His will that stands above all.
❬Joseph could not have taken his brother Under the King's law, But Allah had so
willed.❭ 376 —Quran 12:76
Thus, the wise-one understands—
To abide in His grace
Is not merely to be blessed,
But to see.
To see the world
Not through human rule,
But through divine presence.
To see victory
Not in action,
But in decree.
To see order
Not in law,
But in wisdom.

When grace illumines the soul,
The wise-one sees through the dust of appearances—
Past actions, past actors—
Into the luminous Hand behind every unfolding.

---

376 This is in agreement with the Quran verse narrating the story of Josef taking his brother by his side even in the presence of his other brothers:

❬Joseph began searching their bags before that of his brother 'Benjamin', then brought it out of Benjamin's bag. This is how We inspired Joseph to plan. He could not have taken his brother under the King's law, but Allah had so willed. We elevate in rank whoever We will. But above those ranking in knowledge is the One All-Knowing. (76)❭ [Quran 12:76]

He no longer judges by surface movements,
But beholds the hidden choreography of Mercy.
I no longer see men moving,
I see the Wind that carries them.
For knowledge among men
Is limited,
But above all ranks
Is the One Who Knows all.
Thus, the wise-one walks forward,
Not governed by the sight of man,
But illuminated
By the presence of the Creator.
And in that vision,
All illusion falls away.
For only He reigns.
Only He elevates.
Only He commands all things.

So the wise-one walks forward,
Not fighting with what the heavens have planned,
He finds in his solace, his peace on this land.
He lets his spirit prostrate to a wisdom unknown,
And finds in His rida a peace all his own.

For only He is the One, the Ever-True,
Whose guidance is always sacred and new.
He is the Lord of both loss and of gain,
And to trust in His will is to go far.

For only He remains the source
Of Serenity, and boundless force.

Wisdom Unveiled

The profound wisdom of this contemplation is the realization that alignment with Divine Will grants a profound clarity of sight, allowing the wise-one to perceive the unseen hand of the Creator in all things. This clarity transcends superficial human appearances and perceptions, and is a manifestation of divine grace (Fadl). The verses from Quran 15:19-25, 8:17, and 12:76 serve as a powerful testament to this, illustrating how the

Creator's will governs everything from the growth of a plant to the outcome of a battle, and even to the laws of kings. This wisdom unveils that true sight is not in judging by surface movements, but in beholding the hidden choreography of divine mercy and wisdom (hikmah), freeing the heart to find peace and gratitude in every circumstance.

Wise-Reflection

Reflect on a time when you achieved a great victory or faced a significant challenge. Did you attribute the outcome to your own efforts, or were you able to see the unseen hand of the Creator? Consider the thought, "I no longer see men moving, I see the Wind that carries them." How can you cultivate this profound clarity of sight, allowing you to see beyond the "ordinance of humanity" and into the presence of divine grace in your own life?

Contemplation: The Imprisonment of Ordinary Life

The wise-one recognizes the imprisonment of ordinary life when lived outside of alignment with Divine Will. This "imprisonment" is characterized by constant striving for control, anxiety over outcomes, attachment to fleeting worldly gains, and grief over losses. The Gateway Verse warns against grieving over what is missed or boasting over what is granted, precisely because these actions indicate a lack of alignment and lead to an internal state of spiritual confinement, veiled from the true freedom of surrender.

The wise-one understands that the absence of divine grace does not lead to a neutral state, but rather a fall into the frail and limiting laws of humanity. This contemplation serves as a powerful warning against mistaking human judgment for ultimate truth and man-made order for divine wisdom. The wise-one learns that true freedom is not found in autonomy, but in the liberation that comes from surrendering to the Creator's unwavering guidance, thereby escaping the spiritual confinement of ordinary life.

The Absence of Divine Grace: The Fall into Human Ordinance

The presence of the Creator's grace
Is the anchor,
The light that guides,

The force that elevates the soul
Beyond the laws of men,
Beyond the blindness
Of earthly judgment.
Yet when that grace is absent,
When His wisdom is ignored,
The world does not remain
Neutral.
It shifts,
It bends,
It conforms to human ordinance—
An imperfect, transient law
Crafted by hands
That cannot see beyond themselves.
"The wise-one knows That if one is in the absence Of the stance of the Creator's grace,
Then the sight of humans And humanity ordinances Should take place."
For He has revealed the path,
Made clear the truth,
Offered guidance
So mankind may walk unburdened.
❲It is Allah's Will To make things clear to you, Guide you to the noble ways Of
those before you, And turn to you in mercy.❳ —Quran 4:26
Yet those who stray,
Who follow desire over wisdom,
Who prefer man-made order
Over divine command,
They do not merely drift.
They fall.
They descend into a system
That does not see clearly,
That does not judge rightly,
That does not elevate,

But rather binds the soul
To its lowest impulses. [377]

David, a man of wisdom,
A ruler blessed,
Was tested—
Not by force,
But by the limitations
Of human sight.
He judged quickly,
Seeing only the surface,
Forgetting that truth
Is not merely what is seen,
But what is revealed
Through divine reflection.

❨Judge between us with truth— Do not go beyond it— And guide us to the right
way.❩ —Quran 38:22
Yet even a prophet,
Without divine reflection,
May misjudge.

❨Then David realized That We had tested him, So he asked for his Lord's
forgiveness, Fell down in prostration, And turned to Him in repentance.❩ —Quran
38:24
For judgment without His guidance
Is an empty verdict.

---

[377] This is in agreement with the Quran verse narrating the inclination of human for degradation of morale with the absence of the Creator's grace and guidance:

📖 ❨It is Allah's Will to make things clear to you, guide you to the ´noble` ways of those before you, and turn to you in mercy. For Allah is All-Knowing, All-Wise. (26) And it is Allah's Will to turn to you in grace, but those who follow their desires wish to see you deviate entirely ´from Allah's Way`. (27) And it is Allah's Will to lighten your burdens, for humankind was created weak. (28) O believers! Do not devour one another's wealth illegally, but rather trade by mutual consent. And do not kill ´each other or` yourselves. Surely Allah is ever Merciful to you. (29) And whoever does this sinfully and unjustly, We will burn them in the Fire. That is easy for Allah. (30) If you avoid the major sins forbidden to you, We will absolve you of your ´lesser¨ misdeeds and admit you into a place of honour. (31)❩ [Quran 4:31]

Law without His wisdom
Is hollow command. [378]

Without the lens of grace,
The world becomes a bewildering maze.
Faces become enemies,
Actions seem random,
The heart tightens into fear and blame.
But grace opens the true seeing:
Every act is a mirror reflecting the hidden decree.
Am I lost in the puppets' dance,
Or have I lifted my gaze to the hidden Hand?
Thus, the wise-one understands—
To abandon His grace
Is to fall
Into the blind workings
Of human ordinance.
To walk without Him
Is not merely to be lost,
But to be bound
To the frailty of mortal judgment.
To stray from His wisdom
Is to submit
Not to justice,
But to illusion.
And when all collapses,

---

[378] This aligns with the sacred words of the Quran, recounting the tale of David, who, in his wisdom, faltered when faced with two disputing souls. He beheld only the surface of their conflict, neglecting to seek the divine guidance that illuminates the path of justice.

📖 ⟨Has the story of the two plaintiffs, who scaled the ˹wall of David's˺ sanctuary, reached you ˹O Prophet˺? (21) When they came into David's presence, he was startled by them. They said, "Have no fear. ˹We are merely˺ two in a dispute: one of us has wronged the other. So judge between us with truth—do not go beyond ˹it˺—and guide us to the right way. (22) This is my brother.[1] He has ninety-nine sheep while I have ˹only˺ one. ˹Still˺ he asked me to give it up to him, overwhelming me with ˹his˺ argument." (23) David ˹eventually˺ ruled, "He has definitely wronged you in demanding ˹to add˺ your sheep to his. And certainly many partners wrong each other, except those who believe and do good—but how few are they!" Then David realized that We had tested him so he asked for his Lord's forgiveness, fell down in prostration, and turned ˹to Him in repentance˺. (24) So We forgave that for him. And he will indeed have ˹a status of˺ closeness to Us and an honourable destination! (25) ˹We instructed him:˺ "O David! We have surely made you an authority in the land, so judge between people with truth. And do not follow ˹your˺ desires or they will lead you astray from Allah's Way. Surely those who go astray from Allah's Way will suffer a severe punishment for neglecting the Day of Reckoning." (26)⟩ [Quran 38:21-26]

[1]: Brother in faith or business partner.

When regret dawns,
When false paths crumble,
Only those
Who turn back to Him
Will stand redeemed.
Thus, the wise-one walks forward,
Not guided by human laws,
But illuminated by divine presence.
For only He elevates.
Only He judges rightly.
Only He remains unshaken.

So the wise-one walks forward,
Not fighting with what the heavens have planned,
He finds in his solace, his peace on this land.
He lets his spirit prostrate to a wisdom unknown,
And finds in His rida a peace all his own.

For only He is the One, the Ever-True,
Whose guidance is always sacred and new.
He is the Lord of both loss and of gain,
And to trust in His will is to go far.
For only He remains the source
Of Serenity, and boundless force.

Wisdom Unveiled

The profound wisdom of this contemplation is the realization that to live outside of alignment with Divine Will is to be spiritually imprisoned, falling into the limited and often misguided laws of human ordinance. The wise-one understands that the absence of the Creator's grace leads to a state where the soul is bound by the frailty of mortal judgment and the bewildering cycles of cause and consequence. The verses from Quran 4:26-31 and the story of David in Quran 38:21-26 serve as a powerful testament to this, illustrating how the Creator offers guidance to lighten our burdens and how even a man of great wisdom can misjudge without divine reflection. This wisdom unveils that true freedom is not found in human autonomy, but in surrendering to the Creator's light, which alone can illuminate the hidden decree behind every act and liberate the soul from the prison of ordinary life.

Wise-Reflection

Reflect on a time when you felt trapped by a situation or a system. Did you attribute your feelings to the "ordinance of humanity," or did you seek to understand the divine reflection within it? Consider the thought, "Am I lost in the puppets' dance, or have I lifted my gaze to the hidden Hand?" How can you cultivate a state of alignment with the Creator's grace so that your judgments and actions are illuminated by His wisdom, and you are freed from the imprisonment of human perception?

Contemplation: The Rule of Headlessness Stems from Needs

The wise-one receives a profound insight into the spiritual sickness of heedlessness (ghaflah), recognizing that its root lies not in a passive state of forgetting, but in the active misdirection of human needs and desires. This contemplation reveals a two-fold danger: first, that a life lived without divine guidance becomes a self-perpetuating cycle of suffering where fleeting cravings multiply and consume the soul; and second, that this heedlessness inevitably devolves into the sin of neglect (takasul), where passive hopes and wishful thinking replace the disciplined action required for true spiritual alignment. This realization calls the wise-one to a higher state of awareness, one that confronts the illusion of worldly fulfillment and seeks contentment not in chasing desires, but in surrendering them to the Source of all true sustenance.

Part 1: The Consequences of Headlessness

This contemplation dissects the root of spiritual heedlessness, linking it to the misdirection of human needs and desires. Human desires and misguided approaches to fulfilling them are often the root of suffering. This rule emphasizes the necessity of addressing needs through divine alignment rather than indulgence in fleeting cravings.

The wise-one understands that the heart's straying is not a sudden, dramatic fall, but a slow descent into heedlessness (ghaflah) fueled by unchecked desires. This contemplation serves as a powerful warning against the illusion that satisfying every worldly need will lead to contentment. Instead, it unveils a profound truth: a life lived in disharmony with Divine Will, preoccupied with fleeting cravings, becomes a self-perpetuating cycle of suffering and spiritual confinement.

The Consequences of Headlessness: The Misguided Pursuit of Need

---

Need, when pursued without wisdom,
Becomes a cycle of suffering.
Desires chased without reflection
Do not fulfill—
They multiply,
They consume,
They leave the soul thirsting
For more."

"The wise-one knows That treating need by headlessness Will cause suffering of more needs.

For hardship arrives,
Not merely as burden,
But as a call—
A moment for humility,
For reflection,
For return to the Creator.
Yet rather than seeking grace,
They hardened their hearts,
Blind to the warning
Within their suffering.

⟨Why did they not humble themselves When We made them suffer? Instead, their hearts were hardened, And Satan made their misdeeds Appealing to them.⟩ —

Quran 6:43

And when the warning was ignored,
When gratitude faded,
When desires became their compass,
Their undoing arrived
Without warning.

⟨We showered them With everything they desired. But just as they became prideful Of what they were given, We seized them by surprise, Then they instantly fell into despair!
—Quran 6:44

For indulgence does not satisfy.
It blinds.

It lures the soul into illusion,
Leading further from truth. [379]

Even those entrusted
With guidance
Fell to the same temptation—
The desire for wealth,
The hoarding of power,
Turning away from the very cause
They were meant to uphold.
❨Indeed, many rabbis and monks Consume people's wealth wrongfully And hinder
others From the Way of Allah.❩ —Quran 9:34
They did not merely fail in duty.
They poisoned the path
For others,
Leading astray
Rather than leading forward.
But the treasure they clung to
Was never theirs to keep.
It was never meant to elevate them.
For what is stored in greed
Will one day burn
As testimony against them.
❨The Day will come When their treasure Will be heated up in the Fire of Hell, And
their foreheads, sides, And backs branded with it. This is the treasure You hoarded
for yourselves. Now taste what you hoarded!❩ —Quran 9:35

When needs drive the soul
Without the compass of surrender,
They multiply like wildfires.

---

[379] This aligns with the verse from the sacred text that recounts how humanity, instead of turning to the mercy and guidance of the Creator in times of hardship, becomes ensnared by the allure of worldly existence, leading to their own downfall:

📖 ❨Indeed, We have sent messengers before you ˹O Prophet˺ to other people who We put through suffering and adversity ˹for their denial˺, so perhaps they would be humbled. (42) Why did they not humble themselves when We made them suffer? Instead, their hearts were hardened, and Satan made their misdeeds appealing to them. (43) When they became oblivious to warnings, We showered them with everything they desired. But just as they became prideful of what they were given, We seized them by surprise, then they instantly fell into despair! (44) So the wrongdoers were utterly uprooted. And all praise is for Allah—Lord of all worlds. (45)❩ [Quran 6:42-45]

To chase one longing without Divine guidance
Is to birth a thousand more thirsts,
Each leading further into the desert. [380]
The wise heart bows its thirst
Before the Source of all waters.
Thus, the wise-one understands—
Need must not be met
Through indulgence alone.
Desire must not be pursued
Without reflection.
For what is gained
Without wisdom
Is never truly gained.
What is taken
Without restraint
Is never truly owned.
And the one
Who abandons guidance
For fleeting fulfillment
Will find themselves trapped—
In endless wanting,
In hollow abundance,
In wealth that does not nourish,
But devours.
Thus, the wise-one walks forward,
Not enslaved by craving,
But guided by grace.
For only He sustains.
Only He elevates need into blessing.
Only He turns hardship into light.

---

[380] This aligns with the sacred verse that recounts how certain devout souls, instead of embodying the virtues they preach, fall prey to the allure of worldly desires, leading them into a state of forgetfulness heedlessness:

📖 ⟨O believers! Indeed, many rabbis and monks consume people's wealth wrongfully and hinder ˹others˺ from the Way of Allah. Give good news of a painful torment to those who hoard gold and silver and do not spend it in Allah's cause. (34) The Day ˹will come˺ when their treasure will be heated up in the Fire of Hell, and their foreheads, sides, and backs branded with it. ˹It will be said to them,˺ "This is the treasure you hoarded for yourselves. Now taste what you hoarded!" (35)⟩ [Quran 9:34-35]

So the wise-one walks forward,
Not fighting with what the heavens have planned,
He finds in his solace, his peace on this land.
He lets his spirit prostrate to a wisdom unknown,
And finds in His rida a peace all his own.

For only He is the One, the Ever-True,
Whose guidance is always sacred and new.
He is the Lord of both loss and of gain,
And to trust in His will is to go far.
For only He remains the source
Of Serenity, and boundless force.

Wisdom Unveiled

The profound wisdom of this contemplation is the realization that spiritual heedlessness (ghaflah) is not a passive state but an active, self-inflicted spiritual suffering rooted in a misguided pursuit of human needs. The wise-one understands that to chase desires without the compass of divine guidance is to enter a cycle of endless wanting and dissatisfaction. The verses from Quran 6:42-45 and 9:34-35 serve as a powerful testament to this, illustrating how those who harden their hearts and become prideful of their worldly gains are seized by surprise and how those who hoard wealth will find it as a source of torment on the Day of Judgment. This wisdom unveils that true fulfillment is not found in indulgence but in turning to the Creator with humility, recognizing that only He can transform need into blessing and hardship into light.

Wise-Reflection

Reflect on a time when you sought to fulfill a need or desire. Did it bring you lasting contentment, or did it only lead to a greater wanting? Consider the thought, "To chase one longing without Divine guidance Is to birth a thousand more thirsts, Each leading further into the desert." How can you cultivate the wisdom to meet your needs not through heedless indulgence, but by turning to the Creator with humility and trust?

Part 2: The Sin of Neglect

Following from heedlessness is the sin of neglect (takasul). This refers to the omission of duties and responsibilities towards Allah and His creation due to preoccupation with "The Else" (as discussed in the previous reflection). The Gateway Verse (57:24) implicitly warns against being "stingy" or "turning away," which are acts of neglect rooted in heedlessness. The wise-one recognizes that neglecting one's spiritual and ethical obligations, even subtle ones, creates further spiritual veils and hinders genuine alignment.

The wise-one understands that heedlessness, when left unchecked, inevitably descends into the sin of neglect. This contemplation serves as a powerful warning against the illusion that passive hope or empty wishes can replace genuine effort and disciplined action. It reveals a profound truth: without conscious striving and steadfastness, the seeds of heedlessness grow into a spiritual rot that consumes the soul, leaving it vulnerable to arrogance and ruin.

The Sin of Neglect: The Pitfall of Passive Hope

Heedlessness, left unchecked,
Becomes its own disease.
Neglect, when ignored,
Spreads like wildfire,
Consuming the spirit,
Leaving only ashes
Of wasted potential.

"In the same manner, The wise-one knows That treating headlessness By wishing Will cause more headlessness."

For wishful hope,
Without action,
Is an empty vessel.
Desiring goodness,
Without striving for it,
Is nothing but illusion.

⟨One never tires Of praying for good. And if touched with evil, They become desperate And hopeless.⟩ —Quran 41:49

Yet when mercy arrives,
Rather than gratitude,
They claim entitlement.
Rather than reflection,
They grow in arrogance.

❬This is what I deserve. I do not think the Hour Will ever come. And if in fact I am returned to my Lord, The finest reward With Him will definitely be mine.❭ —Quran 41:50

They ask,
But do not act.
They believe,
But only when convenient.
They deny,
Yet expect reward.
Thus, when reality crashes,
When illusion crumbles,
The consequences
Cannot be undone. [381]

The man who worshipped
His wealth,
His gardens,
His perceived superiority,
Thought himself invincible.

❬I do not think This will ever perish, Nor do I think The Hour will ever come.❭ —
Quran 18:35-36

Yet the wise-one
Does not measure security
By abundance.
He does not mistake success
For divine favor.
He does not believe
That blessing
Is guaranteed forever.

❬If only you had said, Upon entering your property, 'This is what Allah has willed!

---

[381] This aligns with the sacred verse that speaks of a profound truth about humanity's yearning for reward without the trials and tribulations that lead to the Creator's favor::

❬One never tires of praying for good. And if touched with evil, they become desperate and hopeless. (49) And if We let them taste a mercy from Us after being touched with adversity, they will certainly say, "This is what I deserve. I do not think the Hour will ˹ever˺ come. And if in fact I am returned to my Lord, the finest reward with Him will definitely be mine." But We will surely inform the disbelievers of what they used to do. And We will certainly make them taste a harsh torment. (50) When We show favour to someone, they turn away, acting arrogantly. And when touched with evil, they make endless prayers ˹for good˺. (51) Ask ˹them, O Prophet˺, "Imagine if this ˹Quran˺ is ˹truly˺ from Allah and you deny it: who can be more astray than those who have gone too far in opposition ˹to the truth˺?" (52)❭ [Quran 41:49-52]

There is no power Except with Allah!" —*Quran 18:39*
Thus, the wise-one understands—
Neglect of the self
Cannot be cured
By passive hope.
The absence of discipline
Cannot be replaced
By mere wishing.
For what is built
On arrogance
Will collapse
In ruin.
What is sustained
Without wisdom
Will sink
Into the earth,
Never to be recovered.

And so all his produce Was totally ruined, So he started to wring his hands For all he had spent on it, While it had collapsed On its trellises. He cried, 'Alas! I wish I had never associated Anyone with my Lord in worship!' —*Quran 18:42*
But regret alone
Does not redeem.
Wishing alone
Does not restore. [382]

---

[382] This aligns with the sacred verses that recount the tale of a man who turned away from the truth of the judgment day, claiming to have earned a reward in the hereafter, for he believed his bountiful garden was a gift bestowed upon him by the Creator:

Give them ˹O Prophet˺ an example of two men. To ˹the disbelieving˺ one We gave two gardens of grapevines, which We surrounded with palm trees and placed ˹various˺ crops in between. (32) Each garden yielded ˹all˺ its produce, never falling short. And We caused a river to flow between them. (33) And he had other resources[1] ˹as well˺. So he boasted to a ˹poor˺ companion of his, while conversing with him, "I am greater than you in wealth and superior in manpower." (34) And he entered his property, while wronging his soul, saying, "I do not think this will ever perish, (35) nor do I think the Hour will ˹ever˺ come. And if in fact I am returned to my Lord, I will definitely get a far better outcome than ˹all˺ this." (36) His ˹believing˺ companion replied, while conversing with him, "Do you disbelieve in the One Who created you from dust,1 then ˹developed you˺ from a sperm-drop, then formed you into a man? (37) But as for me: He is Allah, my Lord, and I will never associate anyone with my Lord ˹in worship˺. (38) If only you had said, upon entering your property, 'This is what Allah has willed! There is no power except with Allah!' Even though you see me inferior to you in wealth and offspring, (39) perhaps my Lord will grant me ˹something˺ better than your

Wishing without striving,
Longing without surrender,
Is a seed that bears only weeds.
The wise-one surrenders his wishes
Into the Hands of the All-Knowing (Al-'Aleem),
Trusting the unseen currents that carry them home.
My wishes rise like mist—
But His decree rains as certainty.
Thus, the wise-one acts,
He strives,
He walks forward
Without illusion,
Without arrogance.
For only He sustains.
Only He elevates effort into grace.
Only He turns striving into salvation.
So the wise-one walks forward,
Not fighting with what the heavens have planned,
He finds in his solace, his peace on this land.
He lets his spirit prostrate to a wisdom unknown,
And finds in His rida a peace all his own.

For only He is the One, the Ever-True,
Whose guidance is always sacred and new.
He is the Lord of both loss and of gain,
And to trust in His will is to go far.
For only He remains the source
Of Serenity, and boundless force.

Wisdom Unveiled

The profound wisdom of this contemplation is the realization that heedlessness inevitably gives way to the sin of neglect (takasul), a spiritual

---

garden, and send down upon your garden a thunderbolt from the sky, turning it into a barren waste. (40) Or its water may sink ˹into the earth˺, and then you will never be able to seek it out." (41) And so all his produce was ˹totally˺ ruined, so he started to wring his hands for all he had spent on it, while it had collapsed on its trellises. He cried, "Alas! I wish I had never associated anyone with my Lord ˹in worship˺!" (42) And he had no manpower to help him against Allah, nor could he ˹even˺ help himself. (43) At this time, support comes ˹only˺ from Allah—the True ˹Lord˺. He is best in reward and best in outcome. (44)﴾ [Quran 18:32-44]

[1]: The word "thamar" can mean fruits, gold and silver, etc.

malady that cannot be cured by passive wishing or empty hope. The wise-one understands that genuine spiritual progress requires disciplined action and a conscious rejection of arrogance. The verses from Quran 41:49-52 and the story in Quran 18:32-44 serve as a powerful testament to this truth, illustrating how those who are deluded by worldly success and claim entitlement will find their arrogant hopes shattered, and how a man who boasted of his wealth lost everything, his regret arriving too late to save him. This wisdom unveils that true hope lies not in mere wishes, but in active striving and a humble acknowledgment that all power and sustenance belong to the Creator alone.

Wise-Reflection

Reflect on your own spiritual and ethical duties. Are there areas of your life where you are relying on passive hope or wishful thinking instead of disciplined action? Consider the thought, "My wishes rise like mist— But His decree rains as certainty." Are you building your life on the shifting sands of arrogance and self-entitlement, or on the solid ground of humility and trust in the Creator's will? How can you cultivate the steadfastness to not only wish for good, but to strive for it with a heart surrendered to the All-Knowing?

Conclusion: The Rule of Headlessness Stems from Needs

Thus, the wise-one understands that the path to spiritual clarity is paved with a conscious rejection of heedlessness and a steadfast commitment to action. The heart, when driven by needs without the compass of divine surrender, becomes a desert of endless thirsts. The illusion of passive hope, which promises reward without effort, only leads to further neglect and, ultimately, to ruin. The wise-one, therefore, does not merely wish for salvation; they actively strive for it, knowing that true fulfillment is not a reward to be claimed, but a state of being to be cultivated through humility, discipline, and unwavering trust in the Creator. By abandoning the false comforts of heedlessness and embracing the grace that transforms striving into a form of worship, the wise-one frees their soul from the prison of need and finds ultimate peace in the truth of divine sovereignty.

Contemplation: Divine Alignment as Fulfillment

Ultimately, Divine Alignment is recognized as the epitome of true fulfillment. When the wise-one's personal will dissolves into the Divine Will, they experience profound peace, purpose, and contentment. This is not the annihilation of the self but its perfection, where desires become aligned with what Allah loves, and actions become a pure manifestation of His purpose. This state brings an unshakable inner serenity that transcends all worldly circumstances, leading to the ultimate psychic and spiritual harmony.

The wise-one understands that the search for fulfillment in the material world is a journey into a desert of mirages. This contemplation serves as a powerful revelation that true contentment arises not from feasting on desires, but from the spiritual nourishment of surrender. By aligning with divine will, the wise-one finds an unshakable inner serenity, transcending the restless hunger of the soul and finding ultimate peace in the unyielding promise of the Creator's provision.

The Reality of Fulfillment: The Divine Call to True Contentment

Where does fulfillment lie?
Does it dwell in fleeting pleasures,
In the hollow pursuit of wealth,
In the fragile illusion of power?

No.

The wise-one sees—
True nourishment
Is not in feeding desires,
But in surrendering them to the Creator.

"True nourishment comes Not from feasting on desires, But from drinking The sweet water of surrender. When the soul's needs Are yoked to divine wisdom, They no longer gnaw at the heart— They rest like calm birds Upon the branches of trust."

For the restless heart,
The insatiable hunger,
The constant striving—
These are not signs of success.
They are warnings.
Signs of separation from His grace.

[615]

Thus, patience is commanded.
Detachment is required.

❲*So be patient With what they say. And glorify the praises of your Lord Before sunrise and before sunset, And glorify Him In the hours of the night And at both ends of the day, So that you may be pleased With the reward.*❳ —*Quran 20:130*

For what is the world
If not a test?
What is wealth
If not a fleeting illusion?
What is indulgence
If not a temptation to stray?

❲*Do not let your eyes crave What We have allowed Some of the disbelievers to enjoy; The fleeting splendor of this worldly life, Which We test them with. But your Lord's provision In the Hereafter Is far better And more lasting.*❳ [383] —*Quran 20:131*

Among the honored ones,
Among those who understood
The true nature of fulfillment,
Were the faithful of Madinah—
Who welcomed their brethren
Not with reluctance,
But with open hands,
With unwavering generosity,
With complete trust in divine provision.

❲*They give the emigrants Preference over themselves, Even though they may be in need. And whoever is saved From the selfishness of their own souls, It is they who are truly successful.*❳ —*Quran 59:9*

Thus, the veil is lifted.
The illusion crumbles.
The soul sees.
Fulfillment is not found

---

[383] This aligns with the sacred words of the Quran:

📖 ❲So be patient ˹O Prophet˺ with what they say. And glorify the praises of your Lord before sunrise and before sunset, and glorify Him in the hours of the night and at both ends of the day,[1] so that you may be pleased ˹with the reward˺. (130) Do not let your eyes crave what We have allowed some of the disbelievers to enjoy; the ˹fleeting˺ splendour of this worldly life, which We test them with. But your Lord's provision ˹in the Hereafter˺ is far better and more lasting. (131) Bid your people to pray, and be diligent in ˹observing˺ it. We do not ask you to provide. It is We Who provide for you. And the ultimate outcome is ˹only˺ for ˹the people of˺ righteousness. (132)❳ [Quran 20:130-132]

[1]: This verse refers to the times of the five daily prayers.

In seeking more.
It is found in seeking Him.
Not in craving,
But in gratitude.
Not in indulgence,
But in surrender.
Not in grasping at desires,
But in resting
Upon the unwavering branches
Of divine certainty. [384]

Moses saw this,
When his people were seized in trembling,
When the earth shook beneath them,
When trial revealed
The emptiness of self-reliance.
❬*This is only a test from You— By which You allow Whoever You will to stray And guide whoever You will.*❭ *—Quran 7:155*
Even Moses,
In the presence of fear and failure,
Understood that salvation
Was not found in strength,
Not preserved in command,
But awaited in return—
A return to the Source,
A plea for refuge in divine mercy,
A surrender to the wisdom that weaves through every trembling.
❬*You are our Guardian. So forgive us and have mercy on us. You are the best*

---

[384] In this sacred accord, there exists a revered tale that speaks of the valiant virtues of those who followed the noble prophet Mohammed 🕊, as they embarked on a perilous journey from Makkah, seeking solace and sanctuary in the warm embrace of Madinah. In that moment, they came together with the already dwellers of the city, whose hearts brimmed with compassion and whose hands extended in kindness, ready to lend their support to those in search of refuge::

📖 ❬'Some of the gains will be' for poor emigrants who were driven out of their homes and wealth, seeking Allah's bounty and pleasure, and standing up for Allah and His Messenger. They are the ones true in faith. (8) As for those who had settled in the city and 'embraced' the faith before 'the arrival of' the emigrants, they love whoever immigrates to them, never having a desire in their hearts for whatever 'of the gains' is given to the emigrants. They give 'the emigrants' preference over themselves even though they may be in need. And whoever is saved from the selfishness of their own souls, it is they who are 'truly' successful. (9) And those who come after them will pray, "Our Lord! Forgive us and our fellow believers who preceded us in faith, and do not allow bitterness into our hearts towards those who believe. Our Lord! Indeed, You are Ever Gracious, Most Merciful." (10)❭ [Quran 59:8-10]

forgiver.❭ —*Quran 7:155*
In the shadow of that trembling mountain,
Moses saw beyond the moment—
He glimpsed the coming of mercy,
The answer carried in the footsteps
Of a Messenger yet to be born.
Not one who would command armies,
But one who would lift burdens.
Not one who would increase riches,
But one who would free souls.
He would restore the severed bond
Between soul and truth,
Guide the lost into the embrace
Of divine fulfillment,
And reveal that the weight of religion
Was never meant to crush,
But to cleanse.

❬*He commands them to do good And forbids them from evil, Permits for them what is lawful And forbids to them what is impure, And relieves them from their burdens And the shackles that bound them.*❭ —*Quran 7:157*

Thus, the Prophet of Mercy ﷺ *came—*
Not to deliver wealth,
But to break the chains of the unseen,
To unbind the hearts from worldly anchors,
And to return humanity
To the ease of surrender.
He did not come to magnify self-worth,
But to magnify God.
He did not come to ornament thrones,
But to uplift the prostrating soul.
And in his light,
The trembling of the earth
Gave way to the stillness of hearts.

❬*Say, [O Prophet], 'O humanity! I am Allah's Messenger to you all. To Him* *belongs the kingdom Of the heavens and the earth. There is no god worthy of worship but Him. He gives life and causes death.'*³⁸⁵ *—Quran 7:158*

Thus, the wise-one understands—
Wealth is not fulfillment.
Position is not fulfillment.
Power is not fulfillment.
Only He nourishes.
Only He sustains.
Only He is the True Reward.
*At this time, Support comes only from Allah— The True Lord. He is best in reward And best in outcome.*³⁸⁶ *—Quran 18:44*

When I submit my hunger to the Creator,
Even emptiness becomes fullness.
Thus, the wise-one walks forward—
No longer bound by hunger,
No longer deceived by illusion,

---

³⁸⁵ This aligns with the sacred verse that recounts the tale of Moses and the seventy men, who were seized by trembling due to their misdeeds. In this moment, the Divine revealed the essence of the prophet of mercy (Mohammed ﷺ), who leads humanity toward deliverance by embracing the will of the Creator and dwelling in His grace.

📖 ❨Moses chose seventy men from among his people for Our appointment and, when they were seized by an earthquake,[1] he cried, "My Lord! Had You willed, You could have destroyed them long ago, and me as well. Will You destroy us for what the foolish among us have done? This is only a test from You—by which You allow whoever you will to stray and guide whoever You will. You are our Guardian. So forgive us and have mercy on us. You are the best forgiver. (155) Ordain for us what is good in this life and the next. Indeed, we have turned to You ˹in repentance˺." Allah replied, "I will inflict My torment on whoever I will. But My mercy encompasses everything. I will ordain mercy for those who shun evil, pay alms-tax, and believe in Our revelations. (156) "˹They are˺ the ones who follow the Messenger, the unlettered Prophet, whose description they find in their Torah and the Gospel.[2] He commands them to do good and forbids them from evil, permits for them what is lawful and forbids to them what is impure, and relieves them from their burdens and the shackles that bound them. ˹Only˺ those who believe in him, honour and support him, and follow the light sent down to him will be successful." (157) Say, ˹O Prophet,˺ "O humanity! I am Allah's Messenger to you all. To Him ˹alone˺ belongs the kingdom of the heavens and the earth. There is no god ˹worthy of worship˺ except Him. He gives life and causes death." So believe in Allah and His Messenger, the unlettered Prophet, who believes in Allah and His revelations. And follow him, so you may be ˹rightly˺ guided. (158) There are some among the people of Moses who guide with the truth and establish justice accordingly. (159)❩ [Quran 7:155-159]

[1]: For asking Moses to make Allah visible to them.

[2]: Some Muslim scholars cite Deuteronomy 18:15-18 and 33:2, Isaiah 42, and John 14:16 as examples of the description of Prophet Muḥammad in the Bible. However, Bible scholars interpret these verses differently. The name of Prophet Muḥammad (ﷺ) appears several times in the Gospel of Barnabas, which is deemed apocryphal by Christian authorities.

³⁸⁶ This is derived form the Quran verse of:

📖 ❨At this time, support comes ˹only˺ from Allah—the True ˹Lord˺. He is best in reward and best in outcome. (44)❩ [Quran 18:44]

No longer measuring wealth
By what can be held.
For only He
Elevates effort into grace.
Only He
Transforms need into peace.
Only He
Grants fulfillment beyond desire.

So the wise-one walks forward,
Not fighting with what the heavens have planned,
He finds in his solace, his peace on this land.
He lets his spirit prostrate to a wisdom unknown,
And finds in His rida a peace all his own.

For only He is the One, the Ever-True,
Whose guidance is always sacred and new.
He is the Lord of both loss and of gain,
And to trust in His will is to go far.
For only He remains the source
Of Serenity, and boundless force.

Wisdom Unveiled

The profound wisdom of this contemplation is the realization that true fulfillment is found not in the pursuit of worldly desires but in the complete surrender of the self to the Divine Will. The wise-one understands that this state of alignment brings a profound inner serenity that transcends all worldly circumstances. The verses from Quran 20:130-132, 59:9-10, 7:155-158, and 18:44 serve as a powerful testament to this truth, illustrating how the people of Madinah found success by giving preference to others and how Prophet Muhammad ﷺ came to relieve humanity of their burdens, guiding them to the ease of surrender. This wisdom unveils that true happiness is a divine reward, far better and more lasting than the fleeting splendor of this world, and that by aligning one's needs with the Creator's wisdom, even emptiness can be transformed into a profound sense of spiritual fullness.

Wise-Reflection

Reflect on your own pursuit of happiness. Are you searching for fulfillment in the fleeting pleasures of this world, or in the profound peace of surrender? Consider the thought, "When I submit my hunger to the Creator, Even emptiness becomes fullness." How can you practice patience and detachment, and redirect your desires toward what is truly lasting, so that you may find a contentment that is unshakable by the ups and downs of life?

Conclusion: Alignment with Divine Will

ECHOES OF REALIZATION: THE KINGDOM OF SURRENDER

The very throne of the wise-one's soul is not meticulously built upon the shaky foundations of control or the fleeting sands of worldly ambition. It is, instead, profoundly established upon surrender. Every single act of sincere trust, every conscious relinquishing of the illusion of self-control, meticulously polishes that inner throne, transforming it into a radiant seat. This purification continues until Al-Malik (The Sovereign Himself), in His absolute Majesty, comes to reside within it.

O wise-one, courageously surrender your meticulously crafted plans, your deepest fears, and your subtle clinging to all that is temporary. And then, witness with profound awe how the entire cosmos itself begins to instinctively bow with you before the One Will that eternally was, and perpetually is, and shall forever be..

THE SEEKER'S ASCENT: THE SOVEREIGNTY OF DIVINE WILL

Alignment with the Creator's unyielding Will is the very cornerstone of profound spiritual liberation. By consciously surrendering to Divine authority and by addressing personal needs and desires through the lenses of wisdom and disciplined self-control, the wise-one transcends the inherent constraints of temporal, worldly existence. This sacred alignment transforms the wise-one's entire life into a harmonious reflection of Divine purpose, thereby granting immeasurable peace, ultimate fulfillment, and an enduring, unbreakable connection to the Creator's boundless grace.

The spiritual journey of the wise-one is not, at its core, a strenuous conquest against destiny, but a graceful, continuous yielding to it. It is not a frantic grasping after fleeting earthly crowns, but a profound laying down of all such crowns at the feet of the Absolute Real. When the heart, in its purified state, truly aligns itself with the Creator's perfect decree, life ceases to be a chaotic battlefield of conflicting wants and instead becomes a serene, beautiful unfolding of destined beauty and wisdom.

Surrender, therefore, is not a defeat. It is, in fact, the greatest act of spiritual victory—a sublime moment where the soul transcends its finite self and finds ultimate, eternal rest at last in the boundless embrace of Al-Mutakabbir (The Most Sovereign), the All-Great. This total surrender and alignment signify a complete psychic and spiritual transformation. ❖❖❖

19ᵀᴴ REFLECTION: SINCERITY IN ACTION

(Pure Deeds for the Divine)

THE GATEWAY VERSES

In the sacred words of Allah, a profound description of those who embody ultimate sincerity in their actions, and the magnificent reward awaiting them:

📖 ❮They ˹are those who˺ fulfil ˹their˺ vows and fear a Day of sweeping horror, (7) and give food—despite their desire for it—to the poor, the orphan, and the captive, (8) ˹saying to themselves,˺ "We feed you only for the sake of Allah, seeking neither reward nor thanks from you. (9) We fear from our Lord a horribly distressful Day." (10) So Allah will deliver them from the horror of that Day, and grant them radiance and joy, (11) and reward them for their perseverance with a Garden ˹in Paradise˺ and ˹garments of˺ silk. (12)❯ [Quran 76:7-12]

ILLUMINATION'S DAWN

There comes a transformative moment in the soul's secret unfolding when action ceases to be a mere transaction or a form of bargaining, and becomes, instead, like profound, effortless breathing—a natural, spontaneous outflow. It is when deeds arise not from calculated expectations of gain or loss, but from a boundless love poured out like clear, life-giving water before the Beloved.

Here, the wise-one is profoundly called to act, not primarily for the promise of Paradise, nor solely from the fear of Hellfire, but because the pure, consuming love of Al-Wadud (The Most Loving, The Beloved) has truly become the intrinsic pulse within every offering, animating every fiber of their being. The purest act is, in essence, the act performed with no eye on the spiritual ledger, no thought of repayment—but only on the Beloved Face that watches, silently, and smiles unseen. Let us now walk reverently into this sacred sanctuary, where the wise-one's deeds ascend not by their perceived merit, but by the profound and unadulterated sincerity of their intention.

THE UNFOLDING OF INSIGHTS

This section explores the subtle dynamics of sincerity, highlighting the pitfalls of impure intentions and illuminating the path toward performing deeds solely for the sake of Allah, leading to profound spiritual freedom.

Contemplation: Pitfalls of Self-Centered Actions

(The Unsustainable Nature of Fear and Reward)

The wise-one diligently discerns the subtle yet pervasive pitfalls of self-centered actions that hinder true sincerity. This contemplation reveals that a deed's value is not in its appearance but in its intention. It explores the twin dangers of performing good deeds with a hope for reward (thawab) or a fear of punishment (iqab). The wise-one recognizes that while these motivations may compel action, they ultimately contaminate sincerity, transforming faith into a fragile, transactional relationship with the Divine. By transcending these self-centered drivers, the wise-one seeks a higher form of worship rooted in pure, unconditional love and trust, thereby freeing the soul from a spirituality based on expectation and dread.

Part 1: Hope for Reward

The wise-one diligently discerns the subtle yet pervasive pitfalls of self-centered actions, which hinder true sincerity. The transient nature of actions motivated by self-interest highlights the importance of purifying one's intentions. The wise-one recognizes that such actions, while seemingly virtuous, are ultimately unsustainable and prone to disillusionment.

This first part of the contemplation focuses on the illusion of hope for reward (thawab). The wise-one understands that making rewards the primary motivation for action, rather than pure love for the Creator, contaminates sincerity and reduces faith to a mere transaction. This subtle but profound shift in focus—from the Beloved to His gifts—creates a spiritual veil that prevents true intimacy with the Divine. The wise-one learns to guard against this pitfall, seeking not a return on their deeds, but the pleasure of the One who watches, silently, and smiles unseen.

The Fragility of Self-Interest: The Illusion of Hope for Reward

Hope that is tethered to expectation,
To the fleeting generosity of others,
To the wishful promise of return,
Is a foundation built upon sand.
"Due to wishful hope (of the Creator or others' generosity), Actions shall falter and
grow weary."

[624]

For charity loses its essence
When done to be seen.
Prayer crumbles in hypocrisy
When performed without heart.
And sincerity dissolves
When shackled to personal gain.
❮*Do not waste your charity With reminders of generosity Or hurtful words.*❯ —
Quran 2:246
For what is given
Only to seek status
Is not truly given at all.
It is a transaction,
Not an offering.
A fleeting illusion,
Not an act of devotion.
❮*Their example is that Of a hard barren rock Covered with a thin layer of soil, Hit*
by a strong rain— Leaving it just a bare stone.❯ —*Quran 2:246*
And in the wake of rain,
When the illusion washes away,
There is nothing left—
No reward,
No blessing,
Only emptiness. [387]

So too are those
Whose faith is fractured,
Who stand between belief
And disbelief,
Torn by hesitation,
Ruled by doubt.
❮*When they stand up for prayer, They do it half-heartedly Only to be seen by*
people— Hardly remembering Allah at all.❯ —*Quran 4:142*

---

[387] This is in agreement with the Quran verse of:

📖 ❮O believers! Do not waste your charity with reminders ˹of your generosity˺ or hurtful words, like those who donate their wealth just to show off and do not believe in Allah or the Last Day. Their example is that of a hard barren rock covered with a thin layer of soil hit by a strong rain—leaving it just a bare stone. Such people are unable to preserve the reward of their charity. Allah does not guide ˹such˺ disbelieving people. (246) And the example of those who donate their wealth, seeking Allah's pleasure and believing the reward is certain,1 is that of a garden on a fertile hill: when heavy rain falls, it yields up twice its normal produce. If no heavy rain falls, a drizzle is sufficient. And Allah is All-Seeing of what you do. (247)❯ [Quran 2:246-247]

For what is faith
Without remembrance?
What is devotion
Without sincerity?
It is neither belief
Nor disbelief,
Neither surrender
Nor defiance.
It is a void—
A path to ruin
Disguised as worship. [388]

And those who demand,
Who measure faith
By what they receive,
Find themselves enslaved
To disappointment.

❲There are some of them Who are critical Of your distribution of alms. If they are
given some of it, They are pleased, But if not, They are enraged.❳ —Quran 9:58

For contentment does not exist
In expectation.
It flourishes only
In trust.

❲If only they had been content With what Allah And His Messenger had given them,
And said, 'Allah is sufficient for us!'❳[389] —Quran 9:59

If my hand stretches forth for reward,
Soon it will fall back empty.
For the heart that trades in expectations
Finds itself impoverished

---

[388] This is in agreement with the Quran verse of:

📖 ❲Surely the hypocrites seek to deceive Allah, but He outwits them. When they stand up for prayer, they do it half-heartedly only to be seen by people—hardly remembering Allah at all. (142) Torn between belief and disbelief—belonging neither to these ʿbelieversʾ nor those ʿdisbelieversʾ. And whoever Allah leaves to stray, you will never find for them a way. (143)❳ [Quran 4:142-143]

[389] This is in agreement with the Quran verse of:

📖 ❲There are some of them who are critical of your distribution of alms ʿO Prophetʾ. If they are given some of it they are pleased, but if not they are enraged. (58) If only they had been content with what Allah and His Messenger had given them and said, "Allah is sufficient for us! Allah will grant us out of His bounty, and so will His Messenger. To Allah ʿaloneʾ we turn with hope." (59)❳ [Quran 9:58-59]

When the world does not pay.
Act, O my soul,
As if none but the All-Seeing (Al-Baseer) watches—
And let that be enough.
Thus, the wise-one understands—
Hope rooted in expectation
Is a deception.
Charity, if tainted with self-interest,
Fades into vanity.
Prayer, if done in spectacle,
Loses its meaning.
For true devotion
Is not seeking return,
But surrender.
Not longing for reward,
But finding certainty in grace.
Not demanding more,
But knowing He is sufficient.
And in that knowing,
Actions find purity,
Intentions find elevation,
And the soul stands
Unburdened by expectation,
Upheld by divine certainty.

So the wise-one walks forward,
Not fighting with what the heavens have planned,
He finds in his solace, his peace on this land.
He lets his spirit prostrate to a wisdom unknown,
And finds in His rida a peace all his own.

For only He is the One, the Ever-True,
Whose guidance is always sacred and new.
He is the Lord of both loss and of gain,
And to trust in His will is to go far.
For only He remains the source
Of Serenity, and boundless force.

Wisdom Unveiled

The profound wisdom of this contemplation is the realization that sincerity is a fragile state, easily contaminated by the desire for reward (thawab). The wise-one understands that when hope for reward becomes the primary motivation for good deeds, faith transforms into a transactional relationship, robbing actions of their spiritual essence. The verses from Quran 2:246 and 4:142 serve as a powerful testament to this, illustrating how charity performed to show off is like a hard barren rock, and how those who pray half-heartedly are torn between belief and disbelief. This wisdom unveils that true devotion is not about a return on investment but about a profound and unwavering surrender, and that genuine contentment is found not in demanding more, but in the certainty that the Creator is sufficient.

Wise-Reflection

Reflect on your own good deeds. Do you find yourself performing them with a subtle expectation of reward or recognition? Consider the thought, "Act, O my soul, As if none but the All-Seeing (Al-Baseer) watches— And let that be enough." How can you purify your intentions so that your actions are no longer a means to an end, but a sincere offering of love to the Beloved, allowing you to find a contentment that is unshaken by the world's disappointments?

Part 2: Fear of Punishment

The wise-one diligently discerns the subtle yet pervasive pitfalls of self-centered actions, which hinder true sincerity. The transient nature of actions motivated by self-interest highlights the importance of purifying one's intentions. The wise-one recognizes that such actions, while seemingly virtuous, are ultimately unsustainable and prone to disillusionment.

This second part of the contemplation focuses on the illusion of fear of punishment. The wise-one understands that while fear can be a motivator, allowing it to be the dominant driver of good deeds diminishes sincerity and creates a spiritual burden. Actions performed primarily to avoid Hellfire lack the profound, unconditional love and trust that characterize pure servitude. The wise-one seeks to transcend this fear-based motivation, moving towards a higher state of worship rooted in love and

awe for the Creator, recognizing that true obedience is a surrendering of
the heart, not a forced compliance.

The Failure of Fear: When Actions Falter Without Sincerity

Obedience born of fear
Is neither devotion nor strength.
It is a trembling step,
A hollow act,
A burden that weighs upon the soul
Until it inevitably crumbles.
For what is done in terror
Is never done in faith.
What is practiced out of dread
Is never sustained in certainty.
"Actions and deeds Due to fear of punishment (from the Creator or others) Shall
falter and weary Sooner or later."
Thus, the wise-one sees—
Forced righteousness
Is no righteousness at all.
An act imposed
Is an act empty of spirit.
The people of Moses were commanded,
The mountain raised above them,
The covenant given,
The path revealed.
Yet they followed
Only because they had no choice.
They walked
Not in trust,
But in compulsion.
❨Hold firmly to that Scripture Which We have given you, And observe its teachings
So perhaps you will become mindful.❩ —Quran 2:63
But fear does not create faith.
And the moment the pressure lifted,
They turned back
To their old ways.

For what is forced upon the heart
Will never take root. [390]

So too are those
Who claim submission
Yet resist the truth
When it does not serve them.
❨They will never be true believers Until they accept you As the judge in their disputes,
And find no resistance Within themselves Against your decision.❩ —Quran 4:65
For belief is not half-hearted.
It does not bend
To convenience.
It does not follow
When it benefits
And abandon
When it does not. [391]

Yet the hypocrites say,
❨We believe in Allah and the Messenger, And we obey.❩ —Quran 24:47
But their obedience
Is an illusion.
For when judgment is sought,
When truth demands allegiance,
They turn away.

---

[390] This is in agreement with the Quran verse narrating story of Moses's people forced to follow the right path then the faced backward to the their sinful deeds:

📖 ❨And ˹remember˺ when We took a covenant from you and raised the mountain above you ˹saying˺, "Hold firmly to that ˹Scripture˺ which We have given you and observe its teachings so perhaps you will become mindful ˹of Allah˺." (63) Yet you turned away afterwards. Had it not been for Allah's grace and mercy upon you, you would have certainly been of the losers. (64) You are already aware of those of you who broke the Sabbath. We said to them, "Be disgraced apes!"[1] (65) So We made their fate an example to present and future generations, and a lesson to the God-fearing. (66)❩ [Quran 2:63-66]

[1]: Although many scholars believe that these individuals were turned into real apes, others interpret this verse in a metaphorical sense. This style is not uncommon in the Quran. See 62:5 regarding the donkey that carries books and 2:18 regarding the deaf, dumb, and blind.

[391] This is in agreement with the Quran verse of:

📖 ❨But no! By your Lord, they will never be ˹true˺ believers until they accept you ˹O Prophet˺ as the judge in their disputes, and find no resistance within themselves against your decision and submit wholeheartedly. (65) If We had commanded them to sacrifice themselves or abandon their homes, none would have obeyed except for a few. Had they done what they were advised to do,[1] it would have certainly been far better for them and more reassuring, (66) and We would have granted them a great reward by Our grace (67) and guided them to the Straight Path. (68)❩ [Quran 4:65-68]

[1]: i.e., obeying Allah and His Messenger.

❨*Is there a sickness in their hearts? Or are they in doubt? Or do they fear That Allah and His Messenger Will be unjust to them?*❩ —*Quran 24:50*

Fear may spark the first steps,
But it cannot carry the soul through deserts.
It is love—love alone—
That gives the wings strength for the endless flight.
Let fear teach me vigilance,
But let love teach me flight.
When I act for a reward,
I chain my spirit to disappointment.
When I act from fear,
I shackle my joy.
Both hopes and fears are fragile lamps—
They sputter and die in the winds of trials.
But deeds rooted in love alone
Burn with a flame the tempests cannot quench.
O my soul,
Seek not reward—
Seek the Giver Himself.
Thus, the wise-one understands—
Fear is a fleeting master.
It may compel,
But it does not inspire.
It may demand action,
But it does not grant conviction.
For true obedience
Is not submission in terror,
But surrender in trust.
True devotion
Is not walking a path
To avoid punishment,
But walking it
Because it is right.
Thus, the only response
Of the true believer,
When called to divine judgment,
Is to say—
❨*We hear and obey.*❩ —*Quran 24:51*

And in that obedience,
Not born of fear,
But of certainty,
The soul finds peace.
Not ruled by terror,
But upheld by trust.
And the wise-one walks forward,
Not in the shackles of forced righteousness,
But in the freedom of true surrender. [392]

So the wise-one walks forward,
Not fighting with what the heavens have planned,
He finds in his solace, his peace on this land.
He lets his spirit prostrate to a wisdom unknown,
And finds in His rida a peace all his own.

For only He is the One, the Ever-True,
Whose guidance is always sacred and new.
He is the Lord of both loss and of gain,
And to trust in His will is to go far.
For only He remains the source
Of Serenity, and boundless force.

Wisdom Unveiled

The profound wisdom of this contemplation is the realization that a spirituality driven primarily by the fear of punishment (iqab) is ultimately fragile and unsustainable. The wise-one understands that while fear can serve as a deterrent, it cannot inspire the profound, unconditional love and trust that define true devotion. The verses from Quran 2:63 and 24:47-51 serve as a powerful testament to this, illustrating how the people of Moses, who were compelled to follow, quickly turned away, and how the

---

[392] This is in agreement with the Quran verse of:

📖 ⟨And the hypocrites say, "We believe in Allah and the Messenger, and we obey." Then a group of them turns away soon after that. These are not ʾtrueʾ believers. (47) And as soon as they are called to Allah and His Messenger so he may judge between them, a group of them turns away. (48) But if the truth is in their favour, they come to him, fully submitting. (49) Is there a sickness in their hearts? Or are they in doubt? Or do they fear that Allah and His Messenger will be unjust to them? In fact, it is they who are the ʾtrueʾ wrongdoers. (50) The only response of the ʾtrueʾ believers, when they are called to Allah and His Messenger so he may judge between them, is to say, "We hear and obey." It is they who will ʾtrulyʾ succeed. (51)⟩ [Quran 24:47-51]

hypocrites, who claim obedience, reveal their lack of sincerity when called to judgment. This wisdom unveils that true obedience is not a forced compliance but a willing surrender of the heart, where the believer says, "We hear and obey." It is in this state of pure submission, rooted in love and certainty rather than fear, that the soul finds true peace and the freedom to act with genuine, unwavering sincerity.

Wise-Reflection

Reflect on your own acts of worship and good deeds. Are you performing them out of a deep love for the Creator, or are you primarily motivated by a fear of punishment? Consider the thought, "Let fear teach me vigilance, But let love teach me flight." How can you cultivate a deeper connection to the Divine that allows you to transcend a fear-based motivation, so that your actions are not a burden, but a joyful expression of your love and trust in the Beloved?

Conclusion: Pitfalls of Self-Centered Actions

Thus, the wise-one understands that a spiritual life built on self-centered intentions is a house built on sand. Hope for reward, if made the primary motivation, leads to a heart enslaved by disappointment when expectations are not met. Similarly, a spirituality driven solely by fear of punishment may compel action but cannot sustain the soul through the trials of life. The wise-one, therefore, strives to transcend these pitfalls by purifying their intentions, performing deeds not for a spiritual ledger, but for the pleasure of the Beloved. It is in this state of pure, selfless devotion that actions find their true value, and the soul finds a profound and unshakable peace. The wise-one's ultimate goal is not to gain a reward or escape a punishment, but to be a sincere and unwavering lover of the Divine.

Contemplation: The Nature of Serene Deeds

For the wise-one, sincerity transforms actions into serene deeds. These are acts performed with inner peace, detachment from outcome, and an unwavering focus on Allah. They are free from ostentation (riya'), self-admiration ('ujb), and the desire for human praise. The Gateway Verses beautifully describe this: "We feed you only for the sake of Allah, seeking neither reward nor thanks from you." Such deeds flow from a tranquil heart, radiating a unique spiritual light and profoundly impacting both the doer and the environment. This psychic serenity is a direct outcome of purified intention.

The wise-one understands that true serenity is not a passive state but an active product of purified intentions. This contemplation serves as a powerful testament to the endurance and purity of deeds performed solely for the Creator's sake. By shedding the burdens of self-interest and worldly expectations, the wise-one's actions become infused with a spiritual light that endures beyond time and circumstance, leading to a profound inner peace and a closeness to the Divine that is the ultimate fulfillment.

The Nature of Serene Deeds: The Endurance of Sincere Actions

Not all deeds endure.
Not all efforts remain.
For actions born of fear
Fade with time,
And those rooted in self-interest
Wither in exhaustion.
But actions carried
As a serene offering
For the sake of the Creator's grace—
They do not falter,
They do not weary,
They stand,
Unshaken by trial,
Untouched by decay.
"The wise-one knows That only the one Who carries his own actions and deeds As a serene doing For the sake of the Creator's grace Shall his actions and deeds Never falter or grow weary."
Thus, the devoted ones persevered,
Standing firm beside their prophets,
Enduring hardship,
Losing much,
Yet never wavering.
They sought not worldly return,
Not fleeting gains,
But only His favor—
Only His mercy,
Only His guidance.
[634]

❨How many devotees Fought along with their prophets And never faltered Despite whatever losses They suffered in the cause of Allah! Allah loves those who persevere.❩
—Quran 3:146
And in moments of struggle,
Their prayer was simple,
Their longing pure:
❨Our Lord! Forgive our sins and excesses, Make our steps firm, And grant us victory Over the disbelieving people.❩ —Quran 3:147
For the reward of sincerity
Is not merely strength in hardship,
But tranquility in devotion. [393]

When the soul listens,
When the heart stills,
When the divine words
Are heard with reverence—
There, in that silence,
Mercy descends.
❨When the Quran is recited, Listen to it attentively And be silent, So you may be shown mercy.❩ —Quran 7:204
Not in distraction.
Not in heedlessness.
Not in arrogance.
For even the angels,
Near to the Creator,
Bow without hesitation.
They glorify without pride.

---

[393] This is in agreement with the Quran verse of:

📖 ❨'Imagine' how many devotees fought along with their prophets and never faltered despite whatever 'losses' they suffered in the cause of Allah, nor did they weaken or give in! Allah loves those who persevere. (146) And all they said was, "Our Lord! Forgive our sins and excesses, make our steps firm, and grant us victory over the disbelieving people." (147) So Allah gave them the reward of this world and the excellent reward of the Hereafter. For Allah loves the good-doers. (148)❩ [Quran 3:146-148]

❨Surely those angels Nearest to your Lord Are not too proud To worship Him. They glorify Him. And to Him they prostrate.❩ [394] —Quran 7:206

O my soul,
Actions offered in serenity,
In the secret hush of pure intention,
Are etched into eternity.
Deeds fueled by yearning for His gaze,
Not for His gardens,
Deeds poured out without bargaining—
These never falter,
These never tire.
When I work for His sake alone,
Even the smallest gesture glows with immortality.
Thus, the wise-one understands—
That sincerity is not simply belief,
But a way of being.
It is the abandoning of rest
To invoke Him in the night.
It is the offering of wealth
Without hesitation.
It is the quiet surrender
In moments unseen.
❩The true believers,
When revelation is recited to them,
Fall into prostration
And glorify the praises of their Lord
And are not too proud.❩ —Quran 32:15
And to these—
To those who give without seeking,
To those who kneel without question,
To those who carry deeds
Not for reward,

---

[394] This is in agreement with the Quran verse of:

📖 ❨When the Quran is recited, listen to it attentively and be silent, so you may be shown mercy. (204) Remember your Lord inwardly with humility and reverence and in a moderate tone of voice, both morning and evening. And do not be one of the heedless. (205) Surely those ʿangelsʾ nearest to your Lord are not too proud to worship Him. They glorify Him. And to Him they prostrate. (206)❩ [Quran 7:204-206]

But for devotion—
Unimaginable wonders await.
⟨No soul can imagine What delights are kept in store for them As a reward For
what they used to do.⟩³⁹⁵ —Quran 32:17
Thus, the wise-one walks forward,
Not weighed by expectation,
Not burdened by desire,
But carrying every action
As a serene devotion.
For only He sustains sincerity.
Only He rewards the endurance of purity.
Only He grants the fulfillment of eternal grace.

So the wise-one walks forward,
Not fighting with what the heavens have planned,
He finds in his solace, his peace on this land.
He lets his spirit prostrate to a wisdom unknown,
And finds in His rida a peace all his own.
For only He is the One, the Ever-True,
Whose guidance is always sacred and new.
He is the Lord of both loss and of gain,
And to trust in His will is to go far.

For only He remains the source
Of Serenity, and boundless force.

Wisdom Unveiled

The profound wisdom of this contemplation is the realization that sincerity transforms actions into serene deeds, which are characterized by their endurance, purity, and detachment from worldly outcomes. The wise-one understands that these deeds are not driven by fear or the hope of reward but by a pure love for the Creator, resulting in an unshakable inner peace. The verses from Quran 3:146-148 and 7:204-206 serve as a

---

³⁹⁵ This is in agreement with the Quran verse of:

📖 ⟨The only 'true' believers in Our revelation are those who—when it is recited to them—fall into prostration and glorify the praises of their Lord and are not too proud. (15) They abandon their beds, invoking their Lord with hope and fear, and donate from what We have provided for them. (16) No soul can imagine what delights are kept in store for them as a reward for what they used to do. (17) Is the one who is a believer equal 'before Allah' to the one who is rebellious? They are not equal! (18)⟩ [Quran 32:15-18]

powerful testament to this truth, illustrating how the sincere devotees persevered without faltering and how a quiet, attentive heart is the vessel for divine mercy. This wisdom unveils that serene deeds are the direct outcome of a heart that is free from pride and ostentation, and that it is in this state of pure devotion that the soul finds its ultimate reward—a peace that transcends all worldly circumstances and leads to a spiritual fulfillment beyond human imagination.

Wise-Reflection

Reflect on your most cherished deeds. Were they performed with a tranquil heart, detached from the outcome, or were they burdened by expectation or fear? Consider the thought, "When I work for His sake alone, Even the smallest gesture glows with immortality." How can you cultivate a heart so serene that your actions become a pure offering of devotion, free from the desire for human praise or worldly gain, allowing you to find a profound and enduring peace in your worship?

Contemplation: The Path to Pure Deeds

The wise-one actively cultivates the path to pure deeds (al-'amal al-salih al-khalis). This path involves continuous self-purification, mindful intention-setting before every action, and relentless introspection to examine motivations. It is a journey of gradually shedding all 'other-than-Allah' from one's intentions. This path requires unwavering spiritual discipline (mujahadah) and constant remembrance (dhikr) to ensure that every deed, whether grand or small, external or internal, is solely directed towards seeking the pleasure and proximity of the Divine, embodying the concept of ihsan (doing good as if you see Allah, and if you don't see Him, knowing He sees you).

The wise-one understands that sincerity is not merely a passive state but an active, disciplined practice. This final contemplation serves as a powerful guide, outlining the path to purifying one's deeds and intentions. By moving beyond fear and reward and embracing a love-based devotion, the wise-one's actions become a serene offering, radiating a spiritual light that emanates from a heart dedicated solely to the Creator. This path leads to the ultimate reward: a profound and lasting serenity that is a direct outcome of living in His presence.

The Path to Pure Deeds: The Radiance of a Heart Devoted to the
Creator

The wise-one gathers no ledger of good deeds.
He does not count, measure, or seek recompense.
For his hands do not move
To secure reward,
Nor do his feet walk
In fear of punishment.
He carries only a single lantern—
Lit not by promises,
But by longing.
His every act whispers:
"I did this because You are beautiful, O my Lord—
And beauty calls to be served."
For the heart that knows the Creator's beauty
Does not wait for incentive.
It does not waver in doubt.
It does not ask,
"Will this be weighed in my favor?"
It only moves toward Him,
As the river flows toward the sea,
As the dawn breaks toward the light.
Thus, among the honored ones,
Among those whose very lives
Were an offering,
Stood those who dedicated everything
For Allah's pleasure.
❨And there are those Who would dedicate their lives To Allah's pleasure. And Allah
is Ever Gracious To His servants.❩[396] —Quran 2:207

In the stillness of the night,
When the world sleeps,
When silence cloaks the earth,
The devoted remain awake,

---

[396] This is in agreement with the Quran verse of:

📖 ❨And there are those who would dedicate their lives to Allah's pleasure. And Allah is Ever Gracious to
ʿHisʾ servants. (207)❩ [Quran 2:207]

Not for recognition,
Not for status,
But for the love of their Lord.
❨Are they better— Or those who worship Their Lord devoutly In the hours of the
night, Prostrating and standing, Fearing the Hereafter And hoping for the mercy Of
their Lord?❩ —Quran 39:9
Their longing is greater
Than their fear.
Their devotion stronger
Than hesitation.
Their surrender
Is serene,
Because it is absolute. [397]

I seek no crown,
No applause.
I seek only the nearness
Of the One whose nearness
Is Paradise itself.
Thus, the wise-one understands—
Love is the greatest force of devotion.
Not obligation.
Not transaction.
Not calculation.
For what the devoted seek
Is not merely acceptance,
But the touch of divine love.
And in their hearts,
Where faith flourishes,
Where sincerity breathes,
Allah sends down serenity,
Rewarding them
Not with wealth,
But with unshakable peace.

---

[397] This is in the agreement with the Quran verse of:

📖 ❨Are they better˸ or those who worship ˹their Lord˺ devoutly in the hours of the night, prostrating and standing, fearing the Hereafter and hoping for the mercy of their Lord? Say, ˹O Prophet,˺ "Are those who know equal to those who do not know?" None will be mindful ˹of this˺ except people of reason. (9)❩ [Quran 39: 9]

❨*Indeed, Allah was pleased With the believers When they pledged allegiance to you*
Under the tree. He knew what was in their hearts, So He sent down serenity upon
them And rewarded them With a victory at hand.❩ *398* —*Quran 48:18*

And to them,
To those whose deeds flow
Without expectation,
Without hesitation,
Without concern for worldly recognition,
Allah promises—
❨*As for those who believe And do good, The Most Compassionate Will certainly bless*
them With genuine love.❩ *399* —*Quran 19:96*

Thus, the wise-one walks forward,
Not weighed by accounts,
Not burdened by self-interest,
But carrying a single lantern,
Burning only with longing.
For only He sustains sincerity.
Only He transforms devotion into serenity.
Only He grants fulfillment beyond measure.

So the wise-one walks forward,
Not fighting with what the heavens have planned,
He finds in his solace, his peace on this land.
He lets his spirit prostrate to a wisdom unknown,
And finds in His rida a peace all his own.

For only He is the One, the Ever-True,
Whose guidance is always sacred and new.
He is the Lord of both loss and of gain,
And to trust in His will is to go far.

---

[398] This is in agreement with the Quran verse of:

📖 ❨Indeed, Allah was pleased with the believers when they pledged allegiance to you ˹O Prophet˺ under the
tree. He knew what was in their hearts, so He sent down serenity upon them and rewarded them with a
victory at hand. (18)❩ [Quran 48:18]

[399] This is in agreement with the Quran verse of:

📖 ❨As for those who believe and do good, the Most Compassionate will ˹certainly˺ bless them with
˹genuine˺ love. (96)❩ [Quran 19:96]

For only He remains the source
Of Serenity, and boundless force.

Wisdom Unveiled

The profound wisdom of this contemplation is the realization that the path to pure deeds (al-'amal al-salih al-khalis) is an active journey of self-purification, driven not by fear or reward, but by a deep and abiding love for the Creator. The wise-one understands that a heart devoted to the Divine finds its greatest motivation in the longing for His beauty and nearness. The verses from Quran 2:207 and 39:9 serve as a powerful testament to this, illustrating how those who dedicate their lives to Allah's pleasure and worship Him with both hope and fear are granted an elevated status. This wisdom unveils that a heart that moves with this kind of selfless devotion is rewarded not with worldly treasures, but with a divine serenity and a genuine love from the Most Compassionate, which is the ultimate fulfillment.

Wise-Reflection

Reflect on your own spiritual journey. Is your devotion rooted in a love for the Creator, or is it still driven by a ledger of rewards and punishments? Consider the thought, "I seek no crown, No applause. I seek only the nearness Of the One whose nearness Is Paradise itself." How can you actively cultivate a heart so filled with longing that every action becomes a pure offering, and you find a peace that transcends all worldly circumstances?.

Conclusion: Sincerity in Action

ECHOES OF REALIZATION: THE SILENT OFFERING

The purest deed, whispered only in the deepest chambers of the heart, makes no audible sound when it gracefully falls at the foot of the Divine Throne. It does not clamor for worldly recognition, nor does it demand a prestigious place among the ranks of the outwardly righteous.

It is, instead, a hidden, unassuming flame—a subtle fragrance that rises unseen by human eyes, and is known, intimately and profoundly, only to the One for whom it was lovingly kindled. O wise-one, strive to make your entire life a vibrant garden of such silent offerings—deeds performed not for the approval of eyes, nor for the fleeting promise of rewards, but solely for the sake of pure, unadulterated Divine love. There, in that unseen garden of the heart, you will find Him waiting, ever-Present.

THE SEEKER'S ASCENT: THE ENDURANCE OF SINCERE ACTIONS

Sincerity in action fundamentally transforms what might otherwise be ordinary deeds into profound, sacred acts of pure devotion. By liberating actions from the subtle constraints of fear of punishment and the desire for reward, the wise-one intentionally aligns their every effort with boundless Divine Grace, thereby achieving profound spiritual elevation and lasting inner fulfillment. This absolute purity of intention ensures that every single act becomes a living testament to the Creator's constant Presence, beautifully reflecting the inherent harmony and radiant beauty of a heart wholly devoted to the Divine.

Sincerity is the secret, underground river that silently, yet powerfully, carries deeds into the everlasting gardens of Divine acceptance. To act with no bargaining, to love with no meticulous ledger, to give with no expectation of reciprocity—this is to build not with perishable stone, but with eternal light. The wise-one who courageously surrenders both the fear of wrath and the hope for reward, and acts solely for the luminous Face (Wajhullah) of the Creator, has already, in essence, begun to live eternity even within the finite folds of time. This profound state of sincerity marks a vital step in " The Triumph of Self-Mastery."

20ᵀᴴ REFLECTION: SEEING BEYOND THE SURFACE

(Clairvoyant Wisdom)

THE GATEWAY VERSES

In the sacred words of Allah, a profound challenge to human perception, revealing His absolute sovereignty over all creation and affairs, and distinguishing between spiritual blindness and true insight:

📖 ⟨*Ask ˹them, O Prophet˺, "Who provides for you from heaven and earth? Who owns ˹your˺ hearing and sight? Who brings forth the living from the dead and the dead from the living? And who conducts every affair?" They will ˹surely˺ say, "Allah." Say, "Will you not then fear ˹Him˺'? (31) That is Allah—your True Lord. So what is beyond the truth except falsehood? How can you then be turned away?" (32)*⟩ [Quran 10: 31-32]

And further affirming the distinction:

📖 ⟨*Those blind ˹to the truth˺ and those who can see are not equal, nor are those who believe and do good ˹equal˺ to those who do evil. Yet you are hardly mindful.*⟩ [Quran 40 :58]

ILLUMINATION'S DAWN

There comes a transformative moment in the spiritual journey when the intricate veil of worldly causality suddenly shatters, and the wise-one's soul sees—not through the limited eyes of flesh, but through the profound, expansive gaze of pure spirit. Here, all external forms lose their tyranny over perception. Here, perceived effects no longer desperately beg for a linear explanation. The wise-one no longer anxiously asks: "Why did this specific event happen by that specific cause?" but instinctively bows, with profound submission, instead to the One Who Wills All (Al-Mureed), recognizing His Hand in every unfolding.

To truly see beyond the surface is to perceive with unwavering certainty that every solitary leaf that gently falls from a tree, every distant star that fiercely burns in the cosmos, is suspended and actuated solely by the precise, all-encompassing decree of Al-Haqq (The Absolute Truth, The Real). Let us now step reverently beyond the limited horizon of fleeting appearances, where the wise-one no longer counts superficial causes, but only profoundly witnesses the singular, ultimate Source.

THE UNFOLDING OF INSIGHTS

This section guides the wise-one towards developing profound spiritual insight, emphasizing the dissolution of perceived causality in favor of direct apprehension of Allah's Will as the ultimate origin of all phenomena, fostering true 'clairvoyant wisdom.'

Contemplation: A Comparison to Worldly Validation

The wise-one initially engages in a critical comparison to worldly validation. Ordinary human perception relies on external evidence, logical sequence, and tangible proofs to validate reality. This leads to seeking explanations through chains of cause and effect, focusing on created means rather than the Creator. True spiritual insight, or "clairvoyant wisdom," transcends this dependence on worldly validation, relying instead on inner certainty and direct spiritual apprehension of the Divine source behind all events, thereby freeing the psychic self from external validation.

The wise-one understands that human knowledge, while useful, is a fragile construct built on footnotes and citations. In contrast, divine insight rests on an unshakable foundation: the word of the Author of existence Himself. This contemplation serves as a powerful testament to the superiority of spiritual certainty over worldly validation. The wise-one learns that a soul that has tasted this direct knowledge no longer needs to seek confirmation from the fleeting authorities of men, for its truth is self-sustaining and immutable, rooted in the very fabric of creation.

The Divine Source of Knowledge: When Certainty Needs No
Signatures

Just as human knowledge
Seeks authority in names and citations,
Just as men anchor their truths
In endless footnotes,
Divine insight
Rests its case
In the Author of existence Himself.
For the wise-one smiles
At the meticulous documentation of men—
For they have tasted a certainty

[645]

That needs no signatures.
Man writes.
He records.
He traces every word,
Every thought,
Every conclusion
Back to authority—
To sources,
To names,
To the validation of peers.
Yet the wise-one sees—
Knowledge among men is borrowed,
While divine knowledge is self-sustaining.

For when revelations descend,
When guidance is granted,
When truth is unveiled,
It is not traced back
To earthly authorities,
Nor measured by human authentication,
But attributed only
To the One
Who shaped the heavens and the earth.
For those granted divine wisdom,
For those enveloped in truth,
There is no need to verify.
They do not seek confirmations
From the scholars of the world.
They do not need endorsements
From those who doubt.
They do not require
The chain of transmission—
For they see,
As the Creator sees,
That all occurrences,
All revelations,
All truths
Originate from Him alone.
《Alif-Lām-Mīm. Allah! There is no god Worthy of worship Except Him— The

Ever-Living, All-Sustaining.》 —Quran 3:1-2
He speaks.
And through His command,
Knowledge descends—
Unshaken, unquestioned,
Without need of authentication.

《He has revealed to you The Book in truth, Confirming what came before it, As He revealed the Torah And the Gospel previously As a guide for people.》 —Quran 3:3-4

Thus, no decree,
No scripture,
No guidance
Bears witness
To any but Him.
For He is the One
Who knows all things,
Who sees all things,
Who grants wisdom
To whom He wills.

《Surely nothing On earth or in the heavens Is hidden from Allah. He is the One Who shapes you in the wombs Of your mothers As He wills. There is no god Worthy of worship Except Him—the Almighty, All-Wise.》 —Quran 3:5-6

Even when men seek to twist truth,
Even when they chase knowledge
For power rather than guidance,
Even when they attempt
To cast doubt
Upon divine wisdom—
Only those grounded in knowledge
Understand.

《As for those Well-grounded in knowledge, They say, 'We believe in this Quran— It is all from our Lord.' But none will be mindful Except people of reason.》 —Quran 3:7

For human knowledge
May be debated,
May be reinterpreted,
May be lost in endless analysis.
But divine decree

Is immutable.
Unshaken.
Beyond alteration.
His words
Are not weighed by human desire,
Nor reshaped by doubt,
Nor subject to hesitation
For what knowledge
Could be more certain
Than the Word
Of the One who created knowledge itself? [400]

When the Author Himself speaks into the heart,
What need has the soul for any other witness?
Just as worldly validation relies on chains of authentication, divine insight renders such
processes unnecessary, focusing directly on the ultimate truth.
For His promise
Is truth itself.
❨Allah's promise Is always true. And whose word Is more truthful Than Allah's?❩
—Quran 4:122
And to those who believe,
To those who live in sincerity,
To those who carry the weight
Of good deeds—
Their reward is decreed,

---

[400] This aligns with the sacred verses that declare the Creator of the heavens and the earth as the giver of all divine revelations, with these truths being solely ascribed to Him. Those who are graced with wisdom recognize this profound reality:

📖 ❨Alif-Lām-Mīm. (1) Allah! There is no god ˹worthy of worship˺ except Him—the Ever-Living, All-Sustaining. (2) He has revealed to you ˹O Prophet˺ the Book in truth, confirming what came before it, as He revealed the Torah and the Gospel (3) previously, as a guide for people, and ˹also˺ revealed the Decisive Authority.[1] Surely those who reject Allah's revelations will suffer a severe torment. For Allah is Almighty, capable of punishment. (4) Surely nothing on earth or in the heavens is hidden from Allah. (5) He is the One Who shapes you in the wombs of your mothers as He wills. There is no god ˹worthy of worship˺ except Him—the Almighty, All-Wise. (6) He is the One Who has revealed to you ˹O Prophet˺ the Book, of which some verses are precise—they are the foundation of the Book—while others are elusive.[1] Those with deviant hearts follow the elusive verses seeking ˹to spread˺ doubt through their ˹false˺ interpretations—but none grasps their ˹full˺ meaning except Allah. As for those well-grounded in knowledge, they say, "We believe in this ˹Quran˺—it is all from our Lord." But none will be mindful ˹of this˺ except people of reason. (7) ˹They say,˺ "Our Lord! Do not let our hearts deviate after you have guided us. Grant us Your mercy. You are indeed the Giver ˹of all bounties˺. (8) Our Lord! You will certainly gather all humanity for the ˹promised˺ Day—about which there is no doubt. Surely Allah does not break His promise." (9)❩ [Quran 3:1-9]

[1]: The Decisive Authority (Al-Furqān) is one of the names of the Quran.

Unchanging, eternal.
◁And those who believe And do good, We will soon admit them Into Gardens Under
which rivers flow, To stay there forever. Allah's promise is always true.▷ —Quran
4:122

Thus, the wise-one understands—
Certainty does not dwell
In sources or footnotes,
In revisions or calculations,
But in the unshakable decree
Of the One who governs all things. [401]
To submit to Him
Is to anchor oneself
In truth beyond time.
To trust His wisdom
Is to walk forward
Without fear of uncertainty.
To witness His signs
Is to awaken
To a knowledge
That is complete.
For only He sustains wisdom.
Only He unveils true knowledge.
Only He remains
The source of all reality,
Written and unwritten,
Seen and unseen.

So the wise-one walks forward,
Not fighting with what the heavens have planned,
He finds in his solace, his peace on this land.

---

[401] This aligns with the sacred words of the Quran:

📖 ◁And those who believe and do good, We will soon admit them into Gardens under which rivers flow, to stay there for ever and ever. Allah's promise is ˹always˺ true. And whose word is more truthful than Allah's? (122) ˹Divine grace is˺ neither by your wishes nor those of the People of the Book! Whoever commits evil will be rewarded accordingly, and they will find no protector or helper besides Allah. (123) But those who do good—whether male or female—and have faith will enter Paradise and will never be wronged ˹even as much as˺ the speck on a date stone. (124) And who is better in faith than those who ˹fully˺ submit themselves to Allah, do good, and follow the Way of Abraham, the upright? Allah chose Abraham as a close friend. (125) To Allah ˹alone˺ belongs whatever is in the heavens and whatever is on the earth. And Allah is Fully Aware of everything. (126)▷ [Quran 4:122-124]

He lets his spirit prostrate to a wisdom unknown,
And finds in His rida a peace all his own.

For only He is the One, the Ever-True,
Whose guidance is always sacred and new.
He is the Lord of both loss and of gain,
And to trust in His will is to go far.
For only He remains the source
Of Serenity, and boundless force.

Wisdom Unveiled

The profound wisdom of this contemplation is the realization that clairvoyant wisdom transcends the need for worldly validation. The wise-one understands that while human knowledge is a borrowed construct based on citations and sources, divine knowledge is self-sustaining and absolute, rooted in the word of the Creator Himself. The verses from Quran 3:1-9 and 4:122-126 serve as a powerful testament to this truth, illustrating how Allah's revelations are unshaken and immutable, and how those well-grounded in knowledge find certainty in a truth that needs no authentication. This wisdom unveils that to anchor oneself in the Creator's decree is to step beyond the fear of uncertainty and awaken to a knowledge that is complete and eternal.

Wise-Reflection

Reflect on your own sources of truth. Do you primarily rely on external validation and the "endless footnotes of men," or do you seek to anchor your certainty in the Word of the Divine? Consider the thought, "When the Author Himself speaks into the heart, What need has the soul for any other witness?" How can you cultivate a heart that is so grounded in divine wisdom that you can walk forward with unshakable certainty, free from the need for worldly authentication?

Contemplation: The Rule of the Omission of Chains in Descriptions

A pivotal insight for the wise-one is the rule of the omission of chains in descriptions. When Allah describes His actions in the Quran, particularly those seemingly governed by natural laws, He often omits mentioning the intermediate causes or "chains," directly attributing the effect to His Will. For example, "He sends down rain," rather than "He creates the conditions for clouds to form which then release rain." This teaches the wise-one to bypass the perceived material causes and directly attribute all power and action to Allah, strengthening Tawhid (Oneness of God) in perception.

This contemplation serves as a powerful testament to the superior perception of those blessed with divine clairvoyance. Their understanding bypasses the limited framework of cause and effect, resting instead on the direct apprehension of the Creator's will. The story of Moses and the wise servant is a profound guide to this truth, revealing that some knowledge is not acquired through human effort but is a bestowal of grace, one that requires absolute submission to a reality that transcends human logic and earthly validation.

The Omission of Chains in Descriptions: The Vision Beyond Validation

---

Not all knowledge is granted by effort.
Not all wisdom can be attained through seeking.
For beyond the grasp of human understanding,
Beyond the limits of prophecy itself,
There exists a knowledge—
Bestowed, not acquired—
A sight given as an act of pure grace.
"The wise-one knows That those who achieved True clairvoyance As a bestowal From the Creator's grace, Once they describe incidences, Signs, and knowledge, They omit the chain Of authentication Of their sources. They refer all actions And inactions To the Creator's will."
Thus, Moses,
A prophet of the highest rank,
One who had spoken
Directly with the Divine,
Yearned for more.
He sought wisdom beyond his own,
Not through revelation,
But through a man—
A servant bathed in divine mercy,
Enlightened with knowledge
Not of his own making,

[651]

But of Allah's decree.

❮They found a servant of Ours, To whom We had granted mercy from Us And
enlightened With knowledge of Our Own.❯ —Quran 18:65

But knowledge of this nature
Could not be learned.
It could not be studied.
It required submission.
It required patience.
It required complete surrender
To the fact that human logic
Would fail to comprehend it.

❮You certainly cannot be patient With me. And how can you be patient With what is
beyond Your realm of knowledge?❯[402] —Quran 18:67-68

Thus began the journey,
One that would test the limits
Of human understanding,
One that would force Moses
To confront the fragility of perception.
The acts were perplexing,
Unfathomable,
Even terrifying.
For Moses,
Though steadfast in faith,
Was still bound
By the limitations of knowability.
He still sought reason.
He still searched for justice
Within the frame of human wisdom.

---

[402] This aligns with the sacred verses that recount the tale of Moses and the sage, bestowed with divine wisdom from the Creator:

📖 ❮Moses responded, "That is ˹exactly˺ what we were looking for."[1] So they returned, retracing their footsteps. (64) There they found a servant of Ours, to whom We had granted mercy from Us and enlightened with knowledge of Our Own. (65) Moses said to him, "May I follow you, provided that you teach me some of the right guidance you have been taught?" (66) He said, "You certainly cannot be patient ˹enough˺ with me. (67) And how can you be patient with what is beyond your ˹realm of˺ knowledge?" (68) Moses assured ˹him˺, "You will find me patient, Allah willing, and I will not disobey any of your orders." (69) He responded, "Then if you follow me, do not question me about anything until I ˹myself˺ clarify it for you." (70)❯ [Quran 18:64-70]

[1]: Moses was given a sign: when he and his assistant Joshua (or Yûsha' ibn Nûn) lost their food (a salted fish), this would be the place where they would find the man of knowledge.

The ship damaged.
An innocent boy slain.
A crumbling wall rebuilt
Without recompense.
And Moses,
Could not endure it.
He questioned.
He protested.
He broke the vow of patience,
Not out of doubt,
But out of human limitation.
❨Did I not tell you That you cannot be patient with me?❩ —Quran 18:72
Until at last,
He had to part ways.
For not even prophecy
Was enough to withstand
This level of divine insight.
The wise-one revealed—
Not reasoning,
But divine necessity.
❨I did not do it All on my own.❩ —Quran 18:82
Each act,
Though seemingly unjust,
Was a mercy beyond human sight.
And in those words,
The truth of divine knowledge
Became clear.
It is not logic.
It is not experience.
It is grace—
A gift,
Given to whom Allah wills,
Beyond the measures of learning,
Beyond the systems of validation,
Beyond the structure of comprehension

That even the greatest of prophets
Must abide by. [403]

O my soul,
Those touched by the light of unveiled knowing
No longer lean on the crutches of worldly proofs.
Their words spill from the river of divine certainty,
Untethered to human validations.
They do not cite the stars to describe the sun—
They point directly to its blazing reality.
The purest knowing needs no footnotes—
For its author is the Real (Al-Haqq) Himself.
Thus, the wise-one understands—
Some truths are never taught.
Some wisdom is never studied.
Some sight is never earned.
For only He grants vision
Beyond the veil.
Only He bestows knowledge
That exceeds all earthly wisdom.
Only He remains the true source
Of all understanding,
Seen and unseen.

So the wise-one walks forward,
Not fighting with what the heavens have planned,
He finds in his solace, his peace on this land.

---

[403] The quest began with a most bewildering event, one that no mortal could fully comprehend nor withstand the weight of its evident repercussions:

📖 ❨So they set out, but after they had boarded a ship, the man made a hole in it. Moses protested, "Have you done this to drown its people? You have certainly done a terrible thing!" (71) He replied, "Did I not say that you cannot have patience with me?" (72) Moses pleaded, "Excuse me for forgetting, and do not be hard on me." (73) So they proceeded until they came across a boy, and the man killed him. Moses protested, "Have you killed an innocent soul, who killed no one? You have certainly done a horrible thing." (74) He answered, "Did I not tell you that you cannot have patience with me?" (75) Moses replied, "If I ever question you about anything after this, then do not keep me in your company, for by then I would have given you enough of an excuse." (76) So they moved on until they came to the people of a town. They asked them for food, but the people refused to give them hospitality. There they found a wall ready to collapse, so the man set it right. Moses protested, "If you wanted, you could have demanded a fee for this." (77) He replied, "This is the parting of our ways. I will explain to you what you could not bear patiently. (78)❩ [Quran 18:71-78]

He lets his spirit prostrate to a wisdom unknown,
And finds in His rida a peace all his own.

For only He is the One, the Ever-True,
Whose guidance is always sacred and new.
He is the Lord of both loss and of gain,
And to trust in His will is to go far.
For only He remains the source
Of Serenity, and boundless force.

Wisdom Unveiled

The profound wisdom of this contemplation is the realization that true spiritual insight, or "clairvoyant wisdom," bypasses the need for conventional chains of causality and worldly validation. The wise-one understands that some knowledge is a bestowal of divine grace, not an acquisition through human effort. The story of Moses and the wise servant from Quran 18:64-82 serves as a powerful testament to this truth, illustrating how a prophet of the highest rank was unable to endure the seemingly unjust actions of a servant who was acting on divine knowledge. This wisdom unveils that true sight is a gift that allows one to perceive the ultimate cause behind every event, directly attributing all power and action to the Creator, thereby strengthening Tawhid in perception and fostering an understanding of a reality that transcends human logic.

Wise-Reflection

Reflect on your own perception of the world. Do you primarily seek to understand events through the chains of cause and effect, or do you seek to see the hand of the Creator behind every occurrence? Consider the thought, "They do not cite the stars to describe the sun—They point directly to its blazing reality." How can you cultivate a heart so surrendered that you can accept the wisdom that lies beyond your realm of knowledge, and a sight that omits the chains of causality in favor of direct apprehension of the Divine?

Contemplation: Immersion in Divine Grace

This 'seeing beyond' leads to a profound immersion in Divine Grace (Fadl). When the wise-one perceives Allah as the direct Actor in all affairs, they also realize that every moment, every breath, every unfolding, is a manifestation of His grace and wisdom, regardless of its appearance. This immersion dissolves resentment over perceived misfortunes and boasts over perceived successes, leading to a state of perpetual gratitude and contentment, as the heart recognizes the Divine Hand in all things.

The wise-one understands that the highest form of knowledge is not acquired through human effort but is a divine bestowal. This contemplation serves as a powerful testament to the serenity and contentment that comes from a heart submerged in the tide of divine grace. By recognizing the Creator as the direct Actor in all affairs, the wise-one is freed from the need to understand worldly causality, finding profound peace and satisfaction in the unshakable certainty that all waters flow from Him.

> The Bestowal of Divine Clairvoyance: Knowledge Beyond Prophetic Comprehension

The highest wisdom
Is not merely learned—
It is bestowed.
It is poured into the heart
Of those whom the Creator chooses,
Those whom He envelops in His grace,
Those whom He submerges
In divine knowing.
Thus, when they speak,
When they describe,
They do not trace their words
Back to earthly validation.
For their knowledge
Is not gathered
Through tradition,
Nor memorized from books.
It is simply given.
"This omission is not due to ignorance Or misconception, But an accustomed habit Established by their clairvoyance, As they become immersed In the grace stance of the Creator."
Thus stood the wise-one—
Whom Moses was to meet,
Whom Moses sought out,

[656]

Not knowing that he was approaching
One already immersed
In a wisdom beyond prophecy itself.
❨*There they found a servant of Ours, To whom We had granted mercy from Us And*
enlightened With knowledge of Our Own.❩[404] —*Quran 18:65*

For even prophets,
Even those closest to the Divine,
Must surrender
To patience
When seeking knowledge.
For revelation itself
Must be received in clarity,
Not rushed in eagerness,
Not grasped before it is properly delivered.
❨*Exalted is Allah, The True King! Do not rush to recite A revelation of the Quran*
Before it is properly conveyed to you, And pray, 'My Lord! Increase me in
knowledge.'❩ —*Quran 20:114*
For knowledge
Is not merely a pursuit.
It is a granting—
An unfolding into greater understanding
By the will of the Creator alone.
Thus, even the chosen ones
Are guided slowly,
Steadily,
With wisdom unfolding
As He wills. [405]

---

[404] This aligns with the sacred words of the Quran, which speak of the wise-one, Moses' companion, who was already steeped in the Creator's grace long before their fateful encounter, a depth of understanding that even Moses struggled to grasp.:

📖 ❨There they found a servant of Ours, to whom We had granted mercy from Us and enlightened with knowledge of Our Own. (65)❩ [Quran 18:65]

[405] This is in accordance with the sacred verse that recounts how the Almighty urged His prophet to exercise patience in grasping the divine revelations and beseeched the Lord for an increase in wisdom:

📖 ❨Exalted is Allah, the True King! Do not rush to recite ˹a revelation of˺ the Quran ˹O Prophet˺ before it is ˹properly˺ conveyed to you,[1] and pray, "My Lord! Increase me in knowledge." (114)❩ [Quran 20:114]

[1]: The Prophet ﷺ was eager to recite the Quran while it was being revealed to him through the angel Gabriel. So he ﷺ was told to take his time to learn it by heart once the verses are properly delivered to him.

When the heart swims in the sea of grace,
It no longer asks which river brought the water.
It drinks—
And is satisfied.
The wise-one, submerged in the tide of divine vision,
Sees causality as but foam upon the waves.
Drink, O soul,
And forget the names of the rivers—
For all waters flow from Him.
Forms melt into formlessness,
Events bow to decrees unseen,
And every whisper of creation
Traces back to the mouth
Of the Uncreated.
For causality—
The endless search for origins,
The fixation on material explanations—
Is but foam upon the waves
To the wise-one,
Who sees only the tide
Of divine vision.
For the ones granted prophecy
Were not selected by chance.
They were chosen
Because they honored the Creator,
Because their souls longed
For His favor,
Because their hearts
Were open to the truth
Before they even received it.
Among them,
Abraham, Moses, Ishmael, Enoch—
Each blessed,
Each raised in status,
Each showered in mercy.

❨And mention in the Book, The story of Abraham. He was surely A man of truth And a prophet…❩ ❨…And mention in the Book, The story of Moses. He was truly A chosen man, And was a messenger And a prophet…❩ ❨…And mention in the Book, The story of Enoch. He was surely A man of truth And a prophet. And We

elevated him To an honorable status. —*Quran 19:41-57*
Thus, the wise-one understands—
Divine grace is not earned.
It is not found in books.
It is bestowed,
A gift beyond human seeking,
A truth beyond the surface.
For only He lifts the ones He wills. 406
Only He grants wisdom beyond comprehension.
Only He remains
The source of knowledge
Not written, but revealed.
Knowledge is not merely an accumulation.
It is a bestowal,
A grace,
A gift beyond measure.
And those who receive it,
Those who bathe in its divine essence,
Speak not in citation,
But in certainty.
Not tracing their sources,
But pointing only to the Creator.

---

406 This aligns with the sacred words of the Quran, which proclaim that the choosing of prophets is not a matter of chance, but rather a divine gift bestowed upon them, rooted in their innate virtue of honoring the Creator and seeking His favor. This also speaks of various attributed of selected prophets including Enoch, known as Idrîs, who has been bestowed with great honor among them, both in stature and wisdom:

📖 ⟨And mention in the Book ʿO Prophet, the story ofˋ Abraham. He was surely a man of truth and a prophet. (41) ... So after he had left them and what they worshipped besides Allah, We granted him Isaac and Jacob, and made each of them a prophet. (49) We showered them with Our mercy, and blessed them with honourable mention.[1] (50) And mention in the Book ʿO Prophet, the story ofˋ Moses. He was truly a chosen man, and was a messenger and a prophet. (51) We called him from the right side of Mount Ṭûr, and drew him near, speaking ˋwith himˋ directly. (52) And We appointed for him—out of Our grace—his brother, Aaron, as a prophet. (53) And mention in the Book ʿO Prophet, the story ofˋ Ishmael. He was truly a man of his word, and was a messenger and a prophet. (54) He used to urge his people to pray and give alms-tax. And his Lord was well pleased with him. (55) And mention in the Book ʿO Prophet, the story ofˋ Enoch. He was surely a man of truth and a prophet. (56) And We elevated him to an honourable status.[2] (57) Those were ˋsome ofˋ the prophets who Allah has blessed from among the descendants of Adam, and of those We carried with Noah ˋin the Arkˋ, and of the descendants of Abraham and Israel,[3] and of those We ˋrightlyˋ guided and chose. Whenever the revelations of the Most Compassionate were recited to them, they fell down, prostrating and weeping. (58)⟩ [Quran 19:41 and 49-58]

[1]: On a daily basis, Muslims invoke Allah's blessings upon Prophet Muḥammad 🌟 and his family and Prophet Abraham 🌟 and his family, in both obligatory and optional prayers.

[2]: Prophet Enoch (Idrîs) 🌟 is said to be in the fourth heaven.

[3]: Israel is another name for Jacob 🌟.

For only He grants wisdom.
Only He bestows vision beyond knowing.
Only He remains the source
Of all understanding,
Seen and unseen.

So the wise-one walks forward,
Not fighting with what the heavens have planned,
He finds in his solace, his peace on this land.
He lets his spirit prostrate to a wisdom unknown,
And finds in His rida a peace all his own.

For only He is the One, the Ever-True,
Whose guidance is always sacred and new.
He is the Lord of both loss and of gain,
And to trust in His will is to go far.
For only He remains the source
Of Serenity, and boundless force.

Wisdom Unveiled

The profound wisdom of this contemplation is the realization that clairvoyant wisdom is a direct result of being immersed in Divine Grace (Fadl). The wise-one understands that this grace is not earned but is a bestowal from the Creator, a gift that allows them to perceive His hand in all affairs, transcending the need for worldly causality and intellectual validation. The story of Moses and the wise servant from Quran 18:65 and the reminder from Quran 20:114 serve as powerful testaments to this truth, illustrating that even prophets must surrender to divine timing and that the highest wisdom is a gift. This wisdom unveils that a heart submerged in this grace finds a profound contentment and gratitude, recognizing that every unfolding is a manifestation of the Creator's will, thereby dissolving resentment and boasts and leading to a state of perpetual serenity.

Wise-Reflection

Reflect on your own heart's contentment. Do you find yourself resentful of perceived misfortunes or boastful of perceived successes? Consider the thought, "When the heart swims in the sea of grace, It no longer asks which river brought the water. It drinks— And is satisfied." How can you cultivate a state of perpetual gratitude and contentment, immersing your heart so deeply in divine grace that you see the hand of the Creator in all things and find a profound serenity that transcends all worldly circumstances?

Contemplation: Referring All to the Creator's Will

To see beyond the surface is to embark on a journey that shatters the very foundations of worldly perception. The culmination of this spiritual ascent is the profound and liberating realization that all phenomena and events are a direct referral to the Creator's Will. This is not merely a belief, but a clairvoyant wisdom that invalidates the illusion of independent causality. The wise-one, through this heightened sight, no longer sees the fire as the agent of burning, or the rain as the cause of growth, but rather as mere instruments in the hands of the Divine. This contemplation guides the seeker from the shadow of cause and effect to the blazing reality of the Divine Source, where every particle and every movement is a direct expression of Allah's power and command. It is a journey from the fragmented, chaotic world of man-made explanations to the unified, serene universe of divine orchestration, where every event becomes a direct revelation of a Divine Name and Attribute, and the heart finds its ultimate refuge in the certainty of the One who wills all.

Part 1: Invalidation of Causality

The culmination of this reflection is the complete referral of all phenomena and events to the Creator's Will (Mashī'ah/Irādah). This is the essence of true clairvoyant wisdom.

The wise-one's clairvoyance leads them to attribute all occurrences to the Creator's will, bypassing the superficial layers of cause and effect that dominate worldly thinking.

This first part of the contemplation focuses on the invalidation of independent causality. The wise-one understands that while Allah establishes causes and effects in the created world, these causes have no inherent power of their own. Their effect is solely by Allah's continuous permission and creation. This deepens the understanding that the fire does not burn, the knife does not cut, and sustenance does not nourish, except by Allah's direct Will. This contemplation serves as a powerful testament to the illusion of independent causes, revealing a deeper reality where every event is a direct manifestation of the Creator's unwavering will.

> The Invalidity of Worldly Causality: The Divine Orchestration
> Behind All Occurrences

Lightning does not strike because of clouds.
Birds do not soar because of wings.
Rain does not fall because of heavy air.
All things are whispers—
Uttered by the Divine Will (Al-Mureed).
All causes dissolve
At the foot of His command.
For the wise-one sees—
Cause and effect
Are but illusions of limited understanding,
Mere shadows of a deeper reality,
Where every unfolding event,
Every movement,
Every force of nature
Bows only to the decree
Of the Creator.
The disbelievers mock,
Dismissing the notion
Of divine orchestration.
They reduce the workings of the universe
To coincidence,
To mere natural processes,
Blind to the hidden hand
Guiding all things.
They scoff at resurrection,
Laughing at the promise
That what has turned to dust
Can be restored to life.
❰Shall we show you a man Who claims that when you have been Utterly disintegrated
You will be raised As a new creation?❱ —Quran 34:7
Yet their skepticism
Is ignorance itself.
For if they truly observed,

If they truly perceived
All that surrounds them,
They would witness—
In the heavens,
In the earth,
In the unfolding of calamities—
The signs of divine power
That leave no room for doubt.
❨*If We willed, We could cause the earth To swallow them up, Or cause deadly pieces*
Of the sky To fall upon them.❩⁴⁰⁷ —*Quran 34:9*

And still,
They insist upon their blindness,
Stripping away
The Creator's hand from existence itself.
But He reveals
The reality of creation,
Showing how nothing unfolds
Except by His will.
The earth—
Dead and barren,
Only to spring forth
In grain and sustenance
By His command.
The gardens,
The palm trees,
The rivers,
The life-giving springs—
None of these
Are the result of random chance,

---

⁴⁰⁷ This aligns with the sacred verses that speak of the Creator's grasp in the seemingly natural events of landslides, earthquakes, and calamities, which, by divine decree, serve as both a punishment for His wayward servants and a profound lesson...and all that arises from the fury of lightning and the chaos of horizontal disasters is likewise a manifestation of retribution. And by His decree, the return of humanity is nigh:

📖 ❨The disbelievers say ˊmockingly to one anotherˋ, "Shall we show you a man who claims that when you have been utterly disintegrated you will be raised as a new creation? (7) Has he fabricated a lie against Allah or is he insane?" In fact, those who do not believe in the Hereafter are bound for torment and have strayed farthest ˊfrom the truthˋ. (8) Have they not then seen all that surrounds them of the heavens and the earth? If We willed, We could cause the earth to swallow them up, or cause ˊdeadlyˋ pieces of the sky to fall upon them. Surely in this is a sign for every servant who turns ˊto Allahˋ. (9)❩ [Quran 34:7-9]

But a sign
Of divine orchestration.

❨*There is a sign for them In the dead earth: We give it life, Producing grain For them
to eat. And We have placed in it Gardens of palm trees And grapevines, And caused
springs To gush forth in it.* —Quran 36:33-34

Yet the blind
Continue in their arrogance.
They do not bow,
They do not acknowledge,
They do not give thanks.
Even when the universe itself
Moves in perfect harmony,
Its design unfaltering,
Its paths ordained,
They refuse to see.

❨*The sun travels For its fixed term. That is the design Of the Almighty, All-
Knowing. As for the moon, We have ordained precise phases for it, Until it ends up
Looking like an old, curved palm stalk.*❩ —Quran 36:38-39

The stars,
The celestial bodies,
The cosmic movements—
None collide,
None outrun their course,
None falter.
For they follow
An order decreed
By the One
Who sustains all reality.

❨*It is not for the sun To catch up with the moon, Nor does the night Outrun the day.
Each is travelling In an orbit of their own.*❩[408] —Quran 36:40

---

[408] This aligns with the sacred verse that speaks of the cosmic events, which, beyond the grasp of mortal
understanding, are but a grand design woven by the will of the Creator, culminating in a harmonious whole
from what appears to be a myriad of occurrences within this realm:

📖 ❨There is a sign for them in the dead earth: We give it life, producing grain from it for them to eat. (33) And
We have placed in it gardens of palm trees and grapevines, and caused springs to gush forth in it, (34) so

But despite the grandeur
Of these divine signs,
They refuse.
They turn away.
They dismiss the truth
When it is placed before them.
Even when disaster strikes,
Even when the sky splits open,
Even when the earth trembles,
They claim it is
Nothing but nature.

❰*If they were to see A deadly piece of the sky Fall down upon them, Still they would*
say, 'This is just A pile of clouds.'❱ —*Quran 52:44*

To see beyond the chain
Is to see the Hand that moves all things. [409]
Thus, the wise-one understands—
Nothing moves except by Him.
No force exists
Independent of His will.
No occurrence
Is outside His knowledge.

---

that they may eat from its fruit, which they had no hand in making. Will they not then give thanks? (35) Glory be to the One Who created all ˹things in˺ pairs—˹be it˺ what the earth produces, their genders, or what they do not know! (36) There is also a sign for them in the night: We strip from it daylight, then—behold!—they are in darkness. (37) The sun travels for its fixed term. That is the design of the Almighty, All-Knowing. (38) As for the moon, We have ordained ˹precise˺ phases for it, until it ends up ˹looking˺ like an old, curved palm stalk. (39) It is not for the sun to catch up with the moon,[1] nor does the night outrun the day. Each is travelling in an orbit of their own. (40) Another sign for them is that We carried their ancestors ˹with Noah˺ in the fully loaded Ark, (41) and created for them similar things to ride in. (42) If We willed, We could drown them: then no one would respond to their cries, nor would they be rescued— (43) except by mercy from Us, allowing them enjoyment for a ˹little˺ while. (44) ˹Still they turn away˺ when it is said to them, "Beware of what is ahead of you ˹in the Hereafter˺ and what is behind you ˹of destroyed nations˺ so you may be shown mercy." (45) Whenever a sign comes to them from their Lord, they turn away from it. (46)❱ [Quran 36:33-46]

[1]: The moon completes a cycle every month (waxing and waning), while the sun takes a whole year to complete its cycle (resulting in the spring, summer, fall, and winter seasons).

[409] This aligns with the sacred verse that speaks of the disbeliever, lost in a haze, unable to perceive the signs and the divine presence woven into the fabric of creation:

📖 ❰Or do they have access to ˹the Record in˺ the unseen, so they copy it ˹for all to see˺? (41) Or do they intend to scheme ˹against the Prophet˺? Then it is the disbelievers who will fall victim to ˹their˺ schemes. (42) Or do they have a god other than Allah? Glorified is Allah far above what they associate ˹with Him˺! (43) If they were to see a ˹deadly˺ piece of the sky fall down ˹upon them˺, still they would say, "˹This is just˺ a pile of clouds." (44) So leave them until they face their Day in which they will be struck dead— (45) the Day their scheming will be of no benefit to them whatsoever, nor will they be helped. (46)❱ [Quran 52:41-46]

For every earthquake,
Every storm,
Every shift in the cosmos
Is a decree,
Not a happenstance.
Nothing unfolds
Without purpose.
Nothing exists
Without His design.
Thus, the wise-one walks forward,
Not bound by illusion,
Not weighed by earthly reasoning,
But carrying only the certainty
That every movement,
Every breath,
Every unfolding event
Is by His decree alone.
For only He sustains reality.
Only He commands existence.
Only He remains the source
Of all that was, is, and will be.

So the wise-one walks forward,
Not fighting with what the heavens have planned,
He finds in his solace, his peace on this land.
He lets his spirit prostrate to a wisdom unknown,
And finds in His rida a peace all his own.

For only He is the One, the Ever-True,
Whose guidance is always sacred and new.
He is the Lord of both loss and of gain,
And to trust in His will is to go far.
For only He remains the source
Of Serenity, and boundless force.

Wisdom Unveiled

The profound wisdom of this contemplation is the realization that clairvoyant wisdom leads to the invalidation of independent causality. The wise-one understands that while Allah establishes causes and effects in the created world, these causes have no inherent power of their own; their effect is solely by His continuous permission and creation. The verses from Quran 34:7-9, 36:33-40, and 52:44 serve as a powerful testament to this truth, illustrating how the disbelievers are blind to the divine orchestration behind natural phenomena, attributing them to mere coincidence. This wisdom unveils that a heart that sees beyond the chain of worldly causality finds an unshakable certainty, recognizing that every event, from the movement of the celestial bodies to the growth of a seed, is a direct manifestation of the Creator's will.

Wise-Reflection

Reflect on your own perception of cause and effect. When you see a beautiful sunset, a flourishing garden, or a powerful storm, do you attribute the event to natural processes alone, or do you see the hand of the Creator behind it? Consider the thought, "To see beyond the chain Is to see the Hand that moves all things." How can you cultivate a vision that invalidates the illusion of independent causality, allowing you to find a profound certainty in the divine orchestration of all occurrences?

Part 2: The Divine Source of All Things

This leads directly to the realization of the Divine Source of all things. Every particle, every movement, every event originates directly from Allah's power and command. The "clairvoyant wisdom" is to see the One in the many, the Creator in His creation, without any intermediary truly possessing independent power. The Quranic questions in 10:31-"Who provides... Who owns... Who brings forth... Who conducts every affair?"-all point to Allah as the singular Source.

The wise-one understands that all apparent forms and events are merely manifestations of an Unseen Will. This contemplation serves as a powerful testament to the spiritual insight that sees beyond the surface of creation to its singular Divine Source. By recognizing that all things, from the creation of a human being to the movement of the celestial bodies, are a direct result of the Creator's will, the wise-one is freed from the illusion of independent causation, finding profound serenity in the absolute certainty that all of existence traces back to the mouth of the Uncreated.

The Divine Source of All Things: The Unfolding Decree Behind All Existence

The wise-one sees—
Forms melt into formlessness,
Events bow to decrees unseen,
And every whisper of creation
Traces back to the mouth
Of the Uncreated.
"The wise-one knows That all appeared forms and incidences Stem from the
knowability Of the Truth-Maker— The Creator's own will."
For behind all appearances,
Beneath all forms,
Beyond every seemingly independent cause,
Lies the Truth-Maker,
The one source
From which all emerges,
By which all moves,
To which all returns.
Thus, when mankind wonders,
When doubt settles upon their hearts,
When they gaze upon scattered bones
And question their return to life,
They forget—
Creation itself
Was already an unfathomable miracle.
❨O humanity! If you are in doubt About the Resurrection, Then know that We did
create you From dust, Then from a sperm-drop, Then developed you Into a clinging
clot, Then a lump of flesh— Fully formed or unformed— In order to demonstrate
Our power to you.❩ —Quran 22:5
From the unseen depths of the womb,
From the smallest seed of existence,
From the silent formation
Of human life itself—
Who can claim
These were works of chance?
Who can deny
The One who wrote the decree

Of every transition,
Every phase,
Every hidden process
Long before time itself began?
❬That is because Allah alone Is the Truth, He alone gives life to the dead, And He
alone Is Most Capable of everything.❭[410] *—Quran 22:6*

And yet,
Despite the clarity of creation,
Despite the unfolding of His signs
Through every breath,
Every drop of rain,
Every rising dawn,
Mankind refuses to acknowledge
The hand that gives them all.
The heavens expand,
The earth thrives,
The rain nourishes,
The rivers carve their paths—
All signs,
All reminders
Of the Giver.
❬He created humans From a sperm-drop, Then—behold!— They openly challenge
Him.❭ —Quran 16:4

---

[410] This aligns with the sacred verse that recounts the tale of human creation in a meticulously woven manner, a narrative that eluded understanding until this present age:

▱ ❬O humanity! If you are in doubt about the Resurrection, then ˹know that˺ We did create you from dust[1], then from a sperm-drop,[2] then ˹developed you into˺ a clinging clot,[3] then a lump of flesh[4]—fully formed or unformed[5]—in order to demonstrate ˹Our power˺ to you. ˹Then˺ We settle whatever ˹embryo˺ We will in the womb for an appointed term, then bring you forth as infants, so that you may reach your prime. Some of you ˹may˺ die ˹young˺, while others are left to reach the most feeble stage of life so that they may know nothing after having known much. And you see the earth lifeless, but as soon as We send down rain upon it, it begins to stir ˹to life˺ and swell, producing every type of pleasant plant. (5) That is because Allah ˹alone˺ is the Truth, He ˹alone˺ gives life to the dead, and He ˹alone˺ is Most Capable of everything. (6) And certainly the Hour is coming, there is no doubt about it. And Allah will surely resurrect those in the graves. (7)❭ [Quran 22:5-7]

[1]: Your father, Adam.

[2]: Nuṭfah refers to the union of male and female gametes (sperm and egg) which results in the zygote after fertilization.

[3]:'Alaqah, meaning the embryo resembles a leech.

[4]: Muḍghah, meaning it resembles a chewed morsel.

[5]: Fully formed or defected, evolving into a healthy embryo or ending in miscarriage.

What blindness causes one
To stand beneath the rain,
To drink from the rivers,
To walk upon the firm earth,
To sail the seas,
To witness the motion of the stars,
And yet deny the One
Who holds all of it in place?

⟨*He has placed Into the earth Firm mountains, So it does not shake with you, As well as rivers, And pathways So you may find your way. Also by landmarks And stars Do people find their way.*⟩ —*Quran 16:15-16*

Even when the night merges into day,
Even when the sun and moon
Move in perfect harmony,
Even when the universe itself
Obeys its unseen command—
They do not reflect.
They fail to grasp
That nothing moves,
Nothing exists,
Nothing survives
Outside His decree.
And if they counted
His favors,
If they attempted
To measure His mercy,
They would never
Reach its end.

⟨*If you tried To count Allah's blessings, You would never Be able to number them.*⟩
[411] —*Quran 16:18*

---

[411] This resonates with the sacred words that speak of the Creator's bountiful gifts bestowed upon humankind, and yet, despite such abundant grace, many remain shrouded in the darkness of denial.

📖 ⟨The command of Allah is at hand, so do not hasten it. Glorified and Exalted is He above what they associate ˹with Him in worship˺! (1) He sends down the angels with revelation by His command to whoever He wills of His servants, ˹stating:˺ "Warn ˹humanity˺ that there is no god ˹worthy of worship˺ except Me, so

Behind every curtain,
Behind every cause,
There stands the Only Cause (Al-Saboor),
Patient, perfect, and supreme.
The ultimate truth lies in the Creator's authority, even when diverse forms and events
appear in varying shapes, times, or causes.
Thus, the wise-one understands—
The visible
Is merely the veil
Over the invisible decree.
Every breath,
Every movement,
Every drop of rain,
Every trembling leaf
Is a manifestation
Of the Unseen Will.
For only He sustains creation.
Only He moves existence forward.
Only He remains

---

be mindful of Me ˹alone˺." (2) He created the heavens and the earth for a purpose. Exalted is He above what they associate with Him ˹in worship˺! (3) He created humans from a sperm-drop, then—behold!— they openly challenge ˹Him˺. (4) And He created the cattle for you as a source of warmth, food, and ˹many other˺ benefits. (5) They are also pleasing to you when you bring them home and when you take them out to graze. (6) And they carry your loads to ˹distant˺ lands which you could not otherwise reach without great hardship. Surely your Lord is Ever Gracious, Most Merciful. (7) ˹He also created˺ horses, mules, and donkeys for your transportation and adornment. And He creates what you do not know. (8) It is upon Allah ˹alone˺ to ˹clearly˺ show the Straight Way. Other ways are deviant. Had He willed, He would have easily imposed guidance upon all of you. (9) He is the One Who sends down rain from the sky, from which you drink and by which plants grow for your cattle to graze. (10) With it He produces for you ˹various˺ crops, olives, palm trees, grapevines, and every type of fruit. Surely in this is a sign for those who reflect. (11) And He has subjected for your benefit the day and the night, the sun and the moon. And the stars have been subjected by His command. Surely in this are signs for those who understand. (12) And ˹He subjected˺ for you whatever He has created on earth of varying colours.[1] Surely in this is a sign for those who are mindful. (13) And He is the One Who has subjected the sea, so from it you may eat tender seafood and extract ornaments to wear. And you see the ships ploughing their way through it, so you may seek His bounty and give thanks ˹to Him˺. (14) He has placed into the earth firm mountains, so it does not shake with you, as well as rivers, and pathways so you may find your way. (15) Also by landmarks and stars do people find their way. (16) Can the One Who creates be equal to those who do not? Will you not then be mindful? (17) If you tried to count Allah's blessings, you would never be able to number them. Surely Allah is All-Forgiving, Most Merciful. (18) And Allah knows what you conceal and what you reveal. (19) But those ˹idols˺ they invoke besides Allah cannot create anything—they themselves are created. (20) They are dead, not alive—not even knowing when their followers will be resurrected. (21) Your God is ˹only˺ One God. As for those who do not believe in the Hereafter, their hearts are in denial, and they are too proud. (22) Without a doubt, Allah knows what they conceal and what they reveal. He certainly does not like those who are too proud. (23)❫ [Quran 16:1-23]

[1]: The verse refers to the diverse creatures that have been created for the service of humanity.

The source of all that was,
Is, and will be.

So the wise-one walks forward,
Not fighting with what the heavens have planned,
He finds in his solace, his peace on this land.
He lets his spirit prostrate to a wisdom unknown,
And finds in His rida a peace all his own.

For only He is the One, the Ever-True,
Whose guidance is always sacred and new.
He is the Lord of both loss and of gain,
And to trust in His will is to go far.
For only He remains the source
Of Serenity, and boundless force.

Wisdom Unveiled

The profound wisdom of this contemplation is the realization that clairvoyant wisdom leads to the direct apprehension of the Divine Source of all things. The wise-one understands that all forms and events, though seemingly disparate, originate from the singular will and power of the Creator. The verses from Quran 22:5-7 and 16:1-23 serve as a powerful testament to this truth, illustrating how the creation of humanity and the harmonious orchestration of the cosmos are irrefutable signs of Allah's singular authority. This wisdom unveils that a heart that sees the One in the many is liberated from the blindness of doubt, finding an unshakable peace in the knowledge that every breath, every movement, and every unfolding of existence is a direct manifestation of the Unseen Will, and that no intermediary possesses independent power.

Wise-Reflection

Reflect on the many blessings in your life. Do you attribute them to your own efforts, to luck, or to the generosity of others? Consider the thought, "Behind every curtain, behind every cause, there stands the Only Cause (Al-Saboor)." How can you cultivate a vision that sees the Divine Source behind every gift and every unfolding event, allowing you to find a profound gratitude that dissolves the illusion of independent causes and an ultimate contentment in the knowledge that all blessings flow from Him?

Part 3: The Names of the Creator

The culmination of this reflection is the complete referral of all phenomena and events to the Creator's Will (Mashī'ah/Irādah). This is the essence of true clairvoyant wisdom.

The wise-one's clairvoyance leads them to attribute all occurrences to the Creator's will, bypassing the superficial layers of cause and effect that dominate worldly thinking.

This final part of the contemplation, "The Names of the Creator," affirms that true spiritual sight recognizes the active manifestations of Allah's Names and Attributes in every phenomenon. Instead of seeing 'nature' or 'circumstance' as causes, the wise-one sees the direct work of Al-Khaliq (The Creator), Al-Razzaq (The Provider), Al-Muhyi (The Giver of Life), and Al-Mureed (The One Who Wills). This profound realization is the ultimate refuge, freeing the heart from the illusion of uncertainty and allowing it to rest in the unwavering certainty of Al-Haqq (The Absolute Truth) and Al-Wakeel (The Ultimate Trustee), upon whom every single thing relies.

The Divine Sovereignty: The Ultimate Refuge Beyond All Uncertainty

---

He is Al-Haqq—The Absolute Truth.
He is Al-Wakeel—The Ultimate Trustee.
Upon Him,
Every trembling leaf rests,
Every soaring soul leans,
Every whisper of existence traces its origin.
To know this is to find rest—
For one no longer leans on the shifting winds.
To recognize Him
Is to awaken.
"This understanding aligns With the Creator's names, Such as 'The Truth' And
'The Proxy.'"
Thus, the wise-one sees—

The foundation of all reality
Is not formed by men,
Nor written by time,
Nor bound by mortal comprehension.
It is He—
The Ever-Living,
The All-Sustaining,
Who neither tires nor sleeps,
Whose knowledge is beyond grasp,
Whose command is unfaltering.

❴*Allah! There is no god Worthy of worship Except Him, The Ever-Living, All-Sustaining. Neither drowsiness Nor sleep overtakes Him. To Him belongs Whatever is in the heavens And whatever is on the earth.*❵[412] —Quran 2:255

He is the Supreme Provider.
The Source of Power.
The Eternal Majesty.

❴*I did not create Jinn and humans Except to worship Me. I seek no provision from them, Nor do I need them to feed Me. Indeed, Allah alone Is the Supreme Provider— Lord of all Power, Ever Mighty.*❵[413] —Quran 51:56-58

And yet, despite His grandeur,
Despite the signs placed
In the heavens and the earth,
Despite His omnipresence
Surrounding every whisper,

---

[412] This aligns with the sacred words that speak of the supreme dominion of the Creator over all that has been wrought:

📖 ❴Allah! There is no god ˹worthy of worship˺ except Him, the Ever-Living, All-Sustaining. Neither drowsiness nor sleep overtakes Him. To Him belongs whatever is in the heavens and whatever is on the earth. Who could possibly intercede with Him without His permission? He ˹fully˺ knows what is ahead of them and what is behind them, but no one can grasp any of His knowledge—except what He wills ˹to reveal˺. His Seat[1] encompasses the heavens and the earth, and the preservation of both does not tire Him. For He is the Most High, the Greatest.[2] (255)❵ [Quran 2:255]

[1]: The Arabic word kursi can either mean seat or knowledge. There are some narrations attributed to Prophet Muḥammad ﷺ that describe Allah's Throne ('Arsh) as being greater than His Kursi.

[2]: According to Muslim belief, this is the greatest verse in the Quran.

[413] This aligns with the sacred scripture that recounts the Names and Attributes of the Creator, revealing their earthly significance to grasp their essence:

📖 ❴I did not create jinn and humans except to worship Me. (56) I seek no provision from them, nor do I need them to feed Me. (57) Indeed, Allah ˹alone˺ is the Supreme Provider—Lord of all Power, Ever Mighty. (58)❵ [Quran 51:56-58]

Every hidden thought,
Every private conversation—
Mankind still doubts.

❨*Do you not see That Allah knows Whatever is in the heavens And whatever is on*
the earth? If three converse privately, He is their fourth. If five, He is their sixth.
Whether fewer or more, He is with them Wherever they may be.❩ —*Quran 58:7*

He is Al-Aleem—The All-Knowing.
Nothing escapes Him.
Nothing unfolds beyond His sight.
Nothing is concealed from His decree.
And when men attempt to deny,
When nations rise against His truth,
When arrogance blinds the hearts
Of those who reject—
His will prevails.

❨*Allah has decreed, 'I and My messengers Will certainly prevail.' Surely Allah Is*
All-Powerful, Almighty.❩[414] —*Quran 58:21*

For who can defy
The One to whom
All dominion belongs?
Who can rewrite fate
When He has already spoken?
Who can undo
What He has ordained?

❨*To Allah belongs Whatever is in the heavens And the earth. Allah is truly The*
Self-Sufficient, Praiseworthy.❩ —*Quran 31:26*

Even if all trees
Became pens,
Even if all oceans
Turned to ink,

---

[414] This aligns with the sacred verse that speaks of the Creator's ever-watchful presence, bearing witness to the quietest of human murmurs:

📖 ❨Do you not see that Allah knows whatever is in the heavens and whatever is on the earth? If three converse privately, He is their fourth. If five, He is their sixth. Whether fewer or more, He is with them[1] wherever they may be. Then, on the Day of Judgment, He will inform them of what they have done. Surely Allah has ˹perfect˺ knowledge of all things. (7)❩

And then His supreme might that His messengers and their followers are the victorious:

📖 ❨Allah has decreed, "I and My messengers will certainly prevail." Surely Allah is All-Powerful, Almighty. (21)❩ [Quran 58:7 and 21]

[1]: By His knowledge.

[675]

His words,
His knowledge,
His decree
Could never be exhausted.

❲*If all the trees on earth Were pens And the ocean were ink, Refilled by seven other oceans, The Words of Allah Would not be exhausted.*❳ [415] —*Quran 31:27*

Thus, the wise-one understands—
It is He alone
Who commands all things.
Every breath,
Every movement,
Every hidden destiny
Is known only to Him.
Tomorrow remains unknown
To every living soul,
Yet He sees beyond the veil
Of the unseen.

❲*No soul knows What it will earn for tomorrow, And no soul knows In what land it will die. Surely Allah Is All-Knowing, All-Aware.*❳ [416] —*Quran 31:34*

---

[415] This resonates with the sacred scripture, which ascribes various names to the Almighty, reflecting His grandeur in creation, allowing humanity a glimpse of understanding the names of the Creator:

📖 ❲To Allah belongs whatever is in the heavens and the earth. Allah is truly the Self-Sufficient, Praiseworthy. (26) If all the trees on earth were pens and the ocean ˹were ink˺, refilled by seven other oceans, the Words of Allah would not be exhausted. Surely Allah is Almighty, All-Wise. (27) The creation and resurrection of you ˹all˺ is as simple ˹for Him˺ as that of a single soul. Surely Allah is All-Hearing, All-Seeing. (28) Do you not see that Allah causes the night to merge into the day and the day into the night, and has subjected the sun and the moon, each orbiting for an appointed term, and that Allah is All-Aware of what you do? (29) That is because Allah ˹alone˺ is the Truth and what they invoke besides Him is falsehood, and ˹because˺ Allah ˹alone˺ is the Most High, All-Great. (30) Do you not see that the ships sail ˹smoothly˺ through the sea by the grace of Allah so that He may show you some of His signs? Surely in this are signs for whoever is steadfast, grateful. (31)❳ [Quran 31:26-31]

[416] This aligns with the verse that speaks of the Creator's boundless wisdom and understanding of all that lies beyond the grasp of mortal minds:

📖 ❲Indeed, Allah ˹alone˺ has the knowledge of the Hour. He sends down the rain,[1] and knows what is in the wombs.[2] No soul knows what it will earn for tomorrow, and no soul knows in what land it will die. Surely Allah is All-Knowing, All-Aware. (34)❳ [Quran 31:34]

[1]: He knows precisely when, where, and how much rain falls, and whether it is going to be drunk by people and animals or used for irrigation, or absorbed by the earth, etc.

[2]: The Prophet ﷺ was reported in a ḥadîth collected by Bukhârî and Muslim to have said, "Indeed, the creation of each one of you is brought together in the womb of one's mother as a drop of ˹male and female˺ discharges for forty days, then one becomes a clinging clot for a similar period, then a lump of flesh for a similar period. Then an angel is sent to blow the breath of life into the embryo. The angel is then commanded to write four things: one's destined provisions, lifespan, actions, and whether one will be happy or miserable ˹in the Hereafter˺."

Lean only upon Him—
And you will never fall.
These divine attributes reinforce the wise-one's trust in the Creator's will as the origin
of all existence.
Thus, the wise-one walks forward,
No longer fearful of uncertainty,
No longer searching for shelter
In the fleeting promises of the world,
But resting only
In the hands of the Ultimate Trustee.
For only He sustains certainty.
Only He unveils the unseen.
Only He remains the refuge
Of all who seek the truth beyond illusion.

So the wise-one walks forward,
Not fighting with what the heavens have planned,
He finds in his solace, his peace on this land.
He lets his spirit prostrate to a wisdom unknown,
And finds in His rida a peace all his own.

For only He is the One, the Ever-True,
Whose guidance is always sacred and new.
He is the Lord of both loss and of gain,
And to trust in His will is to go far.
For only He remains the source
Of Serenity, and boundless force.

Wisdom Unveiled

The profound wisdom of this contemplation is the ultimate realization that true spiritual sight, or "clairvoyant wisdom," is the complete affirmation of the Names of the Creator as the ultimate agents behind all phenomena. The wise-one understands that every event, from the provision of sustenance to the manifestation of death, is a direct expression of a Divine Name and Attribute. The verses from Quran 2:255, 51:56-58, 58:7-21, and 31:26-34 serve as powerful testaments to this truth, illustrating His supreme dominion, His all-encompassing knowledge, and His unwavering power. This wisdom unveils that to see the Creator in His creation is to find a profound rest, for the heart no longer leans on the shifting winds of worldly causation but finds its ultimate refuge and certainty in Al-Haqq and Al-Wakeel, the Absolute Truth and Ultimate Trustee.

Wise-Reflection

Reflect on the events in your life. Do you see them as a result of 'luck' or 'circumstance,' or do you see them as a direct manifestation of a Divine Name? Consider the thought, "Lean only upon Him— And you will never fall." How can you cultivate a heart that is so grounded in the knowledge of the Creator's Names that every event, whether seemingly good or bad, becomes a source of profound trust, gratitude, and a complete surrender to His will?

Conclusion: Referring All to the Creator's Will

In the end, the wise-one's journey culminates in an unshakeable certainty that every occurrence, every blessing, and every trial is a direct manifestation of the Creator's Will. By transcending the illusion of independent causality, the heart is freed from the tyranny of worldly explanations and the shifting winds of circumstance. The wise-one no longer leans on created means but rests entirely in the unwavering embrace of the Ultimate Trustee, Al-Wakeel. This spiritual clarity affirms the Names of the Creator as the true agents behind all phenomena—whether it is the provision of sustenance (Al-Razzaq) or the unfolding of destiny (Al-Mureed). The heart finds its ultimate peace and contentment in this submission, for it understands that all existence traces its origin back to the One, Al-Haqq, the Absolute Truth. To live in this state is to find rest, to move with a profound sense of purpose, and to witness a reality where every event is a testament to His infinite wisdom and boundless power.

Conclusion: Seeing Beyond the Surface

ECHOES OF REALIZATION: THE EYE BEYOND EYES

There exists a transcendent eye beyond the limited eyes of mere flesh—an eye that perceives not merely the ripple of an effect, but the very pebble cast by the Majestic Hand of the Creator. The wise-one who consistently gazes with this profound spiritual eye ceases entirely to blame superficial causes, ceases to frantically chase after fleeting effects, and ceases to cling to the temporary tyranny of forms.

They move through existence as the unburdened wind moves at His subtle decree—silent in their acceptance, certain in their surrender, and completely yielded to the Divine Flow. For they have witnessed with absolute clarity: all roads, all rivers, all ruins, and indeed, all resurrections, begin and ultimately end at His singular command alone.

THE SEEKER'S ASCENT: THE ESSENCE OF CLAIRVOYANT WISDOM

Clairvoyant wisdom is a truly divine gift that profoundly elevates the wise-one beyond limiting worldly constructs, illuminating the Creator's singular Will as the ultimate, true Source of all existence. By consciously omitting the perceived "chains of validation" and focusing solely on the Divine Act, the wise-one aligns their understanding completely with the Creator's timeless truth. This enlightened perspective fosters immense clarity, deep humility, and an ever-deepening connection to the Creator, enabling the wise-one to navigate the complexities of life with unwavering trust in boundless Divine Grace.

To truly see beyond the surface is to become spiritually blind to the fleeting illusions of appearances and to become, simultaneously, utterly clear-sighted to the Only Absolute Reality. True clairvoyance strips away, layer by layer, the deceptive illusions of independent causality, false autonomy, and self-generated striving, and reveals with pristine clarity that all things— whether perceived as beautiful or broken—are but perfect, precise strokes of the same singular, Divine Pen. The wise-one who sees in this profound, all-encompassing way, becomes a pure mirror reflecting the Creator's Will, living not by fear, nor by intricate calculation, but solely by the luminous light of unveiled, absolute trust. This deep psychic transformation is crucial for navigating " The Triumph of Self-Mastery."

CONCLUSION FOR PART IV: THE TRIUMPH OF SELF-MASTERY

(The Soul's Ascendancy...)

ECHO WITHIN THE HEART... (THE SELF REFINED, THE VISION CLEAR)

The Manifestation of The Triumph of Self-Mastery does not conclude; rather, it elevates, like a mountain peak piercing the clouds, revealing the vastness of the sky beyond. The wise-one, having navigated the active disciplines and overcome the inner obstacles, now stands at the threshold of an even more profound, more luminous realization: true self-mastery is not a static achievement, but a dynamic state of continuous vigilance and profound inner freedom, to be lived in every breath. Each reflection meticulously laid along this pathway has not served merely as a signpost; it has wrought a profound empowerment—a meticulous dismantling of self-limiting beliefs, a burning away of subtle impurities, and a sacred unveiling of the inherent authority intrinsically woven into the soul's very essence.

THRESHOLD OF AWE

The Unveiling of Inner Authority

As the veils gently lift upon this Manifestation of The Triumph of Self-Mastery, the wise-one transitions from effort to effortless grace. The contemplations engaged within this part—of embracing trials with acceptance, of breaking the chains of ingrained habits, of aligning one's entire being with the Divine Will, of cultivating a profound sincerity in every action, and of seeing beyond the superficial surface to the underlying Reality—do not merely add to one's store of information. Rather, they fundamentally reshape the very faculties that are capable of perceiving Divine truths and embodying spiritual excellence, preparing the wise-one for the ultimate zenith of liberation.

Pillars of Realization

Embraced Trials as Pathways:

The heart no longer resists challenges; it welcomes them as divinely appointed opportunities for growth, understanding that true strength lies in accepting the Divine decree with patience and contentment.

Habits as Broken Chains:

The discerning soul has recognized the subtle tyranny of ingrained patterns and actively loosened their grip, paving the way for conscious choices guided by divine principles rather than unconscious impulses.

Alignment as Resonant Being:

Every intention, every action, every thought now resonates with the Divine Will, creating a profound inner harmony where personal desires dissolve into the universal purpose, bringing peace and fulfillment.

Sincerity as Pure Radiance:

Deeds are no longer performed for external validation or internal reward, but solely for the sake of the Creator's Face, transforming ordinary actions into acts of profound worship and inner light.

Seeing Beyond as True Perception:

The eyes of the wise-one now perceive the Divine Hand in every occurrence, transcending the illusions of causality and recognizing Allah as the singular Source and ultimate Actor in all of existence.

The Seeker Reflects

"I have sharpened my inner sword, not to fight the world, but to master my own self. Where I once saw overwhelming temptations, I now perceive veiled opportunities for deeper surrender. My habits, once my masters, are now my servants, disciplined by conscious choice. The very rhythm of my heart has shifted, beating in alignment with a Will vaster than my own. My actions, once a blend of motives, are now purified, flowing from a sincere spring. And my vision, once clouded by appearances, now pierces through the surface, seeing the Divine in every unfolding. I stand, not just as one transformed by trials, but as one who actively co-creates my inner reality, ready for the ultimate freedom."

INVITATION TO THE NEXT MANIFESTATION

With this profound triumph of self-mastery, the sacred path now unfolds to its final, most exalted station: The Zenith of Liberation. If this Manifestation revealed the active discipline and purification of the inner being, the next invites the soul to experience the ultimate freedom that transcends all earthly attachments and limitations. The wise-one, having mastered the self, must now fully release all that binds, ascending towards a state of pure, unadulterated spiritual liberation.

Call to Action

"The self has been triumphed over; will you now take the final, liberating step into boundless freedom?"

FIFTH STATION

PART V: THE ZENITH OF LIBERATION

❖ ❖ ❖

﴿ ذَٰلِكَ هُدَى ٱللَّهِ يَهْدِى بِهِۦ مَن يَشَآءُ مِنْ عِبَادِهِۦ ۚ وَلَوْ أَشْرَكُواْ لَحَبِطَ عَنْهُم مَّا كَانُواْ يَعْمَلُونَ (88) أُوْلَـٰٓئِكَ ٱلَّذِينَ ءَاتَيْنَـٰهُمُ ٱلْكِتَـٰبَ وَٱلْحُكْمَ وَٱلنُّبُوَّةَ ۚ فَإِن يَكْفُرْ بِهَا هَـٰٓؤُلَآءِ فَقَدْ وَكَّلْنَا بِهَا قَوْمًا لَّيْسُواْ بِهَا بِكَـٰفِرِينَ (89)﴾

 ❨This is Allah's guidance with which He guides whoever He
wills of His servants. Had they associated others with Him ⸢in
worship⸣, their ⸢good⸣ deeds would have been wasted. (88) Those were
the ones to whom We gave the Scripture, wisdom, and prophethood.
But if these ⸢pagans⸣ disbelieve in this ⸢message⸣, then We have
already entrusted it to a people who will never disbelieve in it. (89)❩
[Quran 6:88-89]

"When the heart is detached, it finds wings." – Anonymous Sufi saying

❖ ❖ ❖

Having meticulously cultivated self-mastery and purified intentions, the wise-one now stands at the very summit of their spiritual ascent: The Zenith of Liberation. This final, profound part unveils the ultimate freedom that arises from a complete detachment from the transient world, revealing a state of being where the soul, unburdened by attachments, resides in perfect harmony with Divine Will.

This station invites the seeker to transcend the final vestiges of worldly concerns, surrendering fully to the Creator's all-encompassing plan. Here, every perceived burden dissipates, every fleeting desire loses its grip, and every attachment to temporal forms gives way to an enduring connection with the Eternal. It meticulously guides the wise-one through reflections that reveal the profound peace found in ultimate surrender, and the boundless joy that accompanies complete spiritual freedom.

Each reflection within this profound section acts like a final key, unlocking the gates to the highest spiritual realization. From achieving ultimate Mastery Over the Self, where every internal struggle is resolved, to experiencing the absolute Liberation from Attachments, allowing the soul to soar unhindered by worldly concerns. These culminate in a state of unparalleled inner peace and alignment, where the wise-one lives in the world yet is not of the world, truly embodying the essence of Divine grace.

At its core, this Manifestation beckons the discerning soul to shed all remaining veils, even the subtle ones of personal will and perceived autonomy. It explores profound shifts in being: from striving to effortless living, from clinging to release, and from seeking external validation to finding ultimate fulfillment within the Divine embrace. It challenges the wise-one to relinquish all that binds, to embrace unwavering trust, and to cultivate a heart that is light, boundless, and eternally directed towards its true Origin.

This Zenith is not an endpoint of growth, but the ultimate state of being from which all future growth flows. It is an invitation to perceive the boundless freedom in complete surrender, to discern the infinite joy in ultimate detachment, and to apprehend the eternal companionship born of total liberation. To walk this path is to initiate the ultimate unveiling, transcending the final veils of temporal existence, and to stand, utterly free, in the brilliance of Divine grace—a profound realization where the soul apprehends its true nature as irrevocably intertwined with the Eternal, living in the world with a heart in Paradise.

21ST REFLECTION: MASTERY OVER THE SELF

(The Triumph of Restraint)

THE GATEWAY VERSE

In the sacred words of Allah, a profound reminder of individual accountability and the personal nature of spiritual guidance::

📖 ⟨*O believers! You are accountable only for yourselves. It will not harm you if someone chooses to deviate—as long as you are ˹rightly˺ guided. To Allah you will all return, and He will inform you of what you used to do.*⟩ *[Quran 5:105]*

ILLUMINATION'S DAWN

There comes a sacred, pivotal hour in the profound journey of the soul when the wise-one realizes that the true spiritual battlefield is no longer the vast world outside—but the intricate, challenging inner terrain of the self. Here, in this intimate arena, the true jihad al-akbar (the greater struggle) commences: not against external enemies of flesh and blood, but against the restless appetites, the insidious whispering desires, and the pervasive illusions cunningly spun by the ego's deceptive hand.

The wise-one understands with profound clarity: true victory is not found in outward conquest or worldly dominance, but in rigorous restraint (zuhd, nafs-control). True spiritual greatness is not seized by exerting control over others or circumstances, but by absolute, willing surrender to the Higher Divine Command. Let us now walk, with courage and unwavering resolve, into this inner crucible, where deliberate mastery over the lower self becomes the very first key to unlocking the boundless treasures of Divine intimacy and liberation.

THE UNFOLDING OF INSIGHTS

This section delves into the disciplined process of mastering the self, exploring the dangers of unchecked desires, the importance of inner struggle, and the ultimate triumph found in aligning one's will with the Divine.

Contemplation: Terrifying Magnitude of Punishment

The wise-one, in understanding self-mastery, first reflects upon the terrifying magnitude of punishment (iqab) not merely for overt sins, but for spiritual heedlessness (ghaflah) and unchecked desires that lead to deviation. This contemplation is not to instill paralyzing fear, but to awaken the soul to the grave consequences of neglecting the inner struggle. It is a stark reminder that true harm often comes from within, from a self unbridled by spiritual discipline, ultimately affecting one's return to Allah, as implied by [417]❲To Allah you will all return, and He will inform you of what you used to do❳ [Quran 5:105].

The wise-one understands that the greater the spiritual gift, the greater the responsibility. This contemplation serves as a powerful testament to the gravity of spiritual betrayal. The stories of the people of Moses and Thamûd illustrate that those who have witnessed divine signs and tasted grace face a punishment of a far greater magnitude when they turn away. The wise-one's fear is not born of despair, but of reverence and a profound understanding that neglecting the inner struggle is a betrayal of the divine light that was once entrusted to them. This realization is the first step towards the rigorous self-restraint necessary for true liberation.

> The Terrifying Magnitude of Punishment: Betrayal Against Divine Light

The wise-one
Who sins after witnessing the signs
Bears the weight of betrayal—
Not only against the self,
But against the Light
That once trusted them.
Their fall
Echoes louder
In the halls of unseen worlds.
Thus, the wise-one fears—
Not in despair,
But in reverence,

---

[417] This is derived from the Quran verse of:

📖 ❲ O believers! You are accountable only for yourselves.[1] It will not harm you if someone chooses to deviate—as long as you are ˹rightly˺ guided. To Allah you will all return, and He will inform you of what you used to do. (105)❳ [Quran 5:105]

[1]: After fulfilling their obligation of delivering the truth, enjoining what is good, and forbidding what is evil.

Lest they trample
The gift of divine nearness.
Hence, their punishment
Shall be more terrifying
Than what punishment
Could be explained by.

For those
Who are close to the truth,
For those
Who have seen the signs,
For those
Who have tasted the grace—
Their failure resounds
With a magnitude beyond comprehension.

So it was
With the people of Moses,
Granted the covenant,
Witnesses to divine miracles,
Recipients of sacred law.
Yet they transgressed,
They schemed,
They twisted the command
To serve their desires.
❨During the Sabbath, Abundant fish Would come to them clearly visible, But on other days The fish were never seen. In this way We tested them For their rebelliousness.❩ —Quran 7:163

They did not simply err.
They did not merely slip.
They sought ways
To twist the command,
To circumvent the truth,
To justify deception.
❨But when they stubbornly Persisted in violation, We said to them, 'Be disgraced apes!'❩ —Quran 7:166

Thus, the wise-one understands—
Betrayal after grace
Is not simply a mistake,
But a rejection of the divine gift itself.
The sacred verses unfold the tale,
Detailing the defiance of Moses's people
Against the Creator's order
And the dire consequence
That befell them as a result.
Warnings were given.
Advisors urged them to stop.
Yet arrogance prevailed.

❲When they ignored the warning They were given, We rescued those Who used to warn against evil And overtook the wrongdoers With a dreadful punishment For their rebelliousness.❳ —Quran 7:165

Had they stopped,
Had they repented,
Had they honored the decree,
Their fate would have been different.
But instead,
They persisted.
And when rebellion
Became their only path,
When they rejected the covenant,
When they violated the trust,
Punishment descended
Beyond measure.

❲And remember, O Prophet, When your Lord declared That He would send against them Others who would make them suffer terribly Until the Day of Judgment.❳[418] —Quran 7:167

---

[418] This is in agreement with the Quran verses narrating the story of Moses's people who trespassed the Creator's orders not to fish on Saturday and sanctuary it for the sake of the Creator. Yet they trespass in a deceitful aggression toward the Creator's command, so they brought doom upon themselves:

So it was
With the people of Thamûd,
Whose hearts were hardened
By their worldly goods.
They lived in conceit,
In gardens and springs,
And carved out great homes,
Proud of all their things.
They mocked their own prophet,
Their brother Ṣâliḥ,
And asked for a sign,
If his truth was of Allah.

❲*Do you think You will be forever Left secure In what you have here— Amid gardens and springs, And crops, And palm trees Loaded with tender fruit?*❳ —
Quran 26:146-148

📖 ❲You are already aware of those of you who broke the Sabbath. We said to them, "Be disgraced apes!"[1] (65) So We made their fate an example to present and future generations, and a lesson to the God-fearing. (66)❳ [Quran 2:65-66]

[1]: Although many scholars believe that these individuals were turned into real apes, others interpret this verse in a metaphorical sense. This style is not uncommon in the Quran. See Quran 62:5 regarding the donkey that carries books and Quran 2:18 regarding the deaf, dumb, and blind.

This tale unfolds within the sacred verses, recounting the treachery and defiance of Moses's kin against the divine decree, and the dire retribution that befell them as a result of their transgressions.

📖 ❲Ask them ˹O Prophet˺ about ˹the people of˺ the town which was by the sea, who broke the Sabbath.[1] During the Sabbath, ˹abundant˺ fish would come to them clearly visible, but on other days the fish were never seen. In this way We tested them for their rebelliousness. (163) When some of ˹the righteous among˺ them questioned ˹their fellow Sabbath-keepers˺, "Why do you ˹bother to˺ warn those ˹Sabbath-breakers˺ who will either be destroyed or severely punished by Allah?" They replied, "Just to be free from your Lord's blame, and so perhaps they may abstain." (164) When they ignored the warning they were given, We rescued those who used to warn against evil and overtook the wrongdoers with a dreadful punishment for their rebelliousness. (165) But when they stubbornly persisted in violation, We said to them, "Be disgraced apes!"[2] (166) And ˹remember, O Prophet,˺ when your Lord declared that He would send against them others who would make them suffer terribly until the Day of Judgment. Indeed, your Lord is swift in punishment, but He is certainly All-Forgiving, Most Merciful. (167) We dispersed them through the land in groups—some were righteous, others were less so. We tested them with prosperity and adversity, so perhaps they would return ˹to the Right Path˺. (168)❳ [Quran 7:163-168]

[1]: The people of Aylah, an ancient town by the Red Sea, were forbidden to catch fish on the Sabbath. However, on Saturdays fish were everywhere, whereas on weekdays no fish were seen. To get around the prohibition, some decided to lay their nets on Fridays and collect the fish caught in their nets on Sundays. Those opposed to this practice were divided into two groups: one group tried to convince the offenders to honour the Sabbath, but soon gave up when their advice was not taken seriously. The second group was persistent in giving advice to the Sabbath-breakers. Eventually, the Sabbath-breakers were punished whereas the other two groups were saved.

[2]: Although many scholars believe that these individuals were turned into real apes, others interpret this verse in a metaphorical sense. This style is not uncommon in the Quran. See Quran 62:5 regarding the donkey that carries books and Quran 2:18 regarding the deaf, dumb, and blind.

A sign was then granted,
A she-camel of grace,
To share the water with them,
Each on an appointed day.

❮*Here is a camel. She will have her turn To drink As you have yours, Each on an*
appointed day. And do not Ever touch her with harm, Or you will be overtaken By
the torment Of a tremendous day.❯[419] —*Quran 26:155-156*

But arrogance grew,
And malice took hold,
They defied the command,
In a manner so bold.

❮*Then they killed the she-camel—defying their Lord's command—and challenged*
ˋ*Ṣâliḥ* ˋ, *"Bring us what you threaten us with, if you are* ˋ*truly* ˋ *one of the*
messengers.❯—*Quran 7:77*

They killed her,
They extinguished the sign.
They betrayed the trust,
And in their malice did they intertwine.
A dreadful punishment was set,
A fate they could not deny.
A mighty blast, a shock of death,
Fell from a vengeful sky.

---

[419] This aligns with the sacred verses that recount the tale of Thamûd, the people of the prophet Ṣâliḥ. They turned against the faith of their seer after demanding a sign of his divine message, yet their malice knew no bounds as they took the life of the sacred camel, the very sign they had sought from the above. Thus, they remained oblivious to the fact that they were unwittingly pursuing their own ruin and annihilation, a consequence of their brazen transgressions.

📖 ❮The people of Thamûd rejected the messengers (141) when their brother Ṣâliḥ said to them, "Will you not fear ˋAllah`? (142) I am truly a trustworthy messenger to you. (143) So fear Allah, and obey me. (144) I do not ask you for any reward for this ˋmessage`. My reward is only from the Lord of all worlds. (145) Do you think you will be ˋforever` left secure in what you have here: (146) amid gardens and springs, (147) and ˋvarious` crops, and palm trees ˋloaded` with tender fruit; (148) to carve homes in the mountains with great skill? (149) So fear Allah, and obey me. (150) And do not follow the command of the transgressors, (151) who spread corruption throughout the land, never setting things right." (152) They replied, "You are simply bewitched! (153) You are only a human being like us, so bring forth a sign if what you say is true." (154) Ṣâliḥ said, "Here is a camel. She will have her turn to drink as you have yours, each on an appointed day. (155) And do not ever touch her with harm, or you will be overtaken by the torment of a tremendous day." (156) But they killed her, becoming regretful. (157) So the punishment overtook them. Surely in this is a sign. Yet most of them would not believe. (158) And your Lord is certainly the Almighty, Most Merciful. (159)❯ [Quran 26:141-159]

❲*Then an ˹overwhelming˺ earthquake struck them, and they fell lifeless in their homes.*❳*420* —*Quran 7:78*

For they were shown the path,
The grace and light of truth,
Yet they chose to walk in blindness,
A tragic, bitter proof.

❲*As for Thamûd, We showed them guidance, but they preferred blindness over guidance. So the blast of a disgracing punishment overtook them for what they used to commit.*❳ —*Quran 41:17*

Thus, a heavy weight of warning,
The wise-one does perceive,
That to betray the given light,
Is a lesson to receive.
And so the word is carried,
A truth that must be said,
A mighty blast awaits the blind,
Just as it did the dead.

❲*If they turn away, then say, ˹O Prophet,˺ "I warn you of a ˹mighty˺ blast, like the one that befell 'Âd and Thamûd.*❳*421* —*Quran 41:13*

Thus, the wise-one understands—
There is no greater failure
Than rejecting what is granted in mercy.

---

420 This is derived from the Quran verses of:

📖 ❲Then they killed the she-camel—defying their Lord's command—and challenged ˹Ṣâliḥ˺, "Bring us what you threaten us with, if you are ˹truly˺ one of the messengers." (77) Then an ˹overwhelming˺ earthquake struck them, and they fell lifeless in their homes. (78)❳ [Quran 7:77-78]

421 This is derived from the Quran verse of:

📖 ❲If they turn away, then say, ˹O Prophet,˺ "I warn you of a ˹mighty˺ blast, like the one that befell 'Âd and Thamûd." (13) The messengers had come to them from all angles, ˹proclaiming,˺ "Worship none but Allah." They responded, "Had our Lord willed, He could have easily sent down angels ˹instead˺. So we totally reject what you have been sent with." (14) As for 'Âd, they acted arrogantly throughout the land with no right, boasting, "Who is superior to us in might?" Did they not see that Allah ˹Himself˺, Who created them, was far superior to them in might? Still they persisted in denying Our signs. (15) So We sent against them a furious wind,[1] for ˹several˺ miserable days, to make them taste a humiliating punishment in this worldly life. But far more humiliating will be the punishment of the Hereafter. And they will not be helped. (16) As for Thamûd, We showed them guidance, but they preferred blindness over guidance. So the blast of a disgracing punishment overtook them for what they used to commit. (17) And We delivered those who were faithful and were mindful ˹of Allah˺. (18)❳ [Quran 41:17]

[1]: lit., a bitter and screaming wind.

For knowledge demands responsibility.
For proximity demands purity.
For divine wisdom
Requires unwavering obedience.

The greater the love bestowed,
The deeper the sorrow when it is spurned.
O soul,
Cling fiercely to what you have been shown—
Lest it be sealed away.

Thus, the wise-one walks forward,
Not fearing loss,
But fearing betrayal,
Not in despair,
But in reverence,
Not burdened by punishment,
But humbled by responsibility.
For only He sustains justice.
Only He magnifies consequence
For those who were entrusted.
Only He remains the source
Of ultimate judgment,
Perfect accountability,
And boundless mercy.

So the wise-one walks forward,
Not fighting with what the heavens have planned,
He finds in his solace, his peace on this land.
He lets his spirit prostrate to a wisdom unknown,
And finds in His satisfaction (rida) a peace all his own.

For only He is the One, the Ever-True,
Whose guidance is always sacred and new.
He is the Lord of both loss and of gain,
And to trust in His will is to go far.
For only He remains the source
Of Serenity, and boundless force.

Wisdom Unveiled

The profound wisdom of this contemplation is the realization that true self-mastery begins with a reverent fear of spiritual heedlessness (ghaflah) and the terrifying magnitude of punishment (iqab) that befalls those who betray the divine trust. The wise-one understands that a person who has witnessed divine signs and tasted grace bears a far heavier responsibility. The stories from Quran 7:163-168 regarding the people of the Sabbath and Quran 26:141-159 concerning the people of Thamûd serve as powerful testaments to this truth. This wisdom unveils that spiritual failure after being shown the light is a rejection of a divine gift, leading not merely to punishment but to an enduring consequence that echoes louder in the unseen worlds. It is this profound understanding that compels the wise-one to a continuous and rigorous inner struggle for self-restraint.

Wise-Reflection

Reflect on your own spiritual journey. Do you see spiritual heedlessness as a minor failing, or do you recognize it as a profound betrayal of the divine light you have been granted? Consider the thought, "O soul, Cling fiercely to what you have been shown—Lest it be sealed away." How can you use the stories of those who transgressed after receiving divine signs as a motivation for greater vigilance and self-discipline, and what steps can you take today to honor the spiritual gifts you have been given?.

Contemplation: The Rule of Low of Magnified Punishment (for responsibility)

(For Those in the Creator's Grace)

The wise-one recognizes the rule of magnified punishment as one ascends in spiritual proximity and knowledge. For those blessed with greater insight and closer connection to the Divine, the subtle errors of the self, if left unchecked, carry a heavier spiritual consequence. This is not arbitrary; it is because greater knowledge brings greater responsibility. This motivates the wise-one to even greater vigilance over their inner state, knowing that their 'minor' deviations can be magnified in the Divine estimation, urging impeccable self-mastery.

The proximity to the Creator's grace elevates the wise-one to a position of heightened accountability. With greater knowledge and spiritual awareness comes a deeper responsibility to uphold divine principles. This contemplation serves as a powerful testament to the spiritual weight of nearness to the Divine. The stories of Prophet Muhammad and Prophet Jonah illustrate that those entrusted with divine knowledge are held to an unshakable standard. Their missteps, though human, are magnified in significance due to their elevated station. This realization is what drives the wise-one to a state of trembling vigilance, understanding that divine favor is not just an honor but a test of the soul that requires unwavering obedience and impeccable self-mastery.

The Magnified Consequence: Accountability for Those in the Creator's Grace

---

To be raised in wisdom
Is not merely to receive honor,
But to bear its weight.
To be granted divine knowledge
Is not simply a gift,
But a responsibility.
For the wise-one understands—
Proximity to the Creator's grace
Elevates accountability,
For with greater awareness
Comes a greater duty to uphold
Divine principles.
The wise-one knows
That the one
Who shall achieve clairvoyance
To the Creator
And then commit sin,
Such sin
Shall be greater than the universe
In magnitude
In the sight of the Creator.

For the chosen ones,
For the messengers,
For the vessels of divine revelation,
Deviation from the path

Carries the gravest consequence.
Even the noblest of souls,
Even those entrusted
With the highest wisdom,
Are held to an unshakable standard.
Thus, when revelation descended,
When the divine words
Were granted to mankind
Through the Prophet,
No doubt could be tolerated,
No deception could be excused,
No falsehood could be permitted.

❮*Indeed, this Quran Is the recitation Of a noble Messenger. It is not the prose of a poet, Nor the mumbling of a fortune-teller. It is a revelation From the Lord of all worlds.*❯ —*Quran 69:40-43*

Had the Messenger
Altered a single word,
Had he spoken on behalf of the Divine
Without truth,
Had he introduced falsehood
To what was pure—
His punishment would have been severe.

❮*Had the Messenger Made up something In Our Name, We would have certainly Seized him by his right hand, Then severed his aorta, And none of you Could have shielded him from Us!*❯[422] —*Quran 69:44-47*

Thus, the wise-one understands—

---

[422] This aligns with the sacred words of the Quran, which speak of the profound purity of the prophet Mohammed, declaring that the revelation contained within is the pinnacle of divine gifts bestowed upon humanity. Though the revered messenger stands as the nearest to the divine, there lies a solemn admonition that none shall dare to encroach upon this sacred revelation. Should he, as some would claim, transgress this hallowed decree, it would herald the gravest of sins, bringing forth dire repercussions for himself and all of humanity:

📖 ❮Now, I do swear by whatever you see, (38) and whatever you cannot see! (39) Indeed, this ˹Quran˺ is the recitation of a noble Messenger. (40) It is not the prose of a poet ˹as you claim˺, ˹yet˺ you hardly have any faith. (41) Nor is it the mumbling of a fortune-teller, ˹yet˺ you are hardly mindful. (42) ˹It is˺ a revelation from the Lord of all worlds. (43) Had the Messenger made up something in Our Name, (44) We would have certainly seized him by his right hand, (45) then severed his aorta, (46) and none of you could have shielded him ˹from Us˺! (47) Indeed, this ˹Quran˺ is a reminder to those mindful ˹of Allah˺. (48) And We certainly know that some of you will persist in denial, (49) and it will surely be a source of regret for the disbelievers. (50) And indeed, this ˹Quran˺ is the absolute truth. (51) So glorify the Name of your Lord, the Greatest. (52)❯ [Quran 69:38-51]

Purity in revelation
Is uncompromising.

And yet,
Even among the chosen,
Even among the messengers,
There were moments
Of human error,
Where the burden of calling mankind
To the path of righteousness
Grew heavy upon the soul.
So it was with Jonah,
Who abandoned his mission,
Who fled from his people,
Who did not persevere
In delivering the call
For the sake of the Creator.
And for this,
His consequence was magnified.

❨And Jonah Was indeed one of the messengers. Remember when he fled To the overloaded ship. Then he drew straws With other passengers. He lost And was thrown overboard. Then the whale engulfed him While he was blameworthy.❩ —Quran 37:139-142

For had he not glorified His Lord,
Had he not sought forgiveness,
Had he not remembered
The weight of his responsibility,
His punishment would have been absolute.

❨Had he not constantly Glorified Allah, He would have certainly Remained in its belly Until the Day of Resurrection.❩ —Quran 37:143-144

Yet in mercy,
His Lord spared him.
His Lord restored him.
His Lord returned him
To the people
He once abandoned.

❨We later sent him back To his city Of at least one hundred thousand people, Who

then believed in him, So We allowed them enjoyment For a while.❳ *423*   —*Quran*
37:147-148

Thus, the wise-one understands—
The closer one stands to the Creator,
The greater the accountability.
For knowledge demands action.
For proximity demands purity.
For divine wisdom
Requires unwavering obedience.

O soul,
The closer you draw to the Radiance,
The greater your shadow looms if you turn away.
With every unveiling of divine nearness,
Your accountability deepens.
A crack in the cup of the ignorant may be overlooked;
But a crack in the chalice held near the King's hand—
How grievous it becomes!
Thus, the wise-one walks forward,
With the weight of awareness,
With the burden of responsibility,
With the certainty
That divine favor
Is not simply an elevation—
But a test of the soul.

---

[423] In harmony with the sacred verses, the tale unfolds of the prophet Jonah, who, in a moment of despair, departed from his kin, forsaking them in their time of need. Yet, in the eyes of the Almighty, this act was not without consequence. A trial was set before him, a crucible meant to cleanse his spirit and compel him to reflect upon his choices. Thus, he was called to rise anew, steadfast in his mission to lead his people back to the righteous path laid forth by the Divine:

📖 ❲And Jonah was indeed one of the messengers. (139) ˹Remember˺ when he fled to the overloaded ship. (140) Then ˹to save it from sinking,˺ he drew straws ˹with other passengers˺. He lost ˹and was thrown overboard˺. (141) Then the whale engulfed him while he was blameworthy.[1] (142) Had he not ˹constantly˺ glorified ˹Allah˺,[2] (142) he would have certainly remained in its belly until the Day of Resurrection.[3] (144) But We cast him onto the open ˹shore˺, ˹totally˺ worn out, (145) and caused a squash plant to grow over him.[4] (146) We ˹later˺ sent him ˹back˺ to ˹his city of˺ at least one hundred thousand people, (147) who then believed ˹in him˺, so We allowed them enjoyment for a while. (148)❳ [Quran 37:139-148]

[1]: For abandoning his city without Allah's permission.

[2]: Before being swallowed and while inside the whale (see 21:87). The lesson is: good deeds are of great help during difficult times.

[3]: The belly of the whale would have become his grave.

[4]: The squash plant provided Jonah with shade and repelled harmful insects.

For only He sustains those He chooses.
Only He magnifies the consequence
For those entrusted.
Only He remains the source
Of ultimate accountability,
Absolute justice,
And infinite mercy.

So the wise-one walks forward,
Not fighting with what the heavens have planned,
He finds in his solace, his peace on this land.
He lets his spirit prostrate to a wisdom unknown,
And finds in His satisfaction (rida) a peace all his own.

For only He is the One, the Ever-True,
Whose guidance is always sacred and new.
He is the Lord of both loss and of gain,
And to trust in His will is to go far.
For only He remains the source
Of Serenity, and boundless force.

Wisdom Unveiled

The profound wisdom of this contemplation is the realization of the Rule of Magnified Punishment, a principle that states that as one draws closer to the Divine in knowledge and spiritual proximity, their accountability (musaba) for even subtle errors increases. The wise-one understands that divine favor is not just an honor but a solemn trust. The verses from Quran 69:44-47 concerning the Prophet Muhammad (peace be upon him) and Quran 37:139-148 regarding Prophet Jonah (peace be upon him) serve as powerful testaments to this truth. This wisdom unveils that a misstep from a vessel of divine light is far more grievous than that of an ignorant person. It is this profound understanding that compels the wise-one to an impeccable state of self-mastery, knowing that the "burden of beauty" carried in divine nearness requires a constant, trembling vigilance.

Wise-Reflection

Reflect on your own spiritual journey and the gifts of knowledge and insight you have been given. Do you see them as a source of pride, or as a heavy trust? Consider the thought, "A crack in the cup of the ignorant may be overlooked; But a crack in the chalice held near the King's hand—How grievous it becomes!" How can you cultivate a state of greater vigilance and self-mastery, knowing that your actions are magnified in the divine estimation? What would it mean for you to carry the "burden of beauty" with the humility and accountability of those who have been chosen?.

Contemplation: Overcoming Self-Centered Desires

The core of self-mastery is overcoming self-centered desires (hawa al-nafs) and attachments. These desires, rooted in the lower self (nafs al-ammarah), constantly pull the individual away from Divine Will and higher spiritual aspirations. The wise-one engages in continuous mujahadah (struggle) against these desires, not by suppression, but by redirecting them towards what is pleasing to Allah. This involves developing zuhd (abstinence from worldly luxuries) and wara' (scrupulousness), gradually purifying the heart of its cravings and dependencies.

The wise-one understands that desires are a fleeting mirage, glittering like stars but ultimately dying fires compared to the sun of Divine Light. This contemplation serves as a powerful testament to the spiritual discipline of "fasting with the heart and soul." It is not a call for deprivation, but a path to profound purification, where the eyes are trained not to wander, the heart is stilled from yearning after the temporary, and the soul is liberated from the pursuit of that which will never satisfy. The verses from Quran 18:28-31 and 79:34-41 beautifully lay out the clear choice between succumbing to worldly desires and earning the eternal reward of Paradise through inner restraint and awe of the Lord.

Overcoming Self-Centered Desires: Fasting with the Heart and Soul

Desires glitter
Like scattered stars,
But they are dying fires
Compared to the sun
Of Divine Light.
For the wise-one sees—
What the world calls brilliance
Is but fleeting radiance,
What the self covets

Is but passing indulgence,
What temptation whispers
Is but illusion.
Yet the soul longs.
It reaches.
It clings.
And so, the wise-one learns—
To fast not only with the stomach,
But with the eyes,
With the heart,
With the soul.
To master oneself
Is not simply to abstain from food,
But to train the gaze
Not to wander toward distraction,
To still the heart
From yearning after the temporary,
To silence the soul
From pleading after what will never satisfy.
❨And patiently stick with those Who call upon their Lord Morning and evening,
Seeking His pleasure. Do not let your eyes Look beyond them, Desiring the luxuries
Of this worldly life.❩ —Quran 18:28
For the eyes deceive,
The heart wavers,
The soul whispers.
Yet the wise-one remains firm—
For desire is but a fleeting shadow,
While the eternal reward
Is unshaken.
❨And do not obey those Whose hearts We have made heedless Of Our remembrance,
Who follow only their desires, And whose state is total loss.❩ [424] —Quran 18:28

---

[424] This aligns with the sacred words that recount the divine command bestowed upon the cherished prophet and his followers, guiding them and all true believers toward the path of the chosen ones. These steadfast souls, unwavering in their quest for the Creator's favor, remain impervious to the temptations of worldly splendor and distractions, as they journey toward the grace of the Almighty:

> *Thus, the wise-one understands—*
> *There is a choice before every soul.*
> *To surrender to longing,*
> *To indulge the cravings*
> *Of the moment,*
> *To prefer the fleeting life*
> *Of this world.*
>
> *Or to remember,*
> *To restrain,*
> *To stand in awe*
> *Before the One*
> *Who commands all things.*

❮Then as for those Who transgressed, And preferred The fleeting life Of this world, The Hellfire Will certainly be their home.❯ —Quran 79:37-39

❮And as for those Who were in awe Of standing before their Lord And restrained themselves From evil desires, Paradise will certainly Be their home.❯[425] —Quran 79:40-41

> *Thus, the wise-one understands—*
> *Fasting is not deprivation,*
> *But purification.*
> *For desire may promise satisfaction,*

📖 ❮And patiently stick with those who call upon their Lord morning and evening, seeking His pleasure.[1] Do not let your eyes look beyond them, desiring the luxuries of this worldly life. And do not obey those whose hearts We have made heedless of Our remembrance, who follow ˹only˺ their desires and whose state is ˹total˺ loss. (28) And say, ˹O Prophet,˺ "˹This is˺ the truth from your Lord. Whoever wills let them believe, and whoever wills let them disbelieve." Surely We have prepared for the wrongdoers a Fire whose walls will ˹completely˺ surround them. When they cry for aid, they will be aided with water like molten metal, which will burn ˹their˺ faces. What a horrible drink! And what a terrible place to rest! (29) As for those who believe and do good, We certainly never deny the reward of those who are best in deeds. (30) It is they who will have the Gardens of Eternity, with rivers flowing under their feet. There they will be adorned with bracelets of gold, and wear green garments of fine silk and rich brocade, reclining there on ˹canopied˺ couches. What a marvellous reward! And what a fabulous place to rest! (31)❯ [Quran 18:28-31]

[1]: lit., seeking His Face.

[425] This aligns with the sacred verses that recount the fates of those who seek to mend their ways and those who succumb to the temptations of their own desires, serving as a solemn warning to all of humanity against the deceit of self-indulgence. It is a tribute to those who remain unwavering in their quest for the grace of the Creator:

📖 ❮But, when the Supreme Disaster[1] comes to pass— (34) the Day every person will remember all ˹their˺ striving, (35) and the Hellfire will be displayed for all to see— (36) then as for those who transgressed (37) and preferred the ˹fleeting˺ life of this world, (38) the Hellfire will certainly be ˹their˺ home. (39) And as for those who were in awe of standing before their Lord and restrained themselves from ˹evil˺ desires, (40) Paradise will certainly be ˹their˺ home. (41)❯ [Quran 79:34-41]

[1]: This is the second Blast which will cause the dead to come to life for judgment. See 39:68.

But it delivers only emptiness.
Temptation may offer brilliance,
But it fades into darkness.
Indulgence may whisper fulfillment,
But it leaves the soul thirsting.
Yet in restraint,
There is light.
In patience,
There is peace.
In obedience,
There is elevation.

They deny the self's cravings
So that the heart may feast upon the Real (Al-Haqq).
True wealth is the emptying of the self—
That the Infinite may fill it.
Thus, the wise-one walks forward,
Not chasing desires,
Not weighed by longing,
But carrying only the certainty
That discipline leads to clarity,
Restraint leads to freedom,
And surrender leads to the Divine.
For only He sustains the patient.
Only He grants victory over temptation.
Only He remains the source
Of all true satisfaction,
Eternal and unshaken.

So the wise-one walks forward,
Not fighting with what the heavens have planned,
He finds in his solace, his peace on this land.
He lets his spirit prostrate to a wisdom unknown,
And finds in His satisfaction (rida) a peace all his own.

For only He is the One, the Ever-True,
Whose guidance is always sacred and new.
He is the Lord of both loss and of gain,
And to trust in His will is to go far.

For only He remains the source
Of Serenity, and boundless force.

Wisdom Unveiled

The profound wisdom of this contemplation is the realization that true wealth is the emptying of the self, a process achieved by overcoming self-centered desires (hawa al-nafs) through continuous spiritual struggle (mujahadah). The wise-one understands that the heart must fast not only from food but from the allure of worldly distractions and the cravings of the lower self (nafs al-ammarah). The verses from Quran 18:28-31 and 79:34-41 serve as a clear and powerful testament to the eternal choice: a life of indulgence leading to loss, or a life of restraint and awe leading to the ultimate reward of Paradise. This wisdom unveils that true liberation from the constraints of ego and worldly attachments is found in the discipline of redirecting desires toward the satisfaction (rida) of the Divine, allowing the heart to be filled with the unshakeable reality of Al-Haqq (the Real).

Wise-Reflection

Reflect on the desires that most pull you away from your spiritual path. Do you see them as harmless or as "dying fires" that distract from the Divine Light? Consider the thought, "True wealth is the emptying of the self—That the Infinite may fill it." How can you practice "fasting with the heart and soul" in your daily life? What specific steps can you take to cultivate zuhd (abstinence from worldly luxuries) and wara' (scrupulousness), gradually purifying your heart so that it no longer yearns for the temporary but finds its sole fulfillment in the Eternal?.

Contemplation: Rule of Triumph Over Oneself

The wise-one internalizes the fundamental rule of triumph over oneself. True victory, in the spiritual sense, is not achieved by external conquests or accumulating worldly power, but by the successful subjugation of one's own ego, passions, and negative inclinations. This inner triumph is the greatest and most enduring of victories, for it is the conquest of the greatest enemy—the lower self that prevents sincere devotion and alignment with the Divine. This is the essence of psychic empowerment.

The first step in mastering the self lies in recognizing its inherent tendencies toward desires and attachments. Conquering these inclinations is a prerequisite for spiritual growth and alignment with the Creator's will. This contemplation serves as a powerful testament to the spiritual truth that the greatest battlefield is within. The verses from Quran 3:14-18 and 74:1-7 beautifully illustrate the choice between the fleeting pleasures of this world and the eternal reward of Allah's pleasure (rida). By understanding that discipline is not deprivation but liberation, the wise-one learns to school the self until it longs for the Creator (Al-Khaliq) alone, thus achieving the true zenith of liberation.

Mastery Over the Self: Triumph Over Desire and Attachment

The path to divine grace
Begins not with knowledge,
Nor with external conquest,
But with mastery over the self.
For the first battle
Is always within.
The wise-one understands—
The soul leans toward desire,
Gravitates toward attachment,
Clings to the comforts
Of the material world.
But to ascend,
To grow,
To align oneself
With the will of the Creator,
One must first conquer
The inclinations of the self.
"The wise-one knows
That to triumph over self,
One must abstain from its calling,
As it usually calls
For desires and earthly wishes."

Worldly pleasures have been made appealing,
Their allure woven into
The fabric of human existence—

Wealth, status, family,
Power, indulgence.
Yet the wise-one sees—
They are fleeting,
Mere adornments upon a temporary stage.

❨*The enjoyment of worldly desires— Women, children, Treasures of gold and silver, Fine horses, cattle, And fertile land— Has been made appealing to people. These are the pleasures of this worldly life, But with Allah Is the finest destination.*❩ —*Quran 3:14*

For beyond the pull of the material,
Beyond the whispers of the self,
There exists something greater—
The eternal reward.
A life of discipline,
A heart purified,
An existence anchored
Not in fleeting indulgence,
But in divine purpose.

❨*Shall I inform you Of what is better Than all of this? Those mindful of Allah Will have Gardens With their Lord, Under which rivers flow, To stay there forever, And pure spouses, Along with Allah's pleasure.*❩ —*Quran 3:15*

Thus, the wise-one understands—
Discipline is not deprivation,
But liberation.
For to master oneself
Is not to suffer in restraint,
But to rise above
The chains of worldly longing.
For patience, sincerity, obedience,
And humility
Lead not to loss,
But to clarity, redemption, and fulfillment.

❨It is they Who are patient, Sincere, obedient, And charitable, And who pray For forgiveness before dawn.❩[426] —*Quran 3:17*

> *Even the chosen ones,*
> *Even the messengers,*
> *Are called upon*
> *To stand firm,*
> *To remain vigilant,*
> *To guard themselves*
> *Against distraction.*
> *For revelation itself*
> *Is received through discipline,*
> *Through perseverance,*
> *Through sustained dedication*
> *To the Creator's command.*

❨O you covered up In your clothes! Arise and warn all. Revere your Lord alone. Purify your garments. Continue to shun idols. Do not do a favor Expecting more in return. And persevere For the sake of your Lord.❩[427] —*Quran 74:1-7*

> *Thus, the wise-one understands—*
> *The conquest of self*
> *Is the first step*

---

[426] This aligns with the sacred words that speak of mankind's yearning for the fleeting pleasures of this realm, often forsaking the virtue of patience. It is the steadfast souls, those who seek the favor of their Creator, who shall inherit the eternal grace and find their abode among the heaves:

📖 ❨The enjoyment of ´worldly` desires—women, children,[1] treasures of gold and silver, fine horses, cattle, and fertile land—has been made appealing to people. These are the pleasures of this worldly life, but with Allah is the finest destination. (14) Say, ´O Prophet,` "Shall I inform you of what is better than ´all of` this? Those mindful ´of Allah` will have Gardens with their Lord under which rivers flow, to stay there forever, and pure spouses,1 along with Allah's pleasure." And Allah is All-Seeing of ´His` servants, (15) who pray, "Our Lord! We have believed, so forgive our sins and protect us from the torment of the Fire." (16) ´It is they` who are patient, sincere, obedient, and charitable, and who pray for forgiveness before dawn.[2] (17) Allah ´Himself` is a Witness that there is no god ´worthy of worship` except Him—and so are the angels and people of knowledge. He is the Maintainer of justice. There is no god ´worthy of worship` except Him—the Almighty, All-Wise. (18)❩ [Quran 3:14-18]

[1]: Banîn means sons. In the ancient Arab culture, sons were a source of pride for their parents and tribes. This is because they provided for their families and took up arms in defence of their tribes.

[2]: Optional prayers before dawn are recommended and are more likely to be accepted.

[427] This aligns with the sacred verses that recount the divine command given to His cherished messenger, urging him to remain steadfast in reflection, to summon others, and to uphold a vigilant and obedient heart towards the Creator:

📖 ❨O you covered up ´in your clothes`! (1) Arise and warn ´all`. (2) Revere your Lord ´alone`. (3) Purify your garments. (4) ´Continue to` shun idols. (5) Do not do a favour expecting more ´in return`.[1] (6) And persevere for ´the sake of` your Lord. (7)❩ [Quran 74:1-7]

[1]: It was a common practice to give someone a gift, hoping to receive a more valuable gift in return. This practice is disliked in Islam.

To spiritual maturity.
For only through discipline
Can the soul transcend attachment.
Only through patience
Can desire be tamed.
Only through humility
Can the self be mastered.
And once the self is conquered,
Once the heart is freed,
Once the soul is purified,
The path to divine grace
Is laid bare.

O my soul,
Your greatest adversary wears your own face.
It calls you toward fleeting desires,
It whispers of ease and indulgence,
It entices you to trade eternity for a moment's sweetness.
But the wise-one hears another call—
A higher summons that sings beyond the tongue of appetite.
To conquer the self
Is to wrest the heart from the tyranny of yearning,
To offer every impulse at the threshold of Divine Will (Al-Mureed).
Mastery is not silencing the self—
But schooling it
Until it kneels in longing for the Creator (Al-Khaliq) alone.
Thus, the wise-one walks forward,
Not chasing desires,
Not weighed by longing,
But carrying only the certainty
That discipline leads to clarity,
Restraint leads to freedom,
And surrender leads to the Divine.
For only He sustains discipline.
Only He grants victory over the self.
Only He remains the source
Of all strength, wisdom, and guidance.

So the wise-one walks forward,
Not fighting with what the heavens have planned,
He finds in his solace, his peace on this land.
He lets his spirit prostrate to a wisdom unknown,
And finds in His satisfaction (rida) a peace all his own.

For only He is the One, the Ever-True,
Whose guidance is always sacred and new.
He is the Lord of both loss and of gain,
And to trust in His will is to go far.
For only He remains the source
Of Serenity, and boundless force.

Wisdom Unveiled

The profound wisdom of this contemplation is the realization that true victory is the conquest of the self, a triumph over the ego, desires, and attachments. The wise-one understands that the greatest adversary wears one's own face, and that worldly pleasures, while appealing, are mere fleeting adornments. The verses from Quran 3:14-18 and 74:1-7 serve as a powerful testament to the spiritual truth that a life of discipline and perseverance is not one of deprivation but of ultimate liberation. This wisdom unveils that psychic empowerment is the result of schooling the self until it no longer longs for the temporary but kneels in devotion for the Creator (Al-Khaliq) alone. The conquest of the self, therefore, is the first and most crucial step toward spiritual maturity, paving the way for a heart purified and an existence anchored in divine purpose.

Wise-Reflection

Reflect on your own spiritual battles. Do you often seek victory in external circumstances, or do you recognize that the greatest war is the one fought within yourself? Consider the thought, "Mastery is not silencing the self— But schooling it Until it kneels in longing for the Creator (Al-Khaliq) alone." What specific steps can you take to "school" your lower self? How can you reframe your daily acts of discipline and restraint not as a burden, but as a path to true freedom and enduring peace?

Contemplation: Balancing Grace and Responsibility

Finally, the wise-one finds balance between Divine Grace (Fadl) and personal responsibility. While all guidance and strength come from Allah's grace, the Gateway Verse emphasizes individual accountability: "You are accountable only for yourselves." This means the wise-one must actively engage in the struggle for self-mastery, exercising free will and disciplined effort, while simultaneously recognizing that success in this struggle is ultimately a gift from Allah. This balanced perspective prevents both arrogance (thinking it's solely one's own effort) and fatalism (passively awaiting grace without striving).

The wise-one understands that while proximity to divine grace is a gift, it also comes with the responsibility to act in alignment with divine will, ensuring that actions reflect the wise-one's elevated spiritual state. This contemplation serves as a powerful testament to the spiritual truth that being a recipient of divine favor means being a guardian of it. The stories of the poets and messengers in the Quran show the profound difference between those who wield their gifts for self-serving pursuits and those who honor their trust with sincerity and truth. The journey of self-mastery culminates in this final balance, where striving and surrender become two sides of the same sacred coin, leading the soul to a state of complete devotion until the inevitable certainty arrives.

Balancing Grace and Responsibility: A Crown of Stars or Thorns

"Proximity to divine grace
Is a crown—
But a crown of thorns
For the heedless,
And a crown of stars
For the vigilant."
For the wise-one moves now
Not by habit,
Nor by ease,
But by awe.
Each breath
Becomes an act of worship.
Each step,

A testimony.
For closeness to the Divine
Is not merely an elevation—
It is a burden.
It is a responsibility.
It is a summons to absolute devotion.
Thus, the wise-one understands—
The weight of divine favor
Demands purity of heart,
Clarity of purpose,
And unwavering obedience.

So do not ever Call upon any other god Besides Allah, Or you will be One of the punished. —*Quran 26:213*

For guidance itself
Is not simply a gift—
It is a test.
How does one wield it?
How does one carry it?
How does one reflect
Its divine brilliance?
For to be chosen
Is to be watched,
To be entrusted
Is to be judged.

And warn all, Starting with your closest relatives, And be gracious To the believers who follow you. But if they disobey you, Say, 'I am certainly free Of what you do.'
—*Quran 26:214-216*

The wise-one knows—
The call to righteousness
Demands separation
From corruption.
The heart must anchor
Only in truth.
For falsehood masquerades
As knowledge,
Whispers in empty wisdom,
Parades itself
In half-truths and deception.

❰Shall I inform you Of whom the devils Actually descend upon? They descend upon Every sinful liar, Who gives an attentive ear To half-truths, Mostly passing on Sheer lies.❱ —Quran 26:221-223

Thus, the wise-one understands—
Knowledge must be pure.
Truth must be guarded.
Divine favor
Must not be tarnished
By vanity, arrogance,
Or self-serving pursuits.
For poetry is elevated
When carried with righteousness,
But diminished
When wielded for deception.

❰As for poets, They are followed Merely by deviants. Do you not see How they rant In every field, Only saying What they never do?❱ —Quran 26:224-226

And yet, the wise-one knows—
Words have power,
But power must serve truth.
For only those
Who speak with sincerity,
Who use wisdom
To uplift rather than deceive,
Who wield words
In defense of righteousness,
Carry the favor of the Divine.

❰Except those Who believe, Do good, Remember Allah often, And poetically avenge The believers After being wrongfully slandered.❱ —Quran 26:227

Thus, the wise-one understands—
Grace must be balanced
With responsibility. [428]

---

[428] This aligns with the sacred verses that recount the divine guidance bestowed upon the prophet, illuminating the path of responsibility in conveying the message and the manner of engagement with both the faithful and the unfaithful. Then, it unfolds to reveal the folly of those who claim to possess the gift of foresight, asserting that the mysteries of the future and the arcane truths should never be reduced to mere

For even the most blessed souls,
Even the messengers,
Even those closest to the Divine,
Are commanded
To uphold their trust with precision.

❲*We have not created The heavens and the earth And everything in between Except for a purpose. And the Hour Is certain to come, So forgive graciously.*❳ —*Quran 15:85*

Thus, the wise-one moves—
Not led by fleeting pleasures,
Not swayed by distractions,
But steadfast
In divine devotion.

❲*Do not let your eyes Crave the fleeting pleasures We have provided For some of the disbelievers, Nor grieve for them. And be gracious To the believers.*❳ —*Quran 15:88*

For revelation is a trust,
Not a privilege.
Divine favor is a summons,
Not simply a gift.
It must be upheld
With patience,
With truth,
With unwavering sincerity.

❲*So proclaim What you have been commanded, And turn away From the polytheists. Surely We will be sufficient For you against the mockers.*❳ —*Quran 15:94-95*

---

conjecture or declarations made for the sake of exploiting the unwary. Then, proceed to recount the plight of mortals who summon bards for both noble and nefarious purposes, exploring their virtues and vices, and the measure of their worth in the eyes of the Creator, as well as the nature of poetic deception:

❲So do not ever call upon any other god besides Allah, or you will be one of the punished. (213) And warn ˹all, starting with˺ your closest relatives, (214) and be gracious to the believers who follow you. (215) But if they disobey you, say, "I am certainly free of what you do." (216) Put your trust in the Almighty, Most Merciful, (217) Who sees you when you rise ˹for prayer at night˺, (218) as well as your movements ˹in prayer˺ along with ˹fellow˺ worshippers. (219) He ˹alone˺ is indeed the All-Hearing, All-Knowing. (220) Shall I inform you of whom the devils ˹actually˺ descend upon? (221) They descend upon every sinful liar, (222) who gives an ˹attentive˺ ear ˹to half-truths˺, mostly passing on sheer lies.[1] (223) As for poets, they are followed ˹merely˺ by deviants. (224) Do you not see how they rant in every field, [2] (225) only saying what they never do? (226) Except those who believe, do good, remember Allah often, and ˹poetically˺ avenge ˹the believers˺ after being wrongfully slandered. The wrongdoers will come to know what ˹evil˺ end they will meet. (227)❳ [Quran 26:213-227]

[1]: This refers to fortune-tellers who listen to Satanic whispers, adding more lies as they pass on the information to people.

[2]: lit., roam aimlessly in every valley.

Thus, the wise-one walks forward,
Not merely as a recipient of grace,
But as its guardian.
For divine favor is not merely received—
It must be honored.
For the closeness to Allah is not simply bestowed—
It must be upheld.
Thus, the wise-one worships
Until the certainty arrives,
Until the final test is completed,
Until the soul returns
To its Creator in purity.

❴*So glorify the praises Of your Lord And be one of those Who always pray. And worship your Lord Until the inevitable Comes your way.*❵[429] —*Quran 15:98-99*

The wise-one reflects:
To walk in the garden of grace
Is to tread barefoot upon roses—and thorns—
Knowing both are gifts from the Beloved.
Thus, the wise-one walks forward,
With the balance of grace and responsibility,
Not in arrogance,
But in humility,
Not in fatalism,
But in steadfast striving.
For only He sustains justice.

---

[429] This aligns with the sacred verse that recounts the divine command bestowed upon the prophet, urging him to pursue the highest virtues in his quest for the Creator's favor:

📖 ❴We have not created the heavens and the earth and everything in between except for a purpose. And the Hour is certain to come, so forgive graciously. (85) Surely your Lord is the Master Creator, All-Knowing. (86) We have certainly granted you the seven often-repeated verses[1] and the great Quran. (87) Do not let your eyes crave the ˹fleeting˺ pleasures We have provided for some of the disbelievers, nor grieve for them. And be gracious to the believers. (88) And say, "I am truly sent with a clear warning"— (89) ˹a warning˺ similar to what We sent to those who divided ˹the Scriptures˺, (90) who ˹now˺ accept parts of the Quran, rejecting others. (91) So by your Lord! We will certainly question them all (92) about what they used to do. (93) So proclaim what you have been commanded, and turn away from the polytheists. (94) Surely We will be sufficient for you against the mockers, (95) who set up ˹other˺ gods with Allah. They will soon come to know. (96) We certainly know that your heart is truly distressed by what they say. (97) So glorify the praises of your Lord and be one of those who ˹always˺ pray, (98) and worship your Lord until the inevitable[2] comes your way. (99)❵ [Quran 15:85-99]

[1]: Sûrah 1 of the Quran.

[2]: i.e., lit., what is certain—death.

Only He magnifies consequence
For those entrusted.
Only He remains the source
Of ultimate judgment,
Perfect accountability,
And boundless mercy.

So the wise-one walks forward,
Not fighting with what the heavens have planned,
He finds in his solace, his peace on this land.
He lets his spirit prostrate to a wisdom unknown,
And finds in His satisfaction (rida) a peace all his own.

For only He is the One, the Ever-True,
Whose guidance is always sacred and new.
He is the Lord of both loss and of gain,
And to trust in His will is to go far.
For only He remains the source
Of Serenity, and boundless force.

Wisdom Unveiled

The profound wisdom of this contemplation is the realization of the crucial balance between Divine Grace (Fadl) and personal accountability. The wise-one understands that all success in the struggle for self-mastery is a gift from the Divine, yet this does not negate the need for human effort and free will. The verses from Quran 26:213-227 and 15:85-99 serve as a powerful testament to this truth, highlighting the responsibility that comes with receiving a divine trust. This wisdom unveils that spiritual gifts, such as prophetic messages and poetic talent, are not privileges to be used for self-gain but trusts to be wielded with sincerity and in the service of truth. The wise-one lives in a state of continuous, active devotion, understanding that the closeness to the Creator is not merely a destination but a journey of unwavering vigilance until the "inevitable" certainty arrives.

Wise-Reflection

Reflect on your own spiritual journey. Do you ever fall into the traps of arrogance, believing your success is solely due to your own effort, or fatalism, passively waiting for divine intervention? Consider the thought,

"To walk in the garden of grace Is to tread barefoot upon roses—and thorns— Knowing both are gifts from the Beloved." How can you cultivate a balanced perspective, actively striving for self-mastery while simultaneously recognizing that all strength and guidance are gifts of Divine Grace? What would it mean for you to not just be a recipient of grace, but a guardian of it in your own life?

Conclusion: Mastery Over the Self

ECHOES OF REALIZATION: THE CRUCIBLE OF THE SELF

There is a fire, more intensely purifying than any worldly trial—it is the subtle, internal fire that tests the very metal of the soul against its own lower self. In this crucible of relentless restraint, the self is either consumed by its own impurities or profoundly refined into pure, unadulterated essence.

The wise-one who achieves true mastery over the self emerges not merely outwardly victorious, but inwardly luminous. They become a sacred vessel painstakingly emptied of egoic self, exquisitely filled with the fragrant essence of profound surrender, bearing within their profound inner silence the roaring echo of Divine Harmony.

THE SEEKER'S ASCENT: THE TRIUMPH OF RESTRAINT

Mastery over the self is a transformative, lifelong process that rigorously demands unwavering discipline, profound humility, and an unshakeable commitment to higher spiritual principles. By courageously overcoming the insidious grip of lower desires and limiting attachments, the wise-one aligns ever more closely with the Creator's pure Will, thereby achieving ultimate liberation and profound spiritual elevation. The wise-one's growing proximity to Divine Grace amplifies the inherent significance of their every action, urging them to act with greater, more conscious responsibility and profound reverence. Through the consistent practice of inner restraint and relentless self-mastery, the wise-one ascends towards an ultimate state of absolute purity and harmonious alignment, beautifully embodying the very principles of Divine Harmony.

Mastery over the self is not a victory that vociferously shouts from grand mountaintops, but a silent, profound triumph that whispers in the hidden, sacred places of the soul. By diligently restraining desires, by consistently answering Divine love over fleeting worldly pleasure, and by standing firm and patient under the spiritual weight of Divine Nearness, the wise-one deeply enters into the sacred, timeless dance of Divine Companionship. Through unwavering discipline, profound awe, and serene accountability, the wise-one no longer lives for the confines of the individual self—but profoundly through the Universal Self that is beyond all temporal selves: Al-Ahad (The One), As-Samad (The Eternal Refuge), the Ultimate Reality.

This is the essence of psychic and spiritual completion within " The Zenith of Liberation."

22ND REFLECTION: THE LIBERATION FROM ATTACHMENTS

(Freedom from the Temporal)

THE GATEWAY VERSES

In the sacred words of Allah, a vivid depiction of the transient nature of worldly life and the contrasting eternity of the Abode of Peace for the righteous:

❲The life of this world is just like rain We send down from the sky, producing a mixture of plants which humans and animals consume. Then just as the earth looks its best, perfectly beautified, and its people think they have full control over it, there comes to it Our command by night or by day, so We mow it down as if it never flourished yesterday! This is how We make the signs clear for people who reflect. (24) And Allah invites ˹all˺ to the Home of Peace and guides whoever He wills to the Straight Path. (25) Those who do good will have the finest reward and ˹even˺ more. Neither gloom nor disgrace will cover their faces. It is they who will be the residents of Paradise. They will be there forever.❳ [Quran 10:24-26]

ILLUMINATION'S DAWN

There comes a profound day, often subtly hidden within the ordinary course of time, when the wise-one awakens to a distinct, sacred trembling within: a deep, ineffable restlessness that no accumulation of wealth, no chorus of praise, and no worldly conquest can ever truly soothe. It is then that they perceive with crystal clarity—how all the seemingly gilded towers of life, all its fleeting glories, are but ephemeral reflections on transient water, instantly vanishing when touched by the hand of reality.

The wise-one learns a liberating truth: ultimate freedom is not found in gaining more, but in courageously releasing all that binds. True, enduring peace is not held securely in possessions, but in complete surrender to Al-Malik (The Possessor of all). Let us now walk, with hearts unburdened, into this profound, liberating unveiling, where the chains of worldly attachments gracefully fall away, and the wise-one's soul rises—unburdened, light, and eternally directed toward its true and ultimate Home.

THE UNFOLDING OF INSIGHTS

This section explores the nature of attachment, its inherent burdens, and the interconnected virtues that lead to profound liberation, culminating in a balanced life lived in harmony with Divine Will.

Contemplation: Rule of Affixion to Life as the Source of Hardship

---

The wise-one understands the fundamental rule: affliction (excessive attachment) to life is the primary source of human hardship and suffering. The Gateway Verse vividly illustrates the fleeting nature of worldly beauty and human illusion of control. When the heart becomes overly attached to transient things—wealth, status, relationships, desires—their inevitable loss or decline leads to immense grief and despair. Liberation begins with recognizing this attachment as the true 'affliction,' not the worldly event itself, initiating a crucial psychic detachment.

The concerns of worldly life, when overly emphasized, become the primary source of human suffering. Liberation lies in detaching from these concerns and trusting in the Creator's plan. The wise-one understands that the human heart's burdens stem not from external circumstances but from its internal grasping. The verses from Quran 90:4-7, 24:39-40, 9:55, and others serve as profound warnings against the allure of worldly possessions and the false sense of security they provide. This contemplation unveils the liberating truth that true peace and freedom are found not in accumulating the world, but in surrendering it to the Hands of the Eternal (Al-Baaqi).

The Liberation from Attachments: The Hidden Burden Beneath the Glitter of Life

---

The wise-one sees—
Affixion to life
Is the greatest deception,
An alluring mirage,
A silent weight that crushes
Those who grasp too tightly.
For when the heart
Clings too fiercely
To the world,
The world itself

Becomes its torment.
"The wise-one knows
That all humans' heart burdens
Stem from the concern
About life."
Mankind chases,
Strives,
Gathers wealth,
Hoards status,
Competes in fleeting grandeur.
Yet, their souls
Are restless.
Their hearts
Are heavy.
Their journey
Is endless.

❪Indeed, We have created Humankind in constant struggle.❫ —Quran 90:4

They believe
They have triumphed,
That their conquests
Have secured them,
That their riches
Have protected them.
But the wise-one sees—
No wealth can shield the soul
From suffering.

❪Do they think That no one sees them?❫ —Quran 90:7

For life seduces,
It whispers promises
Of fulfillment,
It entangles the heart
In golden chains,
It blinds the heedless
To the reality
Beneath its veil.

❪As for the disbelievers, Their deeds Are like a mirage In a desert, Which the thirsty
Perceive as water, But when they approach it, They find it to be nothing.❫ —Quran
24:39

For those
Who surrender to life's seduction,
Who build upon its shifting sands,
Who anchor their hopes
In its fleeting pleasures,
Their ruin is hidden
Beneath its gold.

❨*Or their deeds are like the darkness in a deep sea, covered by waves upon waves, topped by dark clouds. Darkness upon darkness! If one stretches out their hand, they can hardly see it. And whoever Allah Does not bless with light Will have no light!*❩
[430] *—Quran 24:40*

Even those
Whom the world adores,
Whom it elevates in wealth,
Whom it showers with children—
Their fortune
May be their downfall.

❨*So let neither Their wealth nor children Impress you. Allah only intends To torment them Through these things In this worldly life, Then their souls Will depart While they are disbelievers.*❩[431] *—Quran 9:55*

And so,
There are those

---

[430] This aligns with the sacred verse that recounts the tale of humanity's struggle to seize this ephemeral existence, adorned with the splendor of opulence:

❨Indeed, We have created humankind in ῾constant῾ struggle. (4) Do they think that no one has power over them, (5) boasting, "I have wasted enormous wealth!"? (6) Do they think that no one sees them? (7)❩ [Quran 90:4-7]

Yet, they remain blind to the shadows they have summoned upon themselves via the trials of this life and the realms beyond. Moreover, these verses from the Quran reveal the profound shadows that envelop their existence as they turn away from the illuminating guidance bestowed by the Creator:

❨As for the disbelievers, their deeds are like a mirage in a desert, which the thirsty perceive as water, but when they approach it, they find it to be nothing. Instead, they find Allah there ῾in the Hereafter, ready῾ to settle their account. And Allah is swift in reckoning. (39) Or ῾their deeds are῾ like the darkness in a deep sea, covered by waves upon waves,[1] topped by ῾dark῾ clouds. Darkness upon darkness! If one stretches out their hand, they can hardly see it. And whoever Allah does not bless with light will have no light! (40)❩ [Quran 24:39-40]

[1]: This is another scientific fact mentioned in the Quran: the existence of underwater waves, like layers.

[431] Thus, the Almighty has cautioned His messenger, Mohammed, against the seductions of worldly distractions that lead the faithful astray from His divine wisdom. For in the matters of offspring and riches, these temptations may become their bane in this life and the harbinger of their downfall:

❨So let neither their wealth nor children impress you ῾O Prophet῾. Allah only intends to torment them through these things in this worldly life, then their souls will depart while they are disbelievers. (55)❩ [Quran 9:55]

Who boast in their arrogance,
Believing their wealth and children
Shall follow them beyond the veil,
Believing their power
Shall secure them in the Hereafter.

❲Have you seen, O Prophet, The one who rejects Our revelations Yet boasts, 'I will definitely be granted Plenty of wealth and children If there is an afterlife'?❳ —*Quran 19:77*

But has he seen the unseen?
Has he gazed into fate
To ensure his claim?
Has he sought a pact
With the Most Merciful?
No—
His words become his downfall,
His arrogance becomes his ruin.

❲Not at all! We certainly record Whatever he claims And will increase his punishment extensively. And We will inherit What he boasts of, And he will come before Us All by himself.❳ —*Quran 19:79-80*

For life tempts with power.
It deceives with false security.
It whispers self-sufficiency.
But the wise-one understands—
Power that is not anchored in truth
Becomes the weight that sinks its bearer.
And when they
Seek refuge in idols,
Turning their backs on the Creator,
Trusting false gods
For strength and protection,
Those gods shall betray them.

❲They have taken other gods, Instead of Allah, Seeking strength and protection Through them. But no! Those gods will deny their worship And turn against them.❳

[432] —*Quran 19:81-82*

Thus, the wise-one understands—
What is held too tightly
Becomes the source of suffering.
What is chased too desperately
Becomes the very thing
That destroys.
What is treasured
Above truth
Becomes the burden
That pulls the soul downward.

And yet, mankind still deceives itself,
Still competes over dust,
Still raises monuments
In boasting vanity.

❨*Know that this worldly life Is no more than play, Amusement, Luxury, Mutual boasting, And competition In wealth and children. Like rain That causes plants to grow, To the delight of the planters, But later, The plants dry up, And you see them wither, Then they are reduced to chaff.*❩ —*Quran 57:20*

But the wise-one sees beyond—
They strive for what does not decay,
They seek what does not diminish,
They chase not the world,
But the favor of the Divine.

❨*So compete with one another For forgiveness from your Lord And a Paradise As vast as the heavens and the earth, Prepared for those Who believe in Allah And His*

---

[432] This is also consistent with Quranic passages relating the story of one who became disgraced for Allah's providing and challenge, only to be rewarded later, implying that it was his words that brought him down. Then proceed to tell the account of disbelievers seeking alternative idols from Allah, and how these idols led to their demise:

📖 ❨Have you seen ʿO Prophetʾ the one[1] who rejects Our revelations yet boasts, "I will definitely be granted ʿplenty ofʾ wealth and children ʿif there is an afterlifeʾ."? (77) Has he looked into the unseen or taken a pledge from the Most Compassionate? (78) Not at all! We certainly record whatever he claims and will increase his punishment extensively. (79) And We will inherit what he boasts of, and he will come before Us all by himself. (80) They have taken other gods, instead of Allah, seeking strength ʿand protectionʾ through them. (81) But no! Those ʿgodsʾ will deny their worship and turn against them. (82) Do you ʿO Prophetʾ not see that We have sent the devils against the disbelievers, constantly inciting them? (83) So do not be in haste against them, for indeed We are ʿcloselyʾ counting down their days. (84)❩ [Quran 19:77-84]

[1]: This statement was made by Al-ʿĀṣ ibn Wāʾil, a Meccan pagan who staunchly disbelieved in resurrection.

messengers. This is the favor of Allah. He grants it To whoever He wills.❭⁴³³ —
Quran 57:21

For beyond the world's distractions,
Beyond its fleeting pleasures,
Beyond its trials—
Lies the eternal promise.

❬*Then We granted the Book To those We have chosen From Our servants. Some of them Wrong themselves, Some follow a middle course, And some are foremost In good deeds By Allah's Will. That is truly The greatest bounty. They will enter The Gardens of Eternity, Where they will be adorned With bracelets of gold And pearls, And their clothing Will be silk. And they will say, 'Praise be to Allah, Who has kept away from us All causes of sorrow. He is the One Who—out of His grace— Has settled us In the Home Of Everlasting Stay, Where we will be touched By neither fatigue Nor weariness.'❭⁴³⁴ —Quran 35:32-35*

O my soul,
The more tightly you grip the world,
The more its weight bends your back.
Every concern over loss or gain,
Every fear for tomorrow,
Every hope anchored in passing things—
Each is a rope that tethers the heart to sinking ground.

---

⁴³³ This is in agreement with the Quran verse of:

📖 ❬Know that this worldly life is no more than play, amusement, luxury, mutual boasting, and competition in wealth and children. This is like rain that causes plants to grow, to the delight of the planters. But later the plants dry up and you see them wither, then they are reduced to chaff. And in the Hereafter there will be either severe punishment or forgiveness and pleasure of Allah, whereas the life of this world is no more than the delusion of enjoyment. (20) ʹSoʹ compete with one another for forgiveness from your Lord and a Paradise as vast as the heavens and the earth, prepared for those who believe in Allah and His messengers. This is the favour of Allah. He grants it to whoever He wills. And Allah is the Lord of infinite bounty. (21) No calamity ʹor blessingʹ occurs on earth or in yourselves without being ʹwrittenʹ in a Record before We bring it into being. This is certainly easy for Allah. (22) ʹWe let you know thisʹ so that you neither grieve over what you have missed nor boast over what He has granted you. For Allah does not like whoever is arrogant, boastful— (23) those who are stingy and promote stinginess among people. And whoever turns away ʹshould know thatʹ Allah ʹaloneʹ is truly the Self-Sufficient, Praiseworthy. (24)❭ [Quran 57:20-24]

⁴³⁴ This is consistent with the Quran verse that tells the narrative of those who won Allah's mercy after recalling the past days in this world and their efforts in it, therefore they received a lot of recompense afterwards:

📖 ❬The Book We have revealed to you ʹO Prophetʹ is the truth, confirming what came before it. Surely Allah is All-Aware, All-Seeing of His servants. (31) Then We granted the Book to those We have chosen from Our servants. Some of them wrong themselves, some follow a middle course, and some are foremost in good deeds by Allah's Will. That is ʹtrulyʹ the greatest bounty. (32) They will enter the Gardens of Eternity, where they will be adorned with bracelets of gold and pearls, and their clothing will be silk. (33) And they will say, "Praise be to Allah, Who has kept away from us all ʹcauses ofʹ sorrow. Our Lord is indeed All-Forgiving, Most Appreciative. (34) ʹHe is the Oneʹ Who—out of His grace—has settled us in the Home of Everlasting Stay, where we will be touched by neither fatigue nor weariness." (35)❭ [Quran 35:31-35]

The wise-one knows:
True liberation is not in mastering the world,
But in surrendering it into the Hands of the Eternal (Al-Baaqi).

Thus, the wise-one walks forward,
Not weighed by the world,
Not shackled by its illusions,
But free,
Purified,
Liberated from attachments,
And aligned
With the Divine Will.
For only He grants true freedom.
Only He lifts the burdens of the heart.
Only He remains the source
Of peace, clarity, and eternal grace.

So the wise-one walks forward,
Not fighting with what the heavens have planned,
He finds in his solace, his peace on this land.
He lets his spirit prostrate to a wisdom unknown,
And finds in His satisfaction (rida) a peace all his own.

For only He is the One, the Ever-True,
Whose guidance is always sacred and new.
He is the Lord of both loss and of gain,
And to trust in His will is to go far.
For only He remains the source
Of Serenity, and boundless force.

Wisdom Unveiled

The profound wisdom of this contemplation is the realization that affixion to life is the primary source of all human hardship and suffering. The wise-one understands that true liberation is a psychic detachment from the fleeting allure of this world. The verses from Quran 90:4-7, 24:39-40, and 57:20-21 serve as a clear and powerful testament to the deceptive nature of worldly wealth and the fleeting pleasure of life, which is likened to a mirage or a fleeting crop. This wisdom unveils that the heart's burdens are not caused by the external world but by its grasping nature. The wise-one seeks not to gain more but to release what it was never meant to carry, finding true freedom and eternal peace in surrendering all to the Hands of the Eternal (Al-Baaqi).

Wise-Reflection

Reflect on the things in your life you feel most attached to—your wealth, your status, your relationships. Do you see these attachments as a source of security or as a potential source of sorrow? Consider the thought, "The more tightly you grip the world, The more its weight bends your back." How can you begin the process of psychic detachment? What would it mean for you to surrender your concerns and hopes for tomorrow into the Hands of the Eternal (Al-Baaqi), and what practical steps can you take to anchor your heart in divine purpose rather than worldly possessions?

Contemplation: The Trial of Human Existence

This leads to a deep understanding of the trial of human existence. Life in this world is inherently designed as a test (fitnah) of attachment and sincerity. Every blessing and every challenge serve as opportunities to choose between the temporary and the Eternal. The wise-one recognizes that the fleeting nature of this life (as depicted in 10:24) is not a flaw but a deliberate design to constantly redirect the soul's gaze towards Al-Baaqi (The Everlasting) and the Home of Peace.

The wise-one comprehends that life is a trial, a journey of choices where each individual is solely responsible for their own path. The verses from Quran 35:15-24, 91:7-10, and 29:1-7 serve as powerful and clear testaments to this truth. They illustrate that no one can bear another's burden, and that success or ruin is a direct consequence of one's own efforts to purify or corrupt the soul. This contemplation unveils the liberating truth that a life anchored in the certainty of the Real (Al-Haqq) provides a security that the shifting sands of the worldly life can never offer. The wise-one does not wait for salvation but actively builds it through a life of striving and accountability.

The Trial of Human Existence: The Responsibility of One's Own Path

The wise-one comprehends—
Life is a trial,

A passage of choices,
A journey sculpted
By each individual's own hand.
The wise-one comprehends
That those who uprighted their own lives
Could upright themselves,
And those who ruined their own lives
Would ruin themselves.
For no one bears another's burden,
No soul carries another's sins,
No wrongdoing is shifted—
Each path is walked alone.

❨*O humanity! It is you Who stand in need of Allah, But Allah alone Is the Self-Sufficient, Praiseworthy. If He willed, He could eliminate you And produce a new creation. And that is not difficult For Allah at all.*❩ —*Quran 35:15-17*

Thus, the wise-one understands—
Success is carved by purity,
Ruin is carved by corruption,
And every soul
Shapes its own destiny. [435]

❨*And by the soul And the One Who fashioned it, Then with the knowledge Of right and wrong Inspired it! Successful indeed Is the one Who purifies their soul, And doomed Is the one Who corrupts it!*❩ —*Quran 91:7-10*

For life

---

[435] This is in agreement with the Quran verses of:

📖 ❨O humanity! It is you who stand in need of Allah, but Allah ˹alone˺ is the Self-Sufficient, Praiseworthy. (15) If He willed, He could eliminate you and produce a new creation. (16) And that is not difficult for Allah ˹at all˺. (17) No soul burdened with sin will bear the burden of another. And if a sin-burdened soul cries for help with its burden, none of it will be carried—even by a close relative. You ˹O Prophet˺ can only warn those who stand in awe of their Lord without seeing Him[1] and establish prayer. Whoever purifies themselves, they only do so for their own good. And to Allah is the final return. (18) Those blind ˹to the truth˺ and those who can see are not equal, (19) nor are the darkness and the light, (20) nor the ˹scorching˺ heat and the ˹cool˺ shade.[2] (21) Nor are the dead and the living equal. Indeed, Allah ˹alone˺ makes whoever He wills hear, but you ˹O Prophet˺ can never make those in the graves hear ˹your call˺. (22) You are only a warner. (23) We have surely sent you with the truth as a deliverer of good news and a warner. There is no community that has not had a warner.[3] (24)❩ [Quran 35:15-24

[1]: This can also mean that they are in awe of their Lord as much in private as they are in public.

[2]: This implies Hell and Paradise.

[3]: According to a Prophetic narration collected by Ibn Ḥibbân, the total number of prophets sent around the world, from Adam ﷺ to Muhammad ﷺ, is 124 000—of which only twenty-five are mentioned in the Quran.

Is not simply given—
It is formed,
It is tested,
It is revealed through trials.
No words alone
Carry weight.
No claims of faith
Stand unchallenged. [436]

❨Do people think Once they say, 'We believe,' That they will be left Without being put to the test? We certainly tested Those before them. And in this way Allah will clearly distinguish Between those Who are truthful And those Who are liars.❩ —
Quran 29:2-3
Thus, the wise-one understands—
One's life is a reflection
Of one's choices.
One who strives
For purification
Finds elevation.
One who embraces corruption
Finds destruction.
❨Whoever hopes For the meeting with Allah, Let them know That Allah's appointed time Is sure to come. He is the All-Hearing, All-Knowing. And whoever strives In Allah's cause, Only does so For their own good. Surely Allah Is not in need Of any of His creation.❩ —*Quran 29:5-6*
Thus, the wise-one walks forward,
Not waiting for salvation,
But building it.
Not fearing judgment,
But embracing accountability.

---

[436] This is in agreement with the Quran verses of:

📖 ❨And by the soul and ˹the One˺ Who fashioned it, (7) then with ˹the knowledge of˺ right and wrong inspired it! (8) Successful indeed is the one who purifies their soul, (9) and doomed is the one who corrupts it! (10)❩ [Quran 91:7-10]

Not lost in uncertainty,
But anchored in truth. [437]

O traveler on the road of dust,
Understand:
You cannot upright yourself
By clutching the ruins of a collapsing world.
Those who imagine that life's fortunes are the measure of their worth
Build their homes on shifting sand.
But the wise-one builds in the unseen—
On the certitude of the Real (Al-Haqq),
Where storms do not reach.
True security lies not in the flourishing of worldly gardens,
But in the hand that plants them—and uproots them in wisdom.

For only He watches all trials.
Only He distinguishes sincerity from deception.
Only He remains the source
Of ultimate justice, mercy, and reward.

So the wise-one walks forward,
Not fighting with what the heavens have planned,
He finds in his solace, his peace on this land.
He lets his spirit prostrate to a wisdom unknown,
And finds in His satisfaction (rida) a peace all his own.

For only He is the One, the Ever-True,
Whose guidance is always sacred and new.
He is the Lord of both loss and of gain,
And to trust in His will is to go far.

---

[437] This aligns with the sacred verses that recount the essence of the Creator shaping existence and placing humanity in an eternal test, guiding them to discern His will in their choices between virtue and vice::

⌕ ⟨Alif-Lām-Mīm. (1) Do people think once they say, "We believe," that they will be left without being put to the test? (2) We certainly tested those before them. And ˹in this way˺ Allah will clearly distinguish between those who are truthful and those who are liars. (3) Or do the evildoers ˹simply˺ think that they will escape Us? How wrong is their judgment! (4) Whoever hopes for the meeting with Allah, ˹let them know that˺ Allah's appointed time is sure to come. He is the All-Hearing, All-Knowing. (5) And whoever strives ˹in Allah's cause˺, only does so for their own good. Surely Allah is not in need of ˹any of˺ His creation. (6) As for those who believe and do good, We will certainly absolve them of their sins, and reward them according to the best of what they used to do. (7)⟩ [Quran 29:1-7]

For only He remains the source
Of Serenity, and boundless force.

Wisdom Unveiled

The profound wisdom of this contemplation is the realization that human existence is a deliberate and eternal trial (fitnah) designed to test one's sincerity and attachments. The wise-one understands that every individual is solely responsible for their own spiritual destiny, a principle powerfully articulated in Quran 35:18, where it states, "No soul burdened with sin will bear the burden of another." This wisdom unveils that true liberation is not a passive gift but an active, continuous struggle to purify the soul, as highlighted in Quran 91:9-10: "Successful indeed is the one who purifies their soul, and doomed is the one who corrupts it!" The wise-one, therefore, builds their security not on the fleeting fortunes of this world but on the unshakeable foundation of the Real (Al-Haqq), which provides true peace and resilience against the storms of life.

Wise-Reflection

Reflect on your own perception of life's challenges. Do you see them as random hardships, or as deliberate tests (fitnah) designed to purify your heart and strengthen your connection to the Divine? Consider the thought, "You cannot upright yourself By clutching the ruins of a collapsing world." Where are you building your home—on the "shifting sand" of worldly attachments or the "certitude of the Real (Al-Haqq)"? What specific actions can you take today to live with a greater sense of personal responsibility and spiritual accountability, knowing that your every choice shapes your ultimate destiny?

Contemplation: Rule of Adherent Pairs Characteristics

The wise-one discerns the rule of adherent pairs characteristics—that spiritual virtues often function most powerfully in complementary pairs. Just as Divine Attributes are perfectly balanced (e.g., Justice with Mercy), so too must human virtues be cultivated in harmony. This prepares for the following section, emphasizing that true liberation comes from a balanced cultivation of interconnected qualities, rather than isolated efforts.

The wise-one understands that certain virtues are inherently connected, existing in a symbiotic relationship that strengthens the spiritual

foundation. The verses from Quran 23:1-9, 23:57-61, and 25:63-73 serve as a powerful testament to this truth, depicting the ideal believer not as a collection of disjointed qualities but as a cohesive, harmonious whole. This contemplation reveals that the path to spiritual liberation is not a solitary effort but a symphony of surrender, where humility and honesty, prayer and purity, all rise together. The wise-one knows that to cultivate one virtue is to nurture its counterpart, for to sever one strand of the spiritual vine is to weaken the entire structure of the soul.

The Law of Adherent Pairs: A Contemplation on the Interwoven
Nature of Virtue

The wise-one sees—
That the soul does not bloom
By isolated seeds,
But by a garden
Where virtues grow in pairs.
That sincerity must walk beside humility,
And humility must guard the hand
As it stretches to give.
That the one who kneels in prayer
With reverence
Cannot rise
With idle speech.
That the one who guards their gaze
Will also guard their tongue.
That the one who fulfills their trusts
Will speak with dignity—
For integrity is never half-formed.

❦Successful indeed are the believers: those who humble themselves in prayer, those who avoid idle talk, those who pay alms-tax, those who guard their chastity, those who are true to their trusts and covenants, and those who are properly observant of their

prayers.⟩⁴³⁸ —Quran 23:1-9
And so the wise-one understands—
That these traits do not scatter
Like leaves in the wind.
They form a vine.
And if one strand is cut,
The others begin to unravel.
The one who truly prays
Will not indulge in corruption.
The one who fasts with devotion
Will not bear false witness.
The one who trembles before the Lord
Will race toward acts of mercy,
Never away from them.

⟨Surely those who tremble in awe of their Lord, and who believe in the revelations of their Lord, and who associate none with their Lord, and who do whatever good they do with their hearts fearful, knowing that they will return to their Lord, it is they who race to do good deeds, always taking the lead.⟩⁴³⁹ —Quran 23:57-61

Because the soul that fears its return
Does not delay its obedience.
Because fear without hope
Is despair—
But fear with love
Is a call to motion,

---

⁴³⁸ This is in agreement with the Quran verses narrating the characteristic virtues of the real believers whom their doing for specific tasks and orders are always associated with non-separated pure emotions and strive for the Creator's acceptance or avidance of corrupting human traits:

📖 ⟨Successful indeed are the believers: (1) those who humble themselves in prayer; (2) those who avoid idle talk; (3) those who pay alms-tax;[1] those who guard their chastity [2] (5) except with their wives or those ´bondwomen` in their possession, for then they are free from blame, (6) but whoever seeks beyond that are the transgressors; (7) ´the believers are also` those who are true to their trusts and covenants; (8) and those who are ´properly` observant of their prayers. (9) These are the ones who will be awarded (10) Paradise as their own.[3] They will be there forever. (11)⟩ [Quran 23:1-11]

[1]: Zakâh means purification and growth. Paying alms-tax and charity are forms of purifying one's wealth.

[2]: lit., private parts.

[3]: Al-Firdaws, the highest place in Paradise.

⁴³⁹ Then the Quranic tale unfolds, revealing their qualities:

📖 ⟨Surely those who tremble in awe of their Lord, (57) and who believe in the revelations of their Lord, (58) and who associate none with their Lord, (59) and who do whatever ´good` they do with their hearts fearful, ´knowing` that they will return to their Lord1— (60) it is they who race to do good deeds, taking the lead. (61) We never require of any soul more than what it can afford. And with Us is a record which speaks the truth. None will be wronged. (62)⟩ [Quran 23:57-62]

A breath drawn before every good deed.
So the wise-one understands—
These traits must feed each other,
Must lift each other,
Must coexist with harmony,
For light that is scattered
Loses its power to illuminate.

And so the Most Compassionate
Describes His true servants
Not with one trait,
But with entire rhythms of character:

❲*They walk humbly upon the earth. And when the foolish address them improperly,*
they respond with peace. They spend a portion of the night prostrating and standing
before their Lord. They spend moderately—neither wastefully nor stingily. They do not
bear false witness. They do not turn a blind eye or deaf ear to His revelation.❳ —

Quran 25:63-73

None of these stand alone.
Their speech echoes their silence.
Their prayer guards their spending.
Their restraint shapes their dignity.
Their reverence governs their relationships.
Their repentance reconfigures their past.

❲*As for those who repent, believe, and do good deeds, they are the ones whose evil deeds*
Allah will change into good deeds.❳[440] —*Quran 25:70*

---

[440] Other qualities are unveiled in the verses of the Quran:

📖 ❲The ˹true˺ servants of the Most Compassionate are those who walk on the earth humbly, and when the foolish address them ˹improperly˺, they only respond with peace. (63) ˹They are˺ those who spend ˹a good portion of˺ the night, prostrating themselves and standing before their Lord. (64) ˹They are˺ those who pray, "Our Lord! Keep the punishment of Hell away from us, for its punishment is indeed unrelenting. (65) It is certainly an evil place to settle and reside." (66) ˹They are˺ those who spend neither wastefully nor stingily, but moderately in between. (67) ˹They are˺ those who do not invoke any other god besides Allah, nor take a ˹human˺ life—made sacred by Allah—except with ˹legal˺ right,[1] nor commit fornication. And whoever does ˹any of˺ this will face the penalty. (68) Their punishment will be multiplied on the Day of Judgment, and they will remain in it forever, in disgrace. (69) As for those who repent, believe, and do good deeds, they are the ones whose evil deeds Allah will change into good deeds. For Allah is All-Forgiving, Most Merciful. (70) And whoever repents and does good has truly turned to Allah properly. (71) ˹They are˺ those who do not bear false witness, and when they come across falsehood, they pass ˹it˺ by with dignity. (72) ˹They are˺ those who, when reminded of the revelation of their Lord, do not turn a blind eye or a deaf ear to

Thus, the wise-one understands—
The presence of one virtue
Summons another,
And the absence of one
Weakens the whole.
The wise-one does not seek one without cultivating its companion—
For to sever one is to wound them both.
For the soul is not healed
By fragments of righteousness,
But by a whole symphony of surrender.
To claim belief
Is to walk in its reflection.
To kneel in prayer
Is to speak in mercy,
Act in honesty,
And guard the soul like a fortress.
❲They are the ones who will be rewarded with elevated mansions in Paradise, for their
perseverance, received with salutations and greetings of peace, staying there forever.❳ —
Quran 25:75
So the wise-one walks forward—
Not gathering scattered deeds,
But cultivating a structure
Where every virtue
Holds another aloft.

The wise-one reflects:
In the garden of the soul,
No flower blooms alone.
These paired virtues reflect the interconnectedness of spiritual qualities, emphasizing
that true growth involves nurturing all reflections of the soul.
Thus, the wise-one walks forward,
Not fighting with what the heavens have planned,

---

it. (73) ˹They are˺ those who pray, "Our Lord! Bless us with ˹pious˺ spouses and offspring who will be the
joy of our hearts, and make us models for the righteous." (74) It is they who will be rewarded with ˹elevated˺
mansions ˹in Paradise˺ for their perseverance, and will be received with salutations and ˹greetings of˺
peace, (75) staying there forever. What an excellent place to settle and reside! (76) Say, ˹O Prophet,˺ "'You
˹all˺ would not ˹even˺ matter to my Lord were it not for your faith ˹in Him˺. But now you ˹disbelievers˺ have
denied ˹the truth˺, so the torment is bound to come." (77)❳ [Quran 25:63-77]

[1]: For example, in retaliation for intentional killing through legal channels.

He finds in his solace, his peace on this land.
He lets his spirit prostrate to a wisdom unknown,
And finds in His satisfaction (rida) a peace all his own.
For only He is the One, the Ever-True,
Whose guidance is always sacred and new.
He is the Lord of both loss and of gain,
And to trust in His will is to go far.
For only He remains the source
Of Serenity, and boundless force.
For only He knits the traits together.
Only He reads the fabric of the heart.
Only He remains the source
Of wholeness, purity, and reward.

Wisdom Unveiled

The profound wisdom of this contemplation is the realization of the Rule of Adherent Pairs Characteristics, where spiritual virtues do not exist in isolation but in a harmonious, interconnected relationship. The wise-one understands that to sever one virtue is to weaken the entire fabric of the soul. The verses from Quran 23:1-9 and 25:63-73 serve as a powerful testament to this, painting a picture of the ideal believer as a unified whole whose prayers are connected to their speech, whose humility is linked to their charity, and whose reverence for the Divine fuels their race toward good deeds. This wisdom unveils that true spiritual growth is a holistic process, a "symphony of surrender," where every quality is cultivated in harmony with its counterpart, leading to a state of internal wholeness and a life that is a complete reflection of faith.

Wise-Reflection

Reflect on your own virtues. Do you find yourself focusing on one quality while neglecting others? Consider the thought, "In the garden of the soul, No flower blooms alone." What virtues do you see as a pair in your own life? How can you consciously cultivate the counterpart of a virtue you are already striving for, understanding that your spiritual growth depends on their interconnected harmony? What would it mean to live your life not as a collection of scattered deeds, but as a cohesive structure where every virtue holds another aloft?

Contemplation: Liberation Through Surrender

The ultimate goal is liberation through total surrender (istislam). This is not a passive giving up, but an active, conscious relinquishing of the ego's desire for control over outcomes, events, and possessions. It is the understanding that true freedom comes when one's will merges with the Divine Will, acknowledging Allah's absolute sovereignty and trust in His wisdom. This profound surrender frees the wise-one from the anxieties of the future, the regrets of the past, and the burdens of the present, leading to unparalleled psychic peace.

The wise-one understands that fate is a river set in motion by the will of the Creator, and to swim against it is to drown in exhaustion, while to surrender to it is to be carried by the breath of His Mercy. This contemplation serves as a powerful testament to the spiritual truth that true peace is found in acknowledging the divine orchestration of all events. The stories of Prophet Jacob and Prophet Joseph, as told in the Quran, illustrate that every trial and tribulation is a thread in a divine tapestry, designed to cleanse and guide the soul. The verses from Quran 9, 3, and 12 beautifully reinforce the importance of trusting in the divine will, finding hope in mercy, and surrendering the desire for control in the face of the unknown.

Liberation Through Surrender: Flowing with Fate into Divine Mercy

The wise-one knows—
Fate is not to be defied,
Nor to be chiseled like stone
In anxious certainty.
Rather, fate is a river,
Set in motion
By the will of the Creator.
To swim against it
Is to drown in exhaustion.
To surrender to it
Is to be carried
By the breath of His Mercy.
The wise-one knows

That overcoming fate
Is not by challenging it
But by embracing it
And surrendering to the Creator's will,
While never ceasing hope,
Nor giving up trying,
But holding firmly
In the grace stance of the Creator.
My soul,
Cease your restless carving of fate into stone.
Surrender to the flow of His will,
And you will find
That the river carries you farther
Than all your anxious paddling ever could.
Lay down the burden of control—
And rise on the breath of His Mercy.
For the heedless mistake
Both joy and hardship
As products of their own design.
They grieve at loss,
They boast in gain,
Never seeing the hand
That orchestrates all events
For the trial of the soul.

❨*Say, 'Nothing will ever befall us Except what Allah has destined for us. He is our Protector.' So in Allah Let the believers Put their trust.*❩[441] —*Quran 9:51*

They are blind
To the meaning behind the moment.

---

[441] This aligns with sacred texts that speak of those who are oblivious, believing that joyful and sorrowful experiences are merely the result of human actions, unaware of the deeper significance of such events as trials for the spirit, distinguishing the faithful from the false-hearted. This verse speaks of destiny or divine will, as the Almighty has foreseen what shall come to pass for humankind. It highlights the importance of placing faith in the divine as the Guardian and surrendering to the will of the Maker. It also upholds the notion that destiny is guided by a higher power.

❨If a blessing befalls you ˹O Prophet˺, they grieve, but if a disaster befalls you, they say, "We took our precaution in advance," and turn away, rejoicing. (50) Say, "Nothing will ever befall us except what Allah has destined for us. He is our Protector." So in Allah let the believers put their trust. (51) Say, "Are you awaiting anything to befall us except one of the two best things: ˹victory or martyrdom˺? But We are awaiting Allah to afflict you with torment either from Him or at our hands. So keep waiting! We too are waiting with you. (52)❩ [Quran 9: 50-52]

But the wise-one sees—
Every outcome,
Whether victory or martyrdom,
Ease or hardship,
Is a sign
And a mercy
For the surrendered soul.

❮Do not be like the unfaithful Who say about their brothers Who travel or engage in battle, 'If they had stayed with us, They would not have died or been killed.' Allah makes such thinking A cause of agony in their hearts. It is Allah Who gives life And causes death.❯[442] —Quran 3:156

For the wise-one understands—
Destiny is not cruelty,
But refinement.
A trial,
Yes.

But a trial designed to cleanse,
To teach,
To guide,
To awaken.

So they do not grieve
Over what they miss,
Nor boast
Over what they gain.

❮No calamity or blessing Occurs on earth Or in yourselves Without being written In a Record Before We bring it into being. This is certainly easy For Allah.❯ —Quran 57:22

Thus, even in the darkest depths,

---

[442] This aligns with the sacred texts that recount how individuals are relieved from the weight of life's trials and their own decisions by placing their trust in the divine, surrendering the outcomes of their choices to the all-knowing wisdom of a higher power, whose will shall inevitably prevail.

📖 ❮O believers! Do not be like the unfaithful[1] who say about their brothers who travel throughout the land or engage in battle, "If they had stayed with us, they would not have died or been killed." Allah makes such thinking a cause of agony in their hearts. It is Allah who gives life and causes death. And Allah is All-Seeing of what you do. (156) Should you be martyred or die in the cause of Allah, then His forgiveness and mercy are far better than whatever ˹wealth˺ those ˹who stay behind˺ accumulate. (157) It is out of Allah's mercy that you ˹O Prophet˺ have been lenient with them. Had you been cruel or hard-hearted, they would have certainly abandoned you. So pardon them, ask Allah's forgiveness for them, and consult with them in ˹conducting˺ matters. Once you make a decision, put your trust in Allah. Surely Allah loves those who trust in Him. (159) If Allah helps you, none can defeat you. But if He denies you help, then who else can help you? So in Allah let the believers put their trust. (160)❯ [Quran 3:156-160]

[1]: i.e., the hypocrites.

The wise-one holds on.
Never abandoning hope.
Never forsaking devotion.

As did Jacob,
Who in anguish over the unknown
Clung not to despair,
But to faith and surrender.
❨I complain Of my anguish and sorrow Only to Allah. And I know from Allah
What you do not know. Do not lose hope In the mercy of Allah, For no one loses
hope Except those with no faith.❩ —Quran 12:86-87
And Joseph,
Cast into the pit,
Sold into slavery,
Wrongfully imprisoned—
Yet he surrendered
To the unseen decree.
And in the end,
He saw that every tragedy
Had been a thread
In the Divine tapestry.

❨My Lord has made it come true. He was truly kind to me When He freed me from
prison, And brought you all from the desert After Satan had ignited rivalry Between
me and my siblings. Indeed my Lord Is subtle in fulfilling what He wills. Surely He
alone Is the All-Knowing, All-Wise.❩ 443 —Quran 12:100

---

443 This aligns with the sacred verses recounting the tale of a father (prophet Jacob ﷺ) urging his sons to seek their lost kin (prophet Joseph ﷺ and Benjamin), reminding them to hold steadfast in their faith and never despair of divine compassion:

📖 ❨He replied, "I complain of my anguish and sorrow only to Allah, and I know from Allah what you do not know. (86) O my sons! Go and search ˹diligently˺ for Joseph and his brother. And do not lose hope in the mercy of Allah, for no one loses hope in Allah's mercy except those with no faith. (88)). And the replay of Josef that what they done to him and his brother in adversity was in fact a blissing at the end: ❨When they entered Joseph's presence, they pleaded, "O Chief Minister! We and our family have been touched with hardship, and we have brought only a few worthless coins, but ˹please˺ give us our supplies in full and be charitable to us. Indeed, Allah rewards the charitable." (88) He asked, "Do you remember what you did to Joseph and his brother in your ignorance?" (89) They replied ˹in shock˺, "Are you really Joseph?" He said, "I am Joseph, and here is my brother ˹Benjamin˺! Allah has truly been gracious to us. Surely whoever is mindful ˹of Allah˺ and patient, then certainly Allah never discounts the reward of the good-doers." (90) They admitted, "By Allah! Allah has truly preferred you over us, and we have surely been sinful." (91) Joseph

For the wise-one understands—
Fate is not a punishment,
But a pilgrimage.
A flow in which the soul is meant
To be purified,
To be taught surrender,
To be returned to its Source
In dignity.
So let the anxious paddling cease.
Let the craving for control dissolve.
Let the spirit float in trust.

The wise-one reflects:
The heavy door swings open
Not by force of hands,
But by the key of surrender.
Detachment from worldly concerns and complete surrender to divine will offer the only
escape from this cycle of hardship. By trusting in the Creator's wisdom, the wise-one
achieves liberation and peace.

For only He arranges all affairs.
Only He grants mercy through tribulation

---

said, "There is no blame on you today. May Allah forgive you! He is the Most Merciful of the merciful! (92)) And the culmination of the Joesph's story as he reminding his father about his childhood dream and what he faced in hardship in the apparent sad fate but to be all are an orchestrated plan form the most merciful Creator so he attain what he become as a honored advisor: (Then he raised his parents to the throne, and they all fell down in prostration to Joseph,[1] who then said, "O my dear father! This is the interpretation of my old dream. My Lord has made it come true. He was truly kind to me when He freed me from prison, and brought you all from the desert after Satan had ignited rivalry between me and my siblings.[2] Indeed my Lord is subtle in fulfilling what He wills. Surely He ˺alone˹ is the All-Knowing, All-Wise." (100) "My Lord! You have surely granted me authority and taught me the interpretation of dreams. ˹O˺ Originator of the heavens and the earth! You are my Guardian in this world and the Hereafter. Allow me to die as one who submits[3] and join me with the righteous." (101)). Finally, Allah remind his prophet (Mohammed) to take lesson form this story as it a revelation form the past times to steadfast him in striving for Allah's cause: (That is from the stories of the unseen which We reveal to you ˹O Prophet˺. You were not present when they ˹all˺[4] made up their minds, and when they plotted ˹against Joseph˺. (102) And most people will not believe—no matter how keen you are— (103) even though you are not asking them for a reward for this ˹Quran˺. It is only a reminder to the whole world. (104)》 [Quran 12:86-104]

[1]: Joseph's ﷺ parents and his eleven brothers prostrated before him out of respect, not as an act of worship. This was permissible in their tradition, but in Islam, Muslims prostrate only to Allah.

[2]: Joseph ﷺ did not mention how Allah saved him from the well because he did not want to embarrass his brothers after forgiving them.

[3]: lit., as a Muslim.

[4]: This includes Joseph's brothers, the travellers who picked him up from the well and sold him into slavery, and the Chief Minister's wife and other women in the city.

Only He remains the source
Of hope, guidance, and everlasting peace.

So the wise-one walks forward,
Not fighting with what the heavens have planned,
He finds in his solace, his peace on this land.
He lets his spirit prostrate to a wisdom unknown,
And finds in His satisfaction (rida) a peace all his own.

For only He is the One, the Ever-True,
Whose guidance is always sacred and new.
He is the Lord of both loss and of gain,
And to trust in His will is to go far.
For only He remains the source
Of Serenity, and boundless force.

Wisdom Unveiled

The profound wisdom of this contemplation is the realization that liberation is achieved through total surrender (istislam) to the Divine Will. The wise-one understands that fate is not an arbitrary force but a divinely orchestrated river, and that true peace lies in trusting its flow. The verses from Quran 9:51 and 3:156 serve as a powerful testament to this, teaching that every event, whether a blessing or a calamity, is a sign and a trial for the soul. The stories of Prophets Jacob and Joseph, as recounted in Quran 12:86-100, beautifully illustrate that surrender in the face of seemingly tragic circumstances ultimately reveals the hidden wisdom and mercy of the All-Knowing Creator. This wisdom unveils that a life of surrender is a pilgrimage designed to purify the soul, freeing it from the burdens of past regrets and future anxieties by anchoring it in the unshakeable certainty of divine purpose.

Wise-Reflection

Reflect on your own struggle for control. Do you find yourself anxious about the future or burdened by the past? Consider the thought, "The heavy door swings open Not by force of hands, But by the key of surrender." What is one area of your life where you can actively practice surrender today, relinquishing your need for control and trusting in the Divine Will? How can you learn from the stories of the prophets, seeing your own trials not as random misfortunes but as threads in a grand, beautiful tapestry of divine design?

Contemplation: The Three Pillars of Inner Harmony

(Certitude, Endurance, and Divine Intimacy)

In the final act of this sacred journey, the wise-one turns inward, no longer seeking to master the external world, but to establish a harmonious kingdom within. This is not a journey to a distant land, but a descent into the depths of the soul. For in its profound stillness, the wise-one discovers that the key to true liberation lies not in a single virtue, but in the perfect synergy of sacred pairs. These are the three pillars that hold up the heavens of the soul: a fortress built on Certitude and Devoutness, a garden that blossoms with Patience and Contentment, and a sanctuary that finds peace in Seclusion and Worship. With these pillars, the heart becomes a home, the spirit takes flight, and the wise-one finds their ultimate solace in the unfading light of the Eternal.

Part 1: Certitude and Devoutness: Foundations of the Fortress

Certitude (Yaqeen) is an unshakeable conviction in Allah's Oneness, His promises, and His ultimate control over all things. It is the inner fortress of faith. Hand-in-hand with this is Devoutness (Taqwa), which is a conscious awareness of Allah's presence leading to righteousness, vigilance against sin, and obedience to His commands. Yaqeen provides the inner strength and Taqwa provides the protective discipline, together forming the impenetrable foundation for liberation.

The wise-one understands that these two virtues are not separate but function as a single, cohesive force. Yaqeen (Certitude) is the bedrock upon which the entire spiritual life is built, while Taqwa (Devoutness) is the light-bearing canopy that protects and adorns it. The verses from Quran 2:2-5 and 27:1-3 serve as a profound testament to this sacred pairing, linking belief in the unseen and the Hereafter directly to the righteous actions of establishing prayer and giving charity. This contemplation unveils the liberating truth that true faith is not a passive mental state, but an active, embodied reality where unshakable conviction in the heart naturally flows into a life of disciplined obedience.

Certitude and Devoutness: Foundations of the Fortress

In the quiet chamber of the heart,
Certitude settles like bedrock—
Unmoved by the tides of doubt,
Unshaken by the winds of trial.
Upon it rises Devoutness—
A light-bearing canopy,
Shade for the striving soul,
Shelter from the tempests of temptation.
Certitude anchors the heart.
Devoutness adorns it.
Together, they build a fortress of unshakable faith.

The wise-one knows—
When the soul grasps certainty in what it cannot see,
The limbs follow in righteousness without resistance.
Faith in the unseen is not blindness—
It is clarity beyond sight,
A lens polished by devotion,
Focused on the Hereafter.
❲This is the Book! There is no doubt about it— A guide for those mindful ˋof
Allah ˋ, Who believe in the unseen, Establish prayer, And donate from what We have
provided for them...❳ — Quran 2:2–3
Certitude does not stand idle.
It plants roots.
And those roots
Birth prayer—
Steady, luminous, inwardly bowed.
They bear charity—
Silent, pure, released without demand.
They crown belief—
Not just in revelation,
But in the unseen eternity
That awaits beyond time.
❲...And who believe in what has been revealed to you ˋO Prophet ˋ And what was
revealed before you, And have sure faith in the Hereafter. It is they who are ˋtruly ˋ

guided by their Lord, And it is they who will be successful.❯❯❯444 — *Quran 2:4–5*

The wise-one understands—
Certitude without Devoutness
Is theory without embodiment.
And Devoutness without Certitude
Is motion without direction.
Thus, when prayer is sincere,
It points back to Certitude.
When Zakah flows,
It is not just social justice—
It is proof of the unseen,
Acted out in the realm of the seen.

❮*These are the verses of the Quran; The clear Book. It is a guide and good news For the believers— Those who establish prayer, Pay alms-tax, And have sure faith in the Hereafter.*❯445 — *Quran 27:1-3*

In the soul of the wise-one,
These two traits do not walk apart.
One strengthens the other.
One lights the other's path.
One shapes intention,
The other refines action.
Together, they make the believer
Rooted in vision,

---

444 This aligns with the sacred texts that directly connect devoutness (the reverence and effort for the acceptance of the Creator) with certitude (unwavering faith and belief in the afterlife and the unseen) and delineates the actions that arise from this union (faith in the unseen, devotion in prayer, acts of charity). It unmistakably reveals the deep bond that exists, serving as the very bedrock for authentic direction and triumph:

📖 ❮Alif-Lãm-Mĩm. (1) This is the Book! There is no doubt about it[1]—a guide for those mindful ʿof Allahʾ,[2] (2) who believe in the unseen,[3] establish prayer, and donate from what We have provided for them, (3) and who believe in what has been revealed to you ʿO Prophetʾ and what was revealed before you, and have sure faith in the Hereafter. (4) It is they who are ʿtrulyʾ guided by their Lord, and it is they who will be successful. (5)❯ [Quran 2:1-5]

[1]: i.e., there is no doubt regarding its authenticity or consistency.

[2]: The word muttaqi (plural muttaqûn) can be translated as one who is mindful ʿof Allahʾ, devout, pious, God-fearing, righteous, or God-conscious.

[3]: i.e., the belief in Allah, the angels, and the Day of Judgment.

445 In a manner reminiscent of the earlier passage, this verse intertwines the sacred practices of devotion with unwavering faith in the afterlife, portraying them as essential traits of the genuine faithful who are bestowed with enlightenment and joyful news:

📖 ❮Tã-Sĩn. These are the verses of the Quran; the clear Book. (1) ʿIt isʾ a guide and good news for the believers: (2) ʿthoseʾ who establish prayer, pay alms-tax, and have sure faith in the Hereafter. (3)❯ [Quran 27:1-3]

Active in virtue.
Not swayed by the mirage of doubt,
Nor stalled by the illusions of this world.
The heart holds truth.
The limbs enact surrender.
The soul rests
In a fortress
Built not of stone—
But of certainty and devoutness,
Guarded by the gaze of the Most Merciful.

So the wise-one walks forward,
Not fighting with what the heavens have planned,
He finds in his solace, his peace on this land.
He lets his spirit prostrate to a wisdom unknown,
And finds in His satisfaction (rida) a peace all his own.

For only He is the One, the Ever-True,
Whose guidance is always sacred and new.
He is the Lord of both loss and of gain,
And to trust in His will is to go far.
For only He remains the source
Of Serenity, and boundless force.

Wisdom Unveiled

The profound wisdom of this contemplation is the realization that
**Certitude (Yaqeen) and Devoutness (Taqwa) are an inseparable pair,
forming the foundation of a truly liberated spiritual life. The wise-one
understands that Yaqeen is the inner conviction in the unseen realities of
faith, while Taqwa is the outward manifestation of that conviction in
righteous deeds. The verses from Quran 2:2-5 and 27:1-3 serve as a
powerful testament to this, showing that the successful believer is defined
by this integrated state of being—a heart with sure faith in the Hereafter
and hands that establish prayer and give charity. This wisdom unveils that
a fortress of faith is not built on one virtue alone, but on the
complementary synergy of an unwavering internal belief and a disciplined,
conscious external practice.

Wise-Reflection

Reflect on the connection between your beliefs and your actions. Do you find yourself acting in a way that reflects your deepest convictions? Consider the thought, "Certitude without Devoutness Is theory without embodiment. And Devoutness without Certitude Is motion without direction." What is one area of your life where you can strengthen your inner Yaqeen (Certitude) and allow it to manifest in a more conscious act of Taqwa (Devoutness)? How can you cultivate a heart that is not only rooted in faith but also expressed in a life of righteous deeds?

Part 2: Patience and Contentment: Blossoming Beneath the Storm

Patience (Sabr) is steadfast endurance in the face of adversity and perseverance in obedience. It is a state of active waiting with trust. Complementing this is Contentment (Rida), which is a profound acceptance and satisfaction with whatever Allah has decreed, whether an apparent blessing or a trial. While Sabr is enduring the storm, Rida is finding a garden blossoming beneath it, a state of deep inner peace regardless of external circumstances.

The wise-one understands that Patience and Contentment are not merely passive virtues but are active states of being that transform hardship into spiritual growth. The verses from Quran 2:155-157 beautifully articulate how a whispered declaration of "Surely to Allah we belong and to Him we will all return" is an act of deep surrender that brings divine blessings and guidance. Furthermore, Quran 65:2-3 illustrates that this profound trust in the divine decree, even in the most difficult of personal trials, unlocks unforeseen provision and brings a way out of difficulty. This contemplation unveils the liberating truth that true serenity is found not in the absence of pain, but in the unwavering faith that every trial has a divine purpose, and that a heart rooted in patience and contentment will always find its solace.

Patience and Contentment: Blossoming Beneath the Storm

The wise-one knows—
Not all gardens are planted in spring.
Some bloom
Under thunder.

Some sprout
Where tears once fell."
Patience holds steady in storms.
Contentment dances under the rain.
Together, they turn trials into gardens.

These are not merely virtues—
They are survival.
They are soul-alchemy.
They are the shade
And the sanctuary
For the one walking through fire.

❨*We will certainly test you With a touch of fear and famine And loss of property, life, and crops. Give good news To those who patiently endure— Those who say, when struck by a disaster, 'Surely to Allah we belong And to Him we will ˹all˼ return.'*❩
— Quran 2:155–156

This surrender—
This whispered declaration in calamity—
Is not passive despair.
It is the breath
Of deepest strength:
Contentment with fate,
Faith in decree,
Patience with timing,
And trust in return.

And what does this surrender bring?

❨*They are the ones Who will receive Allah's blessings and mercy. And it is they Who are ˹rightly˼ guided.*❩[446] *— Quran 2:157*

Contentment is not the absence of pain—
It is standing firm within it

---

[446] This passage weaves together the essence of trials with the virtue of patience, proclaiming a deep allegiance to the Divine, an act of profound contentment and unwavering surrender to His will. It reveals that enduring trials with steadfastness summons celestial favor and compassion, ushering one into a realm of enlightenment that embodies tranquility and fulfillment.

📖 ❨We will certainly test you with a touch of fear and famine and loss of property, life, and crops. Give good news to those who patiently endure— (155) who say, when struck by a disaster, "Surely to Allah we belong and to Him we will ˹all˼ return." (156) They are the ones who will receive Allah's blessings and mercy. And it is they who are ˹rightly˼ guided. (157)❩ [Quran 2:155-157]

And seeing Divine purpose
Where others see only ruin.

Even in the most intimate fracture,
In the trial between hearts,
Where love fades and homes fracture—
Even there,
Patience and contentment
Are the mark
Of those who know their Lord.

❲*Then when they have ʿalmostʾ reached The end of their waiting period, Either retain them honourably Or separate from them honourably…*❳

To act with dignity,
To speak with grace,
To release with respect—
This is patience clothed in honor.
And to accept what was written,
Without bitterness,
To trust what remains unseen—
This is contentment
Bathed in light.

❲*And whoever is mindful of Allah, He will make a way out for them, And provide for them From sources they could never imagine. And whoever puts their trust in Allah, Then He alone Is sufficient for them…*❳[447] — *Quran 65:2–3*

---

[447] This aligns with the sacred verse that instructs the faithful on how to conduct themselves in the most trying of times between partners. What is the separation, and how even in such a trial, patience stands as the noble virtue of those who place their trust in the Divine, a true testament of the faithful. Thus, placing trust in the Almighty here embodies a profound endurance in the anticipation of His aid and a serene acceptance of His bounty and will. It suggests that genuine patience and contentment guide one towards celestial abundance.

📖 ❲O Prophet! ʿInstruct the believers:ʾ When you ʿintend toʾ divorce women, then divorce them with concern for their waiting period,1 and count it accurately. And fear Allah, your Lord. Do not force them out of their homes, nor should they leave—unless they commit a blatant misconduct. These are the limits set by Allah. And whoever transgresses Allah's limits has truly wronged his own soul. You never know, perhaps Allah will bring about a change ʿof heartʾ later.[2] (1) Then when they have ʿalmostʾ reached the end of their waiting period, either retain them honourably or separate from them honourably.[3] And call two of your reliable men to witness ʿeither wayʾ—and ʿlet the witnessesʾ bear true testimony for ʿthe sake ofʾ Allah. This is enjoined on whoever has faith in Allah and the Last Day. And whoever is mindful of Allah, He will make a way out for them, (2) and provide for them from sources they could never imagine. And whoever puts their trust in Allah, then He ʿaloneʾ is sufficient for them. Certainly Allah achieves His Will. Allah has

Where patience is rooted,
Contentment flowers.
Where the heart holds still,
Provision arrives
From doors that had no hinges.

So the wise-one understands—
These virtues are not parallel lines.
They are the warp and weft
Of a soul's strength.
One does not truly exist
Without the other.
For the one who is patient
But resents fate
Has not yet tasted surrender.
And the one who is content
But restless in hardship
Has not yet learned endurance.
True grace
Is to endure the hardship
While smiling at its meaning.
True beauty
Is to suffer loss
And still whisper,

---

already set a destiny for everything. (3) As for your women past the age of menstruation, in case you do not know, their waiting period is three months, and those who have not menstruated as well. As for those who are pregnant, their waiting period ends with delivery.1 And whoever is mindful of Allah, He will make their matters easy for them. (4) This is the commandment of Allah, which He has revealed to you. And whoever is mindful of Allah, He will absolve them of their sins and reward them immensely. (5)❭ [Quran 65:1-5]

[1]: Meaning, when a husband intends to divorce his wife—after the consummation of marriage—he should divorce her outside her monthly cycle, provided that he has not touched her after her period. This makes it easy for the wife to observe her 'iddah (waiting period for around three months, see 65:4). Otherwise, things will be complicated for her. For example, if divorce happens after sexual intercourse, she might get pregnant, which delays the end of 'iddah until the end of her pregnancy. If divorce happens during a monthly cycle, scholars are in disagreement as to whether the divorce counts or not. If it does not, she has to wait until her menstruation is over to see if her husband still wants to divorce her.

[2]: Perhaps the husband who has divorced his wife may change his mind and restore the marriage before the end of her waiting period (after the first or second count of revocable divorce).

[3]: A husband may separate from his wife after each of the first two counts of divorce or at the end of her waiting period with dignity. If he chooses to stay with her after the first two counts of divorce then divorces her a third time, the marriage is terminated at the end of her third waiting period. The wife will have to marry and divorce another man before she can be remarried to her ex-husband (see 2:230). However, a woman marrying someone with the intention of getting divorced, in order to return to her first husband, is forbidden.

"To Allah we belong,
And to Him we return."

The wise-one reflects:
Patience holds steady in storms.
Contentment dances under the rain.
Together, they turn trials into gardens.
This reflects the symbiotic relationship between patient endurance and a serene heart.
Thus, the wise-one walks forward,
Shielded not by circumstance,
But by patience rooted in contentment,
And contentment strengthened by patience.
For only He brings gardens from storms.
Only He makes the soul flourish in hardship.
Only He remains the source
Of tranquility, healing, and divine reward.

So the wise-one walks forward,
Not fighting with what the heavens have planned,
He finds in his solace, his peace on this land.
He lets his spirit prostrate to a wisdom unknown,
And finds in His satisfaction (rida) a peace all his own.

For only He is the One, the Ever-True,
Whose guidance is always sacred and new.
He is the Lord of both loss and of gain,
And to trust in His will is to go far.
For only He remains the source
Of Serenity, and boundless force.

Wisdom Unveiled

The profound wisdom of this contemplation is the realization that Patience (Sabr) and Contentment (Rida) are an inseparable pair that allow the soul to not only endure but also flourish amidst life's trials. The wise-one understands that while patience is the active endurance of a storm, contentment is the profound acceptance of the divine purpose behind it. The verses from Quran 2:155-157 serve as a powerful testament to this, teaching that a heart that surrenders to divine decree in calamity is blessed with mercy and guidance. This wisdom unveils that true strength is not found in controlling external events but in cultivating an internal state where trust in the Divine is so deep that it transforms loss into a source of peace, and hardship into a garden of spiritual growth.

Wise-Reflection

Reflect on a recent challenge in your life. Did you meet it with Sabr (Patience) alone, or did you also find Rida (Contentment) in its decree? Consider the thought, "Patience holds steady in storms. Contentment dances under the rain." What is one specific trial you are currently facing where you can consciously practice both patience and contentment? How can you reframe your perception of hardship, seeing it not as a punishment but as a divinely orchestrated test designed to bring you closer to peace and an unexpected provision from the Creator?

Part 3: Seclusion and Worship: The Sanctuary of Stillness

Seclusion (Khulwah) refers to intentional withdrawal from worldly distractions and the clamor of people to create a space for intimate communion with Allah. It's an inner and sometimes outer quietude. This is married with profound Worship (Ibadah), which encompasses all acts of devotion done out of love and obedience to Allah, particularly the prescribed rituals (prayer, remembrance) performed with presence. Together, Khulwah provides the sanctuary, and Ibadah fills it with Divine connection, cultivating the heart's direct link to Al-Qayyum (The Sustainer of All).

The wise-one understands that a heart cannot truly hear the divine whisper until it is first hushed. The verses from Quran 73:1-9 beautifully illustrate this, portraying the night as a sacred time for intimacy and profound worship, where the soul, stripped of worldly distractions, becomes receptive to a "weighty revelation." Furthermore, Quran 17:78-79 shows that this deliberate act of night prayer is not just an obligation but a path to a "station of praise," an elevated state of being. This contemplation unveils the liberating truth that solitude is not isolation but an invitation to a deeper relationship with the Creator, and that true peace is found not in the noise of the world but in the quiet of a heart filled with devotion.

Seclusion and Worship: The Sanctuary of Stillness

The wise-one knows—
That the heart,
To truly hear,
Must first be hushed.
That worship,
To truly soar,
Must rise from silence.
Seclusion hushes the noise.
Worship raises the soul's song.
Together, they weave
A secret communion with the Creator.
It is not escape—
But invitation.
Not isolation—
But immersion.
For in stillness,
The soul becomes fertile.
In aloneness,
The spirit becomes receptive.
And in the hush of the night,
When the world sleeps,
The servant awakes—
To whisper with eternity.
❲O you wrapped in your clothes! Stand all night in prayer—except a little, pray half
the night, or a little less, or a little more—and recite the Quran In a measured way.❳
— Quran 73:1–4
The wise-one sees—
This is no ordinary call.
This is the summons to intimacy,
When revelation descends
Upon the soul clothed in night,
Lit not by lamps
But by longing.
❲Indeed, worship in the night Is more impactful And suitable for recitation.❳ —
Quran 73:6
For the world

Claims the day.
Responsibilities shout,
Voices swirl,
Duties clamor.
But the night is sacred.
It clears the chamber of distraction.
It bathes the seeker in solitude.
It is then the Quran
Is not just spoken—
But heard.
Not just recited—
But absorbed.
And this worship?
It is not rote.
It is devotion in its purest form.
⟨Always remember the Name of your Lord, And devote yourself to Him
wholeheartedly.⟩ — Quran 73:8
Tabattul—devotion by detachment.
Worship that requires
Leaving the world behind.
Letting go of noise,
Identity,
Even effort—
And simply being with Him. [448]

The wise-one sees—
That every soul needs Khulwah.
Not to flee,
But to return.

---

[448] This aligns with the sacred verses that call forth a solemn duty for prayer under the cloak of night, a time set apart from the clamor of the world. It clearly intertwines the act of rising for the night prayer, a profound expression of reverence, with deep devotion, showcasing how the worship of the Creator thrives in solitude. The expression "dedicate thyself to Him with unwavering commitment" suggests a retreat into solitude for the purpose of reverent worship.

📖 ⟨O you wrapped 'in your clothes'! (1) Stand all night 'in prayer' except a little— (2) 'pray' half the night, or a little less, (3) or a little more—and recite the Quran 'properly' in a measured way. (4) 'For' We will soon send upon you a weighty revelation. (5) Indeed, worship in the night is more impactful and suitable for recitation. (6) For during the day you are over-occupied 'with worldly duties'. (7) 'Always' remember the Name of your Lord, and devote yourself to Him wholeheartedly. (8) 'He is the' Lord of the east and the west. There is no god 'worthy of worship' except Him, so take Him 'alone' as a Trustee of Affairs. (9)⟩ [Quran 73:1-9]

That the Prophet himself
Was instructed not only to pray,
But to rise beyond obligation,
Seeking in the quiet of night
The station of praise reserved
For those who make worship their secret companion.
❨Observe the prayer from the decline of the sun Until the darkness of the night And
the dawn prayer... And rise at the last part of the night, Offering additional prayers,
So your Lord may raise you To a station of praise.❩ — Quran 17:78–79
Such prayer is not public,
Not proclaimed.
It is a murmur between creation and Creator.
It lifts the soul
Not in eyes of others—
But in the gaze of the Most Merciful. 449

The wise-one reflects:
Seek not the seed without the water,
Nor the lamp without the flame.
For the virtues of the soul bloom only together—
And together they lead you Home.
Thus, the wise-one walks forward,
Not alone—
But accompanied by stillness.
Not idle—
But immersed in worship.
For seclusion is the door,
Worship is the passage,
And praise is the light
Found at the end.

---

449 This aligns with the sacred verse that beckons the faithful to engage in the noble practice of night prayer (in Islam referred to as tahajjud), often undertaken in the stillness of solitude, heralding the promise of elevated spiritual realms. This underscores the significance of devotion carried out in solitude (in Islam, referred to as halwa).

📖 ❨Observe the prayer from the decline of the sun until the darkness of the night and the dawn prayer, for certainly the dawn prayer is witnessed ˹by angels˺.[1] (78) And rise at ˹the last˺ part of the night, offering additional prayers, so your Lord may raise you to a station of praise.[2] (79)❩ [Quran 17:78-79]

[1]: This verse gives the times of the five daily prayers: the decline of the sun refers to the afternoon and late afternoon prayers, the darkness of night refers to sunset and late evening prayers, then the dawn prayer.

[2]: This refers to the time when the Prophet ﷺ will make intercession (shafâ'ah) on the Day of Judgment.

For only He beckons in silence.
Only He meets in stillness.
Only He remains the source
Of secret intimacy, elevation, and peace.

So the wise-one walks forward,
Not fighting with what the heavens have planned,
He finds in his solace, his peace on this land.
He lets his spirit prostrate to a wisdom unknown,
And finds in His satisfaction (rida) a peace all his own.

For only He is the One, the Ever-True,
Whose guidance is always sacred and new.
He is the Lord of both loss and of gain,
And to trust in His will is to go far.
For only He remains the source
Of Serenity, and boundless force.

Wisdom Unveiled

The profound wisdom of this contemplation is the realization that Seclusion (Khulwah) and Worship (Ibadah) are the ultimate pillars of inner harmony and liberation. The wise-one understands that intentional withdrawal from worldly noise and distraction is not an escape but a necessary step to create space for a direct, intimate connection with the Creator. The verses from Quran 73:1-9 and 17:78-79 serve as a powerful testament to this, revealing that night prayer, performed in stillness and with deep devotion, is the path to an elevated spiritual state and a true sense of purpose. This wisdom unveils that the heart's deepest fulfillment is not found in the clamor of the world but in the quiet sanctuary of worship, where the soul finds its ultimate peace and alignment with Al-Qayyum (The Sustainer of All).

Wise-Reflection

Reflect on the amount of noise and distraction in your life. Do you intentionally create space for stillness and solitude? Consider the thought, "Seclusion hushes the noise. Worship raises the soul's song." What is one practical step you can take today to cultivate more Khulwah (Seclusion) in your daily routine? How can you make your acts of Ibadah (Worship), such as prayer or remembrance, more than just a routine, transforming them into a profound and intimate conversation with your Creator?

Conclusion

And so, the journey concludes not with a final destination, but with a new beginning—a life lived in a state of continuous harmony. The wise-one, now liberated from the temporal, walks forward with a heart that is a fortress, a soul that is a garden, and a spirit that is a sanctuary. They understand that Certitude is the light that guides their steps, while Devoutness is the robe that protects them. They have learned that Patience is the enduring root, and Contentment is the sweet fruit it bears. Most importantly, they have found that Seclusion is the door, and Worship is the private dialogue that leads them to a peace that surpasses all worldly understanding. With these three pillars, the wise-one is no longer a traveler burdened by the world, but a liberated soul, aligned with the divine will, and forever directed toward its true and ultimate Home.

Conclusion: The Liberation from Attachments

ECHOES OF REALIZATION: THE LIGHTNESS OF THE UNBOUND HEART

There exists a profound freedom, so vast and boundless that even the majestic mountains would envy its unburdened lightness—yet it resides, intimately and powerfully, within the heart that has learned to utterly let go. The wise-one who lovingly surrenders all temporal attachments walks lightly upon the earth, for their true, eternal treasure is not buried here in this transient world, but is kept safely and securely beyond the veil, with Al-Ghaniy (The Self-Sufficient).

They are not weighed down by the ephemeral scales of human praise nor by the passing shadows of blame, by the fleeting thrill of gain nor by the transient sting of loss. They drink from a deeper, inexhaustible well—the wellspring of Divine proximity—where the waters of contentment and peace never, ever dry. Their every step upon the earth is a silent hymn of gratitude. Their every breath is a conscious prayer of remembrance. Their gaze is set—not on the fleeting illusions of the temporal—but unswervingly on the Eternal Presence of the Creator.

THE SEEKER'S ASCENT: FREEDOM FROM THE TEMPORAL

The Liberation from Attachments profoundly calls the wise-one to transcend life's inherent burdens by consciously detaching from worldly concerns and ultimately surrendering fully to Divine Will. By embracing and cultivating the deeply interconnected virtues of certitude and devoutness, patience and contentment, and seclusion and worship, the wise-one meticulously builds a balanced, harmonious, and truly fulfilling spiritual life. This profound detachment fosters an immense sense of inner peace, allowing the wise-one to rise far above temporal distractions and align completely with the Creator's boundless grace.

The Liberation from Attachments is not a mere flight from the responsibilities or experiences of life, but rather a profound sanctification of it. By meticulously loosening the binding chains of worldly concerns, and by cultivating the sacred, adherent pairs of certitude and devoutness, patience and contentment, and seclusion and worship, the wise-one ascends to unparalleled spiritual heights. They live actively in the world—yet are profoundly not owned or defined by it. They touch its fleeting beauty—yet are not captured or enslaved by it. Their heart beats in the serene rhythm of constant surrender, and their soul moves gracefully in the pure, irresistible current of the Infinite (Al-Awwal wa Al-Aakhir). Through this profound detachment, they find enduring peace. Through this complete surrender, they find boundless joy. And through the relinquishment of all else, they find the One Who is beyond all. This final reflection beautifully culminates " The Zenith of Liberation," demonstrating ultimate psychic and spiritual freedom.

"As the crucible cools, what truth, forged in fire, now illuminates the path to your inner sanctuary?"

CONCLUSION FOR PART V: THE ZENITH OF LIBERATION

(The Soul'd Eternal Return...)

ECHO WITHIN THE HEART... (THE DAWN OF INNER LIGHT AND UNBOUND PEACE)

The Manifestation of The Zenith of Liberation does not conclude; rather, it is the culmination, the full blossoming of the soul's journey, merging like a pure stream into the boundless ocean of Divine Presence. The wise-one, having navigated every trial, triumphed over every internal struggle, and shed every attachment, now embodies a profound, unshakeable state of spiritual freedom. This liberation is not a destination to be reached, but an inherent reality to be lived in every breath. Each reflection meticulously laid along this final pathway has not served merely as a signpost; it has wrought an ultimate emancipation—a complete dissolution of all perceived boundaries, an infinite expansion of the heart, and a sacred unveiling of the timeless unity intrinsically woven into the soul's very essence.

THRESHOLD OF AWE

The Unveiling of Ultimate Freedom

As the final veils gently lift upon this Manifestation of The Zenith of Liberation, the wise-one transcends all earthly limitations and embraces a state of pure, unadulterated freedom. The contemplations engaged within this part—of achieving mastery over the self, vanquishing its desires and inclinations, and ultimately experiencing complete liberation from all worldly attachments—do not merely add to one's store of information. Rather, they fundamentally transform the wise-one into a living testament to Divine grace, a soul that moves in the world but belongs wholly to the Eternal.

Pillars of Realization

Mastery Over Self as Inner Sovereignty:

The wise-one has achieved true kingship over their inner domain, subduing the ego and aligning every faculty with the Divine, becoming a vessel of pure intention and spiritual power.

Liberation from Attachments as Boundless Peace:

By shedding all clinging to temporal forms and outcomes, the heart finds an unshakeable serenity, a profound peace that transcends all worldly fluctuations, resting solely in the Eternal.

The Seeker Reflects

"I have journeyed through the veils, battled the self, and tasted the sweetness of surrender. My spirit, once burdened by worldly concerns, now soars, light and free, guided by an unseen hand. The illusions of separation have dissolved, and I perceive only the One, in all and through all. My heart beats in perfect rhythm with Divine Will, my actions flow from pure sincerity, and my vision sees beyond the surface, recognizing the Source of all. I have released all that does not serve the Eternal, and in doing so, I have found myself, not as a limited being, but as an infinite reflection of the Divine. I am home, even while I walk this earth."

INVITATION TO THE EVER-UNFOLDING HORIZON

With this profound liberation from attachments, the wise-one does not reach an end, but a new beginning: The Ever-Unfolding Horizon. This book has been a guide through the stations of awakening, connection, transformation, mastery, and liberation. Now, the path continues infinitely, for the journey into Divine proximity knows no ultimate end. The wisdom gained here is a key, not a destination.

Call to Action

"The path to liberation has been traversed; will you now step into the boundless, ever-unfolding horizon of eternal companionship?"

"Before the next station unfolds, let the heart quiet itself. In the profound silence, discern the echo of what has been revealed, and prepare for the deeper current."

EPILOGUE: THE EVER-UNFOLDING HORIZON

A REFLECTION ON THE INFINITE JOURNEY AND THE THRESHOLD OF UNPRECEDENTED AWAKENING

As the final echoes of this first sacred journey, "The Lantern of the Wise: Sailing Beyond the Horizon of Knowing," resonate through the halls of time, the wise-one stands not at an endpoint, but at the luminous gateway to an ever-expanding eternity. The horizon stretches boundlessly before them, where the veils of conventional perception gently dissolve, and the known converges seamlessly with the profound unknown. This book has been far more than a mere assemblage of words; it has manifested as a meticulously crafted guide, a profound revelation, and a ceaseless whisper of Divine Remembrance, calling the wise-one home to their true origin.

Through the vast expanse of wisdom presented within these pages, the discerning traveler has courageously embarked upon The Dawn of Belief and Knowledge, journeyed along The Pathway to Divine Connection, entered The Crucible of Inner Transformation, ascended towards The Triumph of Self-Mastery, and finally embraced The Zenith of Liberation. They have deeply delved into the hidden realm of profound wisdom, arrived at the precipice of intimate Divine connection, and stood, awestruck, at the very Threshold of the Infinite. Each arduous station traversed, each reflection meticulously engaged, has served not as a final destination, but as a consecrated gateway, compelling the wise-one beyond the confines of the temporal self, beyond mere form, and into the boundless embrace of the Eternal.

The wise-one now apprehends a deeper truth: there was never truly a 'journey' in the conventional sense, but an ever-present, continuous awakening to what always was. The sacred reflections of creation were not separate from the Divine, but intrinsically woven within the very fabric of His manifestation. Every hardship encountered was a divine refinement, every test an unveiling of deeper realities, every moment of silence a profound conversation with the Beloved. As the stars whisper celestial melodies and the rivers sing their timeless currents, the ultimate truth resounds: there is no isolated wise-one, no separate seeking—only the ceaseless, majestic unfolding of Divine Will, within and without.

This volume, "The Lantern of the Wise: Sailing Beyond the Horizon of Knowing," has been a testament to that magnificent unfolding—a journey from veiled knowing to unveiled witnessing, from transient selfhood to eternal Presence. It has illuminated the Dawn of Belief, unveiled the Sanctuary of Devotion, forged strength in the Crucible of Transformation, established the foundation for the Sphere of Higher Wisdom, and beckoned towards the ultimate dissolution into the luminous Grace of the Creator. In every reflection, the reader has been invited to step beyond the page, beyond mere intellectual thought, and into the living, transformative experience of Divine Remembrance.

THE BREATH AT THE THRESHOLD: PREPARING FOR THE DEEPER CURRENT

This comprehensive journey, however, serves as a crucial foundation, a perceptual threshold that conditions the wise-one for the profound spiritual and psychic awakenings yet to come. The experiences within these pages have served as a breath-catching moment, a vital preparation for the unprecedented unveiling of the soul's deepest potentials. Having meticulously laid the groundwork for spiritual insight and transformation, the wise-one is now poised, mind, heart, and soul, to venture into the second, more intricate stage of this inner odyssey.

The path ahead beckons with the promise of an even deeper current, an intensive exploration of the self and the Divine within. The upcoming Second Part of this series, "Illuminating the Soul's Infinite Core," will lead the wise-one into the very essence of silence, certitude, patience, and the profound mastery over internal landscapes. It promises an encounter with the essence of appearance and reality, the piercing gaze of true insight, the quenching of the soul's deepest thirst, and ultimately, an everlasting stance in Divine Grace, unveiling the inner core of being and the profound courtesy of abiding with the Creator.

As we close these pages of "The Lantern of the Wise: Sailing Beyond the Horizon of Knowing," the journey does not cease. For the wise-one, there is no end—only the next, ever-unfolding horizon, where new revelations, new trials, and unimaginable depths of understanding and spiritual-psychic potentials await. The wise-one does not look back in longing, nor do they look forward with anticipation. They stand as the purest mirror of the Divine, reflecting the Infinite in the fleeting, eternal moment. The voice of eternity whispers:

> *The path has no end, only unfolding.*
> *The witness becomes the light.*
> *The light becomes the horizon.*
> *And the horizon—*
> *—is boundless.*

Call to Action

"Having embraced the dawn of creation and traversed its trials, will you now brave the whispers of your inner world, where deeper light awaits?"

END OF THE FIRST PART OF THE LANTERN OF THE WISE...

THE EPIC SAGA: THE JOURNEY OF THE WISE-ONE

A Tale of Divine Revelation and Eternal Contemplation

In the beginning, before the dawn of time,
Before the first breath of creation stirred,
The wise-one was but a whisper in eternity,
A longing unspoken, a light yet unshaped.

There was a path, and yet, no path at all—
Only footsteps dissolving into the wind,
Only echoes vanishing into silence.
What once was sought has always been,
What was distant was never apart.

O Wise-one, did you think you would arrive?
Did you believe the journey would grant you an end?
There are no destinations where the Infinite calls,
Only unfolding, only becoming, only return.

Through the corridors of time, the wise-one walked,
Gathering the echoes of lost ages,
Drinking from the wells of forgotten wisdom,
Reading the silent scripture etched in the stars.

You have walked the labyrinth of knowing,
You have drowned in the depths of unknowing.
Beyond names, beyond veils, beyond forms—
You have seen that the face you sought
Was the face within you all along.

The book of creation stands open before all,
Yet it bears no binding, no parchment, no ink.

It is written upon the fabric of existence,
Inscribed in the dance of galaxies, the whisper of the wind.
No scribe's hand has touched its script,
For its Author is the Eternal, the One beyond words.

It is penned in the ink of light,
With the quill of divine command,
Upon the scroll of infinity.
It is written with the pulse of time,
With the rhythm of waves crashing upon ancient shores,
With the song of stars echoing through the abyss.

The letters of wisdom dissolved in the ether,
The questions unasked before they were answered.
For the lips of the Divine whisper not in words,
But in the stillness between heartbeats.

The book of creation is read by all who live,
Not with eyes alone, but with soul and breath,
Not with voice alone, but with silence and surrender.
It is read in the laughter of a newborn,
In the sorrow of the dying,
In the trembling of hands raised in prayer.

The wise-one ascends the mountain of knowing,
Each step an offering, each breath a prayer.
The stars become scrolls, the winds become scripture,
And the heavens unfold their luminous decree.

The book of creation holds the tales of the ages,
The rise and fall of empires,
The birth and decay of civilizations.
It tells of prophets ※ who walked the desert,
Of saints who wept in the night,
Of warriors who wielded justice as their blade.

The book of creation is a map for the lost,
A beacon for the wandering,
A hymn for the wise-one of truth.

It does not whisper, it does not cry,
It roars with the voice of revelation,
It calls with the breath of eternity.

Did you not hear? The silence was calling.
Did you not see? The unseen was watching.
Did you not know? There was never a journey,
Only awakening from a dream of separation.

The book of creation is a temple without walls,
A sanctuary without borders,
A testament that endures beyond death.
It is the call to worship in the song of the birds,
The rhythm of devotion in the waves of the sea,
The eternal remembrance written upon the heart.

The wise-one kneels at the threshold of mystery,
No longer asking, no longer seeking,
But surrendering to the great unfolding.
The final veil lifts, the last horizon shatters,
And they become the silence, the light, the eternal witness.

The book of creation reveals both mystery and mastery,
It veils the secrets of the unseen,
Yet unfolds the wonder of all that is.
Its verses are carved into the veins of mountains,
Sung by the rivers as they race to the ocean,
Echoed by the heavens in their endless turning.

O Witness of the One, now you stand at the edge—
Not of a precipice, not of an abyss,
But at the threshold of a sky that has no ceiling,
At the horizon that only expands.

The wise-one becomes the sign,
The mirror in which the Divine reflects.
No longer a mariner lost at sea,
But the ocean itself, embracing all.

The book of creation is a call to the bold,
An invitation to the wise,
A promise to the faithful.
It does not end with the closing of eyes,
For every sunset is a prelude to dawn,
And every death is a gateway to life.

Step forward, if you must, but know this:
There is no forward, no backward, no beyond.
You are already here. You have always been.
The path does not lead to the Divine,
The path is the Divine.

So go forth, yet remain still.
Seek, yet abandon seeking.
Speak, yet embrace silence.
For in all things, in every breath, in every moment,
The Eternal is calling, unfolding,
Drawing you deeper into the Infinite embrace.

O Wise-one, have you read the signs?
O Witness, have you seen the path?
O Wayfarer, have you heard the call?

For the book of creation has no end—
Only the next horizon awaits...

www.ingramcontent.com/pod-product-compliance
Lightning Source LLC
Chambersburg PA
CBHW061128120626
46546CB00005B/1706